MILITARY JETS

MILITARY JETS

JIM WINCHESTER

amber
BOOKS

This Amber edition published in 2019

First edition published in 2010

Published by Amber Books Ltd
United House
North Road
London N7 9DP
United Kingdom
www.amberbooks.co.uk
Instagram: amberbooksltd
Facebook: www.facebook.com/amberbooks
Twitter: @amberbooks

ISBN: 978-1-78274-728-4

Project Editor: James Bennett
Picture Research: Terry Forshaw
Design: Zoe Mellors

Printed in China

Contents

Classic Jets 1945–60

Modern Jets 1960–present

Classic Jets 1945–1960

"Only the spirit of attack born in the brave heart can bring the success to any fighter plane, no matter how developed it may be."
– Lieutenant General Adolf Galland, *The First and the Last*

Above: The Messerschmitt Me 262 was the first and last jet many Allied airmen ever saw, but it was too late and too unreliable to influence the outcome of World War II or win back even local air superiority for the Germans.

In 1945, when Adolf Galland was flying his last missions in the Messerschmitt Me 262, only six countries (United Kingdom, United States, Germany, Japan, Sweden and the Soviet Union) had active jet fighter aircraft programmes, and two of those were soon closed down by the Axis defeat. In the 1950s and 1960s, various other countries tried, often with the help of former German designers, to build indigenous fighters, including Switzerland, India, Egypt and Argentina. But the great cost of such programmes and the increasing sophistication of avionics and missiles meant that they usually turned out both more expensive and less competitive than their contemporaries. Almost every Western or non-aligned nation except the United Kingdom, France and Sweden gave up on totally home-grown fighters, and chose to buy outright or produce under licence the products of Lockheed, Dassault or Hawker. Communist or Moscow-leaning nations had a choice of Mikoyan-Gurevich MiGs (or their Chinese copies) or Sukhois. India, Pakistan and some Arab nations hedged their bets by buying aircraft of both Western and Soviet or Chinese origin.

Above: The F-86 Sabre pilot had an excellent outside view when he was not busy monitoring the multitude of instruments typical of first-generation jets.

THE FIGHTER'S GOLDEN AGE

The 1950s, in particular, proved to be a golden age for fighter design, with new prototypes appearing seemingly every month. Some of these even made it into production, a process in those days which could often achieved in a relatively short time and reasonably close to budget. Increasing capability, sophistication and more rigorous testing and evaluation, as well as political interference, have helped to extend development programmes close to two decades between design freeze and initial operational capability.

Today's analysts and marketing depatments recognize five generations of jet fighters. The term "fifth-generation fighter" was coined in Russia in the 1990s as a way of describing the top-secret programme to develop a competitor to the Joint Strike Fighter of the United States and its allies. It seems to have stuck, and postwar fighters can be allocated to previous generations, although the placement of some is debatable.

The first-generation fighters were characterized by gun and occasionally rocket armament, straight or swept wings, single unaugmented (non-afterburning) engines and hence

Above: Mikoyan-Gurevich's MiG-21 proliferated through the 1960s and 1970s, and is the last second-generation fighter still to be found in large numbers.

subsonic speeds in all flight regimes except a dive from altitude. Radar, if present, was usually a simple ranging set for gun aiming. Examples of first-generation fighters include the North American F-86 Sabre, Gloster Meteor, Mikoyan-Gurevich MiG-15, Grumman F9F Panther/Cougar and de Havilland Vampire/Venom. Today, the only survivors of the era remaining airworthy fly in air shows, not air combat.

EVER-GROWING SOPHISTICATION

Supersonic performance in level flight came with second-generation jets, as did basic guided missiles and air-to-air radar. Some fighters such as the Convair F-102 Delta Dagger and F-106 Delta Dart could be flown hands-off to an interception by signals from ground control. Swept or delta wings became universal and afterburning engines widespread. Second-generation fighters included all of the "Century Series" from the North American F-100 Super Sabre to the F-106 Delta Dart, Mikoyan-Gurevich MiG-19 and MiG-21, Vought F-8 Crusader, Saab 35 Draken, Dassault Mirage III/V, Hawker Hunter, English Electric Lightning and Gloster Javelin. Apart from some MiGs and their Chinese equivalents, the second generation has all but vanished from active service.

Third-generation fighters sometimes eliminated gun armament all together in favour of "fire-and-forget" and beyond-visual-range missiles. In actual combat, rules of engagement often prevented firing until positive visual identification was made, which drew the missile-armed fighter into a close-in fight with smaller, nimbler enemies and their cannon. In Vietnam, the United States prevailed in the air-to-air arena, but not before it was taught some important lessons. Representative third-generation fighters include the McDonnell Douglas F-4 Phantom, Panavia Tornado, Mikoyan-Gurevich MiG-23, Saab 37 Viggen and others with analog control systems, conventional dial cockpit instrumentation and in many cases different variants for different roles such as air interdiction and suppression of enemy air defences.

TESTED IN ACTION

The third generation saw significant combat in Southeast Asia and over the Middle East. Considerable numbers remain in service, particularly Phantoms, Dassault Mirage F1s and Northrop F-5s. Upgrade programmes have kept these older aircraft viable with multi-mode radars, "glass" cockpits and integration of precision weapons such as AMRAAMs (advanced medium-range air-to-air missiles) and the later versions of the venerable Sidewinder. Often the technical advances developed for the next generation have

Above: Marking the peak of single-seat fighter size and mechanical complexity, the F-105's main defence was its speed at low level.

Above: For smaller air arms such as Brazil's navy, the purchase and eventual upgrade of older aircraft such as the Douglas A-4 Skyhawk is a way to maintain a fairly cheap fighter capability.

been fed back into the existing fighter fleets, which on one hand has served to keep fighters competitive while the air arms await their (often delayed) replacements, but on the other sometimes reduces the need for the planned number of new fighters. In this way, some fighter manufacturers have found their biggest competitor is their own "legacy" products. Controlling access to the software codes that allow export customers to upgrade their expensive fighters has become as important to the balance sheet as the supply of spare parts has traditionally been for the few remaining fighter makers.

The 1950s, in particular, proved to be a golden age for jet fighter design, with new prototypes appearing seemingly every month.

Messerschmitt Me 262

The Me 262 was the world's first operational jet fighter. Politics and technical difficulties prevented the 262 from reaching its full potential, and only a small number actually saw combat in the last months of World War II.

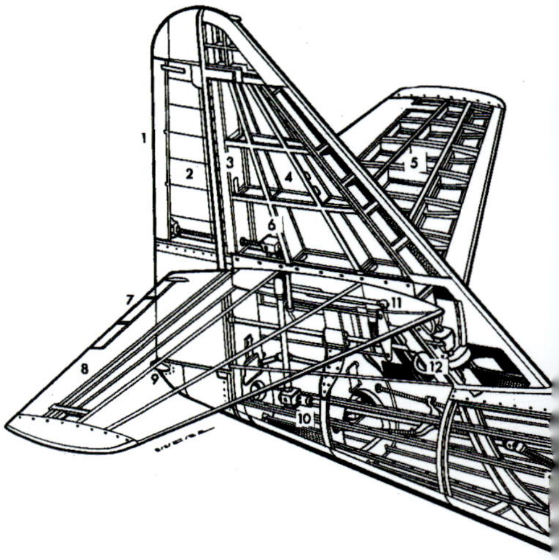

ME 262 A-1A/B SPECIFICATION

Dimensions

Length: 34 ft 9 in (10.58 m)
Height: 12 ft 7 in (3.83 m)
Span: 40 ft 11 in (12.5 m)
Wing area: 234 sq ft (21.73 m²)
Wing leading-edge sweepback: 18° 32′

Powerplant

Two Junkers Jumo 004B-1, -2 or -3 axial-flow turbojets each rated at 1,984 lb st (8.83 kN)

Weights

Empty: 3,778 lb (3795 kg)
Empty equipped: 9,742 lb (4413 kg)
Maximum takeoff: 14,080 lb (6387 kg)

Performance

Maximum speed at sea level: 514 mph (827 km/h)
Maximum speed at 9,845 ft (3000 m): 530 mph (852 km/h)
Maximum speed at 19,685 ft (6000 m): 540 mph (869 km/h)
Maximum speed at 26,245 ft (8000 m): 532 mph (856 km/h)
Initial climb rate: 3,937 ft (1200 m) per minute
Service ceiling: over 40,000 ft (12,190 m)
Range: 652 miles (1050 km) at 29,530 ft (9000 m)
Landing speed: 109 mph (175 km/h)

Armament

Four 30-mm Rheinmetall-Borsig Mk 108A-3 cannon with 100 rounds per gun for the upper pair and 80 rounds per gun for the lower pair, and aimed with a Revi 16.B gunsight or EZ.42 gyro-stabilized sight. Provision for 12 R4M air-to-air rockets under each wing (Me 262A-1b).

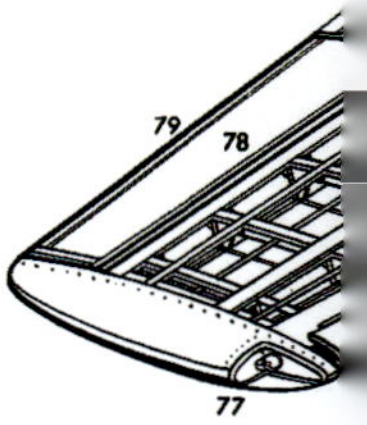

Cutaway Key

1 Flettner-type geared trim tab
2 Mass-balanced rudder
3 Rudder post
4 Tail fin structure
5 Tailplane structure
6 Rudder tab mechanism
7 Flettner-type servo tab
8 Starboard elevator
9 Rear navigation light
10 Rudder linkage
11 Elevator linkage
12 Tailplane adjustment mechanism
13 Fuselage break point
14 Fuselage construction
15 Control runs
16 FuG 25a loop antenna (IFF)
17 Automatic compass
18 Aft auxiliary self-sealing fuel tank (159-US gal/600-litre capacity)
19 FuG 16zy R/T
20 Fuel filler cap
21 Aft cockpit glazing
22 Armoured aft main fuel tank (238-US gal/900-litre capacity)
23 Inner cockpit shell
24 Pilot's seat
25 Canopy jettison lever
26 Armoured 0.59-in (15-mm) headrest
27 Canopy (hinged to starboard)
28 Canopy lock
29 Bar-mounted Revi 16B sight (for both cannon and R4M missiles)
30 Armourglass windscreen 3.54 in (90 mm)
31 Instrument panel
32 Rudder pedal
33 Armoured forward main fuel tank (238-US gal/900-litre capacity)
34 Fuel filler cap

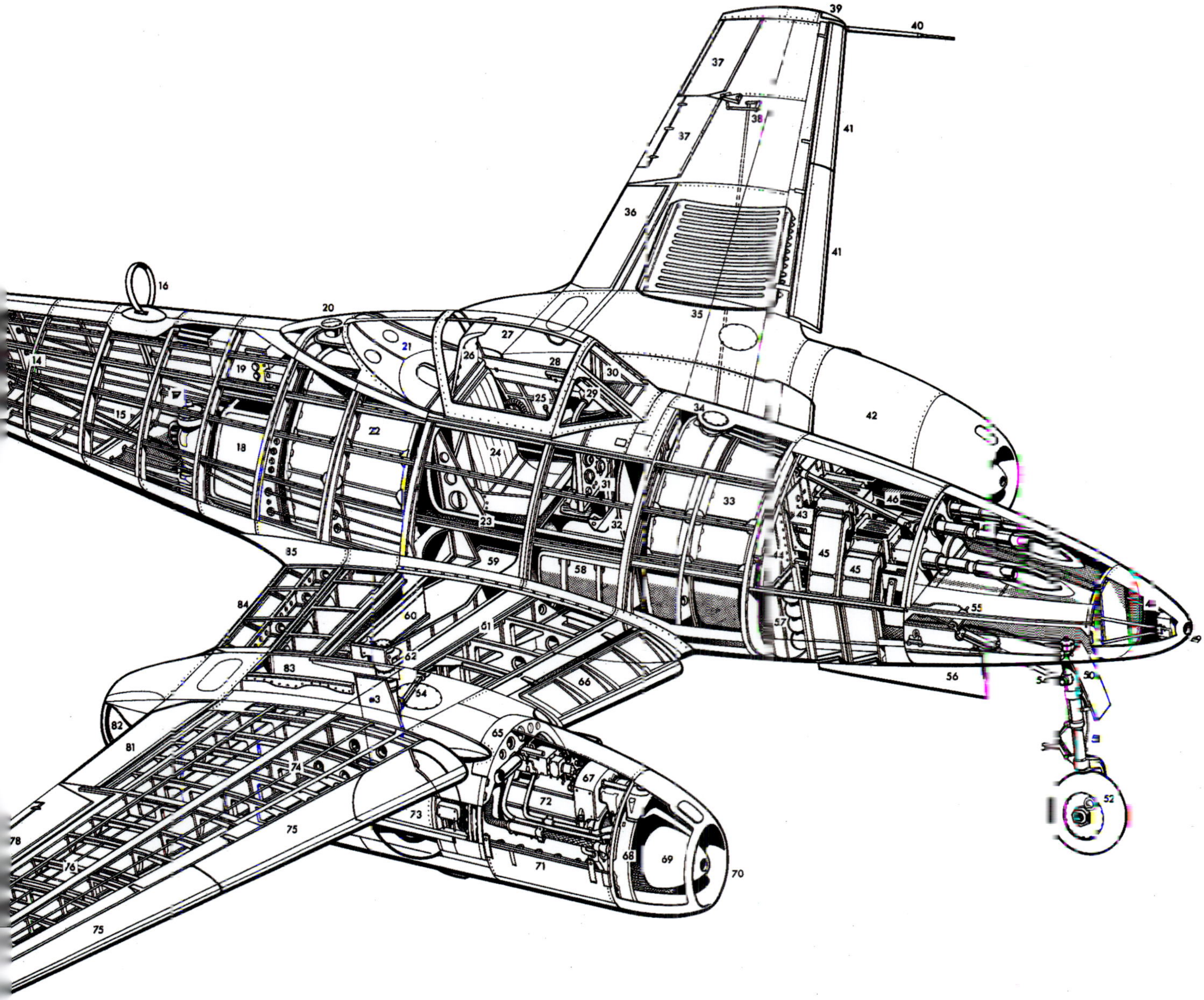

35 Underwing wooden rack for 12 R4M 2.17-in (55-mm) rockets (Me 262A-1b)
36 Port outer flap section
37 Frise-type aileron
38 Aileron control linkage
39 Port navigation light
40 Pitot head
41 Automatic leading-edge slats
42 Port engine cowling
43 Electrical firing mechanism
44 Firewall
45 Spent cartridge ejector chutes
46 Four 30-mm Rheinmetall Borsig Mk 108 cannon (100 rpg belt-fed ammunition for upper pair and 80 rpg for lower pair)
47 Cannon muzzles
48 Combat camera
49 Camera aperture
50 Nosewheel fairing
51 Nosewheel leg
52 Nosewheel
53 Torque scissors
54 Retraction jack
55 Hydraulic lines
56 Main nosewheel door (starboard)
57 Compressed air bottles
58 Forward auxiliary fuel tank (45-US gal/170-litre capacity)
59 Mainwheel well
60 Torque box
61 Main spar
62 Mainwheel leg pivot point
63 Mainwheel door
64 Mainwheel retraction rod
65 Engine support arch
66 Leading-edge slat structure
67 Auxiliaries gearbox
68 Annular oil tank
69 Riedel starter motor housing
70 Engine air intake
71 Hinged cowling section
72 Junkers Jumo 004B-2 axial-flow turbojet
73 Starboard mainwheel
74 Wing structure
75 Automatic leading-edge slats
76 Mainspar
77 Starboard navigation light
78 Frise-type ailerons
79 Trim tab
80 Flettner-type geared tab
81 Starboard [illegible] flap section
82 Engine exhaust orifice
83 Engine support bearer
84 Starboard [illegible] flap structure
85 Faired wing root

"It was as if an angel were pushing me."
– Major General Adolf Galland after his first flight in the Me 262

FACTS

- The Jumo 004 engines of the Me 262 had an estimated operating life of ten hours before failing.
- A handful of Me 262B two-seat night fighters was delivered.
- About 1,400 Me 262s were built, and they accounted for around 500 Allied aircraft against 100 losses in combat.

MESSERSCHMITT ME 262 – VARIANTS

WARTIME VARIANTS

Me 262 A-0: Pre-production aircraft fitted with two Jumo 004B turbojet engines.

Me 262 A-1a "Schwalbe": Production version, fighter and fighter-bomber.

Me 262 A-1a/R-1: Equipped with provisions for R4M air-to-air rockets.

Me 262 A-1a/U1: Single prototype with six nose-mounted guns.

Me 262 A-1a/U2: Single prototype with FuG 220 Lichtenstein SN-2 90 MHz radar transceiver and Hirschgeweih antenna array, for trials as a night fighter.

Me 262 A-1a/U3: Reconnaissance version.

Me 262 A-1a/U4: Bomber-destroyer version.

Me 262 A-1a/U5: Heavy jet fighter with six MK 108s in the nose.

Me 262 A-1b: As A-1a but powered with BMW 003 engines.

Me 262 A-2a "Sturmvogel": Definitive bomber version.

Me 262 A-2a/U1: Single prototype with advanced bombsight.

Me 262 A-2a/U2: Two prototypes with glazed nose for accommodating a bombardier.

Me 262 A-3a: Proposed ground-attack version.

Me 262 A-4a: Reconnaissance version.

Me 262 A-5a: Definitive reconnaissance version.

Me 262 B-1a: Two-seat trainer.

Me 262 B-1a/U1: Me 262 B-1a trainers converted into provisional night fighters, FuG 218 Neptun radar, with Hirschgeweih antenna array.

Me 262 B-2: Proposed night-fighter version with stretched fuselage.

Me 262 C-1a: Single prototype of rocket-boosted interceptor (Heimatschützer I) with Walter HWK 109-509 rocket in tail.

Me 262 C-2b: Single prototype of rocket-boosted interceptor (Heimatschützer II).

Me 262 C-3a: Never completed. Possible Heimatschützer III prototype of rocket-boosted interceptor with Walter rocket motor in belly pack.

Me 262 S: Zero-series model for Me 262 A-1a.

Me 262 V: Test model for Me 262.

POSTWAR VARIANTS

Avia S-92: Czechoslovak-built Me 262A.

Avia S-92: Czechoslovak-built Me 262 A-1a.

Avia CS-92: Czechoslovak-built Me 262 B-1a (fighter trainer, two seats).

MESSERSCHMITT ME 262

The Me 262 A-1a was the first production model of the "Schwalbe" (Swallow), followed by the Me 262 A-2a "Sturmvogel" (Stormbird) fighter-bomber. This Me 262 A-1a of 3./JG 7 was found by Allied forces in April 1945 in a hangar at Stendal, Germany, having been damaged by anti-aircraft fire, possibly German. Although it was considered for repair and evaluation, better examples were available and it was scrapped. Jagdgeschwader 7 was the only wing to fully equip with Me 262s and claimed more than 135 victories against Allied aircraft before the war's end. On 18 March 1945, it managed to get 37 Me 262s airborne for the type's biggest mission, during which it used the R4M rocket for the first time.

German research into jet engines began in the late 1930s, leading to the first flight of the Heinkel He 178 and He 180 test aircraft in 1939 and 1940, respectively. By 1942, Ernst Heinkel had fallen out of favour with the Nazi hierarchy, and the war seemed to be going well enough for Germany that defensive fighters would be unnecessary, no matter how superior. Willi Messerschmitt was working on his own design, to be powered by either a BMW or Junkers axial-flow turbojet.

Above: With two bombs mounted under the fuselage, the Me 262A-2a "Sturmvogel" was a fast but inaccurate fighter-bomber.

In ground testing, the proposed powerplants failed to produce enough thrust, but Messerschmitt proceeded with the airframes regardless, and the first Messerschmitt 262 with a Junkers Jumo 210G piston engine fitted in the nose flew in April 1941.

PROTOTYPE CONFIGURATIONS

The fully jet-powered Me 262 V3 with BMW 003s retained the tailwheel undercarriage of the V1. This proved a mistake because the thrust line and wing incidence combined to prevent enough airflow over the wing to allow flying speed. The temporary solution required the pilot to tap the brakes during the takeoff roll, which raised the tail and allowed liftoff. Subsequent aircraft had the undercarriage changed to a nosewheel configuration. The first flight on jet power alone was in July 1942.

The production model Me 262 A was powered by Jumo 004s, and it was armed with either two or four 30-mm

Above: Me 262s belonging to a test unit in the summer of 1944. Soon the aircraft would have to be dispersed and camouflaged, to avoid roaming Allied ground-attack aircraft on the lookout for German targets.

Above: The simple and well-laid out instrument panel of an Me 262. The engine instruments on the right-hand side had to be carefully watched so that the pilot could take measures to prevent the turbines overheating.

MK 108 cannon. Later aircraft were capable of carrying racks of R4M unguided rockets. The leading-edge sweep of 18.5 degrees was not enough to really call it a swept-wing aircraft by later standards.

When shown the Me 262 in November 1943, Adolf Hitler asked if it could carry bombs. Willi Messerschmitt lied, but immediately set his engineers to modifying the Me 262 to carry a pair of bombs under the forward fuselage. It is debatable whether this actually delayed its service entry appreciably, but it proved harder than anticipated and produced a very short-ranged and inaccurate bomber that was to have no effect on the Allied invasion of France.

The first test unit began business in May 1944, and spawned the first operational jet squadron in September, called Kommando Nowotny after its leader, 283-victory ace Walter Nowotny. Nowotny himself lived only until November 1944, before he was brought down by P-51 Mustangs. Despite their superiority at high speed and altitude, the Me 262s were extremely vulnerable on their landing approaches, and their concrete-paved runways were easy for roving Allied fighters to find.

DEVASTATING EFFECT

Several units were formed, but the largest rarely had more than 30 aircraft operational at one time. The Me 262 scored its first confirmed victories in August 1944. Where they were able to be concentrated against USAAF bombers, their effect could be devastating. A total of 27 Luftwaffe pilots became jet aces by scoring five or more kills with the Me 262, although many were already experten on propeller-driven fighters. One such was Adolf Galland, who added seven U.S. aircraft to his total score of 104.

The Me 262 was in the end hampered by Allied attacks on its supply lines, particularly fuel for support vehicles, and by its unreliable engines, made with materials unsuitable for prolonged high temperatures.

Gloster Meteor

The Meteor was the Allies' first operational jet fighter and the only one to see active combat in World War II. Later variants were used in Korea and served well into the 1960s.

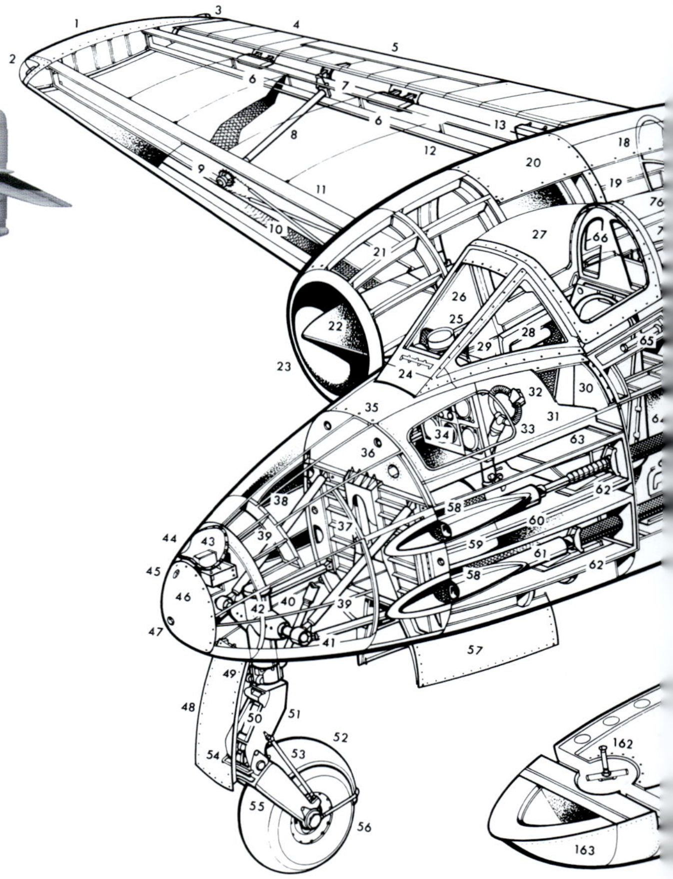

METEOR F.MK 8 SPECIFICATION

Dimensions

Length: 44 ft 7 in (13.59 m)
Wingspan: 37 ft 2 in (11.33 m)
Height: 13 ft (3.96 m)
Wing area: 350 sq ft (32.515 m²)
Aspect ratio: 3.9
Root chord: 11 ft 9 in (3.6 m)

Powerplant

Two 3,500-lb (15.5-kN) thrust Rolls-Royce Derwent 8 turbojets

Weights
Empty: 10,684 lb (4846 kg)
Maximum overload: 15,700 lb (7122 kg)

Performance

Maximum speed at sea level: 592 mph (953 km/h)
Maximum speed at 30,000 ft (9144 m): 550 mph (885 km/h)
Climb to 30,000 ft (9144 m): 6 minutes 30 seconds
Service ceiling: 44,000 ft (13,410 m)
Range without wing drop tanks: 690 miles (1111 km)
Endurance at 40,000 ft (12,192 m) with 504 US gal (1909 litres) of fuel: 592 mph (953 km/h)

Armament

Four fixed 20-mm British Hispano cannon in the nose with 195 rounds per gun

Cutaway Key

1 Starboard detachable wingtip
2 Starboard navigation light
3 Starboard recognition light
4 Starboard aileron
5 Aileron balance tab
6 Aileron mass balance weights
7 Aileron control coupling
8 Aileron torque shaft
9 Chain sprocket
10 Crossover control runs
11 Front spar
12 Rear spar
13 Aileron (inboard) mass balance
14 Nacelle detachable tail section
15 Jet pipe exhaust
16 Internal stabilizing struts
17 Rear spar "spectacle" frame
18 Fire extinguisher spray ring
19 Main engine mounting frame
20 Engine access panel(s)
21 Nacelle nose structure
22 Intake internal leading-edge shroud
23 Starboard engine intake
24 Windscreen de-icing spray tube
25 Reflector gunsight
26 Cellular glass bulletproof windscreen
27 Aft-sliding cockpit canopy
28 Demolition incendiary (cockpit starboard wall)
29 RPM indicators (left and right of gunsight)
30 Pilot's seat
31 Forward fuselage top deflector skin
32 Gun wobble button
33 Control column grip
34 Main instrument panel
35 Nosewheel armoured bulkhead
36 Nose release catches (10)
37 Nosewheel jack bulkhead
38 Nose ballast weight location
39 Nosewheel mounting frames
40 Radius rod (link and jack omitted)
41 Nosewheel pivot bearings
42 Shimmy-damper/self-centring strut
43 Gun camera
44 Camera access
45 Aperture
46 Nose cone
47 Cabin cold-air intake
48 Nosewheel leg door
49 Picketing rings
50 Tension shock absorber
51 Pivot bracket
52 Mudguard
53 Torque strut
54 Doorhoop
55 Wheel fork
56 Retractable nosewheel
57 Nosewheel doors
58 Port cannon trough fairings
59 Nosewheel cover
60 Intermediate diaphragm
61 Blast tubes

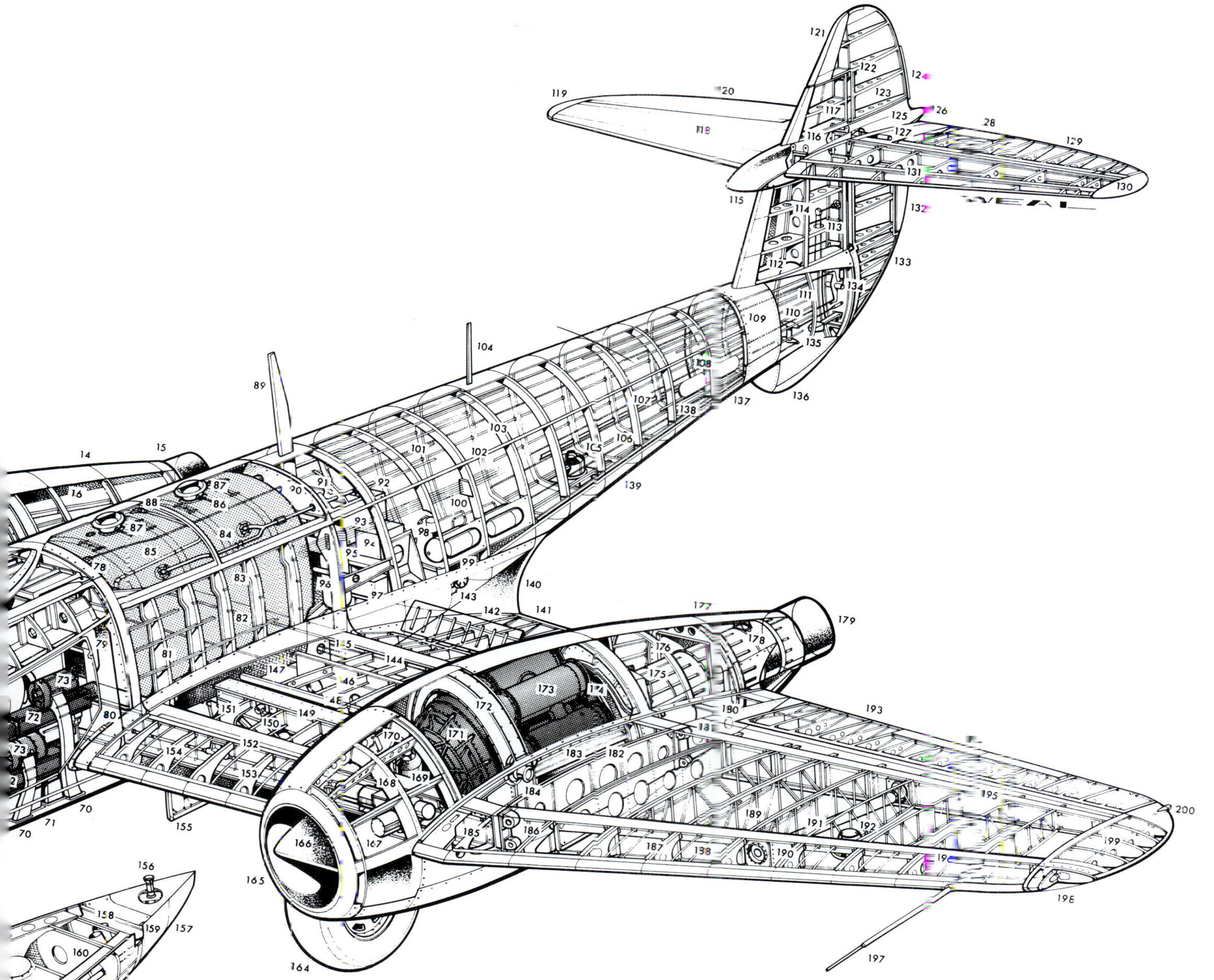

62 Gun front mount rails
63 Pilot's seat pan
64 Emergency crowbar
65 Canopy demisting silica gel cylinder
66 Bulletproof glass rear-view cutouts
67 Canopy track
68 Seat bulkhead
69 Entry step
70 Link ejection chutes
71 Case ejection chutes
72 20-mm Hispano Mk II cannon
73 Belt-feed mechanism
74 Ammunition feed necks
75 Ammunition tanks
76 Aft glazing (magazine bay top door)
77 Leading ramp
78 Front spar bulkhead
79 Oxygen bottles (2)
80 Front spar carry-through
81 Tank bearer frames
82 Rear spar carry-through
83 Self-sealing (twin compartment) main fuel tank, capacity 198 US gal (750 litres) in each half
84 Fuel connector pipe
85 Return pipe
86 Drain pipes
87 Fuel filler caps
88 Tank doors (2)
89 T.R.1143 aerial mast
90 Rear spar bulkhead (plywood face)
91 Aerial support frame
92 R.3121 (or B.C.966A) IFF installation
93 Tab control cables
94 Amplifier
95 Fire extinguisher bottles (2)
96 Elevator torque shaft
97 T.R.1143 transmitter/receiver radio installation
98 Pneumatic system filler
99 Pneumatic system (compressed) air cylinders
100 Tab cable fairlead
101 Elevator control cable
102 Top longeron
103 Fuselage frame
104 IFF aerial
105 DR compass master unit
106 Rudder cables
107 Starboard lower longeron
108 Cable access panels (port and starboard)
109 Tail section joint
110 Rudder linkage
111 Tail ballast weight location
112 Fin spar/fuselage frame
113 Rudder tab control
114 Fin structure
115 Torpedo fairing
116 Tailplane spar/upper fin attachment plates
117 Upper fin section
118 Starboard tailplane
119 Elevator horn and mass balance
120 Starboard elevator
121 Rudder horn and mass balance
122 Rudder upper hinge
123 Rudder frame
124 Fixed tab
125 Rear fairing
126 Tail navigation light
127 Elevator torque shaft
128 Elevator trim tab
129 Elevator frame
130 Elevator horn and mass balance
131 Tailplane structure
132 Rudder combined balance trim tab
133 Rudder lower section
134 Elevator push-rod linkage
135 Rudder internal/lower mass balance weight
136 Emergency landing tailskid
137 Tail section riveted joint
138 Port lower longeron
139 Fuselage stressed skin
140 Wingroot fairing
141 Inboard split flap
142 Airbrake (upper and lower surfaces)
143 Flap indicator transmitter
144 Rear spar
145 Inter-coupler cables (airbrake/airbrake and flap/flap)
146 Port mainwheel well
147 Roof rib station
148 Front diaphragm
149 Undercarriage beam
150 Undercarriage retraction jack
151 Undercarriage sidestay/downlock
152 Front spar
153 Nose ribs
154 Aileron control runs
155 Mainwheel door inner section
156 Ventral tank
157 Tank rear fairing
158 Filler stack pipes
159 Ventral tank attachment strap access doors
160 Anti-surge baffles
161 Fixed ventral fuel tank, capacity 126 US gal (477 litres)
162 Air pressure inlet
163 Tank front fairing
164 Port mainwheel
165 Starboard engine intake
166 Intake internal leading-edge shroud
167 Auxiliary gearbox drive (vacuum pump, generator)
168 Nacelle nose structure
169 Starter motor
170 Oil tank
171 Rolls-Royce W.2B/23C Derwent I
172 Main engine mounting frame
173 Combustion chambers
174 Rear spar 'spectacle' frame
175 Jet pipe heat-shrouding
176 Nacelle aft frames
177 Nacelle detachable aft section
178 Jet pipe suspension link
179 Jet pipe exhaust
180 Gap fairing tail section
181 Rear-spar outer wing fixing
182 Outer wing rib No.1
183 Engine end rib
184 Engine mounting/removal trunnion
185 Gap fairing nose section
186 Front-spar outer wing fixing
187 Nose ribs
188 Intermediate riblets
189 Wing ribs
190 Aileron drive chain sprocket
191 Aileron torque shaft
192 Retractable landing lamp
193 Port aileron
194 Aileron balance tab
195 Rear spar
196 Front spar
197 Pitot head
198 Port navigation light
199 Outer wing rib No. 10/wingtip attachment
200 Port recognition light

"All I want for Christmas is my wings swept back."
– song sung by Australian Meteor pilots in Korea, 1951

"It's a very sweet aeroplane. It's beautiful to fly, lovely to operate, a real honey."
– Meteor ejection-seat testbed pilot Dan Griffith

FACTS

- A modified Meteor became the first aircraft to fly on turboprop power alone.
- None of the two-seat trainer or night-fighter Meteors possessed ejection seats.
- 44 RAF squadrons flew the Meteor, as did 12 of the Royal Navy's Fleet Air Arm squadrons.

GLOSTER METEOR – VARIANTS AND MILITARY OPERATORS

VARIANTS

F: First production aircraft built between 1943 and 1944.

F 1: One-off engine testbed, built 1945, designated EE227, for the new and highly successful Rolls-Royce Trent turboprop engine, making it the world's first turboprop-powered aircraft.

F 2: One model built of alternative-engined version.

F 3: Derwent I powered version with sliding canopy.

F 4: Derwent 5 powered version with strengthened fuselage.

FR 5: One-off fighter reconnaissance version of the F 4.

T 7: Two-seat trainer.

F 8: Greatly improved from the F 4. Longer fuselage, greater fuel capacity, standard ejection seat and modified tail.

F 8 Prone Pilot: One-off experimental prone pilot F8, WK935 modified by Armstrong Whitworth. The sole "prone pilot" experimental testbed.

FR 9: Fighter reconnaissance version of the F 8.

PR 10: Photo reconnaissance version of the F 8.

NF 11: Night-fighter variant with Airborne Intercept radar.

NF 12: Longer-nosed version of the NF 11 with American radar.

NF 13: Tropicalized version of the NF 11 for overseas service.

NF 14: NF 11 with new two-piece canopy.

U 15: Drone conversion of the F 4.

U 16: Drone conversion of the F 8.

TT 20: High-speed target towing conversion of the NF 11.

U 21: Drone conversion of the F 8.

MILITARY OPERATORS

Argentine Air Force
Royal Australian Air Force
Belgian Air Force
Brazilian Air Force
Royal Canadian Air Force
Royal Danish Air Force
Ecuadorian Air Force
Royal Egyptian Air Force
French Air Force
Israeli Air Force
Royal Netherlands Air Force
Royal New Zealand Air Force
Royal Norwegian Air Force
South African Air Force
Swedish Air Force
Syrian Air Force
UK Royal Air Force and Royal Navy Fleet Air Arm

GLOSTER METEOR

The Meteor night fighters were developed and built by Armstrong Whitworth at Coventry, England. The NF 14 was the last to enter service. Unlike earlier models, which inherited a heavily framed canopy from the T 7 trainer, the NF 14 had a clear bubble canopy for the pilot and radar operator. Compared to the original Meteor NF 11, the Mk 14 had a taller tail, longer wings and a longer nose. WS800 was delivered to the RAF in 1954. In 1959, it was serving with No. 60 Squadron at Tengah, Singapore. When 60 Squadron re-equipped with Gloster Javelins, it was struck off charge in August 1961 at RAF Seletar and later scrapped.

Jet-engine pioneer Sir Frank Whittle worked through the 1930s to develop a practical gas turbine (jet) aircraft engine. The British Air Ministry issued a request for an operational fighter based around a Whittle W.2 engine in 1940, and this was preceded by the E.28/39 test aircraft, sometimes called the Gloster Whittle, which flew in May 1941. The low power and questionable reliability of Whittle's original engine suggested that a twin-engined layout would be wise for an operational aircraft. Whittle's own small Power Jets company was not in a position to build aircraft or mass-produce engines. Gloster proposed an aircraft called the G.41, and Rolls-Royce took on engine development and produced the W.2 as the Welland, although the prototype G.41, soon named Meteor, flew in March 1942 with de Havilland Halford H.1 engines.

Above: The Meteor T 7 remained in use as an advanced trainer long after the fighter versions were retired from the RAF. They suffered a high accident rate when training pilots to cope with engine failures.

Two years of testing and training followed before the Meteor F 1 entered service with the RAF in July 1944 at Manston in Kent. Immediately they were thrown into action against the V-1 flying bombs being launched against London. More than a dozen were destroyed by the Meteor's four 20-mm cannon or by tipping them out of control with their wingtips. At first Meteors were forbidden from flying over enemy-held territory in order to preserve their secrets, but this restriction was soon abandoned. By World War II's end, Meteors had had a few inconclusive encounters with manned Luftwaffe aircraft, but had scored no victories nor suffered any losses, being mostly used for ground attack. On these missions, they destroyed numerous aircraft and vehicles on the ground.

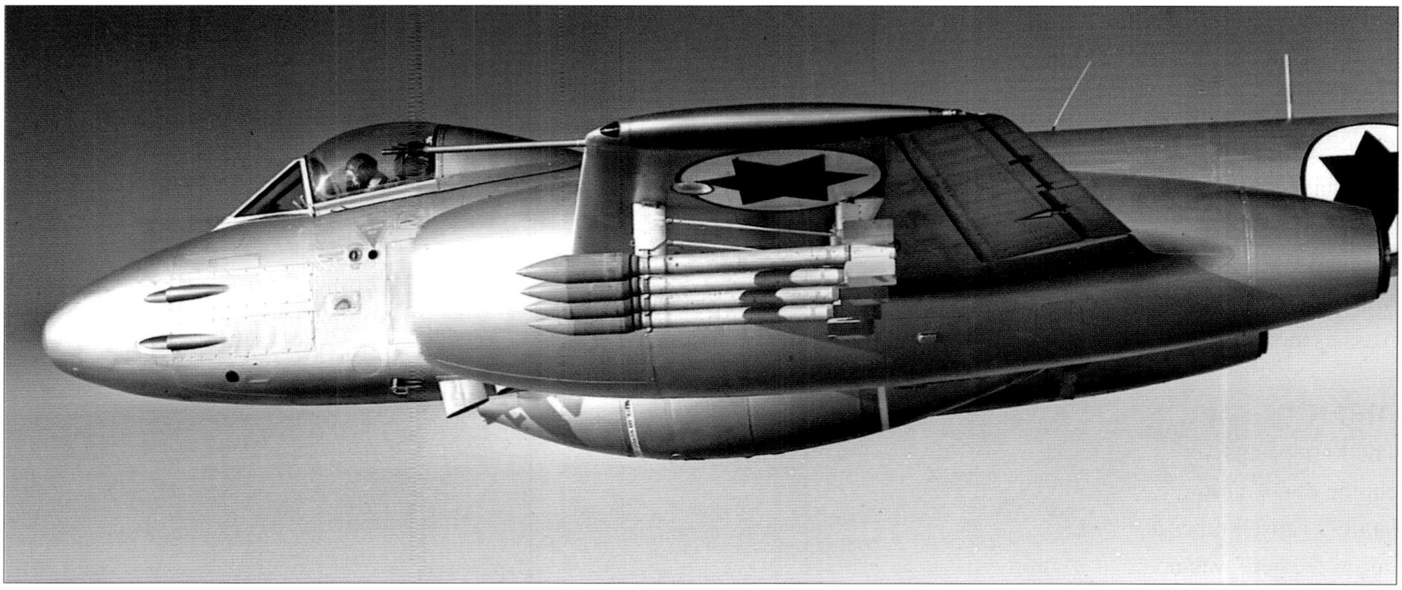

Above: Israel's Meteor F 8s fought with and defeated Egyptian Vampires in 1955. From 1956 until 1961, when they were retired, the aircraft were mainly used in the ground-attack role, with rockets (seen here) and bombs.

Above: A factory-fresh Meteor F 3, the first version produced in large quantities. This F 3 was later converted into a U 15 target drone.

Meteors were developed through a succession of fighter/ground-attack and reconnaissance models. The most important was probably the F 8, with Derwent 8 engines, a taller tail and longer fuselage. The Royal Australian Air Force used them in Korea, but by then the swept-wing Mikoyan-Gurevich MiG-15 was on the scene, and the Aussies suffered a poor kill-to-loss ratio.

DIFFICULT HANDLING

The Meteor had very poor handling at low speed with one engine out. Training for an engine failure on takeoff or landing caused more accidents than did actual engine failures. There was no radar in most models, and flying into bad weather followed by the ground caused further accidents The two-seat models lacked ejection seats, as did the early fighters. In RAF service alone, there were 890 Meteors lost in total, 150 of them in 1952 alone.

A series of night-fighter variants were produced by Armstrong Whitworth from 1949. The NF 11 had a long nose with an American-built radar inside, a second seat for a radar operator, and cannon in the outer wings rather than the fuselage. An NF 13 model suited to tropical conditions and an improved NF 14 followed. As well as the RAF, Israel, Egypt and Syria used the night-fighter Meteors. Single-seaters and trainers were exported to nine countries: Australia, Belgium, Denmark, Ecuador, Egypt, France, Israel, the Netherlands and Syria. Others were used by civilian organizations as target tugs and ejection-seat testbeds. The last fully military Meteors were probably those of the Israeli Air Force, used as trainers until 1970.

Lockheed P-80 Shooting Star

The P-80 was the United States' first successful jet fighter, although it was quickly superseded by swept-wing aircraft. It was adapted to become the most successful jet trainer ever built and eventually evolved into the Lockheed F-94 Starfire.

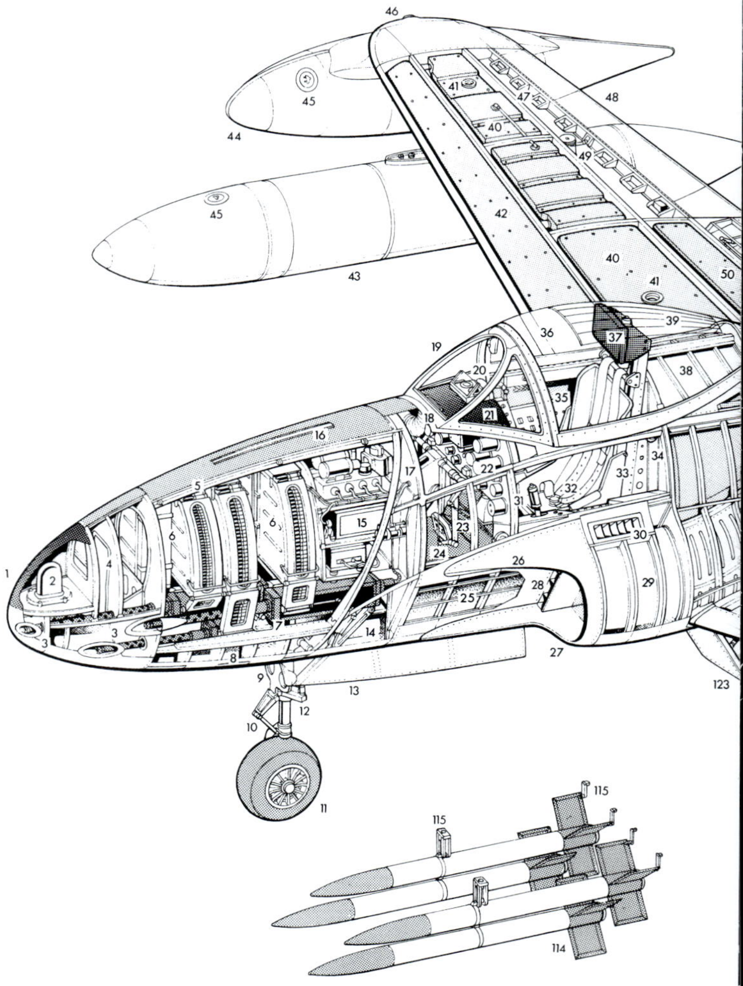

F-80C SHOOTING STAR (EARLY) SPECIFICATION

Dimensions

Length: 34 ft 5 in (10.49 m)
Height: 11 ft 3 in (3.42 m)
Wingspan: 38 ft 9 in (11.81 m)
Wing area: 237.5 sq ft (22.07 m^2

Powerplant

One Allison J33-A-23/35 turbojet rated at 4,600 lb st (20.7 kN) dry, and 5,200 lb st (23.4 kN) with water injection

Weights

Empty: 8,420 lb (3819 kg)
Gross: 12,200 lb (5534 kg)
Maximum takeoff: 16,856 lb (7646 kg)

Fuel

Fuel (normal): 425 US gal (1609 litres)
Fuel (maximum): 755 US gal (2858 litres) including drop tanks

Performance

Maximum level speed at sea level: 594 mph (956 km/h)
Maximum level speed at 25,000 ft (7620 m): 543 mph (874 km/h)
Cruising speed: 439 mph (707 km/h)
Landing speed: 122 mph (196 km/h)
Climb to altitude: climb to 25,000 ft (7620 m) in 7 minutes
Rate of climb: 6,870 ft (2094 m) per minute
Service ceiling: 46,800 ft (14,265 m)

Range

Range: 825 miles (1328 km)
Maximum range: 1,380 miles (222[illegible] km)

Armament

Four 0.50-in (12.7-mm) Colt-Browning M3 machine guns each with 300 rounds, plus ten 5-in (127-mm) HVARs or two 1,000-lb (454-kg) bombs

Cutaway Key

1 Nose antenna fairing
2 D/F loop aerial
3 Machine-gun muzzles
4 Oxygen tank
5 Nose compartment access panel
6 Port and starboard ammunition boxes, 300 rounds per gun
7 0.5-in (12.7-mm) machine guns
8 Spent cartridge case and link ejector chutes
9 Landing and taxiing lamps
10 Nosewheel leg torque scissors
11 Nosewheel
12 Steering linkage
13 Nosewheel doors
14 Retraction strut
15 Radio and electrical equipment bay
16 External canopy-release handle
17 Cockpit front bulkhead
18 Windscreen heater duct
19 Bulletproof windscreen panel
20 Reflector gunsight
21 Instrument panel shroud
22 Instrument panel
23 Rudder pedals
24 Cockpit floor level
25 Nosewheel bay
26 Intake lip fairing
27 Port air intake
28 Boundary layer bleed air duct
29 Intake ducting
30 Boundary layer air exit louvres
31 Engine throttle control
32 Safety harness
33 Pilot's ejection seat
34 Cockpit rear bulkhead
35 Starboard side console panel
36 Sliding cockpit canopy cover
37 Ejection seat headrest
38 Canopy aft decking
39 D/F sense antenna
40 Starboard wing fuel tanks
41 Fuel filler caps
42 Leading-edge tank
43 Fletcher-type tip tank, capacity 265 US gal (1003 litres)
44 Tip tank, capacity 165 US gal (625 litres)
45 Tip-tank filler cap
46 Starboard navigation light
47 Aileron balance weights
48 Starboard aileron
49 Aileron hinge control

50 Trailing-edge fuel tank
51 Starboard split trailing-edge flap
52 Flap control links
53 Fuselage fuel tank, total internal capacity 657 US gal (2487 litres)
54 Fuselage main longeron
55 Centre fuselage frames
56 Intake trunking
57 Main undercarriage wheel well
58 Wing spar attachment joints
59 Pneumatic reservoir
60 Hydraulic accumulator
61 Control access panel
62 Spring-loaded intake pressure relief doors
63 Allison J33-A-23 centrifugal-flow turbojet engine
64 Rear fuselage break point
65 Rear fuselage attachment bolts (three)
66 Elevator control rods
67 Jet pipe bracing cable
68 Fin-root fillet
69 Elevator control link
70 Starboard tailplane
71 Starboard elevator
72 Fin construction
73 Pitot tube
74 Fintip communications antenna fairing
75 Rudder mass balance
76 Rudder construction
77 Fixed tab
78 Elevator and rudder hinge control
79 Tail navigation light
80 Jet pipe nozzle
81 Elevator tabs
82 Port elevator construction
83 Elevator mass balance
84 Tailplane construction
85 Fin/tailplane attachment joints
86 Tailplane fillet fairing
87 Jet pipe mounting rail
88 Rear fuselage frame and stringer construction
89 Gyrosyn radio compass flux valve
90 Fuselage skin plating
91 Jet pipe support frame
92 Trailing-edge wingroot fillet
93 Flap drive motor
94 Port split trailing-edge flap
95 Flap shroud ribs
96 Trailing-edge fuel tank bay
97 Rear spar
98 Trailing-edge ribs
99 Port aileron tab
100 Aileron hinge control
101 Upper-skin panel aileron hinge line
102 Aileron construction
103 Wingtip fairing construction
104 Tip tank
105 Port navigation light
106 Tip-tank mounting and jettison control
107 Detachable lower wing-skin panels
108 Port wing fuel-tank bays
109 Inter-tank bay ribs
110 Front spar
111 Corrugated leading-edge inner skin
112 Port stores pylon
113 1,000-lb (454-kg) HE bomb
114 5-in (127-mm) HVAR ground-attack rockets (10 rockets maximum load)
115 HVAR mountings
116 Port mainwheel
117 Mainwheel doors
118 Wheel brake pad
119 Main undercarriage leg strut
120 Retraction jack
121 Upper skin panel wing stringers
122 Wingroot leading-edge extension
123 Port ventral airbrake

"The name 'Shooting Star' fit the P-80 well. I felt that I was riding on a shooting star, that all my training and flying up to now were to prepare me for this airplane."
– Don Lopez, USAAF test pilot

FACTS

- Shooting Stars were the first U.S. jets to see operational service.
- Early P-80s had no ejection seats and a number of wartime aces were killed in test flying accidents.
- Many F-80s ended their careers by being turned into QF-80 pilotless drones, to act as targets and take air samples from atomic test sites.

P-80 SHOOTING STAR – VARIANTS

EF-80: Prone-pilot test aircraft.

XP-80: Prototype, one built.

XP-80A: Second prototype variant, two built.

YP-80A: 12 pre-production aircraft built.

XF-14: One built from YP-80A order. USAAF photo-reconnaissance prototype.

P-80A: 344 block 1-LO aircraft; 180 block 5-LO aircraft. Block 5 and all subsequent Shooting Stars were natural metal finish.

F-80A: USAF designation of P-80A.

EF-80: Modified to test "prone pilot" cockpit positions.

F-14A: Conversions from P-80A, all redesignated FP-80A.

XFP-80A: Modified P-80A 44-85201 with hinged nose for camera equipment.

F-80A: Test aircraft with twin 0.5-in (12.7-mm) machine guns in oblique mount (similar to World War II German Schräge Musik), to study the ability to attack Soviet bombers from below.

F-80: With Schräge Musik configuration at full elevation.

FP-80A: 152 block 15-LO; operational photo-reconnaissance aircraft.

RF-80A: USAF designation of FP-80A; 66 F-80As modified to RF-80A standard.

ERF-80A: Modified P-80A 44-85042 with experimental nose contour.

XP-80B: Reconfigured P-80A with improved J-33 engine. One model built as a prototype for the P-80B.

P-80B: 209 block 1-LO; 31 block 5-LO; first model fitted with ejection seat.

F-80B: USAF designation of P-80B.

XP-80R: Modification of XP-80B to racer.

P-80C: 162 block 1-LO; 75 block 5-LO; 561 block 10-LO.

F-80C: USAF designation. Major P-80 production version.

RF-80: Upgraded photo-reconnaissance plane.

DF-80A: F-80As converted into drone directors.

QF-80A/QF-80C/QF-80F: Project Bad Boy F-80 conversions to target drones.

TP-80C: First designation for TF-80C trainer prototype.

TF-80C: Prototype for T-33.

TO-1: US Navy variant of F-80C.

LOCKHEED P-80

"Salty Dog" was an F-80C flown by Captain Francis Clark of the 35th Fighter-Bomber Squadron, who shot down a North Korean Yak-9 in one of the opening engagements of the Korean War on 17 July 1950. The Shooting Star was able to deal with North Korean piston-engined aircraft such as the Yak-9 and the Il-10, but 14 aircraft were lost in air combat versus claims of six MiG-15s. The F-80 had a poor gunsight for air combat and was much less agile than the MiG, proving better suited to the ground-attack role. The F-80C had an ejection seat, unlike the older F-80As and RF-80As that served in small numbers in Korea.

The Unites States lagged behind Europe in jet aircraft development during World War II. The Bell XP-59 Airacomet flew in October 1942, before the Gloster Meteor, but was something of a dead end and Bell did not have the capacity to continue development.

In the spring of 1943, Lockheed offered its own design, which was accepted by the USAAF, which called for a flyable prototype in 180 days. Designer Clarence "Kelly" Johnson assembled a top team of engineers and began work in a warehouse in Burbank, Los Angeles. This was the start of the famous "Skunk Works," which was to develop many successful combat and reconnaissance aircraft over the years.

Above: The P-80 pilot's view was dominated by the large gunsight, which proved inadequate for use in air combat at jet speeds.

PROTOTYPE AND DEVELOPMENT

The bottle-green XP-80 prototype, named "Lulu Belle," flew from Muroc Dry Lake (later to become Edwards Air Force Base) in January 1944, only 143 days after the go-ahead. Its appearance was little different to all the P-80s and F-80s to follow, although after early testing the wing and tail tips were rounded off in a move to improve stability. The XP-80 was powered by a British engine, the Halford H.1B, supplied as a goodwill gesture. The following aircraft used the General Electric I-40, a licence-built Whittle engine later mass-produced as the J33 by both GE and Allison. Four YP-80A development aircraft were sent to Europe in late 1944 and two went on to Italy, where they flew a few operational missions before the war's end, although they never met any opposition.

The P-80A was the first major production version. Armament was less than most U.S. piston-engined wartime fighters – four 0.50-in machine guns, with the ability to carry a couple of bombs. The P-80B introduced the first ejection seat in a production U.S. aircraft, as well as other improvements. In June 1948, the new United States Air Force revised its designation system, exchanging "P" for "pursuit" for "F" for "fighter." The P-80C was heavier and more powerful, and the main U.S. jet aircraft in Asia at the time of the outbreak of the Korean War.

F-80s destroyed several North Korean Il-10 propeller-driven attack aircraft in some of the first aerial action of the war in July 1950, and helped to win battlefield air superiority until that situation was reversed with the introduction of Soviet-built MiG-15s in November. The F-80 soon scored the first victory in aerial combat between two jet-propelled

Above: The XP-80R was a modified P-80B used to set the first speed record of more than 1,000 km/h (623 mph) in June 1947.

Above: The F-80 was used for the first U.S. jet display team, the "Acrojets," from 1948 to 1950. These aircraft all have their ventral airbrakes deployed.

aircraft when Lieutenant Russell Brown shot down a MiG-15 over Korea, but generally the MiG outclassed the Shooting Star, which was largely relegated to ground-attack missions.

TWO-SEAT CONVERSION

The F-80 was supplied to a number of Latin American air forces from the late 1940s, including those of Peru, Uruguay and Chile, but was otherwise not widely exported. The T-33 trainer, however, a straightforward two-seat conversion of the F-80, was a huge export success. More than 30 nations used T-33s and, despite its fixed armament of only two machine guns, the aircraft were sometimes used as fighters. While the last F-80s were retired by Uruguay in the 1970s, T-33s continue to serve with a handful of nations.

A development of the T-33 was the Lockheed F-94, which entered service in 1950. The YF-94 prototypes were rebuilt T-33 airframes, but later models diverged from the original design. The ultimate F-94C Starfire had a new wing and tail, and large fixed wingtip tanks and mid-wing rocket pods, as well as rockets and radar mounted in the nose and an afterburning J33 engine. F-94s served only with the USAF's Air Defense Command.

De Havilland Vampire and Venom

The Vampire, the second jet fighter to enter service with the Royal Air Force, may not have seen active combat in World War II, but it achieved several important aviation milestones. The Venom was developed from the Vampire and was intended to be its replacement.

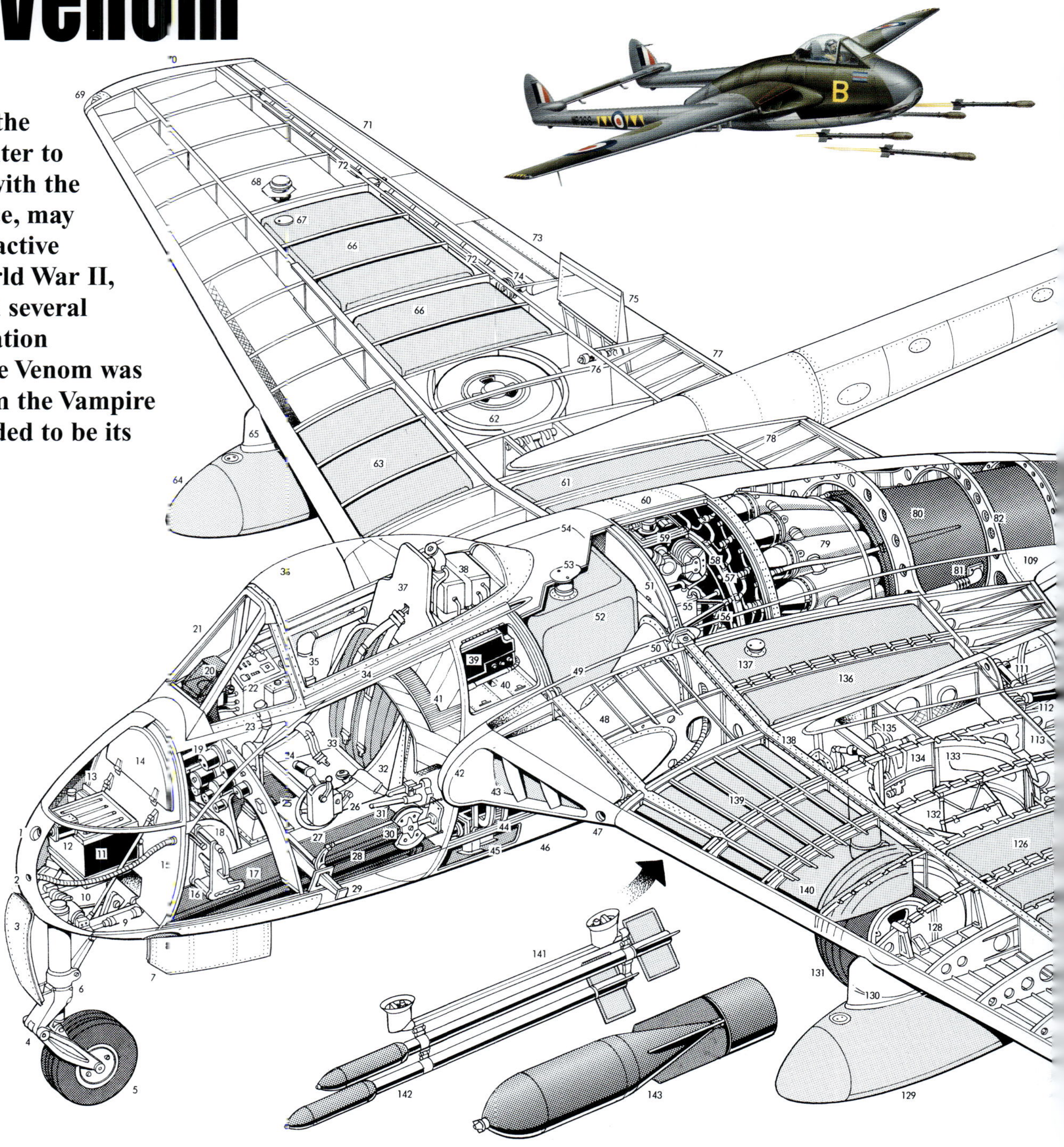

Cutaway Key

1 Ciné camera port
2 Cockpit fresh air intake
3 Nosewheel leg door
4 Pivoted axle nosewheel suspension
5 Anti-shimmy nosewheel tyre
6 Nose undercarriage leg strut
7 Nosewheel door
8 Cannon muzzle blast trough
9 Nosewheel hydraulic jack
10 Nose undercarriage pivot fixing
11 Radio
12 Gun camera
13 Windscreen fluid de-icing reservoir
14 Armoured instrument access panel
15 Cockpit front bulkhead
16 Rudder pedals
17 Cockpit floor level
18 Nosewheel housing
19 Instrument panel
20 Reflector gunsight
21 Windscreen panels
22 Side console switch panel
23 Control column
24 Engine throttle
25 Tailplane trim handwheel
26 Undercarriage and flap selector levers
27 Control linkage
28 Cannon barrels beneath cockpit floor
29 Pull-out boarding step
30 Control system cable compensator
31 Emergency hydraulic handpump
32 Pilot's seat
33 Safety harness
34 Sliding canopy rails
35 Cockpit heater
36 Cockpit canopy cover
37 Pilot's head and back armour
38 Hydraulic system reservoir
39 Radio equipment bay
40 Ammunition tanks (150 rounds per gun)
41 Plywood/balsa/plywood fuselage skinning
42 Boundary layer splitter
43 Port engine air intake
44 Ventral gun bay (4 x 20-mm Hispano cannon)
45 Spent cartridge case and link ejector chute
46 Cannon bay access panel
47 Cockpit heating and pressurizing intake
48 Intake ducting
49 Fuselage/front spar attachment joint
50 Fuselage/main spar attachment joint
51 Engine bay fire wall
52 Fuselage fuel tank (total internal system capacity 480 US gal/1818 litres)
53 Fuel filler cap
54 Wooden skin section fabric covering
55 Cockpit air heat exchanger
56 Engine bearer struts
57 de Havilland Goblin DGn 2 centrifugal-flow turbojet
58 Cabin blower
59 Engine accessories
60 Engine bay access panels
61 Starboard wingroot fuel tank

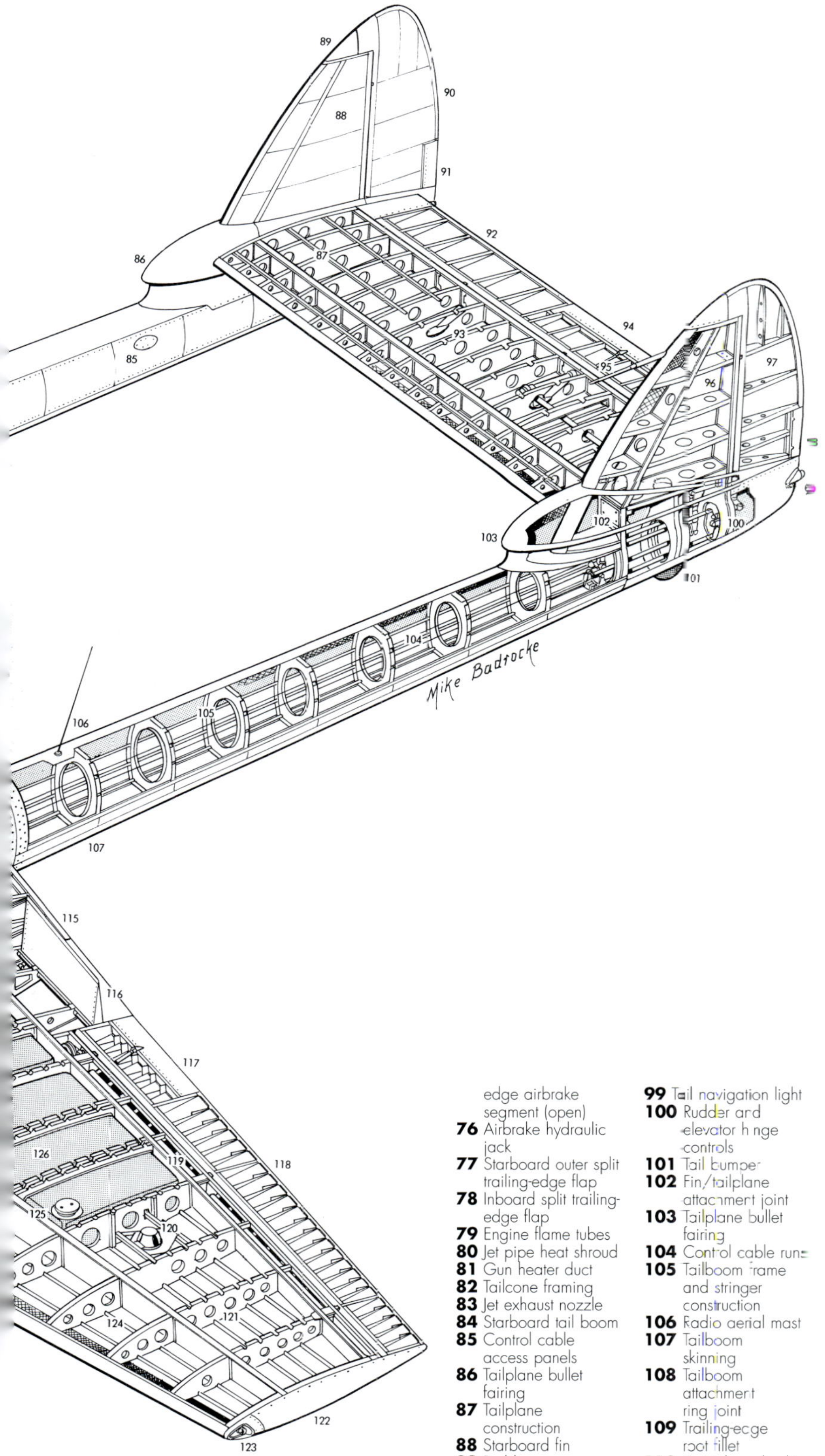

VAMPIRE F MK III SPECIFICATION

Dimensions

Length: 30 ft 9 in (9.37 m)
Height: 8 ft 10 in (2.69 m)
Wingspan: 40 ft (12.19 m)
Wing area: 266 sq ft (24.7 m²)
Wing loading: 39.4 lb/sq ft (192 kg/m²)

Powerplant

One de Havilland Goblin 2 centrifugal-flow turbojet rated at 3,100 lb st ([illegible] kN)

Weights

Empty: 7,134 lb (3236 kg)
Maximum takeoff: 12,[illegible] lb ([illegible] kg)

Fuel

Internal fuel: 636 US gal (2409 litres)
External fuel: 240 US gal ([illegible] litres) in drop tanks

Performance

Maximum level speed at sea level: 531 mph (855 km/h)
Maximum level speed at 17,500 ft (5334 m): 525 mph (845 km/h)
Maximum level speed at 30,000 ft (9144 m): 505 mph (813 km/h)
Rate of climb at sea level: 4,375 ft (1334 m) per minute
Rate of climb at 20,000 ft (6096 m): 2,500 ft (762 m) per minute
Rate of climb at 40,000 ft (12192 m): 990 ft (302 m) per minute
Service ceiling: 43,500 ft (13259 m)
Takeoff run to 50 ft (15.24 m) at maximum weight: 3,540 ft (1079 m)
Landing run from 50 ft (15.24 m): 3,300 ft (1006 m)

Range and endurance

Range at sea level: 590 miles (949 km) at 350 mph (463 km/h)
Range at 30,000 ft (9144 m): 1145 miles (1843 km) at 350 mph (463 km/h)
Patrol duration at sea level: 2 hours at 220 mph (354 km/h)
Patrol duration at 30,000 ft (9144 m): 2 hours 35 mins at 220 mph (354 km/h)

Armament

Four 20-mm Hispano cannon mounted in the front of the lower fuselage. Ammunition of 150 rounds per gun, giving a total of 600 rounds

62 Starboard main undercarriage, retracted position
63 Leading-edge fuel tank
64 Starboard drop tank (134 US gal/509 litres)
65 Drop-tank pylon
66 Starboard wing fuel tanks
67 Fuel filler cap
68 Gyrosyn compass remote transmitter
69 Starboard navigation light
70 Wingtip fairing
71 Starboard aileron
72 Aileron mass balance weights
73 Trim tab
74 Aileron hinge control
75 Starboard trailing-edge airbrake segment (open)
76 Airbrake hydraulic jack
77 Starboard outer split trailing-edge flap
78 Inboard split trailing-edge flap
79 Engine flame tubes
80 Jet pipe heat shroud
81 Gun heater duct
82 Tailcone framing
83 Jet exhaust nozzle
84 Starboard tail boom
85 Control cable access panels
86 Tailplane bullet fairing
87 Tailplane construction
88 Starboard fin
89 Rudder mass balance
90 Starboard rudder
91 Rudder trim tab
92 Elevator construction
93 Ventral elevator mass balance weights
94 Elevator tab
95 Pitot tube
96 Port fin construction
97 Port rudder
98 Rudder trim tab
99 Tail navigation light
100 Rudder and elevator hinge controls
101 Tail bumper
102 Fin/tailplane attachment joint
103 Tailplane bullet fairing
104 Control cable runs
105 Tailboom frame and stringer construction
106 Radio aerial mast
107 Tailboom skinning
108 Tailboom attachment ring joint
109 Trailing-edge root fillet
110 Port inboard split trailing-edge flap
111 Flap interconnection
112 Hydraulic flap jack
113 False rear spar
114 Flap shroud ribs
115 Port outboard split trailing-edge flap
116 Rotating trailing-edge segment airbrake, open
117 Aileron tab
118 Port aileron construction
119 Aileron mass balance weights
120 Retractable landing/taxiing lamp
121 Wingrib and stringer construction
122 Wingtip fairing
123 Port navigation light
124 Leading-edge nose ribs
125 Fuel filler cap
126 Port wing main fuel tanks
127 Fuel tank interconnection
128 Pylon attachment [illegible]
129 Port 134-US gal (509-litre) drop tank
130 Drop-tank pylon
131 Port mainwheel
132 Mainwheel door actuating linkage
133 Port mainwheel bay
134 Retraction linkages and locks
135 Main undercarriage leg strut pivot fixing
136 Wingroot fuel tank
137 Fuel filler cap
138 Main spar
139 Wing stringers
140 Leading-edge fuel tank
141 Rocket launcher rail
142 60-lb (27-kg) unguided ground-attack rocket
143 500-lb (227-kg) HE bomb

"As used by the RAF, the single-seat Vampires were one of the few series-produced jet fighters to not have ejection seats."

Above: The first production Vampire was the F.1. The example seen here is carrying two underwing drop tanks.

FACTS

- The Vampire had a wooden fuselage covered with doped fabric, but the wings and tail section were mainly aluminium.
- In 1948, the Vampire became the first jet aircraft to cross the Atlantic Ocean.
- The Vampire was also the first jet aircraft to land on and take off from an aircraft carrier.

DE HAVILLAND DH 100 VAMPIRE – VARIANTS

DH 100: Three prototypes.

Mk I: Single-seat fighter version for the RAF.

Mk II: Three prototypes, with Rolls-Royce Nene turbojet engine.

F 3: Single-seat fighter for the RAF.

Mk IV: Nene-engined project, not built.

FB 5: Single-seat fighter-bomber version.

FB 6: Single-seat fighter-bomber. Powered by a Goblin 3 turbojet.

Mk 8: Ghost-engined, one conversion from Mk 1.

FB 9: Tropicalized fighter-bomber through air-conditioning a Mk 5.

Mk 10 or DH 113 Vampire: Goblin-powered two-seat prototype.

NF 10: Two-seat RAF night-fighter version.

Sea Vampire Mk10: Prototype for deck trials. One conversion.

Mk 11 or DH 115 Vampire Trainer: Private venture, two-seat jet trainer prototype.

T 11: Two-seat RAF training version for the RAF.

Sea Vampire F 20: Naval version of the FB 5.

Sea Vampire Mk 21: Three aircraft converted for trials.

Sea Vampire T 22: Two-seat training version for the Royal Navy.

FB 25: FB 5 variants.

F 30: Single-seat RAAF fighter-bomber.

FB 31: Nene-engined.

F 32: One Australian conversion with air-conditioning.

T 33: Two-seat training version. Powered by the Goblin turbojet.

T 34: Two-seat training version for the Royal Australian Navy.

T 34A: Vampire T 34s fitted with ejector seats.

T 35: Modified two-seat training version.

T 35A: T33 conversions to T35 configuration.

FB 50: Exported to Sweden as the J 28B.

FB 51: Export prototype (one conversion) to France.

FB 52: Export version of Mk 6.

FB 52A: Single-seat fighter-bomber for the Italian Air Force.

FB 53: Single-seat fighter-bomber for France's Armée de l'Air as the Sud-Est SE 535 Mistral.

NF 54: Export version of Vampire NF 10 for the Italian Air Force.

T 55: Export version of the DH 115 trainer.

DE HAVILLAND VENOM FB MK 4

The Venom was a development of the Vampire with numerous refinements. Obvious recognition features were the swept-wing leading edge and the wingtip fuel tanks. Unlike the RAF's Vampires and the Mk 1 Venom, the FB 4 model, illustrated, had an ejection seat. This FB 4 wears the "Suez" stripes applied to all British and French tactical aircraft as a recognition feature during the Suez Campaign in October 1956, when Venoms were flown from Cyprus and Jordan. It carries eight rocket projectiles (RPs) on rails under the intakes. In 1957, Venom WR410 went on to No. 6 Squadron at RAF Benson, Oxfordshire. It ended its career in 1960, being struck off at RAF Eastleigh (Nairobi), Kenya.

Above: The FB 5 was the definitive RAF Vampire version. The ports for the four 20-mm Hispano cannon can be clearly seen in this view.

While Gloster worked on the twin-engined Meteor, de Havilland was designing a very different single-engined fighter based around the Halford H.1 centrifugal-flow engine. This was another design by Frank Whittle, differing from the axial-flow engines of the Meteor in having a large impeller fan with combustion chambers arranged around the outside, which gave it a large diameter.

The prototype DH 100 was first flown in September 1943, but the second aircraft was delayed when its intended engine was sent to the United States to replace one Lockheed had damaged in early trials of the XP-80. At this time, the aircraft was code-named "Spider Crab," but was officially named "Vampire" in May 1944. The H.1 engine became the de Havilland Goblin.

The pilot, engine and armament were all enclosed in a central pod to which the wings were attached, as were the tail booms, which were connected by a tailplane and elevator. Under the cockpit were four 20-mm Hispano cannon, in the same configuration as the Mosquito fighter-bombers. The same design team was behind both aircraft, and there were many other common features, not least that the fuselage was made of wood. The Vampire nosewheel and leg were the same as the Mosquito tailwheel, and the canopy of the two-seat T 11 was the same as a Mosquito's as well.

As used by the RAF, the single-seat Vampires were one of the few series-produced jet fighters to not have ejection seats. Later export fighters and twin-seaters usually had Martin Baker Mk 3 seats.

OPERATIONAL SQUADRONS

With priority given to getting the Meteor into service, the Vampire did not reach operational squadrons before World War II's end. The first Vampire F 1s joined RAF squadrons from March 1946 as interceptors. F 2s with the Rolls-Royce Nene engine were built under licence in Australia and France (as the Sud-Est Mistral). The F 3 had increased internal fuel and provision for drop tanks.

The definitive single-seater, the FB 5, was intended more as a fighter-bomber, with underside armour plate and pylons for rockets and bombs. As well as being supplied in large numbers to the RAF (more than 1,200), it became the basis of numerous export models such as the FB 6 (Switzerland), FB 51 (France) and FB 52 (India and others.) The FB 9 had an air-conditioner for use in hot climates and was mainly operated by the RAF, although Rhodesia (now Zimbabwe) also used them.

Vampires rarely engaged in actual air-to-air combat. Although they were nimble and delightful to fly, they were quickly outmoded by Mikoyan-Gurevich MiG-15s and other swept-wing jets. Israeli Mystéres claimed a number of Egyptian Vampires over the Sinai in1956. The RAF used them in conflicts in Aden and Kenya against various rebel groups. The rocket armament proved particularly effective in the ground-attack role.

Above: Instrumentation on the Vampire was largely the same as most wartime British fighters, including the standard six-instrument blind flying panel situated in the centre.

TWO-SEAT TRAINER

The two-seat trainer version, the T 11, was first flown in 1950. With side-by-side seats it had a wide nose, which was used for an airborne intercept (AI) radar in the NF 10 night-fighter variant, which was sold to India and Italy, as well as used by the RAF. Armament remained four cannon. T 11s and their derivatives were used by most of the export customers as jet trainers and weapons trainers.

Vampires were phased out of frontline RAF service in the 1960s, but remained with some export customers, including Switzerland, into the 1980s. In many cases, they were replaced by the DH 112 Venom, a larger and more powerful outgrowth of the Vampire design. With its thinner wing with swept leading edge and more powerful engine, the Venom was 100 mph (160 km/h) faster than the Vampire.

Above: The main visual difference between the F 1, seen here, and the FB 5 was found in the tailfin shapes.

Grumman F9F Panther and Cougar

Successor to the great Grumman "cats" of World War II, the F9F Panther was a simple but sturdy fighter-bomber. Its low performance in comparison with the Mikoyan-Gurevich MiG-15 and USAF North American F-86 Sabre was corrected by adding swept wings, to make the F9F-8 Cougar.

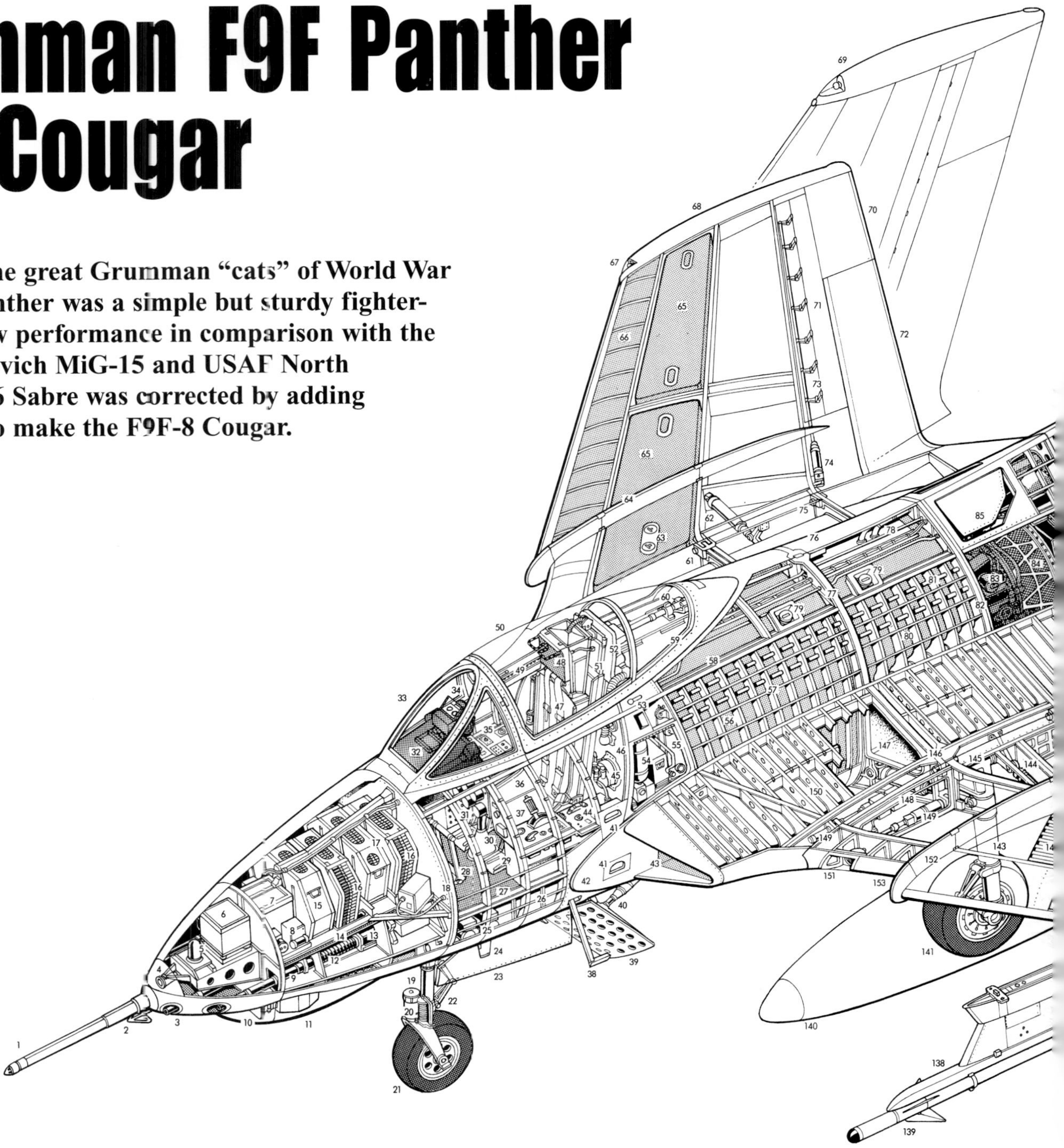

Cutaway Key

1 Flight refuelling probe
2 Deck barricade deflector
3 Cannon muzzles
4 Gun ranging radar antenna (AN/APG-30A)
5 D/F loop aerial
6 D/F transmitter/receiver
7 Battery
8 Voltage regulators
9 Cannon barrels
10 UHF homing adapter antenna
11 Antenna housing
12 Cannon recoil spring
13 M3 20-mm cannon (four)
14 Nose cone withdrawal rail
15 Inboard gun ammunition tanks (190 rpg)
16 Ammunition feed chutes
17 Outboard gun ammunition tanks (190 rpg)
18 Armoured cockpit front pressure bulkhead
19 Nose undercarriage leg strut
20 Shimmy damper
21 Nosewheel
22 Torque scissor links
23 Nosewheel doors
24 VHF aerial on starboard nosewheel door
25 Alternators
26 Nosewheel bay
27 Cockpit floor level
28 Rudder pedals
29 Ejection seat footrests
30 Control column
31 Instrument panel
32 Instrument panel shroud
33 Bulletproof windscreen
34 Radar gunsight (Aero 5D-1)
35 Starboard side console panel
36 Pilot's ejection seat
37 Engine throttle control
38 Retractable boarding step
39 Perforated ventral airbrake (port and starboard)
40 Airbrake hydraulic jack
41 Kick-in boarding steps
42 Boundary layer splitter plate
43 Port air intake
44 Cockpit port side console panel
45 Pressurization and air-conditioning valves
46 Cockpit rear pressure bulkhead
47 Safety harness
48 Face-blind firing handle
49 Sliding canopy rail
50 Cockpit canopy cover
51 Ejection seat launch rails
52 Pilot's back armour
53 Canopy external latch
54 Oxygen bottle
55 Equipment bay access door
56 Forward fuselage fuel tank
57 Fuselage frame and stringer construction
58 Main longeron
59 Canopy aft glazing
60 Sliding canopy jack
61 Wing-fold spar hinge joint
62 Wing-fold hydraulic jack
63 Fuel filler cap
64 Starboard wing fence
65 Wing main fuel tanks (total internal capacity 1,063 U.S. gal/4024 litres)
66 Leading-edge integral fuel tank
67 Starboard navigation light
68 Wingtip fairing
69 Starboard wing folded position
70 Fixed portion of trailing edge
71 Lateral control spoilers divided lengthwise between "flaperons" (forward) and "flaperettes" (aft)
72 Starboard flap
73 Spoiler hinge control links
74 Spoiler hydraulic jack
75 Rear spar hinge joint
76 Fuselage skin plating
77 Wing spar/fuselage main frame
78 Fuel system piping
79 Fuel filler caps
80 Fuselage rear fuel tank
81 Control cable ducts
82 Rear spar/fuselage main frame
83 Engine accessory compartment
84 Compressor intake screen
85 Supplementary air intake doors (open)
86 Pratt & Whitney J48-P-8A centrifugal-flow turbojet
87 Rear fuselage break point (engine removal)
88 Engine mounting main frame
89 Engine flame cans
90 Secondary air intake door open
91 Fireproof bulkhead
92 Jet pipe heat shroud
93 Water injection tank
94 Water filler cap
95 Fuselage/fin root frame construction
96 Fin attachment joint
97 Tailfin construction
98 Starboard tailplane
99 Starboard elevator
100 Fin-tip VHF aerial
101 Rudder construction
102 Rudder mass balance
103 Fin/tailplane fairing
104 Tail navigation lights
105 Lower rudder segment trim tab
106 Elevator trim tab
107 Port elevator
108 Elevator horn balance
109 Port tailplane construction
110 Trimming tailplane hinge joint
111 Tailplane trim jack
112 Exhaust nozzle shroud
113 Jet exhaust nozzle

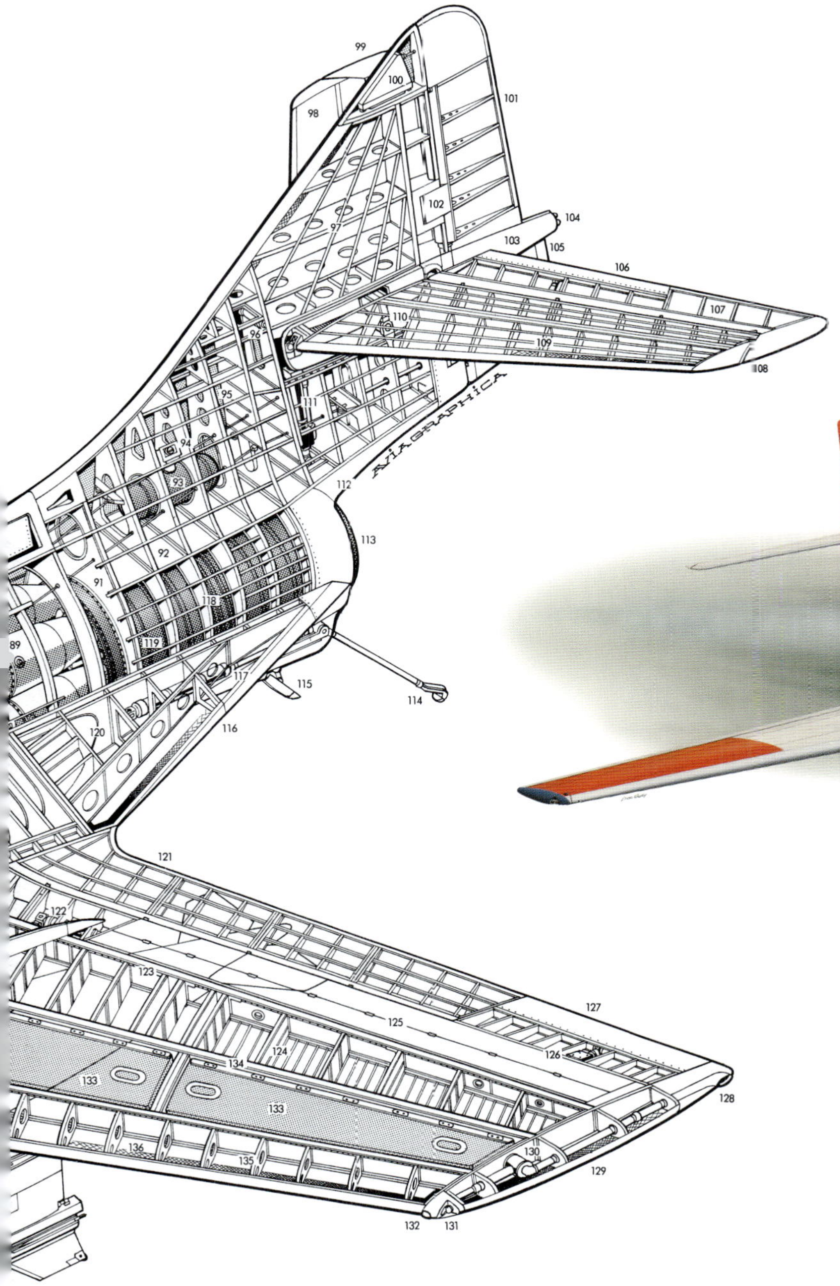

114 Sting-type deck arrester hook
115 Retractable tail bumper
116 Wingroot trailing-edge fillet
117 Arrester hook damper and retraction jack
118 Rear fuselage framing
119 Jet pipe
120 Intake duct aft fairing
121 Port Fowler flap
122 Spoiler hydraulic jack
123 Rear spar
124 Wing rib construction
125 Lateral control spoilers "flaperons" (forward) and "flaperettes" (aft)
126 Trim tab electric actuator
127 Electrically operated trim tab (port only)
128 Fuel jettison vent
129 Port wingtip fairing
130 Fuel vent valve
131 Port navigation light
132 Fuel venting ram air intake
133 Port wing main fuel tanks
134 Main spar
135 Cambered leading-edge ribs
136 Leading-edge integral fuel tank
137 Wing ordnance pylon (four)
138 Missile launch rail
139 AIM-9B Sidewinder air-to-air missile
140 Auxiliary fuel tank (capacity 150 U.S. gal (568 litres)
141 Port mainwheel
142 Fuel-tank bay corrugated double skin
143 Main undercarriage leg strut
144 Wing-fold hydraulic jack
145 Main undercarriage pivot housing
146 Main spar hinge joint
147 Intake duct
148 Undercarriage hydraulic retraction jack
149 Wing-fold locking cylinders
150 Intake duct framing
151 Landing/taxiing lamp
152 Port wing fence
153 Leading-edge dogtooth

F9F-2 PANTHER SPECIFICATION

Dimensions

Length: 37 ft 5⅜ in (11.41 m)
Height: 11 ft 4 in (3.45 m)
Span: 38 ft (11.58 m)
Span (folded): 23 ft 5 in (7.14 m)
Wing area: 250 sq ft (23.23 m²)

Powerplant

One Pratt & Whitney J42-P-4, P-6 or P-8 turbojet rated at 5,000 lb (22.24 kN) thrust dry, or 5,750 lb (25.58 kN) thrust with water injection

Weights

Empty: 9,303 lb (4220 kg)
Loaded: 16,450 lb (7462 kg)
Maximum takeoff: 19,494 lb (8842 kg)

Performance

Maximum speed: 575 mph (925 km/h) at sea level
Cruising speed: 487 mph (784 km/h)
Climb rate: 6,000 ft (1829 m) per minute
Service ceiling: 44,600 ft (13,594 m)
Normal range: 1,353 miles (2177 km)

Armament

Four 20-mm cannon, each with 190 rounds per gun. Most F9F-2s were later modified with four racks under each wing; the inner pair was stressed to carry a 1,000-lb (454-kg) bomb or 150-U.S. gal (568-litre) drop tank, while the outer racks could each carry a 250-lb (114-kg) bomb or a 5-in (127-mm) HVAR. Total external load was 3,000 lb (1361 kg)

"The Panther was just a sweet-flying airplane, like most Grummans. And tough, like all of them."
– Richard Bradberry, F9F Panther pilot in Korea

Above: A formation of four two-seat Cougars shows off the aircrafts' swept wings and tailplanes, which replaced the straight units on the Panther.

FACTS

- In November 1950, the F9F Panther became the first carrier-based jet to score an aerial combat victory.
- Panthers were used by the U.S. Navy, U.S. Marine Corps and Argentine Navy.
- Two-seat Cougars were used by the U.S. Navy as advanced training aircraft up to 1974.

GRUMMAN F9F PANTHER – VARIANTS

XF9F-2: The first two prototypes.

XF9F-3: The third prototype.

F9F-2: First production version, powered by J42 engine.

F9F-2B: Version fitted with underwing racks for bombs and rockets. All F9F-2s were eventually so modified, and the B designation was dropped.

F9F-2P: Unarmed photo-reconnaissance version used in Korea.

F9F-3: Allison J33-powered version produced as insurance against the failure of the J42. All converted to J42 power later.

XF9F-4: Prototype used in the development of the F9F-4.

F9F-4: Version with longer fuselage with greater fuel load and powered by J33 engine. Most re-engined with J42 engines. F9F-4s were the first aircraft to successfully employ blown air, extracted from between the engine's compressor and combustion chambers, to energize the slot flaps, thus achieving a decrease in stalling speed of 9 knots (17 km/h) for takeoff and 7 knots (13 km/h) on power approach for landing.

F9F-5: Variant of F9F-4, but powered by Pratt & Whitney J48 engine.

F9F-5P: Unarmed photo-reconnaissance version with a longer nose.

F9F-5K: After the F9F Panther was withdrawn from operational service, a number of F9F-5s were converted into unmanned target drone aircraft.

F9F-5KD: As drone directors for the F9F-5K drones. Redesignated DF-9E in 1962.

GRUMMAN F9F-2B PANTHER

The F9F-2B Panther illustrated saw combat action in Korea with the U.S. Navy, during which it was struck by ground fire and damaged. After repair it was assigned to the U.S. Marine Corps squadron VMF-311, where it wore this unique "panther's head" marking. Note the open airbrakes and the "stinger"-type tailhook. In 1958, it was supplied to the Argentine Navy, whose 1st Attack Squadron used it as a land-based fighter, becoming one of the last flying Panthers when retired in 1971. After an eventful life, it was donated to the Aero Club Bahía Blanca, and today it is stored awaiting restoration for the National Air Museum.

Due to their lower landing speeds, straight wings were preferred for most early carrier-based jets. As a result, aircraft such as the Grumman Panther and Hawker Sea Hawk had poorer air combat performance than swept-wing Mikoyan-Gurevich MiGs and North American Sabres.

The origins of the Panther, Grumman's first jet fighter, lay in a 1945 concept for the XF9F-1, a four-engined twin-seat night fighter. This proposal was scrapped in 1947 and replaced by one for a single-seat single-engined fighter, which first flew as the XF9F-2 in December 1947.

A variety of engines were proposed for or fitted to the prototypes, including the Pratt & Whitney J42, a development of the British Rolls-Royce Nene, but production F9Fs used the Pratt & Whitney J48, derived from the Rolls-Royce Tay. Range was improved by having two fixed wingtip tanks containing 120 U.S. gallons (445 litres) of fuel.

The Panther's main armament was four 20-mm cannon mounted in the nose, but eight underwing pylons allowed carriage of bombs and/or rockets. A large bubble canopy gave good all-around vision, and was often slid open for carrier takeoffs and landings, to allow easier escape in the event of a ditching. Tests with the Panther included landings on a rubber "flex deck" with the wheels up as part of a concept to save weight by eliminating the undercarriage, and a revolving nose turret holding four guns that could be pointed "off boresight" or away from the flight path.

CHANGING ROLE IN KOREA

The Panther was the most numerous carrier-based jet in the Korean War (1950–53). In early engagements, Panthers destroyed a few piston-engined Yak-9 fighters, but lost more to MiG-15s and were largely relegated to ground-attack missions, where they proved highly effective. U.S. Marine Corps squadrons also flew them from fairly austere bases on land in South Korea. Future astronaut Neil Armstrong flew

Above: With soot around its cannon barrels and airbrakes deployed, a Panther of Carrier Group 7 sits on a Korean airfield.

Above: An F9F-2 Panther of VF-71 flies over the ships of Task Force 77 off the Korean coast. Its own home was the carrier USS Bon Homme Richard.

U.S. Navy Panthers in Korea, and they were the star of the film *The Bridges at Toko-Ri*, alongside Hollywood leading lights William Holden and Mickey Rooney.

After a fairly short career, Panthers were retired from frontline service in 1956, and from reserve squadrons two years later. Two-dozen F9F-2s were sold to Argentina, whose navy used them from land bases into the early 1970s.

ENTER THE COUGAR

The Panther's uncompetitiveness as a fighter led to the quick adaptation of the airframe for swept wings. The F9F-6 shared much with the earlier versions, but had a longer fuselage and swept wings without tip tanks. It was considered different enough to be renamed "Cougar." First flying in late 1951, the Cougar entered service a year later, but was not deployed before the Korean War ended. The later F9F-8 model was lengthened again and had a nose refuelling probe and the ability to carry four AIM-9 Sidewinder missiles. The F9F-8B had provision to deliver a nuclear bomb.

There was no two-seat version of the Panther, but a version of the Cougar was built as the F9F-8T trainer, which was used as an advanced jet trainer by the U.S. Navy's Training Command until 1974, by which time the designation had changed to TF-9J. Some two-seat Cougars were used as fast forward-air-control platforms by the Marines in Vietnam, and Argentina also received two dual-control Cougars to help train Panther pilots.

Above: Wing folding was essential a feature for the Panther, so as to maximize deck space on the crowded straight-deck "Essex"-class carriers.

North American F-86 Sabre

The F-86 Sabre was the classic jet fighter of the early Cold War era. Although it was soon superseded in frontline USAF service, it went on to find use around the world in a myriad different versions.

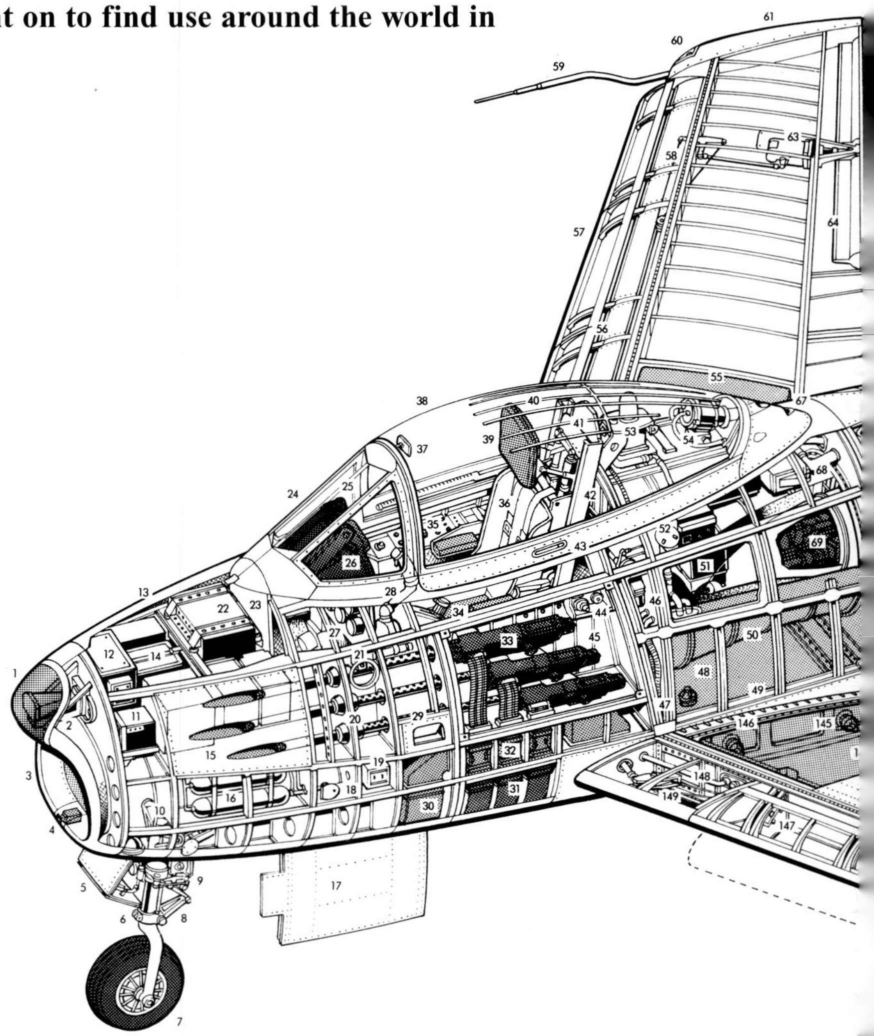

F-86E SABRE SPECIFICATION

Dimensions

Length: 37 ft (11.27 m)
Height: 14 ft (4.26 m)
Wingspan: 37 ft (11.27 m)
Wing area: 288 sq ft (26.75 m^2)

Powerplant

One General Electric J47-GE-13 turbojet rated at 5,450 lb (24.24 kN) static thrust

Weights

Empty: 10,555 lb (4788 kg)
Normal loaded: 16,346 lb (7414 kg)
Maximum takeoff: 17,806 lb (8077 kg)

Fuel

Normal internal fuel: 435 U.S. gal (1646 litres)
Maximum internal fuel: 675 U.S. gal (2555 litres)

Performance

Maximum level speed clean at 35,000 ft (10,688 m): 601 mph (967 km/h)
Maximum level speed clean at low level: 679 mph (1093 km/h)
Cruising speed: 537 mph (864 km/h)
Stalling speed: 123 mph (198 km/h)
Climb to 30,000 ft (9144 m): 6 minutes 18 seconds
Service ceiling: 47,200 ft (14,387 m)
Range: 848 miles (1365 km)
Maximum range: 1,022 miles (1645 km

Armament

Primary armament consisted of six 0.5-in (12.7-mm) Colt-Browning machine guns mounted in the forward fuselage with a total of 1,800 rounds; provision for either two 1,000-lb (454-kg) bombs or 16 0.5-in (12.7-mm) rocket projectiles mounted on underwing racks, in place of two 120-U.S. gal (454-litre) drop tanks, a variety of other ordnance loads could also be carried.

Cutaway Key

1 Radome
2 Radar antenna
3 Engine air intake
4 Gun camera
5 Nosewheel leg doors
6 Nose undercarriage leg strut
7 Nosewheel
8 Torque scissor links
9 Steering control valve
10 Nose undercarriage pivot fixing
11 Sight amplifier
12 Radio and electronics equipment bay
13 Electronics bay access panel
14 Battery
15 Gun muzzle blast troughs
16 Oxygen bottles
17 Nosewheel bay doors
18 Oxygen servicing point
19 Canopy switches
20 Machine-gun barrel mountings
21 Hydraulic system test connections
22 Radio transmitter
23 Cockpit armoured bulkhead
24 Windscreen panels
25 A-1CM radar gunsight
26 Instrument panel shroud
27 Instrument panel
28 Control column
29 Kick-in boarding step
30 Used cartridge case collector box
31 Ammunition boxes (267 rounds per gun)
32 Ammunition feed chutes
33 0.5-in (12.7-mm) Colt Browning machine guns
34 Engine throttle
35 Starboard side console panel
36 North American ejection seat
37 Rear-view mirror
38 Sliding cockpit canopy cover
39 Ejection seat headrest
40 ADF sense aerials
41 Pilot's back armour
42 Ejection-seat guide rails
43 Canopy handle
44 Cockpit pressure valves
45 Armoured side panels
46 Tailplane trim actuator
47 Fuselage/front spar main frame
48 Forward fuselage fuel tank (total internal fuel capacity 435 U.S. gal/1646 litres)
49 Fuselage lower longeron
50 Intake trunking
51 Rear radio and electronics bay
52 Canopy emergency release handle
53 ADF loop aerial
54 Cockpit pressure relief valve
55 Starboard wing fuel tank
56 Leading-edge slat guide rails
57 Starboard automatic leading-edge slat, open
58 Cable drive to aileron actuator
59 Pitot tube
60 Starboard navigation light
61 Wingtip fairing
62 Starboard aileron
63 Aileron hydraulic control unit
64 Aileron balance
65 Starboard slotted flap, down position
66 Flap guide rail
67 Upward identification light
68 Air-conditioning

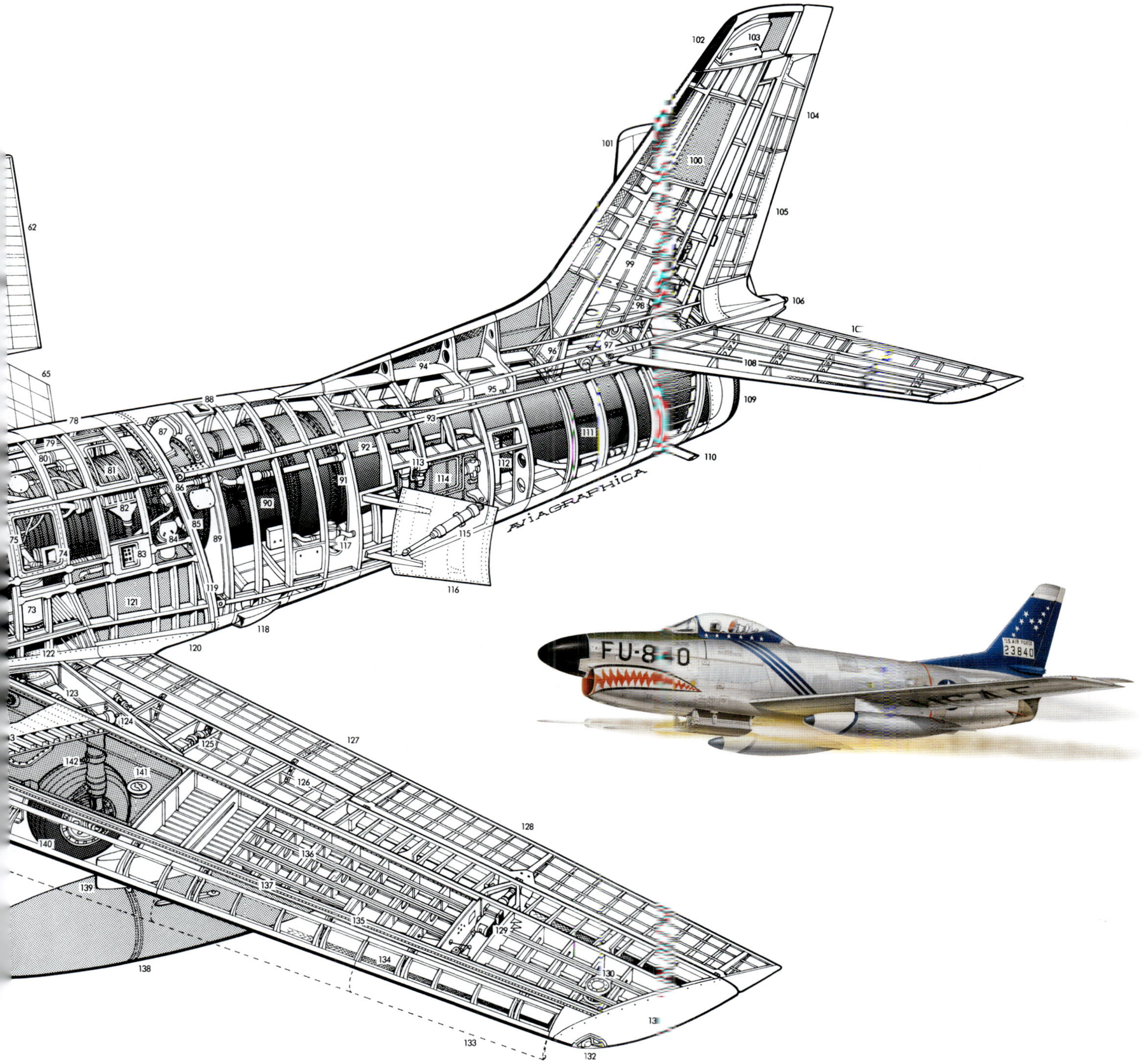

plant
69 Intake fairing starter/generator
70 Fuselage/rear spar main frame
71 Hydraulic system reservoirs
72 Longeron/main frame joint
73 Fuel filter de-icing fluid tank
74 Cooling air outlet
75 Engine equipment access panel
76 Heat exchanger exhaust duct
77 Engine suspension links
78 Fuselage skin plating
79 Engine withdrawal rail
80 Starboard side oil tank
81 General Electric J47-GE-27 turbojet
82 Bleed air system primary heat exchanger
83 Ground power connections
84 Fuel filler cap
85 Fuselage break point sloping frame (engine removal)
86 Upper longeron joint
87 Engine bay air cooling duct
88 Cooling air outlet
89 Engine firewall bulkhead
90 Engine flame cans
91 Rear fuselage framing
92 Fuel jettison pipe
93 Fuselage top longeron
94 Fin/tailplane root fillet fairing
95 Control cable duct
96 Fin spar attachment joint
97 Tailplane/rudder control cables
98 All-moving tailplane hydraulic jack
99 Tailfin construction
100 Flush HF aerial panel
101 Starboard tailplane
102 Fintip dielectric aerial fairing
103 ADF aerial
104 Rudder construction
105 Rudder trim tab
106 Tail navigation light
107 Port elevator/tailplane flap
108 All-moving tailplane construction
109 Engine exhaust nozzle
110 Fuel jettison pipe
111 Heat-shrouded jet pipe
112 Power control compensator
113 Emergency hydraulic valves
114 Air-brake housing
115 Air-brake hydraulic jack
116 Port air-brake (open)
117 Hydraulic system emergency pump
118 Cooling air intake
119 Lower longeron joint
120 Trailing-edge root fillet
121 Aft main fuel tank
122 Main undercarriage wheel bay
123 Hydraulic retraction jack
124 Main undercarriage pivot fixing
125 Hydraulic flap jack
126 Flap shroud ribs
127 Port slotted flaps
128 Port aileron construction
129 Aileron hydraulic power control unit
130 Gyro compass remote transmitter
131 Wingtip fairing
132 Port navigation light
133 Port automatic leading-edge slat, open position
134 Leading-edge slat rib construction
135 Front spar
136 Wing rib and stringer construction
137 Wing skin/leading-edge piano hinge attachment joint
138 120-US gal (454-litre) drop tank
139 Drop-tank pylon
140 Port main wheel
141 Fuel filler cap
142 Main undercarriage leg strut
143 Fuel-tank bay corrugated double skin
144 Port wing fuel tank
145 Tank interconnectors
146 Skin panel attachment joint strap
147 Slat guide rails
148 Fuel feeders
149 Aileron cable drive

"For my money, the F-86E is the greatest jet aircraft I have ever flown from a pure handling aspect. It set standards in stability and control which are still held up as ideals to attain."
– Captain Eric "Winkle" Brown, Royal Navy

FACTS

- Evidence shows that the XP-86 exceeded Mach 1 (in a dive) before the first official supersonic flight was made by the Bell X-1 rocketplane.
- USAF Sabre pilots claimed 792 enemy aircraft for 78 lost in air combat over Korea.
- Korean War–era Sabres had essentially the same armament in place as the North American P-51 Mustang.

NORTH AMERICAN F-86 SABRE – VARIANTS

XF-86: Three prototypes, originally designated XP-86, North American model NA-140.

YF-86A: This was the first prototype fitted with a General Electric J47 turbojet engine.

F-86A: North American model NA-151 and NA-161.

DF-86A: A few F-86A conversions as drone directors.

RF-86A: F-86A conversions with three cameras for reconnaissance.

F-86B: Upgraded A-model with wider fuselage and larger tires, but delivered as F-86A-5, North American model NA-152.

F-86C: Original designation for the YF-93A. North American model NA-157.

YF-86D: Prototype all-weather interceptor originally ordered as YF-95A; two built but designation changed to YF-86D. North American model NA-164.

F-86D: Production interceptor originally designated F-95A.

F-86E: Improved flight control system and an "all-flying tail." North American model NA-170 and NA-172 (essentially the F-86F airframe with the F-86E engine).

F-86E(M): Designation for ex-RAF Sabres diverted to other NATO air forces.

QF-86E: Designation for surplus RCAF Sabre Mk. Vs modified to target drones.

F-86F: Uprated engine and larger "6-3" wing without leading-edge slats. North American model NA-172.

F-86F-2: Designation for aircraft modified to carry the M39 cannon in place of the M3 0.50-calibre machine gun "six-pack."

QF-86F: Former JASDF F-86F airframes converted to drones for use as targets by the U.S. Navy.

RF-86F: F-86F-30s converted with three cameras for reconnaissance.

TF-86F: Two F-86F converted to two-seat training configuration with lengthened fuselage and slatted wings under North American model NA-204.

YF-86H: Extensively redesigned fighter-bomber model with deeper fuselage, uprated engine, longer wings and power-boosted tailplane. Two built as North American model NA-187.

F-86H: Production model with Low Altitude Bombing System (LABS) and provision for nuclear weapon. North American model NA-187 and NA-203.

QF-86H: Target conversion of 29 airframes for use at the United States' Naval Weapons Center.

F-86J: Single F-86A-5-NA flown with Orenda turbojet under North American model NA-167.

F-86E SABRE

This F-86E "Elenore 'E'" in the colours of the 25th Fighter Interceptor Squadron, 51st Fighter Wing, was flown by Major William T. Whisner from Suwon Air Base, South Korea, in 1952. Whisner was credited with 15½ victories in flying P-51s over Europe in World War II and added a further 5½ in Korea for a total of 21, although only 9½ are marked here. "Half" kills were credited when more than one pilot made damaging hits on an enemy that subsequently went down. The F-86E was an improvement on the F-86A, with an all-moving tailplane and leading-edge slats, which enhanced the aircraft's manoeuvrability, particularly at low level.

Above: The F-86F was the ultimate day-fighter Sabre with an all-moving tailplane and an unslatted "hard" wing. The excellent view from the cockpit can be seen well. A basic ranging radar was fitted in the intake lip.

Two different proposals, plus the work of wartime German scientists, led to the F-86 Sabre, one of the classic jet fighters. In 1944, North American Aviation, maker of the P-51 Mustang and B-25 Mitchell, began work on a jet fighter for the U.S. Navy. Configured with a straight wing and a nose-mounted intake, this eventually became the FJ-1 Fury, one of the U.S. Navy's first jets. The U.S. Army Air Force took an interest and ordered a similar model as the XP-86, but before it was complete captured German studies on the superiority of swept wings became available. Using this data, the XP-86 was revised, and emerged with a 35-degree swept wing and tail in 1947, flying in October.

The F-86A reached the USAF in March 1949. It was not immediately dispatched to Korea when fighting broke out in July 1950. When the Mikoyan-Gurevich MiG-15 appeared on the scene in November, Sabres were rushed to bases in the south and were soon engaging enemy jets in what became known as "MiG Alley," around the Yalu River. F-86Es with a "hard" (non-slatted) wing and F-86F fighter-bombers reached U.S. and South African squadrons by the war's end, which saw an official victory-to-loss ratio of 792 to 78 in aerial combat between USAF Sabres and the North Korean Air Force.

PROVING ITS WORTH

The MiG and Sabre were closely matched, with the former having a better climb rate and performance at high altitude, and heavier armament. The Sabre was a more stable gun platform and performed better at lower levels. Crucially, the American pilots were better trained than their North Korean,

Above: "Karen's Kart" was an F-86E assigned to the USAF's 51st Fighter Wing at Suwon Air Base, South Korea. The coloured nose stripe denotes that this is the wing commander's aircraft.

Russian and Chinese adversaries. In fact, the Sabre was probably the most successful jet fighter in terms of both aerial victories and foreign sales and production.

Twenty-two users outside of the United States acquired new American-built F-86s, and they were also built under licence by Canada, Australia and Japan. Canadian-built Sabres were supplied to several countries, including the United Kingdom, West Germany and South Africa. Some were even sold to the United States. Fifteen countries used the radar-equipped F-86D, K and L "Sabre Dog" variants. Pakistani and Taiwanese Sabres also saw air combat. In 1958, Taiwan's F-86s made the first use of guided AAMs in combat, destroying several Chinese MiGs with AIM-9s in fighting over disputed islands.

The F-86D "Sabre Dog" was developed for Air Defense Command, with a Hughes radar in a prominent nose radome and "Mighty Mouse" rockets in a retractable tray under the forward fuselage. The F-86K, built mainly for export, had 30-mm cannon insead. The F-86H, a dedicated strike variant, had a much deeper fuselage and provision for atomic weapons.

MAKING THE SABRE THEIR OWN

Both Australia and Canada developed their own versions of the Sabre. Canadair-built Sabres included the Mk 3, Mk 5 and Mk 6, each with versions of the Canadian-designed Orenda engine. Australia's Commonwealth Aircraft Corporation (CAC) built over 100 "Avon Sabres" in three different marks. To accommodate the Rolls-Royce Avon engine, fuselage depth was increased and the intake widened. Twin 30-mm ADEN cannon were the standard armament. The Mk 31 and 32 versions could carry AIM-9s. Some were later supplied to Malaysia and Indonesia.

Above: The Sabre's cockpit was somewhat cluttered. The large instrument above the control column is the engine temperature gauge.

Lockheed F-94 Starfire

A quickly-developed counter to new Soviet strategic bombers, Lockheed's F-94 was one of the only U.S. jet interceptors of the 1950s to see active combat. Despite this, its career was short-lived because purpose-designed supersonic aircraft were not far behind.

F-94C STARFIRE SPECIFICATION

Dimensions

Length: 44 ft 6 in (13.56 m)
Height: 14 ft 11 in (4.55 m)
Wingspan: 37 ft 4 in (11.38 m)
Wing area: 232.8 sq ft (21.628 m²)

Powerplant

One Pratt & Whitney J48-P-5, -5A or -7A turbojet, rated at 8,750 lb (38.91 kN) thrust with afterburner

Weights

Empty: 12,708 lb (5764 kg)
Loaded: 18,300 lb (8301 kg)
Maximum takeoff: 24,184 lb (10,970 kg)

Performance

Maximum speed at sea level: 640 mph (1030 km/h)
Cruising speed: 493 mph (793 km/h)
Initial rate of climb: 7,980 ft/min (2432 m/min)
Service ceiling: 51,400 ft (15,665 m)
Normal range: 805 miles (1295 km)
Maximum range: 1,275 miles (2050 km)

Armament

Twenty-four 2.75-in (6.99-cm) folding-fin aircraft rockets (FFARs) in four clusters of six arranged around the nose, plus (from the 100th aircraft) 12 FFARs in a pod on the leading edge of each wing

Cutaway Key

1 Radome
2 Radar scanner
3 Radar tracking mechanism
4 Electronics cooling air intake
5 Rocket door hydraulic jack
6 Retractable rocket-launching doors
7 Pitot tube
8 Nose compartment rocket-launching tubes, 24 x 2.75-in (7-cm) folding-fin rockets
9 Battery bay
10 AN/APG-40 radar transmitter
11 AN/APX-6 radar unit
12 Flight data computer
13 AN/ARC-27 radio
14 Nosewheel pivot mounting
15 Landing/taxiing lamps
16 Torque scissors
17 Nosewheel
18 Nose undercarriage leg strut
19 Steering jack and shimmy damper
20 Nosewheel doors
21 Electrical equipment bay
22 Oxygen bottles, port and starboard
23 Nose compartment upper beam construction
24 Front pressure bulkhead
25 Rudder pedals
26 Windscreen demisting air blower
27 Instrument panel
28 Instrument panel shroud
29 Windscreen framing
30 N-3C standby reflector sight
31 Control column
32 Engine throttle control
33 Pressure refuelling connection
34 Air-conditioning plant
35 Port engine air intake
36 Boundary layer bleed air duct
37 Cockpit framing
38 Pilot's ejection seat
39 Cockpit canopy cover
40 Ejection seat headrest
41 AN/ARN-6 radio compass loop antenna
42 Radar operator's AN/APG-40 indicator
43 Accelerometer
44 Intake ducting
45 Side console panel
46 Cockpit pressurization valve
47 Rear pressure bulkhead
48 Radar operator's blackout hood, folded
49 Radar viewing scope
50 Canopy-mounted ADF sense aerial
51 Radar operator's ejection seat
52 Starboard wing main fuel tanks: total one-wing capacity (with 53 and 66), 129 U.S. gal/488 litres)
53 Leading-edge tank
54 Starboard wing rocket pod, 12 x

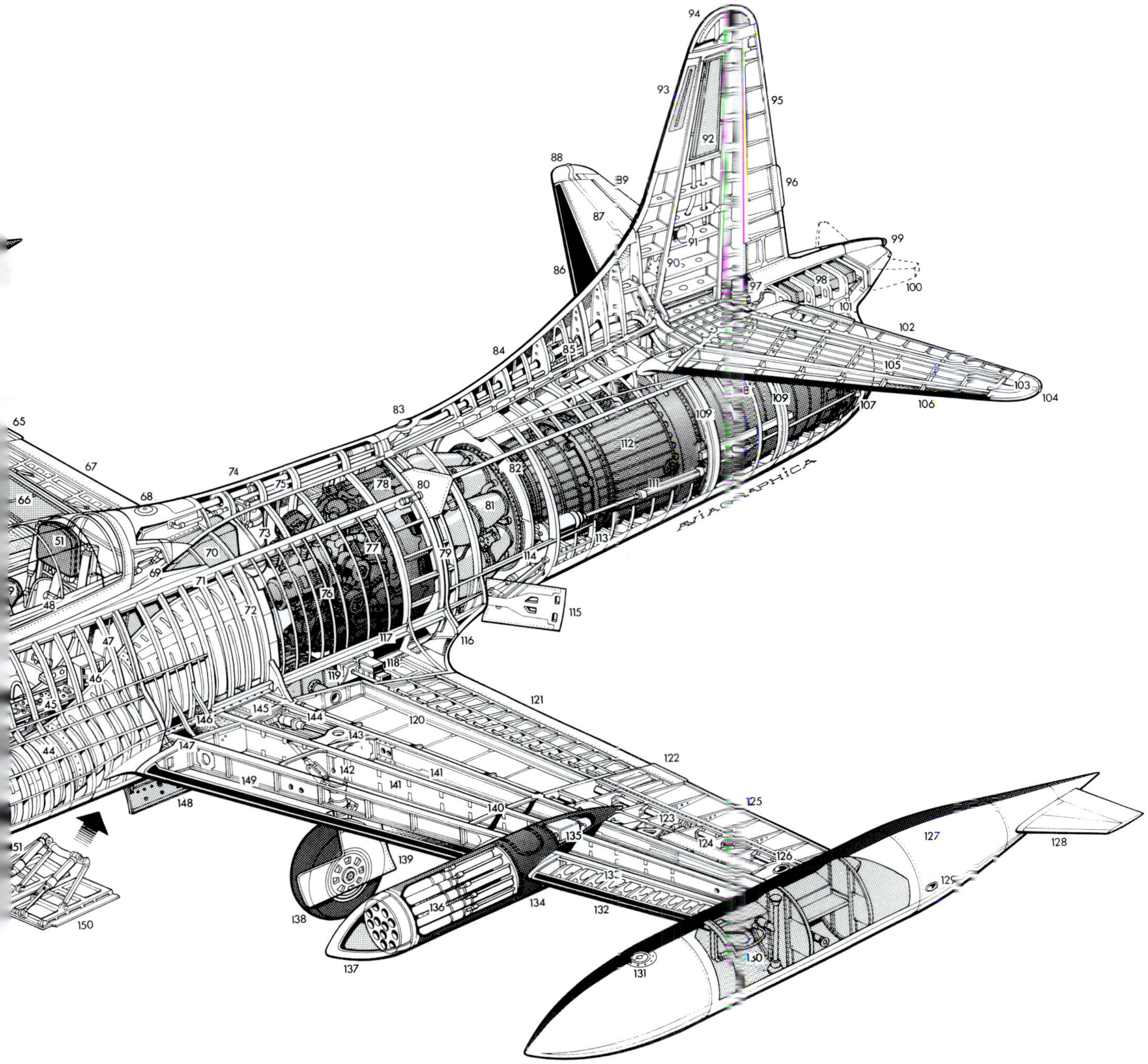

2.75-in (7-cm) rockets
55 Frangible nose cap
56 Leading-edge de-icing boots
57 Tip tank, 250-U.S. gal (946-litre) capacity
58 Fuel filler cap
59 Tip-tank attachment and jettison controls
60 Starboard identification light
61 Aileron spoiler
62 Starboard aileron
63 Aileron hinge control
64 Aileron balance weights
65 Fixed tab
66 Trailing-edge fuel tank
67 Starboard split trailing-edge flap
68 Fuselage fuel tank filler cap
69 Cockpit canopy hinge mechanism
70 Fuselage fuel tank, capacity 65 U.S. gal (246 litres)
71 Fuselage main longeron
72 Centre-section frame construction
73 Hydraulic reservoir
74 Dorsal spine fairing
75 Fuel system vent pipe
76 Engine accessory equipment
77 Engine intake grille
78 Pratt & Whitney J48-P-7A afterburning turbojet
79 Rear fuselage break point
80 Rear fuselage bolted joints (3)
81 Engine flame tubes
82 Firewall
83 Anti-collision light
84 Fin root fairing
85 Fuel jettison valves
86 Tailplane leading-edge de-icing boots
87 Starboard tailplane
88 Fuel jettison pipe
89 Starboard elevator
90 Fin construction
91 Gyrosyn compass transmitter
92 ILS localizer aerial
93 Glideslope antenna
94 AN/ARC-27 radio aerial
95 Rudder construction
96 Fixed rudder tab
97 Rudder and elevator hinge controls
98 Brake parachute housing
99 Tail navigation light
100 Brake parachute doors, open position
101 Elevator trim tab
102 Port elevator construction
103 Elevator mass balance
104 Tailplane tip fuel jettison
105 Tailplane construction
106 Leading-edge de-icing boot
107 Two-position, eyelid-type afterburner exhaust nozzle
108 Tailplane
109 Fin and tailplane attachment frames
110 Jet pipe withdrawal rail
111 Exhaust nozzle control jack
112 Afterburner duct
113 Rear fuselage framing
114 Airbrake hydraulic jack
115 Aft airbrake, open
116 Wing-root trailing-edge fillet
117 Fuselage lower longeron
118 Flap drive motor
119 Fuel feed collector tank
120 Trailing-edge fuel-tank bay
121 Split trailing-edge flap construction
122 Aileron trim tab
123 Aileron hinge control
124 Port coupled spoiler
125 Aileron construction
126 Port identification light
127 Tip tank, 250-U.S. gal (946-litre) capacity
128 Tip-tank stabilizing fin
129 Port navigation light
130 Fuel feed system
131 Filler cap
132 Leading-edge de-icing boots
133 Leading-edge nose ribs
134 Port wing rocket pod
135 Rocket firing control unit
136 Launch tubes
137 Frangible nose cap
138 Port mainwheel
139 Mainwheel leg door
140 Wing spar construction
141 Port wing main fuel-tank bays
142 Main undercarriage leg strut
143 Undercarriage pivot housing
144 Hydraulic retraction jack
145 Mainwheel well
146 Wing skin/fuselage attachment joint
147 Front spar attachment joint
148 Mainwheel door
149 Leading-edge fuel-tank bay
150 Forward ventral airbrakes
151 Airbrake hydraulic jacks

"It was a well-liked warplane that performed an important mission in which everyone believed."
– Robert F. Dorr, U.S. author, columnist and former diplomat

Above: An F-94C lets loose with its wingtip rocket pods. When these were expended, the Starfire had more rockets tucked away in the nose.

FACTS

- Only the F-94C version was officially named the "Starfire."
- The F-94C was the first production aircraft to be fitted with only rocket armament.
- Using radar to guide its interception, an F-94B scored the first known victory against a target that was not seen before its destruction.

LOCKHEED F-94 STARFIRE – VARIANTS & OPERATORS

VARIANTS

YF-94: TF-80Cs converted into YF-94 prototypes, two built.

F-94A: Initial production version, 110 built.

YF-94B: One F-94A modified with new flight director, modified hydraulic systems and two enlarged wingtip tanks.

F-94B: Production model based on YF-94B.

YF-94C: F-94Bs modified with Pratt & Whitney J48 engine, leading-edge rocket pods and swept tailplane. Originally designated YF-97A, two modified.

F-94C: Production version of the YF-94C with longer nose, rocket and gun armament removed and provision for underfuselage JATO rockets. Originally designated F-97A.

EF-94C: Test aircraft for proposed reconnaissance variant.

YF-94D: Prototype single-seat close support fighter version based on the F-94C. One partly built, but construction was abandoned when programme was cancelled.

F-94D: Production version of the YF-94D. 112 were on order, but the model was cancelled and none built.

YF-97A: Original designation of the YF-94C.

F-97A: Original designation of the F-94C.

U.S. AIR DEFENCE UNITS

USAF FIGHTER INTERCEPTOR SQUADRONS
2nd, 4th, 5th, 16th, 27th, 29th, 46th, 48th, 57th, 58th, 59th, 60th, 61st, 63rd, 64th, 65th, 66th, 68th, 74th, 82nd, 84th, 95th, 96th, 97th, 317th, 318th.

U.S. NATIONAL GUARD FIGHTER INTERCEPTOR SQUADRONS

101st: Massachusetts	102nd: New York
103rd: Pennsylvania	109th: Minnesota
114th: New York	116th: Washington
118th: Connecticut	121st: District of Columbia
123rd: Oregon	131st: Massachusetts
132nd: Maine	133rd: New Hampshire
134th: Vermont	136th: New York
137th: New York	138th: New York
139th: New York	142nd: Delaware
148th: Pennsylvania	175th: South Dakota
178th: North Dakota	179th: Minnesota
186th: Montana	190th: Idaho

LOCKHEED F-94C STARFIRE

The midwing rocket pods mark out the F-94 illustrated here as a C-model, or Starfire, the only version of the series that was officially so named (even though all versions of the F-94 tend to be called "Starfire" today). The enlarged afterburner section for the J48 engine is another recognition feature that readily distinguishes the C from the F-94A and B that saw service in Korea. This C was assigned to the 84th Fighter Interceptor Squadron at Hamilton AFB, California, and took part in the 1954 Aerial Gunnery Meet at Yuma, Arizona. As well as the wing pods, the F-94C carried 24 "Mighty Mouse" rockets in launchers behind snap-close doors just behind the radome for the APG-40 radar.

Above: The F-94 pilot's panel included a small radar scope, but the main unit was in the rear cockpit.

In 1948, with piston-engined night fighters such as the Northrop P-61 Black Widow and North American P-82 Twin Mustang rapidly becoming obsolete, the U.S. Air Force urgently sought jet replacements. Lockheed proposed a radar-equipped development of the T-33 trainer, which was ordered as the YF-94.

The first of two YF-94 prototypes started out on the production line as a standard P-80C fighter, before being modified into the prototype for the T-33 trainer family, of which more than 6,500 were eventually built. After testing of the T-33 configuration was complete, the airframe was converted to the aerodynamic testbed for the F-94 and flew as such in April 1949. Modifications included an extended nose with a slightly upturned appearance and the addition of an afterburner to its Allison J333 engine, which required a bulged tailpipe. Production F-94As had a Hughes radar and fire control system and four 0.50-in (12.7-mm) machine guns in the nose. An additional quartet could be carried in underwing pods.

Air Defense Command took delivery of F-94As from late 1949. The F-94B with equipment for bad-weather landings, and large wingtip fuel tanks were to follow soon afterwards.

Above: Although it could carry extra guns in pods on the wings, the F-94A had a standard armament of only four machine guns in the nose.

DEPLOYMENT TO KOREA

With the arrival of Soviet-built Mikoyan-Gurevich MiG-15 jets in Korean airspace in late 1951, F-94s were quickly deployed to the war zone, but fears that the radar technology would fall into enemy hands meant that the aircraft were prohibited from flying over the North. Instead of protecting B-29 bombers against MiG-15s, they were put on alert to chase down North Korean "Bedcheck Charlie" nuisance raids by ancient Polikarpov Po-2 biplanes. The first success, however, was actually against a Lavochkin La-9 fighter,

Above: The definitive F-94 variant and last to be put into production was the F-94C Starfire. With a total of 48 rockets available on the wings and in the nose, it packed a considerable punch.

brought down over the North when restrictions were lifted in early 1953. A MiG-15 and a couple of Po-2s were brought down in the following months, but the final "victory" by an F-94 was the result of a collision with a slow-moving Po-2.

STARFIRE POWER

While fighting in Korea continued, Air Defense Command was receiving the definitive F-94C, officially named the Starfire in line with other astronomically dubbed Lockheed products such as the Shooting Star, Constellation and Neptune. The F-94C had a modified rear fuselage to take an afterburning Pratt & Whitney J48 engine, a development of the Rolls-Royce Tay. The tailplanes were swept back and the fin was taller. The most significant change made was to the armament, with unguided rockets replacing guns. The F-94C could carry 24 rockets in the nose and 12 in each of the wing pods. Hinged doors around the radar would pop open to allow the nose rockets to fire, delivering a devastating blow to enemy bombers.

A BRIEF CAREER

The Starfire served only from 1953–59, when it was phased out in favour of supersonic interceptors such as the McDonnell F-101 and Convair F-102. In that brief time, it helped defend the United States' northern flanks from potential attack by Soviet bombers, which grew in capability year by year.

Mikoyan-Gurevich MiG-17 "Fresco"

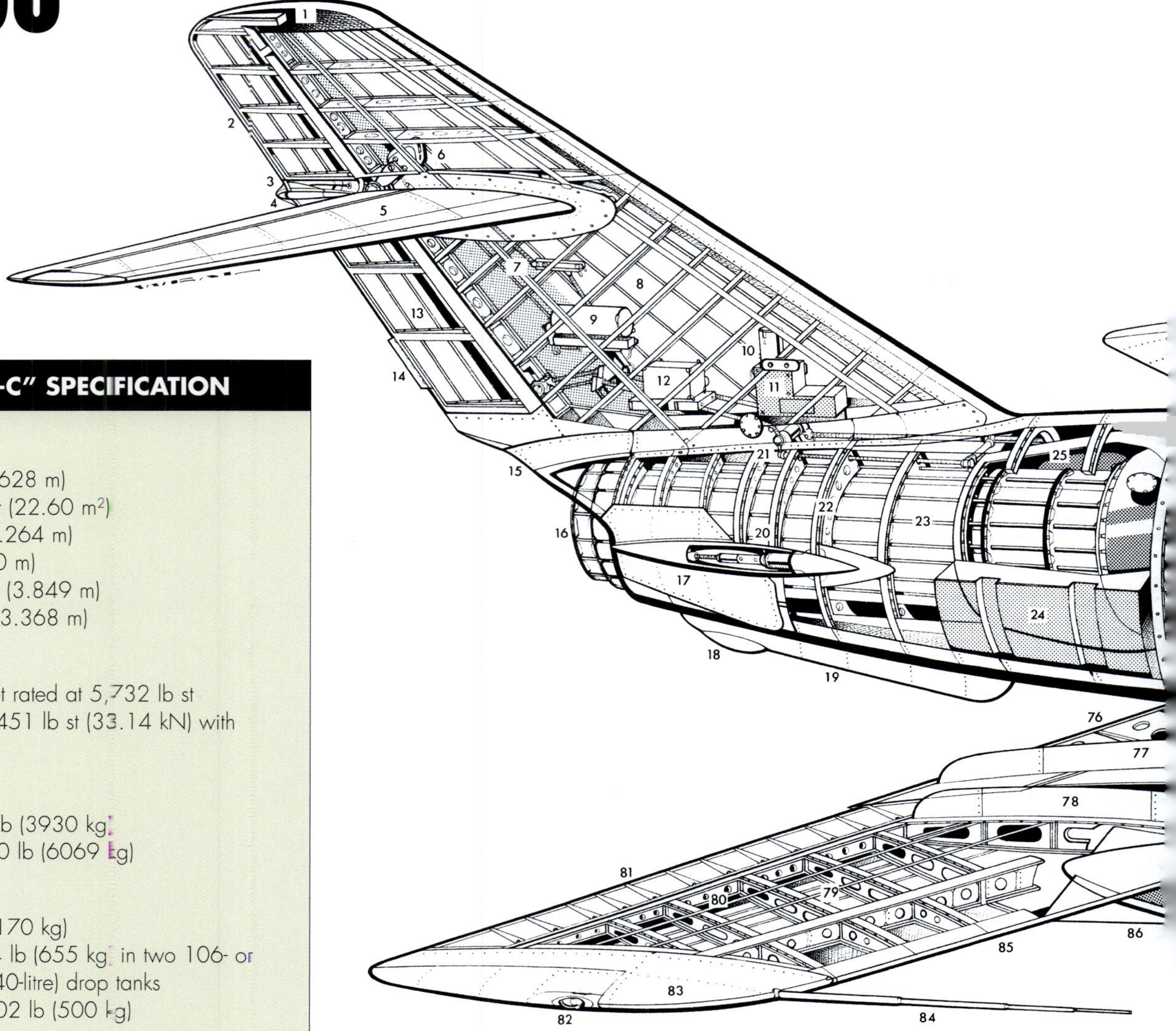

MIG-17F "FRESCO-C" SPECIFICATION

Dimensions

Wingspan: 31 ft 7 in (9.628 m)
Wing area: 243.27 sq ft (22.60 m²)
Length: 36 ft 11½ in (11.264 m)
Height: 12 ft 5½ in (3.80 m)
Wheel track: 12 ft 7½ in (3.849 m)
Wheel base: 11 ft ½ in (3.368 m)

Powerplant

One Klimov VK-1F turbojet rated at 5,732 lb st (29.50 kN) dry and 7,451 lb st (33.14 kN) with afterburning

Weights

Empty equipped: 8,664 lb (3930 kg)
Maximum takeoff: 13,380 lb (6069 kg)

Fuel and load

Internal fuel: 2,579 lb (1170 kg)
External fuel: up to 1,444 lb (655 kg) in two 106- or 63-U.S. gal (400- or 240-litre) drop tanks
Maximum ordnance: 1,102 lb (500 kg)

Performance

Limiting Mach number: 1.03
Maximum level speed "clean" at 9,845 ft (3000 m): 594 kt (684 mph; 1100 km/h)
Maximum level speed "clean" at 32,810 ft (10,000 m): 578 kt (666 mph; 1071 km/h)
Speed limit with drop tanks: 486 kt (559 mph; 900 km/h)
Ferry range: 1,091 nm (1,255 miles; 2020 km) with drop tanks
Combat radius: 378 nm (435 miles; 700 km) on a hi-lo-hi attack mission with two 551-lb (250-kg) bombs and two drop tanks
Maximum rate of climb at sea level: 12,795 ft (3900 m) per minute
Service ceiling: 49,215 ft (15000 m) at dry thrust and 54,460 ft (16600 m) at afterburning thrust
Takeoff run: 1,936 ft (590 m) at normal takeoff weight
Landing run: 2,789 ft (850 m) at normal landing weight

Mikoyan-Gurevich's second MiG jet was only slightly more sophisticated than its predecessor, but nevertheless it gave the United States a run for its money in Vietnam, and saw action in many Middle East and African conflicts from the 1960s onwards.

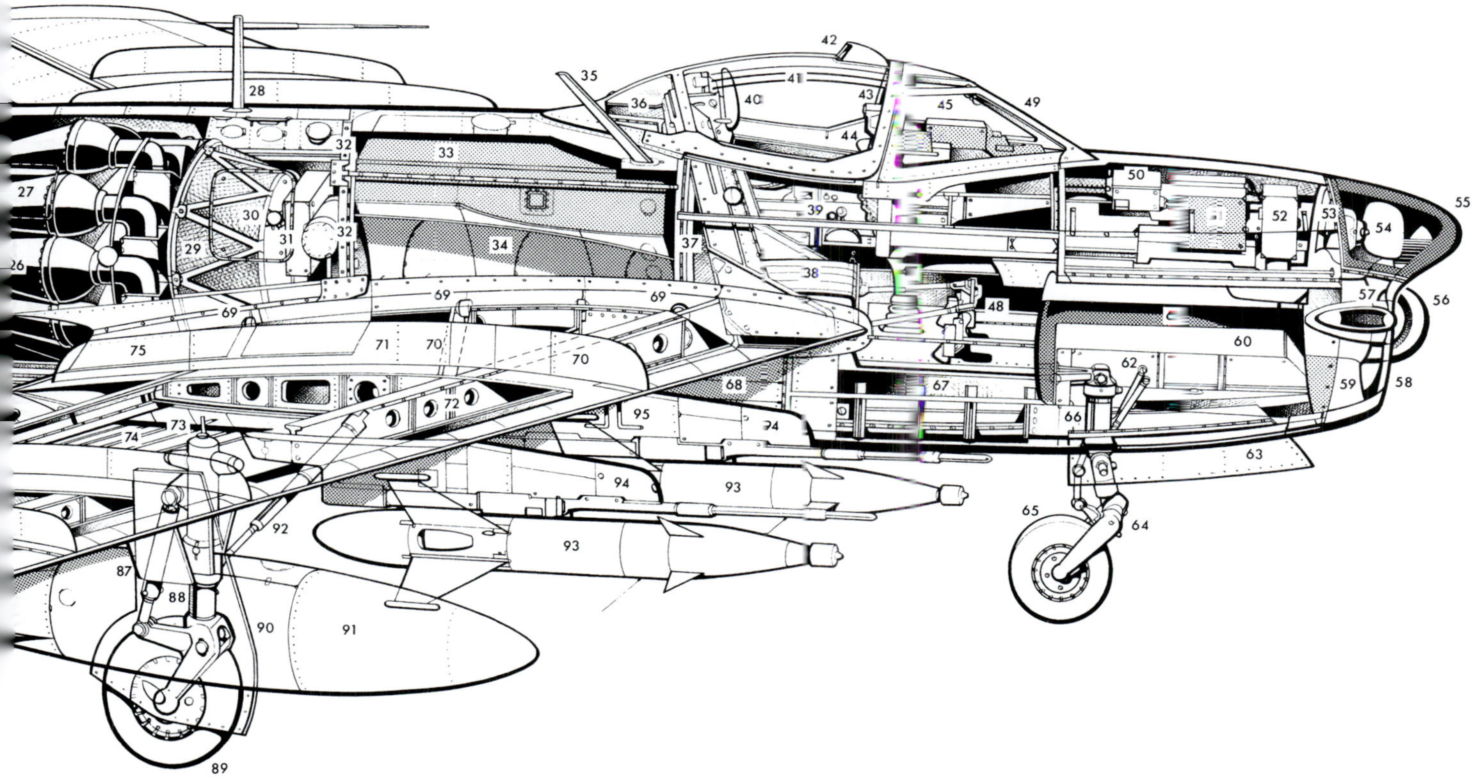

Cutaway Key

1 Rudder upper hinge/balance
2 Rudder (upper section)
3 Passive tail-warning radar unit
4 Rear navigation light
5 Fixed incidence tailplane
6 Elevator control linkage
7 Control lines
8 Tailfin construction
9 Transformer
10 Gyro compass
11 Magnetic amplifier for gyro
12 Tail-warning master unit
13 Rudder (lower section)
14 Rudder trim tab
15 Tailpipe shroud
16 Afterburner nozzle
17 Starboard airbrake
18 Tail skid
19 Ventral strake
20 Airbrake hydraulic activator
21 Control linkage assembly
22 Rear fuselage structure
23 Afterburner pipe
24 Aft fuselage fuel tank
25 Afterburner outer casing
26 Klimov VK-1F turbojet
27 Inspection panel
28 IFF antenna
29 Engine intake grille
30 Inspection panel
31 Engine auxiliaries
32 Aft/forward fuselage breakpoint
33 Main fuselage fuel tank
34 Intake trunking
35 VHF antenna
36 Canopy track
37 Bulkhead
38 Ejector seat
39 Port control console (throttle quadrant)
40 Pilot's headrest
41 Canopy heating web
42 Rear-view mirror
43 Rocket sight
44 Radar-scope shroud
45 Enlarged cockpit quarterlight
46 Instrument panel
47 Control column
48 Rudder pedals
49 Windscreen
50 RDF ranging unit
51 VHF transmitter/receiver
52 Accumulator
53 Radar ranging unit
54 Radar scanner
55 Extended upper intake lip
56 AI scanner in centre intake bullet
57 Combat camera housing
58 Bifurcated intake
59 Intake centre-body
60 Centre-section nosewheel well
61 Intake trunking
62 Nosewheel retraction radii
63 Nosewheel doors
64 Nosewheel fork
65 Forward-retracting nosewheel
66 Nosewheel strut
67 Forward fuselage members
68 Inboard-section wing leading edge
69 Three wing/fuselage attachment points
70 Y-section inner main spar
71 Inboard wing fence
72 Forward main spar
73 Undercarriage indicator spigot
74 Inner wing skinning
75 Split landing flap (inner section)
76 Split landing flap structure (outer section)
77 Centre wing fence
78 Outboard wing fence
79 Wing construction
80 Rear spar
81 Aileron construction
82 Starboard navigation light
83 Wingtip
84 Starboard pitot head
85 Outboard-section wing leading edge
86 Auxiliary tank fin assembly
87 Triple-strut auxiliary-tank bracing
88 Mainwheel leg
89 Starboard mainwheel
90 Mainwheel door
91 Auxiliary tank (106-U.S. gal/400-litre capacity)
92 Mainwheel retraction rod
93 AA-1 "Alkali"-type beam-riding air-to-air missiles
94 Weapon pylons
95 Altimeter radio dipole (port outboard/starboard inboard)

"No matter how good the F-4 is in air-to-air combat, it is no match for the MiG-17 if you fight the way they do – and that's World War II-style dog-fighting."
– Colonel Robin Olds, USAF Wing Commander, Vietnam War

Above: A Mig-17F built in Poland in 1957 and restored by Bill Reesman in 1994. This example served with the Polish Air Force for 25 years during the height of the Cold War, when Poland was part of the Soviet Bloc.

FACTS

- The MiG-17 is slightly longer than the MiG-15, but with a shorter wingspan.
- The majority of MiG-17s were built outside of the USSR, in places such as Poland, Czechoslovakia and China.
- The MiG-17P became Russia's first operational radar-equipped single-seat fighter.

MIG-17F – VARIANTS & OPERATORS

VARIANTS

I-300: Prototype.

MiG-17 ("Fresco-A"): Basic fighter version powered by VK-1 engine ("aircraft SI").

MiG-17A: Fighter version powered by VK-1A engine with longer lifespan.

MiG-17AS: Multirole conversion, fitted to carry unguided rockets and K-13 air-to-air missile.

MiG-17P ("Fresco-B"): All-weather fighter equipped with Izumrud radar ("aircraft SP").

MiG-17F ("Fresco-C"): Basic fighter powered by VK-1F engine with afterburner ("aircraft SF").

MiG-17PF ("Fresco-D"): All-weather fighter version equipped with Izumrud radar and VK-1F engine ("aircraft SP-7F").

MiG-17PM/PFU ("Fresco-E"): Fighter version equipped with radar and K-5 (NATO: AA-1 "Alkali") air-to-air missiles ("aircraft SP-9").

MiG-17R: Reconnaissance aircraft with VK-1F engine and camera ("aircraft SR-2s").

MiG-17SN: Unproduced experimental variant with twin side intakes, no central intake, and nose redesigned to allow cannons to pivot, to engage ground targets.

Shenyang J-5: Some withdrawn aircraft were converted to remotely controlled targets.

OPERATORS

Air Forces
Afghanistan
Albania
Algeria
Angola
Bangladesh
Bulgaria
Burkina Faso
Cambodia
China
Congo
Cuba
Czechoslovakia
East Germany
Egypt
Ethiopia
Guinea
Guinea-Bissau
Indonesia
Iraq
Hungary
Libya
Madagascar
Mali
Mongolia
Morocco
Mozambique
Nigeria
North Korea
Pakistan
Poland
Romania
Somalia
Somaliland
Soviet Union
Sri Lanka
Sudan
Syria
Tanzania
Uganda
Vietnam
Yemen
Zimbabwe

Navies
China
Soviet Union

Anti-Aircraft Defence
Soviet Union

MIKOYAN-GUREVICH MIG-17F "FRESCO"

Indonesia began a re-equipment programme in the late 1950s, obtaining a large amount of Soviet-made equipment, including about 30 MiG-17F "Fresco-Cs," later supplemented with a dozen Shenyang F-6s (Chinese-built versions of the MiG-19 "Farmer"), supplied by Communist China. This MiG-17F belonged to No. 11 Squadron of the Indonesian Air Force (Tentara Nasional Indonesia – Angkatan Udara, or TNI-AU), which operated an aerobatic team at one time.

Indonesia held back its MiG-17s and MiG-21s for the defence of Jakarta during the "Confrontation" with the United Kingdom and its allies over Borneo in 1962–64. RAF fighters including Gloster Javelins and English Electric Lightnings never tangled with the MiGs, although they did intercept Tu-16 bombers, C-130 transports and other TNI-AU aircraft.

Even before the MiG-15 had entered service, an improved follow-up design was being developed. The MiG-17 prototype first flew under the designation SI-1 in January 1950 and, although it crashed on an early test flight, was adopted for production in September 1951.

In side view, the MiG-17 was very similar in appearance to its predecessor, although it had an enlarged tail fin, different-shaped airbrakes and a ventral fin under the lower fuselage. In plan view, the differences were more marked. An all-new wing, sometimes described as being of "scimitar" configuration, was fitted. It was swept at 49 degrees in the inboard section and 45.5 degrees outboard. Three prominent wing fences were fitted.

ADDITIONAL WEAPONRY

The engine fitted to the new version of the MiG was the Klimov VK-1A turbojet, replaced soon after the MiG-17's introduction by the VK-1F with afterburner. The afterburner-equipped aircraft were designated MiG-17F by the Soviet Union and "Fresco-C" by western powers. The MiG-17's gun armament was the same as the MiG-15's: three nose-mounted cannon. Additionally, however, the "Fresco" could carry bombs or rocket pods for ground-attack missions.

Above: Egypt operated nearly 500 MiG-17s over the years. These examples wear the roundel in use by the Egyptian Air Force up to 1958. Many "Frescos" were destroyed on the ground in 1967, as the result of an attack by the Israeli Air Force during the Six-Day War.

Above: In a spin, the MiG-17 pilot began recovery by aligning the joystick with the white stripe running down the centre of the instrument panel.

VARIATIONS ON A THEME

In a similar way to how the North American F-86 Sabre spawned the F-86D derivative with an air interception radar and afterburner, the basic MiG-17 begat the MiG-17PF with a nose-mounted radar. The Izumrud RP-1 radar was in two parts – a search radar in the upper intake lip and a fire control set for weapons aiming in a cone set within the intake. This allowed the aircraft a limited night and bad-weather capability, but had to be used in conjunction with ground-based radar and direction by operators on the ground to get the MiG anywhere near the target. MiG-17PFs were designated "Fresco-D" and usually had three 23-mm cannon The later MiG-21PFU dispensed with the cannon and instead had in its possession up to four AA-1 "Alkali" radar-guided air-to-air missiles.

Like the MiG-15, the MiG-17 was built by factories in the Warsaw Pact countries such as Poland and exported to China, which also built large numbers, initially under licence, and then without one when Sino–Soviet relations soured in 1960. Chengdu-built Chinese MiG-17s were designated J-5 (MiG-17F), J-5A (MiG-17PF) and the two-seat JJ-5. China's J-5s fought a number of air battles with Taiwanese aircraft from the late 1950s onwards, in various skirmishes over the Straits of Taiwan.

CLOSE-COMBAT ADVANTAGE

Vietnam saw the most prominent use of the MiG-17, however. Despite their lack of sophistication and gun-only armament, North Vietnamese Frescos often managed to get the better of both U.S. Air Force and U.S. Navy aircraft, whose pilots were unable to use their long-range missiles due to rules of engagement requiring that they visually identify their targets before firing. This drew them into close combats where the MiGs had superior turning advantage. Although the final tally favoured the Americans, the top ace of the Vietnam War was again a MiG pilot Nguyen van Bay, who as a pilot with the North Vietnamese Air Force is credited with seven kills in the MiG-17F, and who also damaged a U.S. Navy cruiser, USS *Oklahoma City*, in a rare North Vietnamese bombing attack.

MiG-17s and their Chinese counterparts continue to serve with a few nations such as Syria, North Korea and Ethiopia. JJ-5 (export designation FT-5) trainers are used as trainers by nations that have retired their single-seaters.

Republic F-84 Thunderjet and Thunderstreak

Republic's F-84 was one of the most important early Cold War jets. In Korea, Thunderjets undertook the brunt of the U.S. Air Force's ground-attack duties. In Europe, the Thunderstreak formed the backbone of many NATO air forces.

F-84F THUNDERSTREAK SPECIFICATION

Dimensions

Length: 43 ft 4 in (13.23 m)
Wingspan: 33 ft 7 in (10.27 m)
Height: 14 ft 4½ in (4.39 m)
Wing area: 324.70 sq ft (98.90 m²)

Powerplant

One Wright J65-W-3 turbojet delivering 7,220 lb (32.50 kN) of thrust

Weights

Empty: 13,380 lb (6273 kg)
Maximum takeoff: 28,000 lb (12,700 kg)

Performance

Maximum speed at 20,000 ft (6095 m): 658 mph (1059 km/h)
Maximum speed at sea level: 695 mph (1118 km/h)
Initial climb rate: 8,200 ft (2500 m) per minute
Service ceiling: 46,000 ft (14,020 m)
Combat radius (high with two drop tanks): 810 miles (1304 km)

Armament

Six 0.5-in (12.7-mm) Browning M3 machine guns and up to 6,000 lb (2722 kg) of external stores, originally including U.S. tactical nuclear weapons

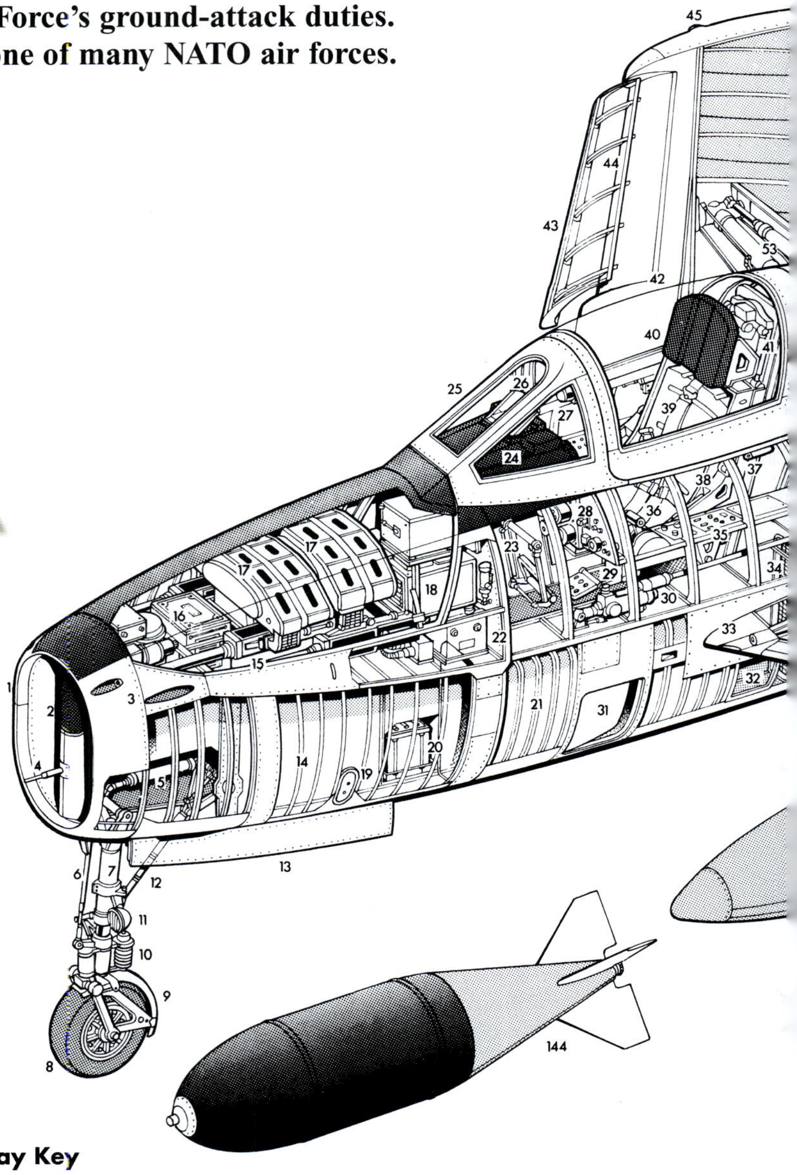

Cutaway Key

1 Engine air intake
2 Gun tracking radar antenna
3 Machine-gun muzzles
4 Pitot tube
5 Nose undercarriage hydraulic retraction jack
6 Leg compression link
7 Nosewheel leg strut
8 Nosewheel
9 Mudguard
10 Steering jack
11 Taxiing lamp
12 Nose undercarriage leg rear strut
13 Nosewheel doors
14 Intake duct framing
15 Nose compartment 0.5-in (12.7-mm) 50 Colt-Browning M3 machine guns (four)
16 Radar electronics equipment
17 Ammunition tanks, total of 1,800 rounds
18 Forward avionics bay, including LABS bombing computer
19 Static ports
20 Battery
21 Intake ducting
22 Cockpit front pressure bulkhead
23 Rudder pedals
24 Instrument panel shroud
25 Windscreen panels
26 A-4 radar gunsight
27 Standby compass
28 Instrument panel
29 Ejection seat footrests
30 Aileron hydraulic booster
31 Intake suction relief door
32 Duct screen clearance access panel
33 Wingroot machine-gun muzzle
34 Intake duct screen
35 Port side console panel
36 Engine throttle
37 External canopy release handle
38 Pilot's ejection seat
39 Safety harness
40 Headrest
41 Ejection seat guide rails
42 Cockpit canopy cover
43 Starboard automatic leading-edge slat, open
44 Slat guide rails
45 Starboard navigation light
46 Wingtip fairing

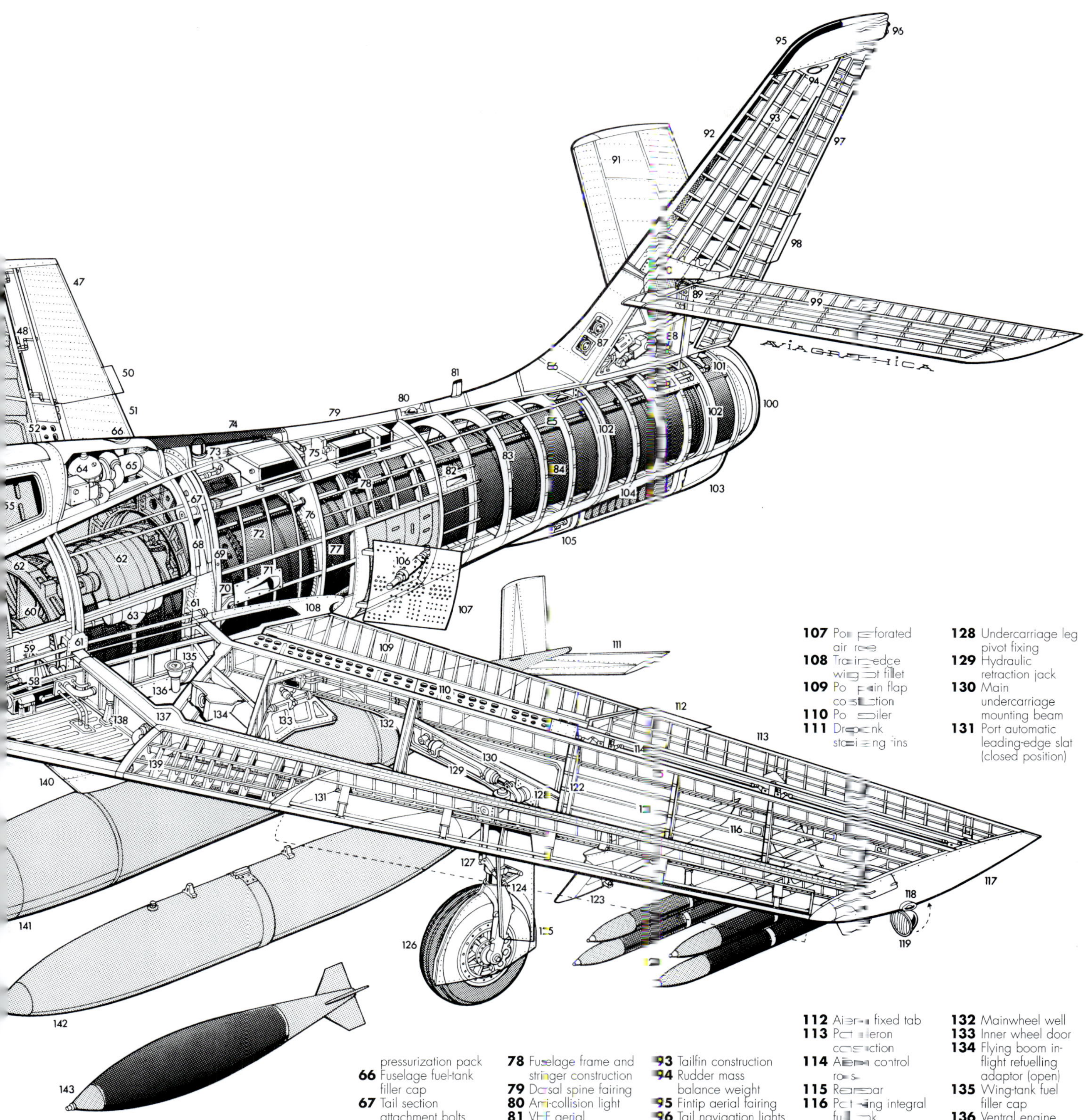

47 Starboard aileron
48 Aileron control rods
49 Starboard wing integral fuel tank; normal maximum fuel capacity 1,475 U.S. gal (5583 litres)
50 Aileron fixed tab
51 Starboard flap
52 Spoiler
53 Starboard main undercarriage leg (retracted position)
54 Canopy rear hinge arm
55 Cockpit aft glazing
56 Ammunition feed chute
57 Cockpit rear pressure bulkhead
58 Wingroot 0.50-in (12.7-mm) Colt Browning M3 machine gun
59 Engine electric starter/generator
60 Intake compressor face
61 Wing/fuselage spar lug attachment bolts (total four)
62 Fuselage main fuel tanks
63 Engine oil tank
64 Oxygen bottle
65 Air-conditioning and pressurization pack
66 Fuselage fuel-tank filler cap
67 Tail section attachment bolts (four)
68 Fuselage double main frames
69 Fuselage break point
70 Main engine mounting
71 Engine bay cooling intake
72 Wright J65-W-3 turbojet engine
73 Radio-compass antenna
74 Flush aerial fairing
75 Aft radio equipment bay
76 Engine firewall
77 Engine turbine section
78 Fuselage frame and stringer construction
79 Dorsal spine fairing
80 Anti-collision light
81 VHF aerial
82 Tailpipe cooling intake
83 Rear fuselage framing
84 Jet pipe
85 Rudder control rod, elevator on starboard side
86 Finroot fillet
87 Aerial tuning units
88 All-moving tailplane control jack
89 Tailplane pivot fixing
90 Fin/tailplane sealing plates
91 Starboard all-moving tailplane
92 Fin leading edge
93 Tailfin construction
94 Rudder mass balance weight
95 Fintip aerial fairing
96 Tail navigation lights
97 Rudder construction
98 Rudder fixed tab
99 Parallel chord all-moving tailplane construction
100 Jet pipe exhaust nozzle
101 Rudder hinge control
102 Tailfin attachment frames
103 Brake parachute fairing doors
104 Parachute stowage
105 Parachute release link
106 Airbrake hydraulic jack
107 Port perforated air brake
108 Trailing-edge wing root fillet
109 Port plain flap construction
110 Port spoiler
111 Drop tank stabilizing fins
112 Aileron fixed tab
113 Port aileron construction
114 Aileron control rods
115 Rear spar
116 Port wing integral fuel tank
117 Wingtip fairing
118 Port navigation light
119 Retractable landing lamp
120 5-in (12.7-cm) HVAR ground-attack rockets
121 Wing stringers
122 Wing rib construction
123 Port outer wing pylon
124 Undercarriage leg torque scissors
125 Mainwheel doors
126 Port mainwheel
127 Main undercarriage leg strut
128 Undercarriage leg pivot fixing
129 Hydraulic retraction jack
130 Main undercarriage mounting beam
131 Port automatic leading-edge slat (closed position)
132 Mainwheel well
133 Inner wheel door
134 Flying boom in-flight refuelling adaptor (open)
135 Wing-tank fuel filler cap
136 Ventral engine access doors
137 Front spar
138 Pylon fixing
139 Fixed leading-edge construction
140 Inboard pylon
141 375-U.S. gal (1420-litre) ferry tank
142 191.5-U.S. gal (725-litre) drop tank
143 Mk 84 1,000-lb (454-kg) HE bomb
144 2,000-lb (907-kg) free-fall nuclear weapon

"Let's admit it – the MiG is all right. It's a damned fine airplane. The F-84 is all right, too. But if we were flying the MiG and they were flying the '84, I think we would be murdering them."
– Captain William Slaughter,
F-84 pilot, Korea 1951

Above: The U.S. Air Force's "Thunderbirds" aerial demonstration team flew the Republic F-84F in 1955 and 1956.

REPUBLIC F-84F THUNDERSTREAK – VARIANTS AND OPERATORS

VARIANTS

YF-84F: Two swept-wing prototypes of the F-84F, initially designated YF-96.

F-84F Thunderstreak: Swept-wing version with Wright J65 engine. Tactical Air Command aircraft were equipped with Low-Altitude Bombing System (LABS) for delivering nuclear bombs. 2711 built; 1301 went to NATO under Mutual Defense Assistance Program (MDAP).

GRF-84F: 25 RF-84Fs were converted to be carried and launched from the bomb bay of a GRB-36F bomber as part of the FICON (FIghter CONveyor) project. The aircraft were later redesignated RF-84K.

RF-84F Thunderflash: Reconnaissance version of the F-84F. 715 were built.

XF-84H: Two F-84Fs were converted into experimental aircraft. Each was fitted with a Allison XT40-A-1 turboprop engine of 5,850 shaft horsepower (4365 kW) driving a supersonic propeller. Ground crews dubbed the XF-84H the "Thunderscreech" due to its extreme noise level.

YF-84J: Two F-84Fs were converted into YF-84J prototypes with enlarged nose intakes and a deepened fuselages for the General Electric J73 engine. The YF-84J reached Mach 1.09 in level flight on 7 April 1954. The project was cancelled due to the excessive cost of conversion of existing F-84Fs.

OPERATORS

Belgium
Denmark
France
Greece
Iran
Italy
Netherlands
Norway
Portugal
Taiwan
Thailand
Turkey
United States
West Germany
Yugoslavia

FACTS

- The F-84 was the first tactical aircraft capable of carrying a nuclear weapon.
- In the 1950s, the U.S. Air Force "Thunderbirds" display team used both the F-84G and F-84F.
- Nearly 2,000 F-84Gs were supplied to NATO, and more than 1,300 F-84Fs and RF-84Fs.

REPUBLIC F-84F THUNDERSTREAK

The 81st Tactical Fighter Wing was based at the airfields of Bentwaters and nearby Woodbridge in Suffolk, England, for many years. In 1958, its equipment was the F-84F Thunderstreak, and this example flew with the 78th Tactical Fighter Squadron. The F-84Fs were used as nuclear-capable fighter-bombers, as illustrated by the 78th TFS's mushroom-cloud emblem. 52-6675, which features a brake parachute housing under the tail as retrofitted to many F-84Fs in service, was later sold to the Luftwaffe, then passed on to Greece. After serving its career almost exclusively outside the United States, it found its way back to Peoria, Arizona, where it is displayed on a pole downtown.

With more than 18,000 delivered, the Republic P-47 Thunderbolt was the most numerous American fighter of all time. It was equally effective as a fighter and a ground-attack platform, and was renowned for its toughness and ability to withstand battle damage.

An attempt to redesign the P-47 for jet power failed, and Republic went back to the drawing board, producing an all-new design. Its new proposal was offered with six 0.50-in machine guns (two fewer than the P-47) or four 15.2-mm machine guns. The USAAF awarded Republic a contract for a jet fighter-bomber in 1944, and increased the order before the prototype XP-84A flew in February 1946.

NEWLY INDEPENDENT ROLE

The U.S. Air Force was created as an independent arm of the military in 1937. The same year, P for "Pursuit" was replaced with F for "Fighter" in the Pentagon's designation system. The P-84 therefore entered service in December

Above: As on most fighters at the time, the instrument panel of the F-84 was crowded with dials, which occupied every inch of available space.

Above: Large external fuel tanks were needed to give the F-84F a reasonable radius of action.

Above: An F-84F fires an AGM-12 Bullpup missile during tests at Edwards Air Force Base California. In service, the Thunderstreak almost exclusively used unguided bombs, rockets and guns.

1947 as the F-84B Thunderjet. A fairly conventional-looking machine, it had an unswept wing and a "straight-through" intake in the nose leading to an Allison J35 axial-flow turbojet. A bubble canopy gave the pilot a good all-around view.

Early Thunderjets had a number of structural and performance issues. The F-84B, C and D all came and went fairly quickly, before the much improved F-84E arrived in 1949, followed by the definitive F-84G. By now the bubble canopy had gone, replaced by a heavily framed reinforced unit. Provision for both boom and probe-and-drogue refuelling was fitted, and a Mk 7 nuclear weapon could be carried.

TACTICAL ATTACK

In Korea, the F-84 followed the traditions of its predecessor the P-47, becoming the primary tactical-attack aircraft. Although technically outclassed by the Mikoyan-Gurevich MiG-15, Thunderjets brought down eight MiGs during the conflict.

Nearly 4,500 straight-wing F-84s were built. As well as the U.S. Air Force, it was operated by 15 foreign nations, including Portugal, Taiwan, West Germany and Iran. The F-84F Thunderstreak was intended to be a swept-wing version with few other differences. In reality, it was almost totally new by the time the first production aircraft flew in November 1952. The fuselage was deeper, with an oval cross section, and contained a Wright J65 engine. The canopy was faired into the spine and opened upwards and to the rear. Six machine guns were fitted. The F-84F served with Tactical Air Command from 1954, but had been mostly passed to Air National Guard service by the late 1950s.

COLD WAR TENSIONS

The regular USAF reintroduced the F-84F during tensions over Berlin in the early1960s. A mass deployment of more than 200 US F-84Fs was made to Europe, to bolster defences against a possible Soviet attack in 1961.

The Thunderstreak spawned the RF-84F Thunderflash with a camera nose and side-mounted intakes. As with the F-84G, the swept-wing models were supplied in large numbers to NATO and other U.S. allies. French F-84Fs claimed at least one Egyptian aircraft during the 1956 Suez crisis. More than 450 served with the newly reformed Luftwaffe. The last F-84s in service were RF-84Fs retired by Greece in 1991.

Dassault Mystère and Super Mystère

Dassault's Mystère and Super Mystère helped to get the French aviation industry back on its feet after World War II and were the workhorses of three air forces through the 1960s and early 1970s.

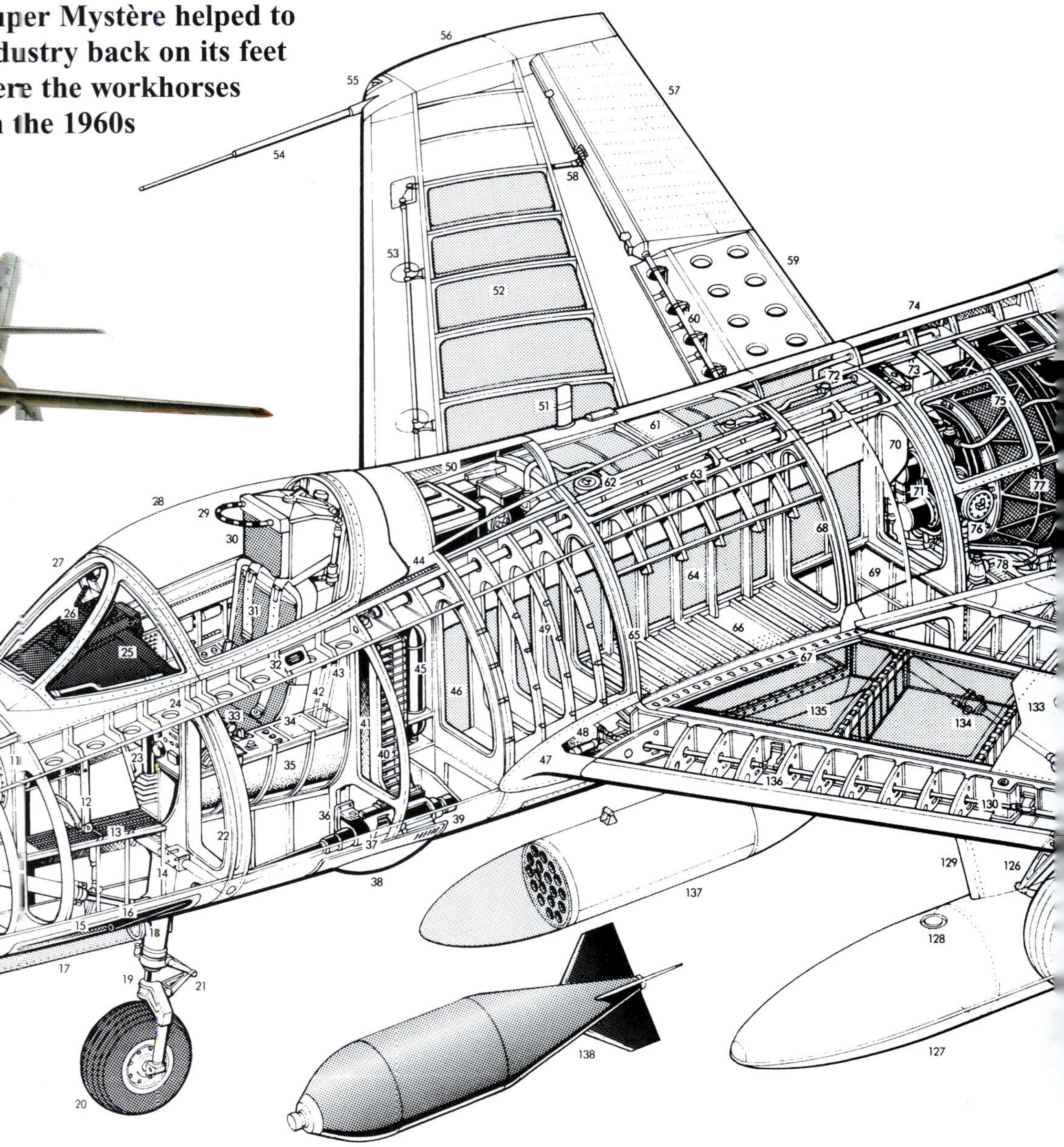

Cutaway Key

1 Engine air intake
2 Radar rangefinder antenna
3 Intake divider
4 Gun camera
5 Nose electronics compartment access door
6 Radar transmitter
7 Radar receiver
8 Nose undercarriage wheel bay
9 Hydraulic retraction jack
10 Battery
11 Cockpit front pressure bulkhead
12 Rudder pedals
13 Cockpit floor level
14 Nose undercarriage pivot fixing
15 Cannon blast trough
16 Cannon muzzle
17 Nosewheel leg door
18 Landing/taxiing lamp
19 Nose undercarriage leg strut
20 Nosewheel
21 Torque scissor links
22 Bifurcated intake duct framing
23 Control column
24 Cockpit coaming
25 Instrument panel shroud
26 Gyro gunsight
27 Windscreen panels
28 Cockpit canopy cover
29 Ejection-seat face blind firing handle
30 Headrest
31 Pilot's ejection seat
32 Canopy emergency release lever
33 Engine throttle lever
34 Port side console panel
35 Cockpit pressurized enclosure
36 Cannon mounting
37 DEFA 30-mm cannon
38 Spent cartridge case collector box
39 Gun bay access panel
40 Ammunition feed chute
41 Ammunition box (150 rounds per gun)
42 Control rod runs
43 Cockpit armoured rear pressure bulkhead
44 Sliding canopy rail
45 Oxygen bottle
46 Forward fuselage fuel tank (total internal capacity 476 U.S. gal/ 1800 litres)
47 Wingroot fillet
48 Aileron hydraulic booster
49 Intake duct framing
50 Radio and electronics equipment bay
51 UHF aerial
52 Starboard wing fuel cells
53 Aileron push-pull control rods
54 Pitot tube
55 Starboard navigation light
56 Wingtip fairing
57 Starboard aileron
58 Aileron hinge control
59 Split trailing-edge flap
60 Flap torque shaft actuator

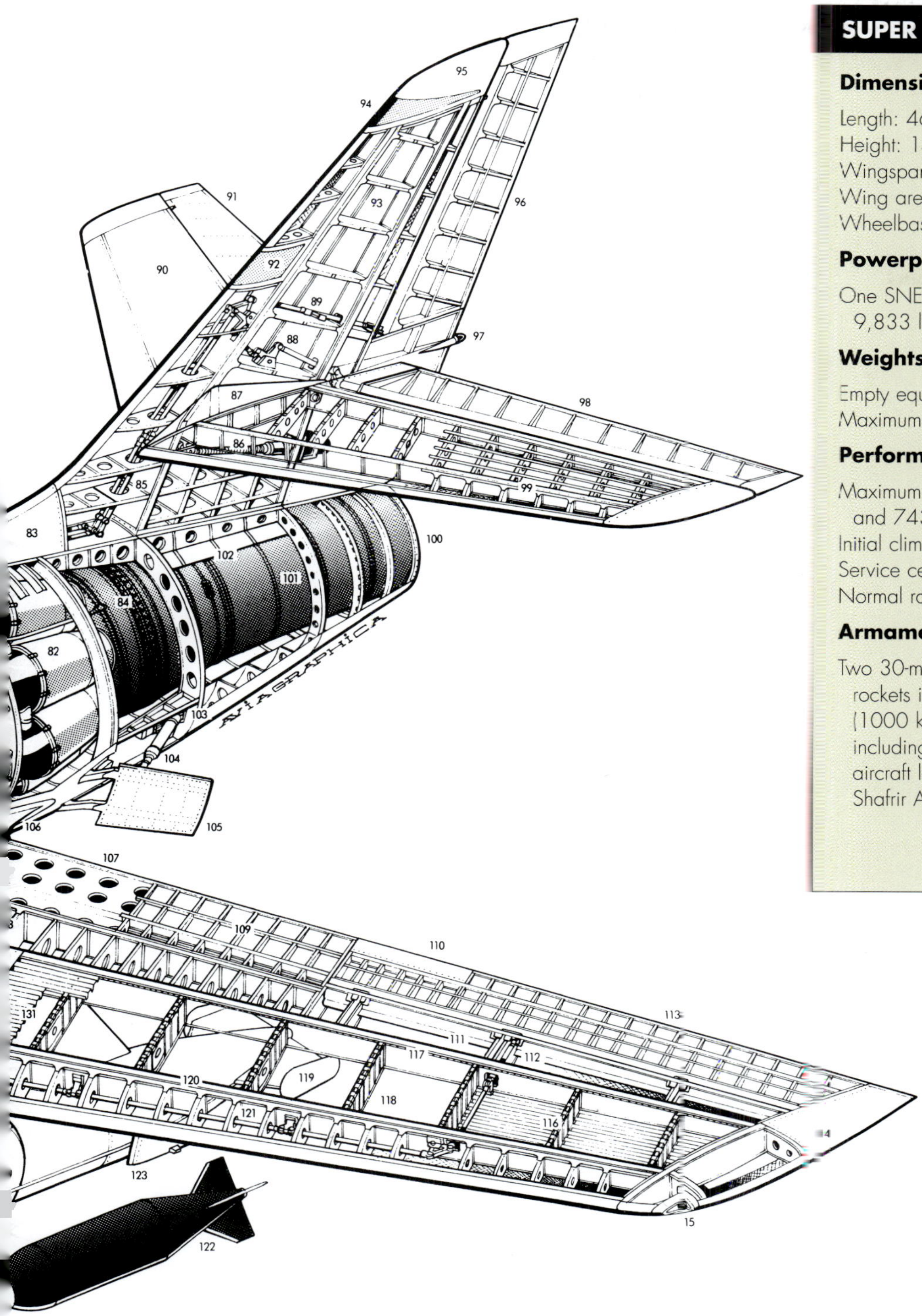

SUPER MYSTÈRE B2 SPECIFICATION

Dimensions

Length: 46 ft 4¼ in (14.13 m)
Height: 14 ft 11 in (4.55 m)
Wingspan: 34 ft 6 in (10.52 m)
Wing area: 376.75 sq ft (35.00 m²)
Wheelbase: 14 ft 11½ in (4.56 m)

Powerplant

One SNECMA Atar 101G-2/-3 turbojet rated at 9,833 lb (43.76 kN) thrust with afterburning

Weights

Empty equipped: 15,282 lb (6932 kg)
Maximum takeoff: 22,046 lb (10,000 kg)

Performance

Maximum speed: 646 mph (1040 km/h) at sea level and 743 mph (1195 km/h) at 39,370 ft (12,000 m)
Initial climb rate: 17,505 ft (5335 m) per minute
Service ceiling: 55,775 ft (17,000 m)
Normal range: 540 miles (870 km)

Armament

Two 30-mm DEFA 551 cannon plus 35 68-mm SNEB rockets in retractable pack plus up to 2,205 lb (1000 kg) of stores on four underwing hardpoints, including bombs up to 1,102 lb (500 kg); some aircraft later upgraded to carry AIM-9 Sidewinder or Shafrir AAMs

61 Fuel tank access door
62 Fuel filler cap
63 Control rod duct
64 Centre fuselage fuel tank
65 Wing front spar/fuselage main frame
66 Wing centre-section carry-through
67 Wing skin bolted root joint
68 Rear spar/fuselage main frame
69 Main undercarriage wheel bay
70 Hydraulic reservoir
71 Engine accessory compartment
72 Fuel system piping
73 Control rod runs
74 Dorsal spine fairing
75 Engine bay access door
76 Generator
77 Compressor intake filter screens
78 Intake plenum chamber
79 Main engine mounting
80 Hispano-Suiza Verdon 350 centrifugal-flow turbojet
81 Rear fuselage break point (engine removal)
82 Engine flame cans
83 Fin-root fillet
84 Engine turbine section
85 Tailplane control rods
86 Tailplane electric screwjack
87 Tailplane sealing plate
88 Elevator control linkage
89 Rudder push-pull control rod
90 Starboard tailplane
91 Starboard elevator
92 IFF aerial
93 Tailfin construction
94 VHF aerial
95 Fin-tip aerial fairing
96 Rudder construction
97 Tail navigation light
98 Port elevator construction
99 All-moving tailplane construction
100 Engine exhaust nozzle
101 Jet pipe
102 Jet pipe heat shroud
103 Airbrake housing
104 Hydraulic jack
105 Port airbrake, open
106 Wingroot trailing-edge fillet
107 Port split trailing-edge flap
108 Main undercarriage leg pivot fixing
109 Flap shroud ribs
110 Port aileron tab
111 Aileron mass balance weights
112 Aileron hinge control
113 Port aileron construction
114 Wingtip fairing
115 Port navigation light
116 Wing rib construction
117 Rear spar
118 Port wing fuel-tank bays
119 Drop-tank stabilizing fins
120 Front spar
121 Leading-edge nose ribs
122 500-lb (227-kg) bomb
123 Outboard stores pylon
124 Port mainwheel
125 Mainwheel hydraulic brake unit
126 Torque scissor links
127 Drop tank (127-US gal/480-litre capacity)
128 Fuel filler cap
129 Fuel tank pylon
130 Inboard pylon fixing
131 Corrugated wing skin sandwich panel
132 Main undercarriage leg strut
133 Wing skin panelling
134 Main undercarriage hydraulic retraction jack
135 Inboard fuel cells
136 Aileron push-pull control rod
137 18 x 68-mm (2.68-in) rocket launcher
138 1,000-lb (454-kg) HE bomb

"The [Improved Super Mystère] had the advantage of speed. It was a lot faster than the [Douglas] A-4, even though it had the same engine, but the French aircraft was slicker."
– Shlomo Shapira, Israeli Air Force pilot

FACTS

- The Mystère series had a radar-ranging gunsight but no air-intercept radar, except on some experimental models.
- The Dassault Ouragan and Mystère IV were both used by the Patrouille de France aerobatic team.
- The Israelis named the Super Mystère B2 or SMB2 the "Sambad."

DASSAULT MYSTÈRE – VARIANTS

M.D. 450 Ouragan: Original design on which the Mystère series is based.

M.D. 452 Mystère I: Initial prototype model designation; total of three examples produced; fitted with Rolls-Royce Tay turbojet engine.

Mystère IIA: Prototype model; two examples produced.

Mystère IIB: Prototype mode; four examples produced.

Mystère IIC: Pre-production model designation fitted with SNECMA Atar 101 6,614-lb (3000-kg) turbojet engine.

Mystère IV: Production prototype model designation. Modified tail, refined aerodynamic features, longer fuselage, Tay powerplant.

Mystère IVA: Pre-production and production models, of which nine examples were produced. Production run led to 480 fighters fitted with Tay and Hispano-Suiza powerplants.

Mystère IVB: Further development of IVA fitted with Rolls-Royce Avon turbojet. Revised fuselage.

Super Mystère B1: Production prototype model of the IVB with an afterburning turbojet.

Super Mystère B2: Production model designation of the B1; 185 were produced. It was fitted with SNECMA Atar 101G-2/3 afterburning turbojet engines.

Above: A Mystére pilot illustrates the relatively basic flying equipment supplied to the first generation "jet jockeys."

DASSAULT MYSTÈRE IVA

Mystère IVA No. 83 belonged to the last unit of the Armée de l'Air to operate the type. Escadron de Chasse 1/8 "Saintonge" at Cazaux, southwest of Borde flew the Mystère IVA from 1964 until 1982, when it re-equipped with the Dassault/Dornier Alphajet. Its role was as an advanced trainer for pilots destined to fly higher performance fighters. Part of 8 Escadre de Transformation (ET 8), EC 1/8 was further divided into two *escadrilles* (flights), which used the insignia of historic units. The winged arrow was that of 3C2. On the reverse side was a leaping lion, the insignia of 4C1. This Mystère was donated to the Newark Air Museum in England in 1978, and has been displayed there ever since.

In 1945, the French aviation industry was in ruins and years behind those of the United Kingdom, United States and Soviet Union. The Armée de l'Air was forced to continue producing Focke-Wulf 190s and other German designs in the factories that had been taken over for Luftwaffe production during the war.

Above: The Mystère IVN was a one-off attempt to produce a two-seat radar-equipped night-fighter variant with cannon armament.

Pre-war designer Marcel Bloch returned from Nazi captivity, changed his name to Dassault and drew up a design for a simple Rolls-Royce Nene–powered jet fighter. This was accepted for production as the Ouragan (Hurricane), and a prototype was flown in February 1949.

OPTING FOR SWEPT WINGS

By this time Dassault was already working on a swept-wing successor. The Mystère (Mystery) with 30-degree wing sweep and a Rolls-Royce Tay engine flew in early 1951. The Mystère IIC was the production version, with a SNECMA Atar 101C turbojet.

Although similar in appearance, the Mystère IV was an all-new design with 41-degree wing sweep, a new tail and an oval fuselage section and intake, and first flew in September 1952. Mystère IVs were fitted with either a Rolls-Royce Tay or a licence-built Hispano-Suiza version called the Verdon

Above: A Mystère IV shows off the range of bombs, rockets, fuel tanks and cannon ammunition that it could carry.

350. The Mystère IVA was a rather conventional aircraft with a thin wing that lacked any fancy high-lift devices. Underneath were four pylons, two of which usually carried fuel tanks, while the others sported either a bomb or a rocket pod. The main armament was a pair of 30-mm DEFA cannon.

In French service, the Mystère IVA was initially used as an interceptor, before reassignment as a ground-attack fighter as the Mirage III entered service.

COMBAT TESTED

The Mystére IV was exported to Israel and India. With India it saw action in both the 1965 and 1971 wars with Pakistan. In an engagement in the former war, a Mystère IV was damaged by a Lockheed F-104, but succeeded in shooting it down before it crashed itself. Israel's Mystères saw combat against Egyptian Mikoyan-Gurevich MiG-15s in 1956, scoring seven victories with cannon, and were again used in 1967, by which time Shafrir missiles were in limited use.

The Super Mystère B1 with an Avon engine flew in 1955, but production B2 models had afterburning Atar 101 engines. The Super Mystère had 45-degree sweep and became the first fighter in Western Europe to exceed Mach 1 in level flight. Again, Israel was the main user.

Israeli Super Mystères saw most action in the ground-attack role, fighting in the Six Day War of 1967 and Yom Kippur War of 1973. To get more from the aircraft, which was becoming obsolescent by the early 1970s, Israel re-engined a number with the Pratt & Whitney J52 engine, as used in the Douglas A-4 Skyhawk. This version was the Improved Super Mystère or in Hebrew the *Sa'ar* (Tempest), and was faster than the heavier A-4. Again, it was used mainly for ground-attack missions in 1973. Some upgraded Super Mystères were supplied to Honduras, which used them as late as the 1990s.

A CONTINUED ROLE IN TRAINING

The Armée de l'Air continued to use the Mystère IVA in the advanced training role until the early 1980s, by the 8th Fighter Wing at Cazaux in southwest France. Many of the Mystères were paid for by the United States under the Mutual Defense Assistance Program (MDAP), and survivors on display in museums today are technically on loan from the National Museum of the U.S. Air Force.

Above: A flight of some of the last Mystère IVs, used in the fighter conversion training role into the 1980s by the Armée de l'Air.

Hawker Hunter

The Hawker Hunter was a delight to fly, simple to maintain and reliable. Although outclassed as a day fighter fairly quickly, it soldiered on for decades as a ground attacker and trainer with many nations.

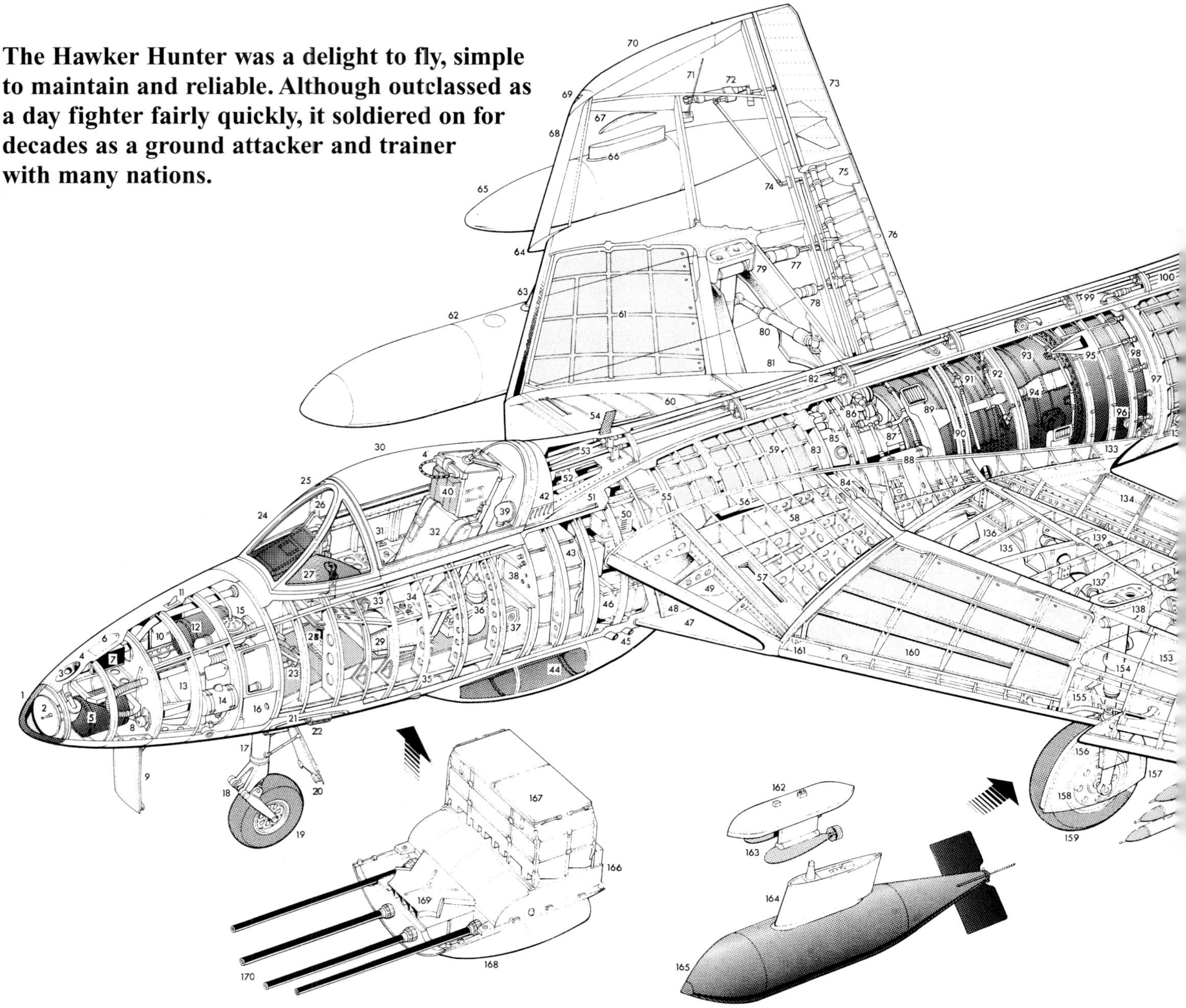

Cutaway Key

1 Radome
2 Radar scanner dish
3 Ram air intake
4 Camera port
5 Radar-ranging equipment
6 Camera access panel
7 Gun camera
8 Ground pressurization connection
9 Nosewheel door
10 Oxygen bottles
11 IFF aerial
12 Electronics equipment
13 Nosewheel bay
14 De-icing fluid tank
15 Pressurization control valves
16 Cockpit front bulkhead
17 Nose landing gear leg
18 Nosewheel forks
19 Forward retracting nosewheel
20 Nosewheel leg door
21 Cannon muzzle port
22 Gun blast cascade deflectors
23 Rudder pedals
24 Bulletproof windscreen
25 Cockpit canopy framing
26 Reflector gunsight
27 Instrument panel shroud
28 Control column
29 Cockpit section fuselage frames
30 Rearward sliding cockpit canopy cover
31 Pilot's starboard side console
32 Martin Baker Mk 3H ejector seat
33 Throttle control
34 Pilot's port side console
35 Cannon barrel tubes
36 Pneumatic system air bottles
37 Cockpit canopy emergency release
38 Cockpit rear pressure bulkhead
39 Air-conditioning valve
40 Ejector-seat headrest
41 Firing handle
42 Air louvres
43 Ammunition tanks
44 Ammunition link collector box
45 Cartridge case ejectors
46 Batteries
47 Port air inlet
48 Boundary layer splitter plate
49 Inlet lip construction
50 Radio and electronics equipment bay
51 Sliding canopy rail
52 Air-conditioning supply pipes
53 Control rod linkages
54 Communications aerial
55 Fuselage double frame bulkhead
56 Boundary layer air outlet
57 Secondary air inlet door, spring-loaded
58 Inlet duct construction
59 Forward fuselage fuel tank
60 Starboard inlet duct
61 Starboard wing fuel tank
62 276-U.S. gal (1045-litre) drop tank
63 Inboard pylon mounting
64 Leading-edge dogtooth
65 120-U.S. gal (455-litre) drop tank
66 Outboard pylon mounting
67 Wing fence
68 Leading-edge extension
69 Starboard navigation light
70 Starboard wingtip
71 Whip aerial
72 Fairey hydraulic aileron booster jack
73 Starboard aileron
74 Aileron control rod linkage
75 Flap cutout section for drop-tank clearance
76 Starboard flap construction
77 Flap hydraulic jack
78 Flap synchronizing jack
79 Starboard main landing gear mounting
80 Retraction jack
81 Starboard landing gear bay
82 Dorsal spine fairing
83 Main wing attachment frames
84 Main spar attachment joint
85 Engine-starter fuel tank
86 Air-conditioning system
87 Engine inlet compressor face
88 Air-conditioning pre-cooler
89 Cooling air outlet louvres
90 Rear spar attachment
91 Aileron control rods
92 Front engine mountings
93 Rolls-Royce Avon 207 engine
94 Bleed air duct
95 Engine bay cooling flush air Intake

96 Rear engine mounting
97 Rear fuselage joint ring
98 Joint ring attachment bolts
99 Tailplane control rods
100 Fuel piping from rear tank
101 Rear fuselage fuel tank
102 Fuel collector tank
103 Jetpipe mounting rail
104 Fin-root fairing
105 Hydraulic accumulator
106 Tailplane trim jack
107 Fairey hydraulic elevator booster
108 Tailplane mounting pivot
109 Rudder hinge control rods
110 Starboard tailplane
111 Starboard elevator
112 Tailfin construction
113 Fin-tip aerial fairing
114 Rudder construction
115 Rudder trim tab
116 Trim tab control jack
117 Tailplane anti-buffet fairing
118 Tail navigation light
119 Brake parachute housing
120 Tailpipe fairing
121 Port elevator construction
122 Tailplane construction
123 Detachable tailcone
124 Tailplane spar mounting frames
125 Jetpipe
126 Jetpipe access doors
127 Rear fuselage frame and stringer construction
128 Airbrake jack housing
129 Airbrake retracted position
130 Airbrake operating jack
131 Airbrake open position
132 Engine bearing cool air outlet
133 Wingroot trailing edge fillet
134 Flap housing construction
135 Port main landing gear bay
136 Main wheel door
137 Port main landing gear retraction jack
138 Main landing gear leg pivot mounting
139 Flap synchronizing jack
140 Hydraulic flap jack
141 Port flap
142 Rear spar
143 Aileron control rods
144 Aileron trim tab
145 Port aileron construction
146 Fairey hydraulic aileron booster
147 Wingtip construction
148 Port navigation light
149 Pitot tube
150 3-in (7.62-cm) rocket projectiles
151 Leading-edge extension ribs
152 Wing rib construction
153 Main spar
154 Dowty main landing gear leg
155 Shock absorber torque links
156 Leading-edge dogtooth
157 Mainwheel doors
158 Dunlop-Maxaret anti-skid wheel brakes
159 Port mainwheel
160 Port wing fuel tank: total internal fuel capacity 471 U.S. gal (1782 litres)
161 Leading edge pin joint
162 ML twin stores carrier
163 20-lb (9-kg) practice bombs
164 Inboard wing pylon
165 1000-lb (454-kg) bomb
166 Four 30-mm ADEN gun pack
167 Ammunition boxes, 150 rounds per gun
168 Link collector box
169 Gun gas-purging air duct
170 Cannon barrels remaining in aircraft when gun pack is withdrawn

HUNTER FGA.MK 9 SPECIFICATION

Dimensions

Length overall: 45 ft 10½ in ([illegible]3.98 m)
Height: 13 ft 2 in (4.01 m)
Wingspan: 33 ft 8 in (1[illegible] m)
Aspect ratio: 3.25
Wing area: 349 sq ft (3[illegible] m²)
Tailplane span: 11 ft 10 in (3.61 m)
Wheel track: 14 ft 9 in ([illegible] m)
Wheelbase: 15 ft 9 in ([illegible] m)

Powerplant

One Rolls-Royce Avon RA[illegible] Mk 207 turbojet rated at 10,150 lb st (45.1[illegible] kN)

Weights

Empty equipped: 14,40[illegible] (6532 kg)
Normal takeoff: 18,00[illegible] lb ([illegible]165 kg)
Maximum takeoff: 24,6[illegible] lb (1[illegible],158 kg)

Fuel and load

Internal fuel: 3,144 lb ([illegible] kg)
External fuel: two 276- or [illegible]20-U.S. gal (1045- or 455-litre) drop tanks
Maximum ordnance: 7,[illegible] lb (3357 kg)

Performance

Maximum level speed "clean" at 36,000 ft (10,975 m): 538 kt (620 mph; 97[illegible] km/h)
Maximum level speed "clean" at sea level: 616 kt (710 mph; 1144 km/h)
Maximum cruising speed at 36,000 ft (10,975 m): 481 kt (554 mph; 8[illegible] km/h)
Economical cruising speed at optimum altitude: 399 kt (460 mph; 740 km/h)
Service ceiling: 50,00[illegible] ft ([illegible]5,240 m)
Maximum rate of climb at sea level: about 8,000 ft (2438 m) per minute
Takeoff run: 2,100 ft ([illegible] m) at normal takeoff weight
Takeoff distance to 50 ft (15 m): 3,450 ft (1052 m) at normal takeoff weight
Landing run: 3,150 ft ([illegible] m) at normal landing weight

Range

Ferry range with two drop tanks: 1,595 nm (1,840 miles; 2961 km)
Combat radius: 385 nm ([illegible]43 miles; 713 km) on hi-lo-hi attack mission with typical warload and two drop tanks

Armament

Four 30-mm Aden cannon mounted in a pack beneath the forward fuselage with up to 150 rounds of ammunition per gun. Inboard pylons could carry either British or foreign bombs of up to 1,000 lb (454 kg), 2-in (5.08-cm) multiple rocket batteries, 120-U.S. gal (455-litre) Napalm bombs, practice bomb carriers and a variety of other stores. Outboard pylons could carry launchers for 24 3-in (7.62-cm) rocket projectiles with various warheads or other types of rocket projectile

"When I first sat in the Hunter, I knew instinctively that I was about to fly a thoroughbred."
– Air Chief Marshal Sir Patrick Hine, quoted in *Cockpits of the Cold War*

"A real pilot's aeroplane, which handled beautifully and was a delight to fly."
– Neville Duke, Hunter test pilot

FACTS

- Hunters are still in service in Lebanon, more than 55 years since they first entered service with the Royal Air Force.
- The Hunter was the first swept-wing British fighter to enter production.
- Hunters equipped numerous aerobatic display teams, including the RAF's "Blue Diamonds," the Indian "Acro Hunters" and the "Patrouille Swiss" of the Swiss Air Force.

HAWKER HUNTER – BRITISH VARIANTS

P.1067: Prototype. First flight 20 July 1951. Three built with the first later modified as a Mark 3 for the successful World Speed Record attempts.

P.1083: Prototype. Supersonic design based on the P.1067 with 50-degree wing sweep and afterburning Avon engine.

P.1101: Two-seat trainer prototype. Two built.

F 1: Avon 113 engine. First flight 16 March 1953. 139 built.

F 2: Sapphire 101 engine. First flight 14 October 1953. 45 built.

Mk 3: Sometimes mistakenly called F 3, but it carried no weapons. The first prototype fitted with afterburning Avon RA.7R with 9,600 lbf (42.70 kN) engine, pointed nose, airbrakes on the sides of the fuselage, and a revised windscreen. Raised the world's absolute air speed record to 727.6 mph (1,171 km/h) off the English coast on 7 September 1953.

F 4: Additional bag-type fuel tanks in the wings, provision for underwing fuel tanks, Avon 115 (later Avon 121) engine, blisters under the nose for ammunition links. First flight 20 October 1954. 349 built.

F 5: F 4 with Sapphire 101 engine. 105 built.

F 6: Single-seat clear-weather interceptor fighter. Powered by one 10,150 lbf (45.17 kN) Rolls-Royce Avon 203 turbojet engine, revised wing with a leading-edge "dogtooth." First flight 22 January 1954.

F 6A: Modified F 6 with brake parachute. 276-U.S. gal (1045-litre) inboard drop tanks.

T 7: Two-seat trainer with side-by-side seating nose section. Engine and systems as for the F 4; some were rebuilt F 4s, others were new-build.

T 7A: T 7 modified with the Integrated Flight Instrumentation System (IFIS). Used by the RAF as a Blackburn Buccaneer conversion training aircraft.

T 8: Two-seat trainer for the Royal Navy. Fitted with an arrestor hook for use on Royal Navy airfields, but otherwise similar to the T 7.

T 8B: T 8 with TACAN radio-navigation system and IFIS fitted, cannon and ranging radar removed. Used by the Royal Navy as a Blackburn Buccaneer conversion training aircraft.

T 8C: T 8 with TACAN fitted.

T 8M: T 8 fitted with the Sea Harrier's Blue Fox radar, used by the Royal Navy to train Sea Harrier pilots.

FGA 9: Single-seat ground-attack fighter version for the RAF.

FR.10: Single-seat reconnaissance version. All 33 were rebuilt F 6 airframes, with three F95 cameras, revised instrument panel layout, brake parachute and 276-U.S. gal (1045-litre) inboard drop tanks.

GA 11: Single-seat weapons training version for the Royal Navy. 40 ex-RAF Hunter F 4s were converted into the Hunter GA11. The GA 11 was fitted with an arrestor hook and some later had a Harley light.

PR 11: Single-seat reconnaissance version for the Royal Navy. The Harley light has been replaced by a camera.

Mk 12: Two-seat test aircraft for the Royal Aircraft Establishment. One built, converted from an F 6 airframe.

HAWKER HUNTER T8 C

The Hunter is known as the Royal Air Force's main day fighter of the 1950s, but the Royal Navy used many for different purposes, including pilot training, weapons training, missile simulation and target towing. The T 8C shown was built in 1958, and wears the markings of No. 738 Naval Air Squadron, the training unit with which it served from 1962 until 1970. Some T 8s were modified with a Blue Fox radar in the nose to train Sea Harrier pilots in its use, and became T 8Ms, but XL598 remained a standard trainer without radar and armed with a single 30-mm Aden cannon for basic weapons training. After retirement in 1994, XL598 was sold to a South African company.

Although Britain had led the United States with development of a practical jet fighter, the Gloster Meteor, the Korean War showed that straight-winged jets no longer had a place as fighters when faced by opponents such as the Mikoyan-Gurevich MiG-15. Through a series of evolutionary steps, Hawker Aircraft took what was to become their straight-winged Sea Hawk from a small, straight-winged naval fighter prototype to the Hunter, which was to become one of the most important second-generation land-based day fighters.

Above: The Sapphire-engined Hunter F 2 equipped only two RAF squadrons, Nos 258 (illustrated) and 263, both based at RAF Wattisham, in Suffolk, England.

In July 1951, the Hawker P.1067, prototype of the Hunter, flew. In April 1952, it was flown through the sound barrier, although in practice the Hunter was supersonic only in a dive. Two early production Hunter versions were developed, varying only in the engine used. The F 1, which entered service in July 1954, had the Rolls-Royce Avon; the F 2 had the Armstrong Siddeley Sapphire. There were a number of teething troubles. F 1s suffered from flame-outs when the cannon were fired, and the aircraft became unstable when the flaps were used as airbrakes. Flight endurance was very short. The F 4 and F 5 introduced some improvements, including a separate airbrake and more fuel. Like the F 2, the F 5 was Sapphire-powered, but subsequent models settled on the Avon engine.

SERVING THE RAF

The Hunter was issued to the squadrons of RAF Fighter Command and provided the main daylight air defence of the United Kingdom before missile-armed interceptors such as the English Electric Lightning replaced them. The Hunter's only air-to-air armament in RAF service was its four cannon, which soon made it obsolete in an era of missiles.

The RAF first used Hunters in action during the Suez Crisis of 1956, when F 5s attacked Egyptian ground targets. Hunters were sent to the Middle East and Far East. With cannon, rockets and bombs, the Hunter proved effective against rebels and terrorists in places such as Aden and Borneo. The main ground-attack version was the FGA.9, which remained in RAF service until 1970 and formed the basis of several export versions.

WIDENING ITS APPEAL

The Hunter was a great export success for the British aviation industry. Beginning with India in 1957, some 18 countries purchased new or refurbished Hunters, including Belgium, Denmark, Sweden, Switzerland, Oman, Jordan, Lebanon, Iraq, Kuwait and Switzerland. Several nations received Hunters that were surplus to their original owner's requirements, then returned, refurbished and resold by Hawker (later Hawker Siddeley, then British Aerospace). Dutch, Belgian and Swiss companies also produced Hunters under licence.

IN COMBAT

The Indo-Pakistan wars of 1965 and 1971 saw heaviest use of the Hunter in combat. India's Hunters were closely matched with Pakistan's North American F-86 Sabres, and air combat spoils between the two types were roughly equal in both wars, although the Hunters were outclassed when they met MiG-19s and Dassault Mirage IIIs in 1971. Jordan's Hunters had little effect against Israel's Mirages in the Six-Day War in 1967, and many were lost on the ground before being able to take an active part in the fighting.

Switzerland was the last European Hunter user, retaining the type until 1995, having introduced it in 1959. In the intervening years, it had equipped its FGA.58 models with AIM-9 Sidewinder and AGM-58 Maverick capabilities, although they still lacked radar and other modern avionics.

Hunters are still used by a number of private companies to provide simulated targets for missile operators, and a fairly large number are used for private enjoyment and air shows. In 2009, the Lebanese Air Force returned a few of its stored Hunters to frontline service, preparatory to re-equipping with more modern fighters such as the MiG-29.

Above: India's Hunters played important roles in the wars with Pakistan. A few remained in use in anciliary roles such as target towing into the first decade of the twenty-first century.

Above: Switzerland operated Hunters for more than 35 years. The Hunter was always regarded as something of a "sports car" and was well loved by its pilots.

North American F-100 Super Sabre

The first of the "Century Series" fighters, the F-100 was also the first U.S. Air Force fighter capable of supersonic speed in level flight. The needs of the Vietnam conflict meant it was largely used in the ground-attack role.

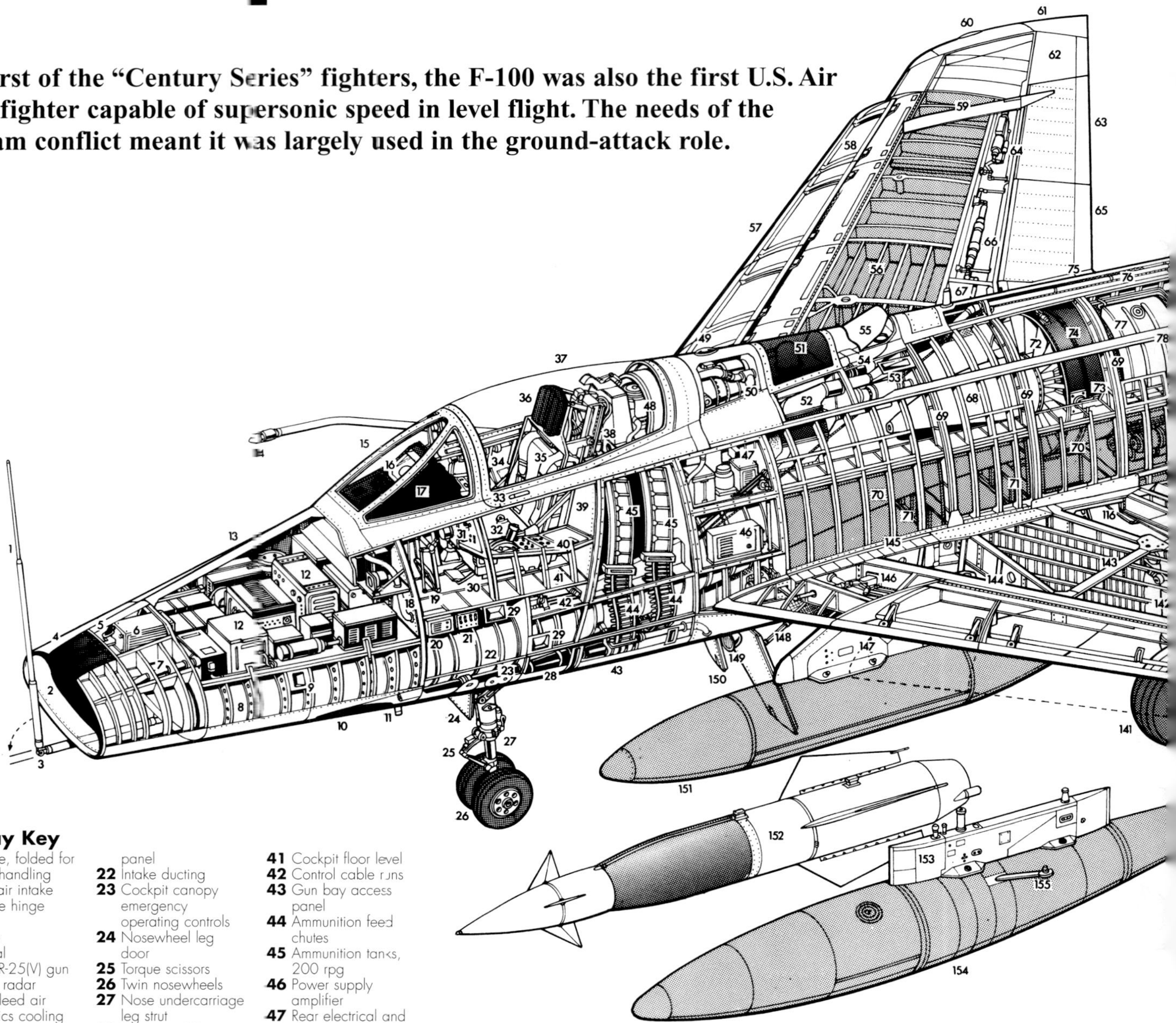

Cutaway Key

1 Pitot tube, folded for ground handling
2 Engine air intake
3 Pitot tube hinge point
4 Radome
5 IFF aerial
6 AN/APR-25(V) gun tracking radar
7 Intake bleed air electronics cooling duct
8 Intake duct framing
9 Cooling air exhaust duct
10 Cannon muzzle port
11 UHF aerial
12 Nose avionics compartment
13 Hinged nose compartment access door
14 Inflight refuelling probe
15 Windscreen panels
16 A-4 radar gunsight
17 Instrument panel shroud
18 Cockpit front pressure bulkhead
19 Rudder pedals
20 Gunsight power supply
21 Armament relay panel
22 Intake ducting
23 Cockpit canopy emergency operating controls
24 Nosewheel leg door
25 Torque scissors
26 Twin nosewheels
27 Nose undercarriage leg strut
28 Pontiac M39 20-mm cannon (four)
29 Kick-in boarding steps
30 Ejection-seat footrests
31 Instrument panel
32 Engine throttle
33 Canopy external handle
34 Starboard-side console panel
35 Ejection seat
36 Headrest
37 Cockpit canopy cover
38 Ejection-seat guide rails
39 Cockpit rear pressure bulkhead
40 Port-side console panel
41 Cockpit floor level
42 Control cable runs
43 Gun bay access panel
44 Ammunition feed chutes
45 Ammunition tanks, 200 rpg
46 Power supply amplifier
47 Rear electrical and electronics bay
48 Cockpit pressurization valve
49 Anti-collision light
50 Air-conditioning plant
51 Radio compass aerial
52 Intake bleed air heat exchanger
53 Heat exchanger exhaust duct
54 Secondary air turbine
55 Air turbine exhaust duct (open)
56 Starboard wing integral fuel tank, capacity 209 U.S. gal (791 litres)
57 Starboard automatic leading-edge slat, open
58 Slat guide rails
59 Wing fence
60 Starboard navigation light
61 Wingtip faring
62 Fixed portion of trailing edge
63 Starboard aileron
64 Aileron hydraulic jack
65 Starboard outer plain flap
66 Flap hydraulic jack
67 UHF aerial
68 Engine intake centre-body
69 Wing attachment fuselage main frames
70 Fuselage fuel tanks, total internal capacity 770 U.S. gal (2915 litres)
71 Wing spar centre-section carry-through beams
72 Engine intake compressor face
73 Main engine mounting
74 Pratt & Whitney J57-P-21A afterburning turbojet engine
75 Dorsal spine fairing
76 Fuel vent pipe
77 Engine oil tank
78 Fuselage upper longeron
79 Engine accessory gearbox
80 Compressor bleed air blow-off valve
81 Fuselage break point
82 Rear fuselage attachment bolts (four)
83 Finroot filet
84 Engine turbine section
85 Engine rear mounting ring
86 Afterburner fuel spray manifold
87 Fin attachment sloping frame
88 Rudder hydraulic jack
89 Fin sub-attachment joint
90 Tailfin construction
91 Fin leading edge
92 Fin-tip aerial fairing
93 Upper UHF aerial
94 Fixed portion of trailing edge
95 AN/APR-26(V) radar warning antenna
96 Tail navigation light
97 Fuel jettison pipe
98 Rudder construction
99 Rudder trim control jack
100 Externally braced trailing-edge section
101 Brake parachute cable fixing
102 Variable-area afterburner exhaust nozzle
103 Parachute cable

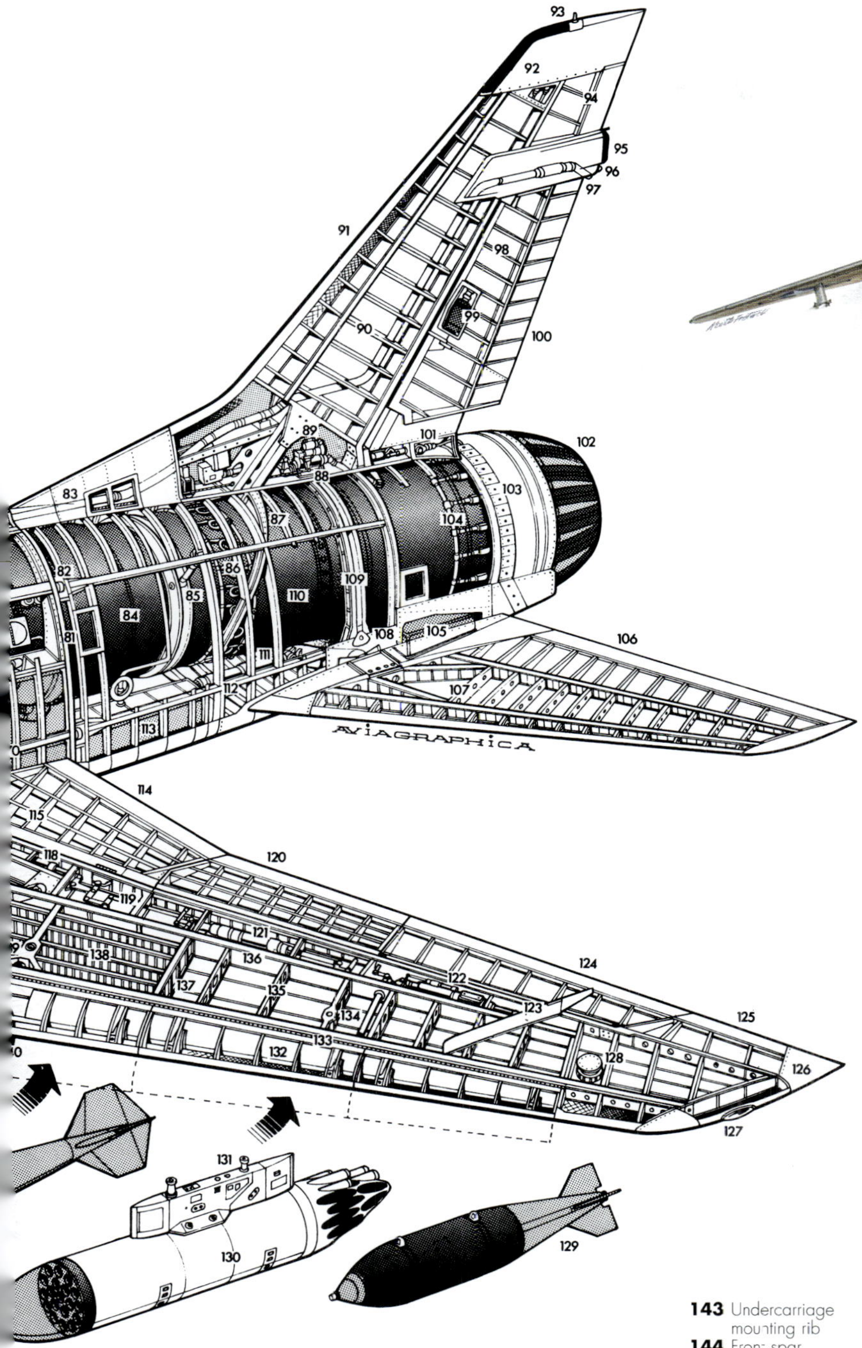

"pull-out" flaps
104 Afterburner nozzle control jacks
105 Brake parachute housing
106 Port all-moving tailplane
107 Tailplane spar box construction
108 Pivot fixing
109 Tailplane mounting fuselage double frames
110 Engine afterburner duct
111 Tailplane hydraulic jack
112 Fuselage lower longeron
113 Rear fuselage fuel tank
114 Port inner plain flap
115 Flap rib construction
116 Main undercarriage wheel bay
117 Undercarriage leg pivot fixing
118 Flap hydraulic jack
119 Flap interconnecting linkage
120 Port outer flap
121 Flap hydraulic jack
122 Aileron jack
123 Wing fence
124 Port aileron
125 Fixed portion of trailing edge
126 Wingtip fairing
127 Port navigation light
128 Compass master transmitter
129 750-lb (340-kg) M117 HE bomb
130 SUU-7A CBU 19-round rocket pod and bomblet dispenser
131 Outboard wing pylon
132 Leading-edge slat rib construction
133 Hinged leading-edge attachment joint
134 Outboard pylon fixing
135 Wing rib construction
136 Rear spar
137 Port wing integral fuel tank, 209 U.S. gal (791 litres)
138 Multi-spar inner wing panel construction
139 Centre pylon fixing
140 Multi-plate disc brake
141 Port mainwheel
142 Main undercarriage leg strut
143 Undercarriage mounting rib
144 Front spar
145 Wing/fuselage attachment skin joint
146 Aileron cable control run
147 Inboard pylon
148 Airbrake hydraulic jacks (two)
149 Retractable landing/taxiing lamps, port and starboard
150 Ventral airbrake
151 200-U.S. gal (757-litre) napalm container
152 AGM-12C Bullpup B tactical missile
153 Centre wing pylon
154 335-U.S. gal (1268-litre) air-refuellable supersonic fuel tank
155 Tank side bracing strut

F-100D SUPER SABRE SPECIFICATION

Dimensions

Length: 49 ft 6 in (15.09 m)
Height: 16 ft 2⅔ in (4.95 m)
Wingspan: 38 ft 9 in (11.81 m)
Wing area: 385.20 sq ft (35.79 m²)

Powerplant

One Pratt & Whitney J57-P-21A turbojet rated at 11,700 lb st (52.02 kN) dry and 16,950 lb st (75.40 kN) with afterburning

Weights

Empty: 21,000 lb (9525 kg)
Loaded: 29,762 lb (13500 kg)
Combat: 30,061 lb (13633 kg)
Maximum takeoff: 38,048 lb (17,256 kg)

Fuel and load

Internal fuel: 1,189 U.S. gal (4500 litres)
External fuel: up to 1,070 U.S. gal (4050 litres)
Drop tanks: usually flown with two 450-U.S. gal (1703-litre) tanks, although 200-U.S. gal (757-litre), 275-U.S. gal (1041-litre) and 335-U.S. gal (1268-litre) tanks were also available
Maximum external load: 7,500 lb (3402 kg)

Performance

Maximum speed at 35,000 ft (10,670 m): 864 mph (1390 km/h)
Rate of climb: 16,000 ft (4875 m) per minute
Climb to 35,000 ft (10,670 m) at combat weight with maximum power: 3 minutes 30 seconds

Range

Combat: 1,500 miles (2415 km)
Ferry: 1,973 miles (3175 km)

Armament

Four 20-mm Pontiac M39E 20-mm cannon with 200 rounds per gun, plus provision for tactical nuclear weapons and a wide range of conventional stores, including Mk 80 series and M117 bombs, cluster munitions, practice bomb dispensers, rocket pods, fire bombs and napalm tanks, AGM-12A/B/C ASMs and AIM-9B AAMs

"The F-100 was a super airplane. [In 1150 flight hours] I never had what could be considered a serious problem in it. It was a pleasure to fly."
– F-100 pilot Don Schmenk

FACTS

- F-100s were used by the U.S. Air Force's "Thunderbirds" and "Skyblazers" aerial demonstration teams.
- Two-seat F-100Fs became the first "Wild Weasel" anti-radar aircraft used in Vietnam.
- The F-100D was the most numerous of the Super Sabres, with 1,273 examples built.

NORTH AMERICAN F-100 SUPER SABRE – VARIANTS & OPERATORS

VARIANTS

YF-100A: Prototype, Model NA-180 two built, s/n 52-5754 and 5755.

YQF-100: Nine test unmanned drone versions: 2 D-models, 1 YQF-100F F-model (see DF-100F) and six other test versions.

F-100A: Single-seat day fighter. 203 built, Model NA-192.

RF-100A (Slick Chick): Six F-100A aircraft modified for photo reconnaissance in 1954. Unarmed with camera installations in lower fuselage bay. Used for overflights of Soviet Bloc countries in Europe and the Far East. Retired from USAF service in 1958; surviving four aircraft transferred to the Republic of China Air Force and retired in 1960.

F-100B: Tactical fighter-bomber with dorsal-mounted variable area inlet duct (VAID).

F-100BI: Proposed interceptor version of F-100B that did not advance beyond mock-up.

F-100C: 70 Model NA-214 and 381 Model NA-217. Additional fuel tanks in the wings, fighter-bomber capability, probe-and-drogue refuelling capability, later uprated J57-P-21engine. 476 built.

TF-100C: One F-100C converted into a two-seat training aircraft.

F-100D: Single-seat fighter-bomber. More advanced avionics, larger wing and tail fin, landing flaps. First flight: 24 January 1956; 1,274 built.

F-100F: Two-seat training version. Armament decreased from four to two cannon. First flight: 7 March 195; 339 built.

DF-100F: This designation was given to one F-100F that was used as drone director.

NF-100F: Three F-100Fs used for test purposes, the prefix "N" indicates that modifications prevented return to regular operational service.

TF-100F: Specific designation given to 14 F-100Fs exported to Denmark in 1974, in order to distinguish them from 10 F-100Fs delivered from 1959 until 1961.

QF-100: 209 D and F models were converted to unmanned radio-controlled FSAT (Full Scale Aerial Target) drone and drone directors for testing and destruction by modern air-to-air missiles used by current USAF fighter jets.

F-100J: Unbuilt all-weather export version for Japan.

F-100L: Unbuilt variant with a J57-P-55 engine.

F-100N: Unbuilt version with simplified avionics.

F-100S: Proposed French-built F-100F with Rolls-Royce Spey turbofan engine.

OPERATORS

French Air Force
Republic of China (Taiwan) Air Force
Royal Danish Air Force
Turkish Air Force
United States Air Force

NORTH AMERICAN F-100 SUPER SABRE

After some initial tussles with North Vietnamese MiGs, the F-100 was largely assigned to areas in South Vietnam and Laos, carrying out close air support missions and interdiction against Ho Chi Minh Trail supply routes from the north. This F-100D of 416th TFS, 37th TFW, carries 500-lb (227-kg) bombs on individual pylons, rather than multiple racks like the F-4 Phantom and F-105 Thunderchief. The large ventral airbrake is shown in the deployed position. "My Gal Sal III" was badly damaged in 1968, when it suffered damage to a hydraulic line and overran the airfield at Phu Cat, South Vietnam. It was repaired to fly again and returned to the United States, where it was later converted to a QF-100D drone for use in missile tests.

Above: Most second-generation USAF jets such as the F-100 featured less cluttered cockpits with light grey panels, making instruments easier to read.

The F-100 began life as a project to make a supersonic Sabre out of the F-86. Refining that aircraft's aerodynamics by sweeping the wing from 30 to 45 degrees did not promise to make enough difference, so North American Aviation's designers started again from scratch. Despite many differences, the new design that was accepted in early 1952 was initially known as the Sabre 45. By May 1953 when it flew, the aircraft had become the YF-100A Super Sabre, and more than 250 had been ordered.

The YF-100A exceeded Mach 1 on its first flight and was soon used for a number of low-level speed record attempts, culminating in a flight at 755.149 mph (1,215.29 km/h) in October 1953 made at an altitude of just 100 ft (30.48 m) above the Mojave Desert in California.

The F-100A had a thin wing with no internal fuel and swept at 45 degrees. The tailplane was mounted lower than the wing to prevent it being blanked by the wing at high angles of attack. A nose intake with sharp lips led to a single Pratt & Whitney J57 turbojet engine. The vertical fin had a single skin with strengthening ribs on the outside. Armament was four 20-mm cannon under the forward fuselage, with two pylons under the wing for fuel tanks or bombs, rockets or missiles. With no radar, the F-100A was intended as a day fighter, but it was decided to modify it for use as a fighter-bomber due to delays with the Republic F-84F Thunderstreak programme.

F-100C AND D

The F-100C introduced fuel tanks within the wings and a detachable inflight refuelling probe. The small fin of the F-100A was inadequate for stability in certain configurations and was replaced by a much larger unit on the F-100C.The F-100D gained more attack capabilities and its pilots trained

Above: The F-100F two-seater (nearest) was combat-capable. Some were modified to become the first "Wild Weasel" defense suppression platforms.

more for close air support than dogfighting. Some were modified to carry AGM-12 Bullpup missiles, and most could carry nuclear free-fall weapons.

The D was the most numerous version of the "Hun" to see service in Vietnam from mid-1964 onwards. F-100s were used as both fighters and fighter-bombers, but were not very effective as the former. With a gun-ranging radar limited only to short-range missiles and cannon, and a relatively poor performance while carrying external stores, F-100s rarely tangled with MiGs. In one of the few aerial engagements, an F-100D pilot claimed a probable victory in April 1965.

EXPORT VARIANTS

F-100s were exported to France, Taiwan, Turkey and Denmark. All of these nations except the last used them in action: the French in the Algerian Civil War; the Taiwanese with RF-100 reconnaissance aircraft over mainland China; and Turkey against Greece over Cyprus in 1974.

Like most fighters in the "Century Series," the F-100D was phased out of the active U.S. Air Force and into the Air National Guard, before serving as pilotless target drones until 1985. Until 2001, civilian company Tracor Flight Systems used some ex-Danish F-100F two-seaters as target tugs in Germany.

Above: Zero-length launch was a largely unsuccessful method for getting F-100s and other fighters into the air quickly and without the need for runways. Until they needed to land, of course.

Mikoyan-Gurevich MiG-19 "Farmer"

Mikoyan-Gurevich's MiG-19 was the first Soviet supersonic fighter. Although rushed into production with many deficiencies, it proved a solid platform and one that remains in service with the Chinese and several other air forces.

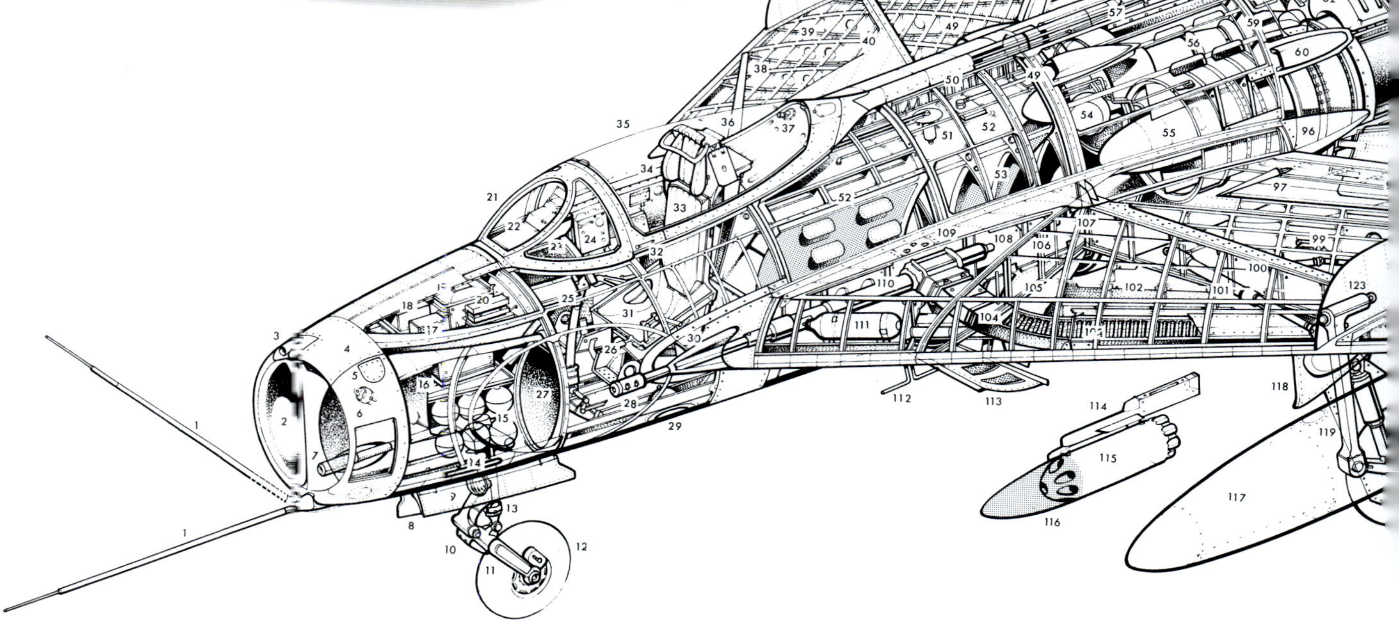

Cutaway Key

1 Pitot tube (hinged)
2 Bifurcated intake
3 Combat camera (offset to starboard)
4 Nose intake ring
5 Access panel
6 Nosewheel retraction cylinder
7 Nudelmann-Richter NR-30 revolver-type cannon (starboard lower fuselage) of 30-mm calibre
8 Nosewheel doors
9 Taxiing light
10 Nosewheel leg assembly
11 Axle fork
12 Forward-retracting nosewheel (500- x 180-mm tyre)
13 Shock absorber
14 Ranging aerial
15 Oxygen bottles
16 Intake trunking (port)
17 RSIU-4 VHF receiver
18 RSIU-4 VHF transmitter
19 Accumulator
20 RV-2 radio altimeter transmitter/receiver
21 Windscreen
22 ASP-5N automatic gyroscopic gunsight (coupled with SRD rangefinder)
23 Instrument panel shroud
24 Starboard console
25 Control column
26 Rudder pedal assembly
27 Intake duct section
28 NR-30 cannon muzzle
29 Landing light
30 NR-30 cannon barrel fairing
31 Ejection seat pan
32 Canopy external release/lock
33 Ejection seat
34 Headrest
35 Single-piece jettisonable canopy
36 ARK-5 radio compass antennas (in canopy)
37 Cabin pressurization compressed air system
38 RSIU-4 VHF antenna
39 Four-spar wing structure (main and three auxiliary)
40 Mainspar (inboard section)
41 Starboard mid-span full-chord boundary layer fence
42 Wire skinning
43 Starboard navigation light
44 Starboard aileron
45 Fuel dump vents
46 Starboard auxiliary fuel tank of 201-U.S. gal (760-litre) capacity
47 Starboard hydraulically powered Fowler-type flap
48 Flap hinge fairing
49 Ram air intakes
50 Dorsal spine housing control rod tunnel
51 Fuel filler cap
52 Main (Nos 1 and 2) fuel tanks of 388-U.S. gal (1470-litre) and 87-U.S. gal (330-litre) capacity
53 Intake cutout frames
54 Hydraulics accumulator
55 Port Tumanskii RD-9B turbojet
56 Slot intakes
57 Air-conditioning system
58 Slab-type tailplane control rod linkage
59 Fuselage break point
60 Air intake
61 Hydraulics tank
62 Oil tanks
63 Rudder control linkage
64 Fuselage aft frames
65 Filler cap for aft tanks (Nos 3 and 4) of 48-U.S. gal (180-litre) and 46-U.S. gal (175-litre) capacity
66 Air intake
67 Tailplane control hydraulic actuator
68 Tailfin front spar
69 Starboard hydraulically actuated one-piece tailplane
70 Anti-flutter weight
71 Tailfin structure
72 ARK-5 radio compass mounting
73 Tail-warning radar amplifier
74 Rudder balance
75 Tailfin antenna fairing
76 Rear navigation light
77 Rudder hinges
78 Tailfin rear spar
79 Rudder tab
80 Pen-nib exhaust fairing
81 Anti-flutter weight
82 One-piece tailplane structure
83 Exhaust nozzle (three-position) hydraulic control
84 Afterburner
85 Afterburner cooling air intakes
86 Tail bumper

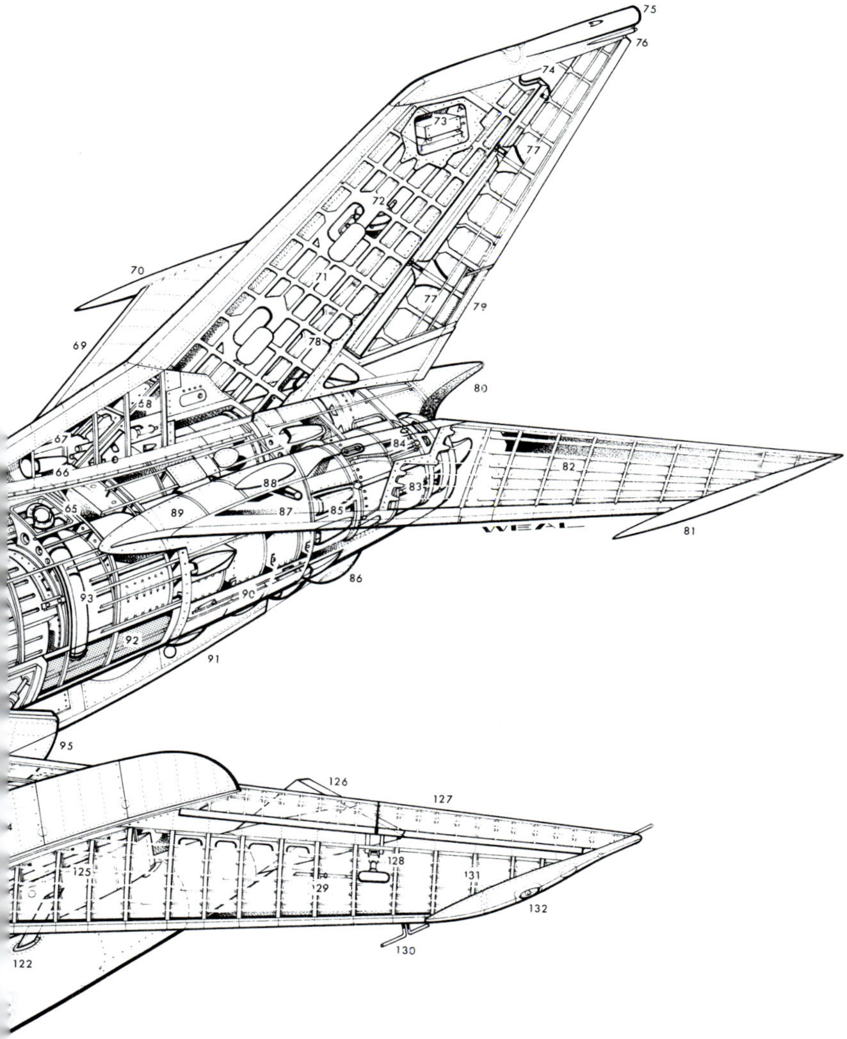

87 Slab tailplane spigot
88 Slab tailplane actuator fairing
89 Tailplane (fixed) fillet
90 PR 19 braking chute packing panel
91 Ventral strake
92 Aft (No. 4) fuel tank of 46-U.S. gal (175-litre) capacity
93 Filler neck
94 Airbrake hydraulic actuating ram
95 Airbrake (port and starboard)
96 Wingroot fillet
97 Flap hinge fairing
98 Port flap structure
99 Aileron control linkage
100 Mainspar (inboard section)
101 Port mainwheel retraction cylinder
102 Port mainwheel well
103 Ammunition track
104 Ammunition feed
105 Undercarriage door (inboard section)
106 Angled rib
107 Mainspar/fuselage attachment
108 Port wingroot cannon bay
109 Cannon cooling louvres
110 Port 30-mm Nudelmann-Richter NR-30 revolver-type cannon
111 Compressed air bottle
112 RV-2 radio altimeter dipole
113 Perforated ventral airbrake
114 Weapons pylon (port and starboard inboard wing)
115 ORO-57K eight-rocket launcher
116 Frangible nose cap
117 Port auxiliary fuel tank of 201-U.S. gal (760-litre) capacity
118 Mainwheel leg fairing
119 Levered suspension mainwheel gear assembly
120 Port mainwheel (660-x 200-mm) tyre
121 Mainwheel door
122 Auxiliary tank bracing struts
123 Mainwheel leg pivot
124 Port mid-span full-chord boundary layer fence
125 Auxiliary tank pylon
126 Fuel-dump vents
127 Port aileron
128 Inspection/access panel
129 Aileron control rod linkage
130 Radio altimeter dipole
131 Wing outboard structure
132 Port navigation light

SHENYANG J-6/F-6 SPECIFICATION

Dimensions

Length with probe: 48 ft 10½ in (14.90 m)
Length without probe: 41 ft 4 in (12.60 m)
Height: 12 ft 8¾ in (3.88 m)
Tailplane span: 16 ft 4¾ in (5.00 m)
Wheel track: 13 ft 7½ in (4.15 m)
Wingspan: 30 ft 2¼ in (9.20 m)
Wing aspect ratio: 3.24
Wing area: 269.11 sq ft (25.00 m²)

Powerplant

Two Liming (LM) Wopen-6 (Tumanskii RD-9BF-811) turbojets each rated at 5,730 lb st (25.49 kN) dry and 7,165 lb st (31.87 kN) with afterburning

Weights

Normal empty: 12,698 lb (5760 kg)
Normal takeoff: 16,634 lb (7545 kg)
Maximum takeoff: 22,046 lb (10,000 kg)

Fuel and load

Internal: 3,719 lb (1687 kg)
External: Up to two 301-U.S. gal (1140-litre) or 201-U.S. gal (760-litre) drop tanks
Maximum ordnance: 1,102 lb (500 kg)

Performance

Maximum rate of climb at sea level: More than 30,000 ft (9145 m) per minute
Service ceiling: 58,725 ft (17,900 m)
Takeoff run with afterburning: 2,198 ft (670 m)
Takeoff distance to 80 ft (25 m) with afterburning: 5,003 ft (1525 m)
Landing distance from 80 ft (25 m) without brake chute: 6,496 ft (1980 m)
Landing run with brake chute: 1,969 ft (600 m)
Never-exceed speed at 35,000 ft (10670 m): 917 kt (1,056 mph; 1700 km/h)
Maximum level speed "clean" at 36,000 ft (10,975 m): 831 kt (957 mph; 1540 km/h)
Cruising speed at optimum altitude: 512 kt (590 mph; 950 km/h)
Ferry range: 1,187 nm (1,366 miles; 2200 km) with two 201-U.S. gal (760-litre) drop tanks
Normal range at 46,000 ft (14020 m): 750 nm (863 miles; 1390 km)
Combat radius: 370 nm (426 miles; 685 km) with two 201-U.S. gal (760-litre) drop tanks

Armament

The J-6 can be used in the air-to-air or the ground-attack roles, although lack of fuel restricts endurance in the close-support role. For the air-to-air role, either AIM-9 Sidewinders or AA-1 "Alkalis" are carried and these are supplemented by the NR-30 cannon. For ground attack, the ORO-57K pod, which fires eight rockets, can be used, although this can be replaced with a single 551-lb (250-kg) bomb or a single rocket of up to 8.35-in (212-mm) calibre. Egypt's F-6s also carry runway-cratering or anti-personnel weaponry

"The Pakistanis had these real cheap [MiG-19s] which could be discarded after 100 hours of flying, but they outclassed the Indians with their more expensive and superior aircraft."
– Chuck Yeager, retired USAF major general and legendary former USAF and NASA test pilot

FACTS

- The MiG-19 has two intakes, separated by a splitter just inside the nose cowling.
- MiG-19s were tested as rocket-boosted interceptors launched from a rail in a scheme similar to the United States' ZELL (Zero-Length Launch) project.
- The AS-3 "Kangaroo" cruise missile was largely based on the MiG-19 airframe.

MIKOYAN-GUREVICH MIG-19 "FARMER" - VARIANTS

MiG-19 (NATO: "Farmer-A"): First production version armed with three 23-mm NR-23 cannons.

MiG-19P (NATO: "Farmer-B"): Version equipped with RP-1 Izumrud radar in the nose and armed with two 23-mm NR-23 (later two 30-mm NR-30) cannons in the wings. Entered production in 1955.

MiG-19PG: MiG-19P equipped with the Gorizont-1 ground control datalink.

MiG-19S (NATO: "Farmer-C"): Development of the MiG-19P equipped with Svod long-range navigation receiver and armed with three 30-mm NR-30 cannons. Entered service in 1956.

MiG-19R: Reconnaissance version of the MiG-19S with cameras replacing the nose cannon and powered by uprated RD-9BF-1 engines.

MiG-19SF: Late-production MiG-19S powered by the same uprated RD-9BF-1 engines as the MiG-19R.

MiG-19SV: High-altitude version for intercepting reconnaissance balloons, reached 68,045 ft (20,740 m) on 6 December 1956.

MiG-19SVK: MiG-19SV with a new wing. Did not warrant production.

MiG-19SU (SM-50): High-altitude version to intercept the Lockheed U-2.

MiG-19PF: Single-seat radar-equipped all-weather interceptor fighter aircraft. Built in small numbers.

MiG-19PM (NATO: "Farmer-E"): Variant with removed cannons, armed with four Kaliningrad K-5M (NATO: AA-1 "Alkali") beam-riding missiles. Entered production in 1957.

MiG-19PML: MiG-19PM with Lazur ground control datalink.

MiG-19PU: Rocket pack fit similar to MiG-19SU.

MiG-19PT: A single MiG-19P equipped to carry Vympel K-13 (NATO: AA-2 "Atoll") missiles.

MiG-19M: Target drone converted from the MiG-19 and MiG-19S.

SM-6: Two MiG-19 Ps converted to flying laboratories for testing the Grushin K-6 developmental AAM (intended for the Sukhoi T-3 jet fighter) and Almaz-3 radar.

SM-12: New fighter prototype, developed into the MiG-21.

SM-20: Missile simulator for testing the Raduga Kh-20 (NATO: AS-3 "Kangaroo") cruise missile.

SM-30: Zero-length launch (ZEL) version with PRD-22 booster rocket.

SM-K: Missile simulator for testing the Raduga K-10 (NATO: AS-2 "Kipper") cruise missile.

Avia S-105: Czechoslovak licence-built MiG-19S.

Shenyang J-6: Chinese-built version of the MiG-19. This version was inducted into the Pakistani Air Force as the F-6. The F-6 was later modified by the Pakistani Air Force to carry U.S.-built AIM-9 Sidewinder missiles.

MIKOYAN-GUREVICH MIG-19 "FARMER"

The MiG-19 was exported to a number of the Soviet Union's allies, and Chinese F-6s were supplied to many more. Top: North Vietnam received more than 50 F-6s from 1968–69. Based on the MiG-19S, they claimed seven American Phantoms, all during May 1972. Middle: Cuba's MiG-19Ps were sent out many times to drive off U.S. military and CIA aircraft. The MiG-19P had two 30-mm cannon and provision for two AA-2 "Atoll" air-to-air missiles. Bottom: Poland was also a user of the MiG-19P, as well as the missile-only MiG-19PM version (seen here) with a basic radar and pylons for four AA-1 "Alkali" beam-riding radar-guided missiles.

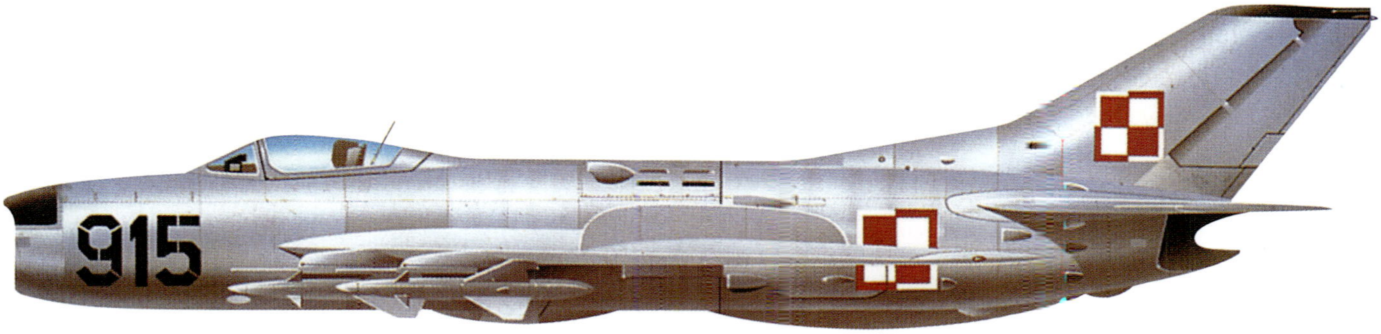

Above: American airmen inspect an Egyptian F-6 during joint exercises. The Shenyang F-6 served with Egypt into the 1990s.

By the early 1950s, supersonic performance was all that seemed to matter in the design of future fighter aircraft. The United States developed the North American F-100 Super Sabre as a supersonic successor to the F-86. In Russia, a similar path created the MiG-19.

The Mikoyan-Gurevich Design Bureau took the sound basic design of the MiG-17 and added two AL-5 engines, producing the I-340. At the same time it trialled the I-350, a MiG-17 with a single engine, but a wing swept back to 60 degrees. Neither prototype offered the hoped-for performance, but the decision to combine the main elements of the two designs produced a third prototype, unsurprisingly named the I-360, which flew in May 1952.

Above: This MiG-19S was modified under the designation SM-9/3T to test the K-13 (AA-2) missile copied from the AIM-9B.

SWIFT TAKE-UP

The I-360 had 37-mm cannon in the wing roots and a T-tail. Again, Mikoyan-Gurevich thought that the design could be improved, and the SM-9 with a new Mikulin AM-9B afterburning turbojet and a low tail was flown in February 1954. Even before testing was completed the Politburo ordered production of the SM-9 as the MiG-19.

The MiG-19 had a thin swept wing with slight anhedral and a large fence on each. The main armament was three 23-mm

Above: Flanked by FT-5s, this Pakistani Air Force formation includes an FT-6 and an F-6. All were part of 25 Squadron, the Pakistani Air Force's Operational Conversion Unit.

cannon, one in each wing root and another under the nose. External fuel tanks were usually carried due to the limited internal fuel tankage.

HASTY SERVICE AND POOR HANDLING

The MiG-19 was somewhat rushed into service and suffered from poor handling. There was a problem with exploding engines. An improved MiG-19S "Farmer-C" entered production in 1956, featuring a long fillet and anti-flutter weights at the tips of the all-moving tailplanes.

A radar-equipped MiG-19B "Farmer-B" interceptor had two 30-mm cannon and a rocket pod as air-to-air armament. The first missile-equipped version was the MiG-19PM with four AA-1 "Alkali" radar-guided weapons and no cannon. The MiG-19 was not particularly popular with pilots. Its highlight in Soviet service was the shooting down of Gary Power's Lockheed U-2 in 1960. One of the intercepting MiGs was itself shot down by a SAM. A number of other USAF and Taiwanese surveillance aircraft such as Boeing RB-47s fell victim to MiG-19s during the 1960s.

China began licence-production of MiG-19PMs in 1958, and later the MiG-19S, both known as the Shenyang J-6. Even though it was obsolescent, about 3,000 were built in all. A two-seat JJ-6 (or FT-6) was the only trainer version, the Soviets relying on MiG-15UTIs for training.

Many were exported (as the F-6) to countries such as Pakistan, Albania, North Korea and Afghanistan. One North Vietnamese regiment used the J-6 and claimed seven McDonnell Douglas F-4 Phantoms during the Vietnam War, in exchange for 10 losses.

Pakistan's F-6s saw combat in 1971 against India, acquitting themselves well. These aircraft were upgraded in the 1980s in Pakistan, receiving Martin Baker ejection seats and the ability to use late-model AIM-9 Sidewinders. F-6s were formally retired from the Pakistani Air Force in 2002. Both Egypt and Syria had many MiG-19s in 1967, but lost large numbers of them when the Israelis attacked their airfields. Both Iran and Iraq used them during the 1980–88 war.

A SPECIAL DERIVATIVE

A very different-looking derivative was the Nanchang Q-5 "Fantan," built as a strike aircraft that used the tail, rear fuselage and undercarriage of the Shenyang J-6 with a new radar nose, side intakes and a similar but redesigned wing. As the A-5, it was exported to a number of countries, including North Korea, Pakistan and Bangladesh.

Gloster Javelin

Among other things, the Javelin was nicknamed the "Flat Iron." Its performance was disappointing in some respects, but it did introduce missiles to Royal Air Force service and was used effectively in the Far East.

1 Detachable flight-refuelling probe, used for overseas deployment
2 Fibreglass radome
3 AI.Mk 22 radar scanner dish (American AN/APQ-43)
4 Scanner tracking mechanism
5 Radar transmitter/receiver
6 Radar mounting bulkhead
7 Instrument venturi
8 Aft-retracting nosewheel
9 Mudguard
10 Torque scissor links
11 Lower IFF antenna
12 Nose equipment bay access door
13 Additional (long-range) oxygen bottles
14 Radar modulator
15 Upper IFF antenna
16 Front pressure bulkhead
17 Rudder pedals
18 Standard oxygen bottle stowage, port and starboard
19 Side console panel
20 Engine throttle levers
21 Control column
22 Pilot's instrument panel
23 Instrument panel shroud
24 Windscreen rain dispersal air duct
25 Starboard engine intake
26 Windscreen panels
27 Pilot's gyro gunsight
28 Rearward-sliding cockpit canopy
29 Ejection-seat face-blind firing handle
30 Pilot's Martin-Baker Mk 4 ejection seat
31 Seat mounting rails
32 Port engine air intake
33 Intake lip bleed air de-icing
34 Intake duct framing
35 Rebecca homing antenna
36 Radar altimeter transmitting antenna
37 Missile cooling system heat exchanger
38 Cold-air unit and compressor
39 Port intake duct
40 Radar operator's instrument console
41 Radar indicator
42 Fixed canopy centre-section
43 Missile cooling system air bottles
44 Radar operator's rearward-sliding canopy
45 Radar operator's Martin-Baker ejection seat
46 Cockpit pressure shell framing
47 Missile control system equipment
48 Engine compressor intake
49 IPN engine starter fuel tank
50 Central equipment bay
51 Engine-driven gearbox with generators and hydraulic pumps
52 Cabin air system heat exchanger
53 Flight control rods
54 Gee antenna
55 Canopy tail fairing with heat exchanger outlet duct
56 Wing spar attachment fuselage main frame
57 Starboard main undercarriage wheel bay
58 Gun heating system air reservoirs
59 Starboard leading edge fuel tanks Nos 1, 2 and 3. Total internal capacity 1,141 U.S. gal (4319 litres)
60 120-U.S. gal (454-litre) external pylon tanks
61 Starboard wing pylons
62 Pylon aerodynamic fairings
63 Cannon muzzle blast fairings with frangible caps
64 Cannon barrel blast tubes
65 30-mm ADEN cannon, four carried for Far Eastern deployment, two only for European operations
66 Link collector boxes
67 Gun camera
68 Aileron control rod and pitch stabilizer
69 Aileron servodyne
70 Vortex generators, three rows
71 Starboard pitot head
72 Starboard navigation light
73 Formation light
74 Starboard aileron
75 Aileron spar
76 Fixed portion of trailing edge
77 Starboard airbrake, upper and lower surfaces
78 Airbrake hydraulic jack (2)
79 Flap hydraulic jack (2)
80 Ventral flap panel
81 Ammunition magazines, 100 rounds per gun
82 Rear fuel tanks, Nos 4 and 5
83 Engine exhaust, zone 3, cooling air intake
84 Artificial feel simulator pressure heads
85 Starboard engine bay
86 Fuselage centre keel structure
87 Rudder feel simulator
88 Port Armstrong Siddeley Sapphire Sa.7R turbojet with 12% limited reheat
89 Engine bay firewall
90 Turbine section
91 Central fuel system collector tanks
92 Engine exhaust duct
93 Fin-mounted bulkhead
94 Fin spar attachment joint
95 Servomotor
96 Rudder servodyne
97 Fin rib structure
98 Leading-edge ribs and control runs
99 Hydraulic accumulators
100 Tailplane hydraulic power control unit
101 Tailplane operating beam
102 Fixed tailplane centre-section

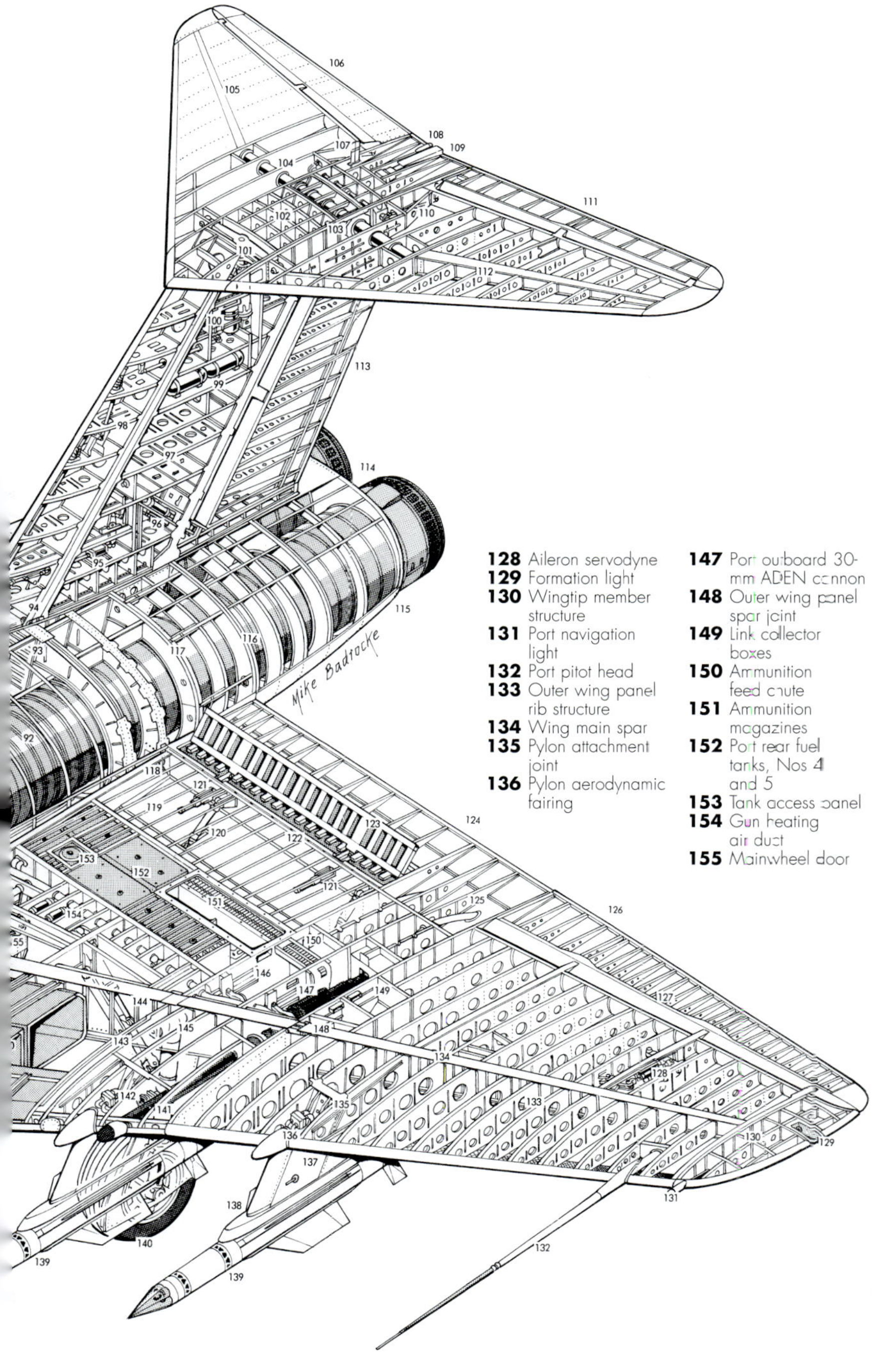

103 Tailplane spar bearing
104 Tubular tailplane spar
105 Starboard trimming tailplane
106 Starboard elevator
107 UHF antenna
108 Tail navigation light
109 Tail warning radar antenna
110 Elevator operating linkage
111 Port elevator rib structure
112 Tailplane single spar and rib structure
113 Rudder rib structure
114 Afterburner nozzles
115 Detachable fuselage tail section, engine removal
116 Afterburner duct
117 Tail section joint frame
118 Wing rear spar attachment joint
119 Port flap housing
120 Flap hydraulic jacks
121 Airbrake hydraulic jacks
122 Semi-span rear spar
123 Port airbrake panel, upper and lower surfaces
124 Fixed trailing-edge rib structure
125 Cartridge-case ejection chutes
126 Port aileron
127 Aileron rib structure
128 Aileron servodyne
129 Formation light
130 Wingtip member structure
131 Port navigation light
132 Port pitot head
133 Outer wing panel rib structure
134 Wing main spar
135 Pylon attachment joint
136 Pylon aerodynamic fairing
137 Port wing pylons
138 Missile shoe
139 De Havilland Propellers Firestreak air-to-air missiles
140 Port mainwheel
141 Cannon barrel blast tube and fairing
142 Mainwheel leg-mounted landing/taxiing light
143 Side stay and breaker strut
144 Hydraulic retraction jack
145 Mainwheel leg pivot mounting
146 Inboard cannon bay, gun deleted for European based operations
147 Port outboard 30-mm ADEN cannon
148 Outer wing panel spar joint
149 Link collector boxes
150 Ammunition feed chute
151 Ammunition magazines
152 Port rear fuel tanks, Nos 4 and 5
153 Tank access panel
154 Gun heating air duct
155 Mainwheel door
156 Door operating torque shaft and linkage
157 Port wheel bay
158 Main spar attachment bolted joint
159 Ventral pressure refuelling connection
160 Port leading-edge fuel tanks, Nos 1 2 and 3
161 Tank access panels
162 Leading-edge rib structure
163 Jettisonable 300-U.S. gal (1137-litre) ventral fuel tank (2)
164 Tank mounting spigots
165 Fuel vent and feed pipes

JAVELIN FAW.MK 7/8/9/9R SPECIFICATION

Dimensions

Length, Mk 7/9/9R: 56 ft 4 in (17.17 m)
Length, Mk 8: 55 ft 2½ in (16.83 m)
Height: 16 ft (4.88 m)
Wingspan: 52 ft (15.85 m)
Wing area: 927 sq ft (86.[illegible]2 m²)
Wheel track: 23 ft 4 in (7.[illegible]1 m)

Powerplant

Mk 7: Two Armstrong Siddeley Sapphire Sa.7 turbojets rated at 11,000 lb st (48.92 kN) dry
Mk 8/9/9R: Two Armstrong Siddeley Sapphire Sa.7R turbojets rated at 11,000 lb st (48.92 kN) dry and 12,300 lb st (54.70 kN) with 12 per cent afterburning at 20,000 ft (6096 m)

Weights

Takeoff, "clean," Mk 7: 3[illegible],690 lb (16,188 kg)
Takeoff, "clean," Mk 8: 3[illegible],410 lb (16,968 kg)
Takeoff, "clean," Mk 9: 3[illegible],100 lb (17,272 kg)
Overload, with two ventral tanks, Mk 7: 40,270 lb (18,266 kg)
Overload, with two ventral tanks Mk 8: 42,510 lb (19,282 kg)
Overload, with two ventral tanks Mk 9: 43,165 lb (19,578 kg)

Fuel and load

Internal fuel, Mk 7: 1,[illegible] U.S. gal (4158 litres)
Internal fuel, Mk 8/9/9R: 1,141 U.S. gal (4319 litres)
External fuel: All variants could carry up two 300-U.S. gal (1137-litre) conformal ventral tanks
Drop tanks, Mk 7/8/9: ventral tanks plus up to four 120-U.S. gal (454-litre) tanks
Drop tanks, Mk 9R: ventral tanks plus up to four 276-U.S. gal (1046-litre) tanks

Performance

Maximum level speed "clean" at sea level, Mk 7: 708 mph (1141 km/h)
Maximum level speed "clean" at sea level, Mk 8/9: 702 mph (1130 km/h)
Climb to 45,000 ft (13 716 m), Mk 7: 6 minutes 36 seconds
Climb to 50,000 ft (15 240 m), Mk 8/9: 9 minutes 15 seconds
Service ceiling, Mk 7: 52,800 ft (16,039 m)
Service ceiling, Mk 8/9: 52,000 ft (15,849 m)
Absolute ceiling, Mk 7: 54,100 ft (16,489 m)
Absolute ceiling, Mk 8/9: 54,000 ft (16,459 m)

Armament

Up to four 30-mm ADEN cannon in the outer wing panels, each with 100 rounds, plus up to four de Havilland Propellers Firestreak IR-homing air-to-air missiles

"The old girl was like the Rock of Gibraltar as a weapons platform."
– Javelin pilot

"A good aircraft; it had its limitations, but did the job for which it was designed. More fuel and more power would have made it a *great* aircraft."
– RAF Wing Commander Brian Carroll, Javelin pilot

FACTS

- The Gloster Aircraft Company built 433 Javelins, but these were to be the last type it built.
- The Javelin was the Royal Air Force's only delta-winged fighter before the Eurofighter Typhoon.
- The Javelin was the first missile-armed interceptor to enter RAF service.

GLOSTER JAVELIN – VARIANTS & OPERATORS

VARIANTS

FAW.1: Initial version with Armstrong Siddeley Sapphire Sa.6 engines with 8,000 lbf (35.6 kN thrust) each, British AI.17 radar, four 30-mm ADEN cannon in wings. 40 produced and the seven prototypes were later fitted to this standard.

FAW 2: Replaced the AI.17 radar with U.S.-made Westinghouse AN/APQ-43 radar (known as the AI-22). 30 produced.

T 3: Dual-control trainer version with no radar, bulged canopy for improved instructor visibility. All-moving tailplane; lengthened fuselage to compensate for altered centre of gravity, adding additional internal fuel. Retained four cannon. 22 produced.

FAW 4: Similar to FAW 2, but with the original AI.17 radar of the FAW.1, and with the addition of vortex generators on wings for improved stall characteristics, as well as an all-moving tailplane. 50 produced.

FAW 5: Based on FAW 4, with revised wing structure incorporating additional fuel tanks, provision for missile pylons (never actually fitted). 64 produced.

FAW 6: Combined FAW 2's American radar with the revised wing of the FAW.5. 33 produced.

FAW.7: Introduced new Sa.7 engines with 11,000 lbf (48.9 kN) thrust each, powered rudder, extended rear fuselage. Armed with two 30-mm ADEN cannon plus four Firestreak air-to-air missiles. 142 produced.

FAW 8: Upgraded Sa.7R engines with reheat, raising thrust to 12,300 lbf (54.7 kN) thrust above 20,000 ft (6100 m); at lower altitudes, the limitation of the fuel pump caused a loss of cold thrust. New "drooped" wing leading edge and auto-stabilizer for better handling.

FAW.9: A total of 76 FAW 7s refitted with the revised wing of the Mk 8.

FAW 9R: R standing for "Range." A total of 40 Mk 9s were refitted with in-flight refuelling probes.

OPERATORS

UNITED KINGDOM – ROYAL AIR FORCE
No. 3 Squadron
No. 5 Squadron
No. 11 Squadron
No. 23 Squadron
No. 25 Squadron
No. 29 Squadron
No. 33 Squadron
No. 41 Squadron
No. 46 Squadron
No. 60 Squadron
No. 64 Squadron
No. 72 Squadron
No. 85 Squadron
No. 87 Squadron
No. 89 Squadron
No. 96 Squadron
No. 137 Squadron
No. 141 Squadron
No. 151 Squadron
No. 1 GWTS RAF Valley (Firestreak Trials)
No. 228 Operational Conversion Unit

GLOSTER JAVELIN FAW.9

This Javelin FAW.9 wears the markings of No. 11 Squadron, based at RAF Geilenkirchen in West Germany. Delivered in 1959, it lasted until 1967, when it was sold for scrap in the United Kingdom. The Javelin could carry four cannon in the wings, although two were usually removed when Firestreak missiles were fitted. A ventral fuel tank and an all-moving tailplane had been added on the FAW.5 model and, although the range and manoeuvrability was improved, the Javelin was still known as the "Dragmaster" because of its unrefined shape and fairly poor performance. No. 11 Squadron went on to fly the much faster English Electric Lightning, Panavia Tornado F.3 and Eurofighter Typhoon.

Above: The Javelin line went through nine marks in a fairly short period, each of them slightly improved over the last. This is an FAW.1 with cannon rather than missile armament.

In the early postwar years, the Royal Air Force fielded fighters in two varieties: visual-combat day fighters and radar-equipped night fighters.

The first RAF jet night fighter that was not adapted from an existing airframe such as the de Havilland Vampire or Gloster Meteor was the Gloster Javelin. A javelin was about the last thing Gloster's fighter resembled, with its deep fuselage and broad, thick wing. Its overall shape brought about the nickname "Flat Iron."

DELTA-WING DESIGN

Following an initial requirement issued in 1947, which was modified several times, Gloster and de Havilland offered competing designs for large radar-equipped missile-armed fighters. De Havilland's twin-boomed D.H. 110 went on to form the basis of the naval Sea Vixen fighter, but lost the RAF order to Gloster's delta-winged design.

In November 1951, the Gloster GA.5 flew. It was outwardly similar to the production Javelin, but without radar or weapons. The second seat was covered by a metal hood with only small portholes to give the navigator an outside view. This was later changed to a conventional Perspex canopy.

Above: A specially designed ladder was essential for getting the pilot and navigator into the lofty cockpit.

Various experimental programmes in the United Kingdom were pointing towards delta wings as the best solution for high-speed flight. Unfortunately, none of these was completed

Above: The prototype GA.5 Javelin shows off its distinctive plan view. It was written off in an accident after seven months of test flying.

before the GA.5 flew, and the aircraft had an overly thick wing, which gave great structural strength but reduced performance. Nonetheless, the GA.5 (named Javelin when it was selected for production) was capable of supersonic flight, unlike production aircraft.

AN AWKWARD EVOLUTION

No fewer than six marks of Javelin were introduced into RAF service before a truly operational aircraft, the FAW.7, was fielded with working radar, weapons control system and missiles, and the first firing of a Firestreak missile took place in 1960.

The FAW.9 version had reheat (afterburners), but these had severe limitations due to the maximum flow rate of the fuel pump. At lower altitudes, including takeoffs, the reheat system's use was forbidden because its high fuel consumption starved the core engine of fuel, leading to an overall reduction in thrust, rather than an increase. An aerodynamic quirk was that, if the nose was pulled up too steeply, airflow over the tailplane could be blanked by the wing, leading to a loss of control. This contributed to a number of accidents.

The FAW.7 and subsequent versions were able to carry four Firestreak infrared-guided missiles, which had a large 50-lb (22.7-kg) warhead. Early Javelin models had four 30-mm Aden cannon, although two of these were removed from the FAW.7 onwards. Even then, the Javelin remained one of the most heavily armed fighters of its day, able to engage targets at a respectable distance and still hold its own when merged in a close-range dogfight.

OVERSEAS DEPLOYMENT

As well as serving in the home-defence role, Javelins were deployed to the Far East and came closest to action during the "Confrontation" with Indonesia. It is said that an Indonesian Air Force Lockheed C-130 Hercules crashed while trying to evade a Javelin in 1964, but details remain elusive. If true, this would be the last aerial victory recorded to date by an RAF pilot flying an RAF aircraft. Javelins were also deployed to Cyprus and Zambia during periods of tension with Turkey and Rhodesia (now Zimbabwe), respectively. The last of the operational Javelins were retired at Tengah, Singapore, in 1968, although one remained in use for trials and testing until 1976.

Convair F-102 Delta Dagger

Convair's F-102 suffered more than the usual number of troubles during its development, but was put right to become the most numerous American interceptor of its day. It also ushered in the era of the fighter as a weapons system.

F-102A DELTA DAGGER SPECIFICATION

Dimensions

Length: 68 ft 4½ in (20.82 m)
Wingspan: 38 ft 1½ in (11.60 m)
Height: 21 ft 2½ in (6.45 m)
Wing area: 695 sq ft (64.56 m²)

Powerplant

One Pratt & Whitney J57-P-23 turbojet developing 11,700 lb (53 kN) of thrust dry and 17,200 lb (77 kN) thrust with afterburning

Weights

Empty: 19,350 lb (8777 kg)
Normal loaded, "clean": 27,700 lb (12,565 kg)
Normal loaded, point interception: 28,150 lb (12,769 kg)
Maximum takeoff: 31,500 lb (14,288 kg)

Fuel

Internal: 1,085 U.S. gal (4107 litres) maximum, with two 215-U.S. gal (814-litre) drop tanks: 1,515 U.S. gal (5735 litres)

Performance

Maximum speed "clean" at 40,000 ft (12,190 m): 825 mph (1328 km/h)
Normal cruising speed at 35,000 ft (10,670 m): 540 mph (869 km/h)
Stalling speed: 154 mph (248 km/h)
Service ceiling: 54,000 ft (16,460 m)
Tactical radius with two 215-U.S. gal (814-litre) drop tanks and full armament: 500 miles (805 km)
Maximum range: 1,350 miles (2173 km)
Initial climb rate: 17,400 ft (5304 m) per minute

Armament

Three AIM-4C Falcon infrared homing AAMs and one AIM-26A Nuclear Falcon AAM, or three AIM-4A/E radar-guided and three AIM-4C/F infrared homing AAMs, or up to 24 unguided 2.75-in (70-mm) folding-fin aircraft rockets in early aircraft (this latter facility was later deleted in service)

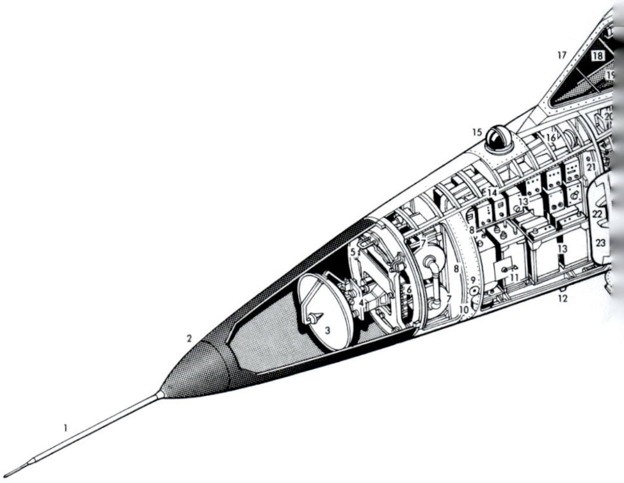

Cutaway Key

1 Pitot head
2 Radome
3 Radar scanner
4 Scanner tracking mechanism
5 ILS glideslope aerial
6 Radar mounting bulkhead
7 Radar pulse generator and modulator units
8 Nose compartment access doors
9 Static port
10 Lower IFF aerial
11 Angle-of-attack transmitter
12 TACAN aerial
13 MG-10 fire control system electronics
14 Nose compartment longeron
15 Infrared detector
16 Electronics cooling air duct
17 Windscreen panels
18 Central vision splitter
19 Instrument panel shroud
20 Rudder pedals and linkages
21 Cockpit front pressure bulkhead
22 Air-conditioning system ram air intake
23 Boundary layer splitter plate
24 Electrical system equipment
25 Port air intake
26 Nosewheel door
27 Taxiing lamp
28 Nosewheel, forward-retracting
29 Nose undercarriage leg strut
30 Torque scissor links
31 Intake duct framing
32 Nose undercarriage pivot mounting
33 Cockpit pressure floor
34 Port side console panel
35 Engine throttle lever
36 Two-handed control grip, radar and flight controls
37 Pilot's ejection seat
38 Canopy handle
39 Starboard-side console panel
40 Radar display
41 Optical sight
42 Cockpit canopy cover, upward-hinging
43 Ejection-seat headrest
44 Boundary layer spill duct
45 Sloping cockpit rear pressure bulkhead
46 Air-conditioning plant
47 Canopy external release
48 Canopy jack
49 Air exit louvres
50 Equipment bay access hatches, port and starboard
51 Canopy hinge
52 Radio and electronics equipment bay
53 Forward position light
54 Intake trunking
55 Missile-bay cooling air duct
56 Missile-bay door pneumatic jacks
57 Canopy emergency release
58 Liquid oxygen converter
59 Electrical system equipment bay
60 Fuselage upper longeron
61 Upper IFF aerial
62 Wing front spar attachment bulkhead
63 Pneumatic system air bottles
64 Bifurcated intake duct
65 Close-pitched fuselage frame construction
66 Engine bleed air duct
67 Anti-collision light
68 Starboard wing forward main fuel tank, total internal

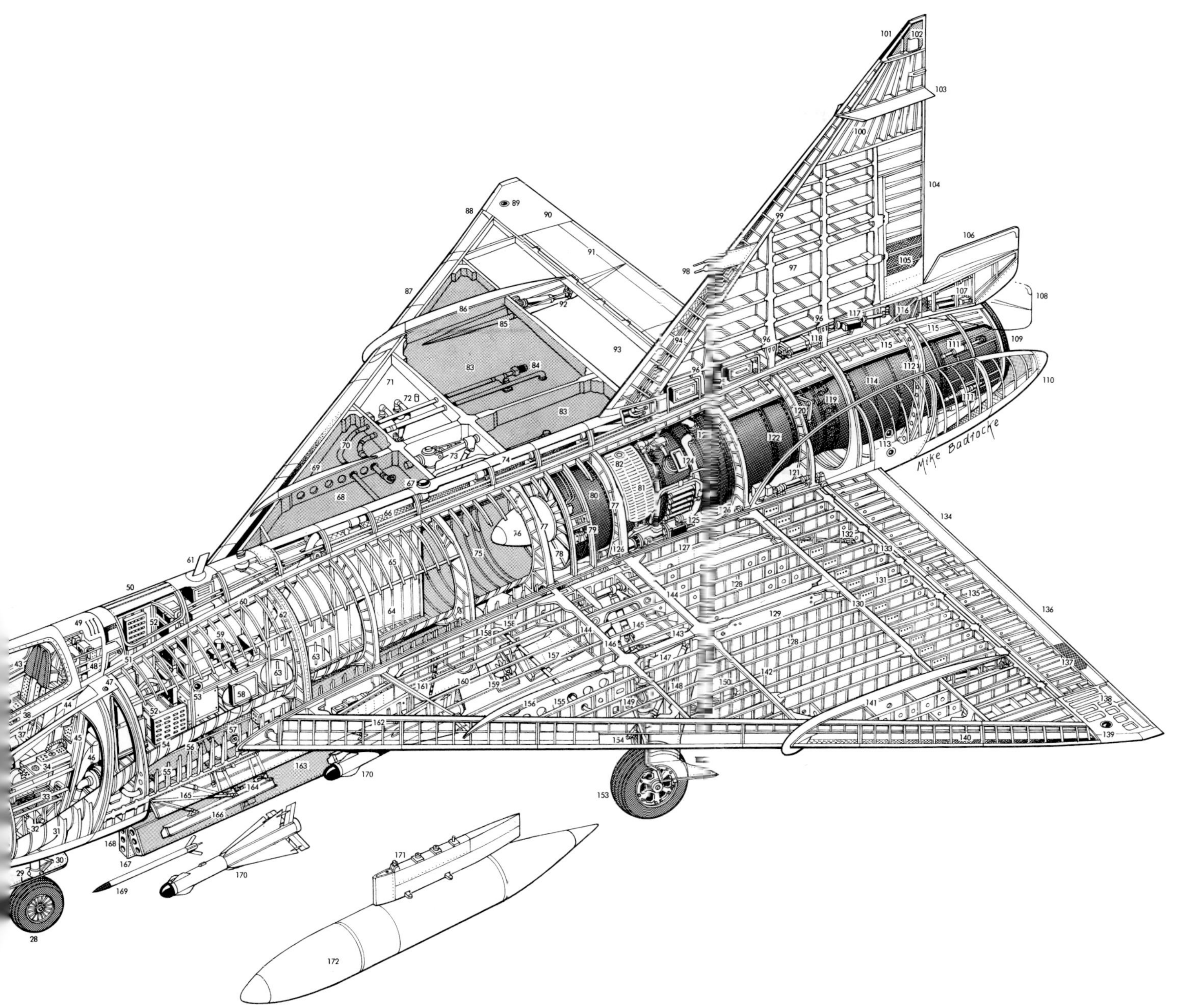

capacity 1,085 U.S. gal (4107 litres)
69 Inboard wing fence
70 Fuel system piping
71 Centre-section wing dry bay
72 Wing pylon mountings and connectors
73 Starboard main undercarriage pivot mounting
74 Dorsal spine fairing
75 Intake duct mixing chamber
76 Engine intake centre-body fairing
77 Wing main spar attachment bulkheads
78 Intake compressor face
79 Forward engine mounting
80 Pratt & Whitney J57-P-23A afterburning turbojet engine
81 Engine oil tank, capacity 5.5 U.S. gal (21 litres)
82 Oil filler cap
83 Starboard wing aft main fuel tanks
84 Fuel feed and vent piping
85 Ventral actuator fairing
86 Outboard wing fence
87 Cambered leading edge
88 Wingtip camber washout
89 Starboard navigation light
90 Fixed portion of trailing edge
91 Starboard outer elevon
92 Elevon hydraulic actuator
93 Trailing-edge dry bay
94 Fin leading-edge rib construction
95 Aerial tuning units
96 Fin attachment joints
97 Tailfin construction
98 Artificial feel system pitot intakes
99 Sloping front spar
100 Upper fin multi-spar construction
101 Fintip aerial fairing
102 UHF aerials
103 VOR localizer aerial
104 Rudder
105 Honeycomb core rudder construction
106 Split airbrake panels
107 Airbrake pneumatic jacks
108 Airbrake, open position
109 Variable-area afterburner exhaust nozzle
110 Aft fuselage aerodynamic (area-rule) fairing
111 Exhaust nozzle control jacks (eight)
112 Tailcone attachment joint frame (engine removal)
113 Rear position lights
114 Afterburner duct
115 Engine bay internal heat shield
116 Brake parachute housing
117 Rudder hydraulic actuator
118 Rudder trim and feel force control units
119 Afterburner fuel manifold
120 Rear engine mounting
121 Inboard elevon hydraulic actuator
122 Engine turbine section
123 Bleed air connections
124 Bleed air blow-off valve
125 Engine accessory equipment gearbox
126 Wing spar/fuselage frame pin joints
127 Wingroot rib
128 Port wing aft integral fuel tanks
129 Fuel-tank dividing rib
130 Rear spar
131 Trailing-edge ribs
132 Runway emergency arrester hook, lowered
133 Elevon spar
134 Inboard elevon
135 Elevon rib construction
136 Outboard elevon
137 Trailing-edge honeycomb
138 Wingtip fairing construction
139 Port navigation light
140 Cambered leading-edge rib construction
141 Outboard wing fence
142 Wing rib construction
143 Main undercarriage mounting rib
144 Twin main spars
145 Main undercarriage side strut
146 Hydraulic retraction jack
147 Main undercarriage leg pivot mounting
148 Drag strut and pneumatic brake reservoir
149 Landing lamp
150 Port wing dry bay
151 Wing pylon mountings and connectors
152 Main undercarriage leg door
153 Port mainwheel
154 Torque scissor links
155 Port wing forward integral fuel tank
156 Inboard wing fence
157 Mainwheel door
158 Hydraulic reservoirs
159 Position of ram air turbine on starboard side
160 Missile-bay aft section doors
161 Retractable overrun barrier probe
162 Wing front spar
163 Port missile bay doors
164 Pantographic action missile displacement gear
165 Displacement gear hydraulic jack
166 Missile launch rail
167 Missile-bay door integral rocket launch tubes
168 Centre missile bay door
169 2.75-in (70-mm) FFAR folding-fin rockets (24)
170 AIM-4D Falcon air-to-air missile (6)
171 Port wing fuel-tank pylon
172 215-U.S. gal (814-litre) external fuel tank

Left: North Dakota's "Happy Hooligans" were typical of the Air National Guard units that flew the F-102A. Note the airbrakes also double as the braking parachute doors.

FACTS

- The F-102A Delta Dagger was the first delta-winged aircraft in operational service.
- The F-102 was designated the "1954 Interim Interceptor" during development, but did not reach service until 1956.
- 1,000 Delta Daggers were ordered in total, including 111 two-seat TF-102As.

CONVAIR F-102 DELTA DAGGER – VARIANTS & OPERATORS

VARIANTS

YF-102: Prototypes. Non-area-ruled fuselage. Powered by 14,500 lbf (64.5 kN) J57-P-11 engine. Two built.

YF-102A: Area-ruled prototypes. 16,000 lbf (71.2 kN) J57-P-23. Four converted from pre-production aircraft.

F-102A: Production model. Initial eight pre-production aircraft built with non-area-ruled fuselage. Remainder (879) with area-ruled fuselage.

TF-102A: Two-seat training version. 111 built.

F-102B: The original designation of the F-106A.

F-102C: Proposed tactical-attack version with J57-P-47 engine. Two converted as YF-102C engineering testbeds.

QF-102A: Target drones converted from the F-102A. Six built.

PQM-102A: Unpiloted target drones. 65 converted.

PQM-102B: Revised target drone conversion, capable of being flown remotely or by pilot in cockpit. 146 converted.

OPERATORS

Greece: 20 F-102A and 6 TF-102A supplied from surplus U.S. stock

Turkey: 35 F-102A and 8 TF-102A supplied from surplus U.S. stock

CONVAIR F-102 DELTA DAGGER

The F-102A was assigned to several squadrons of the U.S. Air Forces in Europe (USAFE), including the 525th Fighter Interceptor Squadron (FIS) of the 86th Air Division, at Bitburg Air Base, Germany. Shown with weapons bay open and AIM-4 Falcon missiles visible, this 525th FIS "Deuce" served in Europe for ten years from late 1959 until it returned to the United States and was transferred to the Air National Guard. In 1978, it was allocated for conversion to a PQM-102A drone, and in May 1980 it was destroyed in a missile test.

Above: An F-102A of the U.S. Air Force's Iceland-based 57th Fighter Interceptor Squadron launches a Falcon from its weapons bay. Air Defense Command Delta Daggers were usually assigned to northern bases to counter Soviet bombers approaching from the Arctic.

In 1948, Convair's XP-92 became the first powered delta-winged aircraft to fly. It was a fairly basic experimental jet with a nose intake and a heavily framed canopy. The configuration was based on designs by the German engineer Alexander Lippisch, who had tested delta-winged gliders during World War II, but never completed any jet projects before the Nazi defeat. The proposed F-92 fighter was cancelled, but in 1951 the U.S. Air Force chose Convair's design for an enlarged and revised version for their new supersonic fighter programme.

The F-102 was intended to be a weapons system rather than a fighter. Onboard electronics working via a datalink with ground radars would guide the pilot to the point of firing its sophisticated missiles. Problems Hughes Electronics had with its part of this ambitious scheme caused delays. More significantly, wind-tunnel testing indicated that the design would not go supersonic in level flight; this proved true when the first of 10 YF-102 test aircraft flew in October 1953.

The solution lay in the newly discovered aerodynamic formula of "area rule," which stated that the cross section of an aircraft along the line of flight should be as constant as possible to minimize drag at transonic speeds. This could be achieved by narrowing the fuselage where it met the wing and widening it at the ends. Bulges were added to several of the YF-102s, allowing them to exceed Mach 1, but the initial plan to build a production aircraft based on the YF-102 with minimal changes had to be scrapped.

REFINING THE DESIGN

The F-102A that eventually emerged and flew in June 1955 (a year after the new interceptor was supposed to be in service) had a longer fuselage with "wasp-waisting" built in, a larger, thinner wing and a new canopy and windscreen. After the first batch was delivered in May 1956, the tail fin was increased in height.

Armament of the F-102A Delta Dagger was four AIM-4 Falcon missiles in the internal weapons bay and 3-in (76-mm)

Above: The instrument panel of the F-102 was dominated by the rubber "boot" shielding the radar display. One arm of the control column was used to adjust the radar display.

or 2.75-inch (70-mm) folding-fin aircraft rockets (FFARs) in launchers within the weapons bay doors. The two-seat TF-102A had an unusual side-by-side seating arrangement, which unsurprisingly reduced the aircraft's performance below Mach 1.0 in level flight. TF-102As did not have the full fire control system of the F-102A, but were capable of carrying the same weapons.

OPERATIONAL HISTORY

Although issued to Air Defense Command (ADC) for the continental defence mission, some F-102As and TF-102As were stationed in Thailand and Vietnam from 1962–69, to defend against possible North Vietnamese attacks on the South. In practice, they mainly provided escorts for B-52 missions and occasionally used their IR Falcon missiles against heat sources such as trucks and campfires on the Ho Chi Minh Trail. One F-102 was shot down by a North Vietnamese Mikoyan-Gurevich MiG-21 during the war.

Greece and Turkey were the Delta Dagger's only export customers, each receiving surplus USAF aircraft in 1968–69. In 1974, the two countries clashed over Cyprus and, although F-102s never fought each other, two Turkish Delta Daggers are believed to have been shot down by Greek Northrop F-5As. By 1979, each air force had retired its F-102s.

In the United States, the last operational Delta Daggers were used by various Air National Guard squadrons until the last was retired in 1977. Many examples went on to be converted to PQM-102 pilotless drones and were expended in missile tests from the mid-1970s until 1986, when the last was shot down.

Above: The prototype YF-102 had only a superficial similarity to the Delta Dagger that followed. When the YF-102 failed to go supersonic in testing, the aircraft's whole design had to be revised.

Douglas A-4 Skyhawk

Originating as a lightweight attack aircraft able to carry the first generation of tactical nuclear weapons, the Skyhawk evolved into a capable multi-role platform, equally at home providing close air support and fighter defence to both carrier- and land-based forces.

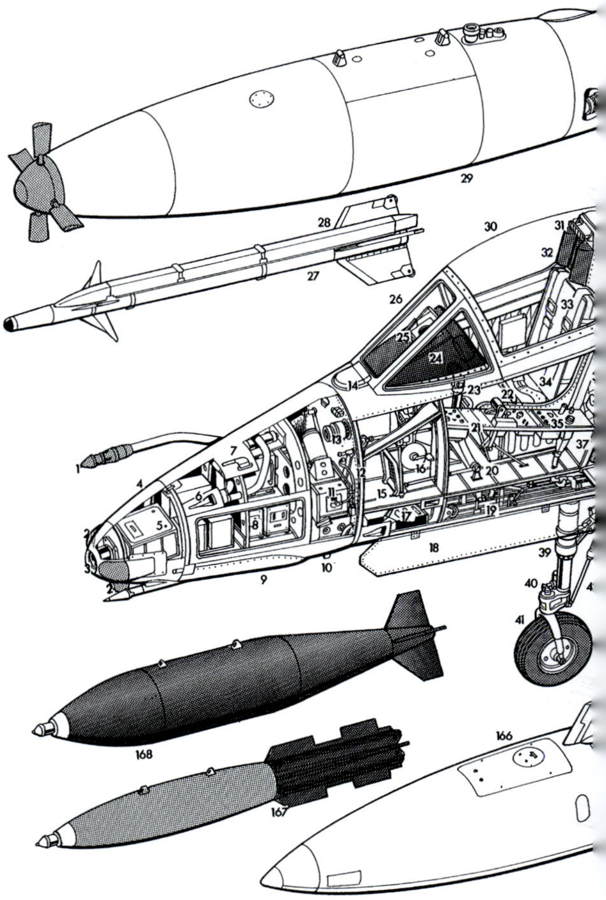

A-4M SKYHAWK SPECIFICATION

Dimensions

Fuselage length: 40 ft 3½ in (12.29 m)
Height: 15 ft (4.57 m)
Wingspan: 27 ft 6 in (8.38 m)
Wing area: 260.00 sq ft (24.15 m²)

Powerplant

One Pratt & Whitney J52-P-408A turbojet rated at 11,200 lb st (49.80 kN)

Weights

Empty: 10,465 lb (4747 kg)
Maximum takeoff: 24,500 lb (11,113 kg)

Fuel and load

Internal fuel capacity: 800 U.S. gal (3028 litres)
External fuel capacity: up to 1,000 U.S. gal (3786 litres)

Performance

Maximum speed at sea level: 685 mph (1102 km/h)
Maximum rate of climb at sea level: 10,300 ft (3140 m) per minute
Service ceiling: 38,700 ft (11,795 m)
Combat radius: 345 miles (547 km) with a 4,000-lb (1814-kg) warload

Armament

Two Colt Mk 12 20-mm cannon, each with 200 rounds of ammunition, plus up to 9,155 lb (4153 kg) of weapons on five external hardpoints

Cutaway Key

1 Fixed inflight refuelling probe
2 Nose ECM recording and suppression aerials
3 Angle-Rate Bombing System (ARBS) laser seeker head
4 Hinged nose compartment access door
5 Laser seeker system electronics
6 Electronics cooling air inlet
7 Pitot tube
8 Avionics access panel
9 APN-153(V) navigation radar
10 Lower TACAN aerial
11 Communications electronics
12 Cockpit front pressure bulkhead
13 Pressurization valve
14 Windscreen rain-dispersal air duct
15 Rudder pedals
16 Angle-of-attack sensor
17 Air-conditioning refrigeration plant
18 Nosewheel door
19 Control system access
20 Cockpit floor level
21 Pilot's side console panel
22 Engine throttle
23 Control column
24 Instrument panel shroud
25 Head-up display (HUD)
26 Windscreen panels
27 AIM-9L Sidewinder air-to-air missile
28 Missile launch rail
29 D-704 flight refuelling pack containing 300 U.S. gal (1135 litres)
30 Cockpit canopy cover
31 Face-blind firing handle
32 Ejection-seat headrest
33 Safety harness
34 McDonnell Douglas ESCAPAC IG-3 "zero-zero" ejection seat
35 Anti-G valve
36 Cockpit insulation and fragmentation blanket
37 Rear pressure bulkhead
38 Emergency canopy-release handle
39 Nose undercarriage leg strut
40 Steering linkage
41 Nosewheel
42 Leg shortening link
43 Hydraulic retraction strut
44 Emergency wind-driven generator
45 Port cannon muzzle
46 Intake gun gas shield
47 Port air intake
48 Boundary layer splitter plate
49 Self-sealing fuselage fuel cell, capacity 240 U.S. gal (908 litres)
50 Fuel system piping
51 Canopy hinge cover
52 Starboard air intake duct
53 Fuel-system gravity filler cap
54 UHF aerial
55 Electronics cooling air inlet
56 Engine-driven generator
57 Constant-speed drive
58 Bifurcated intake duct
59 Reel-type ammunition magazine (200 rounds per gun)
60 Intake compressor face
61 Electrical system power amplifier
62 Engine accessory drive gearbox

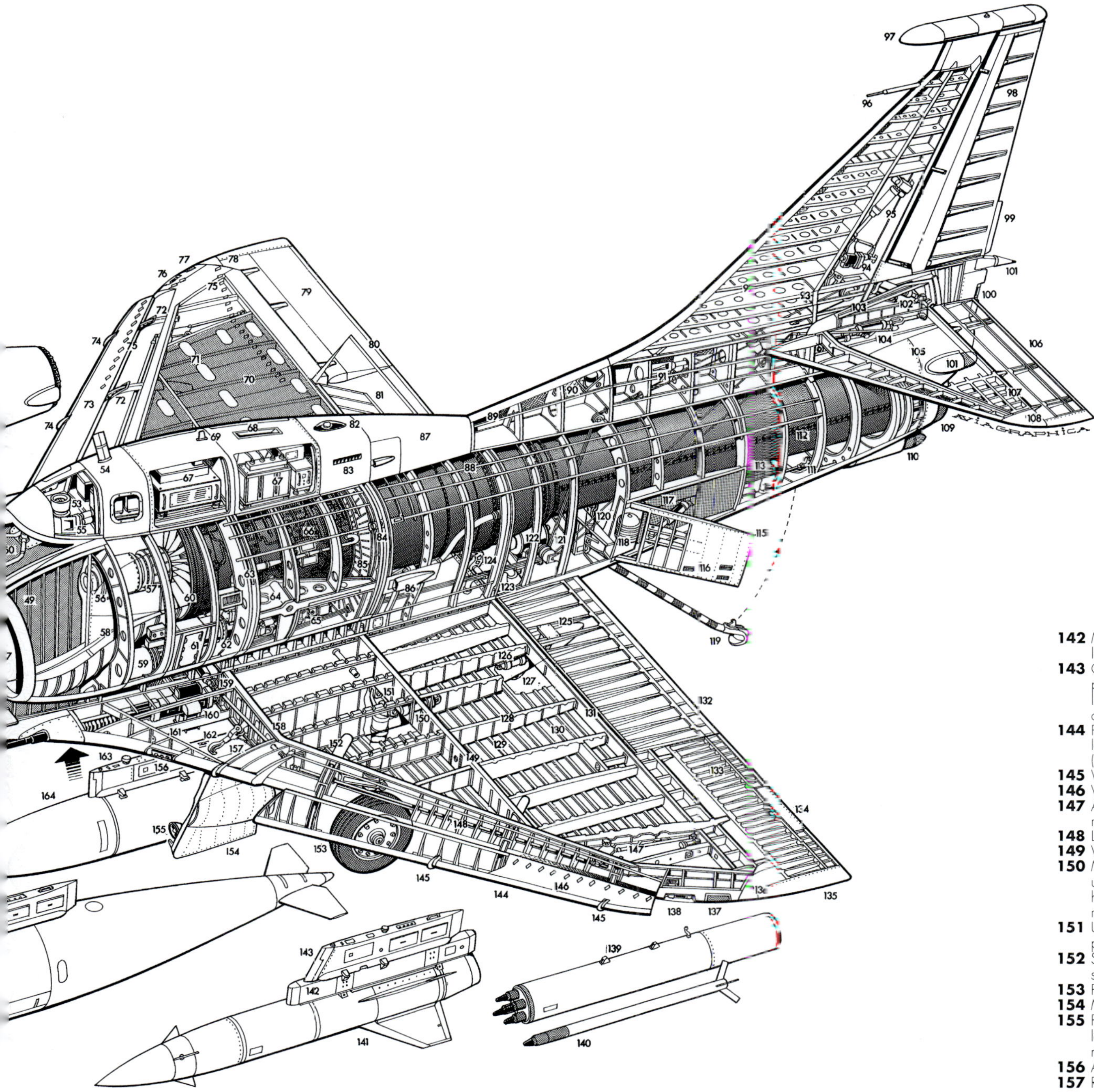

63 Wing spar attachment fuselage double frame
64 Engine mounting trunnion
65 Engine fuel system access panel
66 Pratt & Whitney J52-P-408 turbojet
67 Dorsal avionics bays
68 Compressor bleed air exhaust duct
69 Upper TACAN aerial
70 Starboard wing integral fuel tank (total wing capacity 560 U.S. gal/ 2120 litres)
71 Wing tank access panels
72 Slat guide rails
73 Starboard automatic leading-edge slat (open)
74 Wing fences
75 Vortex generators
76 Starboard navigation light
77 Wingtip communications aerial
78 Aileron horn balance
79 Starboard aileron
80 Split trailing-edge spoiler (open position)
81 Starboard split trailing-edge flap (down position)
82 Anti-collision light
83 Cooling air exit louvres
84 Rear fuselage double frame break point
85 Engine firewall
86 Cooling air intake
87 VHF aerial
88 Upper fuselage stringers
89 Fin-root dorsal fairing
90 Remote compass flux valve
91 Rear electronics bay cooling air inlet
92 Fin rib construction
93 Fin spar attachment joint
94 Rudder hydraulic jack
95 Artificial-feel spring unit
96 Pitot tube
97 Fintip ECM antenna housing
98 Externally braced rudder construction
99 Fixed rudder tab
100 Tail navigation light
101 ECM antennas
102 Tailplane trim jack
103 Tailplane seal plate
104 Elevator hydraulic jack
105 Tailpipe fairing
106 Port elevator
107 All-moving tailplane construction
108 Elevator horn balance
109 Jet pipe exhaust nozzle
110 Brake parachute housing for 16-ft (4.88-m) diameter ribbon-type parachute
111 Brake parachute release linkage
112 Insulated jet pipe
113 Electronics bay heat shield
114 Rear electronics bay, automatic flight control system (AFCS)
115 Port airbrake (open)
116 JATO bottle attachment hardpoints
117 Airbrake hydraulic jack
118 2.65-U.S. gal (10-litre) liquid oxygen (LOX) converter
119 Arrestor hook (down position)
120 Arrestor hook hydraulic jack
121 Control cable runs
122 Inertial platform
123 Central pressure refuelling connection
124 Central hydraulic flap drive linkage
125 Port upper surface spoiler
126 Spoiler hydraulic jack
127 Ventral anti-collision light
128 Wing rib construction
129 Stringer construction
130 Port wing integral fuel tank (single tank tip-to-tip)
131 Rear spar
132 Port split trailing-edge flap
133 Port aileron construction
134 Aileron trim tab
135 Tip fairing
136 Aileron horn balance
137 Wingtip antenna fairing
138 Port navigation light
139 LAU-10A Zuni rocket launcher
140 5-in (12.7-cm) folding-fin rocket
141 AGM-12 Bullpup air-to-ground missile
142 Missile launcher rail
143 Outboard wing pylon (1,000-lb/454-kg capacity)
144 Port automatic leading-edge slat (open)
145 Wing fences
146 Vortex generators
147 Aileron control rod linkage
148 Leading-edge ribs
149 Wing centre spar
150 Main undercarriage hydraulic retraction jack
151 Undercarriage leg pivot mounting
152 Slat guide rail fuel sealing can
153 Port mainwheel
154 Mainwheel door
155 Position of landing lamp on starboard mainwheel door
156 Approach lights
157 Retractable catapult hook
158 Cranked wing front spar
159 Aileron servo control
160 Colt Mk 12 20-mm cannon
161 Spent cartridge case and link ejector chutes
162 Mainwheel well
163 Centreline pylon (3,575-lb/1622-kg capacity)
164 150-U.S. gal (568-litre) fuel tank
165 Inboard wing pylon (2,240-lb/ 1016-kg capacity)
166 400-U.S. gal (1514-litre) long-range fuel tank
167 Snakeye 500-lb (227-kg) retarded bomb
168 Mk 83 1,000-lb (454-kg) HE bomb

"Every pilot I know loved to fly all models of the A-4, even when they were killing us off at a terrible rate."
– US Navy A-4 pilot Meredith "Pat" Patrick

FACTS

- The Skyhawk entered U.S. Navy service in 1954 and was finally retired in 2005.
- The Skyhawk was the only U.S. carrier-based jet to not have folding wings.
- The A-4 was capable of carrying more than its empty weight in weapons and fuel.

DOUGLAS A-4 SKYHAWK – VARIANTS

XA4D-1: Prototype.

YA4D-1 (YA-4A, later A-4A): Prototypes and pre-production aircraft.

A4D-1 (A-4A): Initial production version. 166 built.

A4D-2 (A-4B): Strengthened aircraft with air-to-air refuelling capabilities.

A-4P: Remanufactured A-4Bs sold to Argentine Air Force known as A-4B.

A-4Q: Remanufactured A-4Bs sold to Argentine Navy.

A-4S: 50 A-4Bs remanufactured for Republic of Singapore Air Force.

TA-4S: Seven trainer versions of A-4S.

A4D-3: Proposed advanced avionics version. None built.

A4D-2N (A-4C): Night/adverse-weather version of A4D-2. 638 built.

A-4L: A-4C remanufactured for U.S. Marine Corps Reserve and U.S. Navy Reserve.

A-4S-1: 50 A-4Cs remanufactured for Republic of Singapore Air Force.

A-4SU Super Skyhawk: Modified A-4S for the Republic of Singapore Air Force (RSAF).

A-4PTM: 40 A-4Cs and A-4Ls refurbished for Royal Malaysian Air Force, incorporating many A-4M features. ("PTM" stands for "Peculiar to Malaysia.")

A4D-4: Long-range version with new wings cancelled.

A4D-5 (A-4E): A4D-5 (A-4E): Major upgrade, including new Pratt & Whitney J52-P-6A engine with 8,400 lbf (37 kN) thrust. 499 built.

A4D-6: Proposed version. None built.

A-4F: Refinement of A-4E with extra avionics housed in a hump on the fuselage spine. 147 built.

A-4G: A-4F variation for the Royal Australian Navy.

A-4H: 90 aircraft for the Israeli Air Force based on the A-4F.

A-4K: 10 aircraft for Royal New Zealand Air Force.

A-4M: Dedicated Marine version with improved avionics and more powerful J52-P-408a engine with 11,200 lbf (50 kN) thrust, enlarged cockpit, IFF system. Later fitted with Hughes AN/ASB-19 Angle Rate Bombing System (ARBS) with TV and laser spot tracker. 158 built.

A-4N: 117 modified A-4Ms for the Israeli Air Force.

A-4KU: 30 modified A-4Ms for the Kuwaiti Air Force. Brazil purchased 20 of these second-hand and redesignated them AF-1. Now used in Brazilian Navy on carrier duty.

A-4AR: 36 A-4Ms refurbished for Argentina. Known as Fightinghawk.

A-4Y: Provisional designation for A-4Ms modified with the ARBS. Designation never adopted by the U.S. Navy or Marine Corps.

DOUGLAS A-4E SKYHAWK

The A-4E was the first of the Skyhawks to be powered by the Pratt & Whitney J52 engine, which was more powerful and reliable than the Wright J65 of the A-4A, B and C. The extra power and the addition of two wing pylons allowed a heavier warload. This A-4E of VA-72 "Blue Hawks" of the U.S. Navy is depicted carrying six 500-lb "Snakeye" retarded bombs. In 1965, the aircraft and squadron were flying missions over Vietnam from the carrier USS *Independence*. After service with several other squadrons and at least two more tours of duty in Vietnam, it was lost in May 1970 when its engine failed after an aerial refuelling.

Above: The impressive load-carrying ability of the Skyhawk is demonstrated by this A-4E of U.S. Navy squadron VA-164, the "Ghost Riders." It is seen here carrying AGM-12 Bullpup air-to-surface missiles and racks of 500 lb (227 kg) bombs on a mission over Vietnam.

In 1952, Douglas was awarded a contract for a light attack bomber able to lift one of the new generation of tactical nuclear bombs. Through careful weight-saving measures, Douglas was able to deliver a compact aircraft that could carry more than its own empty weight at a cost under the stipulated $1 million.

The XA4D-1 Skyhawk flew in June 1954. Under the revised designation system introduced in 1962, the A4D-1, A4D-2 and A4D-2N became the A-4A, A-4B and A-4C, respectively. All these early models had the Wright J65 engine, a version of the Armstrong Siddeley Sapphire, and simple navigation and attack avonics. All A-4s had a single-piece wing that did not require wing folding for stowage on aircraft carriers.

FLYING INTO COMBAT

With at least one external fuel tank always carried, the early model A-4s could carry air-to-ground or air-to-air ordnance, but not both, on their remaining pylons. The A-4E (A4D-5) added two outer wing pylons, allowing carriage of missiles as well as bombs or rockets. In the early 1960s, Skyhawks equipped with AIM-9s acted as the fighter defence for the smaller anti-submarine carriers.

Flying conventional attack and close air support missions over Southeast Asia and the Middle East, the Skyhawk tangled with enemy aircraft on a number of occasions. Interestingly, several confirmed kills by the Skyhawk were scored with air-to-ground ordnance. In Vietnam, a pilot on a ground-attack mission destroyed a Mikoyan-Gurevich MiG-17 with a salvo of unguided rockets. In 1970, an Israeli A-4 pilot shot down two Syrian "Frescoes," one with rockets and one with cannon.

PROLONGED SERVICE

Several upgrade programmes in the 1980s and 1990s extended the life span of the A-4, and enhanced its air-to-air credentials. Development of digital electronics allowed the compact nose of the Skyhawk to accept multi-mode radar, and the cockpit to take the display screens and controls usually found in fighters such as the Lockheed Martin F-16. New Zealand's Project "Kahu" incorporated the APG-66 from the F-16A in the Royal New Zealand Air Force's A-4K and TA-4K models, as did Argentina, which designated its radar version the ARG-1 and its Skyhawks A-4AR and TA-4AR. The new radars, combined with a HUD, allowed the A-4 to use newer-generation Sidewinders like the all-aspect AIM-9L.

Brazil's ex-Kuwaiti Skyhawks serve as fighter defence for its sole aircraft carrier, the *São Paulo,* but have no radar. They may in future be upgraded with an Italian Selex radar.

Above: The two-seat TA-4F Skyhawk was combat-capable. The U.S. Marines used it as a fast forward-air-control platform.

Above: When Iraq invaded Kuwait in 1990 at the start of the First Gulf War, Kuwaiti A-4KUs are said to have destroyed several Iraqi helicopters before their base was destroyed and the aircraft and their crew escaped to Saudi Arabia.

Chance Vought F-8 Crusader

The Crusader was regarded as a real fighter pilot's aircraft, with great manoeuverability compared to its contemporaries. It had the best victory-to-loss rate of any U.S. fighter in the Vietnam War, where it served from land and sea throughout the conflict.

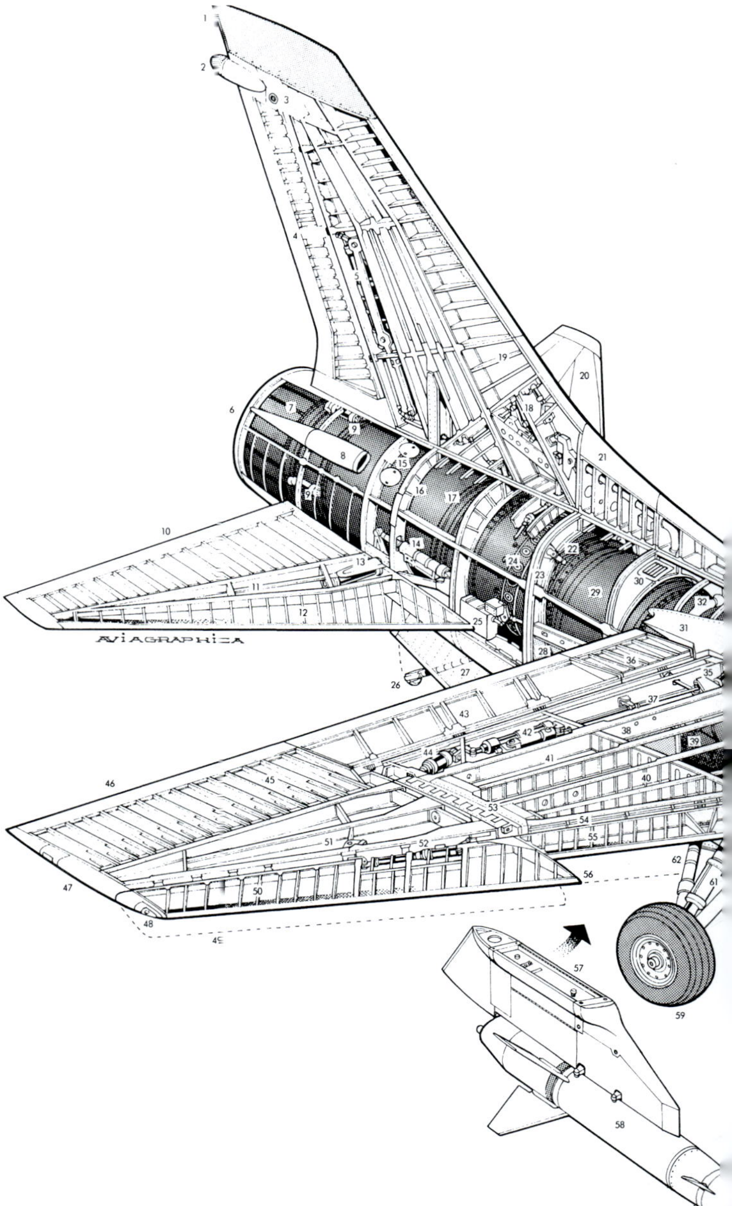

F-8E CRUSADER SPECIFICATION

Dimensions

Length: 54 ft 6 in (16.61 m)
Height: 15 ft 9 in (4.80 m)
Wingspan: 35 ft 2 in (10.72 m)
Wing area: 350 sq ft (35.52 m²)

Powerplant

One Pratt & Whitney J57-P-20A turbojet rated at 10,700 lb (48.15 kN) static thrust or 18,000 lb st (81 kN) with afterburner

Weights

Empty: 17,541 lb (7957 kg)
Gross weight: 28,765 lb (13,048 kg)
Combat weight: 25,098 lb (11,304 kg)
Maximum takeoff: 34,000 lb (15,422 kg)

Performance

Maximum level speed at sea level: 764 mph (1230 km/h)
Maximum level speed at 40,000 ft (12192 m): 1,120 mph (1802 km/h)
Cruising speed: 570 mph (917 km/h)
Stalling speed: 162 mph (261 km/h)
Rate of climb in one minute: 31,950 ft (9738 m)
Service ceiling: 58,000 ft (17678 m)
Combat ceiling: 53,400 ft (16276 m)

Range

Range: 453 miles (729 km)
Maximum range: 1,737 miles (2795 km)

Armament

Four Colt-Browning (20-mm) Mk 12 cannon with 144 rounds per gun; plus up to four AIM-9 Sidewinder AAMs; or 12 250-lb (113-kg bombs); or eight 500-lb (227-kg) bombs; or eight Zuni rockets; or two AGM-12A or AGM-12B Bullpup A AGMs

Cutaway Key

1 Fintip VHF aerial fairing
2 Tail warning radar
3 Tail navigation light
4 Rudder construction
5 Rudder hydraulic jack
6 Engine exhaust nozzle
7 Variable-area nozzle flaps
8 Afterburner cooling air duct
9 Nozzle control jacks
10 Starboard all-moving tailplane construction
11 Tailplane spar box
12 Leading-edge ribs
13 Tailplane pivot fixing
14 Tailplane hydraulic control jack
15 Tailpipe cooling air vents
16 Fin attachment main frame
17 Afterburner duct
18 Rudder control linkages
19 Fin leading-edge construction
20 Port all-moving tailplane
21 Fin-root fillet construction
22 Rear engine mounting
23 Fuselage break point double frame (engine removal)
24 Afterburner fuel spray manifold
25 Tailplane autopilot control system
26 Deck arrestor hook
27 Starboard ventral fin
28 Rear fuselage fuel tank
29 Pratt & Whitney J57-P-20A afterburning turbojet
30 Engine-bay cooling air louvres
31 Wingroot trailing-edge fillet
32 Bleed air system piping
33 Engine oil tank (85 U.S. gal/ 322 litres)
34 Wing spar pivot fixing
35 Hydraulic flap jack
36 Starboard flap
37 Control rod linkages
38 Rear spar
39 Engine accessory gearbox compartment
40 Inboard wing panel multi-spar construction
41 Starboard wing integral fuel tank, total fuel system capacity 1,348 U.S. gal (5103 litres)
42 Aileron power control unit
43 Starboard drooping aileron construction
44 Wing-fold hydraulic jack
45 Trailing-edge ribs
46 Fixed portion of trailing edge
47 Wingtip fairing
48 Starboard navigation light
49 Leading-edge flap, lowered position

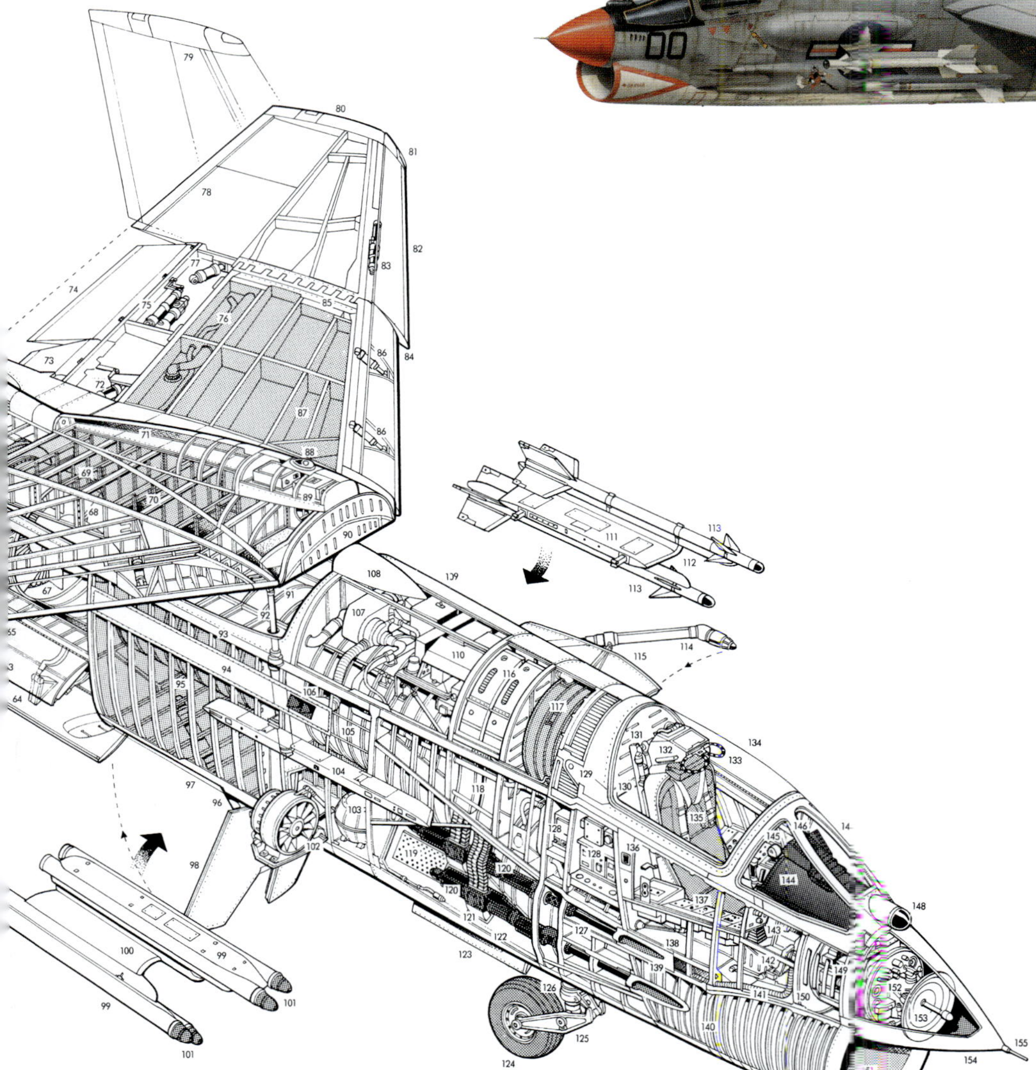

50 Leading-edge flap rib construction
51 Outer wing panel spar construction
52 Leading-edge flap hydraulic jack
53 Wingfold hinge
54 Front spar
55 Leading-edge flap inboard section
56 Leading-edge dogtooth
57 Wing pylon
58 AGM-12B Bullpup A air-to-ground missile
59 Starboard mainwheel
60 Main undercarriage leg strut
61 Shock absorber strut
62 Hydraulic retraction jack
63 Landing lamp
64 Wheel bay doors
65 Main undercarriage pivot fixing
66 Wing spar/front engine mounting main bulkhead
67 Engine compressor intake
68 Wingroot rib
69 Centre-section fuel tank
70 Wing spar carry-through structure
71 Dorsal fairing
72 Port flap jack
73 Port plain flap, lowered position
74 Port drooped aileron, lowered position
75 Aileron power control unit
76 Fuel system piping
77 Wing-fold hydraulic jack
78 Fixed portion of trailing edge
79 Port wing folded position
80 Wingtip fairing
81 Port navigation light
82 Port outboard leading-edge flap, lowered
83 Outboard flap hydraulic jack
84 Leading-edge dogtooth
85 Wing-fold hinge
86 Inboard leading-edge flap hydraulic jacks
87 Port wing integral fuel tank
88 Anti-collision light
89 Missile system avionics
90 Two-position variable-incidence wing, raised position
91 Intake trunking
92 Wing incidence hydraulic jack
93 Fuselage upper longeron
94 Air system exhaus heat shield
95 Main fuselage fuel tank
96 Airbrake hydraulic jack
97 Airbrake housing
98 Ventral airbrake, lowered
99 Rocket launch tube
100 Rocket launcher pylon adaptor
101 Zuni folding-fin ground attack rockets (8)
102 Emergency air-driven generator
103 Liquid oxygen bottle (LOX)
104 Fuselage stores pylon
105 Intake duct
106 Heat exchanger air exhaust
107 Air-conditioning plant
108 Dorsal fairing
109 Upper fuselage access panels
110 Electronics bay and electrical power system
111 Fuselage pylon adaptor
112 Missile launch rails
113 AIM-9 Sidewinder air-to-air missiles (4)
114 Inflight-refuelling probe, extended
115 Refuelling probe housing door
116 Ammunition tanks (144 rounds per gun)
117 Avionics system inertial platform
118 Ammunition feed chutes
119 Gun-bay gas vent panel
120 Mk 12 20-mm cannon
121 Spent cartridge case/link collector chutes
122 Gun compartment access panel
123 Nosewheel doors
124 Nosewheel
125 Pivoted axle beam
126 Nose undercarriage leg strut
127 Cannon barrels
128 Radio and electronics equipment bays
129 Canopy hinge point
130 Cockpit rear pressure bulkhead
131 Ejection seat rails
132 Pilot's Martin-Baker ejection seat
133 Face-blind firing handle
134 Cockpit canopy cover
135 Safety harness
136 Canopy emergency release
137 Pilot's starboard-side console panel
138 Cockpit floor level
139 Cannon muzzle blast troughs
140 Intake duct framing
141 Radar cooling air piping
142 Rudder pedals
143 Control column
144 Instrument panel shroud
145 Engine throttle control
146 Radar gunsight
147 Bullet-proof windscreen
148 Infrared seeker head
149 Radar electronics package
150 Cockpit front pressure bulkhead
151 Engine air intake
152 Radar scanner tracking mechanism
153 Radar antenna
154 Fibreglass radome
155 Pitot tube

"When you are out of F-8s, you are out of fighters."
– Crusader pilots' slogan

FACTS

- The Crusader had a unique variable-incidence wing that allowed it to land on carrier decks at lower speeds.
- The F-8 was the first carrier-based fighter capable of supersonic level flight.
- Nicknames for the F-8 included "MiG-master" and "Last of the Gunfighters."

VOUGHT F-8 CRUSADER – VARIANTS

XF8U-1 (XF-8A): The two original unarmed prototypes – V-383.

F8U-1 (F-8A): First production version. J57-P-12 engine replaced with more powerful J57-P-4A, starting with 31st production aircraft. 318 built.

YF8U-1 (YF-8A): One F8U-1 fighter used for development testing.

YF8U-1E (YF-8B): One F8U-1 converted to serve as an F8U-1E prototype.

F8U-1E (F-8B): Added a limited all-weather capability, thanks to the AN/APS-67 radar. First flight: 3 September 1958. 130 built.

XF8U-1T: One XF8U-2NE used for evaluation as a two-seat trainer.

F8U-2 (F-8C): J57-P-16 engine with 16,900 lbf (75 kN) of afterburning thrust. First flight 20 August 1957. 187 built. This variant was sometimes referred to as Crusader II.

F8U-2N (F-8D): All-weather version, unguided rocket pack replaced with an additional fuel tank, J57-P-20 engine with 18,000 lbf (80 kN) of afterburning thrust. First flight 16 February 1960. 152 built.

YF8U-2N (YF-8D): One aircraft used in the development of the F8U-2N.

YF8U-2NE: One F8U-1 converted to serve as an F8U-2NE prototype.

F8U-2NE (F-8E): J57-P-20A engine, AN/APQ-94 radar in a larger nose cone. First flight 30 June 1961. 286 built.

F-8E(FN): Air-superiority fighter version for the French Navy (Aéronavale), significantly increased wing lift due to greater slat and flap deflection, and the addition of a boundary-layer control system, enlarged stabilators. 42 built.

F-8H: Upgraded F-8D with strengthened airframe and landing gear.

F-8J: Upgraded F-8E, similar to F-8D but with wing modifications. 136 rebuilt.

F-8K: Upgraded F-8C with Bullpup capability and J57-P-20A engines.

F-8L: F-8B upgraded with underwing hardpoints. 61 rebuilt.

F-8P: 17 F-8E(FN) of the Aéronavale underwent a significant overhaul at the end of the 1980s, to stretch their service life another ten years. They were retired in 1999.

F8U-1D (DF-8A): Retired F-8A modified to controller aircraft for testing of the SSM-N-8 Regulus cruise missile.

DF-8F: Retired F-8A modified for target-tug duty.

F8U-1KU (QF-8A): Retired F-8A modified into remote-controlled target drones.

YF8U-1P (YRF-8A): Prototypes used in the development of the F8U-1P photo-reconnaissance aircraft – V-392.

RF-8G: Modernized RF-8As.

XF8U-3 Crusader III: New design loosely based on the earlier F-8 variants, created to compete against the F-4 Phantom II.

CHANCE VOUGHT F-8 CRUSADER

Although not designed with much thought given to ground-attack missions, the F-8 became an effective bomber in Vietnam, mainly with the U.S. Marine Corps. All-weather Marine fighter squadron VMF(AW)-235 with its colourful F-8Es was based at Da Nang, South Vietnam, in 1968. At that time, it was called on to support the besieged Marines at Khe Sanh, in danger of being overrun by the North Vietnamese. This F-8 is shown armed with eight Mk 82 500-lb (227-kg) bombs and eight 5-in (127-mm) Zuni rockets. The rockets are mounted on the so-called "Y" launchers that were developed during the Crusader's service to allow carriage of four AIM-9s.

The Crusader's origins were in a 1952 U.S. Navy requirement for a supersonic carrier-based fighter. In March 1955, the XF8U-1 prototype made its first flight and exceeded the speed of sound. The designation arose from the pre-1962 U.S. Navy system, in which it was the eighth fighter design from Chance Vought (which was assigned "U" as its company designation letter). From October 1962, the system was rationalized and F8Us became F-8s. Testing and evaluation were swift and the F8U-1, soon named "Crusader," was in service two years after first flying. This was in contrast to some other aircraft of the period (including Vought's own F7U Cutlass), which spent longer in development than they did in the fleet.

Above: Commander Dick Bellinger was one of the more colourful F-8 pilots of the Vietnam era. In October 1966, he became the first U.S. Navy pilot to shoot down a MiG-21.

The Crusader had a long fuselage and a short undercarriage. The variable-incidence wing was raised for takeoffs and landings to give a higher angle of attack and thus more lift, while keeping the fuselage level. This prevented the jetpipe scraping the deck and gave the pilot a better forward view. The engine was the Pratt & Whitney J57 turbojet, one of the most successful U.S. jet engines, used in different forms on everything from the North American F-100 Super Sabre to the Boeing B-52 bomber and 707 airliner.

The F-8 was armed with four 20-mm cannon in the forward fuselage. Early models also had a 16-shot rocket pack mounted in the speed brake. Two or four Sidewinders became standard air-to-air armament, and bombs and air-to-ground rockets were widely used in Vietnam, particularly by the U.S. Marines. The AGM-12 Bullpup air-to-ground missile could be carried, but appears to have been rarely used in action.

RECORD-WINNING SPEED

Even before its service entry in December 1956, the Crusader was used to set speed records, both for measured circuits and cross-country point-to-point flights. Crusaders made the first official U.S. flights over 1,000 mph (1609 km/h), flew from carriers off the West Coast to carriers off the East Coast, and flew from Los Angeles to New York in under three and a half hours among other milestones.

The Crusader could fly from the smaller "Essex"-class carriers, unlike the Phantom, although safety margins were

Above: The all-weather F8U-2N Crusader first flew in 1960. Under the post-1962 designation system it became the F-8D.

Above: A photo-reconnaissance RF-8 Crusader makes a touch-and-go landing on an angled deck carrier. The variable-incidence wing that allowed operations from smaller ships can be seen.

small and there were many accidents. In Vietnam, F-8s provided air defence and fighter escort for these carriers and were flown by Marine Corps squadrons from land bases. Photo-reconnaissance RF-8 versions provided targeting information and post-strike battle damage assessment.

SUCCESS IN COMBAT

In air combat, the Crusader acquitted itself well, shooting down 19 North Vietnamese MiGs, four of them with cannon, against the loss of four F-8s in dogfights.

France became the only customer for new-build Crusaders, ordering the first of 42 in 1962. These F-8E(FN)s had a higher wing incidence, larger tailplanes and boundary layer control, a method of blowing engine bleed air over the flaps to give extra takeoff lift. These modifications helped them to fly from the small French carriers *Clemenceau* and *Foch*. From the late 1980s, they were modified as F-8Ps ("P" standing for *prolonge*, or prolonged), and the last squadron kept flying them until 1999.

The Philippines bought 25 F-8Hs (which they also designated F-8Ps) for use from land bases in 1977. Humid conditions were hard on the aircraft, which suffered from poor reliability, and by 1991 the last one had been withdrawn from service.

McDonnell F-101 Voodoo

The Voodoo was one of the biggest and heaviest interceptors ever built. Its long range and nuclear-tipped missiles made it an effective defender of North America's higher latitudes in the depths of the Cold War against the former Soviet Union.

Cutaway Key

1 Radome
2 Scanner dish
3 Radar tracking mechanism
4 Radar mounting bulkhead
5 Refuelling probe doors
6 Radar modulating units
7 Refuelling probe hydraulic jack
8 Flight refuelling probe, extended
9 Forward avionics equipment bay, radar and weapons system equipment
10 Nose compartment access panels
11 Angle of attack transducer
12 Pitot head
13 Nosewheel doors
14 Emergency brake reservoir
15 Cannon muzzles
16 Cockpit pressure floor
17 Cockpit air-conditioning ducting
18 Front pressure bulkhead
19 Rudder pedals
20 Control column
21 Instrument panel
22 Instrument panel shroud
23 K-19 (Mk 7) gunsight
24 Armoured glass windscreen panel
25 MA-7 flight indicator radar scope
26 Canopy cover
27 Canopy-mounted flush aerial
28 Headrest
29 Safety harness
30 Canopy external release
31 Pilot's ejection seat
32 Throttle levers
33 Side console panel
34 Cockpit pressurization valve
35 Cannon barrel seals
36 Nose undercarriage pivot fixing
37 Cannon barrel fairings
38 Nose undercarriage leg strut
39 Landing and taxiing lamps
40 Twin nosewheels
41 Torque scissor links
42 Ventral AW aerial
43 Cannon barrels
44 Control rod runs
45 Anti-G valve
46 Rear pressure bulkhead
47 Canopy hydraulic jack
48 Canopy aft fairing
49 Rear avionics equipment bay, navigation and communications systems
50 Canopy hinge
51 Ammunition access door
52 Ammunition magazine, 375 rounds per gun
53 Feed chutes
54 M39 20-mm cannon (single cannon on starboard side, fourth weapon replaced by transponder equipment)
55 Heat exchanger flush air intake
56 Circuit breaker panel
57 Air-conditioning plant
58 Autopilot rate gyros
59 Control linkages
60 Hydraulic accumulators
61 Boundary layer splitter plate
62 Port engine air intake
63 Intake duct framing
64 Port hydraulic system reservoir
65 Boundary layer bleed air spill duct
66 Wing spar attachment main bulkhead
67 Forward fuselage fuel tanks; total system capacity 2,146 U.S. gal (8123 litres)

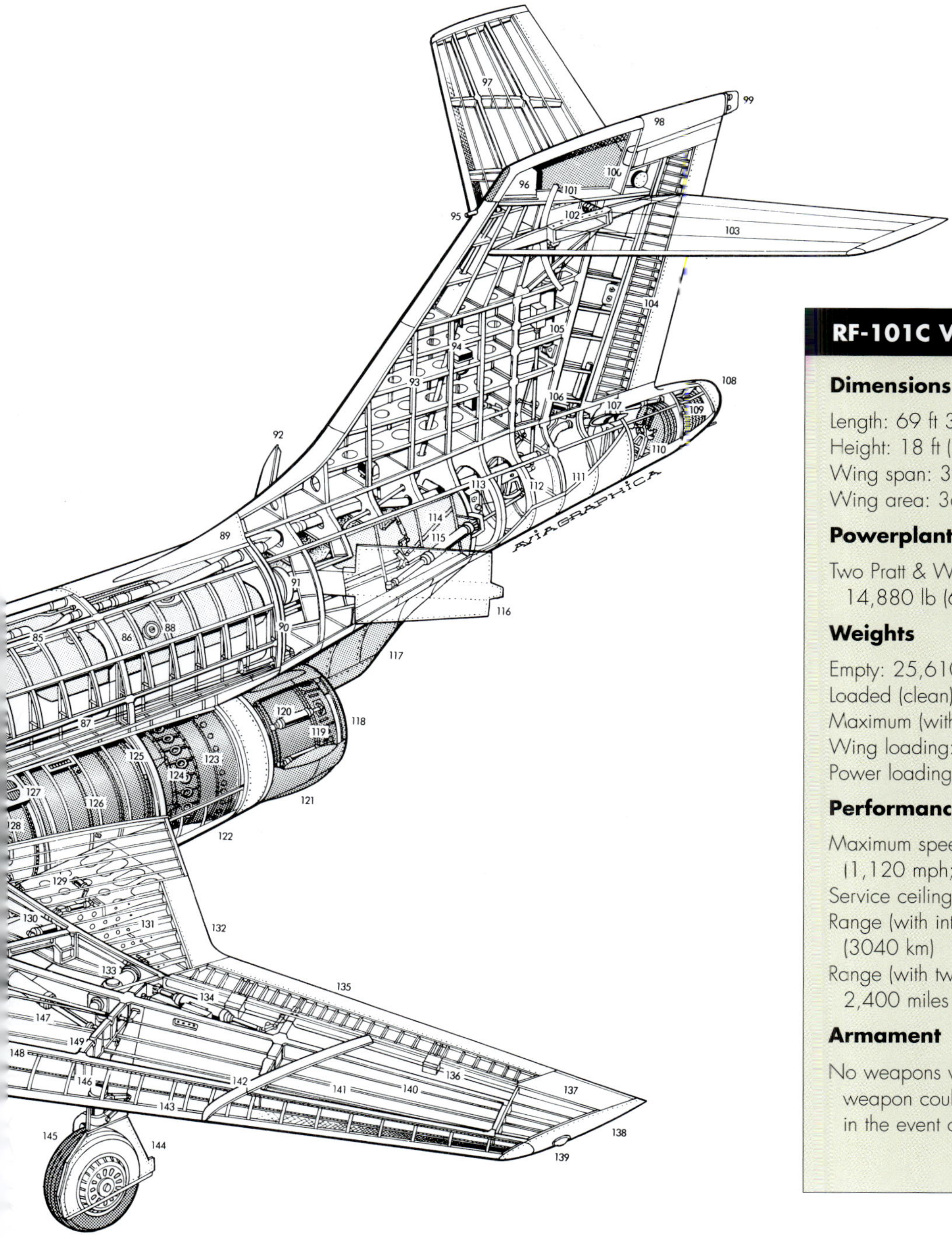

RF-101C VOODOO SPECIFICATION

Dimensions

Length: 69 ft 3 in (21.1 m)
Height: 18 ft (5.49 m)
Wing span: 39 ft 8 in (12.09 m)
Wing area: 368 sq ft (34.19 m²)

Powerplant

Two Pratt & Whitney J57-13 turbojets each rated at 14,880 lb (66.2 kN) with maximum afterburner

Weights

Empty: 25,610 lb (11,617 kg)
Loaded (clean): 42,550 lb (19,300 kg)
Maximum (with two tanks): 48,720 lb (22,099 kg)
Wing loading: 130.8 lb/sq ft (638.6 kg/sq m)
Power loading: 1.6 lb/lb st (1.6 kg/kgp)

Performance

Maximum speed ("clean," at height): Mach 1.7 (1,120 mph; 1802 km/h)
Service ceiling: 52,000 ft (15,850 m)
Range (with internal tanks at high altitude): 1,890 miles (3040 km)
Range (with two 375-U.S. gal (1705-litre) drop tanks: 2,400 miles (3862 km)

Armament

No weapons were carried, although a single nuclear weapon could be mounted on the centreline hardpoint in the event of nuclear war

68 Fuel filler cap, pressure refuelling connector on starboard side
69 Fuel system piping
70 Anti-collision light
71 Starboard wing panel
72 Wing fence
73 Starboard navigation light
74 Fixed portion of trailing edge
75 Starboard aileron
76 Aileron mass-balance weights
77 Aileron hydraulic actuator
78 Main undercarriage pivot fixing
79 Starboard split trailing-edge flap
80 Boom type refuelling receptacle, open
81 Wing spar and engine mounting main bulkheads
82 Centre fuselage fuel tank
83 Fuel vent piping
84 Fuselage upper access panels
85 Fuselage top longeron
86 Aft fuselage fuel tanks
87 Control cable duct
88 Fuel filler cap
89 Fin-root fillet
90 Tailcone joint frame
91 Artificial feel system bellows
92 Starboard airbrake, open
93 Tailfin construction
94 Remote compass transmitter
95 Artificial feel system ram air intake
96 VHF aerial
97 Starboard tailplane construction
98 Fintip fairing
99 Tail navigation lights
100 Rudder mass-balance
101 Tailplane sealing plate
102 Tailplane pivot fixing
103 Port all-moving tailplane
104 Rudder construction
105 Tailplane hydraulic actuator
106 Rudder hydraulic actuator
107 Fuel jettison, port and starboard
108 Parachute door
109 Brake parachute housing
110 Parachute release mechanism
111 Tailboom construction
112 Control system linkages
113 Tailplane autopilot controller
114 Port airbrake housing
115 Airbrake hydraulic jack
116 Port airbrake, open
117 Tailcone heat shield
118 Engine exhaust nozzle
119 Variable-area afterburner nozzle
120 Nozzle control jacks
121 Nozzle shroud
122 Engine bay ventral access panels
123 Afterburner duct
124 Afterburner fuel spray manifold
125 Rear engine mounting frame
126 Port Pratt & Whitney J57-P-13 afterburning turbojet
127 Bleed air spill duct
128 Compressor bleed air spill duct
129 Flap position transmitter
130 Flap hydraulic jack
131 Flap shroud ribs
132 Port split trailing-edge flap
133 Plain undercarriage pivot fixing
134 Aileron hydraulic actuator
135 Port aileron construction
136 Mass-balance weight
137 Fixed portion of trailing edge
138 Wingtip fairing
139 Port navigation light
140 Main spar
141 Lower wing skin/stringer panel
142 Port wing fence
143 Detachable leading-edge access panel
144 Mainwheel doors
145 Port mainwheel
146 Main undercarriage leg strut
147 Hydraulic retraction jack
148 Front spar
149 Wing ribs
150 Aileron control rod linkage
151 Autopilot controller
152 Engine starter/generator
153 Main undercarriage wheel bay
154 Engine oil tank, 5.5 U.S. gal (21 litres)
155 Forward engine mounting
156 Compressor intake
157 Hydraulic pumps
158 Oil cooler
159 Intake conical centre-body
160 Intake duct main frame
161 Wing spar attachment joints
162 Ventral fuel tank 450 U.S. gal (1700 litres)
163 Mk 84 2,000-lb (907-kg) low-drag HE bomb
164 Mk 7 1-megaton free-fall nuclear weapon

"You have a tremendous amount of thrust available to you and plenty of control, but you can't afford to horse this airplane around with wild abandon at low altitudes."
– U.S. Air Force Voodoo pilot Bob Little, 1957

FACTS

- Although an American design, the Voodoo is more remembered for its service in Canada.
- The Voodoo served as a strike aircraft, fighter, reconnaissance aircraft and jamming platform.
- The only Voodoo version to see combat action was the RF-101 reconnaissance model.

MCDONNELL F-101 VOODOO – VARIANTS

F-101A: Initial production fighter bomber. 77 produced.

NF-101A: One F-101A used by General Electric for testing of the General Electric J79 engine.

YRF-101A: Two F-101As built as prototype reconnaissance models.

RF-101A: First reconnaissance version. 35 built.

F-101B: Two-seat interceptor. 479 built.

CF-101B: 112 F-101Bs transferred to Royal Canadian Air Force (RCAF).

RF-101B: 22 ex-RCAF CF-101B modified for reconnaissance use.

TF-101B: Dual-control trainer version of F-101B, redesignated F-101F. 79 built.

EF-101B: Single F-101B converted for use as a radar target and leased to Canada.

NF-101B: F-101B prototype based on the F-101A airframe. The second prototype was built with a different nose.

F-101C: Improved fighter-bomber. 47 built.

RF-101C: Reconnaissance version of F-101C airframe. 166 built.

F-101D & E: Proposed versions with General Electric J79 engines, not built.

F-101F: Dual-control trainer version of F-101B. 79 re-designated TF-101Bs, plus 152 converted F-101B.

CF-101F: RCAF designation for 20 TF-101B/F-101F dual-control aircraft.

TF-101F: 24 dual-control versions of F-101B, redesignated F-101F.

RF-101G: 29 F-101As converted for Air National Guard reconnaissance.

RF-101H: 32 F-101Cs converted for reconnaissance use.

MCDONNELL F-101 VOODOO

This CF-101B of 410 "Cougar" Squadron of the Royal Canadian Air Force was one of 66 Voodoos supplied by the United States in 1961. RCAF Voodoos were armed with the AIR-1 Genie, two of which can be seen mounted here on pylons under the forward fuselage. The missiles were technically the property of the U.S. government and would have only been passed to Canadian control in a crisis. CF-101Bs were the equivalent of the F-101B, with some extra equipment. The CF-101F had dual controls. RCAF's 410 Squadron was based mainly at Bagotville, Quebec, from 1964. In 1971, many of the CF-101Bs were returned to U.S. Air Force inventory, including the aircraft illustrated.

Above: This view of an F-101 being refuelled gives a glimpse into the weapons bay that was capable of carrying Falcon missiles. Two nuclear-tipped AIR-2 Genie rockets could be carried externally.

The F-101 story began as far back as 1945, with a proposal for a jet "penetration fighter" designed to escort bombers all the way to distant targets and back. McDonnell Aircraft was a relative novice on the aviation scene, having been formed in 1939 and not having produced any production aircraft during World War II. McDonnell's XP-88 prototype flew in October 1948, but its intended development, the F-88 escort fighter, did not enter production because the U.S. Air Force's Strategic Air Command (SAC) believed that its new generation of strategic jet bombers, the Boeing B-47 and Boeing B-52, would be fast enough to not require an escort.

Test work continued, however, and one offshoot was the XF-88B, with an Allison T38 turboprop in the nose, as well as two Westinghouse J34 jet engines. This became the first aircraft with a propeller to exceed Mach 1.

ENTER THE VOODOO

In 1953, the F-88 design was revised and offered to the U.S. Air Force as the F-101A Voodoo, with a new wing, revised tailplane and much more powerful afterburning J57 engines. The single-seat F-101A first flew in September 1954. As a strike aircraft, the F-101A's armament was four 20-mm cannon and an externally carried nuclear weapon. The RF-101A reconnaissance aircraft, with cameras instead of cannon, followed before the first true fighter version, the F-101B, entered service in 1959. The two-seat F-101B had an internal weapons bay that allowed it to carry a mix of air-to-air missiles, including the AIM-4 Falcon, available in infrared- and radar-guided forms, and the unguided AIR-2 Genie. The Genie was a unique weapon, an unguided air-to-air rocket with a nuclear warhead.

Voodoos were initially assigned to Tactical Air Command (TAC) as fighter-bombers and North American Air Defense Command (NORAD) as interceptors. After a relatively brief period with regular squadrons, most U.S. F-101 interceptors and RF-101 photo-reconnaissance platforms were passed on to squadrons of the U.S. Air National Guard. TAC did send RF-10Cs to Vietnam, where they undertook dangerous but valuable reconnaissance missions. Their high speed at low level made them very difficult to intercept, but nonetheless nearly 40 aircraft were lost, most of them to anti-aircraft guns and surface-to-air missiles.

A small number of recon Voodoos were supplied to Taiwan, who used them on missions over China. Several are believed to have been shot down over the mainland.

Above: The front cockpit of a Voodoo shows the pilot's attack scope radar repeater; the weapons systems operator had a larger scope in the rear cockpit.

A CONTROVERSIAL NUCLEAR ROLE

Having cancelled the indigenous Avro Arrow fighter programme in favour of U.S.-built Bomarc interceptor missiles, which quickly became obsolescent, Canada ordered Voodoos in 1961. As the CF-101B and F, the Voodoos, variants of the F-101B and dual-control F-101F, replaced the subsonic Avro Canada CF-100 "Clunk" in Royal Canadian Air Force service. Canada's Voodoos were armed initially only with Falcons, but after 1965 could use the nuclear-tipped Genie. The introduction of these weapons, officially under U.S. ownership and control, caused huge political controversy in Canada.

CF-101s remained assigned to NORAD for many years until their eventual replacement by CF-188 Hornets. They intercepted numerous Soviet aircraft approaching over the polar regions or down the eastern coasts of North America en route to Cuba. In late 1984, the last fighter Voodoos were retired, but two were retained a little longer. One of these was converted to the unique EF-101B "Electric Voodoo" and used to simulate enemy jamming during exercises. The EF-101B was finally retired in 1987.

Above: The vast majority of the 805 Voodoos produced were two-seat interceptors such as this F-101B of the Oregon Air National Guard, seen on patrol.

Lockheed F-104 Starfighter

The Starfighter was known as the "missile with a man in it" for its extremely high performance. It became NATO's standard fighter in the 1960s and 1970s, but gained a perhaps undeserved reputation for poor safety due to its high accident rate in European conditions.

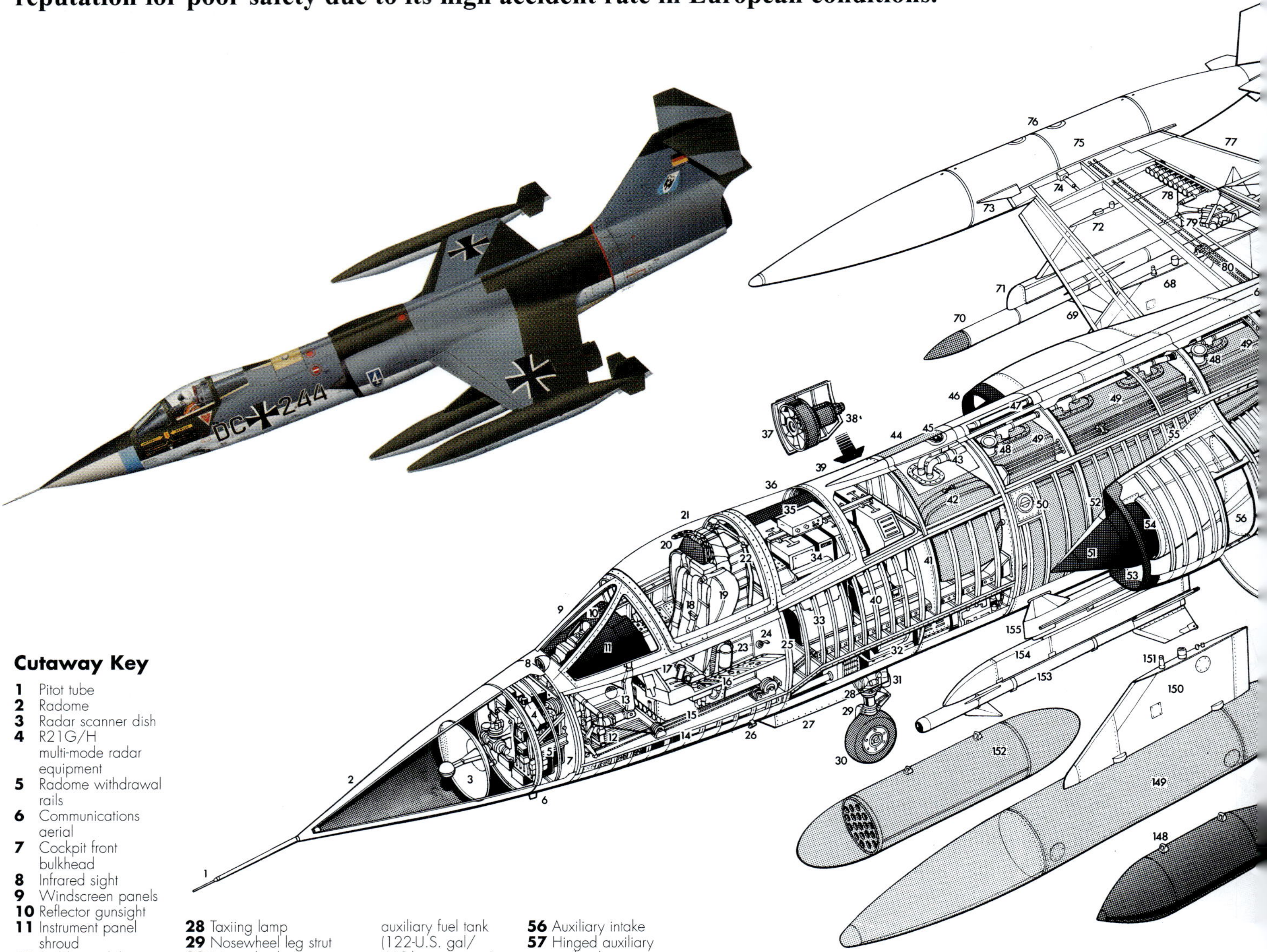

Cutaway Key

1 Pitot tube
2 Radome
3 Radar scanner dish
4 R21G/H multi-mode radar equipment
5 Radome withdrawal rails
6 Communications aerial
7 Cockpit front bulkhead
8 Infrared sight
9 Windscreen panels
10 Reflector gunsight
11 Instrument panel shroud
12 Rudder pedals
13 Control column
14 Nose section frame construction
15 Control cable runs
16 Pilot's side console panel
17 Throttle control
18 Safety harness
19 Martin-Baker IQ-7A ejection seat
20 Face-blind seat firing handle
21 Cockpit canopy cover
22 Canopy bracing struts
23 Seat rail support box
24 Angle-of-attack probe
25 Cockpit rear bulkhead
26 Temperature probe
27 Nosewheel doors
28 Taxiing lamp
29 Nosewheel leg strut
30 Nosewheel
31 Steering linkage
32 AIM-7 Sparrow avionics (replacing M61 gun installation of strike model)
33 Inertial platform
34 Avionics compartment
35 Avionics compartment shroud cover
36 Cockpit aft glazing
37 Ram air turbine
38 Emergency generator
39 Avionics compartment access cover
40 Fuselage frame construction
41 Pressure bulkhead
42 Ammunition compartment auxiliary fuel tank (122-U.S. gal/462-litre capacity)
43 Fuel feed pipes
44 Flush-fitting UHF aerial panel
45 Anti-collision light
46 Starboard intake
47 Engine bleed air supply to air-conditioning
48 Gravity fuel fillers
49 Fuselage main fuel tanks (total internal capacity 896 U.S. gal/3391 litres)
50 Pressure refuelling adaptor
51 Intake shock cone centre body
52 De-iced intake lip
53 Port intake
54 Shock cone boundary layer bleed
55 Boundary layer bleed air duct
56 Auxiliary intake
57 Hinged auxiliary intake door
58 Navigation light
59 Leading-edge flap jack
60 Intake trunking
61 Fuselage main longeron
62 Wingroot attaching members
63 Intake flank fuel tanks
64 Wing-mounting fuselage mainframes
65 Control cable runs
66 Electrical junction box
67 Dorsal spine fairing
68 Starboard inboard pylon
69 Leading-edge flap (lowered)
70 AIM-7 Sparrow AAM
71 Missile launch rail
72 Starboard outer pylon
73 Tip-tank vane
74 Tip-tank latching unit
75 Starboard wingtip tank
76 Fuel filler caps
77 Starboard aileron
78 Aileron power control jacks
79 Power control servo valves
80 Fuel lines to auxiliary tanks
81 Flap blowing duct
82 Starboard blown flap (lowered)
83 Engine intake compressor face
84 Intake spill flaps
85 Aileron torque shaft
86 Hydraulic reservoir
87 Air-conditioning bleed air supply pipe
88 General Electric J-79-GE-19 turbojet
89 Engine withdrawal rail
90 Starboard airbrake (open)
91 Fin-root fillet
92 Elevator servo controls
93 Elevator/all-moving tailplane hydraulic jacks
94 Push-pull control rods
95 Tailfin construction
96 Fintip fairing
97 Tailplane rocking control arm
98 Starboard tailplane
99 One-piece tailplane construction
100 Tailplane spar
101 Tailplane spar central pivot
102 Fin trailing-edge construction
103 Rudder construction
104 Rudder power control jacks
105 Rudder servo valves
106 Exhaust shroud
107 Fully variable afterburner exhaust nozzle
108 Fin attachment joints
109 Fin-carrying mainframes
110 Afterburner duct

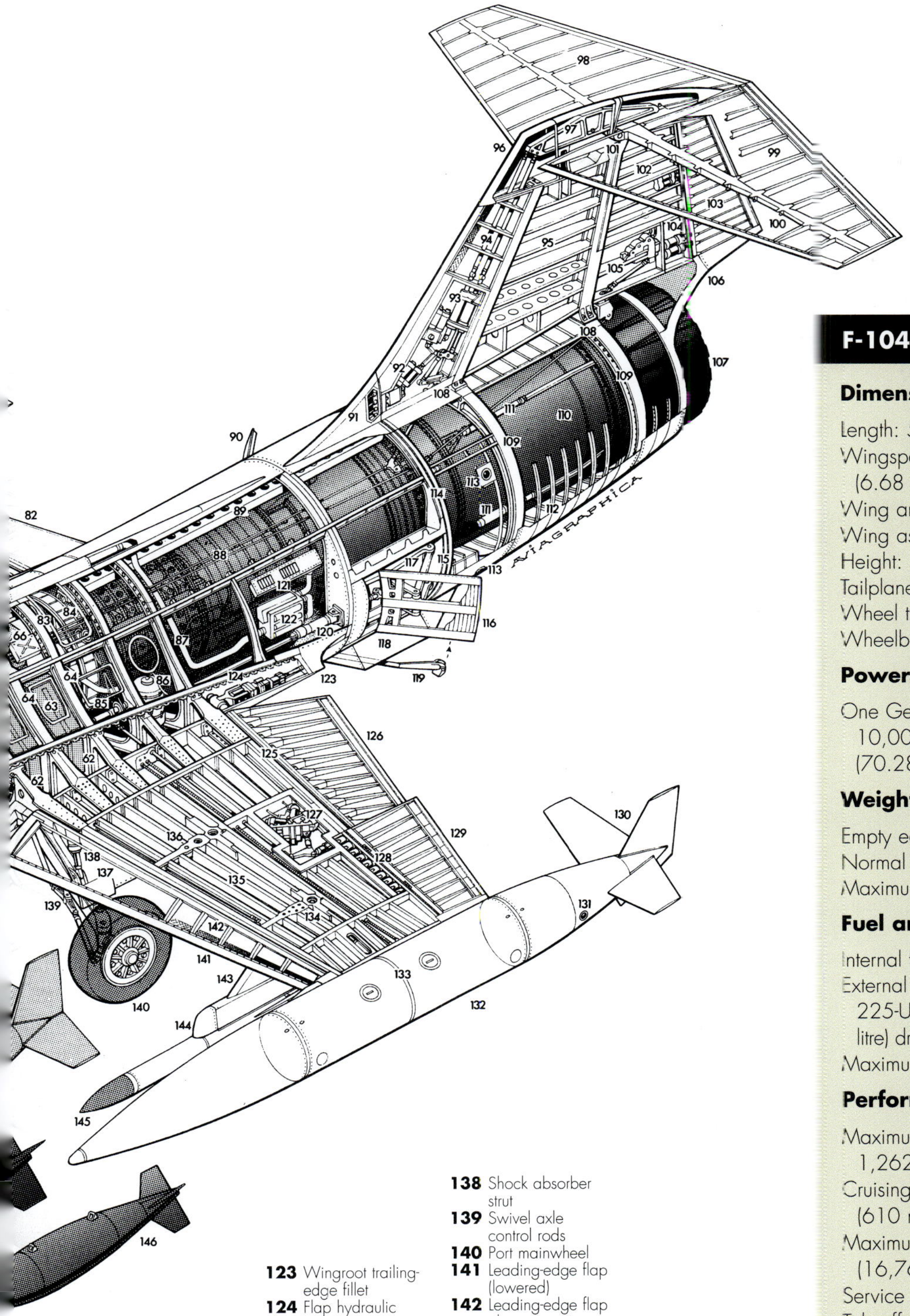

111 Nozzle control jacks
112 Steel and titanium aft fuselage construction
113 Rear navigation lights
114 Aft fuselage attachment joint
115 Brake parachute housing
116 Port airbrake (open)
117 Airbrake scissor links
118 Fuselage strake (both sides)
119 Emergency runway arrestor hook
120 Airbrake jack
121 Air exit louvres
122 Primary heat exchanger
123 Wingroot trailing-edge fillet
124 Flap hydraulic jack
125 Flap blowing slot
126 Port blown flap (lowered)
127 Aileron servo valves
128 Aileron power control jacks
129 Port aileron
130 Tip-tank fins
131 Port navigation light
132 Port wingtip fuel tank (340-U.S. gal/1287-litre) capacity
133 Fuel filler caps
134 Outboard pylon mounting rib
135 Wing multi-spar construction
136 Inboard pylon mounting rib
137 Main undercarriage leg door
138 Shock absorber strut
139 Swivel axle control rods
140 Port mainwheel
141 Leading-edge flap (lowered)
142 Leading-edge flap rib construction
143 Port outboard pylon
144 Missile launch rail
145 Port AIM-7 Sparrow AAM
146 Mk 82 500-lb (227-kg) bomb
147 Mk 83 1,000-lb (454-kg) bomb
148 Bomb mounting shackles
149 Auxiliary fuel tank (195-U.S. gal/ 740-litre capacity)
150 Port inboard wing pylon
151 Pylon attachments
152 LAU-3A 2.75-in (70-mm) FFAR pod (19 rockets)
153 AIM-9 Sidewinder AAM
154 Missile launch rail
155 Fuselage stores pylon adaptor

F-104G STARFIGHTER SPECIFICATION

Dimensions

Length: 54 ft 9 in (16.69 m)
Wingspan (without tip-mounted AAMs): 21 ft 11 in (6.68 m)
Wing area: 196.10 sq ft (18.22 m²)
Wing aspect ratio: 2.45
Height: 13 ft 6 in (4.11 m)
Tailplane span: 11 ft 11 in (3.63 m)
Wheel track: 9 ft (2.74 m)
Wheelbase: 15 ft ½ in (4.59 m)

Powerplant

One General Electric J79-GE-11A turbojet rated at 10,000 lb st (44.48 kN) dry and 15,800 lb st (70.28 kN) with afterburning

Weights

Empty equipped: 14,082 lb (6387 kg)
Normal takeoff: 21,639 lb (9840 kg)
Maximum takeoff: 28,779 lb (13,054 kg)

Fuel and load

Internal fuel: 896 U.S. gal (3392 litres)
External fuel: up to 955 U.S. gal (3615 litres) in one 225-U.S. gal (852-litre) and two 195-U.S. gal (740-litre) drop tanks and two 170-U.S. gal (645-litre) tip tanks
Maximum ordnance: 4,310 lb (1955 kg)

Performance

Maximum level speed "clean" at 36,000 ft (10,975 m): 1,262 kt (1,453 mph; 2338 km/h)
Cruising speed at 36,000 ft (10,975 m): 530 kt (610 mph; 981 km/h)
Maximum rate of climb at sea level: 55,000 ft (16,765 m) per minute
Service ceiling: 58,000 ft (17,680 m)
Takeoff distance to 50 ft (15 m): 4,600 ft (1402 m)
Landing distance from 50 ft (15 m): 3,250 ft (990 m)

Range

Ferry range with four drop tanks: 1,893 nm (2,180 miles; 3510 km)
Combat radius: 648 nm (746 miles; 1200 km)
Combat radius on hi-lo-hi attack mission with maximum warload: 261 nm (300 miles; 483 km)

Armament

Fixed: One General Electric 20-mm M61A-1 Vulcan six-barrelled rotary cannon with 725 rounds
Weapon stations: One underfuselage, four underwing and two wingtip hardpoints for AIM-9 AAMs and a variety of bombs, pods and rockets

"The F-104 was sort of like owning the sharpest knife in the world. It was an honest airplane; you knew what was going on all the time. But like using a sharp knife, you better not make any mistakes."
– Walt "BJ" Bjorneby, U.S. Air Force F-104 pilot

FACTS

- Starfighters were built in Canada, the Netherlands, Germany, Belgium, Italy and Japan, as well as the United States.
- Taiwan used nine different versions of the Starfighter, from the F-104A to the RF-104G reconnaissance aircraft.
- The F-104 was the first production fighter with a boundary layer control (BLC) system that blew air over the wings to improve takeoff and landing performance.

LOCKHEED F-104 STARFIGHTER PRODUCTION

Version	Quantity	Time Period
Lockheed Aircraft Company, Burbank, California		
XF-104	2	1953–1954
YF-104A	17	Oct 1954–1956
F-104A	153	1956–Dec 1958
F-104B	26	1956–Nov 1958
F-104C	77	1958–June 1959
F-104D	21	1958–1959
F-104DJ	20	1962–1964
CF-104D	38	1961
F-104F	30	1959–1960
F-104G	139	1960–1962
RF-104G	40	1962–1963
TF-104G	220	1962–1966
F-104J	3	1961
F-104N	3	1963
Total:	**741**	
Canadair, Cartierville, Montreal, Quebec, Canada		
CF-104	(1 F-104A conv.)	1961
CF-104	200	1961–1963
F-104G	140	1963–1964
Total:	**340**	
Aircraft delivered to Canada (CF-104) and Denmark (F-104G).		
Fiat, Turin, Italy		
F-104G	164	June 1962–1966
RF-104G	35	1963–1966
F-104S	(2 F-104G conv.)	1966
F-104S	245	1968–March 1979
F-104S ASA	(147 conv.)	1986–1992
F-104S ASA/M	(49 conv.)	1998–2000
TF-104G ASA/M	(15 conv.)	1998–2000
Total:	**444**	
Aircraft delivered to Italy, the Netherlands, West Germany and Turkey.		
Fokker, Schiphol, Amsterdam, Netherlands		
F-104G	231	1961–1966
RF-104G	119	1962–1966
Total:	**350**	
Aircraft delivered to the Netherlands and West Germany.		
MBB, Manching, Augsburg, Germany		
F-104G	50	1970–1972
Total:	**50**	
Aircraft delivered to West Germany only.		
Messerschmitt, Manching, Augsburg, Germany		
F-104G	210	1960–1966
Total:	**210**	
Aircraft delivered to West Germany only.		
Mitsubishi Heavy Industries, Komaki, Nagoya, Japan		
F-104J	207*	Apr 1962–Dec 1967
Total:	**207**	
*29 assembled from Lockheed kits plus 178 local. Aircraft delivered to Japan.		
SABCA, Gosselies, Charleroi, Belgium		
F-104G	188	Gosselies 1961–1965
Total:	**188**	
Aircraft delivered to Belgium and West Germany.		

LOCKHEED F-104 STARFIGHTER

West Germany's naval air arm, or Marineflieger, operated this F-104G in the anti-shipping role from 1972 until 1987. Built by Messerschmitt, which assembled 260 of the 1,103 F-104Gs produced as part of the international production pool, 26+65 rolled off the line in December 1972. Fitted with the electronics and weapons pylons to operate the AS-30 Kormoran missile, it is shown when in service with MFG-1 at Schleswig in northern Germany. It is depicted with practice bombs on the centreline pylon, in addition to dummy Kormorans. This aircraft was one of four F-104Gs that flew to the United States as part of a farewell tour for the German Navy's Starfighters in 1986.

In the Korean War, U. S. pilots demanded a simple fighter that was faster and able to outclimb and outmanoeuvre any opposition aircraft. Lockheed took these ideas on board and designed an aircraft with a long fuselage and tiny wings that was ready for flight test by February 1954, too late for Korea, but of interest to the U.S. Air Force, which was evaluating the lessons of the conflict and also looking to counter the first generation of Soviet jet bombers.

Above: With seemingly as many dials as possible crammed onto the instrument panel, and no head-up display, the Starfighter was an aircraft for which pilots valued simulator training for low-level flight.

The XF-104 Starfighter flew in March 1954 and, despite some initial teething problems, soon demonstrated supersonic performance, even with a non-afterburning Wright J65 engine. The production F-104A and subsequent variants had the General Electric J79 engine. The F-104A was an interceptor, and the F-104C was a fighter-bomber with a nuclear role. The F-104 B and D were equivalent two-seaters.

SINGULAR CHARACTERISTICS

The F-104's wings were tiny, only 21 feet (6.4 m) in total span. The leading edges were nearly as slim as the trailing edges and were often fitted with covers to protect both them and ground crew during maintenance. Missiles or fuel tanks could be attached to the wingtips. Until the F-104C model, the ejection seat operated in the reverse way to most seats, being catapulted downwards through a hatch in the underside of the fuselage. This arrangement was chosen because contemporary seats lacked the power to clear the high tail in

Above: Mitsubishi Heavy Industries built 210 F-104Js and 20 F-104DJ two-seaters from 1962–67. Two of the former, in the markings of the 203rd Hikotai of the Japan Air Self-Defence Force, are seen here carrying single Sidewinders on underfuselage pylons.

Above: The 69th Tactical Fighter Training Squadron was a U.S. Air Force unit that trained German Starfighter pilots in the (usually) cloudless skies of Arizona. This F-104G has AIM-9Js on wingtip launchers.

every circumstance. The downward seat was usable above 500 feet (152 m), in practice not a lot worse than the upward-firing seats of the day, but was understandably unpopular.

The U.S. Air Force made comparatively little use of the F-104. By the end of 1967, Tactical Air Command and Air Defense Command had passed their F-104s on to the U.S. Air National Guard, and they were gone by 1975.

From 1965–67, F-104Cs were deployed to Vietnam and Thailand, initially in the air defence role for the South, then as fighter-bombers and escorts for F-105 "Wild Weasels." One of the few air combat actions saw a Chinese MiG-19 (Shenyang J-6) shoot down one Starfighter that wandered over Chinese territory.

EXPORT SUCCESS

The Starfighter was one of the biggest sales successes of its era, serving with 14 international users. The spur for this proliferation was West Germany's selection of the strengthened F-104G model in 1958. The Luftwaffe and Marineflieger took 917 Starfighters in total, a number of which remained in the United States for training. The high performance of the F-104, its use as a low-level fighter-bomber in European weather and the rapid growth of the reborn Luftwaffe all contributed to the high accident rate, with 270 being lost by the time it was retired in 1991. Norway, Denmark, the Netherlands, Belgium, Spain, Italy, Greece and Turkey all operated F-104Gs and other variants. Other users were Jordan, Pakistan, Taiwan, Japan and Canada.

TESTED IN COMBAT

Taiwan's Starfighters fought numerous clashes with Chinese aircraft in the 1960s, and Greek and Turkish aircraft met over Cyprus in 1974. The most extensive combat use was with the Pakistan Air Force in 1965 and 1971, with an estimated 10 victories over Indian aircraft in the two Indo-Pakistan wars. The Indians respected the F-104 and avoided engagement with them wherever possible.

F-104s were finally retired from Italian service in 2004. A civilian group in Florida still operates several Starfighters for display purposes. In 2009, it was awarded a contract to supply F-104 flying hours to NASA for research programmes, including some requiring suborbital vehicle trajectories.

Republic F-105 Thunderchief

Republic's huge F-105 found its niche in high-speed low-level missions over North Vietnam. As well as holding its own against North Vietnamese MiGs, it undertook the hazardous "Wild Weasel" role, dueling with enemy missile batteries.

F-105D THUNDERCHIEF SPECIFICATION

Dimensions

Length: 64 ft 4 in (19.61 m)
Height: 19 ft 7 in (5.97 m)
Wingspan: 34 ft 9 in (10.59 m)
Wing area: 385 sq ft (35.77 m²)

Powerplant

One Pratt & Whitney J75-P-19W turbojet rated at 17,200 lb (76.0 kN) thrust dry and 24,500 lb (110.25 kN) thrust with afterburning; water injection permitted 60-second rating of 26,500 lb (117.7 kN) thrust in afterburner mode

Weights

Empty: 27,500 lb (12474 kg)
Maximum overload takeoff: 52,838 lb (23,967 kg)

Fuel

Normal internal fuel: 435 U.S. gal (1646 litres)
Maximum internal fuel: 675 U.S. gal (2555 litres)

Performance

Maximum level speed "clean" at 36,000 ft (10,970 m): 1,390 mph (2237 km/h)
Initial climb rate: 34,400 ft (10,485 m) per minute in "clean" configuration
Service ceiling: 41,200 ft (12,560 m)
Range: 920 miles (1480 km) with two 450-U.S. gal (1703-litre) drop tanks underwing, one 650-U.S. gal (2461-litre) drop tank on centreline and two AGM-12 Bullpup ASMs; ferry range 2,390 miles (3846 km) with maximum external fuel at 584 mph (940 km/h)

Armament

Combination of 750-lb (340-kg) M117 bombs, 1,000-lb (454-kg) Mk 83 bombs, 3,000-lb (1361-kg) M118 bombs, AGM-12 Bullpup ASMs, AIM-9 Sidewinder AAMs, 2.75-in (70-mm) rocket pods, napalm containers, Mk 28/43 special weapons, chemical bombs, leaflet bombs, 5-in (127-mm) rocket pods and MLU-10/B mines; also one M61 Vulcan 20-mm cannon with 1,028 rounds of ammunition

Cutaway Key

1 Pitot tube
2 Radome
3 Radar scanner dish
4 Radar mounting and tracking mechanism
5 Forward electronic countermeasures (ECM) antenna
6 Aft-facing strike camera
7 Radome hinge
8 ADF sense aerial
9 Fire-control radar transmitter/receiver
10 Cannon muzzle
11 Instrument electronics
12 Inflight refuelling position light
13 Air refuelling receptacle
14 Cannon ammunition drum, 1,028 rounds
15 Liquid oxygen converter
16 Angle-of-attack transmitter
17 Cannon barrels
18 Nosewheel doors
19 M61 20-mm six-barrelled rotary cannon
20 Ammunition feed chute
21 Gun gas venting pipe
22 Air refuelling probe housing
23 Alternator and electrical bay
24 Air-driven turbine
25 Air refuelling probe
26 Windscreen rain-dispersal duct
27 Bulletproof windscreen panels
28 Radar attack sight
29 Instrument panel shroud
30 Navigation radar display
31 Rudder pedals
32 Cockpit front pressure bulkhead
33 Cannon mounting
34 Nosewheel leg strut
35 ILS system radar reflector
36 Taxiing lamps
37 Nosewheel
38 Torque scissor links
39 Hydraulic steering controls
40 Flight control system hydraulics bay
41 Electronics cooling air outlet
42 IFF aerial
43 UHF aerial
44 Underfloor radio and electronics bay
45 Cockpit pressure floor level
46 Pilot's side console panel
47 Engine throttle
48 Control column
49 Pilot's ejection seat
50 Seat back parachute pack
51 Headrest
52 Cockpit canopy cover
53 3,000-lb (1360-kg) HE bomb (inboard pylon)
54 Starboard air intake
55 Cockpit canopy jack
56 Canopy hinge
57 Air-conditioning pack
58 Cockpit rear pressure bulkhead
59 Secondary electronics bay
60 Air data computer
61 Port air intake
62 Bomb bay fuel tank, 390-U.S. gal (1476-litre) capacity
63 Boundary layer splitter plate
64 Intake duct variable-area sliding ramp
65 Forward group of fuselage fuel tanks; total internal fuel capacity 1,160 U.S. gal (4391 litres)
66 Gyro compass platform
67 Bomb-bay fuel tank fuel transfer lines
68 Fuselage/front spar main frame

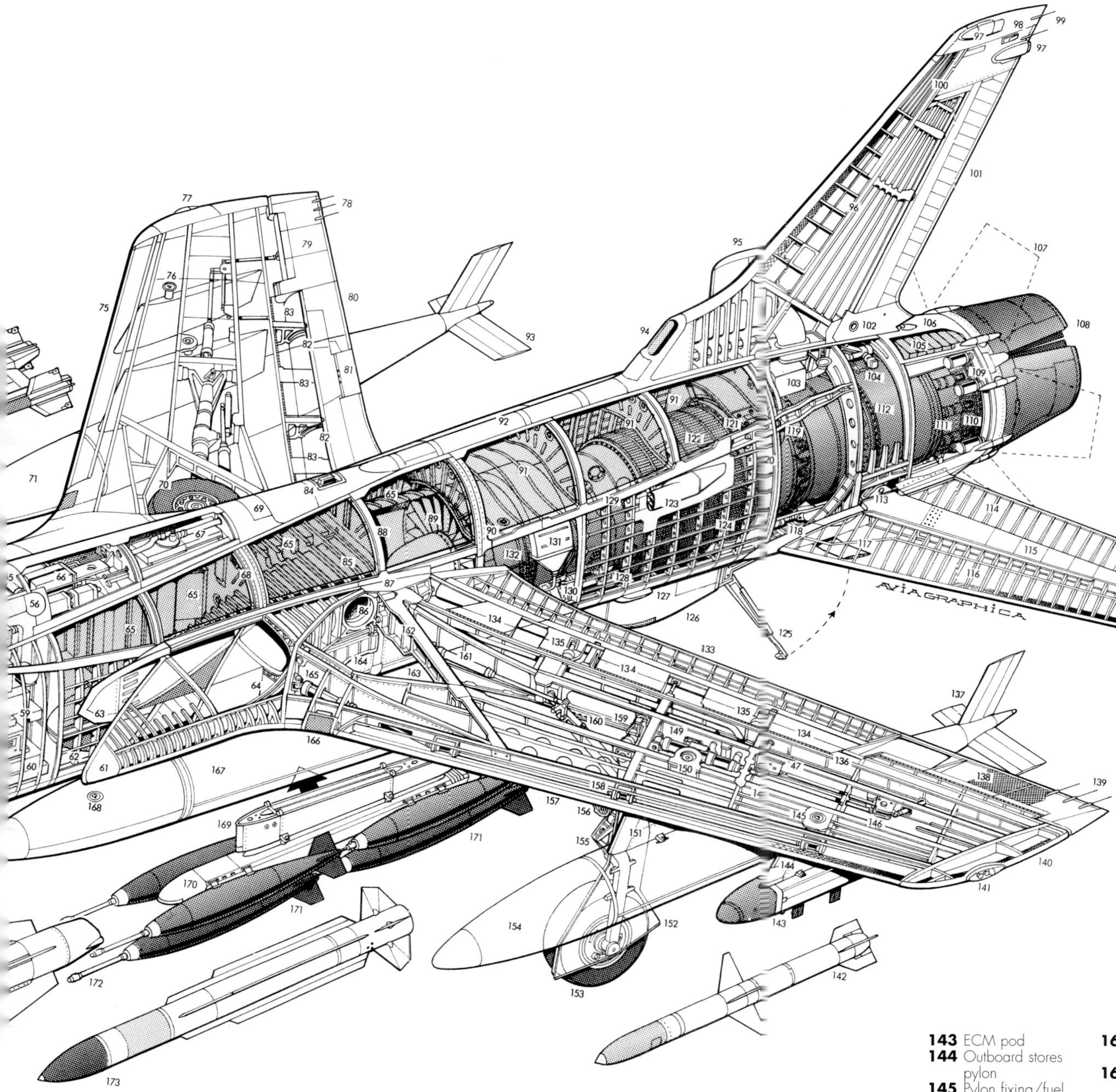

69 Dorsal spine fairing
70 Starboard mainwheel, stowed position
71 450-U.S. gal (1703-litre) external fuel tank
72 AIM-9 Sidewinder air-to-air missile
73 Missile launcher rail
74 Twin missile carrier (outboard pylon)
75 Starboard leading-edge flap
76 Outboard pylon fixing/drop-tank filler cap
77 Starboard navigation light
78 Static dischargers
79 Starboard aileron
80 Starboard fowler flap
81 Trim tab, starboard only
82 Flap guide rails
83 Roll control spoilers
84 Anti-collision light
85 Air intake ducting
86 Ground running secondary air intake
87 Wing spar attachment joint
88 Fuselage/rear spar main frame
89 Engine compressor face
90 Forward engine mounting frame
91 Rear fuselage group of fuel tanks
92 Fuel pipe ducting
93 Drop tank tail fins
94 Afterburner duct cooling ram air intake
95 Starboard all-moving tailplane
96 Tailfin construction
97 Fintip ECM aerials
98 Tail position light
99 Static dischargers
100 Rudder mass balance
101 Rudder
102 Formation light
103 Water injection tank 36-U.S. gal (136-litre) capacity
104 Rudder-power control unit
105 Brake parachute housing
106 Parachute door
107 Petal-type airbrakes, open position
108 Republic convergent/civergent ram air ejector nozzle flaps
109 Airbrake/nozzle flap jacks
110 Internal variable-area afterburner nozzle
111 Afterburner nozzle actuators
112 Afterburner ducting
113 Tailplane pivot fixing
114 Port all-moving tailplane construction
115 Tailplane titanium box spar
116 Leading-edge nose ribs
117 Ventral fuel vent
118 All-moving tailplane control jack
119 Rear fuselage break point
120 Engine firewall
121 Rear engine mounting
122 Engine turbine section heat shroud
123 Engine bay venting ram air intake
124 Rear fuselage frame and stringer construction
125 Runway arrestor hook
126 Ventral fin
127 Accessory cooling air duct
128 Cartridge starter
129 Fuselage top longeron
130 Engine-driven accessory gearbox
131 Oil tank, 4.5-U.S. gal (17-litre) capacity
132 Pratt & Whitney J75-P-19W afterburning turbojet
133 Port Fowler-type flap construction
134 Five-section roll control spoilers
135 Flap screw jacks
136 Aileron mass balance
137 Port drop-tank tail fins
138 Honeycomb aileron construction
139 Static dischargers
140 Wingtip fairing
141 Port navigation light
142 AGM-45 Strike anti-radar missile
143 ECM pod
144 Outboard stores pylon
145 Pylon fixing/fuel filler cap
146 Aileron hinge control
147 Aileron/spoiler mixer linkage
148 Multi-spar wing construction
149 Aileron power control unit
150 Inboard pylon fixing
151 Inboard stores pylon
152 Mainwheel leg door
153 Port mainwheel
154 450-U.S. gal (1703-litre) drop tank
155 Main undercarriage leg torque scissor links
156 Landing lamp
157 Port leading-edge flap
158 Leading-edge flap rotary actuators
159 Main undercarriage pivot mounting
160 Undercarriage side breaker strut
161 Hydraulic retraction jack
162 Diagonal wing spar
163 Mainwheel housing
164 Inner mainwheel door
165 Leading-edge flap actuator
166 Leading-edge flush aerial
167 650-U.S. gal (2461-litre) centreline fuel tank
168 Fuel-tank filler cap
169 Centreline stores pylon
170 Triple ejection rack
171 Six M117 750-lb (340-kg) HE bombs
172 Anti-personnel extended bomb fuse
173 AGM-78 Standard anti-radar missile
174 AGM-12C Bullpup air-to-ground missile

"The F-105 was nothing if not unmistakable, with its distinctive wing planform and backward-looking intakes, stalky undercarriage, oddly shaped fin and bulbous rear end."

FACTS

- The F-105 is the largest single-seat single-engined fighter to enter production.
- More than half of the F-105s built were lost in action in the Vietnam War.
- Nicknames for the Thunderchief included "Thud," "Lead Sled" and "Ultra Hog."

REPUBLIC F-105 THUNDERCHIEF – U.S. AIR FORCE ACTIVE DUTY

WING	SQUADRON	LOCATION	VARIANTS	SERVICE DATES
4th TFW	333rd TFS	Seymour Johnson AFB,	F-105B/D/F	1958–1964
	334th TFS	North Carolina	F-105B/D/F	
	335th TFS		F-105B/D/F	
	336th TFS		F-105B/D/F	
			F-105B/D/F	
8th TFW			F-105D/F	1963–1964
6441st TFW	35th TFS	Itazuke AB, Japan	F-105D/F	
	36th TFS	Yokota AB, Japan	F-105	
	80th TFS		F-105	
			F-105	
18th TFW	12th TFS		F-105D/F/G	
	44th TFS	Kadena AB, Japan	F-105D/F/G	1962, 1966
	67th TFS	Korat RTAFB, Thailand	F-105D/F/G	1964
		Da Nang AB, Vietnam	F-105F/G	1965
			F-105	
			F-105	
36th TFW	22nd TFS		F-105D/F	
	23rd TFS	Bitburg AB,	F-105	1961–1966
	53rd TFS	West Germany	F-105	
			F-105	
49th TFW	7th TFS		F-105D/F	
	8th TFS	Spangdahlem AB,	F-105	1961–1967
	9th TFS	West Germany	F-105	
			F-105	

REPUBLIC F-105 THUNDERCHIEF

This F-105G "Wild Weasel" had an interesting career. Built as an F-105F combat-capable two-seater in 1964, it served from 1967–70 at Takhli, Thailand, during which time its crews claimed three North Vietnamese MiGs in air combat. In 1970, it was one of those F-105Fs modified with radar locating equipment and the ability to fire anti-radiation missiles. It is depicted in the markings of the 333rd TFW, carrying AGM-45 Shrike missiles on the outer pylons and the larger AGM-78 Standard on the inboard ones. These missiles would fly down the radar beam of an enemy radar transmitter to destroy it. After further upgrades and more Vietnam service, it was eventually put on display at the National Museum of the U.S. Air Force in Ohio.

Above: Designed in an era before miniaturized avionics, the F-105 had a reputation for needing intensive maintenance between missions.

From the outset, Republic's F-105 was intended to be a fighter-bomber, rather than a pure fighter. Previous U.S. fighters had been adapted to carry air-ground ordnance, instead of having the capability included in the design from the beginning. The F-105's intended warload was a single nuclear bomb in a ventral bay, but provision for air-to-air combat was built into the aircraft's systems. The design was changed during construction to take account of the problems encountered with the Convair YF-102, which was hampered by drag at transonic speeds. As with the F-102A, the problem was fixed by "wasp-waisting" the fuselage. The intakes were also revised to better function at high Mach numbers.

DISTINCTIVE LINES

Republic was famous for its large aircraft, from the P-47 Thunderbolt to the A-10 Thunderbolt II. It was not, however, known for creating pretty ones. Still, the F-105 was nothing if not unmistakable, with its distinctive wing planform and backward-looking intakes, stalky undercarriage, oddly shaped fin and bulbous rear end. The pilot sat quite high up and had little rearward view. The heavy weight when the aircraft was loaded contributed to the F-105's reputation as a "ground gripper" on takeoff.

The YF-105A prototype flew in October 1955, and the much-revised YF-105B in May 1956. The production model F-105B had a relatively short service career, during which it briefly served with the "Thunderbirds" demonstration team, as well as a few regular squadrons. The most numerous model was the F-105D, with an uprated engine and an improved radar and fire control system that required a lengthened nose. Improved conventional weapons capability allowed carriage of 16 750-lb (340-kg) bombs. An extra fuel tank was fitted in the bomb bay, removing its nuclear capability.

Vietnam became the proving ground for the F-105. With its speed, range and heavy warload, it was ideal for missions against North Vietnam's heavier targets, flown from bases in Thailand. Despite its tasking as an attack aircraft, the Thunderchief regularly did battle with Soviet and Chinese-built MiGs of the North Vietnamese air force. "Thud" pilots claimed 27 MiGs in air combat, all but two of them with the internal cannon. In response, the U.S. Air Force lost at least 17 F-105s to MiGs. The F-105's main defence was its speed at low level, which allowed it to accelerate away from trouble and use terrain to mask it from radar. This speed could usually be achieved only by dumping bombs and fuel tanks, however, which suited the purpose of the defenders.

ADAPTING TO A NEW ROLE

Almost half the F-105s produced were lost in Vietnam, many of them to radar-guided SAMs. This helped to spur the adaptation of the EF-105F and F-105G "Wild Weasels." These were modified two-seat Thunderchiefs equipped with sensitive radar-locating and homing devices and armed with the AGM-45 Shrike and AGM-78 Standard anti-radiation missiles. The Wild Weasels would fly ahead of the strike package, locating the "Fan Song" radars associated with the SA-2 "Guideline" missile, and try to launch their missiles first. The presence of the Wild Weasels was often enough for North Vietnamese radar operators to shut down, thus rendering their missiles ineffective.

The F-105D was retired before the end of the Vietnam War, but the Gs went on to serve with stateside regular units until 1980 and Air National Guard squadrons until 1983.

Above: An F-105G gets airborne carrying a pair of dummy AGM-45 Shrikes, two large fuel tanks and a centreline multiple ejector rack with two large bombs for good measure.

Above: One of the two YF-105B Thunderchiefs in flight. One of these early aircraft reached Mach 2.15 in testing. Operational F-105s with ordnance aboard were considerably slower.

Mikoyan-Gurevich MiG-21F "Fishbed"

The MiG-21 is the most numerous jet fighter ever, with more than 10,000 built in several countries. Hard to spot and nimble, in the hands of a good pilot it was a match for much more sophisticated Western fighters.

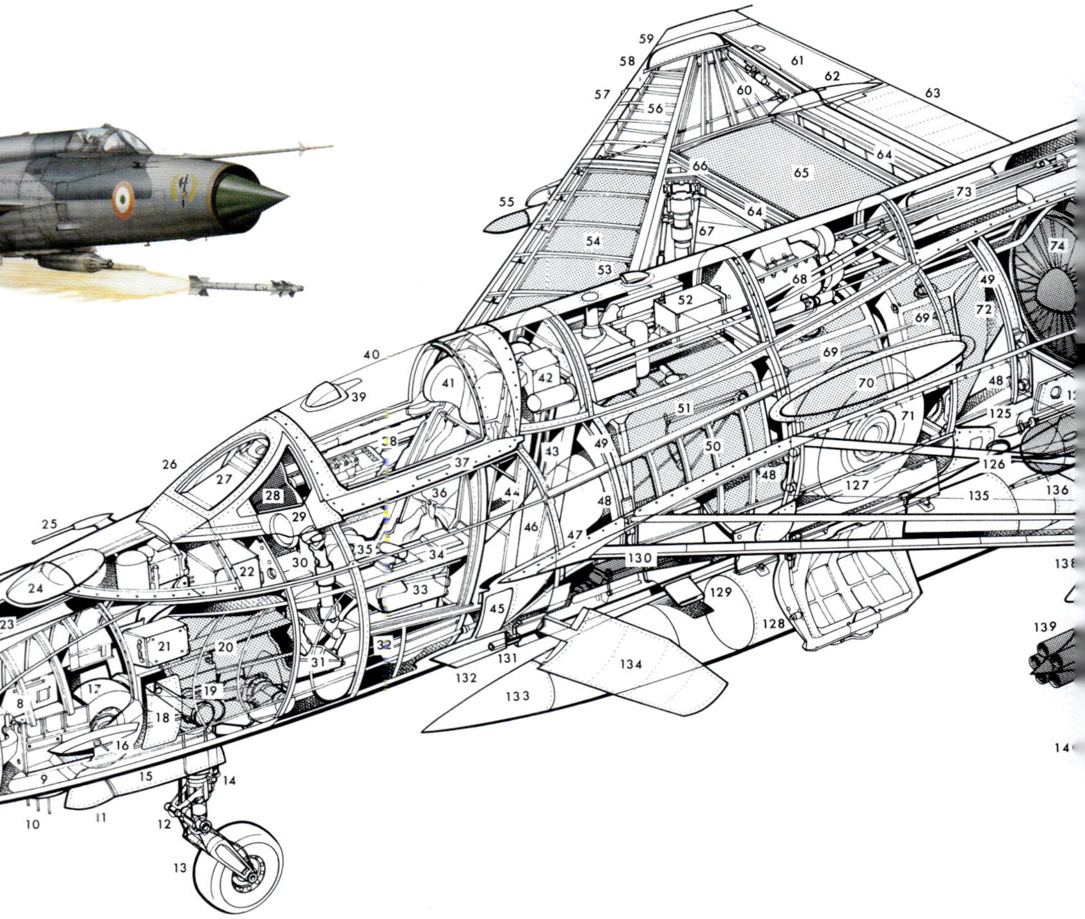

Cutaway Key

1 Pitot static boom
2 Pitch vanes
3 Yaw vanes
4 Conical three-position intake centre-body
5 "Spin Scan" search-and-track radar antenna
6 Boundary layer slot
7 Engine air intake
8 "Spin Scan" radar
9 Lower boundary layer exit
10 IFF antennas
11 Nosewheel doors
12 Nosewheel leg and shock absorbers
13 Castoring nosewheel
14 Anti-shimmy damper
15 Avionics bay access
16 Attitude sensor
17 Nosewheel well
18 Spill door
19 Nosewheel retraction pivot
20 Bifurcated intake trunking
21 Avionics bay
22 Electronics equipment
23 Intake trunking
24 Upper boundary layer exit
25 Dynamic pressure probe for Q feel
26 Semi-elliptical armour glass windscreen
27 Gunsight mounting
28 Fixed quarterlight
29 Radar scope
30 Control column (with tailplane trim switch and two firing buttons)
31 Rudder pedals
32 Underfloor control runs
33 KM-1 two-position zero-level ejection seat
34 Port instrument console
35 Undercarriage handle
36 Seat harness
37 Canopy release/lock
38 Starboard wall switch pane
39 Rear-view mirror fairing
40 Starboard hinged canopy
41 Ejection seat headrest
42 Avionics bay
43 Control rods
44 Air-conditioning plant
45 Suction relief door
46 Intake trunking
47 Wingroot attachment fairing
48 Wing/fuselage spar-lug attachment points (four)
49 Fuselage ring frames
50 Intermediary frames
51 Main fuselage fuel tank
52 RSIU radio bay
53 Auxiliary intake
54 Leading-edge integral fuel tank
55 Starboard outer weapons pylon
56 Outboard wing construction
57 Starboard navigation light
58 Leading-edge suppressed aerial
59 Wing fence
60 Aileron control jack
61 Starboard aileron
62 Flap actuator fairing
63 Starboard blown flap SPS (*sduva pogranichnovo sloya*)
64 Multi-spar wing structure
65 Main integral wing fuel tank
66 Undercarriage mounting/pivot point
67 Starboard mainwheel leg
68 Auxiliaries compartment
69 Fuselage fuel tanks Nos 2 and 3
70 Mainwheel well external fairing
71 Mainwheel (retracted)
72 Trunking contours
73 Control rods in dorsal spine
74 Compressor face
75 Oil tank
76 Avionics pack
77 Engine accessories
78 Tumanskii R-13 turbojet
79 Fuselage break/transport joint
80 Intake
81 Tail surface control linkage
82 Artificial feel unit
83 Tailplane jack
84 Hydraulic accumulator
85 Tailplane trim motor
86 Fin spar attachment plate
87 Rudder jack
88 Rudder control linkage
89 Fin structure
90 Leading-edge panel
91 Radio cable access
92 Magnetic detector
93 Fin mainspar
94 RSIU (*radio-stantsiya istrebitelnaya*

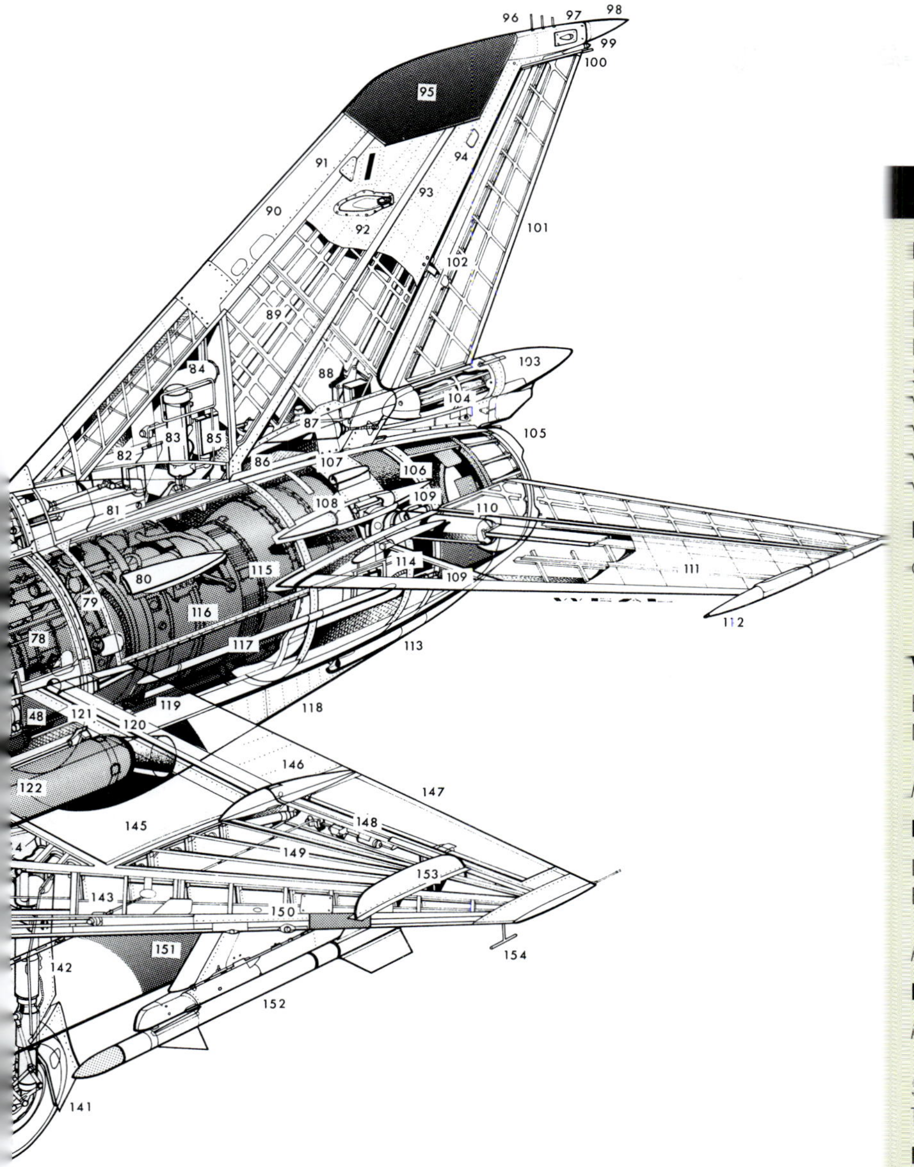

ultrakorotkykh vol'n – very short-wave fighter radio) antenna plate
95 VHF/UHF aerials
96 IFF antennas
97 Formation light
98 Tail warning radar
99 Rear navigation light
100 Fuel vent
101 Rudder construction
102 Rudder hinge
103 Braking parachute hinged bullet fairing
104 Braking parachute stowage
105 Tailpipe (variable convergent nozzle)
106 Afterburner installation
107 Afterburner bay cooling intake
108 Tail plane linkage fairing
109 Nozzle actuating cylinders
110 Tailplane torque tube
111 All-moving tailplane
112 Anti-flutter weight
113 Intake
114 Afterburner mounting
115 Fixed tailplane root fairing
116 Longitudinal lap joint
117 External duct (nozzle hydraulics)
118 Ventral fin
119 Engine guide rail
120 ATO assembly canted nozzle
121 ATO assembly thrust plate forks (rear-mounting)
122 ATO assembly pack
123 Ventral airbrake (retracted)
124 Trestle point
125 ATO assembly-release solenoid (front-mounting)
126 Underwing landing light
127 Ventral stores pylon
128 Mainwheel inboard door
129 Splayed link chute
130 23-mm GSh-23 cannon installation
131 Cannon muzzle fairing
132 Debris deflector plate
133 Auxiliary ventral drop tank
134 Port forward air brake (extended)
135 Leading-edge integral fuel tank
136 Undercarriage retraction strut
137 Aileron control rods in leading edge
138 Port inboard weapons pylon
139 UV-16-57 rocket pod
140 Port mainwheel
141 Mainwheel outboard door section
142 Mainwheel leg
143 Aileron control linkage
144 Mainwheel leg pivot point
145 Main integral wing fuel tank
146 Flap actuator fairing
147 Port aileron
148 Aileron control jack
149 Outboard wing construction
150 Port navigation light
151 Port outboard weapons pylon
152 Advanced "Atoll" R-homing AAM
153 Wing fence
154 Radio altimeter antenna

MIG-21MF "FISHBED-J" SPECIFICATION

Dimensions

Length with probe: 51 ft 8½ in (15.76 m)
Length excluding probe: 40 ft 4 in (12.29 m)
Height: 13 ft 6 in (4.13 m)
Span: 23 ft 6 in (7.15 m)
Wing area: 247.5 sq ft (23 m²)
Wing aspect ratio: 2.23
Wheel track: 9 ft 1¾ in (2.79 m)
Wheelbase: 15 ft 5½ in (4.71 m)

Powerplant

One MNPK "Soyuz" (Tumanskii/Gavrilov) R-13-300 turbojet rated at 8,972 lb st (39.92 kN) dry and 14,037 lb st (63.66 kN) with afterburning

Weights

Empty: 11,795 lb (5350 kg)
Normal takeoff with four AAMs and three 129-U.S. gal (490-litre) drop tanks: 17,967 lb (8150 kg)
Maximum takeoff: 20,723 lb (9400 kg)

Fuel and load

Internal fuel: 687 U.S. gal (2600 litres)
External fuel: up to 387 U.S. gal (1470 litres) in three drop tanks
Maximum ordnance: 4,409 lb (2000 kg)

Performance

Maximum rate of climb at sea level: 23,622 ft (7200 m) per minute
Service ceiling: 59,711 ft (18,200 m)
Takeoff run: 2,625 ft (800 m)

Range

Ferry range: 971 nm (1,118 miles; 1800 km) with three drop tanks
Combat radius: 200 nm (230 miles; 370 km) on a hi-lo-hi attack mission with four 551-lb (250-kg) bombs, or 400 nm (460 miles; 740 km) on a hi-lo-hi mission with two 551-lb (250-kg) bombs and drop tanks

Armament

Standard gun is the GSh-23L which has a calibre of 23 mm and can fire AP or HE ammunition, with 420 rounds being carried. The only guided missiles normally carried are for air-to-air use. The MF is capable of firing the K-13A (AA-2 "Atoll") and the AA-2-2 Advanced "Atoll." As with other MiG-21s, up to eight R-60 (AA-8 "Aphid") infrared missiles can also be carried. There is provision for various FABs (free-fall general-purpose bombs), up to 1,102 lb (500 kg) in weight. A wide range of fragmentation, chemical, cluster bombs and rocket-boosted penetrators for use against concrete can be carried, as well as 57-mm or 240-mm calibre rockets.

"Perhaps the most important lesson on fighting the MiG-21 was that it was very manoeuvrable and that it was better to take care of it before you got into a tussle with it."
– Bob Sheffield, U.S. Air Force fighter pilot

FACTS

- Including Chinese output, the MiG-21 was in production for more than 50 years.
- More than 55 countries operated the original Russian-designed "Fishbed," and more than 20 still use it.
- The canopy on early MiG-21s hinged at the front to provide the pilot with a blast screen if he had to eject.

MIKOYAN-GUREVICH MIG-21 "FISHBED" – MAJOR VARIANTS

Generation Zero (1954–56)
Ye-1: Swept-wing prototype.

Ye-2A/MiG-23: Ye-2 design modified for RD-11 turbojet.

Ye-4: First delta-wing MiG-21.

Ye-50: Swept-wing experimental high-altitude interceptor.

Ye-50A/MiG-23U: A refinement of the Ye-50.

Ye-5: Delta-wing research prototype powered by Mikulin AM-11 turbojet.

MiG-21: The first series of fighters, production version of Ye-5.

Generation One (1957–76)
Ye-6: Three pre-production versions of MiG-21F.

Ye-50P: Rocket-boosted high-altitude interceptor project.

MiG-21F: Single-seat day-fighter aircraft. It was the first production aircraft, with 93 machines being made.

MiG-21P-13: Two MiG-21s were converted to use the K-13 missile system.

MiG-21F-13: Existing MiG-21Fs using K-13 missiles.

Generation Two (1961–66)
MiG-21PF/FL: Production versions of all-weather interceptors. PF was the Warsaw Pact export version; FL the developing nations export version.

MiG-21PFS: Identical to PF variant, but with blown flaps.

MiG-21PFM: A PF model with uprated radar and avionics.

MiG-21R: Combat-capable reconnaissance aircraft.

MiG-21S: Tactical fighter. Delivered only to the Soviet Air Force.

MiG-21N: Variant of the 21S. Capable of delivering the RN-25 tactical nuclear weapon.

Generation Three (1968–72)
MiG-21M: Export variant of MiG-21S.

MiG-21SM: Upgrade of the MiG-21S.

MiG-21MF: Export version of the MiG-21SM.

MiG-21MT: MiG-21MF with increased fuel capacity.

MiG-21SMT: A development of the MiG-21SM with increased fuel capacity. Easily spotted from its larger spine.

MiG-21ST: Rebuilt versions of the unpopular MiG-21SMT with smaller saddle tanks of the MiG-21bis.

MiG-21bis: Ultimate development of the MiG-21. Fitted with a Turmansky R25-300 turbojet and many other advances.

MiG-21bis-D: 2003 upgrade for the Croat Air Force. Modernized for NATO interoperability.

MIKOYAN-GUREVICH MIG-21 "FISHBED"

The Romanian Air Force (Fortele Aeriene Române) is one of the last in Europe to use the MiG-21. In the 1990s, faced with the need but not the finances for new fighters, Romania chose to upgrade its existing fleets of MiG-21s and MiG-29s. The "Fulcrum" upgrade was eventually abandoned, but Aerostar planned to turn MiG-21Ms, MFs and UMs into the modernized Lancer with the help of Israeli firm Elbit. The Lancer A (shown) was optimized for ground attack. New weapons (depicted) include the Opher IR-guided bomb, which resembles a laser-guided bomb, but homes in on infrared emissions such as those from a vehicle engine, and the Python III short-range air-to-air missile. The Lancer B was the two-seat trainer and the Lancer C a dedicated interceptor version.

Above: The Slovak Air Force inherited MiG-21s from the Czech Republic in the 1993 "Velvet Divorce," or dissolution of Czechoslovakia. It retained some, including the MiG-21US trainer, until 2000.

In an effort to develop a lightweight Mach 2 interceptor to replace the MiG-19, Mikoyan-Gurevich started with a clean slate. There was debate as to whether swept or delta wings were the most efficient. The Ye-1 prototype of 1955 had a slender fuselage and highly swept wings, while the Ye-4 used a delta wing. Several further prototypes were ordered in each configuration; the delta-winged Ye-5 was judged marginally superior and chosen as the basis for the MiG-21.

The initial MiG-21 "Fishbed-A" was built in relatively small numbers, but the MiG-21F-13 "Fishbed-C" that entered production in 1960 was produced in its thousands. Like the prototypes, it had a bubble canopy that hinged at the front to provide wind blast protection during an ejection and its radar in a shock cone within the engine inlet. Aerodynamic "fences" on the wing were reduced to two rather than six.

Armament was two R-3S (AA-2 "Atoll") guided missiles, which were copied from the U.S. AIM-9B Sidewinder, and a 23-mm cannon. "Fishbed-Cs" were exported to India, Romania, Finland and China.

IN CHINESE HANDS

In China, the MiG-21F-13 was built by Chengdu as the F-7 and entered service around 1965. Even today nearly 400 are believed to remain in service. The Chinese improved the MiG-21 and offered the F-7M Airguard for export. This had a rearward-opening canopy, a pair of cannon and provision for four air-to-air missiles. A considerable amount of Western equipment was included, including Martin Baker ejection seats. F-7Ms were sold to Iran, Zimbabwe and Pakistan. Older F-7Ps and F-7Ms are the most numerous aircraft in Pakistan's inventory, with nearly 150 in service.

CONTINUED DEVELOPMENT

In the Soviet Union, development continued with the MiG-21S fighter, R reconnaissance aircraft and M and MF fighter-bombers. The latter had enlarged spines containing extra fuel and/or avionics. All these second-generation MiG-21s had smaller canopies that hinged to the side. The next step was the MiG-21bis, which could carry R-60 (AA-8 "Aphid") missiles, plus a wide range of conventional or nuclear air-to-ground weapons. It was exported to over a dozen nations.

Initially employed as an interceptor with very limited endurance, the MiG-21 evolved into the fighter-bomber of choice (limited though that might have been) for the communist nations of the world.

Above: The radar scope was given priority over forward vision in the busy cockpit of the MiG-21.

WIDELY BATTLE-TESTED

MiG-21s and their Chinese derivatives have been involved in almost every area of conflict since the mid-1960s, with an exception being the Falklands War. In several cases, including Iran–Iraq and the Balkans conflicts of the 1990s, MiG-21s or F-7s were used by both sides. Most air-to-air action was seen in the Middle East by Syrian and Egyptian "Fishbeds" against Israel and by the North Vietnamese Air Force against the United States.

Although wealthier countries have been able to replace their "Fishbeds" with MiG-29 "Fulcrums" or Lockheed Martin F-16 Fighting Falcons (although usually not on a one-for-one basis), retaining and upgrading MiG-21s remains the only option for many air forces. Upgrade programmes have included RAC MiG's own MiG-21-93, and Romania's Lancer. The MiG-21-93 formed the basis of India's Bison upgrade, which was applied to more than 100 aircraft. Likewise, around 50 Lancers were modified from MiG-21M, MF and UM airframes.

Above: India acquired around 900 MiG-21s over the years. About 125 of them are being upgraded to remain competitive in the modern era.

Convair F-106 Delta Dart

The F-106 Delta Dart was the last purpose-designed interceptor introduced by the U.S. Air Force, and it served for nearly 30 years guarding the skies of North America before being replaced by more versatile multi-role fighters.

F-106A DELTA DART SPECIFICATION

Dimensions

Length (with probe): 70 ft 8 in (21.55 m)
Wingspan: 38 ft 3½ in (11.67 m)
Wing area: 697.5 sq ft (64.8 m²)
Height: 20 ft 3⅓ in (6.18 m)

Powerplant

One Pratt & Whitney J75-P-17 turbojet rated at 17,200 lb (77.4 kN) dry and 24,500 lb (110.25 kN) with full afterburner

Weights

Empty: 23,814 lb (10,800 kg)
Normal loaded: 35,500 lb (16,012 kg)
Maximum takeoff: 38,250 lb (17,350 kg)

Performance

Maximum speed (without tanks) at 40,000 ft (12,192 m): Mach 2.25 (1,487 mph/2393 km/h)
Sustained ceiling: 58,000 ft (17,680 m)
Combat radius (with internal fuel): 575 miles (925 km)
Combat radius (with external tanks and aerial refuelling): 1,950 miles (3138 km)
Time to 57,000 ft (17,374 m): 4.5 minutes

Armament

Most aircraft had an M61A-1 20-mm cannon. Standard missile armament was four AIM-4E/F and/or AIM-4G Falcon AAMs (Super Falcons), plus one AIR-2A Genie nuclear rocket. The F-106 also tested the XAIM-97A ASAT weapon.

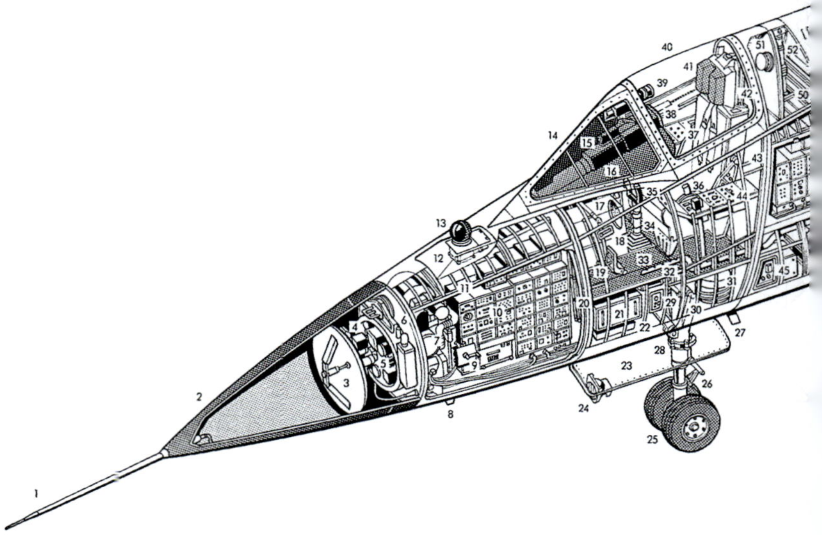

Cutaway Key

1 Pitot head
2 Radome
3 Radar scanner dish
4 Radar tracking mechanism
5 Hughes MA-1 weapons system radar unit
6 Radar mounting bulkhead
7 Pulse generator units
8 TACAN aerial
9 Angle-of-attack transmitter
10 MA-1 weapons system electronics units
11 Electronics bay access door
12 Infrared detector fairing
13 Retractable infrared detector
14 Knife-edged windscreen panels
15 Central vision splitter
16 Instrument panel shroud
17 "Head down" tactical display panel
18 Canopy external release
19 Rudder pedals
20 Cockpit front pressure bulkhead
21 Electrical relay panel
22 Nose undercarriage wheel bay
23 Nosewheel door
24 Taxiing lamp
25 Twin nosewheels
26 Torque scissor links
27 UHF aerial
28 Nose undercarriage leg strut
29 Oxygen filler point and gauge
30 Nosewheel leg pivot fixing
31 Liquid oxygen converter
32 Cockpit air-conditioning ducting
33 Cockpit pressure floor
34 Control column
35 Two-handed control grip, radar and flight controls
36 Engine throttle lever
37 Pilot's ejection seat
38 Radar display
39 Optical sight
40 Cockpit canopy cover
41 Ejection-seat headrest
42 Ejection-seat launch rails
43 Cockpit rear pressure bulkhead
44 Side console panel
45 Ground power supply connections
46 Doppler navigation unit
47 Aft lower electronics compartment
48 Aft upper electronics equipment bays, port and starboard
49 Electronics bay door
50 Cockpit rear decking
51 Overpressurization relief valve
52 Canopy pneumatic jack
53 Canopy hinge
54 Air exit louvres
55 Starboard engine air intake
56 Fuel tank access panel
57 Upper longeron
58 Fuselage fuel tank, total internal capacity 1,514 U.S. gal (5731 litres)
59 Fuselage frame construction
60 Ventral weapons bay
61 Missile pallet hinge arms
62 Bottom longeron
63 Boundary layer splitter plate
64 Port engine air intake
65 Variable-area intake ramp
66 Ramp bleed air louvres
67 Air-conditioning system intake duct
68 Intake duct framing
69 Starboard-side pressure refuelling connection
70 Forward missile pallet pneumatic jack
71 Air-conditioning plant
72 De-icing fluid reservoir
73 Heat exchanger air exit duct
74 Air refuelling ramp door, open
75 Pneumatic system air bottles
76 Bifurcated intake ducting
77 Aft missile pylon pneumatic jacks
78 AIR-2 Genie air-to-air missile housing
79 Hydraulic accumulators
80 Hydraulic reservoirs, duplex systems
81 Intake trunking
82 Wing spar attachment fuselage main frames
83 Oil cooler air duct
84 Intake centre-body fairing
85 Engine intake compressor face
86 Bleed air ducting
87 Dorsal spine fairing
88 Fuel boost pump

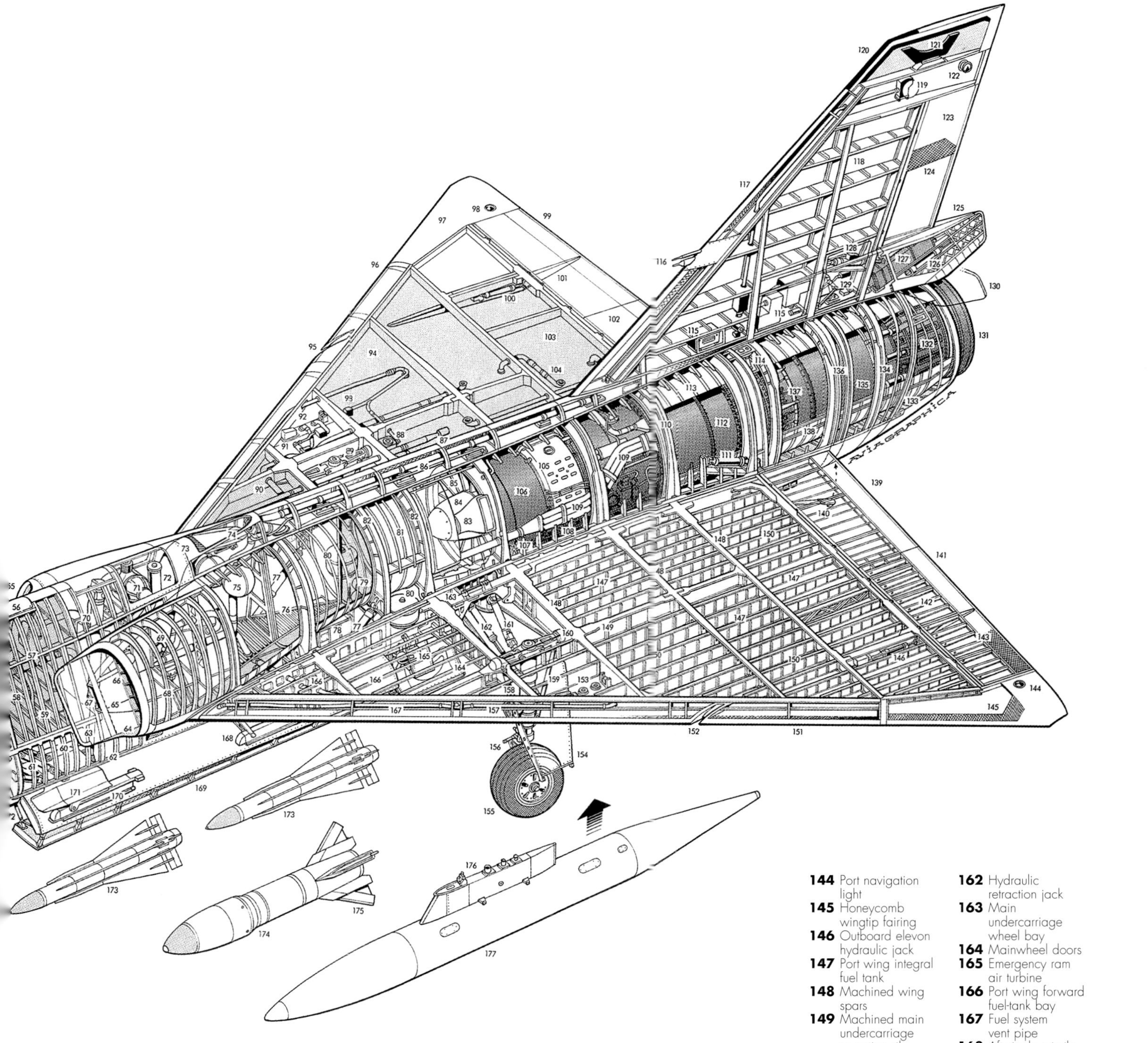

89 Starboard main undercarriage pivot fixing
90 Wing forward fuel tank
91 Dry bay
92 Wing pylon mountings and connectors
93 Fuel system piping
94 Starboard wing main fuel tank
95 Leading-edge slot
96 Cambered leading edge
97 Wingtip fairing
98 Starboard navigation light
99 Outboard elevon
100 Elevon hydraulic jack
101 Elevon jack ventral fairing
102 Inboard elevon
103 Starboard wing aft fuel tank
104 Fuel system vent piping
105 Engine oil tank, 45 U.S. gal (17 litres)
106 Pratt & Whitney J75-P-17 turbojet engine
107 Forward engine mounting
108 Ventral accessory equipment compartment
109 Cooling air ducting
110 Wing and fin spar attachment main frame
111 Inboard elevon hydraulic jack
112 Engine turbine section
113 Exhaust pipe heat shroud
114 Rear engine mounting
115 Aerial tuning units
116 Artificial feel system pitot intakes
117 Fin leading edge
118 Tailfin construction
119 Air-to-air identification (AAI) aerial
120 Fintip aerial fairing
121 UHF/TACAN aerial
122 Tail navigation light
123 Rudder
124 Rudder honeycomb construction
125 Split airbrake panels
126 Airbrake pneumatic jacks
127 Brake parachute housing
128 Rudder hydraulic jack
129 Rudder trim and feel force control units
130 Airbrake, open position
131 Divergent exhaust nozzle
132 Variable-area afterburner exhaust nozzle
133 Detachable tailcone (engine removal)
134 Afterburner nozzle control jacks
135 Afterburner ducting
136 Sloping fin mounting bulkheads
137 Afterburner fuel spray manifold
138 Engine withdrawal rail
139 Port inboard elevon
140 Runway emergency arrestor hook, lowered
141 Port outboard elevon
142 Elevon rib construction
143 Honeycomb trailing-edge panels
144 Port navigation light
145 Honeycomb wingtip fairing
146 Outboard elevon hydraulic jack
147 Port wing integral fuel tank
148 Machined wing spars
149 Machined main undercarriage mounting rib
150 Wing rib construction
151 Cambered leading edge
152 Leading-edge slot
153 Port wing pylon connectors
154 Main wheel leg door
155 Port mainwheel
156 Torque scissor links
157 Landing lamp
158 Main undercarriage leg strut
159 Drag brace and pneumatic brake reservoir
160 Main undercarriage leg pivot fixing
161 Breaker strut
162 Hydraulic retraction jack
163 Main undercarriage wheel bay
164 Mainwheel doors
165 Emergency ram air turbine
166 Port wing forward fuel-tank bay
167 Fuel system vent pipe
168 Aft single missile pylon, port and starboard, lowered position
169 Weapons bay doors, open
170 Missile launch rail
171 Forward twin missile pallet
172 Weapons bay door pneumatic jack
173 AIM-4F Falcon air-to-air missile (4)
174 Single AIR-2A Genie air-to-air nuclear missile
175 Missile folding fins, deployed position
176 Port wing pylon
177 227-U.S. gal (859-litre) external fuel tank

"The responsiveness of the airplane, its capabilities of turn, speed and altitude, and its honesty in feedback, were the seeds of a life-long love affair"
– Lieutenant Colonel Michael "Buddha" Nelson, F-106 pilot

FACTS

- Although designed as an interceptor, Convair's F-106 proved itself to be a highly manoeuvrable dogfighter.
- In the 1980s, many F-106As were fitted with a clear-topped canopy and a 20-mm Vulcan cannon.
- The MB-1 Genie and the AIM-26 Nuclear Falcon used by the F-106 were the only atomic air-to-air weapons ever fielded.

CONVAIR F-106 DELTA DART – VARIANTS & OPERATORS

Normal F-102B: The original designation of the F-106A. Fitted with J-75 afterburning turbojet. Performance was deemed unsatisfactory and modifications were made.

F-106A: Modified F-106 with improved performance. Maximum speed at least Mach 2.5, with some estimates as high as Mach 2.85 in level flight.

F-106B: Two-seat combat-capable training version. Pilot and instructor are seated in tandem.

NF-106B: This designation was given to two F-106Bs used as test aircraft with NASA and associated research facilities from 1966 until 1991.

F-106C: Unbuilt version. Aircraft was intended to have the AN/ASG-18 radar and fire control system fitted originally developed for the XF-108 Rapier. To accommodate this larger radar system, the nose cone was longer and of greater diameter. The F-106C/D project was cancelled on 23 September 1958.

F-106D: Unbuilt two-seat version of the F-106C.

F-106X: Unbuilt version (early 1968). Would have been outfitted with canards and powered by a JT4B-22 turbojet. It was envisioned as an alternative to the Lockheed YF-12.

F-106E: Unbuilt version. It was to be compatible with the upcoming airborne warning and control systems as well as with the "over-the-horizon" radar defence network.

F-106F: Unbuilt two-seat version of the F-106E.

U.S. Air Force Air Defense Command Squadron Assignments
2nd Fighter Interceptor Squadron (1971–72)
5th Fighter Interceptor Squadron (1960–85)
11th Fighter Interceptor Squadron (1960–68)
27th Fighter Interceptor Squadron (1959–82)
48th Fighter Interceptor Squadron (1960–82)
49th Fighter Interceptor Squadron (1968–87)
71st Fighter Interceptor Squadron (1960–71)
83rd Fighter Interceptor Squadron (1971–72)
84th Fighter Interceptor Squadron (1968–81)
87th Fighter Interceptor Squadron (1968–85)
94th Fighter Interceptor Squadron (1960–69)
95th Fighter Interceptor Squadron (1959–73)
318th Fighter Interceptor Squadron (1960–83)
319th Fighter Interceptor Squadron (1960–63 and 1971–72)
329th Fighter Interceptor Squadron (1960–67)
437th Fighter Interceptor Squadron (1968–68)
438th Fighter Interceptor Squadron (1960–68)
456th Fighter Interceptor Squadron (1959–68)
460th Fighter Interceptor Squadron (1968–74)
498th Fighter Interceptor Squadron (1959–68)
539th Fighter Interceptor Squadron (1959–67)

U.S. Air National Guard Squadron Assignments
101st Fighter Interceptor Squadron, Massachusetts (1972–88)
119th Fighter Interceptor Squadron, New Jersey (1972–88)
159th Fighter Interceptor Squadron, Florida (1974–87)
171st Fighter Interceptor Squadron, Michigan (1972–78)
186th Fighter Interceptor Squadron, Montana (1972–87)
194th Fighter Interceptor Squadron, California (1974–84)

CONVAIR F-106 DELTA DART

The U.S. Air Force's Air Defense Command operated 22 squadrons of Delta Darts over the years, all of them at one time or another wearing high-visibility tail markings and trim over a light grey base colour. This F-106 crashed following a lightning strike in May 1973 and never received the "Six Shooter" modifications that gave the F-106 an M61 cannon in the weapons bay, a new gunsight and a clear-topped canopy, all of which enhanced its dogfighting ability. The 49th Fighter Interceptor Squadron was based at Griffiss AFB, New York, and became the last active-duty USAF squadron to operate F-106s, retiring them and disbanding in 1987. It was later re-established as a T-38 Talon training unit.

Above: The air speed and climb rate of the F-106 were displayed on the vertical tape instruments on either side of the central attitude indicator.

The F-106 was a development of the F-102A intended to produce an "ultimate interceptor" for the defence of North American airspace. Initially known as the F-102B, the new fighter deviated enough from the Delta Dagger that it warranted a new name and designation: F-106 Delta Dart. Many of the changes were internal, but on the outside the F-106 was more streamlined, with repositioned intakes, a broader fin and a flat top.

Clamshell airbrakes were added at the base of the fin above the exhaust for the Pratt & Whitney J75 engine, which replaced the J57 of the F-102. Under the skin, the F-106 had an all-new fire-control system called the MA-1. This could be integrated with the SAGE (Semi-Automatic Ground Environment) system of radars and ground control stations, which could control the F-106's autopilot and fly it to a perfect interception of an intruder.

The rockets in the weapons bay doors of the F-102 were left out, but the four Falcon missiles were retained. New to the F-106, however, was the MB-1 Genie nuclear rocket. The

Above: F-106s were used as chase aircraft during the development of the B-1B Lancer strategic bomber in the 1980s.

Above: The New Jersey Air National Guard operated the F-106 from 1972 until 1988. Note the runway arrestor hook under this F-106A.

unguided Genie had a 1.5 kiloton warhead, which was theoretically capable of destroying a formation of Soviet bombers with one shot.

The first F-106A flew in December 1956, and again there were some teething problems that needed addressing before the Delta Dart could reach its full potential. The intakes were redesigned and a more powerful variant of the J75 was fitted before the F-106 reached the speed and acceleration goals promised by Convair. The fire-control system was not as reliable as it should have been, and there were numerous revisions of the instrument layout. All these issues contributed to a reduction in orders from 1,000 (to replace all the F-102s) to just over 300.

AN IMPROVED VERSION

The two-seat F-106B had the more sensible tandem seating arrangement than the side-by-side TF-102A, and thus its performance was not reduced by extra drag, although the second seat did replace a fuel tank. F-106Bs had the weapons and fire-control systems found in the F-106A, although not the cannon that was refitted to the single-seaters late in their careers.

The Delta Dart reached operational service about five years later than originally planned. The aircraft served with 21 squadrons of Air Defense Command and, from the early 1970s on, with Air National Guard units. The "Six" had a long career before finally being phased out in 1988.

KEEPING CLOSE TO HOME

Unlike the F-102, the F-106 was not exported or involved in combat. F-106s were deployed to South Korea during a crisis period in 1968 and saw occasional deployments to West Germany and Iceland, but were never permanently assigned overseas. "Sixes" based in Alaska intercepted many Soviet Tupolev Tu-95 "Bears" and other bombers making probing flights over the Arctic; others on the U.S. East Coast from Maine to Florida tracked Soviet flights en route to Cuba.

When finally retired as interceptors, F-106s followed their predecessors in becoming unmanned drones for target practice and test purposes. Nearly 200 were converted; the last one in service was shot down in 1997. NASA, which had used F-106s for various tasks including astronaut training, conducted a programme in 1998 to test concepts for a delta-wing spacecraft using an F-106B, after which it was retired.

De Havilland Sea Vixen

The Sea Vixen was the only twin-boomed carrier fighter to see service – with the Royal Navy Fleet Air Arm – and one of the largest ever built. Operating from the United Kingdom's small carriers required skilled crews, and the accident rate was high.

SEA VIXEN FAW.1 SPECIFICATION

Dimensions

Length: 55 ft 7 in (16.94 m)
Length (nose folded): 50 ft 2½ in (15.3 m)
Height: 10 ft 9 in (3.28 m)
Wingspan: 50 ft (15.24 m)
Wing area: 648 sq ft (60.20 m^2)

Powerplant

Two Rolls-Royce Avon 208 turbojet engines each rated at 11,230 lb st (49.95 kN)

Weights

Empty: 27,952 lb (12,679 kg)
All-up: 35,000 lb (15,876 kg)
Maximum takeoff: 41,575 lb (18,858 kg)

Fuel and load

External fuel: Provision for two 180-U.S. gal (682-litre) drop tanks
Maximum ordnance: up to 2,000 lb (907 kg) of ordnance on underwing pylons

Performance

Maximum speed at sea level: 690 mph (1110 km/h)
Maximum speed at 10,000 ft (3048 m): 645 mph (1038 km/h)
Time to 10,000 ft (3048 m): 1½ minutes
Time to 40,000 ft (12,192 m): approximately 6½ minutes
Service ceiling: 48,000 ft (14, 630 m)

Armament

Up to four de Havilland Firestreak IR-homing air-to-air missiles on underwing pylons; two retractable Microcell rocket packs under the forward fuselage, each holding 14 2-in (508-mm) rockets; a 500-lb (227-kg) or 1,000-lb (454-kg) GP bomb, napalm tank, rocket pod (carrying either 2-in/50-mm or 3-in/76-mm rockets) or Martin Bullpup A air-to-surface missile on each of the inner pair of AAM pylons

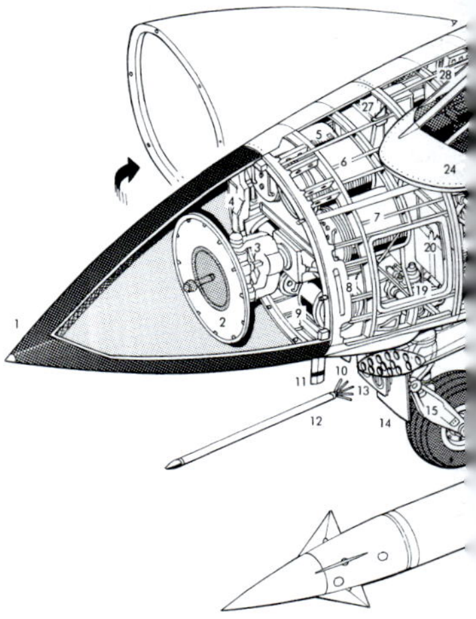

Cutaway Key

1 Fibreglass radome
2 GEC AI radar scanner
3 Scanner gimballing mechanism
4 Radome hinge point, opens to starboard
5 Wave form generator
6 Power pulse unit
7 Radar modulator
8 Radome latch
9 Radar transmitter/receiver
10 Lower IFF aerial
11 UHF aerial
12 2-in (50-mm) folding-fin rocket
13 Landing taxiing and carrier approach lights
14 Nosewheel leg door
15 Levered suspension nosewheel forks
16 Nosewheel, aft-retracting
17 Microcell 14-round rocket launcher, extended
18 Rocket launcher hydraulic jack
19 Nose undercarriage pivot mounting
20 Front pressure bulkhead
21 Rudder pedals
22 Control column
23 Nosewheel housing
24 Cockpit rain-dispersal air duct fairing
25 Instrument panel shroud
26 Ferranti gunsight
27 Upper IFF aerial
28 Knife-edged windscreen panels
29 Observer's instrument panel
30 Sliding cockpit canopy cover
31 Canopy framing, FAW.1 (clear canopy on FAW.2)
32 Observer's instrument console
33 Pilot's Martin-Baker Mk 4 ejection seat
34 Engine throttle levers
35 Fuel cocks
36 Rudder Q-feel dashpot
37 Airbrake hinge point
38 Ventral airbrake, open
39 Airbrake strake
40 Airbrake hydraulic jack
41 Boundary layer splitter plate
42 Electronics equipment racks
43 Port engine air intake
44 Ventral air-conditioning system ram air intake
45 Boundary layer spill duct
46 Canopy-release strut
47 Canopy demisting air duct
48 Observer's ejection seat
49 Bulged hatch fairing (on modified FAW.2 aircraft)
50 Observer's entry hatch
51 Starboard engine air intake
52 Rear pressure bulkhead
53 Electrical and Low-Altitude Bombing System (LABS) equipment bays, port and starboard
54 Boundary layer spill air louvres
55 Centre-section fuel tank
56 Fuel filler, port and starboard
57 Intake de-icing air duct
58 Engine intake ducting
59 Central air-conditioning equipment bay
60 Intake flank fuel tank
61 Ventral catapult strop hook
62 Mainwheel door actuator
63 Engine fire suppression bottle
64 Port main undercarriage wheel bay
65 Engine bleed air ducting
66 Rolls-Royce Avon 208 engine
67 Starter housing intake fairing
68 Bleed air spill duct
69 Air-conditioning controllers
70 VHF aerials
71 Starboard mainwheel, stowed position
72 Starboard intake flank fuel tank
73 Tailboom fuel tank
74 Extended tailboom fairing (FAW.2 only)
75 Outer wing panel integral fuel tank
76 Wing fence
77 Aileron trim actuator
78 Autopilot actuator
79 Extended chord outboard leading edge
80 Pitot head
81 Starboard navigation light

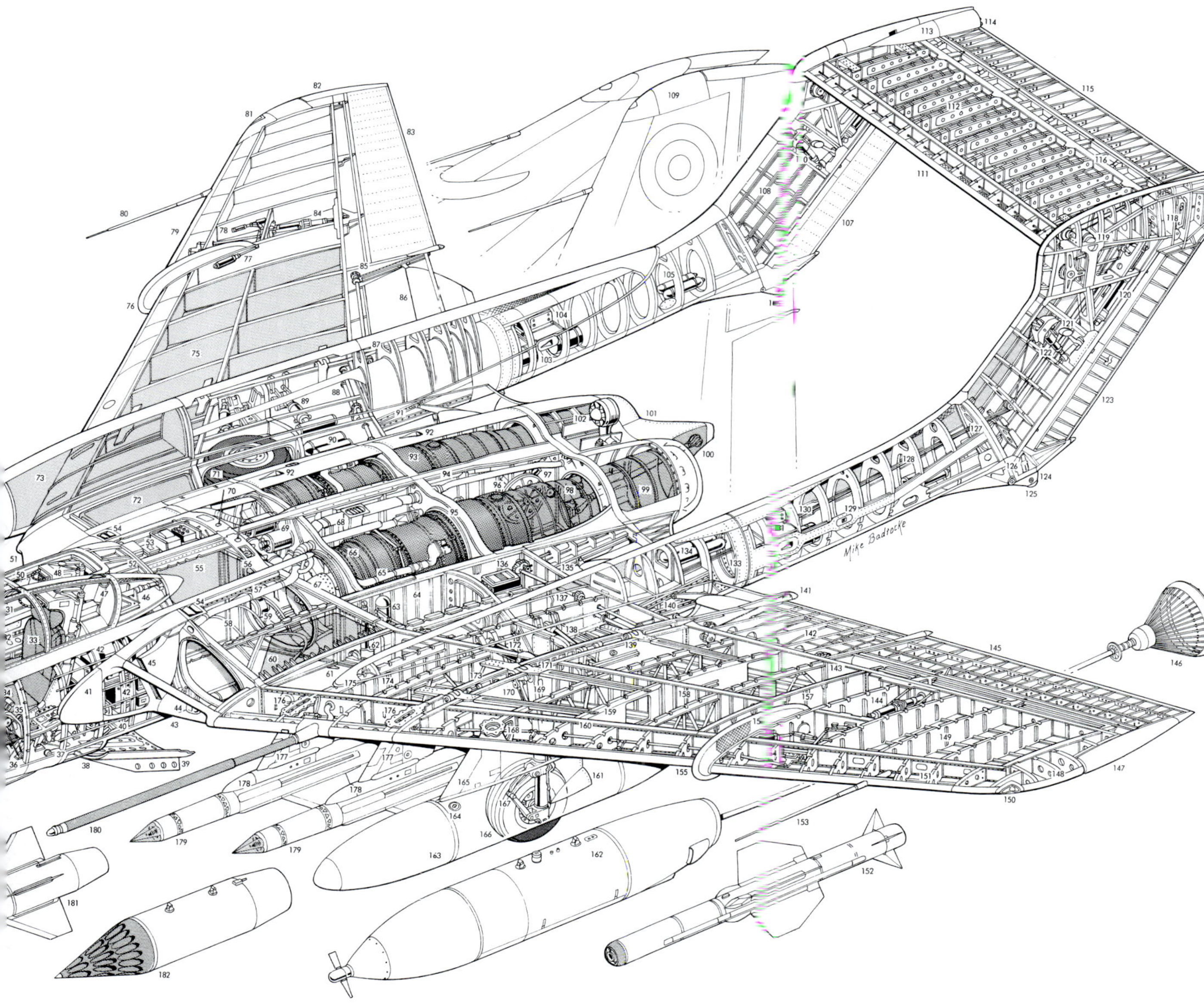

82 Aileron horn balance
83 Starboard aileron
84 Aileron hydraulic actuator
85 Chain and sprocket flap drive
86 Outboard Fowler-type flap
87 Extended tailboom aft fairing
88 Flap drive shafts
89 Wing-fold hydraulic deck
90 Hydraulic reservoir, leader tank and accumulator
91 Inboard flap segment guide rails
92 Engine bay venting air intakes
93 Starboard engine bay
94 Fuselage centre keel member
95 Detachable firewall upper segment (for engine removal)
96 Flap drive cable drum
97 Flap hydraulic actuator
98 Arrestor hook jack and damper
99 Engine jet pipe
100 Arrestor hook stowage
101 Exhaust nozzle fairing
102 Emergency ram air turbine, extended
103 Static inverters
104 Tailboom electrical equipment bay
105 Hydraulic accumulators
106 Tail bumper
107 Starboard rudder
108 Tailplane rib and stringer construction
109 Wing panels, folded position
110 Rudder hydraulic actuator
111 All-moving horizontal tailplane
112 Tailplane rib construction
113 Fin/tailplane fairing
114 Tail navigation lights
115 Tailplane trailing edge
116 Tab balance weights
117 Tailplane tip fairing
118 Tab control linkage
119 Tailplane pivot mounting
120 Tailplane hydraulic actuator
121 Rudder mass balance weight
122 Port rudder hydraulic actuator
123 Rudder rib construction
124 Tie-down point
125 Tail bumper
126 Bumper strut
127 Tailboom/fin joint frame
128 Tailboom frame construction
129 Telebriefing socket
130 Tailplane control cables
131 Port electrical equipment bay
132 Inverter cooling air intake
133 Tailboom joint ring frame
134 Air bottles
135 Port inboard flap segment
136 Autopilot control unit
137 Flap drive shafts and gearboxes
138 Wing-fold hydraulic jack
139 Wing-fold hinge fittings
140 Outboard flap segment guide rails
141 Flap rail fairings
142 Flap shroud ribs
143 Rear spar
144 Aileron hydraulic actuator
145 Port aileron rib construction
146 Refuelling drogue, extended
147 Port aileron horn balance
148 Tip fairing construction
149 Outer wing panel rib construction
150 Port navigation light
151 Leading-edge nose ribs
152 Red Top air-to-air missile (arming FAW.2 only)
153 Pitot head
154 Aileron control rod linkage
155 Leading-edge dogtooth
156 Wing fence honeycomb construction
157 Fuel-tank end rib
158 Semi-span centre spar
159 Port outer wing panel integral fuel tank
160 Front spar
161 Mainwheel leg door
162 "Buddy" refuelling pack
163 180-U.S. gal (682-litre) external fuel tank
164 Fuel filler
165 Fuel tank pylon
166 Port mainwheel
167 Torque scissor links
168 Pylon hardpoint
169 Main undercarriage leg strut
170 Side breaker strut
171 Undercarriage leg pivot mounting
172 Hydraulic retraction jack
173 Wing-fold hinge rib
174 Wing inboard segment integral fuel tank
175 Tailboom forward fairing (FAW Mk 1)
176 Light stores pylon fittings
177 Missile pylons
178 Missile launch rails
179 Firestreak air-to-air missiles (arming FAW.1)
180 Flight refuelling boom
181 Bullpup A air-to-surface missile
182 36 x 2-in (50-mm) rocket pack

"As a weapons system [in the early 1970s], she was long overdue retirement, but as an aircraft to fly and have adventures in, she was ageless."
– Jonathan Whaley, Royal Navy Sea Vixen pilot

FACTS

- The Sea Vixen was the Royal Navy's first swept-wing aircraft.
- One in five Sea Vixens built were lost in crashes.
- The Sea Vixen's AI.18 radar was a version of the AI.17 used in the Gloster Javelin.

DE HAVILLAND SEA VIXEN - OPERATORS

SQUADRON	FORMED	BASED	SERVICE HISTORY
700Y NAVAL AIR SQUADRON: Intense Flying Unit	October 1958	RNAS Yeovilton, Somerset, England	Disbanded in 1960 to form 892 Naval Air Squadron.
766 NAVAL AIR SQUADRON: Operational Flying Training	November 1959	RNAS Yeovilton, Somerset, England	
890 NAVAL AIR SQUADRON: Second Sea Vixen Squadron	February 1960	Embarked on the HMS *Hermes* and then the HMS *Ark Royal* on fourth and fifth commissions.	Equipped with Sea Vixen Mk 1s (1960–66) and Mk 2s (1967–71).
892 NAVAL AIR SQUADRON:	1943	Squadron embarked on HMS *Victorious* (October 1959) and HMS *Ark Royal* (March 1960), HMS *Centaur* (1963–65) and HMS *Hermes* (1967–68).	First Sea Vixen Squadron to form up with FAW.1.
893 NAVAL AIR SQUADRON: Third Sea Vixen Squadron	September 1960	Embarked HMS *Ark Royal* (November 1960), HMS *Centaur* (1960–62), HMS *Victorious* (1963–67), HMS *Hermes* (1967).	Equipped with Sea Vixen Mk 1 (1960–65) and Sea Vixen Mk 2 (1965–70).
899 NAVAL AIR SQUADRON: Fourth Sea Vixen Squadron	February 1961	RNAS Yeovilton, Somerset, England. Embarked HMS *Victorious* (1963) and HMS *Eagle* (1964).	Equipped with Sea Vixen Mk 1s (1961–64), Sea Vixen Mk 2s (1964–72).
"C" SQUADRON:	1968	RAF Boscombe Down, Wiltshire, England	Created for the evaluation of the Martel TV guided air-to-ground missile.

DE HAVILLAND DH.110

The illustrations here represent the prototype DH.110 WG236, which made its maiden flight in September 1951 in the hands of the legendary ex-RAF and test pilot John "Catseye" Cunningham. During tests in February 1952, it became the first twin-engined aircraft to exceed Mach 1, and the first two-seater. This aircraft broke up in flight during a display at Farnborough in September 1952, killing the crew and 29 spectators in the worst accident in British air show history. As a result, the second prototype was modified with new leading edges, stronger wing structure and an all-moving tailplane. These modifications were retained in the production Sea Vixen, which had many other changes, including wing folding, larger flaps, an arrestor hook and radar.

Above: The offset pilot's cockpit of the Sea Vixen was not exactly roomy, but had a better view than the observer's "coal hole."

In 1947, the Royal Air Force issued a requirement for a jet night fighter to replace the de Havilland Mosquito. De Havilland drew up a design for a large twin-boomed twin-engined jet, with provison for a radar in a bulbous nose. The Royal Navy, which was also looking for an all-weather fighter, took an interest in a version of this DH.110 design as well. A combined requirement was issued and revised, eventually calling for 13 prototypes in several different configurations. In the end, only two prototypes were built. One suffered structural failure at the 1952 Farnborough Air Show, crashing into the crowd and killing many spectators.

The RAF decided to buy the Gloster Javelin, but the Royal Navy ordered a navalized version, the prototype of which flew in June 1955. Understandably, the structure was considerably stronger than the prototype's. A definitive version with folding wings and a new nose flew as the Sea Vixen FAW.1 in 1957 and entered Fleet Air Arm service in 1959, 12 years after the original RAF requirement, and made its first cruise on HMS *Ark Royal* in March 1960.

CRAMPED CONDITIONS

The Sea Vixen was a large aircraft with a swept wing, twin tailbooms and a straight tailplane. The pilot's canopy was offset to the left side of the fuselage. The observer (radar operator) sat behind, below and to the right. On the later aircraft, a transparent hatch cover provided light, but not much outside view. Both crew had ejection seats. Armament was a mix of Blue Jay (later called Firestreak) missiles and unguided rockets. Bombs and air-to-ground rocket packs could also be carried.

The FAW.2 introduced a refuelling probe and larger tailbooms that had extensions forward of the wings. Extra fuel could be carried in the booms, and they improved the aerodynamics by conforming to the "area rule." The newer Red Top missile could be carried. Over time, most FAW.1s were upgraded to Mk 2 standard.

The Sea Vixen never saw active combat, but was involved in operations off Mozambique in southern Africa flying combat air patrols to enforce sanctions against Rhodesia in the late 1970s and in the Middle East in 1961 when Iraq threatened to invade Kuwait.

ABYSMAL SAFETY RECORD

The Sea Vixen had a rather poor safety record, proportionally even worse than that of the Luftwaffe's Lockheed F-104 Starfighters. As a large all-weather fighter flying off the small

Top: The second DH.110, WG240 was lighter and more powerful than the one that crashed at Farnborough. On the fateful day, it was unserviceable and was replaced by the first prototype.

Bottom: The Sea Vixen lacked a gun, but could pack a powerful punch using rockets, as seen by this 800 Squadron aircraft unleashing two pods.

British carrier decks, it suffered a large number of landing accidents, as well as crashes while training at night. The original observer's hatch had to be jettisoned before ejection, which took too long at low level. This was replaced by a frangible hatch that could be ejected through, but nonetheless 51 Sea Vixen crew members were killed in 30 crashes between 1962 and 1970. Most Sea Vixens had been retired by 1972 in favour of the McDonnell Douglas Phantom FG.1.

REMOTE-CONTROL TRAINING

A small number of Sea Vixens were converted to D.3 drones to be employed as aerial targets, but they were too expensive to destroy with missiles and so were mainly used to train drone pilots in the art of flying by remote control. They retained normal cockpits and could be flown by an onboard pilot. The last D.3 was retired in 1991 and, after restoration, was put on the UK civil register as a display aircraft.

McDonnell Douglas F-4 Phantom II

The Phantom was the most potent combat aircraft in service through the 1960s and early 1970s. Although superseded in most air arms by more modern types, considerable numbers remain in service.

Cutaway Key

1 Pitot head
2 Radome
3 Radar scanner dish
4 Radar dish tracking mechanism
5 Texas Instruments AN/APQ-99 forward-looking radar unit
6 Nose compartment construction
7 No. 1 camera station
8 KS-87 forward oblique camera
9 Forward radar warning antennas, port and starboard
10 Camera bay access hatches
11 Ventral camera aperture
12 KA-57 low-altitude panoramic camera
13 Lateral camera aperture (alternative KS-87 installation)
14 No. 2 camera station
15 ADF sense aerial
16 Windscreen rain-dispersal air duct
17 Camera viewfinder periscope
18 Nose undercarriage emergency air bottles
19 Recording unit
20 No. 3 camera station
21 KA-91 high-altitude panoramic camera
22 Air-conditioning ram air intake
23 Landing/taxiing lamp (2)
24 Lower UHF/VHF aerial
25 Nosewheel leg door
26 Torque scissor links
27 Twin nosewheels, aft retracting
28 Nosewheel steering mechanism
29 AN/AVQ-26 "Pave Tack" laser designator pod
30 Swivelling optical package
31 Fuselage centreline pylon adaptor
32 Sideways-looking radar antenna (SLAR)
33 Electro-luminescent formation lighting strip
34 Canopy emergency-release handle
35 Air-conditioning plant, port and starboard
36 Cockpit floor level
37 Front pressure bulkhead
38 Rudder pedals
39 Control column
40 Instrument panel
41 Radar display
42 Instrument panel shroud
43 LA-313A optical viewfinder
44 Windscreen panels
45 Forward cockpit canopy cover
46 Face-blind seat firing handle
47 Pilot's Martin-Baker Mk.H7 ejection seat
48 External canopy latches
49 Engine throttle levers
50 Side console panel
51 Intake boundary layer splitter plate
52 APQ-102R/T SLAR equipment
53 AAS-18A infrared reconnaissance package
54 Intake front ramp
55 Port engine air intake
56 Intake ramp bleed air holes
57 Rear canopy external latches
58 Rear instrument console
59 Canopy centre arch
60 Starboard engine air intake
61 Starboard external fuel tank, capacity 370 U.S. gal (1400 litres)
62 Rear-view mirrors
63 Rear cockpit canopy cover
64 Navigator/sensor operator's Martin-Baker ejection seat
65 Intake ramp bleed air spill louvres
66 Avionics equipment racks
67 Rear pressure bulkhead
68 Liquid oxygen converter
69 Variable intake ramp jack
70 Intake rear ramp door
71 Fuselage centreline external fuel tank, capacity 600 U.S. gal (2271 litres)
72 Position of pressure refuelling connection on starboard side
73 ASQ-90B data annotation system equipment
74 Cockpit voice recorder
75 Pneumatic system air bottle
76 Bleed air ducting
77 Fuselage No. 1 fuel cell, capacity 215 U.S. gal (814 litres)
78 Intake duct framing
79 Boundary layer spill duct
80 Control cable runs
81 Aft avionics equipment bay
82 IFF aerial
83 Upper fuselage light
84 Fuselage No. 2 fuel cell, capacity 185 U.S. gal (700 litres)
85 Centre fuselage frame construction
86 Electro-luminescent formation lighting strip
87 Engine intake centre-body fairing
88 Intake duct rotary spill valve
89 Wing spar attachment fuselage main frames
90 Control cable ducting
91 In-flight refuelling receptacle, open
92 Starboard main undercarriage leg pivot fixing
93 Starboard wing integral fuel tank, capacity 315 U.S. gal (1192 litres)
94 Wing pylon mounting
95 Boundary layer control air duct
96 Leading-edge flap hydraulic actuator
97 Inboard leading-edge flap segment, down position
98 Leading-edge dogtooth
99 Outboard wing panel attachment joint
100 Boundary layer control air ducting
101 Hydraulic flap actuator
102 Outboard leading-edge flap
103 Starboard navigation light
104 Electro-luminescent formation light

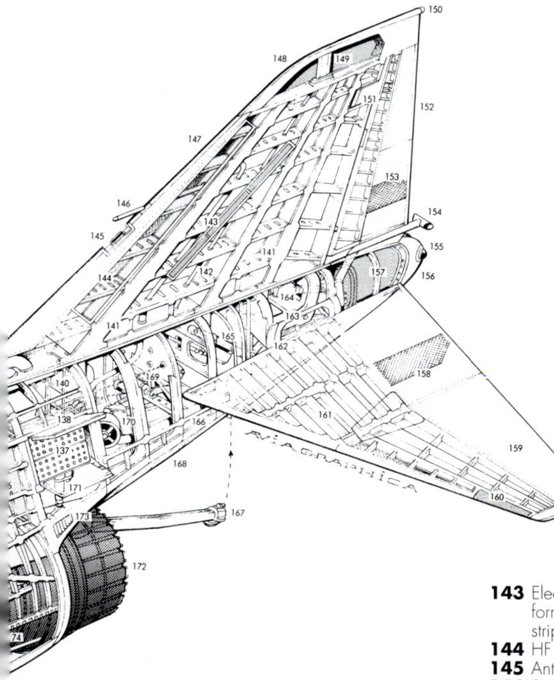

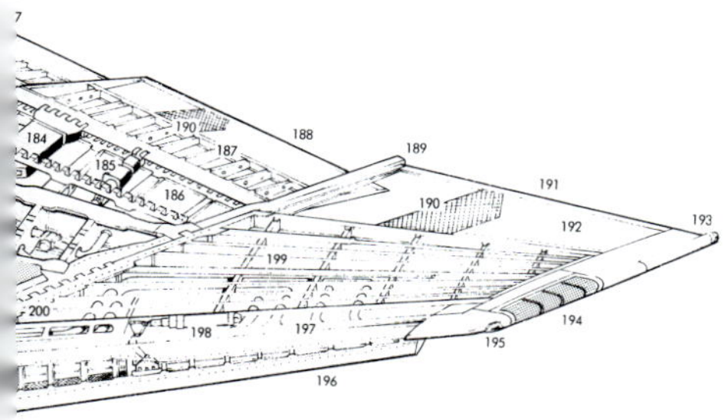

105 Rearward identification light
106 Starboard dihedral outboard wing panel
107 Wing fuel-tank vent pipe
108 Starboard drooping aileron, down position
109 Aileron flutter damper
110 Starboard spoilers, open
111 Spoiler hydraulic actuators
112 Fuel jettison and vent valves
113 Aileron hydraulic actuator
114 Starboard ventral airbrake panel
115 Starboard blown flap, down position
116 TACAN aerial
117 Fuel system piping
118 No. 3 fuselage fuel cell, capacity 150 U.S. gal (566 litres)
119 Engine intake compressor face
120 General Electric J79 GE-15 afterburning turbojet engine
121 Ventral engine accessory equipment gearbox
122 Wing rear spar attachment joint
123 Engine and afterburner control equipment
124 Emergency ram air turbine
125 Ram air turbine housing
126 Turbine doors, open
127 Turbine actuating link
128 Port engine bay frame construction
129 No. 4 fuselage fuel cell, capacity 200 U.S. gal (759 litres)
130 Jet pipe heat shroud
131 No. 5 fuselage fuel cell, capacity 180 U.S. gal (681 litres)
132 Fuel feed and vent system piping
133 LORAN aerial
134 Dorsal access panels
135 Fuel pumps
136 No. 6 fuselage fuel cell, capacity 213 U.S. gal (806 litres)
137 Photographic flare dispenser, port and starboard
138 Flare compartment doors, open
139 Ram air intake, tailcone venting
140 Tailcone attachment bulkhead
141 Three-spar fin torsion box construction
142 Fin rib construction
143 Electro-luminescent formation lighting strip
144 HF aerial panel
145 Anti-collision light
146 Stabilator feel system pressure head
147 Fin leading edge
148 Fintip aerial fairing
149 Upper UHF/VHF aerial
150 Tail navigation light
151 Rudder horn balance
152 Rudder
153 Honeycomb trailing-edge panels
154 Fuselage fuel cell jettison pipe
155 Rear radar warning antennas
156 Tailcone/brake parachute hinged door
157 Brake parachute housing
158 Honeycomb trailing-edge panel
159 Port all-moving tailplane/stabilator
160 Stabilator mass balance weight
161 Stabilator multi-spar construction
162 Pivot sealing plate
163 All-moving tailplane hinge mounting
164 Rudder hydraulic actuator
165 Tailplane hydraulic actuator
166 Heat-resistant tailcone skinning
167 Arrestor hook, lowered
168 Arrestor hook stowage
169 Stabilator feel system balance mechanism
170 Artificial feel system pneumatic bellows
171 Arrestor hook jack and shock absorber
172 Variable-area afterburner exhaust nozzle
173 Engine bay cooling exit louvres
174 Afterburner duct
175 Exhaust nozzle actuators
176 Hinged engine cowling panels
177 Port blown flap, down position
178 Boundary layer control air blowing slot
179 Lateral autopilot servo
180 Airbrake jack
181 Flap hydraulic jack
182 Rear spar
183 Port spoiler hydraulic jack
184 Aileron hydraulic actuator
185 Aileron flutter damper
186 Port spoiler housing
187 Aileron rib construction
188 Port drooping aileron, down position
189 Wing fuel-tank jettison pipe
190 Honeycomb trailing-edge panels
191 Port dihedral outer wing panel
192 Fixed portion of trailing edge
193 Rearward identification light
194 Electro-luminescent formation light
195 Port navigation light
196 Outboard leading-edge flap, lowered
197 Boundary layer control air blowing slot
198 Leading-edge flap actuator
199 Outer wing panel multi-spar construction
200 Outer wing panel attachment joint
201 Leading-edge dogtooth
202 Port mainwheel
203 Mainwheel multi-plate disc brake
204 Mainwheel leg door
205 Outboard wing pylon
206 Inner wing panel outboard leading-edge flap, down position
207 Leading-edge flap rib construction
208 Wing pylon mounting
209 Main undercarriage leg pivot fixing
210 Hydraulic retraction jack
211 Undercarriage uplock
212 Port ventral airbrake panel, open
213 Main undercarriage wheel bay
214 Hydraulic reservoir
215 Hydraulic system accumulator
216 Port wing integral fuel tank, capacity 315 U.S. gal (1192 litres)
217 Two-spar torsion box fuel-tank construction
218 Wing skin support posts
219 Leading-edge boundary layer control air duct
220 Bleed air blowing slot
221 Outboard flap actuator
222 Inboard leading-edge flap, lowered
223 Hydraulic flap actuator
224 Inboard wing pylon
225 AN/ALQ-101 ECM pod
226 Port external fuel tank, capacity 370 U.S. gal (1400 litres)

F-4E PHANTOM II SPECIFICATION

Dimensions

Wingspan: 38 ft 7½ in (11.77 m)
Wingspan (folded): 27 ft 7 in (8.41 m)
Wing aspect ratio: 2.82
Wing area: 530 sq ft (49.2 m²)
Length: 63 ft (19.20 m)
Wheel track: 17 ft 10½ in (5.45 m)
Height: 16 ft 5½ in (5.02 m)

Powerplant

Two General Electric J79-GE-17A turbojets, each rated at 17,900 lb (80 kN) thrust with afterburning

Weights

Empty: 30,328 lb (13,757 kg)
Operating empty: 31,853 lb (14,448 kg)
Combat takeoff: 41,487 lb (18,818 kg)
Maximum takeoff: 61,795 lb (28,030 kg)

Fuel and load

Internal fuel capacity: 1,855 U.S. gal (7022 litres)
Provision for one 600-U.S. gal (2271-litre) tank on centreline and two 370-U.S. gal (1400-litre) tanks under the wings
Maximum weapon load: 16,000 lb (7250 kg)

Performance

Maximum speed: approximately Mach 2.2
Maximum rate of climb: 61,400 ft (18,715 m) per minute
Service ceiling: 62,250 ft (18,975 m)
Takeoff run at maximum takeoff weight: 4,390 ft (1338 m)
Landing run at maximum landing weight: 3,780 ft (1152 m)

Range

Ferry range: 1,978 miles (3184 km)
Area intercept combat radius: 786 miles (1266 km)
Defensive counter-air combat radius: 494 miles (795 km)
Interdiction combat radius: 712 miles (1145 km)

Armament

Fixed internal M61A1 Vulcan 20-mm six-barrelled cannon; standard intercept load of four AIM-7 Sparrow missiles in fuselage recesses and four AIM-9 Sidewinders on wing pylon shoulder stations; four wing pylons and one centreline station available for carriage of wide range of air-to-ground ordnance, including M117 and Mk 80 series bombs, cluster weapons, laser-guided bombs, gun pods, napalm, fuel-air explosives and rocket pods; nuclear weapon options included B28, B43, B57 and B61; various ECM pods, training targets and laser designator pods available; air-to-surface missiles included AGM-12 Bullpup, AGM-45 Shrike, AGM-65 Maverick and AGM-78 Standard

"It was really fun to fly the F-4. It was a big, powerful, stable airplane that would bite an inexperienced guy in a heart beat."
– Colonel Ron "Gunman" Moore, U.S. Air Force

FACTS

- U.S. Navy Phantoms had no rear-seat controls because it was thought that forward vision was too poor to allow the back-seater to fly a carrier landing.
- As well as the 11 export customers who purchased Phantoms outright, Australia leased F-4Es from 1970–73.
- Total Phantom production was 5,195 built in the United States and 138 in Japan.

MCDONNELL DOUGLAS F-4 PHANTOM II – VARIANTS

XF4H-1: Two prototypes for the U.S. Navy, first flown 1958.

F4H-1F (F-4A): Two-seat all-weather carrier-based fighter for the U.S. Navy. Named Phantom II in 1959 and redesignated F-4A in 1962; 45 built.

F4H-1 (F-4B): Two-seat all-weather carrier-based fighter and ground-attack aircraft for the U.S. Navy and Marine Corps. Redesignated F-4B in 1962.

F-110A Spectre: The original U.S. Air Force designation for the F-4C.

F-4C: Two-seat all-weather tactical fighter, ground-attack version for the U.S. Air Force. The aircraft exceeded Mach 2 during its first flight on 27 May 1963. 583 built.

EF-4C Wild Weasel IV: F-4Cs converted into Wild Weasel ECM aircraft.

F-4D: F-4C with updated avionics. First flight June 1965. 825 built.

EF-4D Wild Weasel IV: F-4Ds converted into Wild Weasel ECM aircraft.

F-4E: U.S. Air Force version with an integral M61 Vulcan cannon in the elongated RF-4C nose. First flight 7 August 1965. The most numerous Phantom variant; 1,389 built.

F-4E Kurnass 2000: Modernized Israeli F-4Es.

F-4E Peace Icarus 2000: Greek Air Force modernized F-4Es.

F-4 Terminator 2020: The latest in a long line of F-4 variants, the Terminators are Turkish AF F-4Es, modernized by Israel.

F-4EJ: Two-seat all-weather air-defence fighter version of F-4E. 140 built, 138 of them under licence in Japan.

F-4EJ Kai: Upgraded version of the F-4EJ with improved avionics.

F-4F: F-4E for German Luftwaffe with simplified equipment.

F-4F ICE: Upgraded F-4F.

F-4G: U.S. Navy version; 12 F-4Bs were fitted with the AN/ASW-21 data-link digital communications system for automatic carrier landings.

F-4G Wild Weasel V: F-4E converted to SEAD aircraft for the U.S. Air Force.

F-4J: Improved F-4B version for U.S. Navy and Marine Corps.

F-4J(UK): Designation of 15 low airtime F-4J aircraft purchased by the Royal Air Force from the U.S. Navy in 1984, upgraded to F-4S standard with some British equipment.

F-4K: F-4J version for Fleet Air Arm of the Royal Navy. Operated as the Phantom FG1 (Fighter/Ground attack).

F-4M: Tactical fighter, ground-attack and reconnaissance aircraft developed from F-4K for the Royal Air Force; RAF designation Phantom FGR.Mk.2.

F-4N: F-4B modernized under project Bee Line, the same aerodynamic improvements as F-4J, smokeless engines.

F-4S: F-4J modernized with smokeless engines, reinforced airframe, leading-edge slats for improved manoeuvrability. 302 converted.

MCDONNELL DOUGLAS F-4 PHANTOM II

From 1973, Japan acquired 140 F-4EJ and RF-4EJ Phantoms, all but two built under licence by Mitsubishi. Operated for many years as interceptors, a number were reassigned in the late 1990s to the fighter support role with ground-attack and anti-shipping capabilities. This F-4EJ Kai of the Japan Air Self-Defence Force's 8 Hikotai, 3 Kokudan, at Misawa carries a pair of indigenously designed turbojet-powered ASM-2 anti-shipping missiles. The F-4EJ Kai upgrade programme saw the installation of APG-66J radar, a HUD, new radar warning equipment and a structural life extension programme. Phantoms in the fighter support role are slowly being replaced with the Mitsubishi F-2, derived from the Lockheed Martin F-16.

Above: High above Europe, a Luftwaffe F-4F prepares to receive fuel in its dorsal receptacle. Empty Sidewinder rails can be seen under the wings.

The McDonnell Aircraft Company produced only one aircraft, the XP-67 Bat, in World War II. Its first jets were the FH-1 Phantom and F2H Banshee, the latter seeing considerable action in the ground-attack role in Korea. The F3H Demon was the company's first swept wing and supersonic aircraft, but its inadequate and unreliable Westinghouse engines led to it being regarded as something of a failure.

Several company proposals for a twin-engined fighter-bomber development of the Demon eventually morphed into a larger, all-new two-seat design with the designation F3H-G. The U.S. Navy liked the design, but wanted all-missile armament rather than four 20-mm cannon. With guns deleted and other changes, the XF4H was ordered and a prototype first flew in May 1958, soon being named Phantom II.

ENTERING SERVICE

After extensive testing and several speed and climb records were taken by F4H (later F-4A) test aircraft, the U.S. Navy ordered a large batch of F-4Bs with a larger nose, improved

Above: This F-4 cockpit features a head-up display, a feature added to most upgraded Phantoms.

Above: The F-4D had no built-in gun, but this U.S. Air Force example is carrying a 20-mm Vulcan in an SUU-23 pod under the centreline. It was less accurate than the internal gun on the F-4E.

radar and a larger rear canopy for the Radar Intercept Officer (RIO). In what was then a very unusual move, the U.S. Air Force ordered its own version, which was initially called the F-110A, and later the F-4C.

The Phantom was characterized by the upturn (dihedral) of its outer wing panels and downturn (anhedral) of its all-moving tailplanes, or stabilators. The former corrected roll instability and the latter kept the tail surfaces in clear air at high angles of attack. Under the belly were recesses for four AIM-7 Sparrow missiles, while wing pylons could carry two more, or four AIM-9 Sidewinders, or a combination of fuel tanks and missiles.

DIFFERING ROLES

The U.S. Air Force regarded the Phantom as a fighter-bomber, while the U.S. Navy operated it primarily as a fleet defence interceptor from its larger carriers. In Vietnam, where the F-4 was the workhorse of both forces, USAF Phantoms proved the most successful MiG-killers and the Navy's were often employed as bombers. Vietnam showed up the foolishness of dispensing with guns, as restrictive rules of engagement and poor missile reliability meant that many North Vietnamese enemy MiGs escaped. A centreline gun pod was a partial answer, but a crash programme saw development of the F-4E with a built-in M61 Vulcan cannon under a slimmer nose. It arrived too late to much affect the kill–loss ratio in Vietnam, but became the version of choice for export customers.

EXPORT SUCCESS

The Phantom sold to Israel, West Germany, Greece, Turkey, Iran, Egypt and South Korea. Japan built nearly 140 under licence. The United Kingdom ordered versions powered by the Rolls-Royce Spey turbofan rather than the General Electric J79 turbojet. The F-4Ks (or FG.1s) flew off the Royal Navy's last big deck carrier, HMS *Ark Royal*, joining the Royal Air Force's F-4Ms (FGR.2s) when the "Ark" was retired.

Israel's F-4Es saw the most combat action, scoring 116 victories from 1970 onwards. Iran's saw extensive combat with Iraq in the 1980s and Turkey's have been used in the ground-attack role against Kurdish factions.

A number of upgrades, such as Turkey's Terminator 2020, have kept the Phantom viable into the twenty-first century, by allowing use of weapons such as the AIM-120 AMRAAM, and adding a head-up display and modern multi-mode radar.

Saab J 35 Draken

Sweden's Saab company has become famous for its innovative fighter designs. One of the most unusual was the Draken (Dragon), which was also the first Saab fighter to be exported in reasonable numbers.

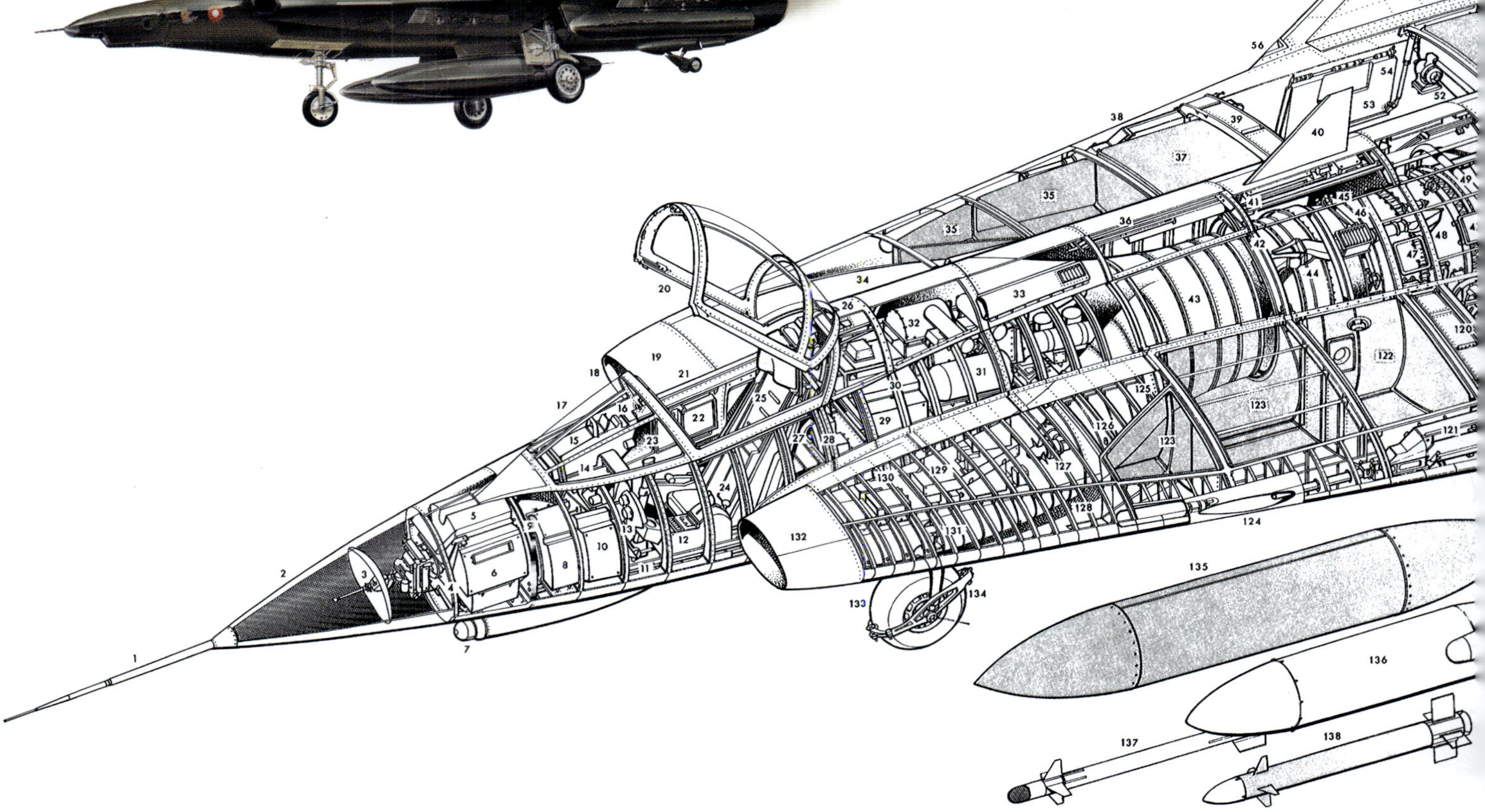

Cutaway Key

1 Nose probe
2 Fibreglass nose cone
3 Radar scanner
4 Scanner mounting frame
5 Radar pack
6 Saab S7-collision-course fire control
7 L.M. Ericsson (Hughes licence) infrared seeker
8 Electronics pack
9 Front pressure bulkhead
10 Data-handling unit
11 Rudder pedal assembly
12 Port instrument console
13 Side panel
14 Instrument panel/radar scope shroud
15 Windscreen frame
16 Weapons sight
17 Windscreen
18 Starboard intake
19 Fibreglass intake lip
20 Aft-hinged cockpit canopy
21 Cockpit sill
22 Control panel
23 Control column
24 Throttle quadrant
25 Pilots Saab RS 35 ejection seat
26 Canopy hinge mechanism
27 Seat support frame
28 Rear pressure bulkhead
29 Navigation computer
30 Forward avionics equipment bay
31 Gyro unit
32 TACAN transmitter-receiver
33 Auxiliary air intake
34 Starboard intake trunk
35 Starboard fuel tanks
36 Dorsal spine
37 Starboard forward bag-type fuel tank
38 30-mm ADEN cannon
39 Ammunition magazine (100 rounds)
40 Dorsal antenna
41 Electrical wiring
42 Mid-fuselage production break line
43 Intake trunking
44 Oil-cooler air intake
45 Volvo Flygmotor RM6C (Rolls-Royce Avon 300 series) turbojet
46 Louvres
47 Access panels
48 Fuselage frames
49 Engine firewall
50 Cooling air inlet scoop
51 Fin-root fairing
52 Fuel transfer
53 Starboard mainwheel door
54 Door actuating rod
55 Inner/outer wing joint strap
56 Starboard navigation light
57 Wing skinning
58 Starboard outer elevon
59 Hinge point
60 Actuating jack access
61 Control hinge
62 Access panels
63 Starboard aft integral fuel tank
64 Starboard aft bag-type fuel tanks (3)
65 Intake grille
66 Jet pipe
67 Engine aft mounting ring
68 Access
69 Tailfin main spar attachment
70 Control stick angle indicator unit
71 Computer amplifier
72 Synchronizer pack
73 Tailfin structure
74 Pitot tube
75 Rudder mass balance
76 Rudder structure
77 Rudder post
78 Tailfin rear spar
79 Rudder servo mechanism and actuator
80 Attachment point
81 Speed brake
82 Fuselage structure
83 Detachable tail cone (engine removal)
84 Access panel
85 Brake parachute housing
86 Aft fairing
87 Afterburner assembly
88 Exhaust
89 Air intake (afterburner housing)
90 Control surface blunt trailing edge
91 Port inner elevon
92 Hinge points
93 Elevon actuator
94 Rear spar

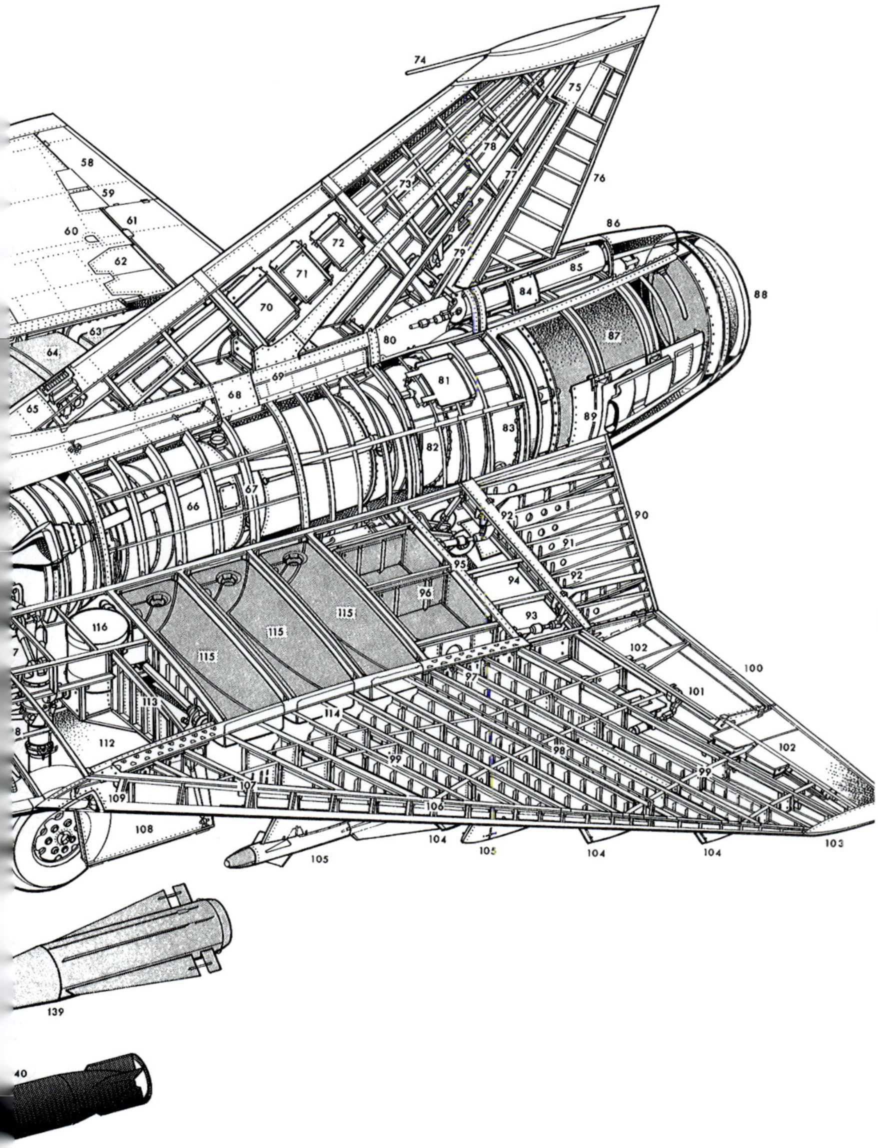

95 Twin (retractable) tailwheels
96 Port aft
97 Inner/outer wing joint
98 Wing outer structure
99 Rib stations
100 Port outer elevon
101 Elevon actuator
102 Hinge points
103 Port wingtip
104 Anti-buffet underwing fences (6)
105 Stores pylons (maximum 8)
106 Nose ribs
107 Forward spar
108 Wheel door
109 Port navigation light
110 Port main wheel
111 Door inboard section
112 Port main wheel well
113 Fuel transfer
114 Wing join strap
115 Port aft bag-type fuel tanks (3)
116 Fuel collector
117 Mainwheel retraction mechanism
118 Mainwheel oleo leg mounting
119 Engine accessory gearbox
120 Port cannon ammunition magazine
121 Port 30-mm ADEN cannon (Saab 35F has starboard gun only, earlier intercept and export 35X versions retaining port gun as illustrated)
122 Port forward bag-type fuel tank
123 Port forward integral fuel tanks
124 Cannon port
125 Inner wing/fuselage integral structure
126 Angled frame member
127 Emergency ventral ram-air turbine
128 Trunking formers
129 Gyro amplifiers
130 Intake trunking
131 Nosewheel leg
132 Fibreglass intake lip
133 Forward retracting nosewheel
134 Steering mechanism
135 Possible stores (including jettisonable tanks)
136 Pod containing 19 x 3-in (75-mm) rockets
137 Rb 28 (Sidewinder) IR-homing missile
138 5.3-in (13.5-cm) rocket
139 Rb 27 (Falcon) radar-homing missile
140 1,102-lb (500-kg) bomb

J 35J DRAKEN SPECIFICATION

Dimensions

Length: 50 ft 4 in (15.35 m)
Wingspan: 30 ft 10 in (9.40 m)
Height: 12 ft 9 in (3.89 m)
Wing area: 529.60 sq ft (49.20 m^2)
Wing aspect ratio: 1.77
Wheel track: 8 ft 10 1/2 in (2.70 m)

Powerplant

One 12,790-lb st (56.89-kN) dry or 17,650-lb st (78.5-kN) with afterburning Volvo Flygmotor RM6C turbojet (licence-built Rolls-Royce Avon Series 300 turbojet fitted with a Swedish-designed afterburner)

Weights

Empty: 18,188 lb (8250 kg)
Normal takeoff: 25,132 lb (11,400 kg)
Maximum takeoff: 27,050 lb (12,270 kg) for interceptor mission or 33,069 lb (17,650 kg) for attack mission

Fuel

Internal fuel: 1,057 U.S. gal (4000 litres)
External fuel: provision for up to 1,321 U.S. gal (5000 litres) in external drop tanks

Performance

Maximum level speed "clean" at 36,000 ft (10,975 m): more than 1,147 kt (1,317 mph; 2119 km/h)
Maximum speed at 300 ft (90 m): 793 kt (910 mph; 1465 km/h)
Maximum climb rate at sea level: 34,450 ft (10,500 m) per minute with afterburning
Service ceiling: 65,600 ft (19,995 m)
Takeoff run: 2,133 ft (650 m) at normal takeoff weight
Takeoff distance to 50 ft (15 m): 3,150 ft (960 m) at normal takeoff weight

Range

Ferry range: 1,533 nm (1,763 miles; 2837 km)
Combat radius: 304 nm (350 miles; 564 km) on a hi-lo-hi attack mission with internal fuel only

Armament

Usual air-to-air armament of two AIM-9J Sidewinder air-to-air missiles on centre-section pylons, two Hughes Falcon air-to-air missiles on wing pylons and one 30-mm ADEN cannon with 90 rounds in starboard wing. Maximum ordnance of 6,393 lb (2900 kg).

"The Draken was the first aircraft that combined low speed and short take-off and landing ability with Mach 2 performance" – Per Pellesberg, Saab test pilot

FACTS

- The Draken's "double delta" configuration is unique among fighter aircraft.
- Swedish Drakens used vertical tape instruments in place of some of the conventional dials.
- A pair of double wheels under the rear fuselage prevented the jet pipe from scraping on the ground during landing.

SAAB J 35 DRAKEN – VARIANTS

J 35A: Fighter version. The J 35As were delivered from 1959–61. The tail section was lengthened. This forced the installation of a retractable tail wheel. The two versions were nicknamed "Adam kort" (Adam short) and "Adam lång" (Adam long). Total production: 90.

J 35B: Fighter version. Built and delivered from 1962–63. This variant had improved radar and gunsights, and was also fully integrated into the Swedish STRIL 60 system (a combat guidance and air surveillance system). Total production: 73.

SK 35C: 25 J 35As with short tail sections rebuilt into a twin-seat trainer version. The minor modification meant that the aircraft could easily be converted back to a J 35A standard if necessary.

J 35D: Fighter version. Delivered from 1963–64. The aircraft had a new and more powerful Rolls-Royce Avon 300 (RM 6C), which could deliver 17,386 lb (77.3 kN) thrust when using its afterburner. This was also the fastest Draken version, capable of accelerating until out of fuel. It was also the last Draken to carry two cannons. Total production: 120.

S 35E: Reconnaissance version. The aircraft was unarmed, but was fitted with a countermeasure system to increase its survivability. A total of 28 aircraft were rebuilt J 35Ds. Total production: 60.

J 35F: Fighter version. Delivered from 1965–72. Improved electronics and avionics (integrated radar, aim and missile systems).

J 35F2: A J 35F produced with a Hughes Aircraft Company N71 infrared sensor, a so-called IR seeker.

J 35J: In 1985, the Swedish government decided to modify 54 J 35F2s to J 35J standard. In 1987, 12 more modifications were ordered. Between 1987 and 1991, the aircraft were given a longer lifespan, more modern electronics, a modernized cannon, an additional two Sidewinder pylons under the air intakes and increased fuel capacity. The final operative J 35J flew for the last time in 1999.

Saab 35H: Proposed export version for the Swiss Air Force.

Saab 35XD: Danish export versions. F-35 single-seat Strike Aircraft, TF-35 two-seat trainer and RF-35 reconnaissance aircraft. The type was heavily modified to make it into a strike aircraft in comparison to the Swedish versions.

Saab 35XS: Fighter version for the Finnish Air Force; built by Saab and assembled under licence by Valmet in Finland.

Saab 35BS: Used J 35Bs sold to Finland.

Saab 35FS: Used J 35F1s sold to Finland.

Saab 35CS: Used SK 35Cs sold to Finland.

Saab 35Ö: In the mid-1980s, Saab purchased back 24 J 35D aircraft from the Swedish Air Force and converted them into the J 35Ö version (also called J 35OE in English literature). These examples were later exported to Austria.

SAAB J 35 DRAKEN

The J 35J Draken was an upgraded version of the J 35F for the Swedish Air Force. The programme was undertaken to keep two squadrons of Drakens operational during a period of delays with Saab's JAS 39 Gripen. To create the J 35J, the nose and cockpit were removed and rebuilt by Saab, while FFV refurbished the rest of the airframe. External changes included an infrared search-and-track sensor unit under the nose and two extra fuselage pylons, shown here carrying AIM-9J Sidewinders. The wing pylons have Rb28 (AIM-4C Falcon) missiles. The modified J 35Js re-entered service between 1987 and 1991. This particular aircraft served with F 10 Wing at Ängelholm in southern Sweden until 1999.

Above: Finland's Drakens operated in all weathers from 1974 until 2000. Austria and Denmark were the other export customers.

The Draken (Dragon) was Saab's first supersonic fighter. The company made a leap ahead in just a few years from the first-generation J 29 Tunnan, equivalent to the North American F-86, and the Hunter-like J 32 Lansen, to a tailless delta capable of Mach 2. The specification that led to the Draken was issued in 1949, when supersonic flight and delta wings were both novelties. As well as high performance and onboard radar, the specification called for the ability to operate from straight stretches of highway as part of Sweden's measures to avoid its fighters being destroyed on the ground in the first hours of war.

The Draken was designed as a "double delta," with its swept wing having different sweep on its inboard and outboard sections. This contrasted with "pure" deltas such as the Convair F-102 and Dassault Mirage III. To test the unique configuration, Saab built a scale testbed called the "Lill Draken," or "Little Dragon," which first flew in 1952. This was about 70 percent the size of the proposed fighter, but the Armstrong Siddeley Adder engine was proportionally much smaller than the one intended for the Draken, and the Lill Draken's performance was very low. Nonetheless, it validated the wing design and proved the need for a longer nose to improve airflow into the intakes.

MATCHING POWER TO PERFORMANCE

The full-size J 35 Draken flew in October 1955, powered by a licence-built Rolls-Royce Avon engine. Production Drakens had the Volvo RM6B, a version of the Avon with a Swedish-designed afterburner. Standard armament was a pair of 30-mm Aden cannon and two AIM-9B Sidewinder missiles (locally designated Rb24). Later models could carry the Hughes AIM-4 Falcon (Rb27 and Rb28), and export versions could use later versions of the Sidewinder.

Several improved versions followed the initial J 35A, among them the J 35D (which was the first to be capable of Mach 2 speeds), the S 35E reconnaissance model and the J 35F with Falcon missile capability. Swedish policy at the time prevented sales of weapons to most nations likely ever to use them, but NATO member Denmark became the first export customer in 1968, taking just over 50 fighters, reconnaissance aircraft and trainers. Finland bought a similar number, all single-seaters. Austria acquired 24 in the 1980s, finally retiring them in 2005.

Above: The two-seat Draken featured a periscope to give the instructor a forward view for landings.

CRUCIAL INNOVATION

One of the less visible but most important features of the Draken was its connection with the Swedish data-link system, one of the first to be used anywhere. The STRIL 60 ground-control network used early digital computer technology and could guide the Draken pilot to a firing solution by presenting him with guidance on his cockpit instruments. It was resistant to electronic jamming.

The unusual shape of the Draken caused one unfortunate flight characteristic – a tendency to "super-stall," when the nose pitched up quickly and the aircraft fell out of control if mishandled. Particular attention was needed to avoid this condition during air combat manoeuvres. Several Drakens were lost in super-stall accidents in training.

The Draken never saw combat, although the user nations frequently intercepted intruding aircraft with them. The first good photographs of many new Soviet aircraft were captured by Draken pilots over the Baltic in the 1970s and 1980s.

Above: A pair of early Flygvapnet (Swedish Air Force) J 35As of F13 Wing show off the Rb 24, the Swedish-produced version of the AIM-9B Sidewinder.

Modern Jets 1960–present

As the Vietnam War came to its conclusion, the fighter rule book was being torn up. Air forces and designers stopped referring to fighters as missile platforms or as the manned component of a weapons system.

Above: The Saab 37 Viggen typified the 1970s approach of different versions for different roles, as illustrated by this AJ 37 of the Swedish Air Force's F 7 Såtenäs, loaded with Mk 81 general-purpose bombs.

Emphasis was placed on air combat again, with agility favoured over pure performance. Features such as bubble canopies returned, the head-up display (HUD) and hands-on-throttle-and-stick (HOTAS) allowed the pilot to concentrate on the target without taking his eyes off it, and there were multifunction displays (MFDs) to manage weapons, sensors and systems in a single-seat cockpit.

Miniaturization and advances in electronics permitted a comparatively tiny fighter such as the Lockheed Martin F-16 to be far more effective than a monster such as the Republic F-105, although turn performance and climb rate were achieved at the expense of range and straight-line speed. For some roles such as fleet defence and long-range interception, a two-man crew was usually deemed necessary.

THE ADVENT OF FLY-BY-WIRE

The most significant advance in the fourth generation was "fly-by-wire." Direct or hydraulically boosted connection between the pilot's hands and feet and the control surfaces was replaced by electrical connections routed through computers. This allowed almost any input, no matter how violent, with the computers (there were usually at least three) regulating the control movement to produce the maximum effect without fear of overstressing the airframe. This meant instantaneous changes of direction and sustained turn rates that put the stress on the pilot. Whereas most third-generation aircraft were stressed to 7 g, their successors were usually rated up to 12. Turns of 9 g became common, and the threat of GLOC, or g-induced loss of consciousness, became a concern and was cited as the cause of many accidents. Pilots were more strictly screened for g tolerance, given improved g-suits and trained to deal with high forces by straining to prevent blood flow away from the upper body under high g.

The first fourth-generation fighter was the F-16 Fighting Falcon. In its initial F-16A form as delivered to the U.S. Air Force in 1978, it was little more than an agile day fighter

Right: The Eurofighter Typhoon lacks obvious stealth features, but is the top-of-the-line fighter in production and on the market in the early 2010s.

Above: The MiG-29 has remained viable through upgrade programmes, including those which make them compatible with NATO systems and procedures.

with a basic ground-attack capability with "dumb" bombs. More than 30 years later, the F-16 remains in production, but under the skin is virtually a new aircraft, offering advanced electronic warfare and self-protection capabilities, as well as an enormous range of precision weapons from numerous U.S. and foreign manufacturers.

ADVANCING A HALF GENERATION

Conformal fuel tanks have boosted the F-16 range, and new radars and sensors are offered to suit the needs of the customer. Not, however, the U.S. Air Force, which long ago accepted its last Fighting Falcon. For the first time, export users (notably Israel and the United Arab Emirates) are fielding a fighter considerably more advanced than the versions in use by the domestic customer. These later F-16s, plus the newer block Super Hornets, the Saab JAS 39C/D Gripen, Eurofighter Typhoon, Dassault Rafale and Sukhoi Su-30/-35 are sometimes called "4.5 generation fighters," having a network-enabled capability allowing to share data from their radars and other sensors (which can be presented on the one display in a process called "sensor fusion") via secure data links.

Today, as in 1945, only six countries have an indigenous jet fighter in production: the United States, Russia, Sweden, France and China, although there are others collaborating on projects such as the Typhoon.

THE FIFTH GENERATION ... OR NOT?

The U.S. Air Force has moved directly on to the fifth generation, fielding (after a long development) the Lockheed Martin/Boeing F-22 Raptor, and progressing with the Lockheed Martin F-35 Lightning II. Each of these embodies stealth technology and unparalleled electronic self-defense systems. The colossal cost of the F-22 (nearing $140 million apiece) and restrictions on technology transfer mean that no

Above: France's Rafale is the only one of the "Eurocanard" fighters built in both land-based (rear) and carrier-capable versions.

Above: The Lockheed Martin/Boeing F-22 Raptor, with its stealth technology, is the only true fifth-generation fighter in service, but rivals from Russia and China can be expected in the next decade.

more than 187 will likely ever be built, all of them for U.S. Air Force use only. The F-35 was conceived as a lower-cost complement to the F-22, with a primary ground-attack role and significant international contribution from risk-sharing partner nations. The programme is highly dependent, however, on sales to the U.S. forces, partner countries and beyond of 4,500–6,000 aircraft. At least one independent analysis of the market suggests that because of delays and cost hikes, and a trend to not replace older fighters at all in some regions, fewer F-35s will be purchased than anticipated and the real figure may be closer to 2,500.

MOVING TOWARD THE FUTURE

In the United States, purchases of increased numbers of 4.5-generation aircraft such as the Boeing F/A-18E/F Super Hornet and the proposed Boeing F-15SE Silent Eagle with some stealth characteristics may be needed to close the U.S. Air Force's and U.S. Navy's "fighter gap" between retiring aircraft and the F-35. In January 2010, Sukhoi finally flew the prototype T-50, the mysterious fifth-generation stealth fighter that had spawned the concept of fighter generations two decades before.

Whereas most third-generation aircraft were stressed to 7 g, their successors were usually rated up to 12. Turns of 9 g became common, and the threat of GLOC, or g-induced loss of consciousness, became a concern and was cited as the cause of many accidents.

English Electric Lightning

The Lightning was the last all-British interceptor and had performance that has rarely been bettered, although this did come at the expense of combat endurance and range.

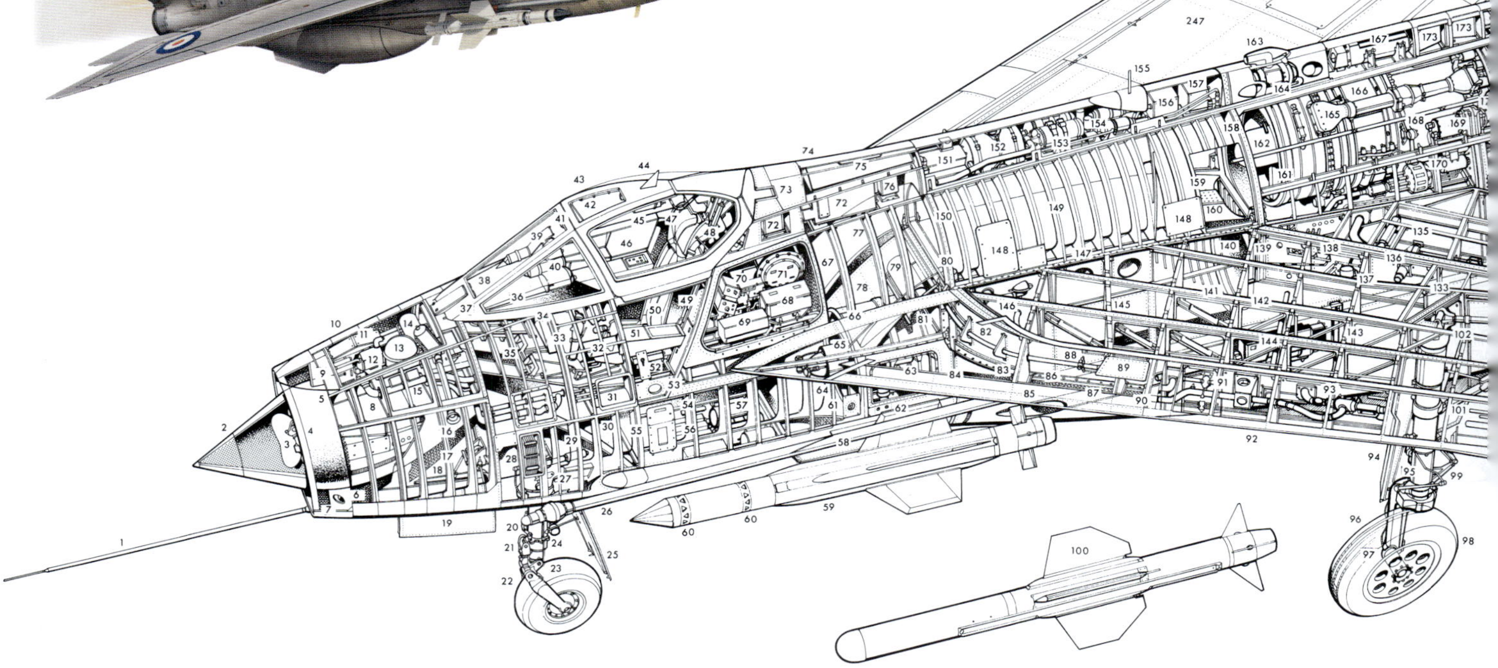

Cutaway Key

1 Pitot head boom
2 Intake bullet fairing
3 Ferranti AIRPASS radar antenna/scanner
4 Engine air intake lip
5 Hot-air de-icing
6 Bullet lower spacer
7 G 90 camera
8 Radar pack
9 Bullet upper spacer (electrical leads)
10 Forward equipment bay
11 Forward fuse box
12 Capacitor box
13 LOX container
14 Light fighter sight control unit
15 De-icing/demister air
16 Radar ground cooling air coupling
17 Nosewheel door mechanism torque shaft and operating rods
18 Nosewheel bay
19 Nosewheel doors
20 Nosewheel strut
21 Roller guide bracket
22 Forward-retracting nosewheel
23 Castor auto-disconnect
24 Shimmy damper and centring unit
25 Aft door (linked to leg)
26 Flight refuelling probe (detachable)
27 Nosewheel strut pivot pin
28 Heat exchanger
29 Nosewheel hydraulic jack
30 Intake ducting
31 Cockpit canted floor
32 Engine power control panel
33 Control column
34 Instrument panel shroud
35 Rudder pedal assembly
36 Canopy column
37 Rain-dispersal duct
38 Windscreen (electro-thermal)
39 CRT display unit (starboard)
40 Airpass (light fighter) attack sight
41 Standby magnetic compass
42 Canopy top panel demisting ducts
43 Magnesium-forged canopy top frame
44 IFF aerial
45 Chemical air driers
46 Starboard (armaments) console
47 Ejection-seat face-blind firing handle
48 Air-conditioning duct
49 Rear pressure bulkhead
50 Martin-Baker ejection seat
51 Port instrument panels
52 Cockpit ladder attachment
53 Cockpit emergency ram air intake
54 Lower (No. 1) engine intake duct frames
55 Firestreak weapons pack
56 Launch sequence units
57 Control units
58 Port missile pylon
59 Firestreak missile
60 Fuse "windows"
61 Armament safety break panel
62 Aileron accumulator pressure gauges
63 Accumulator group bay
64 Plessey LTSA starter in lower (No. 1) engine nosecone
65 Lower (No. 1) engine intake
66 Wingroot inboard fairing
67 Main equipment bay
68 Selector address unit
69 Electronic unit
70 Air data computer
71 Converter signal unit (datalink)
72 Communications T/R (two)
73 Canopy hinge
74 Dorsal spine bays
75 AC fuse and relay box (cold-air unit and water boiler to starboard)
76 28-Volt battery
77 Upper (No. 2) engine intake duct
78 Fuselage frames
79 Water-heater tank and extractor
80 Wing/fuselage main attachment point
81 Aileron idler lever
82 Aileron control push-pull tubes
83 Tube attachment brackets
84 Fuselage multi-bolt forward/centre-section join
85 ADEN gun muzzle
86 Leading-edge integral fuel
87 Muzzle blast tube
88 Aileron tube triple-roller guides
89 Access
90 Fuel lines
91 Non-return valve
92 Detachable leading-edge sections
93 Shuttle valve
94 Undercarriage strut fixed fairing
95 Shock-absorber strut
96 Port mainwheel
97 Brake unit
98 Tubeless tyre
99 Torque links
100 Red Top missile
101 Aft fairing flap
102 Undercarriage pivot
103 Radius rod (inward-breaking)
104 Undercarriage retraction jack
105 Door jack sequence valve
106 Door master locking mechanism
107 Collector tank and booster pumps (two)
108 Aerodynamic leading-edge slot
109 Tank pressurizing intake/vent (in slot)
110 Mainwheel door
111 Undercarriage jack sequence valve
112 Door latch linkage
113 Port mainwheel well
114 Aileron control push-pull tubes
115 Aileron movement restrictor
116 Aileron autostabilizer actuator
117 Aileron control linkage
118 Aileron hydraulic runs
119 Cambered leading-edge extension
120 Localizer aerial
121 Port navigation light
122 Port wingtip
123 Port aileron
124 Aileron powered flying-control units
125 Control linkage
126 Wing outer structure
127 Aileron mass balance
128 Wing outer fixed section
129 Flap outer actuator jack
130 Flap sections
131 Flap integral tank
132 Angled aft spar
133 Undercarriage attachment
134 Refuelling/defuelling valve
135 Flap inner actuator jack
136 Three-way cock (manual)
137 DC transfer pump
138 Gate valves
139 Wing/fuselage rear main attachment point

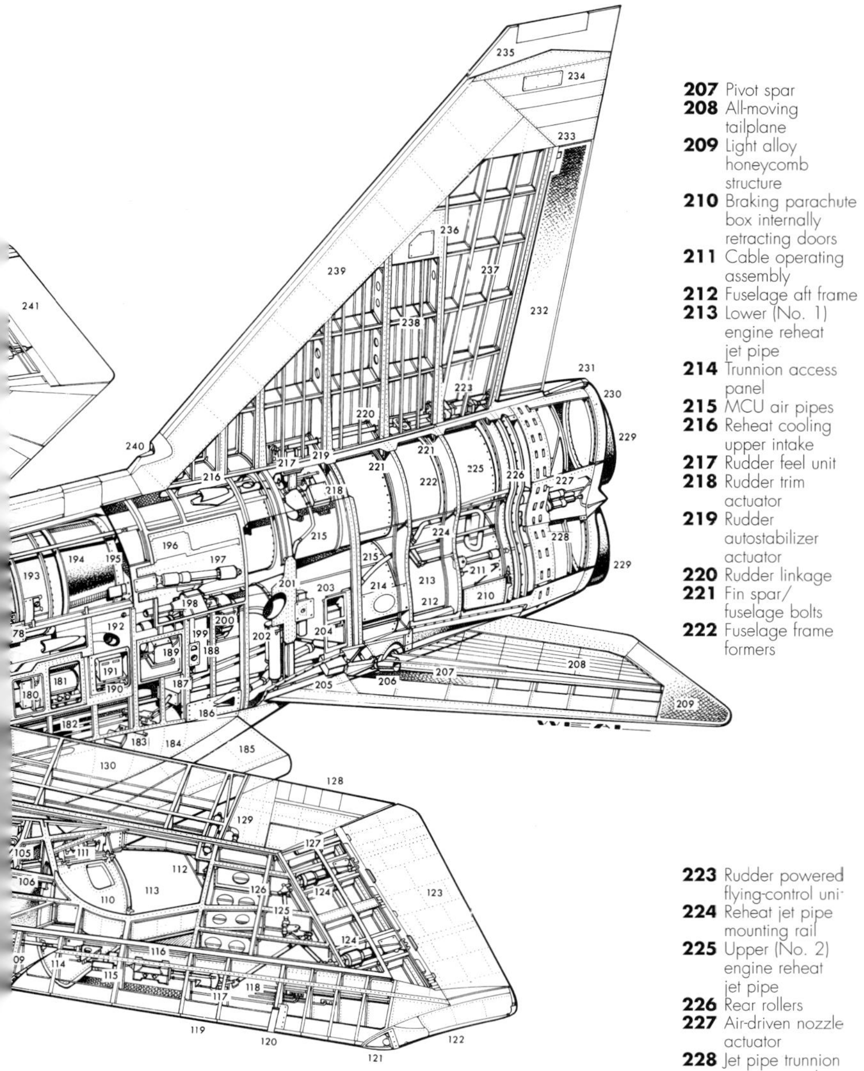

140 Lower (No. 1) engine intermediate jet pipe forward face
141 Wing inboard structure
142 Wing integral fuel
143 Intermediate spar booms (T-section)
144 Port ADEN cannon (forward ventral pack)
145 Wing rib stations
146 Fuel vent pipe
147 Multi-bolt wing attachment plate
148 Access panels
149 Upper (No. 2) engine duct frames
150 Fuselage break frame
151 Voltage regulators
152 Start tank
153 Engine pump units
154 Solenoid valves
155 Communications antenna
156 Starter control unit
157 HF igniter units
158 Fuselage frame
159 Main wing box upper skin
160 Forged centre rib (multi-bolt attachment)
161 Starter exhaust
162 Upper (No. 2) engine nosecone
163 Generator cooling ram-air intake
164 Stand-by generator
165 Anti-icing bleed air
166 Upper (No. 2) Avon 301 turbojet engine and reheat units
167 Airpass recorder unit
168 Engine front mounting point
169 Engine accessories
170 No. 2 engine bleed-air turbopump (reheat fuel)
171 Engine bay firewalls
172 Integral pumps (two)
173 HE ignition units
174 Voltage regulator
175 Current sensing unit
176 Rubber spring feel mechanism
177 Auxiliary intake
178 Main mounting trunnion
179 Aft (port) equipment bays
180 Electronic unit
181 IFF coder
182 Tailplane controls
183 Tailplane trim actuator and feel unit
184 Ventral fuel tank (aft section)
185 Fin
186 Reheat cooling lower intake
187 Tailplane autostabilizer actuator
188 Gearbox oil filler
189 AC generator
190 Glide-path receiver
191 IFF transmit/ receive unit
192 Outlet
193 No. 2 engine intermediate jet pipe
194 Refrasil heat shrouds
195 Stress-bearing upper (No. 2) engine hatch
196 Port airbrake
197 Airbrake hydraulic actuator jack
198 DC generator
199 Main accessory-drive unit
200 Airbrake lower frame
201 Turbine exhaust (from 199)
202 Tailplane accumulator and nitrogen bottle
203 Reheat "hotshot" igniter box
204 Tailplane drive triangular unit
205 Tailplane powered flying-control unit
206 Tailplane spigot
207 Pivot spar
208 All-moving tailplane
209 Light alloy honeycomb structure
210 Braking parachute box internally retracting doors
211 Cable operating assembly
212 Fuselage aft frame
213 Lower (No. 1) engine reheat jet pipe
214 Trunnion access panel
215 MCU air pipes
216 Reheat cooling upper intake
217 Rudder feel unit
218 Rudder trim actuator
219 Rudder autostabilizer actuator
220 Rudder linkage
221 Fin spar/ fuselage bolts
222 Fuselage frame formers
223 Rudder powered flying-control unit
224 Reheat jet pipe mounting rail
225 Upper (No. 2) engine reheat jet pipe
226 Rear rollers
227 Air-driven nozzle actuator
228 Jet pipe trunnion access panel
229 Variable propelling nozzles
230 Streamer cable around rear lip (spring-clipped)
231 Parachute streaming anchor and jettison unit
232 Rudder light-alloy honeycomb structure
233 Flutter damper
234 Communications antenna
235 Dielectric tip
236 Compass unit
237 Angled aft spars
238 Main fin structure
239 Fin leading-edge panels
240 Accessory drive cooling air
241 Starboard aileron
242 Aileron powered flying-control units
243 Control linkage
244 Starboard flap outer actuator jack
245 Starboard flap
246 Wing panels
247 Wing skinning
248 Wing integral fuel
249 Aileron control push-pull tubes
250 Aileron movement restrictor
251 Aileron autostabilizer actuator
252 Starboard navigation light
253 Glide-slope aerial

LIGHTNING F 53 SPECIFICATION

Dimensions

Length overall (including probe): 55 ft 3 in (16.84 m)
Wingspan: 34 ft 10 in (10.62 m)
Wing aspect ratio: 2.65
Tailplane span: 14 ft 6 in (4.42 m)
Wing area: 458.50 sq ft (42.60 m^2)
Overall height: 19 ft 7 in (5.97 m)

Powerplant

Two Rolls-Royce Avon RA.24 Mk 302C turbojets each rated at 11,000 lb (48.92 kN) static military thrust and 16,300 lb (72.49 kN) with afterburning

Weights

Empty operating: 28,040 lb (12,719 kg); 29,600 lb (13,426 kg) with gun pack and missiles
Maximum takeoff (fully armed): 41,700 lb (18,915 kg)

Fuel and load

Maximum internal fuel: 10,608 lb (4812 kg)
Maximum internal fuel capacity: 1534 U.S. gal (5805 litres)
Wing tank capacity: 829 U.S. gal (3137 litres)
Ventral tank capacity: 705 U.S. gal (2668 litres), or 619 U.S. gal (2342 litres) with 30-mm cannon pack fitted
Total external fuel capacity: 625 U.S. gal (2364 litres) in two overwing tanks
Maximum weapon load: 6,000 lb (2722 kg)

Performance

Maximum level speed at high altitude: 1,320 kt (1,520 mph; 2446 km/h) at 40,000 ft (12,190 m) or Mach 2.3
Maximum level speed at low altitude: approximately 723 kt (834 mph; 1340 km/h) or Mach 1.1
Cruising speed for optimum range: 517 kt (595 mph; 958 km/h)
Initial rate of climb: 50,000 ft (15,240 m) per minute
Actual ceiling: in excess of 60,000 ft (18,288 m)
Service ceiling: 60,000 ft (18,288 m)
Time to climb: 150 seconds from brakes release to Mach 0.9 at 40,000 ft (12,192 m)
Acceleration: 210 seconds from Mach 1 to over Mach 2
Landing speed: 160 kt (183mph; 295km/h)

Armament

Fixed: two 30-mm ADEN Mk 4 cannon, each with 120 rounds, in gun pack forward of ventral fuel tank
Forward external stores: standard intercept load of two Red Top or Firestreak infrared-homing short-range air-to-air missiles; in place of missile pack, alternative loads of pack containing twin retractable launchers for total of 44 2-in (51-mm) MicroCell spin-stabilized rockets, or reconnaissance packs
Wing-mounted stores: single hardpoint under outer wing capable of carrying two 1,000-lb (454-kg) HE, retarded or fire bombs, two MATRA Type 155 launchers containing total of 36 2.68-in (68-mm) SNEB rockets, two flare pods or two machine-gun pods; single hardpoint above inner wing capable of carrying single 1,000-lb (454-kg) bomb or other stores

"The Lightning was easy and very pleasant to fly, but not so easy to operate as a weapons system."
– Brian Carroll, Lightning pilot

"In an age now governed by computers and fly-by-wire, there never will be such a charismatic jet again. The Lightning always was – and always will be – the ultimate jet fighter."
– Ian Black, Lightning pilot

FACTS

- The Lightning was the first British aircraft to exceed Mach 2.
- With internal fuel alone and no inflight refuelling, the Lightning had only about 50 minutes' endurance.
- A Lightning was capable of reaching 36,000 ft (10,972 m) in altitude in two and a half minutes from brake release.

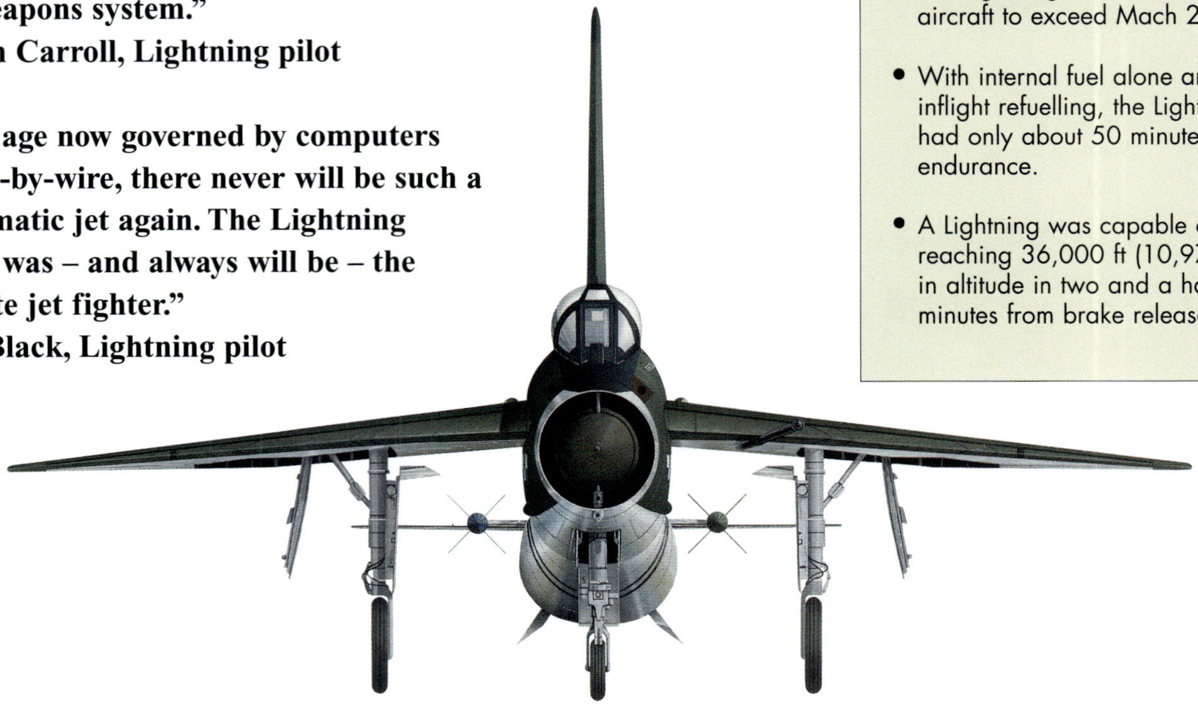

ENGLISH ELECTRIC LIGHTNING – VARIANTS

English Electric P 1A: Single-seat supersonic research aircraft.

English Electric P 1B: Single-seat operational prototypes to meet Specification F23/49.

Lightning F 1: Single-seat fighter. Delivered in 1960. A total of 19 built. Two Rolls-Royce Avon 200R engines. Two 30-mm ADEN cannons in nose. Two Firestreak missiles. Ferranti AI-23 "AIRPASS" radar.

Lightning F 1A: Single-seat fighter. Delivered in 1961. Now the "BAC Lightning." Avon 210R engines. Addition of inflight refuelling probe. A total of 28 built.

Lightning F 2: Single-seat fighter (an improved variant of the F1). Delivered in 1962. A total of 44 built, with 31 later modified to F2A standard. Five later modified to F52 for export to Saudi Arabia.

Lightning F 2A: Single-seat fighter (F2s upgraded to near F6 standard). A total of 31 converted from F2. Avon 211R engines. Retained ADEN cannon and Firestreak of F2 (the Firestreak pack could be replaced with an ADEN cannon pack to give the aircraft four ADEN cannon). Larger ventral tank and arrestor hook.

Lightning F 3: Single-seat fighter. Upgraded radar – AI-23B. Avon 301R engines. Firestreak changed for Red Top missiles. Enlarged and clipped tailfin due to aerodynamics of carriage of Red Top. ADEN cannon removed. A total of 70 built (at least nine were converted to F6 standard).

Lightning F 3A: Single-seat fighter. Extended range of 800 miles (500 km) with large ventral tank. New cambered wings. A total of 16 built at the end of F 3 production, known also as an F 3 Interim version or F6 Interim Version. 15 modified later to full F 6 standard.

Lightning T 4: Two-seat side-by-side training version, based on the F 1A.

Lightning T 5: Two-seat side-by-side training version, based on the F 3.

Lightning F 6: Single-seat fighter (an improved longer-range variant of the F 3). New wings with better efficiency and subsonic performance, increased fuel storage. Overwing fuel tanks and larger ventral fuel tank. Change back to 30-mm cannon. Two Red Top missiles. A total of 39 built (also nine converted from F 3 and 15 from F 3A).

Lightning F 52: Slightly modified ex-Royal Air Force F 2 single-seat fighters for export to Saudi Arabia (five converted from F 2).

Lightning F 53: Export version of the F 6 with pylons for bombs or unguided rocket pods. A total of 46 built and one converted from F 6. 12 F 53Ks for the Kuwaiti Air Force, 34 F 53s for the Royal Saudi Arabian Air Force. Used air-to-ground in dispute near border with South Yemen in 1969 with great success.

Lightning T 55: Two-seat side-by-side training aircraft (export version of the T 5). Eight built (six T 55s for the Royal Saudi Arabian Air Force, two T 55Ks for the Kuwaiti Air Force and one converted from T 5 that crashed before delivery). Total production was 277 single-seat fighters and 52 two-seater trainers, including Royal Air Force and export aircraft.

ENGLISH ELECTRIC LIGHTNING

The Lightning F 2A was a version that only served in the squadrons of RAF Germany, including 19 and 92 Squadrons. Unlike other units, who trained against the threat of Soviet bombers coming down from the North Cape, the RAFG squadrons faced low-level fighter-bombers arriving at high speed from East Germany and other Warsaw Pact nations. Their quick reaction time and good manoeuvrability down low suited them for basing along the Rhine. In this low-level role, a green upper surface camouflage was deemed vital to disguise them from higher adversaries. This F 2A of No 92 Squadron served from 1962 until 1977 when it was retired to ground instructional use at Farnborough. It was eventually scrapped at Foulness Island in 1996.

English Electric (later absorbed into British Aircraft Corporation, then British Aerospace) had not even flown its first military aircraft, the Canberra bomber, by the time it was awarded a contract for a supersonic research aircraft in 1948. Instead of the then-fashionable delta wings, highly swept (60-degree) wings and tailplanes were chosen. A single intake in the nose led to twin Avon engines, one stacked above the other.

The P 1 made its maiden flight in August 1954 and was followed by the P 1A and P 1B, which was substantially different, adding a radar in an intake centre-body, a ventral fuel tank and a larger fin.

An infamous defence review in 1957 called for all British manned combat aircraft development programmes to be cancelled in favour of missile systems. The P 1B escaped because it had progressed too far by this stage.

The Lightning F 1 was essentially the same as the P 1B and entered RAF service in 1960. The F 3 added the ability to fire the Red Top missile and could carry fuel tanks on pylons mounted above the wings, a feature shared only with the SEPECAT Jaguar fighter-bomber. T 4 and T 5s were two-seaters which, like the Convair TF-102A Delta Dagger, had their seats arranged side by side. They had the same weapons and radar capabilities as the equivalent single-seaters, but slightly less endurance due to reduced fuel tank volume.

The definitive Lightning was the F 6, with Red Top or Firestreak missiles, a cannon pack in the ventral tank and a refuelling probe. Lightnings were famed for their rapid climb rate and high ceiling, but very fast fuel use and limited endurance without refuelling meant that the aircraft needed constant tanker support.

AN UNEXPECTED ROLE

Squadrons based in RAF Germany were tasked with a role not envisaged when the Lightning was developed – intercepting low-level intruders such as Warsaw Pact fighter-

Above: With Firestreak missiles and refuelling probe prominent, a camouflaged F 6 flies over the Lightning's last base, RAF Binbrook, in Lincolnshire, which closed when the Lightning retired in 1988.

bombers. The Lightning's quick reaction times and surprisingly good low-level dogfighting ability made it quite suitable for this mission, although the natural metal finish had to be replaced by camouflage greens and greys. Nonetheless, the warload of only two missiles and cannon, as well as the high fuel consumption, gave it limited combat persistence.

Despite sales efforts over the years, Lightnings were sold to only two export customers: Saudi Arabia and Kuwait. The RAF's Lightnings always seemed to be on the verge of going out of service, and potential customers such as Austria and Switzerland feared losing spare parts and maintenance support if the original user retired them.

BARELY REALIZED POTENTIAL

Saudi Lightnings were the only ones to see action, flying ground-attack sorties against Yemeni rebels encamped within Saudi territory in 1969. As well as bombs on underwing pylons, the Saudi and Kuwait Lightnings could carry rocket pods on their overwing pylons. Saudi Arabia retired its Lightnings in 1985 and sold them back to British Aerospace for possible onward sale, but this was never to happen.

The last two RAF Lightning squadrons provided quick-reaction alert (QRA) from Binbrook in Lincolnshire until 1988. BAE retained two flying aircraft until the early 1990s for use as radar targets as part of the Panavia Tornado and Eurofighter Typhoon programmes.

Above: Pilots of RAF 74 Squadron await the call to take off. The heavy canopy provided a relatively poor view.

Left: An RAF 19 Squadron F 2 demonstrates the legendary climbing ability of the Lightning.

Dassault Mirage III/V

Dassault's Mirage III delta was probably the greatest achievement of the postwar French military aircraft industry. Its success on the home and export markets and in combat has allowed France to maintain an indigenous combat aircraft design and production capability to this day.

Cutaway Key

1 Fibreglass fintip aerial fairing
2 VHF aerial
3 Tail navigation and anti-collision lights
4 Tail radar warning antenna
5 Rudder construction
6 Fin main spar
7 Passive radar antenna
8 UHF aerial
9 Rudder hydraulic actuator
10 Magnetic detector
11 Parachute release link
12 Brake parachute housing
13 Parachute fairing
14 Exhaust nozzle shroud
15 Variable-area exhaust nozzle flaps
16 Nozzle jacks
17 Cooling air louvres
18 Jet pipe
19 Rear fuselage frame and stringer construction
20 Wingroot trailing-edge fillet
21 Fin attachment main frame
22 Fin spar attachment joint
23 Control cable runs
24 Engine bay/jet pipe thermal lining
25 Afterburner duct
26 Elevon compensator hydraulic jack
27 Ventral fuel tank
28 Main engine mounting
29 Wing spar/ fuselage main frame
30 Main spar joint
31 Engine gearbox-driven generator

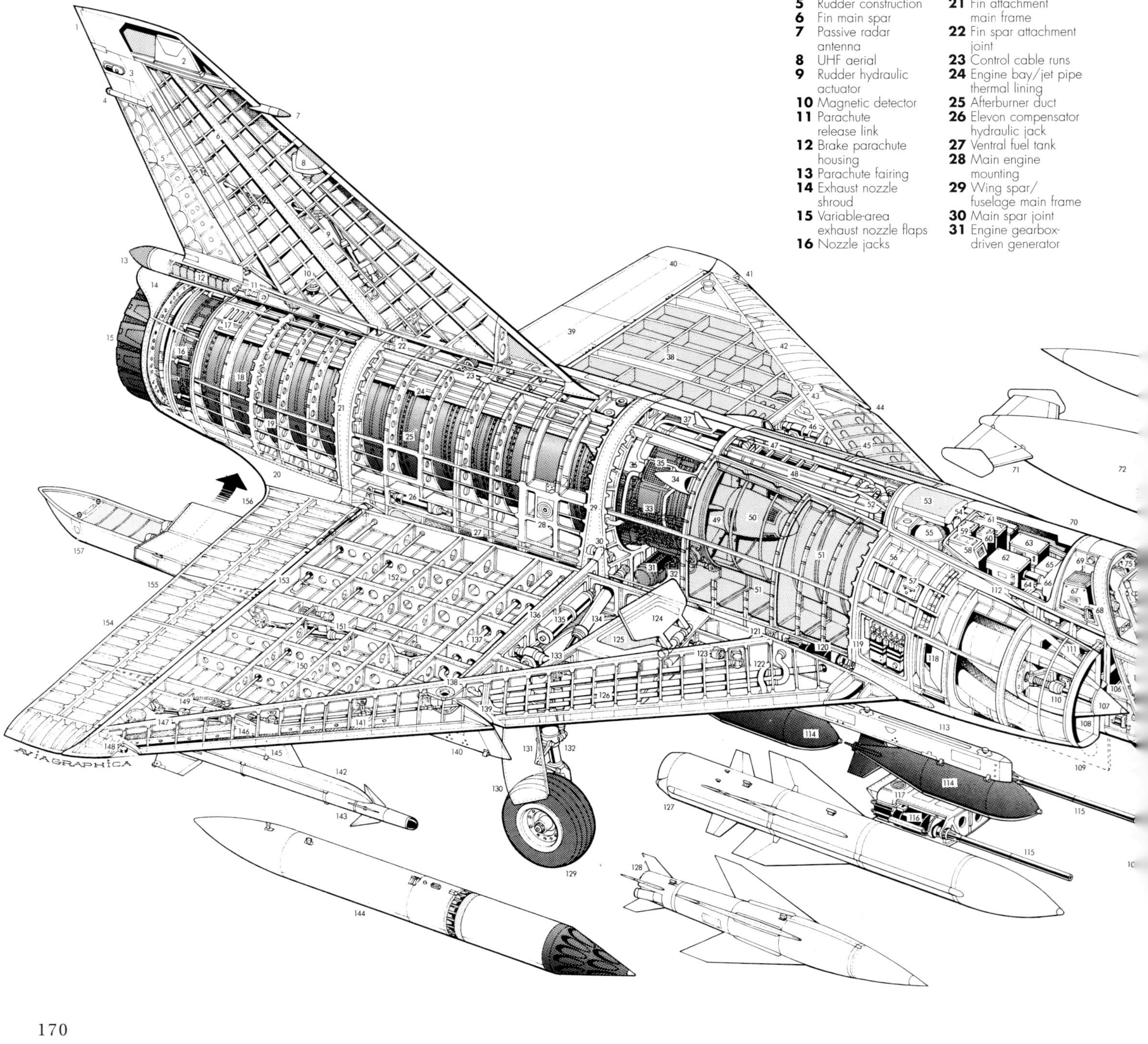

32 Engine accessory compartment
33 SNECMA Atar 9C afterburning turbojet
34 Cooling system air intakes
35 Heat exchanger
36 Engine oil tank
37 IFF aerial
38 Port wing integral fuel tank, total internal capacity 880 U.S. gal (3330 litres)
39 Inboard elevon
40 Outboard elevon
41 Port navigation light
42 Cambered leading-edge ribs
43 Port wing pylon fixing
44 Leading-edge notch
45 Port leading-edge fuel tank
46 Main undercarriage pivot fixing
47 Fuselage dorsal systems ducting
48 Air system piping
49 Turbojet intake
50 Engine starter housing
51 Fuselage fuel tanks
52 Equipment cooling system air filter
53 Computer system voltage regulator
54 Oxygen bottles
55 Inverted flight fuel system accumulator
56 Intake ducting
57 Matra 530 missile computer
58 VHF radio transmitter/receiver
59 Gyro platform multiplier
60 Doppler transceiver
61 Navigation system computer
62 Air data computer
63 Nord missile encoding supply
64 Radio altimeter transceiver
65 Heading and inertial correction computer
66 Armament junction box
67 Radar programme controller
68 Canopy external release
69 Canopy hinge
70 Radio and electronics bay access fairing
71 Fuel-tank stabilizing fins
72 343-U.S. gal (1300-litre) auxiliary fuel tank (449-U.S. gal/1700-litre alternative)
73 165-U.S. gal (625-litre) drop tank
74 Cockpit canopy cover
75 Canopy hydraulic jack
76 Ejection-seat headrest
77 Face-blind firing handle
78 Martin-Baker (Hispano licence) RM4 ejection seat
79 Port-side console panel
80 Canopy framing
81 Pilot's head-up display
82 Windscreen panels
83 Instrument panel shroud
84 Instrument pressure sensors
85 Thomson-CSF Cyrano II fire-control radar
86 Radar scanner dish
87 Fibreglass radome
88 Pitot tube
89 Matra 530 air-to-air missile
90 Doppler radar fairing
91 Thomson-CSF Doppler navigation radar antenna
92 Cockpit front pressure bulkhead
93 Rudder pedals
94 Radar scope (head-down display)
95 Control column
96 Cockpit floor level
97 Starboard-side console panel
98 Nosewheel leg doors
99 Nose undercarriage leg strut
100 Landing/taxiing lamps
101 Levered suspension axle unit
102 Nosewheel
103 Shimny damper
104 Hydraulic retraction strut
105 Cockpit rear pressure bulkhead
106 Air-conditioning ram air intake
107 Movable intake half-cone centre-body
108 Starboard air intake
109 Nosewheel well door (open position)
110 Intake centre-body screw jack
111 Air-conditioning plant
112 Boundary layer bleed air duct
113 Centre fuselage bomb rack
114 882-lb (400-kg) HE bombs
115 Cannon barrels
116 30-mm DEFA cannon (2), 250 rounds per gun
117 Ventral gun pack
118 Auxiliary air intake door
119 Electrical system servicing panel
120 Starboard 30-mm DEFA cannon
121 Front spar attachment joint
122 Fuel system piping
123 Airbrake hydraulic jack
124 Starboard airbrake, upper and lower surfaces (open position)
125 Airbrake housing
126 Starboard leading-edge fuel tank
127 AS37 Martel, radar-guided air-to-ground missile
128 Nord AS30 air-to-air missile
129 Starboard mainwheel
130 Mainwheel leg door
131 Torque scissor links
132 Shock absorber leg strut
133 Starboard main undercarriage pivot fixing
134 Hydraulic retraction jack
135 Main undercarriage hydraulic accumulator
136 Wing main spar
137 Fuel system piping
138 Inboard pylon fixing
139 Leading-edge notch
140 Starboard inner stores pylon
141 Control rod runs
142 Missile launch rail
143 AIM-9 Sidewinder air-to-air missile
144 JL-100 fuel and rocket pack, 66 U.S. gal (250 litres) of fuel plus 18 x 68-mm unguided rockets
145 Outboard wing pylon
146 Outboard pylon fixing
147 Front spar
148 Starboard navigation light
149 Outboard elevon hydraulic jack
150 Starboard wing integral fuel tank
151 Inboard elevon hydraulic actuator
152 Wing multi-spar and rib construction
153 Rear spar
154 Outboard elevon construction
155 Inboard elevon construction
156 Elevon compensator
157 132-U.S. gal (500-litre) auxiliary fuel tanks

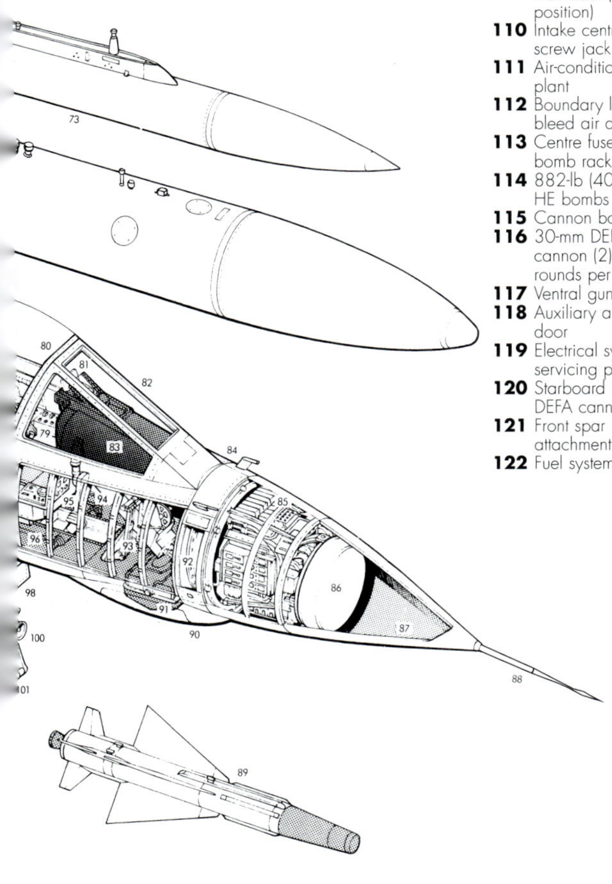

MIRAGE IIIE SPECIFICATION

Dimensions

Length: 49 ft 3½ in (15.03 m)
Height: 14 ft 9 in (4.50 m)
Wingspan: 26 ft 11⅔ in (8.22 m)
Wing area: 376.75 sq ft (35.00 m²)
Aspect ratio: 1.94
Wheel track: 10 ft 4 in (3.15 m)
Wheelbase: 15 ft 11¾ in (4.87 m)

Powerplant

One SNECMA Atar 9C-3 rated at 9,436 lb st (41.97 kN) dry and 13,668 lb st (60.80 kN) with afterburning, and provision for one jettisonable SEPR 84 rocket booster rated at 3,307 lb st (14.71 kN)

Weights

Empty: 15,542 lb (7050 kg)
Normal takeoff: 21,164 lb (9600 kg)
Maximum takeoff: 30,203 lb (13,700 kg)

Fuel and load

Internal fuel: 631.4 U.S. gal (2390 litres)
External fuel: Up to two 449-, 343-, 291- or 165-U.S. gal (1700-, 1300-, 1100- or 625-litre) drop tanks, or two 132-U.S. gal (500-litre) non-jettisonable supersonic tanks, or two 66-U.S. gal (250-litre) JL-100 combined drop tanks/rocket launchers, or two 291-U.S. gal (1100-litre) fuel/electronic equipment tanks
Maximum ordnance: 8,818 lb (4000 kg)

Performance

Maximum level speed "clean" at 39,370 ft (12,000 m): 1,268 kt (1,460 mph; 2350 km/h)
Cruising speed at 36,090 ft (11000 m): 516 kt (594 mph; 956 km/h)
Ferry range with three drop tanks: 2,152 nm (2,486 miles; 4000 km)
Combat radius: 647 nm (746 miles; 1200 km)
Maximum rate of climb at sea level: More than 16,405 ft (5000 m) per minute
Climb to 36,090 ft (11,000 m): 3 minutes
Service ceiling: 55,775 ft (17,000 m) or 75,460 ft (23,000 m) with rocket pack
Takeoff run: Between 2,297 and 5,249 ft (700 and 1600 m), depending on mission-related maximum weight
Landing run: 2,297 ft (700 m) with brake chute

Armament

Cannon armament of two 30-mm DEFA 552 cannon with 125 rounds per gun. Basic IIIC interceptor version with centreline pylon for one radar-guided missile, initially Nord 5103 or MATRA R.511, subsequently MATRA R530 (Hughes AIM-26 Falcon on Swiss aircraft). Two wing pylons for infrared guided missile, either AIM-9B/P Sidewinder or MATRA R550 Magic. Attack capability in form of JL-100 fuel tank/rocket pod. Mirage IIIE multi-role aircraft introduced a maximum of five pylons with a maximum weapon load of 8,818 lb (4000 kg), including most free-fall bombs and rocket pods. Attack missiles include Aérospatiale AS30 and MATRA AS37 Martel. French aircraft wired for 15-kT yield AN52 tactical nuclear free-fall bomb.

FACTS

- The Mirage III was Europe's first delta-winged aircraft to enter production.
- The Mirage III has been in service for more than 50 years, although not continuously with any one air arm.
- Early Mirages had an additional built-in rocket motor to boost speed during an interception.

"The Mirage comes nowhere close to the Viper [Lockheed Martin F-16] in air combat, but for its role, surface attack, it's a beautiful platform." – Squadron Leader Sameen Mazhar, Pakistan Air Force Mirage and F-16 pilot

DASSAULT MIRAGE III – MAJOR VARIANTS

Mirage III-001: Prototype, powered by a 4490-kg (9,900-lb) Atar 101G2 turbojet engine.

Mirage IIIA: Pre-production aircraft, powered by a 6.000 kg (13,228 lb) Atar 9B turbojet engine.

Mirage IIIB: Two-seat tandem trainer aircraft.

Mirage IIIB-1: Trials aircraft.

Mirage IIIB-2(RV): Inflight refuelling training aircraft.

Mirage IIIBE: Two-seat training aircraft for the French Air Force, similar to the Mirage IIID.

Mirage IIIBJ: Export version of the Mirage IIIB for Israeli Air Force. Five built.

Mirage IIIBS: Export version of the Mirage IIIB for the Swiss Air Force. Four built.

Mirage IIIBZ: Export version of the Mirage IIIB for the South African Air Force. Three built.

Mirage IIIC: Single-seat all-weather interceptor fighter aircraft, equipped with a Cyrano Ai radar, powered by a 6000-kg (13,228-lb) thrust Atar 9B-3 turbojet engine. 95 built for the French Air Force.

Mirage IIICJ: Export version of the Mirage IIIC for the Israeli Air Force. 72 built.

Mirage IIICS: One evaluation and test aircraft for the Swiss Air Force.

Mirage IIICZ: Export version of the Mirage IIIC for the South African Air Force. 16 built.

Mirage IIID: Two-seat trainer version of the Mirage IIIE.

Mirage IIIDA: Export version of the Mirage IIID for the Argentine Air Force.

Mirage IIIDBR: Export version of the Mirage IIID for the Brazilian Air Force.

Mirage IIIDE: Export version of the Mirage IIID for the Spanish Air Force.

Mirage IIIDL: Export version of the Mirage IIID for the Lebanese Air Force.

Mirage IIIDP: Export version of the Mirage IIID for the Pakistan Air Force.

Mirage IIIDS: Export version of the Mirage IIID for the Swiss Air Force.

Mirage IIIDZ: Export version of the Mirage IIID for the South African Air Force.

Mirage IIID2Z: Same as IIIDZ, but fitted with an Atar 9K-50 turbojet engine.

Mirage IIIS: Single-seat all-weather interceptor fighter aircraft for the Swiss Air Force.

DASSAULT MIRAGE III

Known as the "Shakak" in Israeli Air Force service, this Mirage IIICJ wears the badge of 116 Tayseet (squadron) on the fin, although this was not a known user of the type. The badge may have been a disinformation ploy to make Mirage numbers seem higher. One of 70 Mirages acquired between 1962 and 1964, Shakak 771 sports 11 victory markings from the 1967 Six-Day War between Israel and the neighbouring states of Syria, Jordan and Egypt. Although 771 is shown sporting Shafrir AAMs, all the Mirage kills in 1967 were scored with cannon. Nearly 20 surviving Mirage IIICJs were sold to Argentina to make up losses suffered in the Falklands conflict.

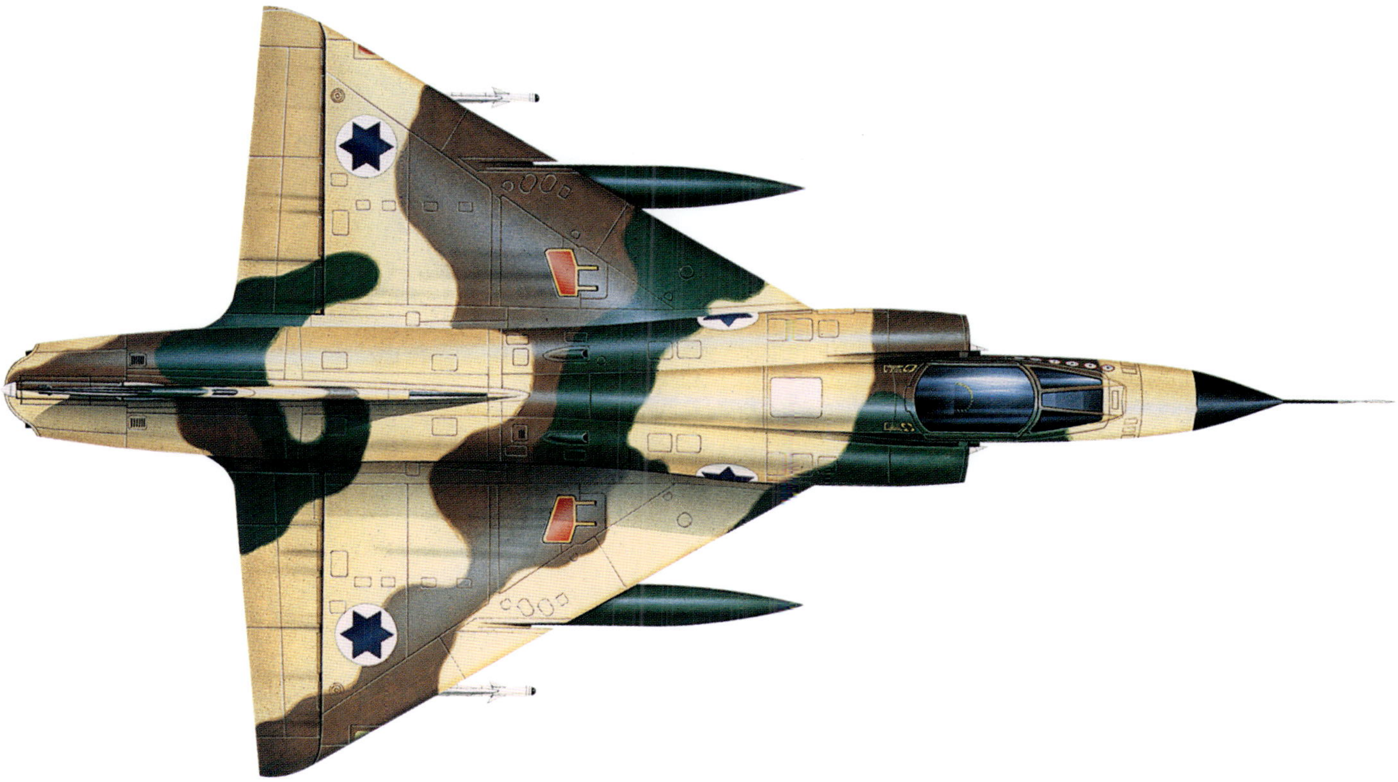

After the straight-winged Ouragan and swept-winged Mystère, Dassault turned to the fashionable new delta wing, which promised low drag and high performance. The Mystère Delta was a small single-engined testbed flown in 1955. It was rebuilt with two jet engines and a rocket motor, becoming the Mirage I, and the design was scaled up into the Mirage III in late 1956.

The operational Mirage IIIA interceptor was fitted with two 30-mm cannon, a single air-to-air missile (usually a Matra R.530 or Nord 5103) and special underwing fuel tanks carrying rockets in the forward ends. The first major version was the Mirage IIIC, which was used by the Armée de l'Air as an interceptor and exported to Israel and South Africa.

In 1967, Israel's Mirages were heavily used in fighting against the air forces of Egypt, Syria, Jordan and Iraq. and claimed more than 60 "kills." Seven Mirage III losses were admitted in return. Most victories were scored with the cannon, although later combats saw use of the AIM-9B Sidewinder and Israeli-designed missiles such as the Shafrir.

A GROWING CUSTOMER LIST

The Mirage IIIE was a version with greater ground-attack capability and was sold to a dozen nations. Switzerland and Australia built their own versions under licences from Dassault. Israel's requirements were behind the Mirage V, which had a slimmer nose and simplified avionics. The V was optimized for longer-range low-level attack missions,

Above: There were dedicated reconnaissance versions of both the Mirage III and V fighters. Distinctions between the IIIE and V were mainly internal.

Above: South Africa's Mirage IIICZs were successful in the "bush wars" of the 1970s and 1980s in both the air-to-air and attack roles.

Above: A few Mirage IIIRs remained in French service with the CEV national test organization at Cazaux into the 2000s.

but in the end never served with Israel because France imposed an arms embargo after the Six-Day War in 1967. Other Middle Eastern countries and a number of African and Latin American ones did, however, become enthusiastic customers for the Mirage V. The V had lower operating costs and maintenance requirements than rivals such as the Lockheed F-104 Starfighter, for example, and was free of restrictions on the export of U.S. technology, which suited many non-aligned nations.

OVERCOMING THE EMBARGO

Frustrated by the French sales ban, Israel managed to obtain the plans of the Mirage V in one of the largest espionage operations ever undertaken. Israel Aircraft Industries (IAI) reverse-engineered the aircraft, producing a modified version called the "Nesher" (Eagle), which was very successful in the 1973 Yom Kippur War. Renamed the Dagger, most of these aircraft were sold to Argentina by 1980 and two years later saw action over the Falkland Islands. Operating at extreme range, Argentina's Mirage IIIs and Daggers had little fuel for dogfighting by the time they reached the islands, and 13 were shot down, most by BAE Sea Harriers firing AIM-9L Sidewinders. Still, the Daggers managed to inflict serious damage on several Royal Navy ships with free-fall bombs.

PROLONGED SERVICE

Switzerland was the last European nation to fly the first-generation Mirages, but they live on in Africa, Pakistan and South America. Several upgrade programmes have been undertaken, resulting in such variants as the Atlas Cheetah in South Africa and ENAER Pantera in Chile, which have longer noses and canard foreplanes, and numerous other derivatives elsewhere with modernized cockpits and avionics, but fewer outward differences from the original design.

Northrop F-5 Freedom Fighter/Tiger II

The Northrop F-5 is a nimble, low-cost fighter and close air support aircraft that has been exported to many nations. Apart from its limited use in Vietnam, the F-5 has mainly been used by U.S. forces to simulate MiGs for air-combat training purposes.

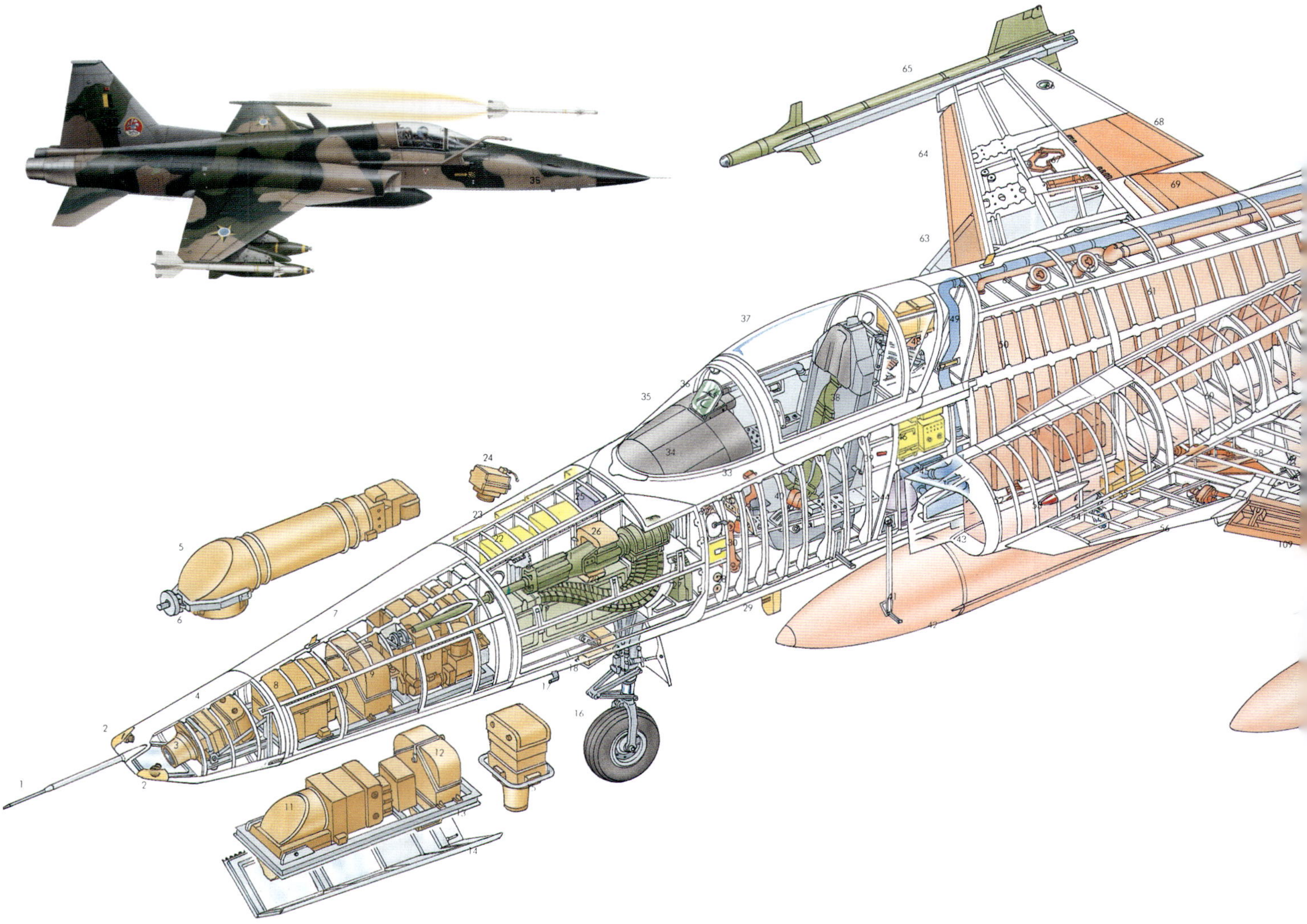

Cutaway Key

1 Pilot head
2 Forward radar-warning antennas
3 KS-87B forward camera, station 1
4 Forward camera compartment
5 Pallet 3, HIAC-1 Long-Range Oblique Photography (LOROP) camera, requires reconfigured window aperture panel
6 LOROP camera rotary drive
7 Main camera compartment
8 Pallet 1 option, KA-95B medium-altitude panoramic camera, station 2
9 KA-56E low-altitude panoramic camera, station 3
10 RS-710 infrared linescanner, station 4
11 Pallet 2 option, KA-93B high-altitude panoramic camera, stations 2 and 3
12 KA-56E low-altitude panoramic camera, station 4
13 Camera-mounting pallet
14 Optical viewing panel, hinged to starboard
15 Optional vertical KS-87B camera replacing IR linescanner at station 4 of pallet 1
16 Forward-retracting nosewheel
17 Temperature probe
18 Gun gas venting retractable air scoop
19 Ammunition magazine, 280 rounds
20 Ammunition feed chute
21 Single M39A2 20-mm cannon
22 Central avionics equipment compartment
23 Avionics equipment relocated to starboard cannon bay
24 Television sighting camera, located at base of starboard cannon bay
25 Windscreen de-icing fluid tank
26 Gun gas venting air ducts
27 Cartridge-case ejector chute
28 Static ports
29 UHF/IFF antenna
30 Rudder pedals
31 Canopy emergency release
32 Position of angle-of-attack transmitter on starboard side
33 Control column
34 Instrument panel shroud
35 Frameless windscreen panel
36 AN/ASG-31 lead computing gunsight
37 Upward-hinged canopy
38 Pilot's lightweight rocket-powered ejection seat
39 External canopy handle
40 Engine throttle levers
41 Fold-out boarding steps
42 275-U.S. gal (1041-litre) centreline fuel tank
43 Port engine air intake
44 Liquid oxygen converter
45 Cabin air-conditioning plant
46 Rear avionics equipment bay, port and starboard access
47 Electro-luminescent formation lighting strip
48 Canopy hinge arms and hydraulic actuator
49 Engine bleed air duct to air-conditioning heat exchanger
50 Forward fuel cell, bag-type tanks, total internal capacity 677 U.S. gal (2563 litres)
51 Inverted flight reservoir
52 Pressure refuelling connection

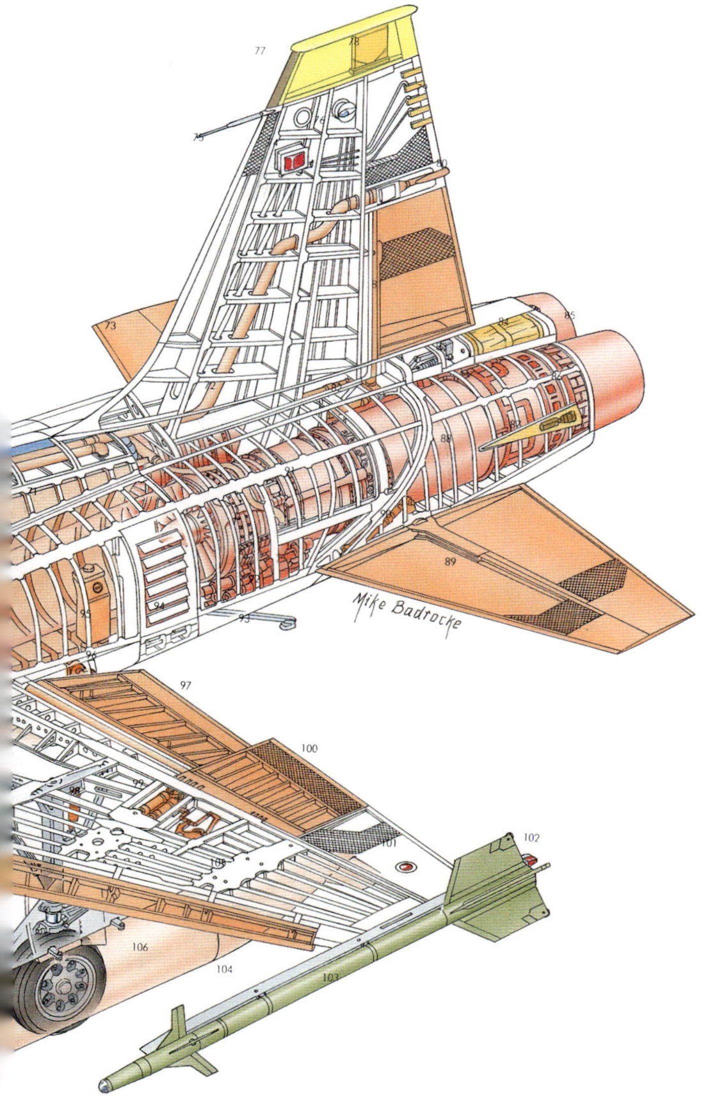

53 Port navigation light
54 Ventral retractable landing light
55 Missile control relay boxes
56 Wing leading-edge root extension
57 Leading-edge flap actuator
58 Ventral airbrake panel, port and starboard
59 Airbrake hydraulic jack
60 Intake ducting
61 Centre fuselage fuel cell
62 Gravity fuel fillers
63 Starboard wing tank pylon
64 Leading-edge manoeuvring flap
65 Wingtip missile installation
66 Starboard position light
67 Aileron control linkage
68 Starboard aileron
69 Starboard plain flap
70 Fuel feed pipes
71 Rear fuselage fuel cell
72 Fuel jettison pipe
73 Starboard all-moving tailplane
74 Anti-collision flashing beacon
75 Pressure head
76 Tail position light
77 Fintip antenna fairing
78 UHF antenna
79 Trailing-edge communications antennas
80 Fuel jettison
81 Rudder
82 Rudder and hydraulic actuators
83 Parachute anchorage and release link
84 Brake parachute housing
85 Exhaust nozzle shrouds
86 Variable-area afterburner nozzle
87 Rear radar warning antenna, port and starboard
88 Afterburner ducting
89 Port all-moving tailplane
90 Tailplane pivot mounting and hydraulic actuator
91 General Electric J85-GE-21 afterburning engine
92 Engine accessory equipment
93 Runway emergency arrestor hook
94 Engine auxiliary air intake doors
95 Hydraulic reservoir, dual systems port and starboard
96 Flap actuator, electro-mechanical
97 Port plain flap
98 Main undercarriage leg mounting and hydraulic retraction jack
99 Aileron tandem hydraulic actuators
100 Port aileron
101 Port position light
102 Navigation light repeater
103 AIM-9L Sidewinder air-to-air missile
104 Missile launch rail
105 Outboard pylon hardpoint (unused)
106 150-U.S. gal (568-litre) external fuel tank
107 Port mainwheel
108 External tank pylon
109 Port leading-edge manoeuvring flap

F-5E TIGER II SPECIFICATION

Dimensions

Length including probe: 47 ft 4¾ in (14.45 m)
Height: 13 ft 4½ in (4.08 m)
Wingspan without wingtip AAMs: 26 ft 8 in (8.13 m)
Wingspan with wingtip AAMs: 28 ft (8.53 m)
Wing area: 186.00 sq ft (17.28 m²)
Wing aspect ratio: 3.82
Tailplane span: 14 ft 1½ in (4.31 m)
Wheel track: 12 ft 5½ in (3.80 m)
Wheelbase: 16 ft 11½ in (5.17 m)

Powerplant

Two General Electric J85-GE-21B turbojets each rated at 3,500 lb st (15.5 kN) dry and 5,000 lb st (22.2 kN) with afterburning

Weights

Empty: 9,558 lb (4349 kg)
Maximum takeoff: 24,664 lb (11,187 kg)

Fuel and load

Maximum internal fuel: 677 U.S. gal (2563 litres)
Maximum external fuel: up to three 275-U.S. gal (1040-litre) auxiliary drop tanks
Maximum ordnance: 7,000 lb (3175 kg)

Performance

Maximum level speed "clean" at 36,000 ft (10,975 m): 917 kt (1,056 mph; 1700 km/h)
Cruising speed at 36,000 ft (10975 m): 562 kt (647 mph; 1041 km/h)
Maximum rate of climb at sea level: 34,300 ft (10 455 m) per minute
Service ceiling: 51,800 ft (15590 m)
Takeoff run: 2,000 ft (610 m) at 15,745 lb (7142 kg)
Takeoff distance to 50 ft (15 m): 2,800 ft (853 m) at 15,745 lb (7142 kg)
Landing run: 2,450 ft (747 m) at 11,340 lb (5143 kg) with brake parachute

Range

Ferry range: 2,010 nm (2,314 miles; 3720 km) with empty auxiliary tanks dropped
Combat radius: 760 nm (875 miles; 1405 km) with two AIM-9 Sidewinder air-to-air missiles

Armament

Two 20-mm Pontiac (Colt-Browning) M39A2 cannon in fuselage nose with 280 rounds per gun; two AIM-9 Sidewinder air-to-air missiles on wingtip launchers and up to 7,000 lb (3175 kg) of mixed ordnance on one underfuselage and four wing hardpoints, including M129 leaflet bombs, 500-lb (227-kg) Mk 82 and Snakeye bombs, 2000-lb (907-kg) Mk 84 bomb, various air-launched rockets, CBU-24, -49, -52 or -58 cluster bomb units and SUU-20 bomb and rocket packs. Can also be adapted to carry AGM-65 Maverick, a centreline multiple ejector rack and laser-guided bombs

"The F-5 could do everything the Super Sabre could do except stay as long over the target."
– Lieutenant Colonel Jim Porter, F-5 "Skoshi Tiger" pilot

FACTS

- The F-5G or F-20 was a single-engined derivative offered in the 1980s that did not enter production.
- The RF-5E Tigereye is a dedicated reconnaissance version with a long camera nose.
- After retiring the F-5E in the mid-1990s, the US Navy re-introduced it for adversary training in 2006.

NORTHROP F-5 FREEDOM FIGHTER/TIGER II – FIGHTER VARIANTS

SINGLE-SEAT VERSIONS

N-156F: Fighter prototype. Only three aircraft were built.

YF-5A: Three prototypes given the U.S. Air Force designation YF-5A.

F-5A: Fighter version.

F-5A (G): Fighter version of the F-5A for the Royal Norwegian Air Force.

A-9: Designation of Spanish-built F-5A.

F-5C Skoshi Tiger: 12 F-5A Freedom Fighters were tested by the U.S. Air Force for four and a half months in Vietnam.

F-5E Tiger II: Fighter version.

F-5E Tiger III: Upgraded F-5E in use by the Chilean Air Force.

F-5G: Temporary designation given to the F-20 Tigershark.

F-5N: Ex-Swiss Air Force F-5Es used by the U.S. Navy.

F-5S: Upgraded F-5E used by the Republic of Singapore Air Force.

F-5T Tigris: Israeli upgrade version of the F-5E of Royal Thai Air Force.

F-5EM: Upgraded F-5E of Brazilian Air Force.

F-5TIII: Upgraded F-5E in service with the Royal Moroccan Air Force.

TWO-SEAT VERSIONS

F-5-21: Temporary designation given to the YF-5B.

F-5B: Fighter version for the Republic of Korea Air Force.

F-5T: Upgraded F-5F in use by the Republic of Singapore Air Force.

FOREIGN VARIANTS – LICENSED VERSIONS

CF-5: Fighter versions for the Canadian Forces Air Command.

NF-5A: Single-seat fighter version of the CF-5A for the Royal Netherlands Air Force. 75 built.

SF-5A: Single-seat fighter version of the F-5A for the Spanish Air Force.

SF-5B: Two-seat training version of the F-5B for the Spanish Air Force.

VF-5A: Single-seat version of the CF-5A for the Venezuelan Air Force.

KF-5E: F-5E built in South Korea for Republic of Korea Air Force.

KF-5F: F-5F built in South Korea for Republic of Korea Air Force.

UNLICENSED VERSIONS

Azarakhsh: F-5E built in Iran with unknown modifications and a mid-wing.

Sa'eqeh: F-5E modified in Iran with canted, twin vertical stabilizers.

NORTHROP F-5 FREEDOM FIGHTER/TIGER II

Under the code name "Skoshi Tiger," a small number of F-5Cs were evaluated in Vietnam by a U.S. Air Force unit called the 10th Fighter Commando Squadron. The F-5C was a version of the F-5A modified on the production line for this mission. Around 200 lb (90 kg) of armour was added to the underside, as were a new gunsight and extra wing pylons. A refuelling probe could be fitted to the left side of the cockpit. This aircraft flew the most missions of any of the Skoshi Tiger aircraft between November 1965 and April 1967, when the aircraft were handed over to South Vietnam. It is shown armed with four BLU-1 napalm tanks.

Above: The U.S. Air Force and U.S. Navy have both used F-5s for dissimilar air combat training. As a small and simple dogfighter, it simulates the Mikoyan-Gurevich MiGs and other light fighters used by many potential adversaries.

Northrop offered various designs for a light fighter to the U.S. Air Force and U.S. Navy under the designation N-156 during the 1950s, but met little interest. The U.S. Air Force did have a requirement for a jet trainer to replace the subsonic T-33, however, and in 1956 selected a version of Northrop's design, which became the T-38 Talon. Northrop revised this design to build a private-venture prototype called the N-156F, which flew in July 1959.

The N-156F suited the needs of the U.S. Military Assistance Program (MAP), which aimed to bolster the armed forces of the United States' allies in the face of nations aligned with the Soviet Union and receiving Soviet military aid. In 1962, Northrop's aircraft, now called the F-5A Freedom Fighter, was chosen to be part of the programme.

The F-5A and two-seat F-5B had two General Electric J85 engines with afterburners, an "area-ruled" fuselage that was pinched in at the midpoint, and a pointed nose with an oval cross section. There was no fire-control radar and the two 20-mm cannon mounted above the nose were aimed with a simple cockpit sight. Wingtip tanks were usually fitted and there were five pylons for bombs, rockets, gun pods or missiles such as the AGM-12 Bullpup under the wings and fuselage.

EXPERIMENTAL DEPLOYMENT

The United States initially showed no interest in the F-5, but a shortfall in tactical aircraft in Vietnam led to an experimental deployment called "Skoshi Tiger," where a dozen F-5As and Bs were used for close-support missions over South Vietnam. While quite effective, they had limited range and faced opposition from generals who preferred to keep their more sophisticated fighters. At the end of the combat evaluation, the surviving F-5s were handed to the South Vietnamese Air Force.

Among other nations that received Freedom Fighters totally or partially funded under MAP were: Iran, South Korea, Turkey, Greece, Norway, Yemen, Jordan, Libya, Morocco, Taiwan and the Philippines. Canadair in Canada produced them under licence as the CF-5A and B, and sold a further 105 to the Netherlands.

Above: Typical of 1970s combat aircraft, the F-5E's cockpit features a lot of mechanical dial instruments.

A NEW VERSION

The second-generation F-5 again began as a private venture of Northrop's. Its F-5A-21 proposal won a U.S. competition for an "international fighter" and was renamed the F-5E Tiger II in 1970. It had a larger wing than the F-5A with leading-edge root extensions, a more powerful version of the J85 engine and a simple radar in a reprofiled nose.

F-5Es and two-seat F-5Fs were produced until 1989 and sold to 20 nations. Some, including Switzerland and South Korea, built them under licence. Probably the most combat action was seen by Iran's F-5s, delivered before the 1979 revolution and used extensively against Iraq in 1980–88.

DISSIMILAR AIR COMBAT TRAINING

The U.S. Air Force, Navy and Marine Corps all acquired F-5Es and Fs, but not for frontline squadrons. The Vietnam experience had shown the need for dissimilar air combat training (DACT) to teach pilots and weapons systems operators how to fight smaller, more manoeuvrable opponents who used Soviet-style tactics. The U.S. Navy started the famous "TOPGUN" school using F-5s and A-4 Skyhawks as adversary aircraft and the U.S. Air Force instigated its own "aggressor" programme, also with F-5s. The Navy and Air Force programmes differed in detail, but each used F-5Es and Fs painted in pseudo-Soviet colour schemes acting as analogs of the MiG-21, which were a similar size with comparable perfomance. Regular fighter units training against F-5s learned lessons that were invaluable in the latter stages of the Vietnam War and in Operation Desert Storm.

Above: The F-5 was a great export success, particularly in the Far East, Middle East and Central and South America.

Sukhoi Su-15 "Flagon"

The Su-15 was a dedicated interceptor that rarely strayed beyond the borders of the Soviet Union, remaining firmly behind the Iron Curtain. It gained international notoriety when one shot down a civilian airliner in 1983, one of the deadliest incidents of the Cold War.

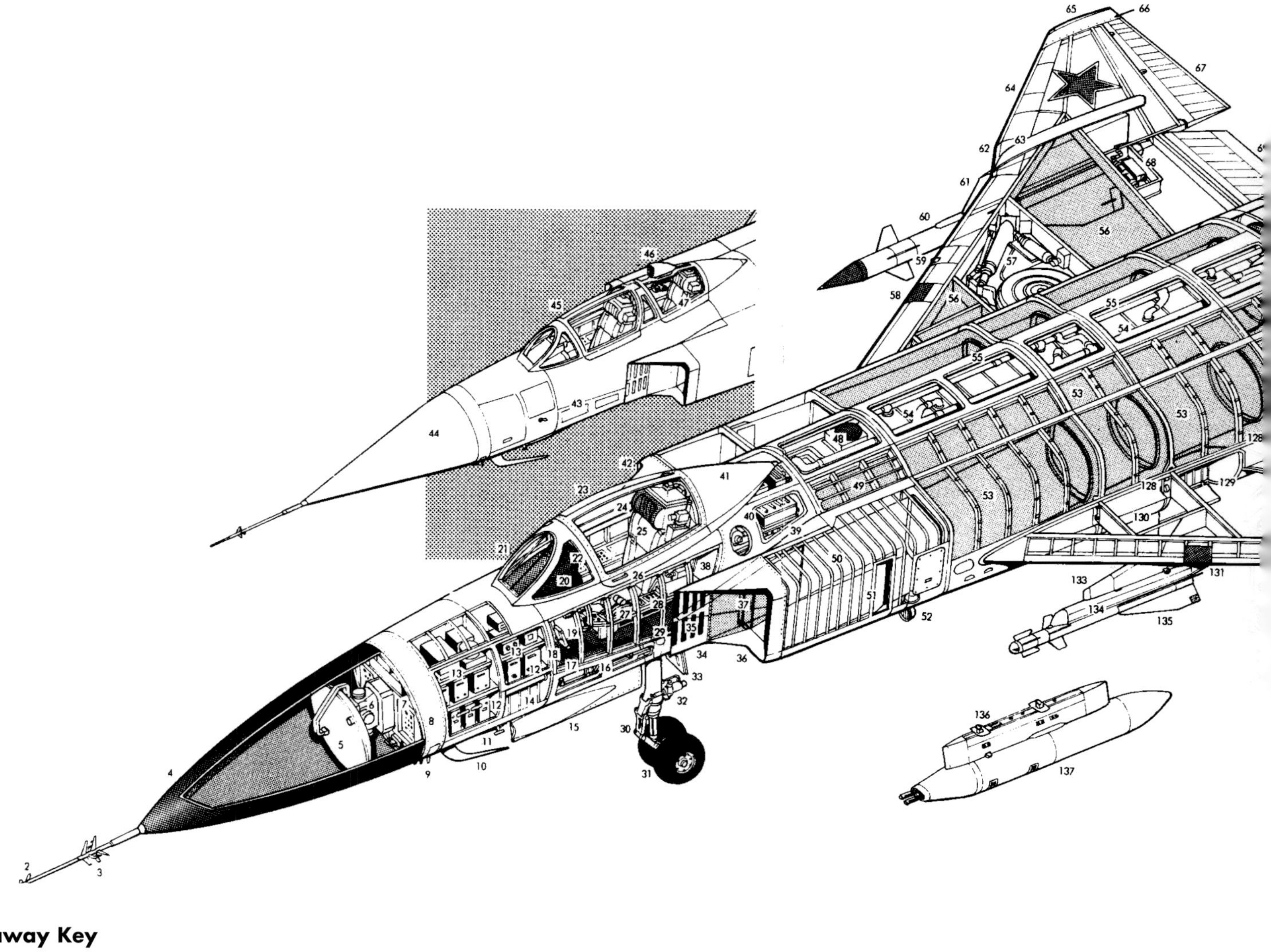

Cutaway Key

1 Instrumentation data probe
2 Yaw and pitch vanes
3 Fire control computer system transducers
4 Ogival-shaped fibreglass radome
5 Radar scanner
6 Scanner tracking mechanism
7 "Twin Scan" X-band radar equipment modules
8 Radar mounting bulkhead
9 SRO-2 "Odd Rods" IFF aerials
10 Communications aerial
11 Temperature probe
12 Nose avionics equipment compartments
13 Avionics equipment racks (SOD-57MATC/SIF navigation system)
14 Nose landing gear wheel bay
15 Nosewheel doors
16 Underfloor control linkages
17 Cockpit pressure floor level
18 Front pressure bulkhead
19 Rudder pedals
20 Instrument panel shroud
21 Armoured glass windscreen panel
22 Pilot's head-up display and attack sight
23 Sliding cockpit canopy cover
24 Ejector-seat headrest
25 Pilot's "zero-zero" ejector seat
26 Canopy latch
27 Engine throttle levers
28 Side console panel
29 Nose landing gear pivot fixing
30 Levered suspension nosewheel forks
31 Twin nosewheels, forward retracting
32 Hydraulic steering unit
33 Nosewheel leg door
34 Boundary layer splitter plate
35 Boundary layer bleed air perforations
36 Port engine variable-geometry air inlet
37 Variable-area movable ramp doors
38 Sloping cockpit rear pressure bulkhead
39 Boundary layer spill duct
40 Aft avionics and equipment bays
41 Canopy tail fairing
42 Starboard engine air inlet
43 SU-15 "Flagon-C" two-seat tandem training variant, nose profile
44 Original pointed radome profile
45 Student pilot's cockpit enclosure
46 Forward vision periscope
47 Instructor's cockpit enclosure
48 ADF aerial
49 Forward fuselage fuel tank
50 Inlet duct close-pitched framing
51 Spring-loaded inlet suction relief door, open
52 Retractable landing/taxiing lamp
53 Centre fuselage main fuel tanks
54 Dorsal control and pipe ducting
55 Dorsal equipment duct access panels
56 Starboard wing integral fuel tanks
57 Starboard main landing gear, retracted position
58 ECM system transmitting aerial
59 Radar warning antenna
60 AA-3 "Anab" air-to-air missile, radar-guided variant
61 Outboard stores pylon
62 Compound sweep leading edge
63 Wing fence
64 Cambered leading-edge section
65 Wingtip fairing
66 Static discharger
67 Port aileron
68 Aileron hydraulic actuator
69 Port plain flap, down position
70 Starboard engine bay
71 Engine bay cooling air intake
72 Fin-root fillet
73 Starboard upper airbake, open
74 Airbrake hydraulic jack
75 Fin-root attachment structure
76 Rudder hydraulic actuator
77 Tailfin construction
78 Starboard all-moving tailplane
79 Anti-flutter weight
80 Fin leading edge
81 Fintip UHF aerial fairing
82 RSIU (very short wave fighter control) aerial

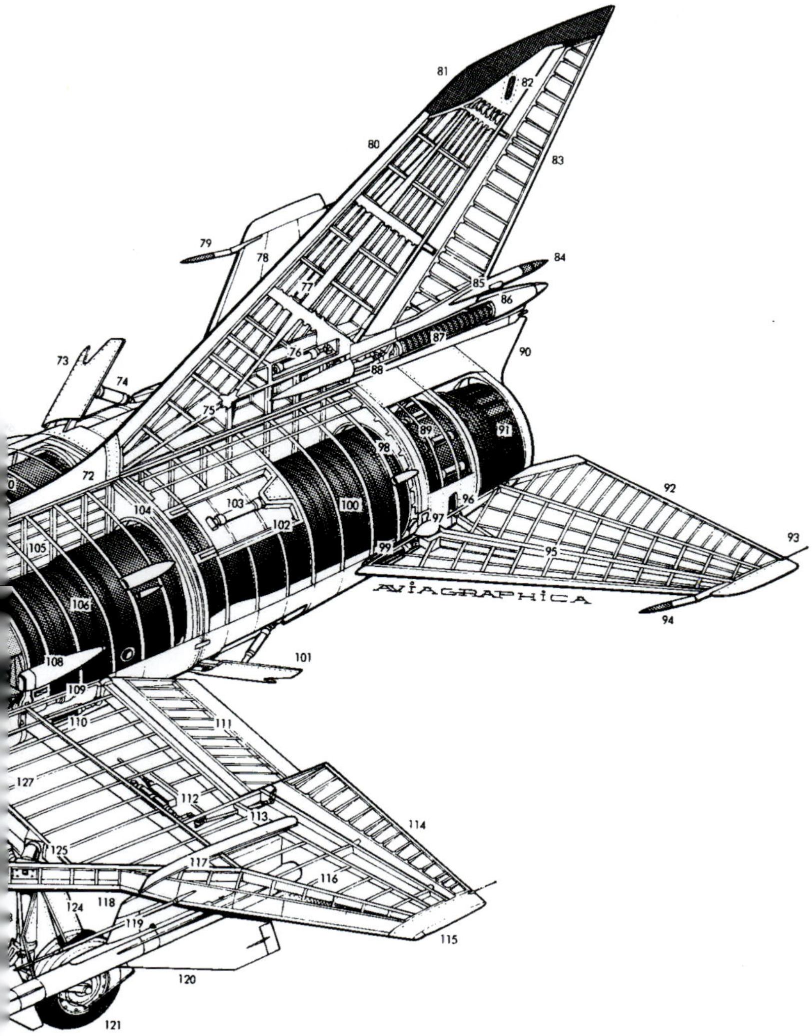

SUKHOI SU-15 "FLAGON"

Dimensions

Length: 67 ft 3 in (20.50 m)
Height: 16 ft 5 in (5.00 m)
Wingspan: 34 ft 6½ in (10.53 m)
Tailplane span: 20 ft ½ in (6.10 m)
Wheel track: 18 ft 4½ in (5.60 m)
Wheelbase: 20 ft 0 in (6.10 m)

Powerplant

Two Lyu'lka ALF-21F-3 afterburning turbojets rated at 22,200 lb (98.7 kN) with afterburner

Weights

Empty operating: 27,007 lb (12250 kg)
Maximum take-off: 35,274 lb (16000 kg)

Fuel and load

Internal fuel: 11,023 lb (5000 kg)
Maximum external weaponload: 3,307 lb (1500 kg)

Performance

Maximum level speed: Mach 2.5 (clean)
Maximum combat radius: 391 nm (450 miles; 725 km)
Initial climb rate: 44,950ft (13700m) per minute

Armament

Two R-98M/AA-3 "Anab" missiles on outer wing pylons; two or four R-60/AA-8 "Aphid" missiles on inner pylons; option of two UPK-23-250 23mm gun pods on fuselage pylons

83 Rudder
84 Sirena-3 tail warning radar
85 Rear ECM aerial
86 Split conic fairing parachute doors
87 Brake parachute housing
88 Parachute release linkage
89 Afterburner nozzle control jacks
90 Exhaust nozzle "Pen Nib" fairing
91 Variable-area afterburner nozzle
92 Port all-moving tailplane construction
93 Static discharger
94 Anti-flutter weight, upward-canted for ground clearance
95 Tailplane main spar
96 Tailplane limit stops
97 Pivot mounting
98 Fin/tailplane attachment main frame
99 Tailplane hydraulic actuator
100 Afterburner ducting
101 Port lower airbrake, open
102 Port upper airbrake housing
103 Airbrake hydraulic jack
104 Rear fuselage break point (engine removal)
105 Fireproof engine bay dividing bulkhead
106 Afterburning turbojet engine
107 Inlet compressor face
108 Engine accessory equipment cooling air intake
109 Accessory equipment gearbox
110 Flap hydraulic jack
111 Port plain flap, down position
112 Aileron hydraulic actuator
113 Aileron control linkage
114 Port aileron
115 Wingtip fairing
116 Extended chord outer wing panel
117 Wing fence
118 Port wing missile pylon
119 Pitot boom
120 AA-3 "Anab" air-to-air missile, infrared-guided version
121 Port mainwheel
122 Levered suspension axle beam
123 Leg rotating and shortening link
124 Mainwheel leg doors
125 Main landing gear leg pivot fixing
126 Hydraulic retraction jack
127 Port wing aft main fuel tank
128 Wing spar attachment joints
129 Mainwheel bay
130 Port wing forward main fuel tank
131 Radar warning antenna
132 ECM transmission aerial
133 Inboard stores pylon
134 Missile launch rail
135 AA-8 "Aphid" short-range air-to-air missile
136 Fuselage pylon (two)
137 GSh-23 gun pod (two)

Above: Few good images of the Su-15 on the ground were seen before the collapse of the USSR.

SUKHOI SU–15/21 "FLAGON" – VARIANTS

T-58: Prototype of Su-15.

Su-15 ("Flagon-A"): First production version.

T-58VD ("Flagon-B"): One-off prototype using three Kolesov lift jets in the centre fuselage to provide STOL capability. Not mass-produced.

Su-15UT ("Flagon-C"): Trainer version without radar and combat capability, in use since 1970.

Su-15 ("Flagon-D"): Version with extended wingtips built since 1969.

Su-15T ("Flagon-E"): Version equipped with Volkov Taifun radar. 10 built.

Su-15TM ("Flagon-F"): Improved Su-15T version equipped with Taifun-M radar and additional aerodynamic modifications, in use since 1971. New radome design for improving radar performances.

Su-15UM ("Flagon-G"): Trainer version of Su-15TM without radar but with combat capability, built between 1976 and 1979.

U-58UM: Prototype of Su-15UM with Taifun-M radar. Not entered into serial production.

Su-15Sh: Proposed supersonic ground-attack aircraft, offered in 1969. Not built.

Su-15-30: Proposed version sharing the radar and missiles of the Mikoyan-Gurevich MiG-25. Not built.

Su-15bis: Converted Su-15TM with R-25-300 engines of 15,652 lb (69.9 kN) afterburning thrust for improved performance; approved for series production, but not built because of a shortage of the engines.

Su-19: Proposed advanced version with R-25-300 engines, ogival wing and additional pylons for missiles. Not built.

"I did not tell the ground that it was a Boeing-type plane," he recalled. "They did not ask me."
– Su-15 pilot Colonel Gennadi Osipovich, who shot down KAL Flight 007 in 1983

SUKHOI SU-15/21 "FLAGON"

The profile view below depicts an Su-15TM "Flagon-F" in an unusual colour scheme. Most were fielded in unpainted natural metal, but three-tone brown and green colours were occasionally seen. The standard armament of the "Flagon" was the AA-3 "Anab" missile, which was used in both infrared- and radar-homing models. Normal practice was to ripple-fire both types at a target to ensure a kill. A 30-mm gun pod was also often carried, as were AA-8 "Aphid" short-range missiles. The "Flagon-F" was distinguished by its radome shape, which was ogival rather than conical. Radar was the Taifun-M system derived from that designed for the Mikoyan-Gurevich MiG-25 "Foxbat."

FACTS

- The "Flagon-C" was a single-seat trainer version that had no radar, weapons system or armament.
- The Taifun-M radar was able to detect a bomber at 37–44 miles (60–70 km) at high altitude.
- Azerbaijan and Georgia inherited Su-15s in the break-up of the Soviet Union, but made little or no use of them.

Following Sukhoi's Su-9 and Su-11 interceptors, which were single-engined and had radars with limited capabilities fitted in the intake shock cones, the Sukhoi Design Bureau began work on a twin-engined development with a large radar in the nose. Several prototypes based on modified Su-11s were tested before the T-58 appeared. This was chosen for production as the Su-15 and flew in May 1962.

Above: A "Flagon" pilot receives some last-minute instruction. Initiative was not highly valued in the Cold War era of the Su-15.

The first public showing of the Su-15 came at the 1967 Moscow Air Show. Official events such as this and flypasts such as on the annual Aviation Day were a deliberate flexing of military might on the part of the Kremlin. These also often represented the first time that outside observers, usually diplomats, were able to see new Soviet hardware, and the aircraft seen, however briefly, were the subject of intense study by Western intelligence agencies.

Dubbed "Flagon-A" by NATO, the Su-15 had two Tumanskii R-11 turbojet engines, a delta wing with 60-degree leading-edge sweep and a bubble canopy, with more rearward view than most contemporary Soviet jet fighters. Armament was only two AA-3 "Anab" missiles. This weapon was available in both radar-guided and infrared-guided forms. Usually one of each was carried, and fired in quick sequence to increase the probability of a kill.

SUCCESSIVE "VERSIONS"

The Su-15T "Flagon-D" appeared in 1969. It had a new, more powerful "Taifun" radar based on that used in the Mikoyan-Gurevich MiG-25 "Foxbat," and a redesigned wing with a noticeable kink in the profile. A boundary layer control system blew air over the flaps to increase their effectiveness and reduce takeoff and landing speeds.

NATO seemed to believe that the Su-15TM with Taifun-M radar was a new type and called it the Su-21, although this designation was never used by the Soviet Union. Su-15s were operated by the Soviet Air Defence Forces (Voyska PVO) and kept out of the limelight, apart from occasional appearances in Soviet magazines, propaganda films and the odd ceremonial flypast.

The Su-15TM "Flagon-F" could be equipped with two underwing 23-mm twin-barrel gunpods or R-60 (AA-8 "Aphid") short-range missiles. The radome shape changed in profile, from a conical shape to an ogival (roundly tapered) one, and the West called these aircraft "Flagon-F," although the Soviet designation remained the same. A more sophisticated data-link allowed ground control to fly the aircraft to an interception. The two-seat Su-15UM "Flagon-G" was the trainer version. Production of the Su-15 ended in 1979, after about 1,250 examples had been built.

AN INFAMOUS RECORD

As a home-defence interceptor, rarely if ever seen outside the Soviet Union, the Su-15 had far less of a public profile in the West than its contemporaries from Mikoyan-Gurevich. All this changed in September 1983, when an Su-15 flying from Sakhalin Island in the Russian far east shot down Korean Airlines Flight 007, a Boeing 747, with two AA-3 missiles. The incident resulted in the loss of 269 lives and an international outcry. It was chillingly similar to one in 1978 when a Korean Boeing 707 was damaged by an Su-15's missile, killing two passengers, but made a successful emergency landing on a frozen lake.

Also, in 1981, a Soviet Air Defence Forces Su-15 based in Baku, Azerbaijan, deliberately rammed an Argentine-registered Canadair CL-44 when it inadvertently strayed into Soviet airspace. The Argentine aircraft was returning to Cyprus via Turkey, on a covert flight to deliver arms from Israel to Iran, to help in the war against Iraq. All four people on board, including the apparent arms broker, were killed when the CL-44 slammed into a mountainside; the Soviet pilot survived after ejecting from his crashing jet.

LIMITED DISTRIBUTION

The "Flagon" was never exported or based in Warsaw Pact countries. Its possible only use outside Soviet borders was in a 1972 deployment to Egypt to boost local defence against Israel, although details are sparse.

The Su-15 was retired from Russian service in 1993, as part of the Conventional Forces in Europe (CFE) Treaty. Ukraine's air force inherited two squadrons' worth, and kept these in service until around 1996.

Above: The "Flagon-F" could be identified in plan view by the kinked wing leading edge. The "Flagon-A" had a smaller, pure delta wing.

Above: Amid the paranoia of the Cold War, the best views of the Su-15 came from encounters with Western fighters and patrol aircraft. This "Flagon-F" has a full load of AA-3 "Anab" and AA-8 "Aphid" missiles.

Mikoyan-Gurevich MiG-23 "Flogger"

Powerful and fast, the MiG-23 was the backbone of the Soviet Union's air-defence squadrons through the 1970s and 1980s, but was fairly soon outmoded by fly-by-wire Western fighters. A wide number of subvariants were supplied to Soviet allies and client states, but it has become increasingly rare in the 2000s.

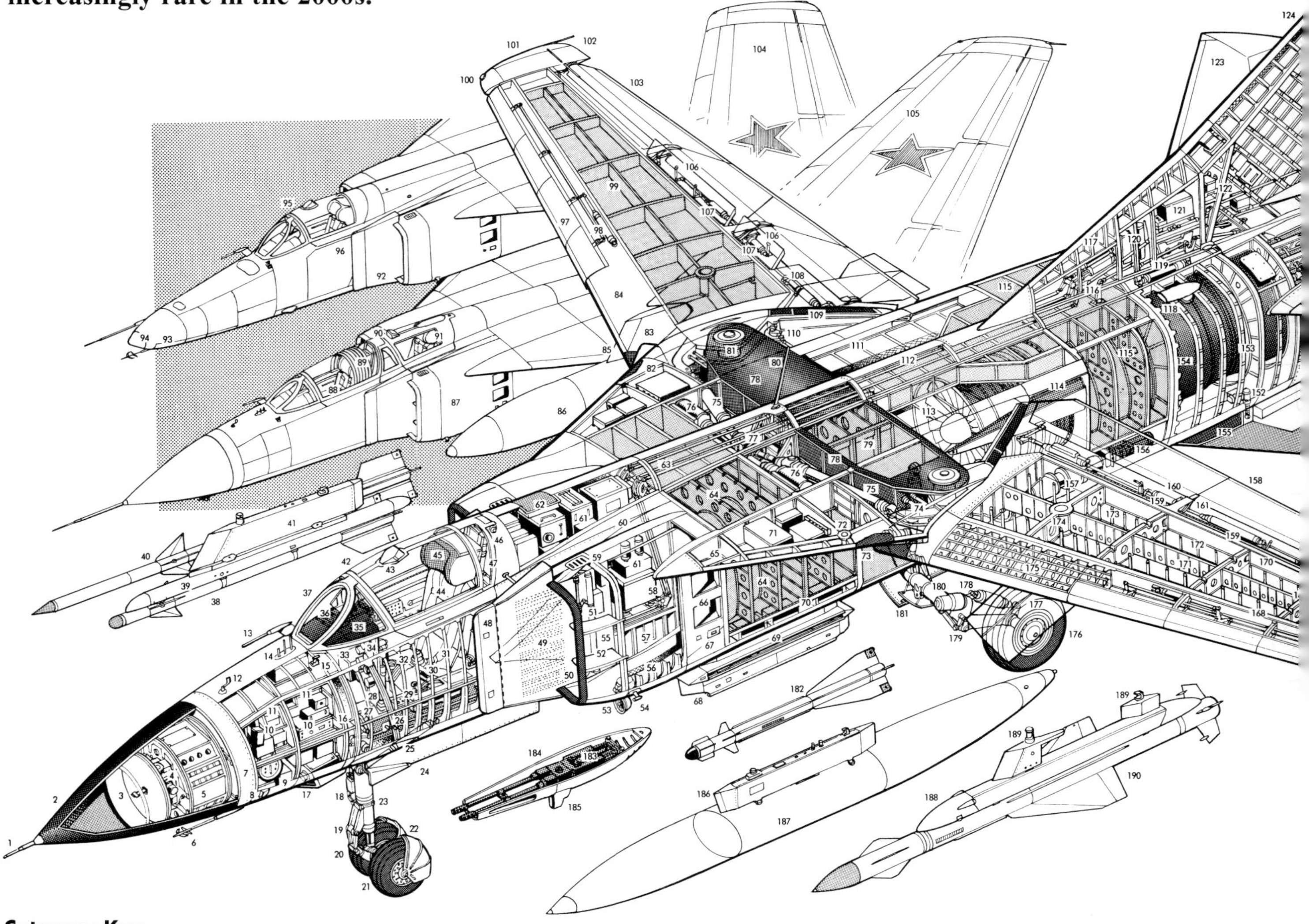

Cutaway Key

1 Pitot tube
2 Radome
3 Flat dish radar scanner
4 Scanner tracking mechanism
5 "High Lark" J-band pulse-Doppler radar module
6 "Swift-Rod" ILS aerial
7 Radar-mounting bulkhead
8 Cooling air scoop
9 Ventral doppler navigation aerial
10 Weapons system avionics equipment
11 Nose compartment access doors
12 Yaw vane
13 Dynamic pressure probe (Q-Feel)
14 SRO-2 "Odd-Rods" IFF antenna
15 Temperature probe
16 Cockpit front pressure bulkhead
17 Ventral laser rangefinder
18 Nosewheel steering control
19 Torque scissor links
20 Pivoted axle beam
21 Twin aft-retracting nosewheels
22 Nosewheel spray/debris guards
23 Shock-absorber strut
24 Nosewheel doors
25 Hydraulic retraction jack
26 Angle-of-attack transmitter
27 Rudder pedals
28 Control column
29 L-position wing sweep control lever
30 Engine throttle lever
31 Cockpit section framing
32 Ejection-seat firing handles
33 Radar "head-down" display
34 Instrument panel
35 Instrument panel shroud
36 Weapons sighting unit "head-up" display
37 Armoured-glass windscreen panel
38 AA-2 "Atoll" K-13A infrared homing air-to-air missile
39 Missile launch rail
40 AA-2-2 Advanced "Atoll" radar homing air-to-air missile
41 Wing glove pylon
42 Cockpit canopy cover, upward-hinging
43 Electrically heated rear-view mirror
44 Pilot's "zero-zero" ejection seat
45 Ejection-seat headrest/drogue parachute container
46 Canopy hinge point
47 Canopy hydraulic jack
48 Boundary layer splitter plate
49 Boundary layer ramp bleed air holes
50 Port engine air intake
51 Adjustable intake ramp screw jack control
52 Intake internal flow fences
53 Retractable landing/taxiing lamp, port and starboard
54 Pressure sensor, automatic intake control system
55 Variable-area intake ramp doors
56 Intake duct framing
57 Ventral cannon ammunition magazine
58 Control rod linkages
59 Intake ramp bleed air ejector
60 Boundary layer spill duct
61 Avionics equipment
62 ADF sense aerial
63 Tailplane control rods
64 Forward fuselage fuel tanks
65 Wing glove fairing
66 Intake duct suction relief doors
67 Ground power and intercomm sockets
68 Twin missile carrier/launch unit
69 Port fuselage stores pylon

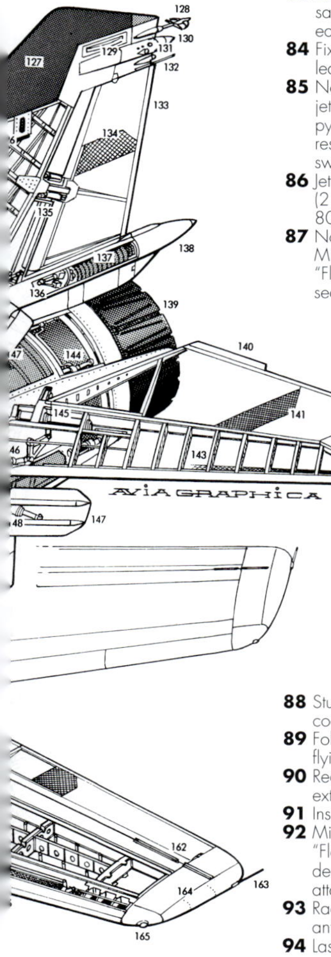

70 Weapons system electronic control units
71 Electronic countermeasures equipment
72 Wing glove pylon attachment fitting
73 SO-69 "Sirena-3" radar warning and suppression aerials
74 Wing sweep control horn
75 Screw jack wing sweep rotary actuator
76 Twin hydraulic motors
77 Central combining gearbox
78 Wing pivot box carry-through unit (welded steel construction)
79 Pivot box integral fuel tank
80 VHF aerial
81 Wing pivot bearing
82 Starboard "Sirena-3" radar warning and suppression aerials
83 Extended-chord sawtooth leading edge
84 Fixed portion of leading edge
85 Non-swivelling, jettisonable wing pylon (wing restricted to forward swept position)
86 Jettisonable fuel tank (211-U.S. gal/ 800-litre capacity)
87 Nose section of MiG-23U "Flogger-C" tandem seat trainer
88 Student pilot's cockpit
89 Folding blind flying hood
90 Rear-seat periscope, extended
91 Instructor's cockpit
92 MiG-23BN "Flogger-F" dedicated ground-attack variant
93 Radar-ranging antenna
94 Laser-ranging nose fairing
95 Raised cockpit canopy
96 Armoured fuselage side panels
97 Starboard wing leading-edge flap (lowered)
98 Leading-edge flap hydraulic actuator
99 Starboard wing integral fuel tank (total fuel capacity 1,519 U.S. gal/ 5750 litres)
100 Starboard navigation light
101 Wing fully forward (16° sweep) position
102 Static discharger
103 Full-span 3-segment plain flap (lowered)
104 Starboard wing intermediate (45° sweep) position
105 Starboard wing full (72° sweep) position
106 Two-segment spoilers/lift dumpers (open)
107 Spoiler hydraulic actuators
108 Flap hydraulic jack
109 Wing glove flexible seal
110 Flap mechanical interconnection and disengage mechanism
111 Wingroot housing
112 Dorsal spine fairing
113 Engine intake compressor face
114 Wingroot housing sealing plate
115 Rear-fuselage fuel tanks
116 Tailplane control linkages
117 Fin-root fillet
118 Afterburner duct cooling air scoop
119 Artificial feel control units
120 Control system hydraulic accumulator
121 Artificial feel and autopilot controls
122 Tailplane trim controls
123 Starboard all-moving tailplane
124 Fin leading edge
125 Tailfin construction
126 Short-wave ground-control communications aerial
127 Fintip UHF aerial fairing
128 ILS aerial
129 ECM aerial
130 "Sirena-3" tail warning radar
131 Tail navigation light
132 Static discharger
133 Rudder
134 Honeycomb core construction
135 Rudder hydraulic actuators, port and starboard
136 Parachute release links
137 Brake parachute housing
138 Split conic fairing parachute doors
139 Variable-area afterburner nozzle
140 Fixed tailplane tab
141 Honeycomb core trailing-edge panel
142 Static discharger
143 Port all-moving tailplane construction
144 Afterburner nozzle control jacks (6)
145 Tailplane pivot bearing
146 Tailplane actuator
147 Airbrakes (4), upper and lower surfaces
148 Airbrake hydraulic jacks
149 Afterburner duct heat shroud
150 Ventral fin, folded (undercarriage down) position
151 Ventral fin down position
152 Screw jack fin actuator
153 Fin attachment fuselage main frame
154 Tumanskii R-29B afterburning turbojet engine
155 Lower UHF aerial
156 Engine accessory equipment compartment
157 Air-conditioning system equipment
158 Port plain flap
159 Spoiler actuators
160 Port spoilers/lift dumpers
161 Flap guide rails
162 Fixed spoiler strips
163 Static discharger
164 Wingtip fairing
165 Port navigation light
166 Port leading-edge flap
167 Leading-edge flap control linkage
168 Front spar
169 Wing rib construction
170 Rear spar
171 Auxiliary centre spar
172 Wing skin support struts
173 Port wing integral fuel tank
174 Wing pylon attachment fitting
175 Leading-edge rib construction
176 Port mainwheel
177 Mainwheel door/ debris guard
178 Shock-absorber strut
179 Pivoted axle beam
180 Articulated mainwheel leg strut
181 Mainwheel leg doors
182 AA-8 "Aphid" (R-60) short-range air-to-air missile
183 GSh-23L twin-barrel 23-mm cannon
184 Ventral cannon pack
185 Gun gas venting air scoop
186 Fuselage centreline pylon
187 Ventral fuel tank (211-U.S. gal/ 800-litre capacity)
188 "Apex" missile launch rail
189 Launch rail attachment hardpoints
190 AA-7 "Apex" (R-23) long-range air-to-air missile

MIG-27 "FLOGGER-D" SPECIFICATION

Dimensions

Wingspan (spread): 45 ft 9⅘ in (13.97 m)
Wingspan (swept): 25 ft 6¼ in (7.78 m)
Wing aspect ratio (spread): 5.22
Wing aspect ratio (swept): 1.77
Tailplane span: 18 ft 10¼ in (5.75 m)
Wing area (spread): 402.05 sq ft (37.35 m²)
Wing area (swept): 367.71 sq ft (34.16 m²)
Length (including probe): 56 ft ¼ in (17.08 m)
Wheel track: 8 ft 8¾ in (2.66 m)
Wheelbase: 18 ft 11¼ in (5.77 m)
Height: 16 ft 5 in (5.00 m)

Powerplant

One Soyuz/Khachaturov R-29B-300 turbojet rated at 17,625 lb st (78.40 kN) dry and 25,335 lb st (112.77 kN) with afterburning

Weights

Empty equipped: 26,252 lb (11,908 kg)
Normal takeoff: 39,903 lb (18,100 kg)
Maximum takeoff: 44,753 lb (20,300 kg)

Fuel and load

Internal fuel: 10,053 lb (4560 kg), or 1,427 U.S. gal (5400 litres)
External fuel: Up to three 209-U.S. gal (790-litre) drop tanks
Maximum weapon load: 8,818 lb (4000 kg)

Performance

Maximum level speed "clean" at 26,245 ft (8000 m): 1,170 mph (1885 km/h)
Maximum level speed "clean" at sea level: 839 mph (1350 km/h)
Maximum rate of climb at sea level: 39,370 ft (12,000 m) per minute
Service ceiling: 45,930 ft (14,000 m)
Takeoff run at maximum takeoff weight: 3,117 ft (950 m)
Landing run at normal landing weight (without brake parachute): 4,265 ft (1300 m)
Landing run at normal landing weight (with brake parachute): 2,953 ft (900 m)

Range

Combat radius: 335 miles (540 km) on a lo-lo-lo attack mission with two Kh-29 ASMs and three drop tanks, or 140 miles (225 km) with two Kh-29 ASMs

Armament

One 23-mm GSh-23L twin-barrelled cannon in underfuselage pack; two bomb or JATO hardpoints either side of rear fuselage, plus five further hardpoints for the carriage of tactical nuclear bombs; Kh-23 (AS-7 "Kerry") and Kh-29 (AS-14 "Kedge") ASMs; 9½-in (240-mm) S-24 rockets, 2¼-in (57-mm) UB-32 or UB-16 rocket packs; 22 110-lb (50-kg) or 220-lb (100-kg) bombs, or nine 551-lb (250-kg) bombs, or eight 1,102-lb (500-kg) bombs; napalm containers or R-3S/K-13T (AA-2D "Atoll-D") and R-13M AAMs

"Iraq's MiG-23s had some success against Iran's Northrop F-5s, McDonnell Douglas F-4 Phantoms and even F-14s."

MIKOYAN-GUREVICH MIG-23 "FLOGGER" – VARIANTS

FIRST GENERATION

MiG-23 ("Flogger-A"): The pre-production model. This model marked the divergence of the MiG-23/-27 and Sukhoi Su-24 from their common ancestor.

MiG-23S ("Flogger-A"): The initial production variant.

MiG-23SM ("Flogger-A"): The second pre-production variant, which was also known as the MiG-23 Type 1971. It was considerably modified compared to the MiG-23S.

MiG-23M ("Flogger-B"): The first truly mass-produced version of the MiG-23, and the first Soviet Air Force (VVS) fighter to feature look-down/shoot-down capabilities. This variant first flew on June 1972.

MiG-23MF ("Flogger-B"): An export derivative of the MiG-23M to Warsaw Pact countries and other allies and clients. Some 1300 MiG-23Ms were produced for the Soviet Air Force (VVS) and Soviet Air Defense Forces (PVO Strany) between 1972 and 1978. It was the most important Soviet fighter type from the mid- to late 1970s.

MiG-23U ("Flogger-C"): A twin-seat training variant.

MiG-23UB ("Flogger-C"): Very similar to MiG-23U except that the R-29 turbojet engine replaced the older R-27 installed in the MiG-23U.

MiG-23MP ("Flogger-E"): Similar to the MiG-23MS, but produced in much fewer numbers and never exported.

MiG-23MS ("Flogger-E"): An export variant, as the 1970s MiG-23M was considered too advanced to be exported to developing countries.

SECOND GENERATION

MiG-23P ("Flogger-G"): A specialized air-defence interceptor variant with the same airframe and powerplant as the MiG-23ML, but with a cutback fin-root fillet instead of the original extended one on other models. Not exported.

MiG-23bis ("Flogger-G"): Similar to the MiG-23P.

MiG-23ML: A considerable redesign of the airframe with refined aerodynamics, manoeuvrability, new engine and thrust-to-weight ratio.

MiG-23MLA ("Flogger-G"): The later production variant of the "ML." Cooperative group search operations were now possible because the radars would not jam each other.

MiG-23MLD ("Flogger-K"): The ultimate fighter variant of the MiG-23 with improved manoeuvrability.

GROUND-ATTACK VARIANTS

MiG-23BM ("Flogger-D"): A MiG-23BK upgrade, with a digital computer replacing the original analog one.

MiG-23BM: The MiG-23BM experimental aircraft served as a predecessor to the MiG-27.

MiG-23B ("Flogger-F"): The MiG-23 appeared suitable for conversion to fit the new requirement for a late 1960s fighter-bomber.

MiG-23BK ("Flogger-H"): Exported to Warsaw Pact countries.

MiG-23BN ("Flogger-H"): The MiG-23BN was the definitive fighter-bomber variant. Extensively exported.

MiG-27: A simplified ground-attack version with simple pitot air intakes, no radar and a simplified engine with two-position afterburner nozzle.

UPGRADES

MiG-23K: A carrier-borne fighter variant based on the MiG-23ML.

MiG-23A: A multi-role variant based on the "K."

MiG-23-9: A late 1990s upgrade.

MiG-23-98-2: An export upgrade including the Saphir radar fitted to their MiG-23MLs.

MiG-23LL (flying laboratory): MiG-23s and MiG-25s were used as the first jet-fighter platforms to test a new in-cockpit warning system with a pre-recorded female voice designed to inform pilots about various flight parameters.

FACTS

- The Mikoyan-Gurevich MiG-23 was the Soviet Union's first variable-geometry fighter.
- Unlike most other "swing-wing" aircraft, the MiG-23 possessed a wing that swept into one of three angles, rather than being fully variable.
- A ventral fin under the rear fuselage was needed for inflight stability, but could be swung out of the way for landing.

Above: A "Flogger" pilot and a mechanic discuss a technical point before a mission is undertaken.

MIKOYAN-GUREVICH MIG-23 "FLOGGER"

Libyan air power is organized along Soviet lines, with interceptors, surface-to-air missiles and radars assigned to Libyan Arab Air Defence Command, and transports, helicopters and fighter-bombers to the Libyan Arab Air Force. The country acquired 54 MiG-23MF and MS fighters in the mid-1970s, and later added a similar number of MiG-23BNs. In January 1989, Libya's "Floggers" repeated the mistake of its Sukhoi Su-22s and tangled with two U.S. Navy Grumann F-14 Tomcats over the Gulf of Sirte. Two MiG-23s were brought down, one by an AIM-9 and one by an AIM-7. Unable for many years to buy Western equipment due to embargoes, Libya has retained its MiG-23s into the 2010s. An Air Defence Command MiG-23MS is illustrated, armed with four AA-2 "Atoll" missiles.

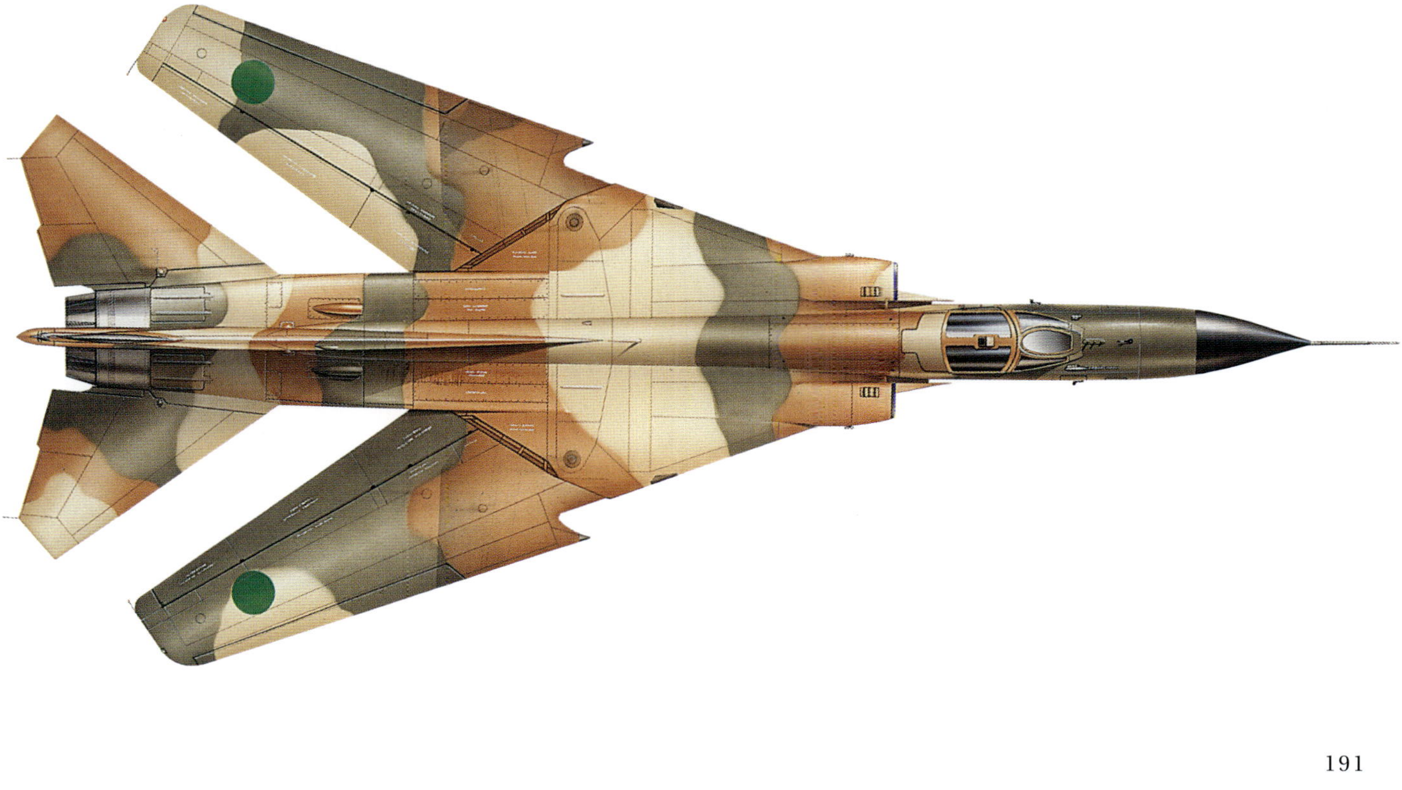

The MiG-23 began as an attempt to replace the MiG-21 with an aircraft that had higher flight performance, but shorter takeoff and landing distances and better handling at low speeds than were possible with the MiG-21's delta wing. Mikoyan-Gurevich first tried two lift jet engines in an enlarged delta-winged airframe, but this aircraft, designated the 23-01, was unsuccessful.

The aircraft regarded as the true MiG-23 prototype flew in June 1967. The 23-11 had variable-geometry wings with three sweep angles and a single Tumansky R-27 turbojet engine. It was soon chosen as the basis for the MiG-23 fighter, which would become known in the West by the NATO reporting name "Flogger."

WORKING TOWARD SUCCESS

The original MiG-23S "Flogger-A" was built in relatively small numbers and issued only to the VVS (Voenno-Vozdushnye Sily – Soviet Air Force), and never achieved full operational status. The MiG-23M "Flogger-B" was the first truly successful model. It had "High Lark" pulse-Doppler radar and an infrared search and track (IRST) system for passive detection of enemy aircraft. This version was used by the VVS and the PVO (Soviet Air Defence Forces).

Above: A close-up of the instruments and HUD of the front cockpit of a Czech Air Force MiG-23 two-seater.

Above: The MiG-23-98 was a upgrade programme offered for export customers. Among other improvements, it enabled the use of R-73 (AA-11 "Archer") and RVV-AE (AA-12 "Adder") missiles.

Above: Although it has retired its MiG-23s, India remains a big user of the MiG-27 "Flogger-M," which it calls "Bahadur" (Valiant).

Downgraded MiG-23MS "Flogger-E" export models went to Algeria, Libya and Syria. They had a simplified radar and no beyond-visual-range missile capability. Syrian "Floggers" were destroyed in large numbers by the Israeli Air Force, mainly during the invasion of Lebanon in 1982. Libya lost two in an engagement with U.S. Navy Grumann F-14s in 1989.

WIDESPREAD EXPORT

The MiG-23 was supplied to all of the Warsaw Pact air forces, plus many communist nations and non-aligned India. In Europe, Bulgaria, Romania, Czechoslovakia, East Germany, Hungary and Poland were MiG-23 users. Since the end of the Cold War, former Soviet republics including Belarus, Ukraine and Kazakhstan have also operated the MiG-23, but the "Flogger" is now gone from Europe and the former Soviet Union. In East Asia, Vietnam and North Korea are the only users, but China did receive several Egyptian MiG-23s in the late 1970s, with a view to reverse-engineering.

Many of Iraq's MiG-23s were lost in the 1991 Gulf War, and two dozen fled to Iran, where they were incorporated into that nation's air force. Ironically, in the Iran-Iraq war (1980–88), Iraq's MiG-23s had some success against Iran's Northrop F-5s, McDonnell Douglas F-4 Phantoms and even F-14s. PVO MiG-23s destroyed several Iranian helicopters that crossed the Soviet Union's borders in the 1980s.

MiG-23s also saw combat in conflicts between South Africa and Angola, Afghanistan and Pakistan, Ethiopia and Eritrea, and in other hotspots around the world. While effective as a ground-attacker, the "Flogger" increasingly lost out when faced by more modern aircraft such as the McDonnell Douglas F-15 and Lockheed Martin F-16.

INTERIM MODEL

MiG-23s, usually regarded as fighters, overlap with dedicated ground-attack MiG-27s. The MiG-23BN "Flogger-F" had a derated engine and improved navigation/attack system. Its radar was replaced by a "duck-bill" nose containing a laser rangefinder and an optical bombsight. Widely exported, the Mig-23BN saw combat in Indian skirmishes with Pakistan. Regarded as an interim type by the Soviets, it evolved into the MiG-27 "Flogger H," used mainly within the Soviet Union and by Cuba, India and Sri Lanka, where they still serve.

SAAB 37 Viggen

The supersonic Viggen was built for the particular requirements of Sweden and served the country well for 25 years. It continued Sweden's traditional posture of independence in military technology and neutrality in defence.

JA 37 VIGGEN SPECIFICATION

Dimensions

Length: 53 ft 9¾ in (16.40 m)
Height: 19 ft 4¼ in (5.90 m)
Wingspan: 34 ft 9¼ in (10.60 m)
Wing area: 495.16 sq ft (46.00 m²)
Canard foreplane span: 17 ft 10½ in (5.45 m)
Canard foreplane area: 66.74 sq ft (6.20 m2)
Wheel track: 15 ft 7½ in (4.76 m)
Wheelbase: 18 ft 8 in (5.69 m)

Powerplant

One Volvo Flygmotor RM8B turbofan (Pratt & Whitney JT8D-22 with Swedish-designed afterburner and thrust reverse) rated at 16,600 lb st (73.84 kN) maximum military dry and 28,109 lb st (125 kN) with afterburning

Weights

Normal takeoff: 33,069 lb (15,000 kg)
Maximum takeoff interceptor: 37,478 lb (17,000 kg)
Maximum takeoff attack: 45,194 lb (20,500 kg)

Fuel and load

Internal fuel: 1,506 U.S. gal (5700 litres)

Performance

Maximum level speed "clean" at 36,000 ft (10,975 m): More than 1,147 kt (1,321 mph; 2126 km/h)
Climb to 32,800 ft (10,000 m): Less than 1 minute 40 seconds from brakes off with afterburning
Service ceiling: 60,000 ft (18,290 m)
Takeoff run at typical takeoff weight: 1,312 ft (400 m)
Landing run: 1,640 ft (500 m) at normal landing weight
Combat radius on hi-lo-hi mission: 539 nm (621 miles; 1000 km)
Combat radius on lo-lo-lo mission: 270 nm (311 miles; 500 km)

Armament

Primary armament consists of six AAMs. The standard beyond-visual-range (BVR) weapon is the medium-range semi-active radar-guided all-weather BAeD Rb 71 Sky Flash. Rb 74 (AIM-9L) IR-homing Sidewinders are fielded for short-range work. The JA 37 also has an integral 30-mm Oerlikon KCA revolver cannon with 150 rounds. Seven to nine pylons accommodate up to 13,000 lb (5987 kg) of external stores. These include four pods each containing six Bofors 5.3-in (135-mm) rockets for air-to-surface use

Cutaway Key

1 Pitot head
2 Fibreglass radome
3 Radar scanner housing
4 LM Ericsson PS-37/A radar equipment module
5 Incidence probe
6 Cockpit pressure bulkhead
7 Forward avionics equipment bay
8 Rudder pedals
9 Instrument panel shroud
10 One-piece frameless windscreen panel
11 Pilot's head-up display
12 Upward-hinging cockpit canopy
13 Ejection seat arming lever
14 Saab rocket-powered ejection seat
15 Engine throttle lever
16 Boundary layer splitter plate
17 Port air intake
18 Landing/taxiing lamp
19 Twin nosewheels, forward retracting
20 Hydraulic steering control
21 Red Baron multisensor reconnaissance pod
22 Centreline external fuel tank
23 Electro-luminescent formation lighting strip
24 Central avionics equipment bay
25 Intake ducting
26 Boundary layer spill duct
27 Forward fuselage integral fuel tank
28 Dorsal avionics equipment bay
29 Starboard canard foreplane
30 Canard flap
31 SATT AQ31 ECM jamming pod
32 SSR transponder aerial
33 Anti-collision light
34 Air-conditioning equipment bay
35 Heat exchanger air exhaust
36 Intake flank fuel tankage
37 Engine compressor face

38 Accessory equipment gearbox
39 Foreplane spar attachment joint
40 Fuselage flank avionics equipment bays, port and starboard
41 Emergency ram air turbine
42 Port canard foreplane flap honeycomb panel
43 Hydraulic reservoirs
44 Formation lighting strip
45 Centre fuselage integral fuel tankage
46 Main engine mounting
47 Volvo Flygmoto RM8A afterburning turbofan engine
48 Engine bleed air pre-cooler
49 Fuel-cooled engine oil cooler
50 Wing spar attachment fuselage main frame
51 Fuel system recuperators
52 ADF aerial
53 Starboard wing panel
54 Outboard missile pylon
55 ECM antenna fairing
56 Extended-chord outboard leading edge
57 Starboard navigation light
58 Starboard elevon panels
59 Artificial feel system pressure head
60 Fin tip aerial fairing
61 Multi-spar fin construction
62 Rudder hydraulic actuator
63 Fin spar attachment joints
64 Hydraulic hand pump for hangaring fin folding
65 Port lateral airbrake
66 Airbrake hydraulic jack
67 Afterburner ducting
68 Variable-area afterburner nozzle control jack
69 Exhaust duct ejector seal (closed at speeds above Mach 1)
70 Ejector seal screw jack
71 Thrust reverser door pneumatic actuator
72 Radar warning antennas
73 Engine/afterburner exhaust nozzle
74 Thrust reverser blocker doors
75 Tail navigation light
76 Lower thrust reverser door pneumatic actuator
77 Port inboard elevon
78 Elevon hydraulic actuators
79 Elevon honeycomb construction
80 Port outboard elevon
81 Port navigation lights
82 Outboard elevon hydraulic actuator
83 Saab Bofors Rb 24 (licence-built Sidewinder) air-to-air self-defence missile
84 Missile launch rail
85 ECM antenna fairing
86 Bofors BOZ-9 flare launcher pod
87 Wing stores pylon
88 Honeycomb wing skin panels
89 Multi-spar wing panel construction
90 Wing panel integral fuel tank
91 Main spar
92 Main undercarriage wheel bay
93 Side breaker strut
94 Hydraulic retraction jack
95 Main undercarriage mounting rib
96 Mainwheel leg strut
97 Torque scissor links
98 Tandem mainwheels
99 Starboard fuselage pylon
100 Long-range camera pod
101 Rb 05A air-to-surface missile
102 Rb 04E air-to-surface anti-ship missile
103 Missile launch adaptor

"The feeling of flying the Viggen can be expressed in one word: force. After flying the Viggen for 18 years I am still impressed by it." – Flygvapnet pilot Major Michael Rosenquist

FACTS

- The Viggen was the first fighter to have a canard-delta configuration.
- "Viggen" is the Swedish name for the thunderclap made by the hammer of the Norse god Thor.
- The JAS 39 Gripen replaced the last operational Viggens in Swedish service in 2006.

SAAB 37 VIGGEN – VARIANTS & OPERATORS

AJ 37: Primarily a single-seat ground-attack fighter aircraft, with a secondary fighter role. First delivery 1971. RM 8A powerplant. PS 37A radar. Partially decommissioned in 1998; some upgraded to AJS 37.

SK 37: Two-seat trainer aircraft; first delivery 1973.

SF 37: Single-seat photographic reconnaissance aircraft; first delivery 1975.

SH 37: Single-seat maritime reconnaissance and strike aircraft; first delivery 1975.

37E Eurofighter: Proposed NATO replacement of Lockheed F-104 Starfighter in 1975. None built.

37X: Proposed export version. None built.

JA 37: Primarily a single-seat all-weather interceptor fighter, with a secondary attack role; first delivery 1979. PS 46A LD/SD radar. Partially decommissioned in 1998; some upgraded to JA 37D.

AJS/AJSF/AJSH 37: Upgrade of some AJ/SF/SH 37 between 1993 and 1998; avionics and software upgrade. Decommissioned in 2005.

JA 37C: Upgrade of older JA 37; avionics and software upgrade.

JA 37D: Upgrade of older JA 37 between 1993 and 1998; avionics and software upgrade.

JA 37Di: Upgrade of older JA 37; avionics and software upgrade.

SK 37E: Electronic warfare trainer.

OPERATIONAL UNITS – SWEDISH AIR FORCE

F 4 Frösön
- 2 squadrons JA 37 1983–2003
- 1 squadron SK 37 1999–2003
- 1 squadron SK 37E 1999–2003

F6 Karlsborg
- 2 squadrons AJ 37 1978–93

F 7 Såtenäs
- 3 squadrons AJ 37 1972–98
- 1 squadron SK 37 1972–74

F 10 Ängelholm
- 1 squadron AJ/SF/SH 37 (combined) 1993–2001

F 13 Norrköping
- 1 squadron SF/SH 37 (combined) 1977–93
- 1 squadron JA 37 1980–93

F 15 Söderhamn
- 2 squadrons AJ 37 1974–98
- 1 squadron SK 37 1974–98

F 16 Uppsala
- 2 squadrons JA 37 1986–2003

F 17 Kallinge
- 1 squadron JA 37 1981–2002
- 1 squadron SF/SH 37 (combined) 1979–93
- 1 squadron JA 37 1993–2002

F 21 Luleå
- 2 squadrons JA 37 1983–2004
- 1 squadron SF/SH 37 1979–2002
- 1 squadron SK 37E (combined) 2003–07

SAAB SF 37 VIGGEN

Viggens were built in a number of specialized versions, including the SF 37 Viggen equipped for all-weather day and night missions (the "SF" denomination stood for "Spaning Foto" – photo reconnaissance). The chisel nose had ports for forward, downward and oblique-facing cameras. The front port was usually occupied by an infrared camera. For night photography, special pods were carried as shown here on this SF 37 of Flygvapnet (Swedish Air Force) F 13 at Norrköping-Bravalla. The pod on the left fuselage pylon contained flares and the right-hand pod the cameras. Usually unarmed, the SF 37 could be equipped with AIM-9Js for self-defence if needed.

The main drivers of the Saab 37 Viggen design were short-field performance and ease of maintenance. Convair and Dassault had proven that the delta wing offered great speed and combat performance, but had the disadvantage of a high landing speed. Saab's solution was to add a canard foreplane ahead of the wing, equipped with trailing-edge flaps. Canards had been used on various experimental aircraft and date back to the Wright Flyer, which had its pitch control surface at the front, but they had not appeared on a production jet fighter before.

The reason for the concentration on takeoff and landing performance was Sweden's dispersed base system, which would see fixed air bases abandoned and combat aircraft dispersed to pre-prepared stretches of straight road supported by a few mechanics and mobile ground equipment.

Above: The upgraded JA 37D cockpit included many features of the JAS 39A Gripen.

LANDING – AND TURNING – ON A DIME

The thrust reverser, powerful brakes on the large double wheels, canard flaps and airbrakes all contributed to the Viggen's short landing distance, even in snowy conditions. A Viggen could land in 1,640 ft (500 m), stop, turn around within the runway width and take off again in the same distance. The wheel arrangement was thinner than standard twin wheels, allowing them to fit inside a thin wing when retracted.

The prototype Saab 37 flew in February 1967; deliveries to the Flygvapnet (Swedish Air Force) began in 1971. Unlike the later Gripen, which incorporated several roles in one airframe, the Viggen was produced in separate versions for different missions. The first was the AJ 37 attack variant armed with bombs, rockets or the Rb 04 anti-shipping and

Above: An early JA 37 Viggen shows off a pair of RB 71 Skyflash missiles, which used the airframe of the U.S. AIM-7, but a British-designed seeker.

Above: The Viggen was famous for its stability at low level. Experienced pilots were cleared to operate down to 30 feet (10 m) in altitude over water, where the splinter camouflage was quite effective.

Rb 75 (AGM-75 Maverick) ground-attack missiles. The SH 37 for maritime reconnaissance had a new radar, but was otherwise similar to the attack Viggen. The SF 37 for day and night overland reconnaissance, however, had a chisel nose for optical cameras and could carry extra camera or sensor equipment in pods. The Sk 37 trainer had an unusual raised cockpit arrangement for the instructor pilot, but also required periscopes to give a forward view on landing. The first pure fighter version was the JA 37 Jakt Viggen (Viggen fighter), which had a new pulse-Doppler radar with better effectiveness against low-flying targets. Armament was Sidewinder and Skyflash missiles, as well as a ventral 30-mm cannon.

In their later years of service, the various Viggen variants were upgraded to meet modern standards. The fighter Viggens were modified to JA 37Ds with the ability to carry the AIM-120 AMRAAM and fitted with many of the avionics and cockpit displays of the JAS 39 Gripen, which was gradually replacing the Viggen. The attack Viggens went through a similar process to create the AJS 37, and some of the trainers became Sk 37E "Erik" electronic warfare training aircraft.

AN UNEXPLOITED EXPORT MARKET

Although it had potential for wide export sales as a Lockheed F-104 replacement, for example, the Viggen was never sold outside of Sweden. Neutrality policies and arms export restrictions of the Swedish government drove away most potential customers in the 1970s. Attempts to lease Viggens to potential Gripen customers such as Austria in the 1990s were also unsuccessful.

Grumman F-14 Tomcat

Grumman's F-14 was the most powerful and heavily armed naval fighter ever built. In the 1990s, precision attack was added to its repertoire, extending its career by a decade.

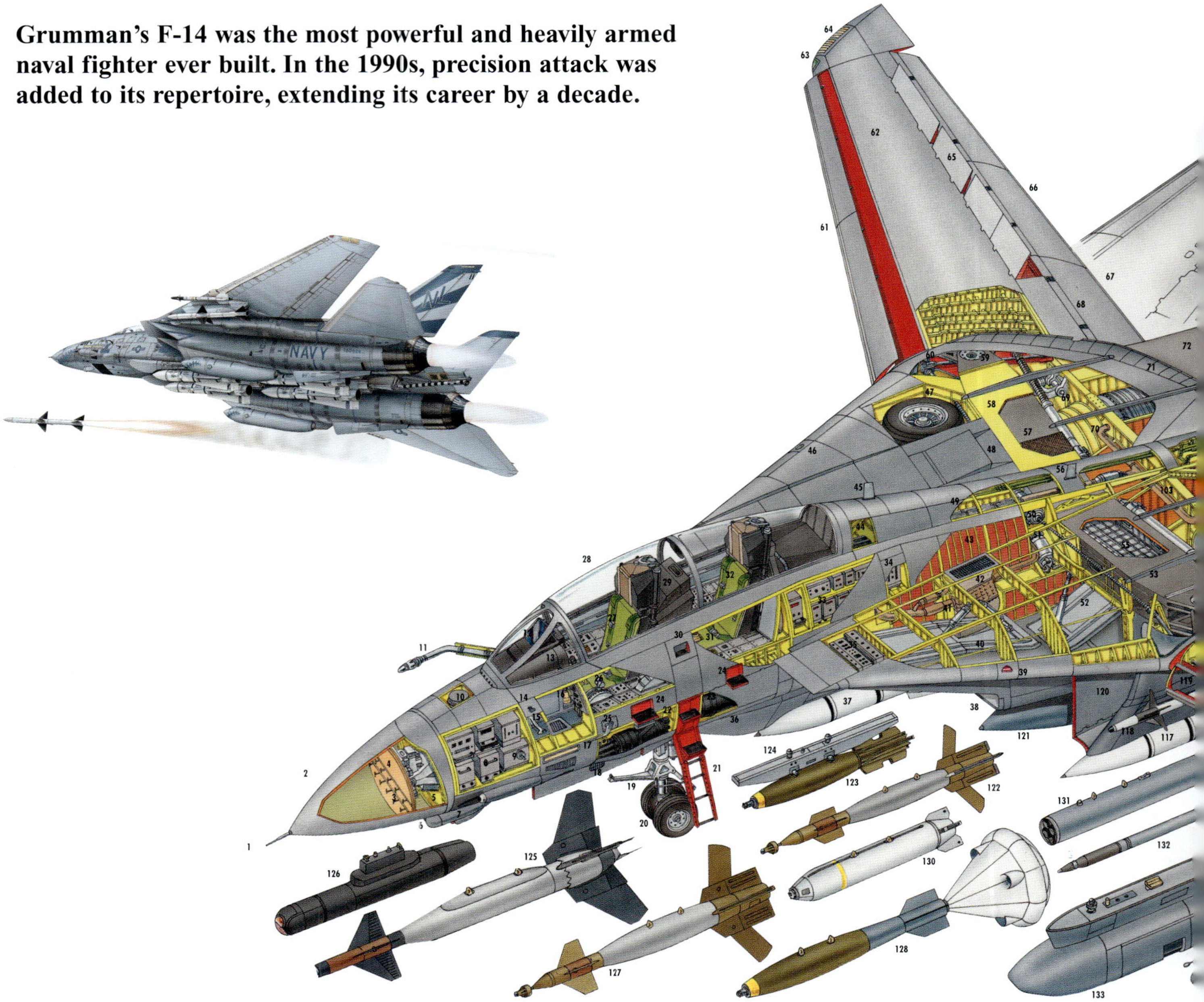

Cutaway Key

1 Pitot head
2 Fibreglass radome
3 IFF aerial array
4 AN/APG-71 flat plate radar scanner
5 Scanner tracking mechanism
6 Infrared search and track sensor (IRST) and television camera housing
7 Cannon port
8 Weapons system avionics equipment bay
9 Angle-of-attack transmitter
10 ADF aerial
11 Flight refuelling probe
12 Pilot's head-up display
13 Instrument panel shroud
14 Temperature probe
15 Rudder pedals
16 Control column
17 Electro-luminescent formation lighting strip
18 Nosewheel doors
19 Catapult strop link
20 Twin nosewheels, forward-retracting
21 Boarding ladder, extended
22 M61A1 Vulcan cannon
23 Ammunition drum
24 Pull-out steps
25 Pitot static head
26 Engine throttle levers
27 Pilot's Martin-Baker Mk 14 Navy Aircrew Common Ejection Seat (NACES)
28 Upward-hinged cockpit canopy cover
29 Naval flight officer's instrument console
30 Kick-in step
31 Tactical information display hand controller
32 NFO's ejection seat
33 Rear avionics equipment bay
34 Air data computer
35 Electrical system relays
36 Fuselage missile pallet
37 AIM-54A Phoenix air-to-air missile
38 Port engine air intake
39 Port navigation light
40 Variable-area intake control ramps
41 Intake ramp hydraulic actuators
42 Air-conditioning pack
43 Forward fuselage fuel tanks
44 Canopy hinge point
45 UHF/TACAN aerial
46 Starboard navigation light
47 Mainwheel stowed position
48 Starboard intake duct spill door
49 Dorsal control and cable duct
50 Central flap and slat drive hydraulic motor
51 Emergency hydraulic generator
52 Intake by-pass door
53 Electron-beam welded titanium wing pivot box
54 Port wing pivot bearing
55 Pivot box beam integral fuel tank
56 UHF datalink/IFF aerial
57 Honeycomb skin panels
58 Wing glove stiffeners
59 Starboard wing pivot bearing
60 Flap and slat drive shaft and gearbox
61 Starboard leading-edge slat
62 Wing panel fully forward position
63 Navigation light
64 Wingtip formation light
65 Roll control spoilers
66 Outboard manoeuvre flaps
67 Inboard high-lift flap
68 Flap sealing vane
69 Mainwheel leg hinge fitting
70 Variable wing-sweep screw jack
71 Wing glove sealing plates
72 Wing glove pneumatic seal
73 Starboard wing fully swept position
74 Starboard all-moving tailplane
75 Fintip aerial fairing
76 Tail navigation light
77 Starboard rudder
78 Rudder hydraulic actuator
79 Variable-area afterburner nozzle control jack
80 Dorsal airbrake (split ventral surfaces)
81 Chaff/flare dispensers
82 Fuel jettison
83 ECM antenna
84 Aluminium honeycomb fin skin panels
85 Anti-collision light
86 Formation lighting strip
87 ECM aerial
88 Port rudder
89 Variable-area afterburner nozzle

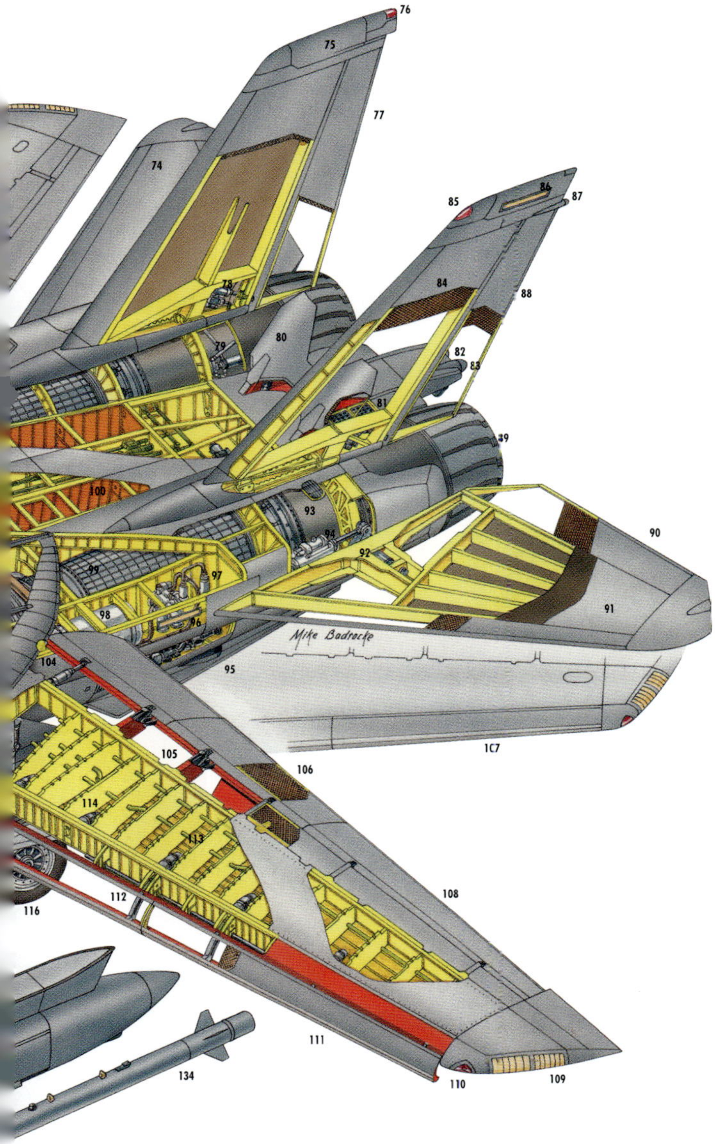

90 Port all-moving tailplane
91 Tailplane boron-fibre skin panels
92 Tailplane pivot bearing
93 Afterburner ducting
94 Tailplane hydraulic actuator
95 Ventral fin
96 Formation lighting strip
97 Hydraulic equipment bay
98 Hydraulic reservoir
99 General Electric F110-GE-400 afterburning turbofan engine
100 Rear fuselage fuel-tank bays
101 Flight control system linkages
102 Engine bleed air ducting
103 Port wing-sweep crew jack
104 Inboard high-lift flap hydraulic jack
105 Flap hinge links
106 Flap honeycomb construction
107 Port wing fully swept position
108 Port manoeuvre flaps
109 Wingtip formation light
110 Navigation light
111 Port leading-edge slat
112 Slat guide rails
113 Wing integral fuel tank
114 Machined wing rib construction
115 Main undercarriage leg strut
116 Port mainwheel, forward-retracting
117 Wing glove mounted AIM-54A Phoenix air-to-air missile
118 AIM-9L Sidewinder air-to-air missile
119 Wing glove pylon
120 Mainwheel door
121 External fuel tank
122 GBU-12D/B Paveway II 500-lb (227-kg) laser-guided bomb
123 Mk 82 Snakeye 500-lb (227-kg) retarded bomb
124 Phoenix pallet weapons adapter
125 GBU-24A/B Paveway III 2,000-lb (907-kg) laser-guided bomb
126 AN/AAQ-14 LANTIRN navigation and targeting pod, carried on starboard glove pylon
127 GBU-16 Paveway II 1,000-lb (454-kg) laser-guided bomb
128 Mk 83 AIR, 1,000-lb (454-kg) retarded bomb
129 Mk 83 AIR inflated ballute
130 Mk 7 submunition dispenser
131 LAU-97 four-round rocket launcher
132 5-in (127-mm) Zuni FFAR (folding-fin air rocket)
133 TARPS reconnaissance pod, carried in centreline tunnel
134 ALQ-167 countermeasures pod, carried on forward fuselage Phoenix pallet station

F-14A TOMCAT SPECIFICATION

Dimensions

Fuselage length (including probe): 62 ft 8 in (19.10 m)
Wing span: (unswept) 64 ft 1½ in (19.54 m); (swept) 38 ft 2½ in (11.65 m); (overswept) 33 ft 3½ in (10.15 m)
Wing aspect ratio: 7.28
Tailplane span: 32 ft 8½ in (9.97 m)
Overall height: 16 ft (4.88 m)
Wheel track: 16 ft 5 in (5.00 m)
Wheelbase: 23 ft 0½ in (7.02 m)

Powerplant

Two Pratt & Whitney TF30-P-412A/414A turbofans rated at 20,900 lb st (92.97 kN) with afterburning

Weights

Empty operating: 40,104 lb (18,191 kg)
Maximum takeoff: 72,000 lb (32,659 kg)

Fuel load

Total internal fuel: 2385 U.S. gal (9030 litres) [approx 16,200 lb/ 7348 kg] in six main tanks, comprising: forward fuselage tank 691 U.S. gal (2616 litres); rear fuselage tank 648 U.S. gal (2453 litres); combined left and right feed tanks 456 U.S. gal (1727 litres); wing tanks 295 U.S. gal (1117 litres) each
External fuel: two 267-U.S. gal (1011-litre) under-intake fuel tanks

Performance

Maximum level speed at altitude: 1,342 kt (1,544 mph; 2485 km/h)
Maximum level speed at low level: 792 kt (912 mph; 1468 km/h)
Limiting Mach numbers: 2.38 at altitude; 2.4 attained, but initially limited to 2.25 in service; 1.2 at low level
Maximum cruising speed: 550 kt (633 mph; 1019 km/h)
Maximum rate of climb at sea level: 30,000 ft (9140 m) per minute
Absolute ceiling: 56,000 ft (17,069 m)
Service ceiling: 50,000 ft (15,240 m) (F-14A); 53,000 ft (16,154 m) (F-14B/D)

Range

Combat air patrol endurance: (with four AIM-54s, two AIM-7, two AIM-9s and external fuel) 90 minutes at 150 nm (173 miles; 278 km); one hour at 253 nm (292 miles; 470 km)
Radius: (deck-launched intercept with four AIM-54s, two AIM-7s, two AIM-9s and external fuel) 171 nm (197 miles; 317 km) at Mach 1.3; 134 nm (154 miles; 248 km) at Mach 1.5
Ferry range: (F-14A with two tanks) 1,730 nm (2,000 miles; 3200 km); (F-14B with two tanks) 2,050 nm (2,369 miles; 3799 km)

Armament

One 0.787 in (20 mm) M61 Vulcan Gatling Gun, with 675 rounds
Ten hardpoints with a capacity of 14,500 lb (6,600 kg) of ordnance and fuel tanks including AIM-54 Phoenix, AIM-7 Sparrow, AIM-9 Sidewinder

"It's a beautiful airplane. It's powerful. It has presence, and it just looks like the ultimate fighter."
– Captain William Sizemore, Commander, Carrier Air Wing 8, U.S. Navy

FACTS

- The F-14 demonstrated the ability to fire six Phoenix missiles at six targets simultaneously, scoring five hits.
- Early Tomcats had "glove vanes," which extended from an area forward of the wings to allow better high-speed manoeuvrability, but these were disconnected to save weight and complexity.
- The F-14 Tomcat was the largest and heaviest fighter aircraft to operate from aircraft carriers.

GRUMMAN F-14 TOMCAT – VARIANTS & OPERATORS

F-14A: Initial two-seat all-weather interceptor fighter variant. The U.S. Navy received 478 F-14A aircraft. 79 were received by Iran.

F-14+ (F-14B): Upgraded engine and new radar. Redesignated F-14B in May 1991. Arrived in time to participate in Desert Storm.

F-14B Upgrade: In the late 1990s, 67 F-14Bs were upgraded to extend airframe life and improve offensive and defensive avionics systems.

F-14D: Final variant of the F-14 was the F-14D Super Tomcat. New engine and new avionics.

F-14D(R): Some F-14Ds received the ROVER III upgrade from 2005.

F-14C: A projected variant of the initial F-14B (F401-powered) with advanced multimission avionics.

UNITED STATES OPERATORS
United States Navy (USN) squadrons
Pacific Fleet
NFWS Navy Fighter Weapons School (TOPGUN) (Merged with Strike U to form Naval Strike and Air Warfare Center (NSAWC) 1996)
VF-1 "Wolfpack" (disestablished 1993)
VF-2 "Bounty Hunters" (redesignated VFA-2 with F/A-18F 2003)
VF-21 "Freelancers" (disestablished 1996)
VF-24 "Fighting Renegades" (disestablished 1996)
VF-51 "Screaming Eagles" (disestablished 1995)
VF-111 "Sundowners" (disestablished 1995; re-established as VFC-111 with F-5F 2006)
VF-114 "Aardvarks" (disestablished 1993)
VF-154 "Black Knights" (redesignated VFA-154 with F/A-18F 2003)
VF-191 "Satan's Kittens" (disestablished 1988)
VF-194 "Red Lightnings" (disestablished 1988)

Atlantic Fleet
VF-11 "Red Rippers" (redesignated to VFA-11 with F/A-18F in 2005)
VF-14 "Tophatters" (redesignated VFA-14 with F/A-18E 2001)
VF-31 "Tomcatters" (redesignated VFA-31 with F/A-18E 2006)
VF-32 "Swordsmen" (redesignated VFA-32 with F/A-18F 2005)
VF-33 "Starfighters" (disestablished 1993)
VF-41 "Black Aces" (redesignated VFA-41 with F/A-18F, 2001)
VF-74 "Bedevilers" (disestablished 1994)
VF-84 "Jolly Rogers" (disestablished 1995)
VF-102 "Diamondbacks" (redesignated VFA-102 with F/A-18F, 2002)
VF-103 "Sluggers"/"Jolly Rogers" (redesignated VFA-103 with F/A-18F, 2005)
VF-142 "Ghostriders" (disestablished 1995)
VF-143 "Pukin' Dogs" (redesignated VFA-143 with F/A-18E in 2005)
VF-211 "Fighting Checkmates" (redesignated VFA-211 with F/A-18F, 2004)
VF-213 "Black Lions" (redesignated VFA-213 with F/A-18F 2006)

Fleet Replacement Squadrons
VF-101 "Grim Reapers" (disestablished 2005)
VF-124 "Gunfighters" (disestablished 1994)

Naval Air Reserve Force Squadrons
VF-201 "Hunters" (redesignated VFA-201 with F/A-18A 1999, disestablished 2007)
VF-202 "Superheats" (disestablished 1999)
VF-301 "Devil's Disciples" (disestablished 1994)
VF-302 "Stallions" (disestablished 1994)

Squadron Augmentation Units
VF-1285 "Fighting Fubijars" (disestablished 1994) augmented VF-301 and VF-302
VF-1485 "Americans" (disestablished 1994) augmented VF-124
VF-1486 "Fighting Hobos" (disestablished 2005) augmented VF-101

GRUMMAN F-14 TOMCAT

The first U.S. Navy fleet squadron to receive the F-14 was VF-1 "Wolfpack," in July 1973. A VF-1 F-41A is seen in the early markings when assigned to the USS *Enterprise*, which represent the last period of widespread colour use on the U.S. Navy's carrier-based aircraft. The standard paint scheme of gull grey over white gave way to a mix of muted greys from the late 1970s. Colour was then mostly restricted to the air wing commander's assigned aircraft in each squadron. This F-14A is depicted "clean" without external weapons or fuel. A VF-1 Tomcat scored the only F-14 kill of the 1991 Gulf War when it destroyed an Iraqi Mi-8 "Hip" helicopter.

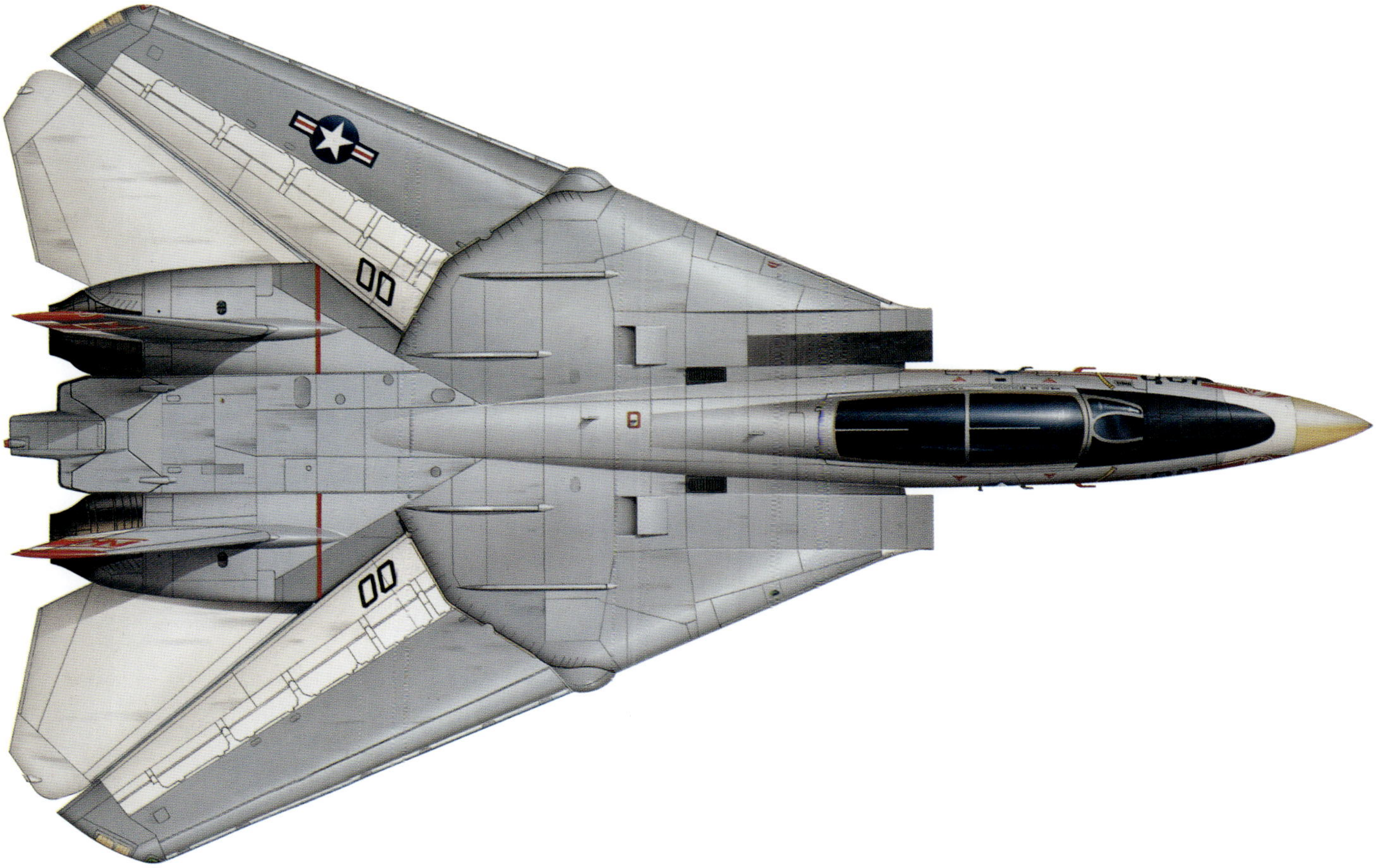

Above: The radar intercept officer (RIO) managed the F-14's complex weapons system from the rear seat. Here, an airman checks the functioning of the RIO's "office" before an evening launch from an aircraft carrier.

The F-14 arose out of a 1968 competition to find a new fleet defence fighter for the U.S. Navy following the failure of the General Dynamics F-111B programme. Although the U.S. Air Force F-111 went on to be a fine strike aircraft, the U.S. Navy's B model proved too heavy and generally unsuitable for a carrier aircraft, and was cancelled in 1968. The F-111B's Phoenix missiles and AWG-9 radar were deemed worthy of further development for use in a new fighter.

Grumman won the contest in 1969 with a two-seat twin-tailed swing-wing design it called the "Tomcat" and the Pentagon designated F-14. The prototype F-14 first flew in December 1970, but was lost on its second flight due to hydraulic failure. This did not delay the test programme greatly, and deliveries to training squadrons began in October 1972. The F-14 made its first operational cruise in September 1974.

The F-14's role was to defend a carrier battle group at long range against missile-carrying bombers such as the Tupolev Tu-22M "Backfire." Using the radar in combination with that aboard the Grumann E-2 Hawkeye to detect and track intruders, the Tomcat could engage them first with the AIM-54 at a range of up to 115 miles (184 km), then deal with any survivors with the AIM-7, AIM-9 and finally the cannon. The F-14 could carry a maximum of six AIM-54s, but in practice would be too heavy to land back aboard a carrier without firing or dumping some of the expensive missiles, which cost $1 million apiece even in the early 1970s.

A FAMLIAR POWERPLANT

As well as the F-111B's radar and missiles, the F-14 used the same Pratt & Whitney TF 30 turbofans. These gave a lot of trouble in the Tomcat's early years, leading to numerous accidents, and handling restrictions were introduced to prevent compressor stalls.

The F-14 had widely spaced engine trunks, and the space between them was used to mount four of the AIM-54s on pallet mounts. These were adapted later in the Tomcat's career to carry bombs. A Tactical Airborne Reconnaissance Pod System (TARPS) camera pod could also be carried by some aircraft.

MULTIPLE COMBAT TESTS

Two F-14 squadrons were involved in covering the final U.S. evacuation from Saigon in 1975, but saw no combat. During the 1980s, they twice tangled with Libyan fighters over Mediterranean waters Libya claimed as its own . In 1981, F-14s from the USS *Nimitz* destroyed two Sukhoi Su-22s and, in 1989, Tomcats from USS *John F. Kennedy* brought down a pair of Libyan MiG-23 "Floggers." In the 1991 Gulf War, however, Tomcats saw little air-to-air action.

Iran was the only export customer for the F-14. In 1976, the Shah's air force received the first of 79 F-14As. One aircraft was yet to be delivered when the Islamic revolution took place in 1979, and the supply of U.S. weapons and spares was stopped. When neighbouring Iraq attacked in 1980, the F-14 played a major part in Iran's air defence. Despite the lack of spare parts, Iran kept about 30 F-14s operational and claimed around 40 kills against Iraqi aircraft against 10 claims against them. Five Iranian pilots scored five or more victories, including several with the AIM-54.

Above: VF-31 "Tomcatters" were the last to fly the F-14. Here, an F-14D "Bombcat" with wings swept back makes a pass at near the speed of sound.

EXTENDED USEFULNESS

The F-14A+ (later redesignated F-14B) was an improved version with General Electric F110 engines, followed by the F-14D with digital radar processing and new cockpit displays among other changes. In the 1990s, the F-14 was given a strike role, which helped to extend its career. Using LANTIRN targeting pods, F-14s could drop a variety of laser-guided bombs, later supplemented by JDAM satellite-guided weapons. "Bombcats" saw action over the Balkans, Iraq and Afghanistan, before finally being retired in 2006. Iran continues to operate F-14s, with an estimated 25 still remaining in service in 2010.

Above: The F-14 Tomcat was to be seen in Iraqi skies from 1991 until 2006, during Operation Desert Storm and Operation Iraqi Freedom. In that time, its role changed from interceptor and escort fighter to that of precision-strike aircraft.

Dassault Mirage F1

The Mirage F1 is a relatively simple fighter and ground-attack aircraft that has seen more action than most of its contemporaries. Upgrade programmes will keep the F1 in service for many years.

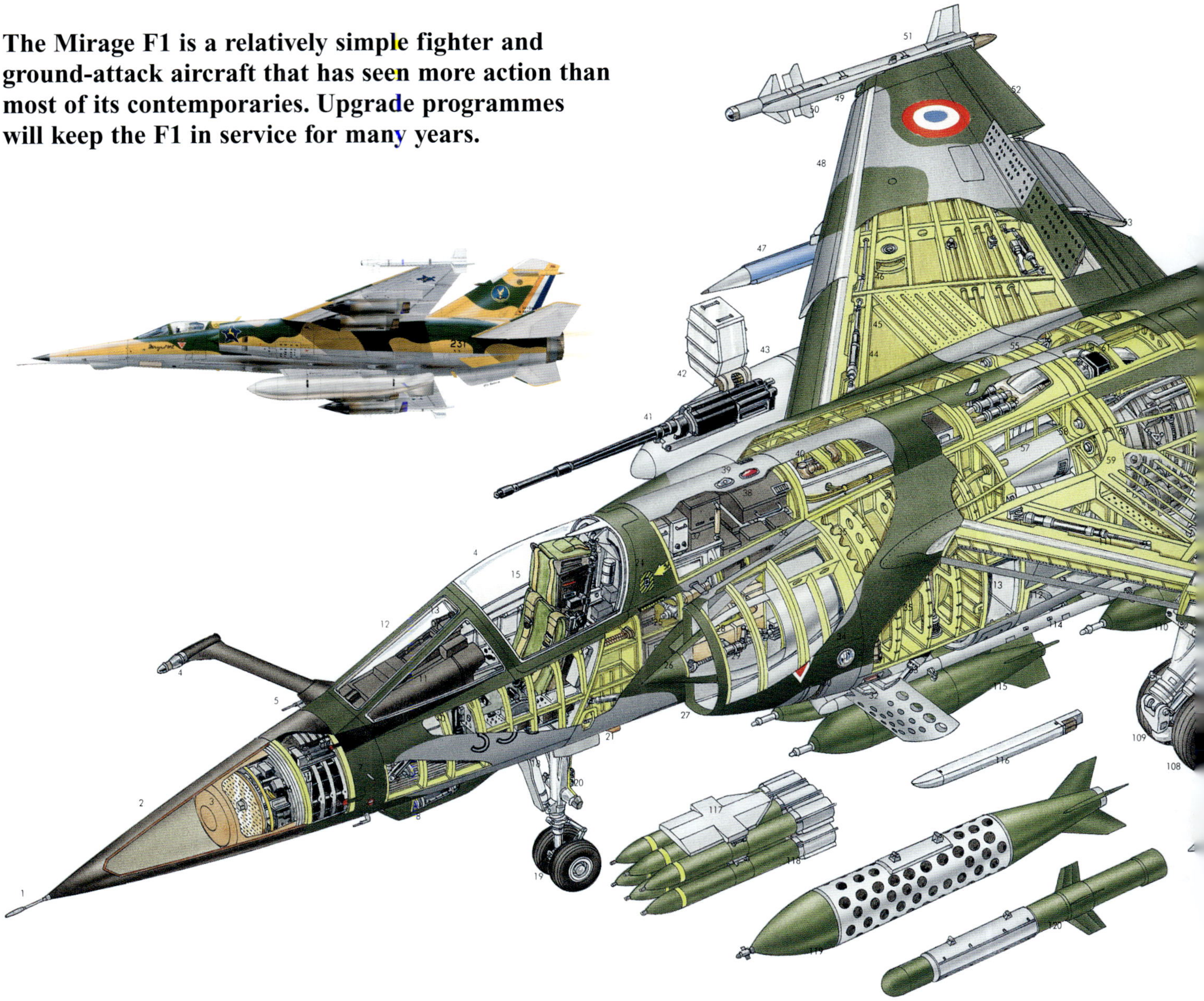

Cutaway Key

1 Pitot head
2 Fibreglass radome
3 Radar scanner housing
4 Inflight refuelling probe
5 Dynamic pressure sensor
6 Thomson-CSF Cyrano IVMR radar equipment module
7 Incidence probe
8 TMV 630A laser rangefinder
9 Rudder pedals
10 Control column
11 Instrument panel shroud
12 Windscreen panels
13 Thomson VE120 head-up display
14 Upward-hinging cockpit canopy cover
15 Martin-Baker F10M zero-zero ejection seat
16 Engine throttle lever
17 Side console panel
18 Nose undercarriage hydraulic retraction jack
19 Twin nosewheels, aft-retracting
20 Hydraulic steering mechanism
21 TACAN aerial
22 Cockpit sloping rear pressure bulkhead
23 Canopy jack
24 Canopy emergency release
25 Central intake control actuator
26 Movable half-cone intake centre-body
27 Port air intake
28 Air-conditioning equipment bay
29 Intake centre-body screw jack
30 Intake suction relief door
31 Pressure refuelling connection
32 Port airbrake panel
33 Airbrake hydraulic jack
34 Retractable landing lamp
35 Forward fuselage integral fuel tank
36 Boundary layer spill duct
37 Avionics equipment bay
38 Power amplifier
39 Strobe light (white) and anti-collision beacon (red)
40 Fuel system inverted flight accumulator
41 30-mm DEFA cannon, starboard side only
42 Ammunition magazine, 135 rounds
43 External fuel tank
44 Starboard wing integral fuel tank
45 Forged-steel wing attachment fitting
46 Inboard pylon attachment hardpoint
47 MATRA-Philips Phimat chaff/flare pod
48 Leading-edge flap
49 Starboard navigation light
50 Wingtip missile launch rail
51 MATRA Magic air-to-air missile
52 Starboard aileron
53 Two-segment double-slotted flaps
54 Spoiler panel (open)
55 Wing panel attachment machined fuselage main frame
56 Fuel system filters
57 Engine intake centre-body/starter housing
58 Wing panel attachment pin joints
59 Engine accessory equipment gearbox
60 SNECMA Atar 9K-50 afterburning engine
61 Engine bleed air pre-cooler
62 Rear spar attachment joint
63 Rear fuselage integral fuel tank
64 Engine turbine section
65 Engine-bay thermal lining
66 Fin spar attachment joint
67 Starboard all-moving tailplane
68 Forward SHERLOC ECM antenna fairing
69 UHF antenna
70 VOR aerial
71 Fintip aerial fairing
72 IFF/VHF 1 aerial
73 Rear navigation light and anti-collision beacon
74 Aft SHERLOC ECM antenna
75 Rudder
76 Rudder hydraulic actuator
77 Rudder trim actuator
78 VHF 2 aerial

79 Brake parachute housing
80 Variable-area afterburner nozzle
81 Nozzle control jacks
82 Port all-moving tailplane
83 Honeycomb trailing-edge panel
84 Multi-spar tailplane construction
85 Tailplane pivot fitting
86 Tailplane hydraulic actuator
87 Autopilot controller
88 Port ventral fin
89 Inboard double-slotted flap segment
90 Flap hydraulic jack
91 Spoiler hydraulic jack
92 Port spoiler housing and actuating linkage
93 Port aileron hydraulic actuator
94 Outboard double-slotted flap segment
95 Port aileron
96 Wingtip missile interface unit
97 Port navigation light
98 Leading-edge flap
99 Port MATRA Magic air-to-air missile
100 68-mm rocket projectile
101 MATRA 18-round rocket launcher
102 Thomson-CSF ECM pod
103 Outer pylon attachment hardpoint
104 Wing panel multi-spar construction
105 Port wing integral fuel tank
106 Main undercarriage hydraulic retraction jack
107 Shock absorber strut
108 Twin mainwheels
109 Levered suspension axle
110 Mainwheel leg strut and leg rotating linkage
111 Leading-edge flap hydraulic jack
112 Main undercarriage wheel bay
113 Port ammunition bay, unused
114 Centre fuselage weapon pylon
115 381-lb (400-kg) HE bombs
116 Underwing MATRA-Corral conformal chaff/flare dispenser
117 Multiple bomb-carrier
118 Thomson-Brandt BAP-100 runway-cratering bomb or BAT-120 area denial/anti-armour munition
119 MATRA Belouga submunition dispenser
120 MATRA Durandal retarded concrete-piercing bomb

MIRAGE F1C SPECIFICATION

Dimensions

Wingspan without tip stores: 27 ft 6¾ in (8.40 m)
Wingspan with tip-mounted Magic AAMs: 30 ft 6¾ in (9.32 m)
Wing aspect ratio: 2.82
Wing area: 269.11 sq ft (25.00 m²)
Length: 50 ft 2½ in (15.30 m)
Wheel track: 8 ft 2½ in (2.50 m)
Wheelbase: 16 ft 4¾ in (5.00 m)
Height: 14 ft 9 in (4.50 m)

Powerplant

One SNECMA Atar 9K-50 turbojet rated at 11,023 lb st (49.03 kN) dry and 15,785 lb st (70.21 kN) with afterburning

Weights

Empty: 16,314 lb (7400 kg)
Operating empty (including pilots): 18,078 lb (8200 kg)
Normal takeoff: 24,030 lb (10,900 kg);
Maximum takeoff: 35,715 lb (16,200 kg)

Fuel and load

Internal fuel capacity: 1,136 U.S. gal (4300 litres)
External fuel capacity: Provision for one 581-U.S. gal (2200-litre) tank on centreline and two 299-U.S. gal (1130-litre) tanks under the wings
Maximum weapon load: 13,889 lb (6300 kg)

Performance

Maximum level speed "clean" at 36,090 ft (11,000 m): 1,453 mph (2338 km/h)
Maximum rate of climb at sea level: 41,930 ft (12,780 m) per minute; Mirage F1B (without afterburning): 13,780 ft (4200 m) per minute
Service ceiling: 65,615 ft (20,000 m); Mirage F1B (stabilized supersonic ceiling): 52,495 ft (16,000 m)
Takeoff run at 25,353 lb (11,500 kg) in weight: 1,969 ft (600 m)
Landing run at 18,739 lb (8500 kg) in weight: 2,198 ft (670 m)

Range

Combat radius: 264 miles (425 km) on a hi-lo-hi attack mission with 14 551-lb (250-kg) bombs, or 373 miles (600 km) on a lo-lo-lo attack mission with six 551-lb (250-kg) bombs and two drop tanks, or 863 miles (1390 km) on a hi-lo-hi attack mission with two 551-lb (250-kg) bombs and three drop tanks
Endurance: 2 hours 15 minutes on a CAP with two Super 530 AAMs and one drop tank

Armament

Two fixed internal DEFA 553 30-mm cannon with 135 rounds per gun; standard air-to-air load of two MATRA Magic or AIM-9 Sidewinder missiles on wingtip rails and either one MATRA R.530 on the centreline station or two Super 530Fs underwing. A limited ground-attack capability is available using various unguided bombs, cluster munitions and rockets

"The Atar engine gave great sea-level performance. Well-balanced flying controls gave the F1 the same positive feel as experienced in the much-loved Sabre." – Dick Lord, South African Air Force Mirage F1 pilot

Above: This Mirage F1CR-200 flew with L'Armée de l'Air's Centre d'Expériences Aériennes Militaires trials unit in France's Aquitane region.

DASSAULT MIRAGE F1 – VARIANTS

F1A: Single-seat ground-attack fighter aircraft.

F1AD: Export version of the Mirage F1A for Libya. 16 built.

F1AZ: Export version of the Mirage F1A for South Africa. 32 built.

F1B: A two-seat operational conversion trainer.

1BE: Export version of the Mirage F1B for Spain. Six built.

F1BJ: Export version of the Mirage F1B for Jordan. Two built.

F1BK: Export version of the Mirage F1B for Kuwait. Two built.

F1BK-2: Four sold to Kuwait as part of a follow-on order.

F1BQ: Export version of the Mirage F1B for Iraq.

F1CE: Export version of the Mirage F1C for Spain. 45 built.

F1CG: Export version of the Mirage F1C for Greece. 40 built.

F1CH: Export version of the Mirage F1C for Morocco. 30 built.

F1CJ: Export version of the Mirage F1C for Jordan. 17 built.

F1CK: Export version of the Mirage F1C for Kuwait. 18 built.

F1CK-2: Nine F1Cs sold to Kuwait as part of a follow-on order.

F1CZ: Export fighter version of the F1C for South Africa. 16 built.

F1D: Two-seat training version, based on the Mirage F1E multi-role fighter and ground-attack aircraft.

F1E: Single-seat all-weather multi-role fighter and ground-attack aircraft.

F1JA: Export version of the Mirage F1E for Ecuador. 16 built.

F1ED: Export version of the Mirage F1E for Libya. 14 built.

F1EE: Export version of the Mirage F1E for Spain. 22 built.

F1EH-200: Moroccan aircraft fitted with an inflight refuelling probe.

F1EQ-2: Single-seat air-defence fighter version for Iraq. 16 built.

F1EQ-4: Single-seat multi-role fighter, ground-attack and reconnaissance version for Iraq. 28 built.

F1EQ-5: Single-seat anti-shipping version for Iraq. 20 built.

F1EQ-6: Single-seat anti-shipping version for Iraq. Built in small numbers.

F1EDA: Export version of the Mirage F1E for Qatar. 12 built.

F1CT: Tactical ground-attack version of the Mirage F1C-200.

Aerosud Mirage F1 AAD2006: Aerosud equipped a Mirage F1 with a Klimov RD-33 engine, the same engine used in the Mikoyan-Gurevich MiG-29. This development was dubbed the "SuperMirage" F1.

DASSAULT MIRAGE F1

The Mirage F1CE entered Spanish Air Force service in 1975, and over the years the Ejército del Aire has operated more than 90 examples. This example is assigned to 142 Escuadrón of Ala de Caza (Fighter Wing) 14 at Albacete in southeastern Spain. In the 1990s, it was one of 40 upgraded to Mirage F1CM standard with new wide-angle HUDs, HoTaS controls, modernized radar, NVG compatibility and a new navigation system. 142 Escuadrón has a sabre-toothed tiger in its squadron badge, qualifying it for membership of the NATO Tiger Association, which runs an annual "Tiger Meet" event. Tiger stripes and elaborate colour schemes often appear on participating aircraft.

FACTS

- The Mirage F1 is the only member of the Mirage family without a delta wing and with a tailplane.
- As well as France, 12 nations have operated the F1.
- Although F1s fought on both sides in the 1991 Gulf War, they never met in combat.

To meet a requirement for an interceptor to replace the Mirage III, Dassault tested various configurations, including one with eight small lift engines and a variable-geometry version called the G8. Another prototype derived from the G8 but with a fixed, high-mounted wing and a conventional tailplane was trialled in 1966. This Mirage F2 was intended as a strike aircraft with two seats. Dassault proposed scaled-down versions, and the multi-role Mirage F1 design proved the most attractive to the Armée de l'Air (French Air Force). The F1 prototype flew in December 1966 and was chosen as the basis of a new interceptor in September 1967.

Above: The conventional wing and large flaps gave the F1 a good landing performance.

Above: Qatar ordered the Mirage F1EDA in 1979, and 14 were in service by 1984. They flew defensive missions in the 1991 Gulf War.

Above: Although the Mirage F1E began as a private venture for export, it was also ordered by France. Subvariants of the F1E were popular in the Middle East, selling to Jordan, Kuwait and Iraq, among others.

The Mirage F1C interceptor reached initial operational status in 1974 with the Armée de l'Air. During C production an inflight refuelling probe was added, as was radar warning equipment on the tailfin. Related versions were the F1B two-seat conversion trainer and the F1CR reconnaissance aircraft.

IMPRESSIVE ARMAMENT

The Mirage F1 had a high wing with leading-edge and trailing-edge flaps, ailerons and spoilers. Under its wings and fuselage were a total of seven stores attachments for fuel tanks, bombs, rockets or missiles, including the large Matra 530 and the smaller Magic air-to-air missiles. A 30-mm cannon was mounted behind each engine intake. There were airbrakes on the fuselage and twin wheels on all undercarriage legs. In the sharply pointed nose was a Cyrano radar. Some export versions had a simplified Aida ranging radar in a slimmer nose.

Like Dassault's Mirage III, the F1 was widely sold abroad. The F1A export version was the basis of South Africa's F1AZ, Ecuador's F1JA, and Libya's F1AD, among other models. Equipment and weapons options varied, but as well as French air-to-air missiles and bombs, export users fitted their F1s with Exocet anti-ship missiles, Israeli and South African air-to-air missiles and even some Russian air-to-surface missiles.

South Africa's F1s saw combat against Angolan MiG-21s and MiG-23s in the bush wars of the 1980s. Against the former, the F1 could hold its own, but a number of South African Air Force Mirages fell to "Floggers." Iraq's F.1s were heavily used in the 1980–88 war with Iran, and reportedly shot down several Grumann F-14s, but they were largely engaged as Exocet launch platforms, damaging numerous oil tankers and the U.S. frigate USS *Stark*.

Against U.S. fighters in 1991's Operation Desert Storm F1s fared poorly, with at least six F1s falling to U.S. Air Force McDonnell Douglas F-15 Eagles. Towards the end of the conflict, the majority of survivors escaped to Iran to avoid destruction, and eventually were integrated into the Islamic Republic's air force.

A CHANGING ROLE

France's F1Cs soon lost the dedicated interceptor mission and were upgraded to F1CT standard, with capability to employ laser-guided bombs and missiles, and improved self-defence measures. The F1CTs and F1CRs have seen operational service over Afghanistan and Chad. A reduced number of F1s remain in French service, but numbers remain in use in Africa and the Middle East. In addition, Spain and Morocco have undertaken upgrade programmes in the 2000s.

Mikoyan-Gurevich MiG-25 "Foxbat"/ MiG-31 "Foxhound"

In terms of pure numbers, no operational fighter has been able to beat the performance of the MiG-25 and its successor, the MiG-31. Neither was built for agility, instead using speed and long-range missiles to defeat enemies, without the need for dogfighting.

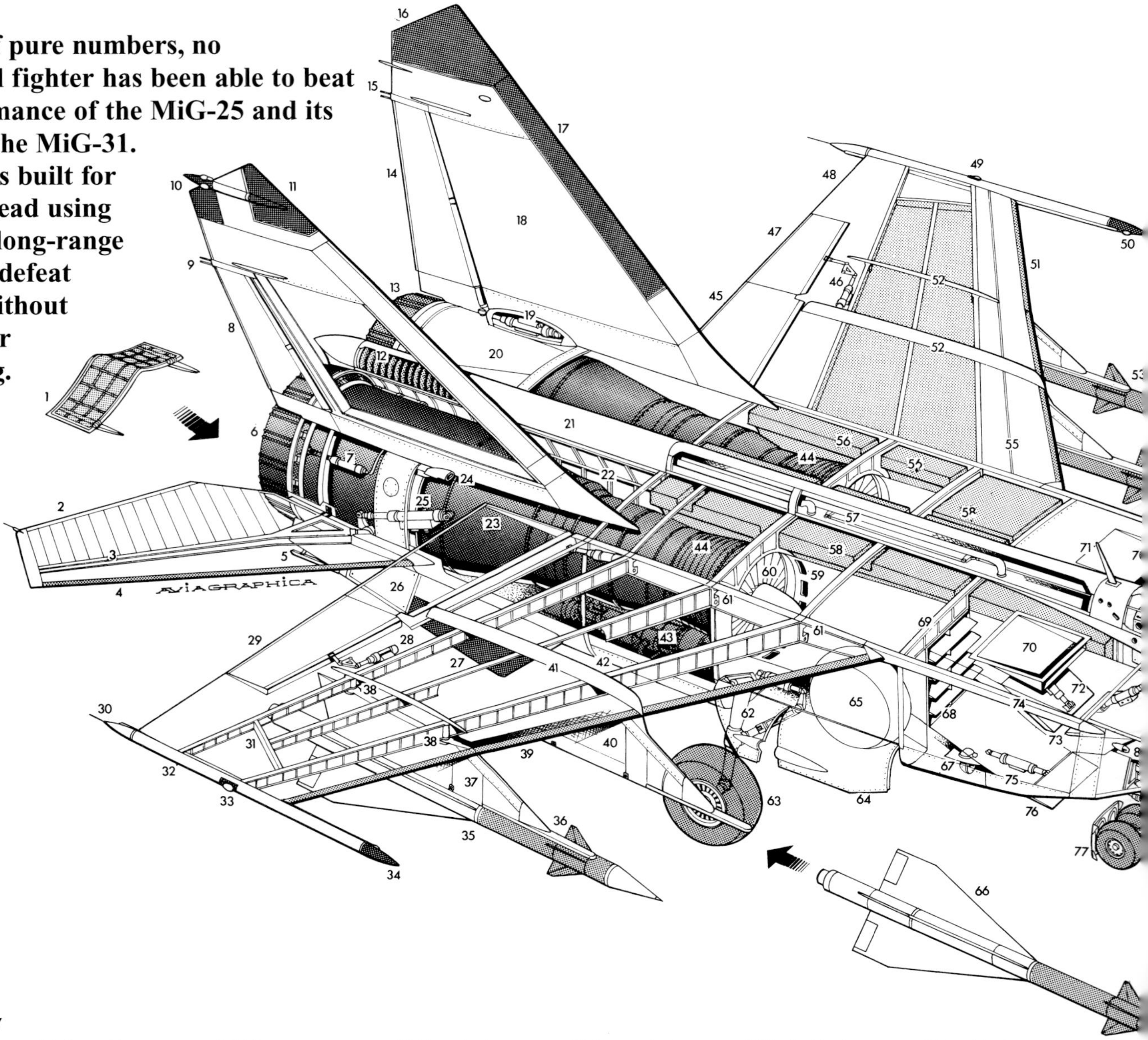

Cutaway Key

1 Ventral airbrake
2 Starboard tailplane (aluminium alloy trailing edge)
3 Steel tailplane spar
4 Titanium leading edge
5 Tail bumper
6 Fully-variable engine exhaust nozzle
7 Exhaust nozzle actuator
8 Starboard rudder
9 Static dischargers
10 Sirena 3 tail warning radar and ECM transmitter
11 Transponder aerial
12 Twin brake parachute housing
13 Port engine exhaust nozzle
14 Port rudder
15 Static dischargers
16 VHF aerial
17 HF leading-edge aerial
18 Port tailfin (steel primary structure)
19 Rudder actuator
20 Titanium rear fuselage skins
21 Dorsal spine fairing
22 Fireproof bulkhead between engine bays
23 Engine afterburner duct
24 Cooling air intake
25 Tailplane hydraulic actuator
26 Starboard ventral fin
27 VHF and ECM aerial housing
28 Aileron actuator
29 Starboard aileron
30 Static discharger
31 All-steel wing construction
32 Wingtip fairing
33 Sirena 3 radar warning receiver and ECM transmitter
34 Continuous-wave target-illuminating radar
35 AA-6 "Acrid" semi-active radar-guided air-to-air missile
36 Missile-launching rail
37 Outboard missile pylon
38 Pylon attachments
39 Wing titanium leading edge
40 Inboard pylon
41 Wing fence
42 Engine access panels
43 Engine accessory gearbox
44 Tumanskii R-31 single-shaft afterburning turbojet engine
45 Port flap
46 Aileron hydraulic actuator
47 Port aileron
48 Fixed portion of trailing edge
49 Sirena 3 radar warning receiver and ECM transmitter
50 Continuous-wave target-illuminating radar
51 Titanium leading edge
52 Port wing fences
53 AA-6 "Acrid" semi-active radar-guided air-to-air missile
54 Infrared-guided AA-6 "Acrid" missile
55 Stainless-steel wing skins
56 Intake flank fuel tanks
57 Controls and systems ducting
58 Main fuel tanks (welded steel integral construction), total system capacity 31,575 lb (14,322 kg), nitrogen-pressurized
59 Intake bleed air ducts engine bay cooling
60 Engine compressor face
61 Wing spar attachments
62 Main undercarriage leg strut
63 Starboard mainwheel
64 Mainwheel doors
65 Mainwheel stowed position
66 Starboard infrared guided AA-6 "Acrid" missile
67 Retractable landing/taxiing lamp
68 Intake duct control vanes
69 Steel fuselage primary structure
70 Intake bleed air outlet ducts
71 UHF communications aerials
72 Variable-intake ramp doors
73 Ramp jacks
74 Intake water/ methanol injection duct
75 Electric intake tip actuator
76 Variable lower intake lip
77 Nose wheel door/ mudguard
78 Twin nose wheels
79 Nose wheel leg doors

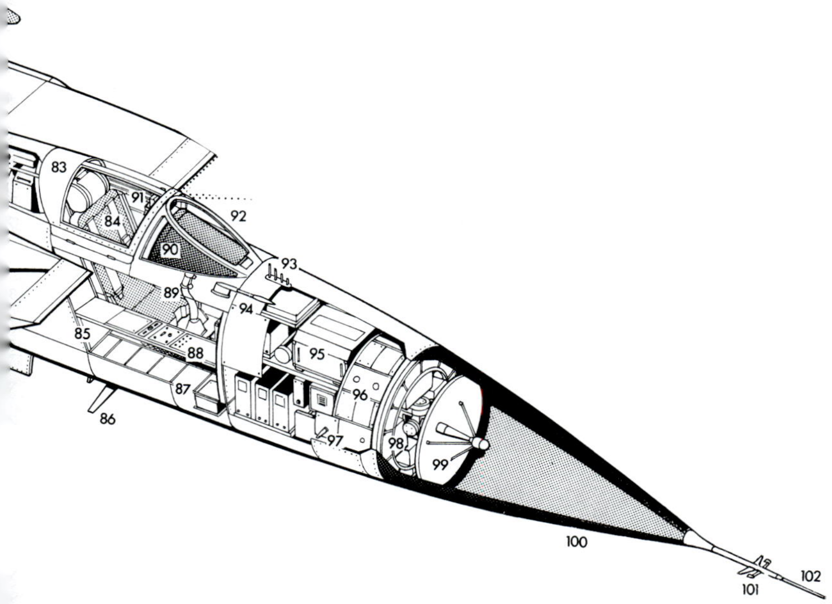

80 Starboard navigation light
81 Curved intake inboard sidewall
82 Rear avionics bay, communications and ECM equipment
83 Cockpit canopy cover, hinges to starboard
84 Pilot's ejection seat
85 Cockpit rear pressure bulkhead
86 UHF communications aerial
87 Radar altimeter
88 Pilot's side console panel
89 Control column
90 Instrument panel shroud
91 Stand-by visual sighting system for infrared missiles
92 Windscreen panels
93 "Odd Rods" IFF aerials
94 Pitot tube
95 Forward avionics compartment, radar and navigation equipment
96 "Fox Fire" fire-control radar system
97 Angle-of-attack probe
98 Scanner tracking mechanism
99 Radar scanner dish, 33½-in (85-cm) diameter
100 Radome
101 "Swift Rod" ILS antenna
102 Pitot tube
103 MiG-25U "Foxbat-C" two-seat operational training variant
104 Student pilot's cockpit enclosure
105 Instructor's cockpit
106 MiG-25R "Foxbat-B" reconnaissance variant
107 Reconnaissance cameras, one vertical and four oblique
108 Sideways-looking airborne radar (SLAR) aperture
109 Ground mapping and Doppler radar antenna
110 "Jay-Bird" forward-looking radar

MIG-25PDS "FOXBAT-E" SPECIFICATION

Dimensions

Length: 78 ft 1¾ in (23.82 m)
Length for aircraft modified with IFR capability: 78 ft 11½ in (24.07 m)
Height: 20 ft ¼ in (6.10 m)
Wingspan: 45 ft 11¾ in (14.02 m)
Wing aspect ratio: 3.2
Wing area: 660.93 sq ft (61.40 m^2)
Wheel track: 12 ft 7½ in (3.85 m)
Wheelbase: 16 ft 10½ in (5.14 m)

Powerplant

Two MNPK "Soyuz" (Tumanskii) R-15BD-300 turbojets each rated at 24,691 lb st (109.83 kN) with afterburning

Weights

Normal takeoff weight with four R-40s (AA-6s) and 100 per cent internal fuel: 80,952 lb (36,720 kg)

Fuel and loads

Internal fuel: 32,121 lb (14,570 kg)
External fuel in an underbelly tank: 9,634 lb (4370 kg)
Maximum ordnance: 8,818 lb (4000 kg)

Performance

Maximum level speed "clean" at 42,650 ft (13,000 m): Mach 2.8 or 1,619 kt (1,864 mph; 3000 km/h)
Maximum level speed "clean" at sea level: Mach 2.8 or 647 kt (745 mph; 1200 km/h)
Climb to 65,615 ft (20,000 m): 8 minutes 54 seconds
Service ceiling: 67,915 ft (20,700 m)
Takeoff run at normal takeoff weight: 4,101 ft (1250 m)
Landing run at normal landing weight with brake chutes: 2,624 ft (800 m)
g limits: + 4.5 supersonic

Range

With internal fuel at subsonic speed: 933 nm (1,075 miles; 1730 km)
With internal fuel at supersonic speed: 675 nm (776 miles; 1730 km)
Endurance: 2 hours 5 minutes

Armament

Standard intercept fit is two or four R-40 (AA-6 "Acrid") missiles. MiG-25PDS aircraft are armed with two R-40s and four R-60 (AA-8 "Aphid") AAMs

"From the height at which we fly, you can see the entire Himalayan range at one go. No aircraft has ever been able to achieve for us what the Foxbat has."
– Wing Commander Sanjeev Taliyan, Indian Air Force

Above: A MiG-25 pulls away from a Western aircraft. The "Foxbat" was virtually immune to interception at its normal operating speeds and heights.

FACTS

- The first close-up view the West had of the "Foxbat" was in 1976, when a Russian pilot defected with one to Japan.
- The MiG-25 was limited to Mach 2.83. If it went faster, the engines were likely to melt.
- For high-altitude flight, "Foxbat" and "Foxhound" pilots are required to wear pressure suits like astronauts.

MIKOYAN-GUREVICH MIG-25 "FOXBAT"/MIG-31 "FOXHOUND" – MAIN VARIANTS & OPERATORS

MAIN VARIANTS
Ye-155-P1: Interceptor fighter prototype.

MiG-25P "Foxbat-A": Single-seat all-weather interceptor fighter aircraft.

MiG-25PU "Foxbat-C": Two-seat trainer aircraft.

MiG-25RB "Foxbat-B": Single-seat reconnaissance-bomber aircraft.

MiG-25RBS "Foxbat-D": Single-seat reconnaissance-bomber aircraft.

MiG-25RBSh: MiG-25RBS Foxbats fitted with new equipment.

MiG-25RBK: Single-seat Elint aircraft, fitted with an airborne radar.

MiG-25RBT: Single-seat Elint aircraft.

MiG-25RBV: Single-seat reconnaissance-bomber aircraft.

MiG-25RU: Two-seat reconnaissance/trainer aircraft.

MiG-25BM "Foxbat-F": Single-seat defence-suppression aircraft.

MiG-25PD "Foxbat-E": Single-seat all-weather interceptor fighter.

MiG-25PDS: Designation applied to all surviving MiG-25P "Foxbat-As."

CURRENT OPERATORS
Algerian Air Force: MiG-25A, PD, PDS, R, RBV, PU, RU.

Armenian Air Force: One MiG-25PD.

Azerbaijan Air Force: MiG-25PD, MiG-25RB and MiG-25 trainers.

Russian Air Force: MiG-25 interceptors and MiG-25RB reconnaissance.

Syrian Air Force: MiG-25PD and MiG-25RB, R and U.

Turkmenistan Air Force: MiG-25PD and MiG-25PU.

FORMER OPERATORS
Bulgarian Air Force: MiG-25RBT, MiG-25RU.

Belarus Air Force: 50 MiG-25s, including 13 MiG-25PD.

Indian Air Force: MiG-25RBK, MiG-25RU.

Iraqi Air Force: Two MiG-25PUs, four MiG-25RBs, five MiG-25RBTs and 11 MiG-25PDs. Seven MiGs were flown over to Iran in 1991, the rest were destroyed in the Gulf War and Operation Southern Watch, or buried during the 2003 invasion of Iraq. A MiG-25 was found buried under the sand at Al Taqaddum Air Base in February 2004.

Libyan Air Force: MiG-25PD, MiG-25RBK, MiG-25PU and MiG-25RU variants.

Soviet Union: The largest operator historically, Soviet aircraft were passed on to its successor states in 1991.

Ukrainian Air Force: Took over 79 aircraft after the break-up of the Soviet Union. They have been withdrawn from service.

MIKOYAN-GUREVICH MIG-25 "FOXBAT"/MIG-31 "FOXHOUND"

The MiG-25BM "Foxbat-F" was a development of the MiG-25RB dedicated to suppression of enemy air defences (SEAD). It was developed for use in the European theatre against NATO radar systems as a platform for the AS-11 "Kilter" anti-radiation missile (ARM). This was the first Soviet ARM able to be carried by tactical aircraft. The MiG-25BM would have cleared a path through the defences for MiG-25 fighters and tactical bombers. Although the prototype flew in 1976, it entered service only in 1988 after many development problems. The nose radome was painted grey to resemble that of the MiG-25PD interceptor and thus disguise the BM's true role. Behind the nose was the Yaguar (Jaguar) electronic warfare and electronic countermeasures suite.

Above: The aircraft's huge inlets and engine trunks are evident in this underside view of a MiG-25 "Foxbat-A."

Development of the MiG-25 was begun in 1961, to counter the proposed North American B-70 Valkyrie bomber. The same year the B-70 itself was cancelled, in part due to its huge cost and also because of the threat of new surface-to-air missiles. Testing of XB-70 protoytypes went ahead and Mikoyan-Gurevich continued MiG-25 development, ostensibly to counter high-altitude reconnaissance aircraft such as the Lockheed U-2 and Lockheed SR-71 Blackbird.

A prototype called the Ye-155P-1 first flew in September 1964. This was followed by several others configured as either interceptors or reconnaissance aircraft. Under the cover designation Ye-266, one was used to set a record for climbing

Above: A Libyan MiG-25PD is seen from an intercepting U.S. Navy aircraft. The missiles are AA-6 "Acrids."

Above: There were a number of specialized reconnaissance models, some with a secondary bombing capability. This is believed to be a MiG-25RBV.

to 98,400 ft (30,000 m) in 4 minutes 3.86 seconds in 1973. The first production MiG-25s (in MiG-25R reconnaissance form) entered Soviet Air Force service in 1969, followed by MiG-25P interceptors in 1972 with the Air Defence Forces, technically a different branch of the Soviet military.

The MiG-25 had huge engine intake ducts with movable inlets to adjust airflow for different speeds. The use of twin vertical fins was one of the first on a jet fighter, although had been seen before on the Vought F7U Cutlass. The use of heat-resistant but very expensive titanium was kept to a minimum, being used only in critical areas. Most of the structure was tempered steel, with some use of aluminium alloys.

COLD WAR DEFECTION

The West had its first close look at the MiG-25 in 1976, when pilot Viktor Belenko defected from the Soviet Union and flew an aircraft to Hakodate, Japan. The aircraft was returned, but only after it had been dismantled and thoroughly studied. U.S. technical experts discovered that the MiG-25 used old-fashioned vacuum tube electronics rather than circuit boards; the forward view was terrible; the surface finish was poor with raised rivet heads; and the aircraft had a poor combat radius and a large turning circle. All of these limitations were understood, however, when the "Foxbat" was built. Vacuum tubes were resistant to jamming or electromagnetic pulse; the radar was powerful enough to burn through enemy jamming; and the rough surfaces were in areas where they had little effect on drag. Flown correctly, the MiG-25 went a fair distance very quickly, reaching a point where intruders could be destroyed by its missiles before they were in range with their own offensive weapons.

EFFECTIVIE ARMAMENT

Main armament of the "Foxbat" was four to six AAMs. The most effective of these were the large AA-6 "Acrid," which was usually fitted in a mix of infrared and semi-active radar homing versions. A pair of each would be fired at a bomber target to outwit countermeasures. AA-7 "Apex" and AA-8 "Aphid" missiles were also carried, but no cannon was fitted.

The MiG-25PD "Foxbat-E" was the definitive interceptor version, with a look-down, shoot-down radar and an IRST system. A small number of MiG-25s were exported to countries including Syria, Iraq, Algeria and Libya. An Iraqi MiG-25 claimed the only aerial victory against a coalition aircraft in the 1991 Gulf War, when it shot down a U.S. Navy F/A-18.

PROPOSED REPLACEMENT

As early as 1975, an intended replacement for the MiG-25 was flying in the form of the Ye-155MP prototype for the MiG-31 "Foxhound." Although outwardly similar, the MiG-31 had few parts in common and a second seat for a radar operator. Unlike the MiG-25, the MiG-31 also had a 30-mm cannon. The improved MiG-31M flew in 1983. Under its belly it could carry four R-37 "Amos" missiles, regarded as the Russian equivalent of the AIM-54 Phoenix. Few if any entered service, but many aspects were retrofitted to existing MiG-31s.

IAI Kfir

Israel took Dassault's Mirage III design and, through a series of steps, improved the original almost beyond recognition into the IAI Kfir, with canard foreplanes and the engine from the McDonnell Douglas F-4 Phantom.

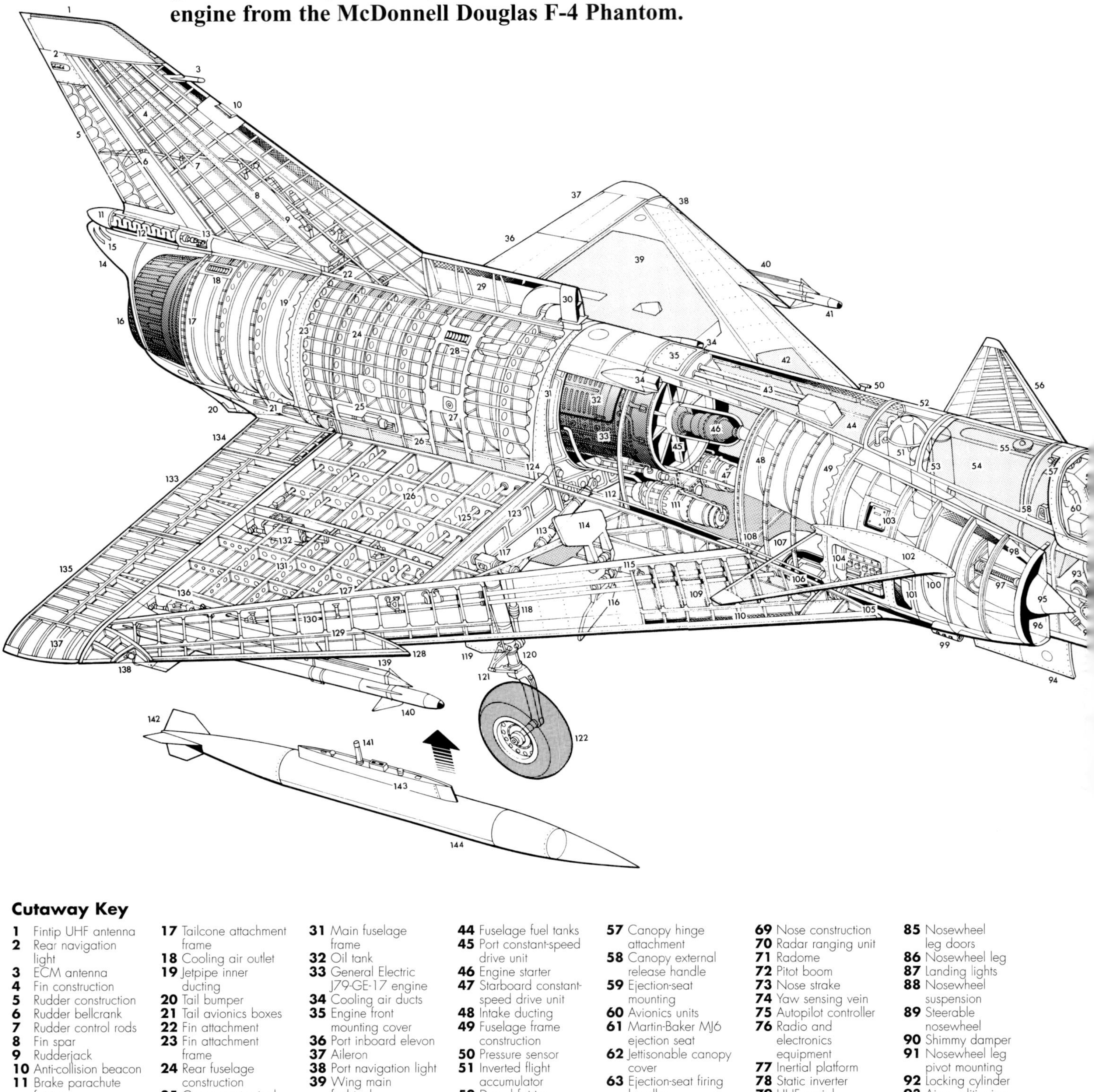

Cutaway Key

1 Fintip UHF antenna
2 Rear navigation light
3 ECM antenna
4 Fin construction
5 Rudder construction
6 Rudder bellcrank
7 Rudder control rods
8 Fin spar
9 Rudderjack
10 Anti-collision beacon
11 Brake parachute fairing
12 Parachute
13 Release mechanism
14 Tailcone fairing
15 Airflow guide vanes
16 Variable exhaust nozzle
17 Tailcone attachment frame
18 Cooling air outlet
19 Jetpipe inner ducting
20 Tail bumper
21 Tail avionics boxes
22 Fin attachment
23 Fin attachment frame
24 Rear fuselage construction
25 Compensator jack
26 Belly fuel tank
27 Engine mounting attachment
28 Cooling air outlet
29 Finroot intake fairing
30 Cooling air intakes
31 Main fuselage frame
32 Oil tank
33 General Electric J79-GE-17 engine
34 Cooling air ducts
35 Engine front mounting cover
36 Port inboard elevon
37 Aileron
38 Port navigation light
39 Wing main fuel tank
40 Missile launch rail
41 Shafrir 2 air-to-air missile
42 Leading-edge fuel tank
43 Fuel supply piping
44 Fuselage fuel tanks
45 Port constant-speed drive unit
46 Engine starter
47 Starboard constant-speed drive unit
48 Intake ducting
49 Fuselage frame construction
50 Pressure sensor
51 Inverted flight accumulator
52 Dorsal fairing
53 Oxygen bottles
54 Forward fuselage fuel tank
55 Fuel filler
56 Canard foreplane construction
57 Canopy hinge attachment
58 Canopy external release handle
59 Ejection-seat mounting
60 Avionics units
61 Martin-Baker MJ6 ejection seat
62 Jettisonable canopy cover
63 Ejection-seat firing handles
64 Pilot's control console
65 Instrument panel
66 Reflector sight
67 Windscreen
68 Instrument pitot
69 Nose construction
70 Radar ranging unit
71 Radome
72 Pitot boom
73 Nose strake
74 Yaw sensing vein
75 Autopilot controller
76 Radio and electronics equipment
77 Inertial platform
78 Static inverter
79 UHF aerial
80 Rudder pedal
81 Radar console
82 Control column
83 Ejection-seat adjusting handle
84 Control rod linkage
85 Nosewheel leg doors
86 Nosewheel leg
87 Landing lights
88 Nosewheel suspension
89 Steerable nosewheel
90 Shimmy damper
91 Nosewheel leg pivot mounting
92 Locking cylinder
93 Air-conditioning plant
94 Nosewheel door
95 Air intake centre-body half-cone
96 Starboard air intake

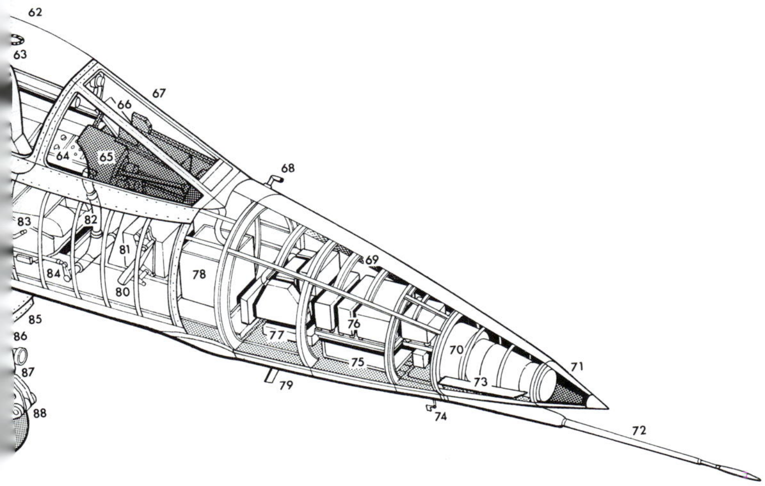

97 Intake half-cone operating jack
98 Boundary layer duct
99 Cannon muzzle blast shield
100 Air intake duct
101 Auxiliary intake
102 Canard foreplane root fairing
103 Electrical control unit
104 Electrical servicing panel
105 Cannon barrel
106 DEFA 30-mm cannon
107 Ammunition feed chute
108 Front spar attachment
109 Leading-edge fuel tank
110 Leading-edge construction
111 Starboard constant-speed drive unit
112 Mainwheel well
113 Main undercarriage jack
114 Upper surface airbrake
115 Airbrake jack
116 Lower surface airbrake
117 Main undercarriage leg pivot
118 Damper strut
119 Main leg door
120 Shock-absorber strut
121 Undercarriage scissors link
122 Mainwheel
123 Main spar
124 Main spar attachment
125 Fuel system piping
126 Main wing fuel tank
127 Leading-edge spar
128 Leading-edge dogtooth
129 Leading-edge construction
130 Control rod linkage
131 Wing construction
132 Inboard elevon jack
133 Inboard elevon construction
134 Elevon compensator
135 Outboard elevon
136 Outboard elevon jack
137 Wingtip profile
138 Navigation light
139 Missile launcher
140 Shafrir 2 air-to-air missile
141 Fuel-tank pylon attachment
142 Fuel-tank fins
143 Tank pylon
144 Fuel tank (132-U.S. gal/500-litre capacity)

KFIR-C7 SPECIFICATION

Dimensions

Length: 51 ft 4¼ in (15.65 m)
Wingspan: 26 ft 11⅔ in (8.22 m)
Wing area: 374.60 sq ft (34.80 m²)
Canard foreplane span: 12 ft 3 in (3.73 m)
Canard foreplane area: 17.87 sq ft (1.66 m²)
Height: 14 ft 11¼ in (4.55 m)
Wheel track: 10 ft 6 in (3.20 m)
Wheelbase: 15 ft 11⅔ in (4.87 m)

Powerplant

One IAI Bedek Division-built General Electric J79-J1E turbojet rated at 11,890 lb st (52.89 kN) dry and 18,750 lb st (83.41 kN) with afterburning

Weights

Empty: about 16,060 lb (7285 kg)
Normal takeoff: 22,961 lb (10,415 kg)
Maximum takeoff: 36,376 lb (16,500 kg)

Fuel and load

Internal fuel: 5,670 lb (2572 kg)
External fuel: up to 8,216 lb (3727 kg) in three 449-, 343-, 218-, 159- or 132-U.S. gal (1700-, 1300-, 825-, 600- or 500-litre) drop tanks
Maximum ordnance: 13,415 lb (6085 kg)

Performance

Maximum level speed "clean" at sea level: 750 kt (863 mph; 1389 km/h)
Maximum level speed "clean" at 36,000 ft (10,975 m): more than 1,317 kt (1,516 mph; 2440 km/h)
Maximum rate of climb at sea level: 45,930 ft (14,000 m) per minute
Climb to 50,000 ft (15,240 m) with full internal fuel and two Shafrir AAMs: 5 minutes 10 seconds
Zoom climb ceiling: 75,000 ft (22,860 m)
Service ceiling: more than 50,000 ft (15,240 m)
Stabilized supersonic ceiling: 58,000 ft (17,680 m)
Ferry range: 1,744 nm (2,000 miles; 3232 km) with one 343-U.S. gal (1300-litre) and two 449-U.S. gal (1700-litre) drop tanks
Combat radius on a hi-hi-hi interception mission with two Shafrir AAMs, one 218-U.S. gal (825-litre) and two 343-U.S. gal (1300-litre) drop tanks: 419 nm (482 miles; 776 km)
Combat radius on a 1-hour CAP with two Shafrir AAMs, one 449-U.S. gal (1700-litre) and two 343-U.S. gal (1300-litre) drop tanks: 476 nm (548 miles; 882 km)
Combat radius on a hi-lo-hi attack mission with two 800-lb (363-kg) and two 400-lb (181-kg) bombs, two Shafrir AAMs, and one 343-U.S. gal (1300-litre) and two 449-U.S. gal (1700-litre) drop tanks: 640 nm (737 miles; 1186 km)

Armament

Two internal 30-mm IAI-built DEFA 552 cannon with 140 rounds per gun, plus a range of stores including M117, M118, Mk 82, Mk 83, Mk 84 and Israeli-designed/derived bombs; CBU-52/58 and Israeli-built TAL-1/2 cluster bombs, LAU-3A, LAU-10A and LAU-32A rocket pods, Python 3 and Shafrir 2 AAMs, and the Elta EL/L-8202 ECM pod

"By the time the Kfir C2 was shown off for the first time in 1976, it was already in service and had gained its most distinctive feature: a pair of swept canard foreplanes."

FACTS

- The Kfir's J79 engine was license-built by the Israeli firm IAI Bedek.
- Kfirs served with the U.S. military as the F-21 "Lion."
- Privately owned Kfirs are used by contractors in U.S. military exercises.

IAI KFIR – VARIANTS & OPERATORS

VARIANTS

Kfir C1: Basic production variant.

F-21A Kfir: 25 upgraded Kfir C1 aircraft were leased to the U.S. Navy and U.S. Marine Corps for an aggressor role and were designated F-21A. These aircraft had been modified and included canards on the air intakes, which improved the aircraft manoeuvrability and slow speed control, and were adopted on later variants.

Kfir C2: An improved C1 that featured many aerodynamic improvements. Changes included "dogtoothed" leading edges on the wings, small strakes under the nose and a larger sweep angle of the canards.

Kfir TC2: A two-seat training variant developed from the C2. It has a longer and lowered nose to improve the pilot's view.

Kfir C7: Vastly modified variant. Most C2 aircraft were modified to this variant. It included an improved J79-GEJ1E engine that offered 1,000 lb st (4445 kN) more thrust at full afterburner (and as a result increasing the maximum takeoff weight by 3,395 lb/1540 kg), two more hardpoints under the air intakes, better avionics such as the Elta EL/M-2021B radar, HOTAS-configured cockpit and inflight refuelling capability.

Kfir TC7: A two-seat training variant developed from the C7.

Kfir C10: An export variant. The most important change is the adaptation of the Elta EL/M-2032 radar. This variant is also known as Kfir CE and Kfir 2000.

Kfir TC10: Upgraded version of the TC7 for the Colombian Air Force.

Kfir C12: Upgraded version of the C7 for the Colombian Air Force; a C10 without the Elta EL/M-2032 radar.

Kfir Tzniut: Reconnaissance version of the C2.

FOREIGN OPERATORS

Fuerza Aérea Colombiana (Colombian Air Force)
Kfir C2s (later upgraded to C7s), one TC2. In 2008, C10s to C12s were added to this force.

Fuerza Aérea Ecuatoriana (Ecuadorian Air Force)
C2s and TC2s, C10s.

Sri Lanka Air Force
C2s, TC2s, C7s.

U.S. Marine Corps
C1 (designated F-21A).

U.S. Navy
C1 (designated F-21A).

IAI KFIR

Israel exported a dozen Kfir C2s to Ecuador in 1981, and they equip the Escuadrón de Combate 2113 at Base Aérea Taura. The Kfirs flew in a combined squadron with Mirage F1s in the brief and inconclusive Alto-Cenepa War with Peru in 1995. The Fuerza Aérea Ecuatoriana C2 illustrated shot down a Peruvian A-37B Dragonfly. U.S. technology used in the Kfir, such as the J79 engines, meant that the United States was able to block further exports to Ecuador. Instead, the FAE upgraded some of its aircraft to Kfir CE standard with a helmet-mounted sight system and provision for Python III and IV air-to-air missiles. As illustrated, this C2 sports Rafael Shafrir 2 infrared-guided AAMs on its outer pylons.

Israel was denied the delivery of 50 Dassault Mirage 5 fighters by a French arms embargo that followed the 1967 Six-Day War. In one of the biggest espionage operations in history, Israeli agents copied the engineering drawings for Swiss licence production of the Mirage III and reverse-engineered a version called the "Nesher" (eagle).

The resulting aircraft was essentially the same as the French Mirage 5, except for Martin-Baker ejection seats and some Israeli avionics. In 1973, the Nesher was the most successful Israel Defence Forces/Israel Air Force type, claiming around 100 victories. About 16 of the 61 Neshers were lost to all causes between 1971 and 1980. Neshers were later sold on to Argentina as the Dagger, and some were upgraded with Israeli help as the Finger in time for the 1982 Falklands War.

AN ALL-NEW DERIVATIVE

In parallel with the Nesher, Israel Aircraft Industries (IAI) created an all-new derivative powered by the J79 engine then in service in the IDF/IAF's Phantoms. Named "Kfir" (lion cub), the new aircraft flew in June 1973. The J79 installation required a shorter rear fuselage, various small scoops on the airframe and a prominent scoop at the base of the fin, which provided cooling air for the afterburner. The undercarriage was stronger and slightly longer. This Kfir C1 model was built in limited numbers, equipping two IAF squadrons from 1974.

By the time the Kfir C2 was shown off for the first time in 1976, it was already in service and had gained its most distinctive feature: a pair of swept canard foreplanes. The C2 had other aerodynamic improvements, including extended panels on the outer wing leading edges, giving a noticeable "dogtooth" appearance and long undernose strakes. All of these features improved manoeuvrability at lower speeds and reduced takeoff and landing runs.

DEFINITIVE VERSION

The Kfir C7 was the definitive version, with a larger-thrust J79 and improved avionics, including HOTAS (hands-on throttle and stick), a new Elta pulse-Doppler radar, and a new weapons management and delivery system. An inflight refuelling capability was added. Two extra weapons hardpoints and the ability to use laser-guided bombs and other smart weapons were other features. The new engine allowed greater takeoff weights, a longer mission radius and a better thrust-to-weight ratio for air combat.

The Kfir was just too late for the Yom Kippur War of 1973, but saw action in various subsequent operations, mainly in the ground-attack role. The type scored its only known victory in Israeli hands in June 1979 when a Kfir C2 shot down a Syrian Mikoyan-Gurevich MiG-21 with a Shafrir II missile. Another Kfir C2 was lost to a Syrian MiG-21 in June 1982 over Lebanon.

Above: The cockpit of a modernized Kfir CE, or C10, as used by Colombia.

SERVICE OUTSIDE ISRAEL

The Kfir found itself in the U.S. inventory when the Navy and Marine Corps leased 25 in the late 1980s for use as adversary aircraft. These C1s were modified before delivery to have the C2's canards and other improvements. Under the designation F-21A Lion, one USN and one USMC squadron used the Kfirs from 1985 to 1989 for dissimilar air combat training before they were returned to Israel.

Kfir C2s and two-seat TC2s were sold to three countries: Colombia, Ecuador and Sri Lanka, each of which has used the type in combat. In a brief 1995 conflict between Peru and Ecuador, a Kfir C2 shot down a Cessna A-37 Dragonfly, Colombia's Kfirs have been used against guerillas, and Sri Lanka's were heavily used in civil war from 1995–2009.

Left: In the 1980s, the U.S. Marine Corps and U.S. Navy leased two squadrons of Kfir C2s for dissimilar combat training.

Above: In their early service, the Israeli Air Force's Kfirs wore large recognition markings to distinguish them from Arab Mirages.

McDonnell Douglas/ Boeing F-15 Eagle

The McDonnell Douglas F-15 Eagle has become the premier air superiority fighter of the modern era. Since the 1970s, it has amassed an unequalled combat record in conflicts in the Middle East and Balkans.

F-15E SPECIFICATION

Dimensions

Length: 63 ft 9 in (19.43 m)
Height: 18 ft 5½ in (5.63 m)
Wingspan: 42 ft 9 ¾ in (13.05 m)
Wing aspect ratio: 3.01
Tailplane span: 28 ft 3 in (8.61 m)
Wheel track: 9 ft ¼ in (2.75 m)
Wheelbase: 17 ft 9 ½ in (5.42 m)

Powerplant

Original F-15E had powerplant of F-15C/D, but with option of General Electric F110-GE-129. Aircraft from 135 onwards (90-0233), built from August 1991, have two Pratt & Whitney F100-PW-229s rated at 29,000 lb st (129 kN)

Weights

Empty operating: 31,700 lb (14,379 kg)
Normal takeoff: 44,823 lb (20,331 kg)
Maximum takeoff: 36,741 lb (81,000 kg)

Fuel and load

Internal fuel: 13,123 lb (5952 kg)
External fuel: 21,645 lb (9818 kg)
Maximum weapon load: 24,500 lb (11,113 kg)

Performance

Maximum level speed: Mach 2.5
Maximum combat radius: 685 nm (790 miles; 1270 km)
Maximum combat range: 2,400 nm (2,765 miles; 4445 km)

Armament

One 20-mm M61A-1 six-barrel gun, with 512 rounds, in starboard wingroot. Wing pylons for AIM-9 Sidewinder, AIM-120 AMRAAM, and AIM-7 Sparrow. Single or triple rail launchers for AGM-65 Maverick on wing pylons. A wide range of guided and unguided weapons including Mk 20 Rockeye, Mk 82, MK 84, BSU-49 and -50, GBU-10, -12, -15, and -24; CBU-52, -58, -71, -87, -89, -90, -92 and -93; LAU-3A rockets; B57 and B61 nuclear weapons

Cutaway Key

1 Fibreglass radome
2 Hughes AN/APG-70 I-band pulse-Doppler radar scanner
3 Radar mounting bulkhead
4 ADF sense antenna
5 Avionics equipment bay, port and starboard
6 UHF antenna
7 Pitot head
8 AGM-130 TV-guided air-to-surface weapon
9 TACAN antenna
10 Formation lighting strip
11 Incidence probe
12 Rudder pedals
13 Instrument panel shroud
14 Pilot's head-up display
15 Frameless windscreen panel
16 B61 tactical nuclear weapon
17 AIM-7F Sparrow air-to-air missile
18 LANTIRN navigation pod, mounted beneath starboard intake
19 FLIR aperture
20 Terrain-following radar
21 Upward-hinging cockpit canopy
22 Pilot's ACES II ejection seat
23 Side console panel
24 Engine throttle levers
25 Boarding steps
26 Extended boarding ladder
27 Forward-retracting nosewheel
28 Landing/taxiing lights
29 Nosewheel leg shock-absorber strut
30 Underfloor control runs
31 Flying controls duplicated in rear cockpit
32 Radar hand controller
33 Weapons systems officer's ACES II ejection seat
34 Canopy hinge point
35 Cockpit air-conditioning pack
36 Port variable capture area "nodding" air intake
37 Boundary layer spill air louvres
38 Nodding intake hydraulic actuator
39 Variable-area intake ramp doors
40 Intake ramp hydraulic actuator
41 Boom-type flight refuelling receptacle, open
42 Air supply duct to conditioning system
43 Ammunition magazine, 512 rounds
44 Forward fuselage fuel tanks
45 Ammunition feed chute
46 Engine intake ducting
47 Centre fuselage fuel tanks (3)
48 Fuel-tank bay access panel
49 Airbrake hydraulic jack
50 Dorsal airbrake honeycomb construction
51 Upper UHF antenna
52 Starboard intake by-pass air spill duct
53 M61A-1 Vulcan 20-mm cannon
54 Anti-collision light
55 Starboard wing pylon carrying GBU-10, AIM-7M and AIM-120
56 Pylon mounting hardpoint
57 Starboard wing integral fuel tank, fire suppressant foam filled
58 Leading-edge flush HF antenna panels
59 Ventral view showing carriage of 12 Mk 82 500-lb (227-kg) bombs
60 610-U.S. gal (2309-litre) external fuel tanks (3)
61 LANTIRN navigation and targeting pods
62 Wing pylon mounted AIM-9M and AIM-120 air-to-air missiles

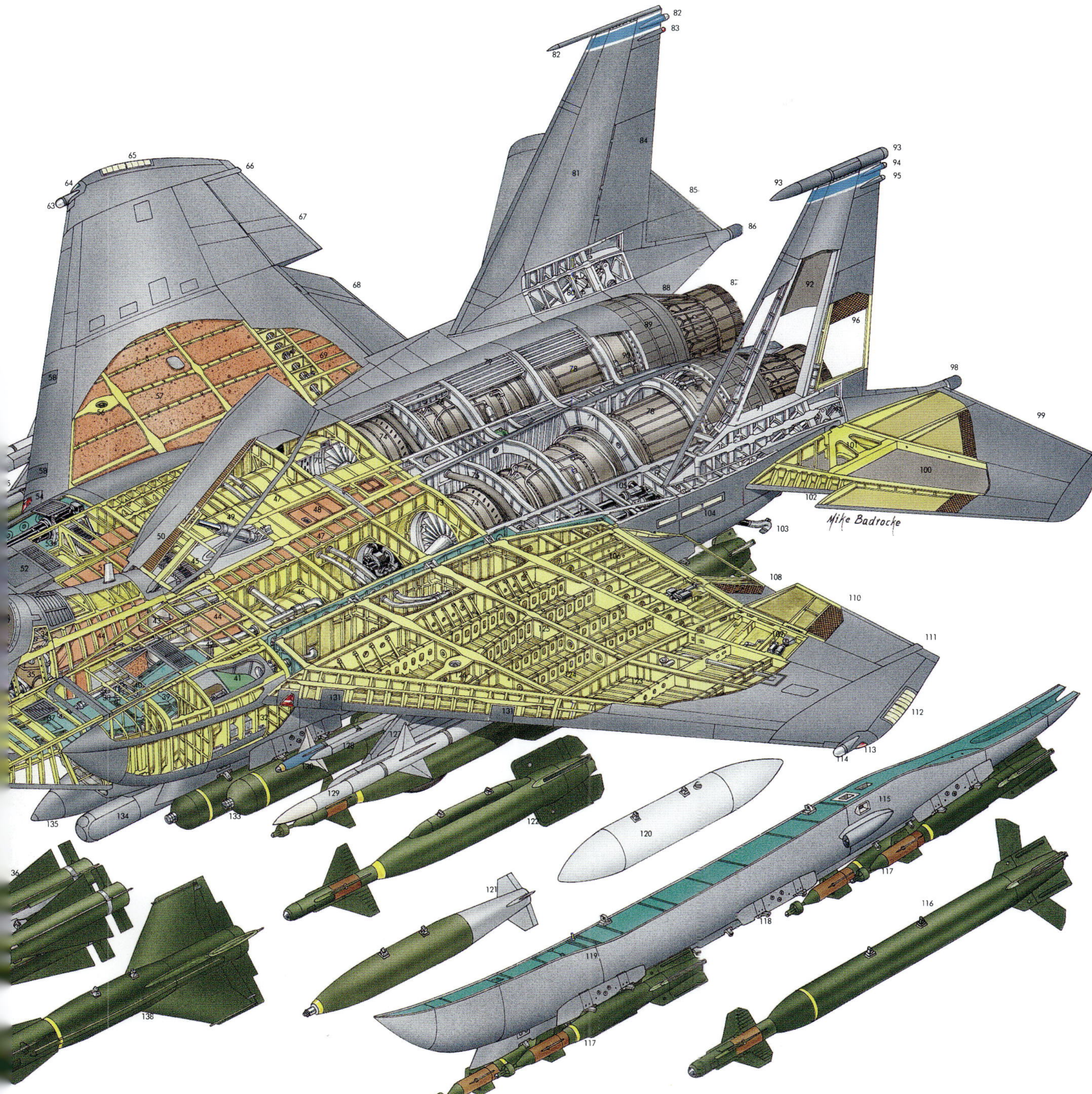

63 Forward ECM transmitting antenna
64 Starboard navigation light
65 Wingtip formation light
66 Fuel jettison
67 Starboard aileron
68 Starboard plain flap
69 Trailing-edge fuel tank
70 Engine-bay cooling intake bleed air louvres
71 Compressor intake
72 Central airframe-mounted engine accessory equipment gearbox
73 Machined main fuselage/wing spar attachment bulkheads
74 Pratt & Whitney F100-PW-229 afterburning turbofan engines
75 Engine bleed air cross-ducting
76 Forward engine mounting
77 Main engine mounting "spectacle" beam
78 Afterburner ducting
79 Rear fuselage/engine bay diffusion-bonded all-titanium structure
80 Tailplane hydraulic actuator
81 Starboard fin
82 Fintip ECM antenna
83 Anti-collision light
84 Starboard rudder
85 Starboard all-moving tailplane
86 Aft ECM transmitting antenna
87 Variable-area afterburner nozzle
88 Nozzle actuating linkage
89 Nozzle shroud panels
90 Fueldraulic afterburner nozzle actuators
91 Two-spar fin torsion box structure
92 Boron-fibre fin skin panelling
93 Radar warning antenna
94 Port rear ECM antenna
95 White strobe light
96 Port rudder honeycomb core construction
97 Tailplane pivot mounting
98 Port aft ECM transmitting antenna
99 Port all-moving tailplane
100 Boron-fibre tailplane skin panelling
101 Machined tailplane trunnion mounting fitting
102 Leading edge dogtooth
103 Runway emergency arrestor hook, lowered
104 Formation lighting strip
105 Engine bleed air primary heat exchangers, port and starboard
106 Port trailing-edge fuel-tank bay
107 Flap hydraulic jack
108 Port plain flap
109 Aileron hydraulic actuator
110 Port aileron honeycomb core construction
111 Fuel jettison
112 Port formation light
113 Port navigation light
114 Forward ECM transmitting antenna
115 Engine bleed air primary heat exchanger air intake and exhaust ducts
116 GBU-28 "Deep Throat" laser-guided bomb
117 GBU-12 laser-guided bombs
118 CFT pylons
119 Port conformal fuel tank (CFT)
120 AXQ-14 datalink pod
121 Mk 84 2,000-lb (907-kg) HE bomb
122 GBU-24 laser-guided bomb
123 Outer wing panel dry bay
124 Port wing integral fuel tankage
125 Multi-spar wing panel structure
126 Port pylon hardpoint
127 Wing stores pylon
128 Missile launch rails
129 AIM-120 AMRAAM
130 AIM-9M Sidewinder air-to-air missile
131 Leading-edge flush HF antenna
132 Stores management system equipment
133 CBU-87 submunition dispensers
134 Port LANTIRN targeting pod
135 Centreline external tank
136 AGM-65 Maverick air-to-surface missiles
137 Triple missile carrier/launch rail
138 GBU-15 electro-optical guided glide bomb

"It's the most powerful air-superiority fighter known to man. It's exceptionally easy to fly, as easy as a Cessna."
– Colonel Doug Dildy (ret.), U.S. Air Force F-15 pilot

FACTS

- The F-15 replaced F-4 Phantoms, F-101 Voodoos and F-106 Delta Darts with both regular and Air National Guard squadrons operating in the air defence role.
- The F-15's wing is sometimes called the "tennis court" due to its large surface area.
- No F-15 has ever been shot down in air-to-air combat, although at least two have been lost in "friendly fire" incidents.

MCDONNELL DOUGLAS F-15 EAGLE – MAJOR VARIANTS & OPERATORS

VARIANTS

F-15A: Single-seat all-weather air-superiority fighter version; 384 built 1972–79.

F-15B: Two-seat training version, formerly designated TF-15A; 61 built 1972–79.

F-15C: Improved single-seat all-weather air-superiority fighter version; 483 built 1979–85.

F-15D: Two-seat training version; 92 built 1979–85.

F-15E Strike Eagle: All-weather ground-attack strike fighter.

F-15J: Single-seat all-weather air-superiority fighter version for the Japan Air Self-Defence Force (JASDF); 139 built under licence in Japan by Mitsubishi 1981–97.

F-15DJ: Two-seat training version for the JASDF.

F-15N Sea Eagle: A carrier-capable variant proposed in the early 1970s to the U.S. Navy.

F-15 Streak Eagle: One stripped and unpainted F-15A, which broke eight time-to-climb world records in January and February 1975.

F-15 S/MTD: The first F-15B was converted into a short-takeoff-and-landing manoeuvre-technology demonstrator aircraft.

F-15 ACTIVE: The F-15 S/MTD was later converted into an advanced flight control technology research aircraft with thrust vectoring nozzles.

F-15 IFCS: The F-15 ACTIVE was converted into an intelligent flight control systems research aircraft.

F-15 MANX: Concept name for a tailless variant of the F-15 ACTIVE, but the NASA ACTIVE experimental aircraft was never modified to be tailless.

F-15 Flight Research Facility: Two F-15A aircraft were acquired in 1976 for use by NASA's Dryden Flight Research Center.

F-15B Research Testbed: Acquired in 1993, it was an F-15B modified and used by NASA's Dryden Flight Research Center for flight tests.

OPERATORS

Israeli Air Force: Two F-15A/B squadrons and one F-15C/D squadron. The IAF had 42 F-15A/Cs, 15 F-15B/D and 25 F-15I aircraft in service as of November 2008.

Japan Air Self-Defence Force: Acquired 203 F-15Js and 20 F-15DJs from 1981. Japan had 157 F-15Js and 45 F-15DJs in use as of November 2008.

Royal Saudi Air Force: Four squadrons of F-15C/D (55/19) since 1981. The RSAF had 139 F-15C/S and 22 F-15D Eagles in operation as of November 2008.

United States Air Force: Operated 630 F-15 aircraft (499 in active duty and 131 in Air National Guard, all variants) as of September 2008.

MCDONNELL DOUGLAS F-15 EAGLE

"Gulf Spirit" was the F-15C assigned to the commander of the U.S. Air Force's 33rd Tactical Fighter Wing (TFW), normally based at Eglin Air Force Base on Florida's Gulf Coast. During Operation Desert Storm, the campaign to remove Iraqi forces from Kuwait in 1991, pilots flying it destroyed three Iraqi Air Force aircraft.

On 29 January 1991, "Gulf Spirit" shot down an Iraqi Mikoyan-Gurevich MiG-23 with an AIM-7M Sparrow. The pilot was Captain David Rose. On 7 February, flown by Captain Anthony Murphy, it destroyed two Sukhoi Su-22M fighter-bombers, again with Sparrows. Colonel Rick Parsons, CO of the 33rd TFW, scored a victory against an Su-22 while flying another F-15, and this is recorded by a green star by his name.

The TFX (Tactical Fighter Experimental) requirement that led to the F-15 was issued in 1968. Experience in Vietnam had shown the need for a fighter with far better manoeuvrability than McDonnell Douglas's F-4 Phantom; improved visibility, particularly to the rear; and a radar that could identify and track targets to be destroyed well beyond visual range. The requirement evolved to specify Mach 2-plus top speed as a counter to Mikoyan-Gurevich's MiG-25 "Foxbat," regarded as a huge threat even though little was factually known about it at the time.

McDonnell Douglas won the TFX contest, and its YF-15A Eagle prototype flew in July 1972, followed in November 1974 by deliveries to the U.S. Air Force.

KEEPING THE WEIGHT DOWN

The F-15A had the same armament as the F-4E Phantom: four AIM-7 Sparrows, four AIM-9 Sidewinders and an M61 Vulcan cannon. Ground attack was very much a secondary consideration, to the extent that "not a pound for air to ground" – in other words, no extra structural weight should be added so that the Eagle could carry bombs – was a frequently heard remark during the design phase.

The F-15A's cockpit was equipped with conventional round dial instruments, but unlike the F-4 had a head-up display (HUD) that displayed flight, radar and weapons information in the pilot's forward vision. Many radar, weapons and communications functions could be controlled by buttons and switches on the throttles and control stick. This was the first application of hands-on-throttle-and-stick, or HOTAS, controls that allowed the pilot to keep his eyes on the enemy without the need to look down.

Avionics equipment was made as accessible as possible, and many items were fitted in line replaceable units or LRUs, which could simply be pulled out and replaced with a fresh unit if the aircraft's built-in test equipment (BITE) detected a fault.

OVERSEAS INTEREST

Israel became the first export customer in 1976 and the only one for the F-15A and two-seat B, which it named Baz (eagle). Later Israeli F-15Cs were the Akef (buzzard) and the F-15I strike aircraft the Ra'am (thunderbolt). In June 1979, Israeli Defence Force/Israeli Air Force Eagles destroyed five Syrian MiG-21s in a skirmish and went on to shoot down many more in 1982 during the Israeli invasion of Lebanon.

Saudi Arabia bought F-15Cs in 1981 and later the F-15S version of the Strike Eagle, eventually acquiring over 140 in total. Saudi Eagles shot down two Iranian Phantoms in 1984. Mitsubishi in Japan built the F-15J and two-seat F-15DJ under licence, while South Korea and Singapore have taken versions of the F-15E designated F-15K and F-15SG, respectively.

In the 1991 Gulf War, U.S. Air Force Eagles were credited with 33 Iraqi aircraft, and a Saudi F-15 destroyed two more. Most kills were scored with the AIM-7. Four MiG-29s fell to U.S. Air Force F-15s over the former Yugoslavia in 1999.

Production of the fighter Eagle has ended, but Boeing has proposed a version of the F-15E called the "Silent Eagle," with canted vertical fins, internal weapons carriage and other stealth features for countries unable to afford or not cleared to receive advanced stealth aircraft such as the F-35 Lightning II.

Above: In the the F-15E Strike Eagle, computer screens have replaced many of the dials found in the F-15A and F-15C.

Above: An F-15C of the U.S. Air Force's 1st Fighter Wing launches an AIM-7 Sparrow. The majority of the F-15s kills have been with AIM-7s.

Above: The F-15 is similar in size to a World War II North American B-25 bomber. Its large wing area is evident here on this Alaska-based aircraft.

Lockheed Martin F-16 Fighting Falcon

F-16C FIGHTING FALCON SPECIFICATION

Dimensions

Fuselage length: 49 ft 4 in (15.03 m)
Wingspan with tip-mounted AAMs: 32 ft 9¾ in (10.00 m)
Wing area: 300.00 sq ft (27.87 m^2)
Wing aspect ratio: 3.0
Tailplane span: 18 ft 3¾ in (5.58 m)
Vertical tail surfaces: 54.75 sq ft (5.09 m^2)
Height: 16 ft 8½ in (5.09 m)
Wheel track: 7 ft 9 in (2.36 m)
Wheelbase: 13 ft 1½ in (4.00 m)

Powerplant

One General Electric F110-GE-100 turbofan rated at 28,984 lb st (128.9 kN) with afterburning, or a Pratt & Whitney F100-PW-220 23,770 lb st (105.7 kN) in Blocks 40/42

Weights

Empty operating: 19,100 lb (8663 kg)
Typical combat takeoff: 21,585 lb (9791 kg)
Max. takeoff for air-to-air mission without drop tanks: 25,071 lb (11,372 kg)
Max. takeoff with max. external load: 42,300 lb (19,187 kg)
g limits: Max. symmetrical design g limit with full internal fuel load ±9

Performance

Max. level speed "clean" at altitude: 1,146 kt (1,320 mph; 2124 km/h)
Max. level speed at sea level: 795 kt (915 mph; 1472 km/h)
Max. rate of climb at sea level: 50,000 ft (15,240 m) per minute
Service ceiling: more than 50,000 ft (15,240 m)
Combat radius: 295 nm (340 miles; 547 km) on a hi-lo-hi mission with six 1,000-lb (454-kg) bombs

Armament

One internal M61 Vulcan 20-mm cannon; max. ordnance of 15,200 lb (6894 kg) on one fuselage pylon and six underwing pylons

Cutaway Key

1 Pitot head/air data probe
2 Fibreglass radome
3 Lightning conducting strips
4 Planar radar scanner
5 Radome hinge point, opens to starboard
6 Scanner tracking mechanism
7 ILS glideslope antenna
8 Radar mounting bulkhead
9 Incidence vane, port and starboard
10 IFF antenna
11 GBU-12B laser-guided bomb
12 AN/APG-68 digital pulse-Doppler multi-mode radar equipment bay
13 Forward oblique radar warning antennas, port and starboard
14 Front pressure bulkhead
15 Static ports
16 Fuselage forebody strake fairing
17 Forward avionics equipment bay
18 Canopy jettison charge
19 Instrument panel shroud
20 Instrument panel, multifunction CRT head-down displays
21 Sidestick controller, fly-by-wire control system
22 Video recorder
23 GEC wide-angle head-up display
24 CBU-52/58/71 submunition dispenser
25 LAU-3A 19-round rocket launcher
26 2.75-in (68-mm) FFAR
27 CBU-87/89 Gator submunition dispenser
28 Starboard intake flank (No. 5R) stores pylon adaptor
29 LANTIRN (FLIR) targeting pod
30 One-piece frameless cockpit canopy
31 Ejection-seat headrest
32 McDonnell-Douglas ACES II zero-zero ejection seat
33 Side console panel
34 Canopy frame fairing
35 Canopy external emergency release
36 Engine throttle lever incorporating HOTAS (hands-on throttle-and-stick) radar controls
37 Canopy jettison handle
38 Cockpit section frame structure
39 Boundary layer splitter plate
40 Fixed-geometry engine air intake
41 Nosewheel, aft retracting
42 LANTIRN (FLIR/TFR) navigation pod
43 Port intake flank (No. 5L) stores pylon adaptor
44 Port position light
45 Intake duct framing
46 Intake ducting
47 Gun gas suppression muzzle aperture
48 Aft avionics equipment bay
49 Cockpit rear pressure bulkhead
50 Canopy hinge point
51 Ejection-seat launch rails
52 Canopy rotary actuator
53 Conditioned-air delivery duct
54 Canopy sealing frame
55 Canopy aft glazing
56 600-U.S. gal (2271-litre) external fuel tank
57 Garrett hydrazine turbine emergency power unit (EPU)
58 Hydrazine fuel tank
59 Fuel-tank bay access panel
60 Forward fuselage bag-type fuel tank, total internal capacity 6972 lb (3162 kg)
61 Fuselage upper longeron
62 Conditioned-air ducting
63 Cannon barrels
64 Forebody frame construction
65 Air system ground connection
66 Ventral air-conditioning system equipment bay
67 Centreline fuel tank, capacity 300 U.S. gal (1136 litres)
68 Mainwheel door hydraulic actuator
69 Mainwheel door
70 Hydraulic system ground connectors
71 Gun-bay ventral gas vent
72 GE M61A1 Vulcan 20-mm rotary cannon
73 Ammunition feed chute
74 Hydraulic gun drive motor
75 Port hydraulic reservoir
76 Centre fuselage integral fuel tank
77 Leading-edge flap drive hydraulic motor
78 Ammunition drum with 511 rounds
79 Upper position light/refuelling floodlight
80 TACAN antenna
81 Hydraulic accumulator
82 Starboard hydraulic reservoir
83 Leading-edge flap drive shaft
84 Inboard, No. 6 stores station, capacity 4,500 lb (2041 kg)
85 Pylon attachment hardpoint
86 Leading-edge flap drive shaft and rotary actuators
87 No. 7 stores hardpoint, capacity 3,500 lb (1588 kg)
88 Starboard forward radar warning antenna
89 Missile launch rails
90 AIM-120 AMRAAM medium-range AAMs
91 MXU-648 baggage pod, carriage of essential ground equipment and personal effects for off-base deployment
92 Starboard leading-edge manoeuvre flap, down position
93 Outboard, No. 8 stores station, capacity 700 lb (318 kg)
94 Wingtip, No. 9 stores station, capacity 425 lb (193 kg)
95 Wingtip AMRAAM
96 Starboard navigation light
97 Fixed portion of trailing edge
98 Static dischargers
99 Starboard flaperon
100 Starboard wing integral fuel tank
101 Fuel system piping
102 Fuel pump
103 Starboard wingroot attachment fishplates
104 Fuel-tank access panels
105 Universal air refuelling receptacle (UARSSI), open
106 Engine intake centrebody fairing
107 Airframe mounted accessory equipment gearbox
108 Jet fuel starter
109 Machined wing attachment bulkheads
110 Engine fuel management equipment
111 Pressure refuelling receptacle ventral adaptor
112 Pratt & Whitney F100-PW-229 afterburning turbofan engine
113 VHF/IFF antenna
114 Starboard flaperon hydraulic actuator
115 Fuel-tank tail fins
116 Sidebody fairing integral fuel tank
117 Position light
118 Cooling air ram air intake
119 Finroot fairing
120 Forward engine support link
121 Rear fuselage integral fuel tank
122 Thermally insulated tank inner skin
123 Tank access panels
124 Radar warning system power amplifier
125 Finroot attachment fittings
126 Flight control system hydraulic accumulators
127 Multi-spar fin torsion box structure
128 Starboard all-moving tailplane (tailplane panels interchangeable)
129 General Electric F110-GE-129 alternative powerplant
130 Fin leading-edge honeycomb core
131 Dynamic pressure probe
132 Carbon-fibre fin skin panelling
133 VHF comms antenna (AM/FM)
134 Fintip antenna fairing

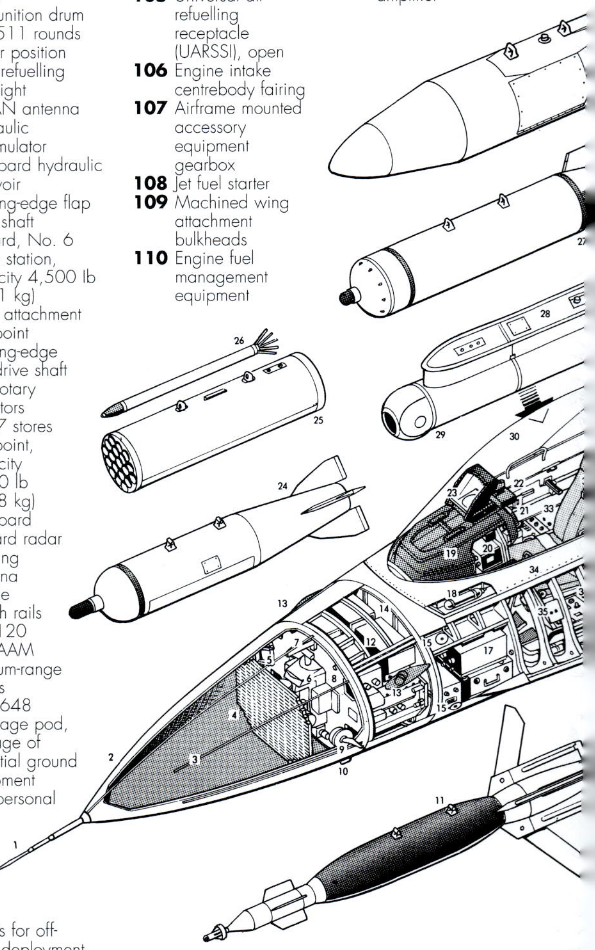

Originally conceived as a "no-frills" lightweight fighter, the F-16 has morphed into a potent multi-role aircraft and one of the great sales successes of the modern era. Constant updating will see this 1970s design remain effective well into the twenty-first century.

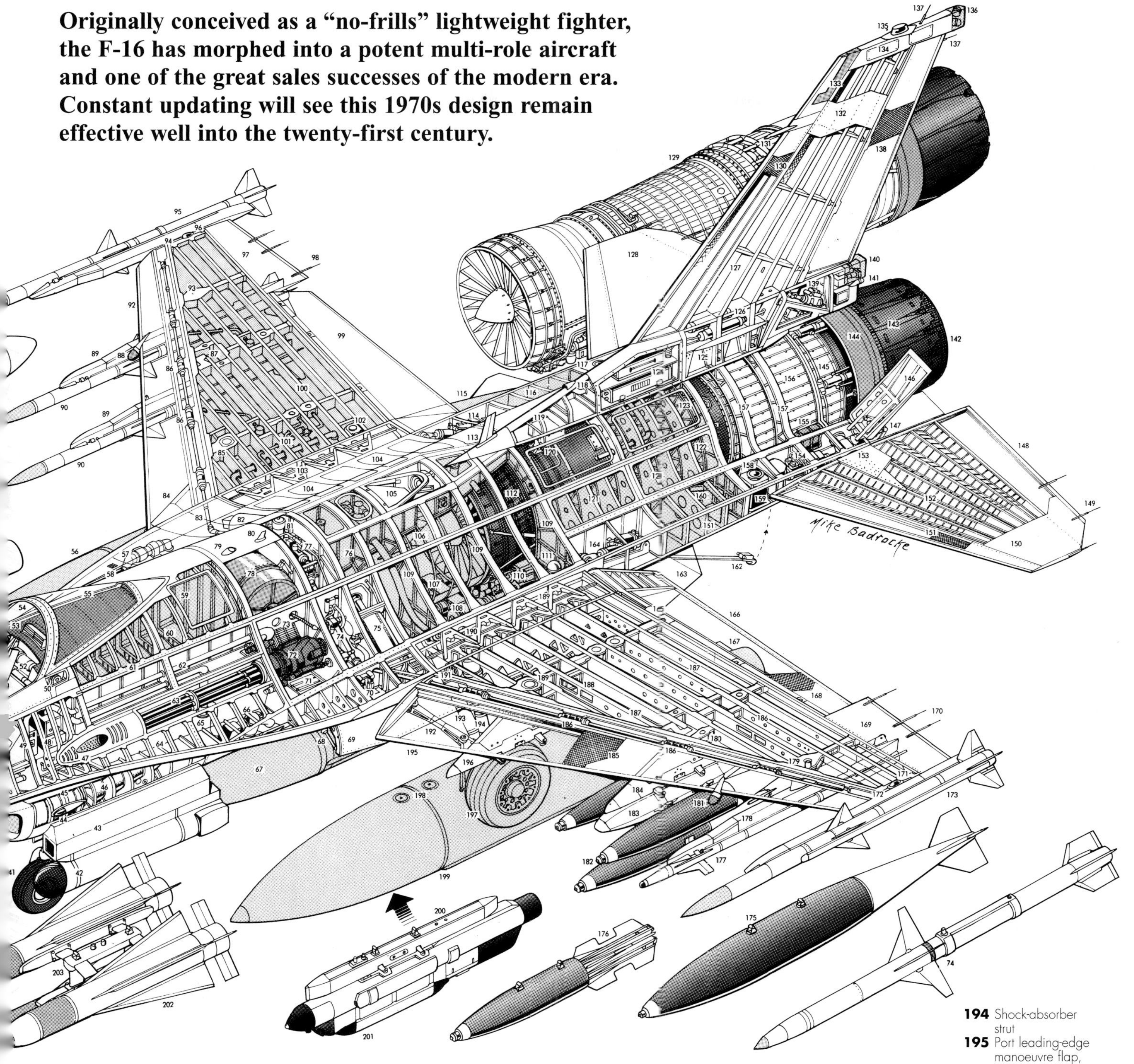

135 Anti-collision light
136 Threat warning antennas
137 Static dischargers
138 Rudder honeycomb core structure
139 Rudder hydraulic actuator
140 ECM antenna fairing
141 Tail navigation light
142 Variable-area afterburner nozzle
143 Afterburner nozzle flaps
144 Nozzle sealing fairing
145 Afterburner nozzle fueldraulic actuators (5)
146 Port split trailing-edge airbrake panel, open, upper and lower surfaces
147 Airbrake actuating linkage
148 Port all-moving tailplane
149 Static dischargers
150 Graphite-epoxy tailplane skin panels
151 Leading-edge honeycomb construction
152 Corrugated aluminium substructure
153 Tailplane pivot mounting
154 Tailplane hydraulic actuator
155 Fuel jettison chamber, port and starboard
156 Afterburner ducting
157 Rear fuselage machined bulkheads
158 Port navigation light
159 AN/ALE-40(VO-4) chaff/flare launcher, port and starboard
160 Main engine thrust mounting, port and starboard
161 Sidebody fairing frame structure
162 Runway arrestor hook
163 Composite ventral fin, port and starboard
164 Port flaperon hydraulic actuator
165 Flaperon hinges
166 Port flaperon, lowered
167 External fuel tank tail fairing
168 Flaperon honeycomb core structure
169 Fixed portion of trailing edge
170 Static dischargers
171 Port navigation light
172 Wingtip, No. 1 stores station, capacity 425 lb (193 kg)
173 Port wingtip AMRAAM
174 AGM-88 HARM (High-speed Anti-Radiation Missile)
175 Mk 84 low-drag 2,000-lb (907-kg) HE bomb
176 Mk 83 Snakeye retarded bomb
177 AIM-9L Sidewinder air-to-air missile
178 Missile launch rails
179 No. 2 stores station, capacity 700 lb (318 Kg)
180 No. 3 stores station, capacity 3,500 lb (1588 Kg)
181 Port forward radar warning antenna
182 Mk 82 500 lb (227 kg) HE bombs
183 Triple ejector rack
184 Intermediate wing pylon
185 Leading-edge manoeuvre flap honeycomb core structure
186 Flap drive shaft and rotary actuators
187 Multi-spar wing torsion box structure
188 Port wing integral fuel tankage
189 No. 4 stores station hardpoint, capacity 4,500 lb (2041 kg)
190 Wing panel root attachment fishplates
191 Undercarriage leg mounted landing light
192 Articulated retraction/drag link
193 Main undercarriage leg strut
194 Shock-absorber strut
195 Port leading-edge manoeuvre flap, down position
196 Inboard wing pylon
197 Port mainwheel, forward-retracting
198 Fuel filler caps
199 Port 370-U.S. gal (1400-litre) external tank
200 Centreline, No. 5 stores pylon, capacity 2,200 lb (998 kg)
201 AN/ALQ-184(V)-2 (short) ECM pod
202 AGM-65 Maverick air-to-surface missiles
203 LAU-88 triple missile carrier/launcher

"The F-16 makes you think there is nothing you can't do. As one [evaluation] pilot said: 'If I'm here and I want to be there, I just sort of *think* there and I *am* there!'"
– Phil Oestricher, F-16 test pilot

FACTS

- More than 4,400 F-16s have been built since 1974, and they are in service with 24 nations.
- F-16s are offered with a choice of General Electric or Pratt & Whitney turbofan engines.
- The pilot's seat is reclined 30 degrees, which helps to increase tolerance to g-forces.

LOCKHEED MARTIN F-16 FIGHTING FALCON – MAJOR VARIANTS

F-16A FSD: Single-seat fighters from full-scale development batch for service testing.

F-16B FSD: Two-seat conversion trainers from full-scale development batch.

F-16A/B Block 1: Initial production version. Distinguished by their black radomes. Most Block 1 aircraft were upgraded to Block 10 standard in a programme called "Pacer Loft" in 1982.

F-16A/B Block 5: Refined production version. Most Block 5 aircraft were upgraded to Block 10 standard.

F-16A/B Block 10: Slightly revised avionics equipment fit.

F-16A/B Block 15: The most numerous version of the F-16. Introduced an enlarged tailplane, which is required when carrying large bomb loads.

ADF F-16A/B Block 15: Conversion of Block 15 aircraft to dedicated Air Defense Fighter role for use by the U.S. Air National Guard.

F-16A/B Block 10/Block 15 OCU: Operational capabilities upgrade programme. Improved avionics and fire-control system and provision for F100-PW-220E engine.

F-16/B MLU: Midlife update programme for the original NATO F-16s.

F-16A/B Block 20: Export version for Taiwan.

F-16C/D Block 25: Introduced the ability to carry AIM-120 AMRAAM, as well as night and precision ground-attack capabilities.

F-16C/D Block 30/32: New engines: Block 30 the General Electric F110-GE-100; Block 32 the Pratt & Whitney F100-PW-220.

F-16C/D Block 40/42 "Night Falcon": Introduced the LANTIRN navigation and targeting pods and extensive air-to-ground loads. Block 40/42 production began in 1988 and went on until 1995.

F-16C/D Block 50/52: Equipped with the APG-68(V)7 radar and F110-GE-229 (Block 50) or F100-PW-220 (Block 52) Improved Performance Engine.

F-16CJ/DJ Block 50D/52D "Wild Weasel": Could carry the AGM-88 HARM and the AN/ASQ-213 HARM Targeting System (HTS) in the suppression of enemy air defences (SEAD) mission.

F-16C/D Block 60: Export to United Arab Emirates.

F-16/79: One F-16A converted to take a General Electric J79 engine.

F-16 CCV: First YF-16 rebuild to test Control Configured Vehicle technology, with twin canards added.

NF-16D VISTA: Dedicated research aircraft.

F-16E/F: Proposed designations for single- and two-seat production versions of F-16XL.

F-16N: Version of the F-16C Block 30 for use by the U.S. Navy as an aggressor aircraft.

TF-16N: Two-seat conversion trainer version of F-16N.

LOCKHEED MARTIN F-16 FIGHTING FALCON

Israel is the largest non-U.S. user of the F-16, with more than 360 having served since 1980. These range from some of the earliest F-16As to the far more sophisticated F-16I. The aircraft illustrated here is an F-16D Block 40 of 105 "Scorpion" Tayseet (Squadron), based at Hatzor Israeli Air Force Base in central Israel. Known as the Brakeet II ("Thunderbolt"), this version was delivered in 1991 under the Peace Marble III programme and features a dorsal spine containing locally designed avionics, probably associated with the "Wild Weasel" defence suppression role. It is armed with a GBU-15 glide bomb on the starboard outer wing, with a Mk 82 500-lb (227-kg) bomb for balance on the port side. Under the port fuselage is an AAW-13 datalink pod for the GBU-15 and a Litening targeting pod on the starboard side.

Above: The F-16CJ is a dedicated defence suppression variant that fulfills the "Wild Weasel" role with the AGM-88 Harm, as seen on the starboard inner pylon here.

Left: This UAE F-16 shows off its large conformal fuel tanks.

U.S. experience in Vietnam showed the need for a small, manoeuvrable fighter able to counter the types of threat posed by aircraft such as the MiG-17 and MiG-21 that were proliferating in Soviet-aligned countries. The trend in fighter aircraft had been towards bigger, heavier and more sophisticated aircraft such as the F-14 and F-15, which even the U.S. military could afford in only relatively small numbers.

A LIGHTWEIGHT FIGHTER

A lightweight fighter (LWF) competition was held by the U.S. Air Force, culminating in 1975 with fly-off evaluations of prototypes from Northrop (the YF-17 Cobra) and General Dynamics (the YF-16). General Dynamics' F-16 design was the victor, while the YF-17 was further developed to become the F/A-18 Hornet for the U.S. Navy and Marine Corps.

Key to the F-16's agility is its fly-by-wire control system, the first to be used in a production aircraft. Instead of moving the control surfaces with mechanical cables and

Above: A feature of many later block F-16C/Ds is a wide-angle holographic head-up display. Note the reclined seat.

hydraulic boosters, the pilot's inputs are carried via wires through flight-control system computers, which allow manoeuvres up to but not beyond the aircraft's physical limits. Designed to be inherently unstable without the computers so that it would easily change direction when commanded to, the F-16 cannot fly without them. Instead of a conventional control column coming up from the cockpit floor, the F-16 pilot uses a sidestick controller on the right console, which has very little physical movement.

SALE OF THE CENTURY

The F-16A entered service with the U.S. Air Force simultaneously with service in several European air forces. In the so-called "fighter sale of the century," Belgium, the Netherlands, Denmark and Norway all ordered F-16s as replacements for their Lockheed F-104 Starfighters even before the programme was still in the testing phase. Turkey, Portugal and Greece, and later Italy and Poland, also joined the club of European F-16 users. The Fighting Falcon, as the F-16 was eventually called, also had sales success in the Middle East (Israel, Jordan, Egypt, United Arab Emirates, Bahrain and Oman); Asia (Pakistan, Singapore, Thailand, Taiwan, Indonesia, South Korea) and South America (Venezuela and Chile). Further countries may become users of new or used F-16s even into the design's fifth decade.

Fighting Falcons have seen action with several users. U.S., Israeli, Pakistani, Venezuelan and Dutch F-16s have all claimed air combat victories in various conflicts. In the air-to-ground role, F-16s have become one of the workhorses of close air support. Many of the NATO users have deployed their F-16s to Afghanistan since 2001.

CONTINUING SERVICE

The main production version has been the F-16C (and its two-seat counterpart the F-16D), which had structural and avionics improvements over the F-16A and B. Production for the U.S. Air Force has ended, but the Falcon is still for sale, mainly in advanced F-16E and F form. Also known as the "Block 60," the F-16E and F have electronically scanned radars, large conformal fuel tanks and the capability to carry a wider range of weapons. The E/F has sold only to the United Arab Emirates, but its features are available for other customers.

British Aerospace Sea Harrier

The Sea Harrier kept British fixed-wing naval aviation alive after the Royal Navy's last big deck carrier was retired. In 1982 they were instrumental in the fight to recover the Falkland Islands from Argentine forces.

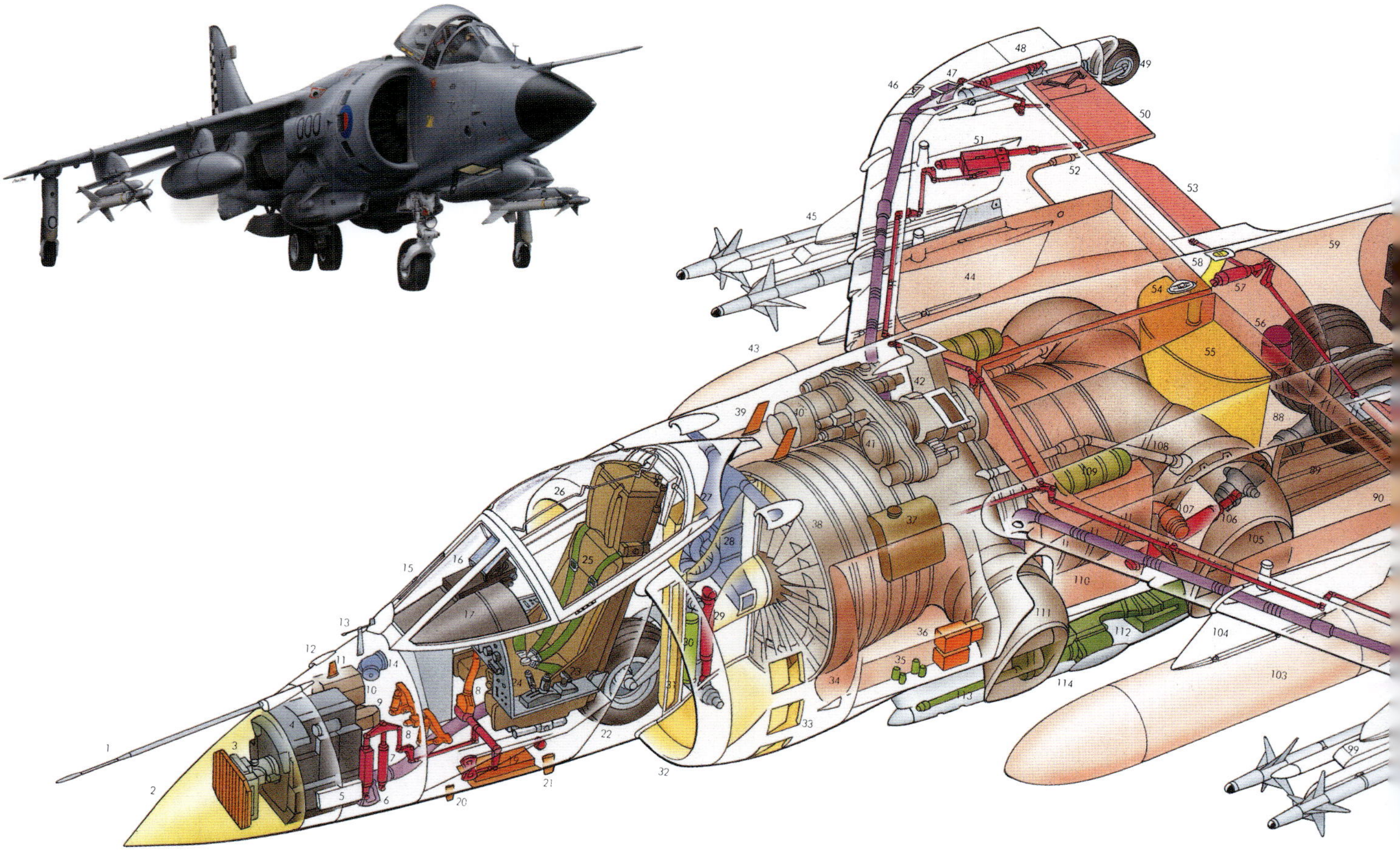

Cutaway Key

1 Pitot head
2 Radome
3 Ferranti Blue Fox radar scanner
4 Radar equipment module
5 Radome hinge
6 Nose pitch reaction control valve
7 Pitch feel and trim control mechanism
8 Rudder pedals
9 Starboard side oblique camera
10 Inertial platform
11 IFF aerial
12 Cockpit ram air intake
13 Yaw vane
14 Pressurization spill valve
15 Windscreen wiper
16 Head-up display
17 Instrument panel shroud
18 Control column and linkages
19 Doppler antenna
20 TACAN aerial
21 UHF aerial
22 Nose undercarriage wheel bay
23 Radar hand controller
24 Throttle and nozzle angle control levers
25 Martin-Baker Mk 10H zero-zero ejection seat
26 Miniature detonating cord (MDC) canopy breaker
27 Boundary layer spill duct
28 Cockpit air-conditioning pack
29 Nose undercarriage hydraulic retraction jack
30 Hydraulic accumulator
31 Boundary layer bleed duct
32 Engine air intake
33 Intake suction relief doors (spring-loaded)
34 Forward fuselage flank fuel tank
35 Hydraulic system ground connectors
36 Engine monitoring and recording equipment
37 Engine oil tank
38 Rolls-Royce Pegasus Mk 104 turbofan engine
39 UHF homing aerials
40 Alternator
41 Accessory equipment gearbox
42 Gas turbine starter/auxiliary power unit (GTS/APU)
43 Starboard external fuel tank
44 Starboard wing integral fuel tank
45 Twin missile pylon
46 Starboard navigation light
47 Roll control reaction air valve
48 Outrigger wheel fairing
49 Starboard outrigger wheel
50 Starboard aileron
51 Aileron hydraulic actuator
52 Fuel jettison valve
53 Starboard plain flap
54 Anti-collision light
55 Water methanol tank
56 Engine-fire suppression bottle
57 Flap hydraulic actuator
58 Water-methanol filler cap
59 Rear fuselage fuel tank
60 Emergency ram air turbine extended
61 Ram air turbine actuator
62 Heat exchanger air intake
63 HF tuner
64 HF notch aerial
65 Rudder control linkage
66 Starboard all-moving tailplane
67 Temperature probe
68 Forward radar-warning antenna
69 VHF aerial
70 Rudder
71 Rudder trim tab
72 Rear rudder-warning antenna
73 Tail pitch control reaction air valve
74 Yaw control reaction air valves
75 Port all-moving tailplane
76 IFF notch aerial
77 Tail bumper

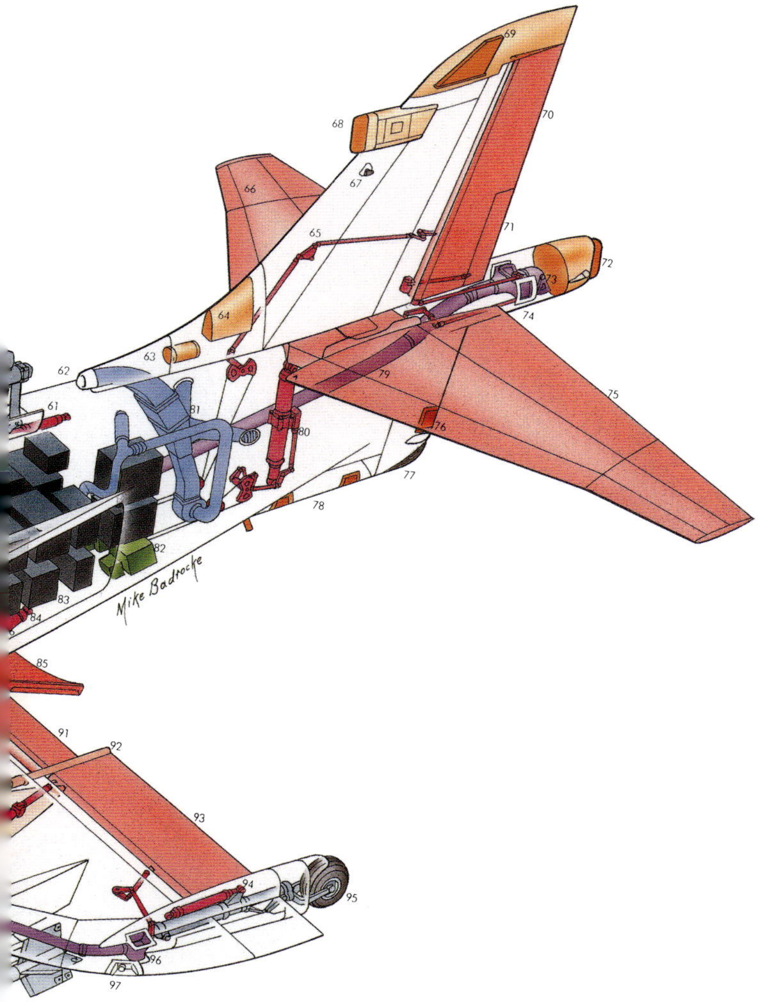

78 Radar altimeter aerials
79 Reaction control air duct
80 Tailplane hydraulic actuator
81 Rear equipment bay air-conditioning pack
82 Chaff/flare dispensers
83 Avionics equipment bay
84 Airbrake hydraulic jack
85 Ventral airbrake
86 Liquid oxygen converter
87 Hydraulic system nitrogen pressurizing bottle
88 Main undercarriage stowage
89 Nozzle blast shield
90 Port wing integral fuel tank
91 Port plain flap
92 Fuel jettison
93 Port aileron
94 Outrigger wheel hydraulic retraction jack
95 Port outrigger wheel
96 Roll control reaction air valve
97 Port navigation light
98 AIM-9L Sidewinder air-to-air missiles
99 Twin missile carrier/launcher
100 Outboard stores pylon
101 Reaction control air duct
102 Port aileron hydraulic actuator
103 External fuel tank
104 Inboard wing pylon
105 Rear (hot-stream) swivelling exhaust nozzle
106 Main undercarriage hydraulic retraction jack
107 Pressure refuelling connection
108 Nozzle bearing cooling air duct
109 Hydraulic system reservoir, port and starboard
110 Centre fuselage flank fuel tank
111 Fan air (cold-stream) swivelling nozzle
112 Ammunition magazine
113 ADEN 30-mm cannon
114 Ventral gun pack, port and starboard

SEA HARRIER FRS1 SPECIFICATION

Dimensions

Overall length: 47 ft 7 in (14.50 m)
Length with nose folded: 41 ft 9 in (12.73 m)
Wingspan: 25 ft 3 in (7.70 m)
Wingspan with ferry tips: 29 ft 8 in (9.04 m)
Wing area: 202.10 sq ft (18.68 m^2)
Wing aspect ratio: 3.175

Powerplant

One Rolls-Royce Pegasus Mk 104 vectored thrust turbofan rated at 21,500 lb st (95.6 kN)

Weights

Basic empty: 13,000 lb (5897 kg)
Operating empty: 14,502 lb (6374 kg)
Maximum takeoff weight: 26,200 lb (11,884 kg)

Fuel load

Maximum internal fuel: 5,060 lb (2295 kg)
Maximum external fuel: 5,300 lb (2404 kg) in two 120-U.S. gal (455-litre) drop tanks or two 396- or 228-U.S. gal (1500- or 864-litre) ferry tanks; maximum ordnance 8,000 lb (3629 kg)

Performance

Maximum speed at high altitude: 825 mph (1328 km/h)
Maximum speed "clean" at sea level: more than 736 mph (1185 km/h)
Cruising speed at 36,000 ft (10,975 m): 528 mph (850 km/h)
Maximum rate of climb at sea level: 50,000 ft (15,240 m) per minute
Service ceiling: 51,000 ft (15,545 m)
Takeoff run: 1,000 ft (305 m) at maximum takeoff weight without "ski jump"; landing run 0 ft (0 m) at normal landing weight

Range

Combat radius: 460 miles (750 km) on a hi-hi-hi interception mission with four AAMs, or 288 miles (463 km) on a hi-lo-hi attack mission.
g limit: +7.8/-4.2

Armament

Underfuselage mounts for two 30-mm ADEN cannon, and four underwing hardpoints stressed for up to 8,000 lb (3629 kg). Standard carrying capabilities as follows: underfuselage and inboard wing hardpoints 2,000 lb (907 kg) each; outboard wing pylons 650 lb (295 kg) each. Cleared for carriage of standard British 1,000-lb (454-kg) free-fall and retarded HE bombs, BAe Sea Eagle ASM, AGM-84 Harpoon ASM, WE177 tactical nuclear free-fall bomb, Lepus flare units, CBLS 100 practice bomb dispenser and most NATO-standard bombs, rockets and flares. Air-to-air armament can comprise four AIM-9L Sidewinders on twin-rail launchers, or MATRA Magic missiles on Indian aircraft.

"The Sea Harrier with the AIM-9L Sidewinder was a very bad system for us, a very good system for the British."
– Argentine Navy pilot Bernado Rotolo

FACTS

- Spain, Thailand and the United States have operated first-generation Harriers from carriers, but the Indian Navy and the Royal Navy were the only Sea Harrier users.
- The two-seat Sea Harriers such as the T8 have more in common with the land-based Harriers.
- The Sea Harrier Mk 2's Blue Vixen radar was regarded as one of the best fitted to any single-seat fighter in the 1990s.

BAE SEA HARRIER – VARIANTS & OPERATORS

VARIANTS

Harrier T4N: Two-seat naval training version of the Harrier T2.

Sea Harrier FRS1: Initial production version of a navalized Harrier. 57 built survivors converted to Sea Harrier FA2.

Sea Harrier FRS51: Indian Navy variant of the FRS1. Single-seat fighter, reconnaissance and attack aircraft. Fitted with Matra R550 Magic air-to-air missiles. The first of 23 FRS51s were delivered in 1983.

Harrier T60: Export version of the T4N two-seat training version for the Indian Navy. At least four Harrier T60s were purchased by the Indian Navy for land-based training.

Sea Harrier FA2: Upgrade incorporating increased air-to-air weapons load, look-down radar, increased range, and improved cockpit displays. The first aircraft was delivered on 2 April 1993, and the first operational deployment was in April 1994 as part of the UN force in Bosnia. The final new-build Sea Harrier FA2 was delivered on 18 January 1999.

Harrier T8: Seven Harrier T4s two-seat trainers updated with Sea Harrier FA2 instrumentation but no radar. Retired from service in March 2006.

OPERATORS

India
Indian Navy
300 Naval Squadron
Still in service.

United Kingdom
Royal Navy
Fleet Air Arm
800 Naval Air Squadron
Operated 12 Sea Harrier FRS1s aboard HMS *Hermes* during the Falklands War (1982).
Disbanded 2006.

801 Naval Air Squadron
Operated eight Sea Harrier FRS1s aboard HMS *Invincible* during the Falklands War (1982).
Disbanded 2006.

809 Naval Air Squadron
Operated Eight Sea Harrier FR1s across HMS *Hermes* and HMS *Invincible* during the Falklands War (1982) and served with HMS *Illustrious* after the Falklands War.
Disbanded 1982.

899 Naval Air Squadron
12 Sea Harriers (10 loaned to 801 Naval Air Squadron and and 809 Naval Air Squadron during the Falklands War).
Disbanded 2006.

BAE SEA HARRIER

The Sea Harrier FA2 first saw operational service flying patrols over Bosnia in August 1994 with the Royal Navy's Operational Evaluation Unit, No. 899 Squadron. Shown here with two Sidewinders and fuel tanks, the FA2 could carry AIM-9s on double launchers or up to four AIM-120 AMRAAMs on the wing pylons and in place of the cannon pods seen fitted here. One drop tank has also been modified to carry a camera. As a Sea Harrier FRS1, Sea Harrier XZ455 shot down two Argentine Daggers in the Falklands War in 1982. It crashed into the Adriatic Sea in February 1996 when returning from a mission over Bosnia, but the pilot was rescued.

Even before the Hawker Siddeley Harrier GR1 Vertical Take-Off and Landing (VTOL) strike aircraft entered Royal Air Force service in 1969, its potential as a shipboard aircraft had been tested on a variety of platforms. Despite factions that said every new fighter had to be large and Mach 2–capable, design work began in 1972 on a basic adaptation of the RAF Harrier into a fighter for operation from light carriers.

The new naval Harrier was intended to be multi-role, able to defend the fleet against Soviet Navy "Bear" bombers, conduct anti-shipping and ground-attack missions, and perform photo-reconnaissance duties. As such, it was designated Sea Harrier FRS1, for "fighter, "reconnaissance" and "strike." The Sea Harrier had a new nose section with a raised canopy and a pointed radome containing a Ferranti Blue Fox radar. A new navigation system and completely revised cockpit were other changes from the GR3, as was a folding nose to allow it to use standard aircraft-carrier elevators.

FALKLANDS FIGHTERS

By the time the Sea Harrier flew in 1978, the last "big deck" Royal Navy carrier, HMS *Ark Royal*, was being retired. The Admiralty had commissioned three so-called "through-deck cruisers" as a way of retaining a carrier capability. The first

Top: The nozzle control lever common to Harriers can be seen on the left console of this Sea Harrier FRS1 cockpit.
Above: One modification made after the 1982 Falklands War was to fit double AIM-9 launchers to Harrier FRS1s such as these No. 800 Squadron aircraft.

of these, HMS *Invincible*, and the older carrier HMS *Hermes* were the only means of providing air protection for the task force that was sent to reclaim the Falkland Islands from Argentina in 1982. Both ships were fitted with "ski-jump" ramps that allowed rolling takeoffs and vertical landings, saving fuel and increasing range.

Flying from HMS *Invincible* and HMS *Hermes*, Sea Harriers destroyed 23 Argentine aircraft with their AIM-9L Sidewinders and 30-mm cannon pods during Operation Corporate, the British name for the Falklands campaign. To keep the carriers safe from Argentine air attack, they had to operate well to the East of the Falklands, giving them little time on station over the islands, and Argentine aircraft were able to successfully attack a number of ships.

VERY LIMITED EXPORT

India became the only export customer for the Sea Harrier when its navy ordered 24 FRS51s, in 1978. Today, the remaining aircraft fly from INS *Vikrant*, the former HMS *Hermes*, and are being upgraded to take newer weapons such as the Rafael Derby AAM.

In 1988 an upgraded version, the Sea Harrier FRS2 (later renamed FA2) was flown. This replaced the Blue Fox radar with the multi-mode Blue Vixen in a new, bulged radome. Four Sidewinders or AIM-120 AMRAAMs replaced the two AIM-9s of the Falklands era. A mix of conversions and new-build aircraft were made for a total of just over 50 aircraft. These served on the "Invincible"-class ships from the mid-1990s and saw action over the Balkans in Operation Deliberate Force in 1995 and Operation Allied Force in 1999, flying both combat air patrol and bombing missions.

The Royal Navy's Sea Harriers were retired somewhat prematurely in 2006 as a money-saving measure, and the Fleet Air Arm's strike capability was merged with the RAF's Harrier GR.7 units to form Joint Force Harrier. The Royal Navy will have a "capability gap" in organic air defence until the Joint Combat Aircraft (F-35 Lightning II) enters service in the mid-2010s.

Above: A Sea Harrier FA2 makes a vertical landing on a Royal Navy "Invincible"-class carrier.

Mikoyan MiG-29 "Fulcrum"

The MiG-29 was the first Soviet fighter design to emphasize manoeuvrability over straight-line performance and pilot initiative over strict ground control. It has continued to sell well even after the fall of the Soviet Union.

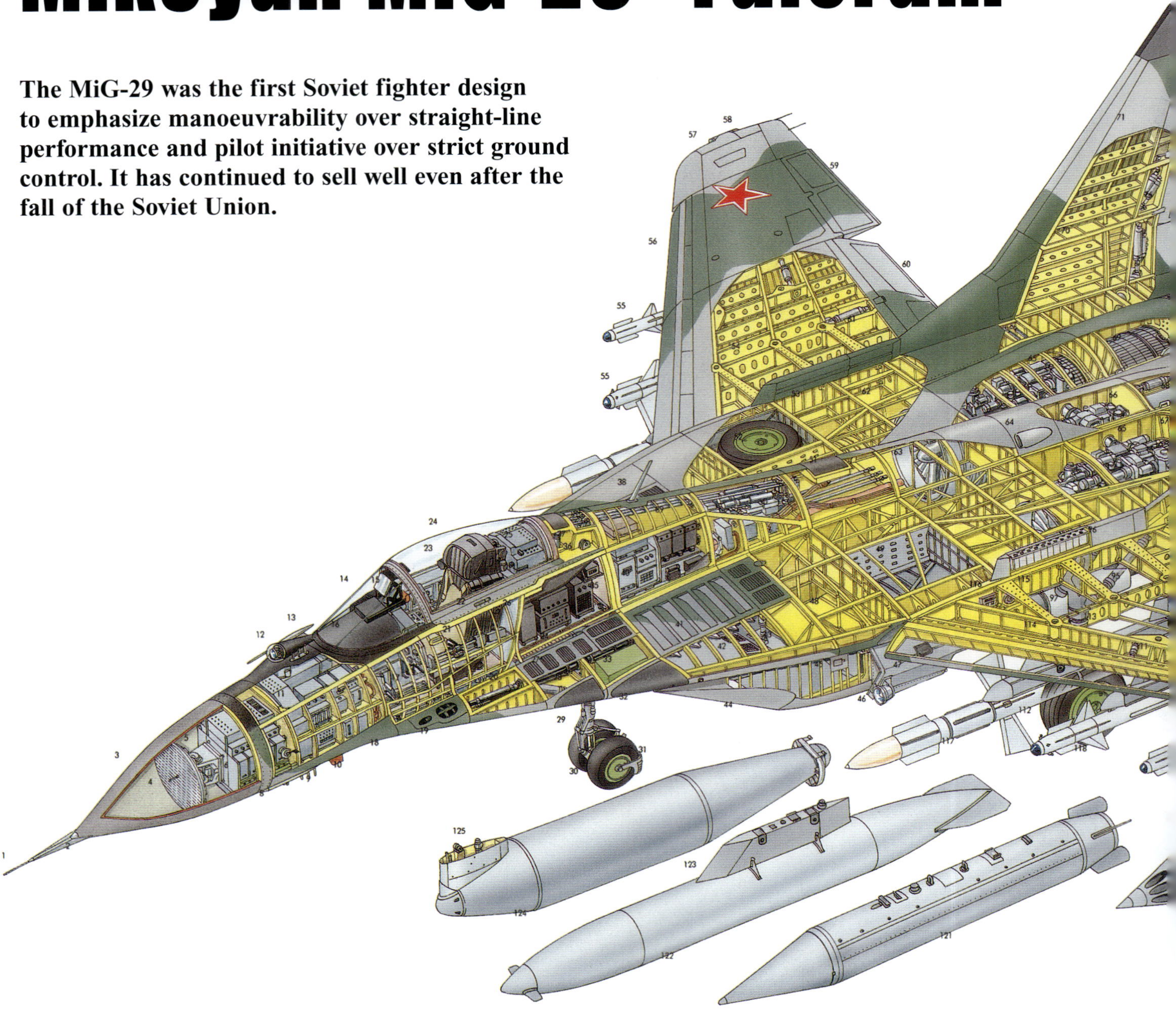

Cutaway Key

1 Pitot head
2 Vortex generating nose strake
3 Fibreglass radome
4 Pulse-Doppler radar scanner
5 Scanner tracking mechanism
6 N-O19 (NATO: "Slot Back") radar equipment module
7 Angle-of-attack transmitter
8 ILS aerial fairing
9 SRO-2 (NATO: "Odd Rods") IFF aerial
10 UHF antenna
11 Forward avionics equipment bay
12 Infrared search and track sensor and laser ranger
13 Dynamic pressure probe
14 Frameless windscreen panel
15 Pilot's head-up-display
16 Instrument panel shroud
17 Rudder pedals and control column
18 Fuselage blended chine fairing
19 Cannon muzzle aperture
20 Cannon barrel
21 Slide mounted engine throttle levers
22 Canopy latch
23 K-36D "zero-zero" ejection seat
24 Upward-hinging cockpit canopy cover
25 Electrical distribution centre
26 Cockpit rear pressure bulkhead
27 Cannon bay venting air louvres
28 Nosewheel retraction jack
29 Levered suspension nosewheel leg
30 Twin nosewheels, aft-retracting
31 Mudguard
32 ECM aerial panels
33 Cartridge case and link collector box
34 Ammunition magazine
35 Centre avionics equipment bay
36 Canopy hinge point
37 Canopy hydraulic jack
38 HF aerial
39 Mechanical control rods
40 Rear avionics equipment bay
41 Air intake louvres/ blow-in doors
42 Variable-area intake ramp doors
43 Ramp hydraulic actuator
44 Port engine air intake
45 Weapons interlock access
46 Landing lamp
47 Mainwheel door
48 Forward fuselage integral fuel tank
49 Port main undercarriage wheel bay
50 Flight-control system hydraulic equipment module
51 ADF aerial
52 Starboard main undercarriage wheel bay
53 Chaff/flare cartridge housing
54 Starboard wing integral fuel tank
55 Starboard wing missile carriage
56 Leading-edge manoeuvre flap
57 Starboard navigation light
58 Radar warning antenna
59 Starboard aileron
60 Plain flap
61 Flap hydraulic jack
62 Centre fuselage integral fuel tank
63 Engine compressor face
64 Cooling air scoop
65 Top-mounted engine accessory equipment gearboxes
66 Central gas turbine starter/APU
67 Engine bay/ tailplane attachment machined main frames
68 Airbrake hydraulic jack
69 RD-33D afterburning turbofan engine
70 Fin rib construction
71 Carbon-fibre fin skin panelling
72 Fintip VHF aerial fairing
73 Radar warning antenna
74 "Swift Rod" ILS aerial
75 Starboard rudder
76 Rudder hydraulic actuator
77 Tailplane hydraulic actuator
78 Starboard all-moving tailplane

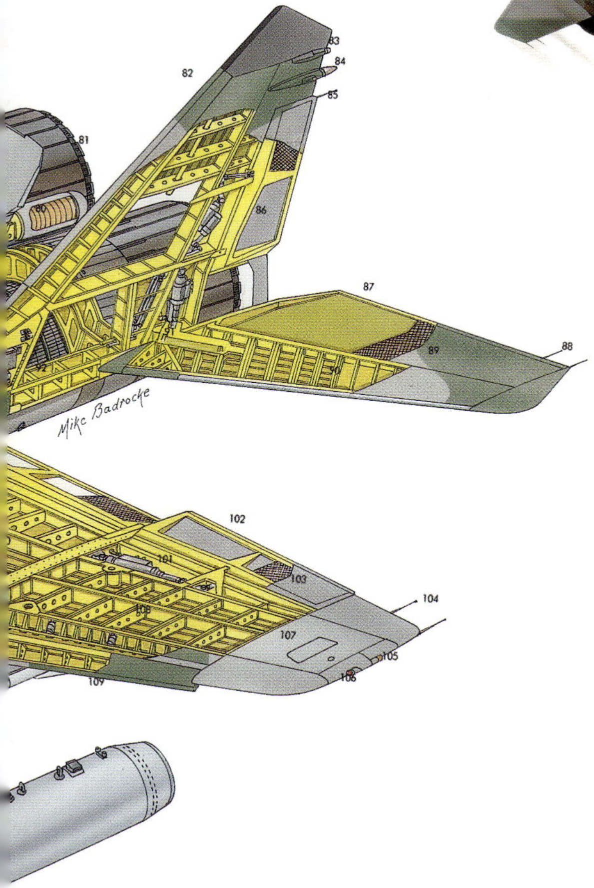

79 Airbrake, upper and lower split surfaces
80 Brake parachute housing
81 Variable-area afterburner nozzle
82 Port tail fin
83 Tail navigation light
84 Sirena-3 ECM aerial fairing
85 Static discharger
86 Port rudder composite construction
87 Port all-moving tailplane
88 Static dischargers
89 Carbon-fibre trailing-edge skin panelling
90 Tailplane spar box construction
91 Tailplane pivot point
92 Fuselage side-body fairing construction
93 Artificial feel system pitot heads and control valves
94 Port plain flap composite construction
95 Main undercarriage hydraulic retraction jack
96 Port chaff/flare cartridge
97 Main undercarriage leg pivot fixing
98 Pylon attachment hardpoints
99 Flap hydraulic jack
100 Port wing integral fuel tank
101 Aileron hydraulic actuator
102 Port aileron composite construction
103 Carbon-fibre skin panelling
104 Static dischargers
105 Port identification light
106 Port navigation light
107 Downward identification light and remote compass housing
108 Outer wing panel rib construction
109 Port leading-edge manoeuvre flap
110 Port wing missile pylons
111 Leading edge flap hydraulic jacks
112 Port mainwheel
113 Main undercarriage leg strut
114 Three-spar wing torsion box construction
115 Spar root attachment joints
116 Undercarriage bay pressure refuelling connection
117 AA-10 "Alamo" long-range air-to-air missile
118 AA-11 "Archer" intermediate-range air-to-air missile
119 AA-8 "Aphid" short-range air-to-air missile
120 57-mm rocket pack
121 Cluster bomb
122 Wing-mounted external fuel tank
123 Tank pylon
124 Centre fuselage "tunnel" fuel tank
125 Tank pylon attachment

MIG-29 "FULCRUM-A" SPECIFICATION

Dimensions

Fuselage length (including probe): 56 ft 10 in (17.32 m)
Wing span: span 37 ft 3¼ in (11.36m)
Wing area: 409.04 sq ft (38 m²)
Tailplane span: 25 ft 6¼ in (7.78m)
Wheel track: 10 ft 2 in (3.10m)
Wheelbase: 12 ft 0.5 in (3.67m)
Height: 15 ft 6.⅕ in (4.73m)

Powerplant

Two Klimov/Leningrad (Isotov/Sarkisov) RD-33 augmented turbofans each rated at 11,111 lb st (49.42 kN) dry and 18,298 lb st (81.39 kN) with afterburning

Weights

Empty operating: 24,030 lb (10,900 kg)
Normal takeoff interceptor: 33,600 lb (15,240 kg)
Maximum takeoff: 40,785 lb (18,500 kg)
Maximum wing loading: 99.71 lb/sq ft (486.8 kg/m²)

Fuel and load

Total internal fuel: 1,153 U.S. gal (4365 litres)
Total external fuel: 402 U.S. gal (1520 litres)
Maximum weapon load: 6,614 lb (3000 kg)

Performance

Maximum level speed "clean" at 36,090 ft (11,000 m): 1,320 kt (1,520 mph; 2445 km/h)
Maximum level speed at low level: 810 kt (932 mph; 1500 km/h)
Limiting Mach numbers: 2.3 at 36,090 ft (11,000 m); 1.22 at sea level
Takeoff speed: 119 kt (137 mph; 220 km/h)
Takeoff run: 820 ft (250 m)
Approach speed: 140 kt (162 mph; 260 km/h)
Landing speed: 127 kt (146 mph; 235 km/h)
Landing run with brake chute: 1,970–2,300 ft (600–700 m)
Service ceiling: 55,780 ft (17,000 m)

Range

With maximum internal fuel: 810 nm (932 miles; 1500 km)
Ferry range with three external tanks: 1,134 nm (1,305 miles; 2100 km)

Armaments

Maximum weapon load: 4,410 lb (2000 kg)
MiG-29 "Fulcrum-C": 6,614 lb (3000 kg) of ordnance on six underwing hardpoints, with provision for two 304-U.S. gal (1150-litre) drop tanks underwing and an optional centreline hardpoint for a 396-U.S. gal (1500-litre) fuel tank
Cannon: one 30-mm GSh-301 cannon in port wingroot leading edge with 150 rounds
Air-to-air missiles: R-60 (AA-8 "Aphid"), R-27 (AA-10 "Alamo"), R-73 (AA-11 "Archer")
Ground-attack weapons: FAB-250 and -500 bombs, KMGU-2 submunitions dispenser, ZB-500 napalm tank, 20 round 80-mm rocket pods, 130-mm and 240-mm rockets; one 30-kT RN-40 nuclear bomb on port inboard pylon

"The ex-Warsaw Pact nations rejected all sorts of ex-Soviet equipment, but kept MiG-29s."
– Vladimir Barkovsky,
Deputy Director General, RAC MiG

FACTS

- Most MiG-29s do not have fly-by-wire controls, unlike their Western contemporaries.
- A carrier-compatible MiG-29K was tested in the 1980s and an improved version sold to the Indian Navy in the 2000s.
- The original MiG-29s were more agile than the Lockheed Martin F-16 Fighting Falcon, but had only half the range.

MIKOYAN-GUREVICH MIG-29 "FULCRUM" – VARIANTS

MiG-29 (Product 9.12): Initial production version. Entered service in 1983. NATO reporting code "Fulcrum-A."

MiG-29B-12 (Product 9.12A): Downgraded export version for non-Warsaw Pact nations. NATO reporting code "Fulcrum-A."

MiG-29UB-12 (Product 9.51): Twin-seat training model. Infrared sensor mounted only, no radar. NATO reporting code "Fulcrum-A."

MiG-29S: Virtually identical in external appearance to MiG-29B airframes. Featured a dorsal "hump" on the upper fuselage (hence the nickname "Fatback").

MiG-29SM: Multi-role fighter variant with the improved avionics necessary to carry and employ precision-guided weapons.

MiG-29S-13 (Product 9.13): Similar to the 9.12, but with an enlarged fuselage spine containing additional fuel and a Gardeniya active jammer. NATO reporting code "Fulcrum-C."

MiG-29S-13 (Product 9.13S): Same airframe as the 9.13, but with an increased external weapons load of 8,818 lb (4000 kg). Radar upgraded. NATO reporting code "Fulcrum-C."

MiG-29SM (Product 9.13M): Similar to the 9.13, but with the ability to carry guided air-to-surface missiles and TV- and laser-guided bombs. NATO reporting code "Fulcrum-C."

MiG-29K (Product 9.31): Naval variant with folding wings, arrestor gear and reinforced landing gear. NATO reporting code "Fulcrum-D."

MiG-29KUB (Product 9.47): Identical characteristics to the MiG-29K, but with tandem twin-seat configuration. It is designed to serve as a trainer for the MiG-29K pilot and is fully combat-capable.

MiG-29M / MiG-33 (Product 9.15): Advanced multi-role variant with a redesigned airframe and mechanical flight controls replaced by a fly-by-wire system. NATO reporting code "Fulcrum-E."

MiG-29M2 / MiG-29MRCA: Two-seat version of MiG-29M. Identical characteristics to MiG-29M, with a slightly reduced ferry range of 1,118 miles (1800 km). Now evolved into the current MiG-35.

MiG-29UBM (Product 9.61): Two-seat training variant of the MiG-29M. Never built. Effectively continued under the designation "MiG-29M2."

MiG-29SMT (Product 9.17): An upgrade package of the first-generation MiG-29s (9.12 to 9.13) containing many enhancements intended for the MiG-29M.

MiG-29UBT (Product 9.51T): SMT Standard upgrade for the MiG-29UB. Main users Algeria and Yemen.

MiG-29OVT: Served as a thrust-vectoring engine testbed and technology demonstrator in various air shows to show future improvement in the MiG-29M. It has identical avionics to the MiG-29M.

MiG-29G/MiG-29GT: Upgrade for the Luftwaffe's MiG-29/29UB, inherited from former East Germany, to NATO standards.

MiG-29AS/MiG-29UBS (MiG-29SD): Slovak Air Force upgrade on its MiG-29/-29UB to ensure NATO compatibility.

MiG-29 Sniper: Upgrade attempt for Romanian Air Force.

MiG-35: Development of the MiG-29M/M2 and MiG-29K/KUB. NATO reporting code "Fulcrum-F."

MIKOYAN-GUREVICH MIG-29 "FULCRUM"

The Fulcrum with "bort" (side) number 156 was one of six MiG-29M prototypes. They had an analog fly-by-wire system, a new "Slot Back" radar with added air-to-ground modes, and two extra wing pylons. This allowed use of new weapons such as the Kh 31 anti-radiation missiles (ARMs) as shown here on the inboard pylons. On the outer pylons are AA-12 "Adder" AAMs, with AA-11 "Archers" with their distinctive lattice fins next to those. Other MiG-29 features were a longer and higher canopy and a lighter structure with more fuel capacity. Although the MiG-29M remedied many of the deficiencies of the original "Fulcrum," the programme was cancelled without a production order.

Left: The original MiG-29A cockpit was less cluttered than that found on earlier-generation MiGs.

Below: The united German Luftwaffe kept MiG-29s longer than any other former Russian equipment. Here, an "Archer" is fired on an exercise in Florida.

In order to replace a number of different aircraft within Frontal Aviation (Frontovaya Aviatsiya), the tactical air arm of the Soviet Union, work began in 1974 at the Mikoyan-Guerevich Design Bureau on a lightweight fighter. Although the MiG-29 prototype, called the "9-12," flew in October 1977, it was not spotted on U.S. satellites until 1979 and was not encountered by Western pilots until 1985. The reporting name "Fulcrum" was applied, one of the first without a slightly derogatory ring to it.

WESTERN CONSTERNATION

Visits to the Farnborough and Paris air shows demonstrated the MiG-29's incredible agility. In particular, the Fulcrum stunned observers by performing a tail slide manoeuvre – climbing vertically at low speed until it ran out of speed and slipped back down the same path before flying away with no loss of control. Some dismissed this as of no value in real combat, but the emergence of Russian aircraft that could challenge the U.S. "teen-series" – in particular, the Lockheed Martin F-16 and McDonnell Douglas F/A-18 – caused great concern in Western defence ministries.

The MiG-29 had twin tail fins and widely spaced engines. Blending of the fuselage into the wing helped to create extra

Above: Poland has increased its "Fulcrum" inventory by acquiring surplus Czech Air Force and Luftwaffe aircraft to give it a total of about 50 MiG-29s.

lift. The raised canopy gave a much better all-round view than previous Soviet fighters and multiple weapons pylons allowed a greater mix of air-to-air and air-to-ground weaponry than before. An interesting feature was a system that closed doors in the intakes and opened louvers above them when the wheels were on the ground, helping to prevent ingestion of foreign objects that would damage the engines.

Large numbers of MiG-29 "Fulcrum-A" fighters, MiG-29UB "Fulcrum-B" trainers and nuclear-capable "Fulcrum-C" fighter-bombers entered service before the Soviet Union's collapse. Slightly simplified versions of the Fulcrum-A and -B were supplied to Warsaw Pact nations, including East Germany, Poland, Hungary, Czechoslovakia and Romania. Aircraft for export farther afield were downgraded further. The "Fulcrum-C" had slightly more internal fuel and a more sophisticated electronic jammer.

A STALLED IMPROVED VERSION

The MiG-29M was a substantially improved version with an analog fly-by-wire system, a modernized cockpit, two more weapons pylons and the ability to carry a range of smart weapons. The end of the Soviet Union put paid to introduction of MiG-29Ms to replace older "Fulcrums," but some elements went into later models for export, including the MiG-29SMT and upgrade packages for Russian and export aircraft.

Although the MiG-29 has seen combat on numerous occasions, its actual air-to-air record has been fairly poor. In the 1991 Gulf War, the Iraqis lost five in the air for no victories against coalition aircraft. The balance sheet in the Kosovo War of 1999 was seven–nil to NATO. Similar results occurred in the Ethiopia–Eritrea conflict of 1998–2000. Most known MiG-29 "kills" have been against unmanned drones, such as in Georgia before the 2008 conflict, or civilian aircraft, such as Cuba's destruction in 1996 of two Cessna 337s belonging to an exile group.

CONTINUING CUSTOMER BASE

Exports of MiG-29s have helped to keep the MiG design bureau (now a semi-private company and part of Russia's United Aircraft Corporation) afloat. Sales money has allowed development of advanced versions to continue. Foreign customers have included Algeria, Cuba, Eritrea, India, Iran, North Korea, Malaysia, Peru, Syria and Yemen, as well as most former Warsaw Pact countries and former Soviet states.

McDonnell Douglas F/A-18 Hornet

The F/A-18 Hornet has become the U.S. Navy's primary fighter and attack aircraft, and the best-selling twin-engined fighter on the export market. It has seen action in all major U.S. military operations since the mid-1980s.

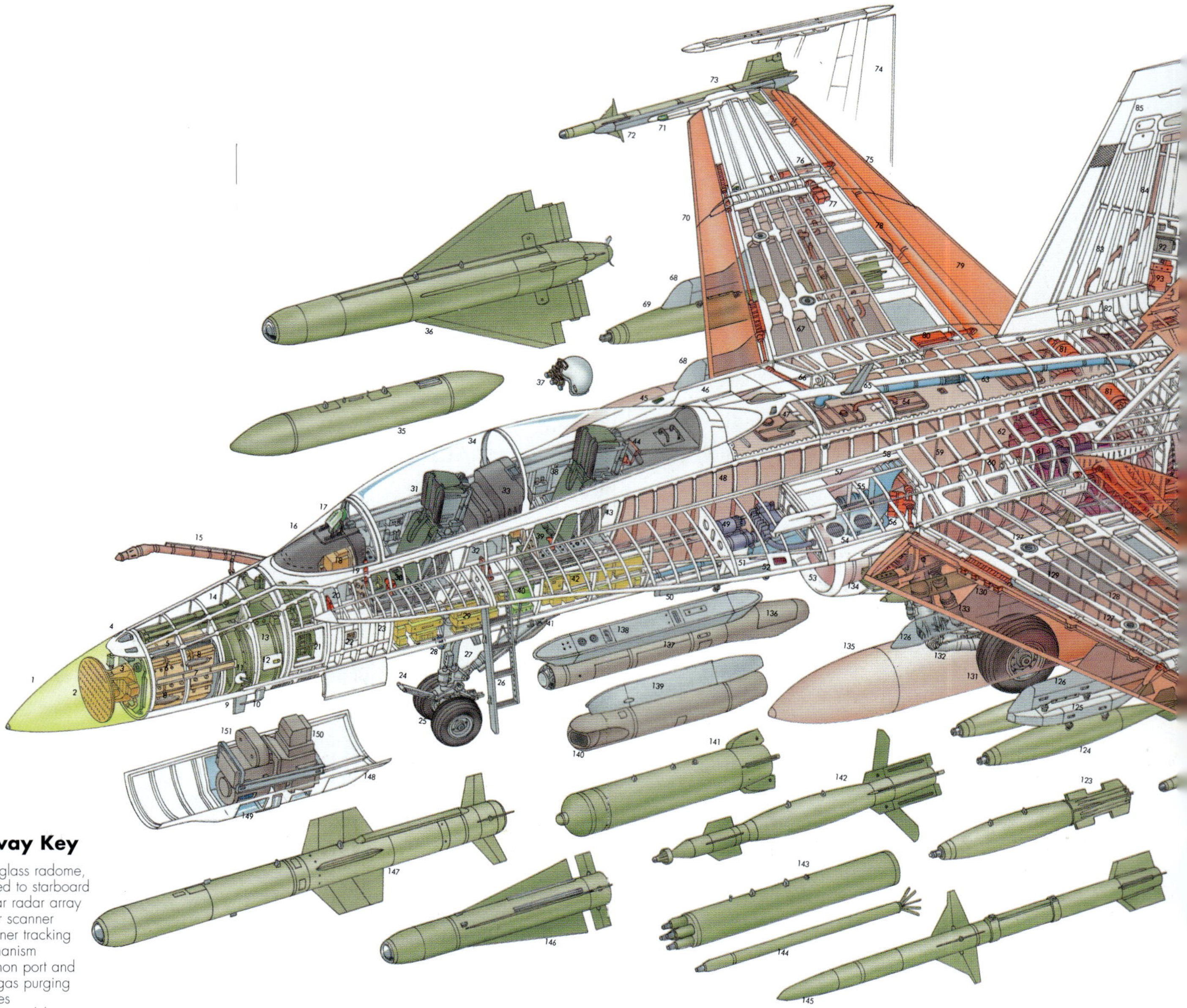

Cutaway Key

1 Fibreglass radome, hinged to starboard
2 Planar radar array radar scanner
3 Scanner tracking mechanism
4 Cannon port and gun gas purging intakes
5 Radar module withdrawal rails
6 Hughes AN/APG-73 radar equipment module
7 Formation lighting strip
8 Forward radar warning antennas
9 UHF/IFF antenna
10 Pitot head, port and starboard
11 Incidence transmitter
12 Canopy emergency release
13 Ammunition drum, 570 rounds
14 M61A1 Vulcan 20-mm rotary cannon
15 Retractable inflight-refuelling probe
16 Single-piece wraparound windscreen
17 Pilot's Kaiser AN/AVQ-28 raster HUD
18 Instrument panel with multifunction colour CRT displays
19 Control column
20 Rudder pedals
21 Ammunition loading chute
22 Ground power socket
23 Nose undercarriage wheel bay
24 Catapult strop link
25 Twin nosewheels, forward-retracting
26 Retractable boarding ladder
27 Nosewheel hydraulic jack
28 Nosewheel leg-mounted deck signalling and taxi lights
29 Forward avionics equipment bays, port and starboard
30 Engine throttle levers
31 Pilot's Martin-Baker SJU-6/A ejection seat
32 Rear cockpit rudder pedals (dual flight-control system interchangeable with radar and weapons controllers)
33 Rear instrument console with multifunction CRT displays
34 Single-piece upward-opening cockpit canopy
35 AWW-7/9 datalink pod for Walleye missile, fuselage centreline pylon-mounted
36 AGM-62 Walleye II ER/DL air-to-surface missile, starboard outboard pylon only
37 Naval flight officer's helmet with GEC-Marconi Avionics Cats Eyes night-vision goggles
38 Naval flight officer's SJU-5/A ejection seat
39 Sidestick radar and weapons controllers, replacing dual flight-control system
40 Liquid oxygen converter

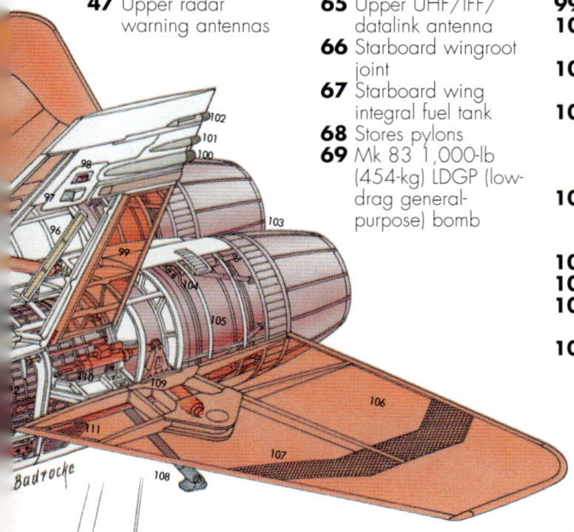

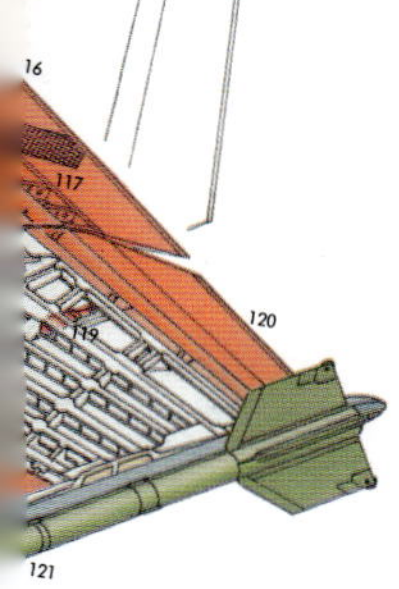

41 Ventral radar warning antenna
42 Rear avionics equipment bays, port and starboard
43 Cockpit rear pressure bulkhead
44 Canopy actuator
45 Starboard navigation light
46 Tailfin aerodynamic load-alleviating strake
47 Upper radar warning antennas
48 Forward fuselage bag-type fuel cell
49 Radar/avionics equipment liquid cooling units
50 Fuselage centreline pylon
51 Boundary layer splitter plate
52 Port navigation light
53 Fixed-geometry engine air intake
54 Cooling air spill louvres
55 Cabin air-conditioning system equipment
56 Leading-edge flap drive motor
57 Boundary layer spill duct
58 Air-conditioning system heat exchanger exhaust
59 Centre fuselage fuel cells
60 Wing panel root attachment joints
61 Central Garrett GTC36-200 auxiliary power unit (APU)
62 Airframe-mounted engine accessory equipment gearbox, port and starboard
63 Engine bleed air ducting to conditioning system
64 Fuel-tank bay access panels
65 Upper UHF/IFF/datalink antenna
66 Starboard wingroot joint
67 Starboard wing integral fuel tank
68 Stores pylons
69 Mk 83 1,000-lb (454-kg) LDGP (low-drag general-purpose) bomb
70 Leading-edge flap
71 Starboard secondary navigation light
72 Wingtip missile launch rail
73 AIM-9L Sidewinder air-to-air missile
74 Outer wing panel, folded position
75 Drooping aileron
76 Aileron hydraulic actuator
77 Wing-fold hydraulic rotary actuator
78 Drooping flap vane
79 Starboard slotted flap, operates as flaperon at low speeds
80 Flap hydraulic actuator
81 Hydraulic reservoirs
82 Reinforced fin-root attachment joint
83 Multi-spar fin structure
84 Fuel jettison pipe
85 Graphite/epoxy tail unit skin panels with fibreglass tip fairings
86 Tail position light
87 AN/ALR-67 receiving antenna
88 AN/ALQ-165 low-band transmitting antenna
89 Fuel jettison
90 Starboard all-moving tailplane
91 Starboard rudder
92 Radar warning system power amplifier
93 Rudder hydraulic actuator
94 Airbrake panel, open
95 Airbrake hydraulic jack
96 Fin formation lighting strip
97 Fuel venting air intake
98 Anti-collision beacon, port and starboard
99 Port rudder
100 Port AN/ALQ-165 antenna
101 AN-ALQ-67 receiving antenna
102 AN/ALQ-165 high-band transmitting antenna
103 Variable-area afterburner nozzles
104 Nozzle actuators
105 Afterburner duct
106 Port all-moving tailplane
107 Tailplane bonded honeycomb core structure
108 Deck arrestor hook
109 Tailplane pivot mounting
110 Tailplane hydraulic actuator
111 Full-authority digital engine controller (FADEC)
112 General Electric F404-GE-400 afterburning turbofan engine
113 Rear fuselage formation lighting strip
114 Engine fuel control units
115 Fuselage side-mounted AIM-7 Sparrow air-to-air missile
116 Port slotted flap
117 Control surface bonded honeycomb core structure
118 Wing-fold rotary hydraulic actuator and hinge joint
119 Port aileron hydraulic actuator
120 Port drooping aileron
121 Wingtip AIM-9L Sidewinder air-to-air missile
122 Port leading-edge flap
123 Mk 82SE Snakeye 500-lb (227-kg) retarded bomb
124 Mk 82 500-lb (227-kg) LDGP bombs
125 Twin stores carrier
126 Port wing stores pylons
127 Pylon mounting hardpoints
128 Multi-spar wing panel structure
129 Port wing integral fuel tank
130 Leading-edge flap-shaft driven rotary actuator
131 Port mainwheel
132 Levered suspension main undercarriage leg strut
133 Shock-absorber strut
134 Ventral AN/ALE-39 chaff/flare launcher
135 330-U.S. gal (1250-litre) external fuel tank
136 Strike camera housing
137 AN/ASQ-173 laser spot tracker/strike camera (LST/SCAM) pod
138 Fuselage starboard side LST/SCAM pylon adaptor
139 Port side FLIR pod adaptor
140 AN/AAS-38 forward-looking infrared (FLIR) pod
141 CBU-89/89B Gator submunition dispenser
142 GBU-12 D/B Paveway II 500-lb (227-kg) laser-guided bomb
143 LAU-10A Zuni four-round rocket launcher
144 5-in (127-mm) FFAR
145 AGM-88 HARM anti-radar missile
146 AGM-65A Maverick air-to-ground anti-armour missile
147 AGM-84 SLAM air-to-surface missile
148 Advanced tactical airborne reconnaissance system (ATARS) unit, interchangeable with gun pack/ammunition magazine (F/A-18D(RC))
149 Sensor viewing apertures
150 Infrared linescanner
151 Low- and/or medium-altitude electro-optical scanner

F/A-18A HORNET SPECIFICATION

Dimensions

Length: 56 ft 0 in (17.07 m)
Height: 15 ft 3½ in (4.66 m)
Wingspan: 37 ft 6 in (11.43 m); 40 ft 4¾ in (12.31 m) with tip-mounted AAMs; 27 ft 6 in (8.38 m) with wings folded
Wing area: 400 sq ft (37.16 m²)
Wheel track: 10 ft 2½ in (3.11 m)
Wheelbase: 17ft 9½ in (5.42 m)

Powerplant

Two General Electric F404-GE-400 turbofans each rated at 16,000 lb st (71.17 kN) with afterburning or, in aircraft built from early 1992, F404-GE-402 turbofans each rated at 17,700 lb st (78.73 kN) with afterburning

Weights

Empty: 23,050 lb (10,455 kg)
Takeoff: 33,585 lb (15,234 kg) on a fighter mission or 48,253 lb (21,888 kg) on an attack mission
Maximum takeoff: about 56,000 lb (25,401 kg)

Fuel and load

Internal fuel: 10,860 lb (4926 kg)
External fuel: up to 6,732 lb (3053 kg) in three 330-U.S. gal (1250-litre) drop tanks
Maximum ordnance load: 15,500 lb (7031 kg) on nine external stores stations

Performance

Maximum level speed "clean" at high altitude: more than 1,033 kt (1,190 mph; 1915 km/h)
Maximum rate of climb at sea level: 45,000 ft (13,715 m) per minute
Combat ceiling: about 50,000 ft (15,240 m)

Range

Ferry range: more than 1,800 nm (2,073 miles; 3336 km) with drop tanks
Combat radius: more than 400 nm (460 miles; 740 km) on a fighter mission; 575 nm (662 miles; 1065 km) on an attack mission; 290 nm (340 miles; 537 km) on a hi-lo-hi interdiction mission

Armament

Gun: M61A1 Vulcan 20-mm cannon with 570 rounds
Air-to-air missiles: AIM-120 AMRAAM; AIM-7 Sparrow; AIM-9 Sidewinder
Precision-guided munitions: AGM-65 Maverick; AGM-84 Harpoon; AGM-84E SLAM; AGM-88 HARM; AGM-62 Walleye EO- (electro-optic) guided bomb; AGM-123 Skipper; GBU-10/12/16 laser-guided bombs
Unguided munitions: B57 and B61 tactical nuclear bombs; Mk 80 series general-purpose bombs; Mk 7 dispenser (including Mk 20 Rockeye II, CBU-59, CBU-72 FAE, CBU-78 Gator mine dispenser); LAU-97 Zuni FFAR pods

Radar

Hughes AN/APG-65 or AN/APG-73
Effective radar range: more than 100 nm (115 miles; 185 km)

"One pilot demonstrated the Hornet's 'swing role' capability by destroying a Mikoyan-Gurevich MiG-21 and carrying on to complete an attack mission, rather than dumping ordnance before engaging."

FACTS

- The F/A-18 began as a Northrop design, was taken over by McDonnell Douglas and is now part of the Boeing stable.
- The U.S. Marine Corps has employed the F/A-18D as a fast forward air control platform and for night attack.
- Swiss and Finnish Hornets are F-18s, used as pure fighters without any ground-attack weapons.

MCDONNELL DOUGLAS F/A-18 HORNET – VARIANTS

U.S. VARIANTS

F/A-18A/B: The F/A 18A is the single-seat variant and the F/A-18B is the two-seat variant. A model Hornets that have been upgraded to the AN/APG-73 radar are designated F/A-18A+.

C/D: The F/A-18C is the single-seat variant and the F/A-18D is the two-seat variant. The D model can be configured for training or as an all-weather strike craft.

E/F Super Hornet: The single-seat F/A-18E and two-seat F/A-18F Super have been extensively redesigned from the original F/A-18, including a 25 percent larger airframe.

EA-18G Growler: An electronic warfare version of the two-seat F/A-18F.

F-18(R): A proposed reconnaissance version of the F/A-18A that included a sensor package that replaced the 20-mm cannon.

RF-18D: Proposed two-seat reconnaissance version for the U.S. Marine Corps. It was to carry a radar reconnaissance pod. This capability was later realized on the F/A-18D(RC).

TF-18A: Two-seat training version of the F/A-18A fighter, later redesignated F/A-18B.

F-18 HARV: Single-seat High Alpha Research Vehicle for NASA.

X-53 Active Aeroelastic Wing: A NASA F/A-18 has been modified to demonstrate Active Aeroelastic Wing technology, and was designated X-53 in December 2006.

EXPORT VARIANTS

F-18L: A proposed, lighter land-based version of the F/A-18 Hornet. Designed to be a single-seat air-superiority fighter/ground-attack aircraft.

(A)F/A-18A: Single-seat fighter/attack version for the Royal Australian Air Force.

(A)F/A-18B: Two-seat training version for the Royal Australian Air Force.

CF-18A: Single-seat fighter/attack version for the Canadian Forces. The Canadian Forces' official designation is CF-188A Hornet.

CF-18B: Two-seat training and combat version for the Canadian Forces. The Canadian Forces' official designation is CF-188B Hornet.

EF-18A: Single-seat fighter/attack version for the Spanish Air Force. The Spanish Air Force designation is C.15.

EF-18B: Two-seat training version for the Spanish Air Force. The Spanish Air Force designation is CE.15.

KAF-18C: Single-seat fighter/attack version for the Kuwait Air Force.

KAF-18D: Two-seat training version for the Kuwait Air Force.

Finnish Air Force: The Finnish Air Force uses F/A-18C/D Hornets, with a Finland-specific midlife update.

Swiss Air Force: The Swiss Air Force uses the F-18C/D, with a later Swiss-specific mid-life update. Swiss F-18s were originally without ground-attack capability until hardware was retrofitted.

MCDONNELL DOUGLAS F/A-18 HORNET

The F/A-18D is a specialist derivative of the Hornet used by the U.S. Marine Corps for night attack and the fast forward air control (FAC) mission. The latter involves spotting targets for other combat aircraft and marking the target for attack. This is more commonly done today using lasers, sensors and datalinks, but in Operation Desert Storm in 1991, the unguided smoke rocket, usually filled with white phosphorus, worked well as a target marker irrespective of the equipment on the attack aircraft. In 1991, VMF(AW)-121 "Green Knights" operated out of Sheikh Isa Air Base in Bahrain. This F/A-18D is armed with AIM-9s and two four-shot LAU-97 rocket pods.

Above: The Hornet had one of the first fighter cockpits where screens mostly replaced dials. This is the rear panel in an F/A-18D.

Left: An F/A-18C catches a wire for a perfect landing aboard a U.S. Navy carrier.

The origins of the F/A-18 Hornet lie in the quest by the U.S. Air Force for a lightweight fighter (LWF) aircraft in the early 1970s. The successful contender for the U.S. Air Force's contract was the General Dynamics YF-16 Fighting Falcon, a single-engined, single-finned aircraft. Northrop's YF-17 Cobra showed enough merit to be selected as the basis for the U.S. Navy's own requirement for a fighter/attack aircraft to replace the Vought A-7 Corsair II and McDonnell Douglas F-4 Phantom. The selection was in fact largely forced upon the Navy by Congress, who directed that the loser of the LWF contest become the new naval combat aircraft.

The YF-17, which truly was lightweight and agile, first flew in June 1974. To make it carrier-capable and suitable for the U.S. Navy's missions, Northrop, which had no experience of carrier aircraft, needed a partner and chose McDonnell Douglas, maker of the Phantom.

Serious changes were needed, and the F-18 design that emerged and flew in November 1978 bore only a superficial resemblance to the Cobra. It was larger and heavier, with a tailhook, a considerably beefed-up landing gear with dual nosewheels, inflight refuelling equipment and folding wings with leading- and trailing-edge flaps.

Northrop worked on a lighter F-18L land-based variant without carrier equipment, but in the end this never entered production. The agreement between Northrop and McDonnell Douglas collapsed, and the Hornet became a "MacAir" product, although legal battles continued for many years.

HIGHLY MANOUEVRABLE

The Hornet's great manoeuvrability was in part due to the large leading-edge root extensions, or LERXs. These helped in particular with handling at lower speeds, as did the digital fly-by-wire control system, the first fitted on a production fighter. Nine weapons stations on the wings and fuselage allowed a wide choice of air-to-air and air-to-ground ordnance.

The aircraft was initially planned to be delivered in separate fighter, attack and trainer models, but the roles were combined into two airframes, designated F/A-18A and F/A-18B, the latter being a combat-capable two-seater. The F/A-18C and D with new ejection seats, an onboard jammer and an improved mission computer followed from 1987.

A POPULAR CHOICE

The U.S. Marine Corps introduced the Hornet into service in August 1982, followed by the U.S. Navy in March 1983. The Hornet proved popular with air arms that wanted two engines for improved safety, longer range and greater load, although its greater expense and complexity than the F-16 restricted sales to Australia, Canada, Spain, Switzerland, Finland, Kuwait and Malaysia.

The Hornet has seen relatively little air-to-air action, although it has conducted attack missions over Libya, Iraq, the former Yugoslavia and Afghanistan. In the 1991 Gulf War, Hornets scored two kills against the Iraqi Air Force. One pilot demonstrated the Hornet's "swing role" capability by destroying a Mikoyan-Gurevich MiG-21 and carrying on to complete an attack mission, rather than dumping ordnance before engaging. A U.S. Navy Hornet became the only victim of the Iraqi Air Force when shot down by a MiG-25.

Above: Firing a flare as a defence against IR-guided missiles, a Hornet shows off its loadout of laser-guided bombs, AIM-9s and a single fuel tank.

Dassault Mirage 2000

Dassault's delta-winged Mirage 2000 has carried on the tradition of elegant and effective fighters from France and been a reasonable export success. In France, it still has considerable life ahead of it, despite the introduction of the Dassault Rafale.

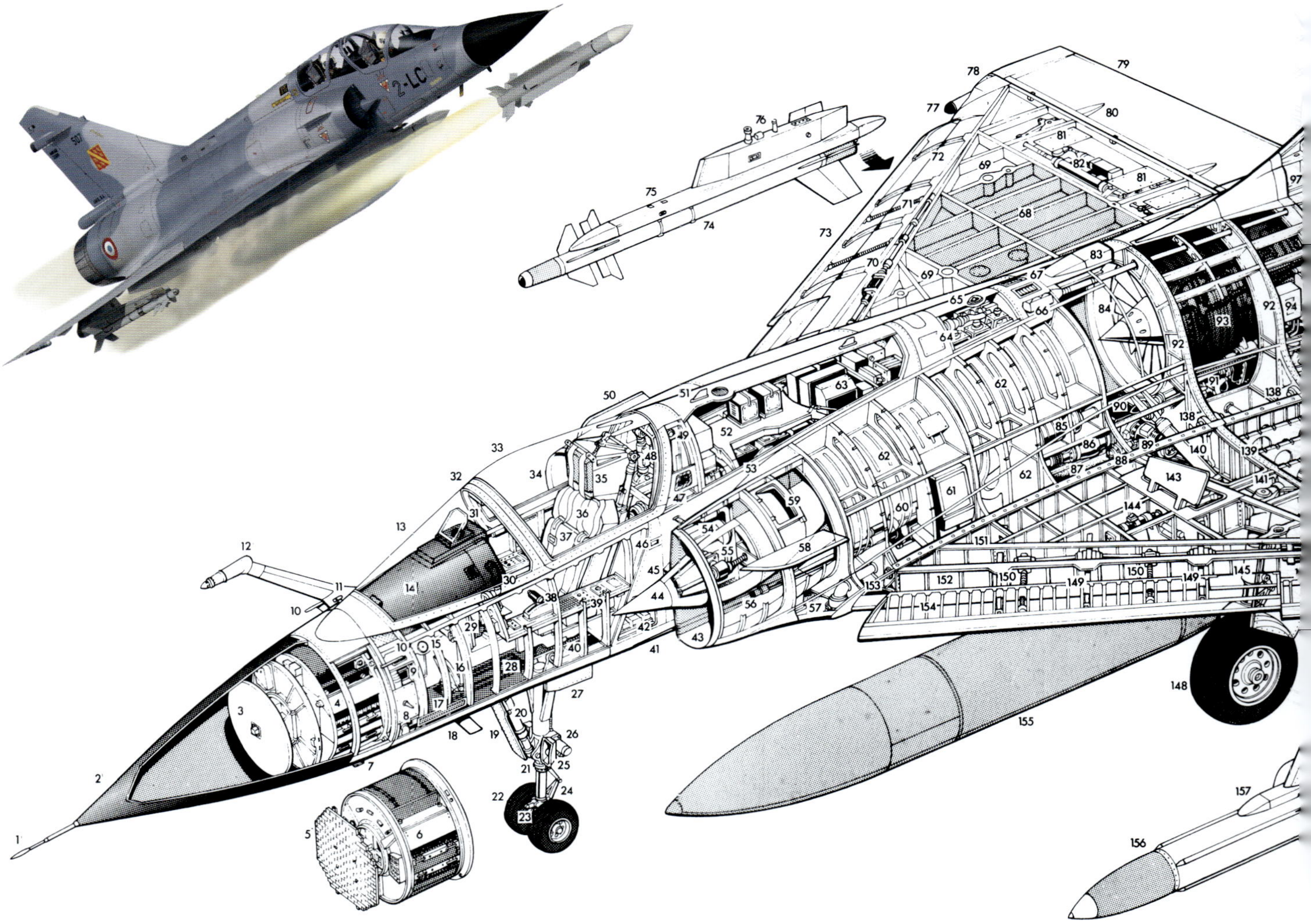

Cutaway Key

1 Pitot tube
2 Fibre radome
3 Flat-plate radar scanner
4 Thomson-CSF RDM multi-role radar unit (initial production aircraft)
5 Cassegrain monopulse planar antenna
6 Thomson-CSF RDI pulse-Doppler radar unit (later production aircraft)
7 Radar altimeter aerial
8 Angle-of-attack probe
9 Front pressure bulkhead
10 Instrument pitot heads
11 Temperature probe
12 Fixed inflight refuelling probe
13 Frameless windscreen panel
14 Instrument panel shroud
15 Static ports
16 Rudder pedals
17 Low-voltage formation light strip
18 VHF aerial
19 Nosewheel jack door
20 Hydraulic retraction jack
21 Nose landing gear leg strut
22 Twin nosewheels
23 Towing bracket
24 Torque scissor links
25 Landing/taxiing lamps
26 Nosewheel steering jacks
27 Nose landing gear leg doors
28 Cockpit flooring
29 Centre instrument console
30 Control column
31 Pilot's head-up display (HUD)
32 Canopy arch
33 Cockpit canopy cover
34 Starboard air intake
35 Ejection-seat headrest
36 Safety harness
37 Martin-Baker Mk 10 zero-zero ejection seat
38 Engine throttle control and airbrake switch
39 Port-side console panel
40 Nosewheel bay
41 Cannon muzzle blast trough
42 Electrical equipment bay
43 Port air intake
44 Intake half-cone centre-body
45 Air-conditioning system ram air intake
46 Cockpit rear pressure bulkhead
47 Canopy emergency-release handle
48 Hydraulic canopy jack
49 Canopy hinge point
50 Starboard intake strake
51 IFF aerial
52 Radio and electronics bay
53 Boundary layer bleed air duct
54 Air-conditioning plant
55 Intake centre-body screw jack
56 Cannon muzzle
57 Pressure refuelling connection
58 Port intake strake
59 Intake suction relief doors (above and below)
60 DEFA 554 30-mm cannon
61 Cannon ammunition box
62 Forward fuselage integral fuel tanks
63 Radio and electronics equipment
64 Fuel system equipment
65 Anti-collision light
66 Air system pre-cooler
67 Air exit louvres
68 Starboard wing integral fuel tank, total internal fuel capacity 1,004 U.S. gal (3800 litres)
69 Wing pylon attachment hardpoints
70 Leading-edge slat hydraulic drive motor and control shaft
71 Slat screw jacks
72 Slat guide rails
73 Starboard wing automatic leading-edge slats
74 Matra 550 Magic "dogfight" AAM
75 Missile launch rail
76 Outboard wing pylon
77 Radar warning antenna
78 Starboard navigation light
79 Outboard elevon
80 Elevon ventral hinge fairings
81 Flight-control system access panels
82 Elevon hydraulic jacks
83 Engine intake by-pass air spill duct
84 Engine compressor face

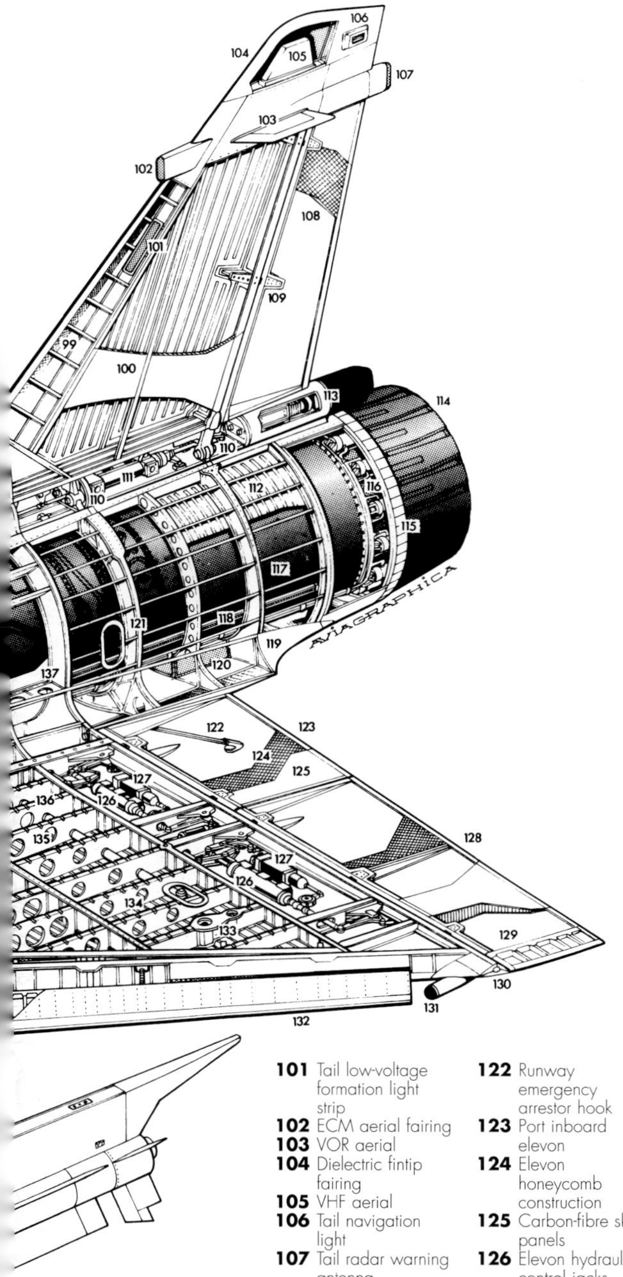

85 Hydraulic accumulator
86 Micro turbo auxiliary power unit
87 Main landing gear wheel bay
88 Hydraulic pump
89 Alternator, port and starboard
90 Accessory gearbox
91 Engine transmission unit and drive shaft
92 Machined fuselage main frames
93 SNECMA M53-5 afterburning turbofan
94 Engine igniter unit
95 Electronic engine control unit
96 Bleed air ducting
97 Engine bleed air blow-off valve spill duct
98 Fin-root fillet construction
99 Leading-edge ribs
100 Boron/epoxy/carbon honeycomb sandwich fin skin panels
101 Tail low-voltage formation light strip
102 ECM aerial fairing
103 VOR aerial
104 Dielectric fintip fairing
105 VHF aerial
106 Tail navigation light
107 Tail radar warning antenna
108 Honeycomb rudder construction
109 Rudder hinge
110 Fin spar attachment joints
111 Rudder hydraulic jack
112 Engine bay thermal lining
113 ECM equipment housing
114 Variable-area afterburner exhaust nozzle
115 Tailpipe sealing flaps
116 Fueldraulic nozzle control jacks
117 Afterburner tailpipe
118 Engine withdrawal rail
119 Wingroot extended trailing-edge fillet
120 Ventral brake parachute housing
121 Rear engine mounting main frame
122 Runway emergency arrestor hook
123 Port inboard elevon
124 Elevon honeycomb construction
125 Carbon-fibre skin panels
126 Elevon hydraulic control jacks
127 Fly-by-wire electronic system command units
128 Outboard elevon
129 Elevon tip construction
130 Port navigation light
131 Radar warning antenna
132 Outboard automatic leading-edge slat
133 Outboard wing pylon attachment hardpoints
134 Machined upper- and lower-wing skin/stringer panels
135 Port wing integral fuel tank
136 Wing rib construction
137 Rear fuselage/wingroot fairing integral fuel tank
138 Wing spar attachment joints
139 Main spars
140 Landing gear hydraulic retraction jack
141 Main landing gear leg pivot fixing
142 Inboard pylon attachment hardpoints
143 Port airbrakes (open) above and beneath wing
144 Airbrake hydraulic jack
145 Main landing gear leg strut
146 Leading-edge slat hydraulic drive motor
147 Mainwheel leg door
148 Port mainwheel
149 Slat guide rails
150 Screw jacks
151 Auxiliary spar
152 Wing front spar
153 Front spar attachment joint
154 Inboard automatic leading-edge slat rib construction
155 449-U.S. gal (1700-litre) auxiliary fuel tank (fuselage centreline or wing inboard stations)
156 MATRA Super 530 medium-range AAM
157 Missile launch rail
158 Inboard wing pylon

MIRAGE 2000C SPECIFICATION

Dimensions

Fuselage length: 47 ft 1¼ in (14.36 m)
Wingspan: 29 ft 11½ in (9.13 m)
Wing area: 441.33 sq ft (41.00 m²)
Wing aspect ratio: 2.03
Height: 17 ft ¾ in (5.20 m)
Wheel track: 11 ft 1¾ in (3.40 m)
Wheelbase: 16 ft 4¾ in (5.00 m)

Powerplant

One SNECMA M53-P2 turbofan rated at 14,462 lb st (64.33 kN) dry and 21,384 lb st (95.12 kN) with afterburning

Weights

Empty: 16,534 lb (7500 kg)
Normal takeoff: 23,534 lb (10,680 kg)
Maximum takeoff: 37,478 lb (17,000 kg)

Fuel and load

Internal fuel: 6,966 lb (3160 kg)
External fuel: 8,201 lb (3720 kg) in one 343-US gal (1300-litre) drop tank and two 449 US-gal (1700-litre) drop tanks.
Maximum ordnance: 13,889 lb (6300 kg)

Performance

Maximum speed at high level: Mach 2.2
Maximum speed at sea level: Mach 1.2
Minimum speed in stable flight: 100 kts (115 mph; 185 km/h)
Range: More than 850 nm (979 miles; 1575 km) with 4,409 lb (2000 kg) of underwing ordnance and external fuel tanks
Service ceiling: 54,000 ft (16,460 m)
Reaction time: Under five minutes, from brakes-off to interception of Mach 3 target at 80,000 ft (24,400 m)

Armament

Two internal DEFA 554 30-mm cannon with 125 rounds per gun. Total of 13,889 lb (6300 kg) of stores carried on five underfuselage and four underwing hardpoints. Standard air-defence load is two Matra Magic 2 infrared missiles and two Super 530D radar-guided missiles. Early aircraft were equipped only to fire the Super 530F. In the ground-attack role, up to 18 551-lb (250-kg) bombs or BAP 100 anti-runway bombs, two 1,984-lb (900-kg) BGL 1000 laser-guided bombs, six Belouga cluster bombs, two AS30L laser-guided air-to-surface missiles, two Armat anti-radiation missiles or two AM39 Exocet anti-ship missiles are options
Mirage 2000D/N/S: The N is dedicated to the carriage of the 1,874-lb (850-kg) ASMP stand-off nuclear missile (150 kT or 300 kT yield). The 2000D/S has provision for the Matra Apache, Durandal, F4 rocket pod or Dassault CC630 gun pod

"In a one-versus-one fight against the highly agile F-16, the Mirage 2000C should win if flown to its strengths … the Mirage can turn on a sixpence, enabling the pilot to bring it into a firing bracket before the F-16 has a chance to escape."
– Ian Black, RAF exchange pilot on the Mirage 2000C

FACTS

- In Indian Air Force service, the Mirage 2000 is known as the "Vajra" (thunderbolt).
- A larger and heavier Mirage 4000 with two engines was tested in parallel with the 2000, but failed to win orders.
- The Mirage 2000C was the first non-U.S. fighter equipped with a fly-by-wire control system.

DASSAULT MIRAGE 2000 – VARIANTS

2000B: A two-seat operational conversion trainer variant which first flew on 11 October 1980.

2000C: Single-seat interceptor. The first production Mirage 2000C flew in November 1982.

2000N: Nuclear-strike variant intended to carry the Aérospatiale Air-Sol Moyenne Portee (ASMP) nuclear stand-off missile. Entered operational service in 1988. 75 were built in total.

Mirage 2000D: A dedicated conventional-attack variant developed from the Mirage 2000N. 86 built in total.

2000-5: A two-seat Mirage 2000B prototype was extensively modified as the first Mirage 2000-5 prototype, and it first flew in October 1990. In 1993, further upgrades meant that it was redesignated as the Mirage 2000-5F.

2000-5 Mark 2: Dassault further improved the Mirage 2000-5.

"2000E": The blanket designation for a series of export variants of the Mirage 2000.

2000M (Egypt): Egypt was the first foreign buyer, ordering 16 single-seat Mirage 2000M and four Mirage 2000BM trainers in late 1981.

2000H (India): The Indian Air Force named the Mirage 2000 "Vajra" (thunderbolt). As India wanted the fighter quickly, the first part of an initial batch of 26 single-seaters and four two-seaters was shipped to the Indian Air Force (IAF) beginning in 1985 with the older M53-5 engines. These aircraft were given the designations of Mirage 2000H5 and Mirage 2000TH5. The second part of this initial batch consisted of ten more single-seaters with the M53-P2 engine, with these aircraft designated Mirage 2000H.

2000P (Peru): Peru placed an order for ten single-seat Mirage 2000Ps and two Mirage 2000DP trainers.

2000-5EI (ROC-Taiwan): In 1992, the Republic of China Air Force ordered 48 single-seat Mirage 2000-5EI interceptors and 12 Mirage 2000-5DI trainers. The programme was given the code name "Fei Lung" (Flying Dragon) and marked the first order by the Chinese of French aircraft since 1937. The Taiwanese ordered 60 2000-5 fighters.

2000-5EDA (Qatar): In 1994, Qatar ordered nine single-seat 2000-5EDAs and three 2000-5DDA trainers.

2000EAD/RAD (UAE): A United Arab Emirates Mirage 2000 multi-role fighter. In 1983, the United Arab Emirates purchased 22 single-seat 2000EADs, eight unique single-seat 2000RAD reconnaissance variants and six 2000DAD trainers.

2000EG (Greece): Beginning in March 1985, Greece ordered 36 single-seat 2000EGs and four 2000BG two-seat trainers, as a part of the "Talos" modernization project.

2000BR (Brazil): Dassault participated in a competition to replace the Brazilian Air Force's aging Mirage IIIEBR/DBRs with the 2000BR, another variant of the 2000–9.

Mirage 2000-9: The export variant of Mirage 2000-5 Mark 2.

DASSAULT MIRAGE 2000

France dispatched 12 Mirage 2000Cs to Saudi Arabia as part of Operation Daguet, its contribution to the 1991 Gulf War. The Mirages from the 5th Escadre de Chasse at Orange were ready for operations only in the final stage of fighting and saw no combat, although they did fly operational patrols from their base at Al Ahsa, Saudi Arabia. The aircraft wore a mix of their normal grey colour schemes and the desert camouflage seen here. As well as a centreline fuel tank, this 2000C carries a pair of infrared-guided Magic II missiles outboard and a pair of Matra Super 530Ds. This semi-active radar-homing (SARH) missile has a range of around 25 miles (40 km).

Above: The two-seat Mirage 2000D and 2000N are dedicated attack aircraft. Two laser-guided bombs and a targeting pod can be seen under the fuselage of this example. The 2000D has seen action over Afghanistan.

From the mid-1960s onwards, in the search for a follow-on to the Mirage III to meet the French government's Avion Combat Futur (ACF) requirement, Dassault considered and tested several configurations for a heavier fighter, including variable-geometry and high-winged two-seat designs. These projects were cancelled by 1975 as being too big or too expensive. Several studies for a super Mirage III were dusted off to offer as a replacement for ACF, and one of these was accepted for further development in 1976 as the Mirage 2000.

The Mirage 2000 did not look too different from the Mirage III, although its proportions differed. A reduced fineness ratio of the fuselage moved the centre of lift ahead of the centre of gravity, which introduced a degree of longitudinal instability. This was deliberate because it allowed greater manoeuvrability when combined with a modern fly-by-wire control system, which constantly adjusted the control surfaces to the most efficient positions for the desired flight path. A large fin and small strakes on the nose helped to preserve control, even at high angles of attack. These features help to reduce the Mirage 2000's takeoff run by lifting the nose earlier. Airbrakes and a brake parachute assist in limiting the landing run.

ONGOING IMPROVEMENTS

The first of five Mirage 2000 prototypes flew in March 1978, and the Mirage 2000C single-seat fighter followed in 1982. During the course of 2000C production, improvements were made to the engine and radar. The definitive Thomson-CSF RDI (Radar Doppler Impulse) radar had the capability to detect low-flying targets and destroy them with Matra Super 530D missiles. This "look-down/shoot-down" ability was advanced for its day and helped to counter the use of terrain, which causes "ground clutter" on radar scopes to avoid interception.

As well as missiles such as the Super 530 and Magic 2, the 2000C was armed with twin DEFA 554 30-mm cannon. The MBDA (formerly Matra) MICA has become the main AAM for the Mirage 2000 in Armée de l'Air (French Air Force) service. Many French 2000Cs have been upgraded to 2000-5 standard, a development originally intended for export with the cockpit displays of the Rafale, new multi-mode RDY radar and improved self-protection systems.

Exports failed to match those of the Lockheed Martin F-16 or indeed the Mirage III, but nonetheless seven air arms acquired new Mirage 2000s: Abu Dhabi, Egypt, Greece, India, Peru, Taiwan and Qatar. New production ended in 2007, but Brazil received a dozen surplus French aircraft from 2006 as an interim measure while they conducted evaluations for a long-term replacement for the Mirage III.

Above: The cockpit of the Mirage 2000-5 incorporates many of the features designed for the Dassault Rafale.

THE MIRAGE 2000 IN OPERATION

Mirage 2000 fighters have seen operational use by France and Abu Dhabi in the 1991 Gulf War; France over the Balkans in the 1990s; and India (in the ground-attack role) in the 1999 Kargil conflict. The destruction of a Turkish F-16D over the Aegean Sea in 1996 by a Greek Mirage 2000EG, in a skirmish over disputed air space, is the only known air-to-air kill to date.

Two specialized attack versions were derived from the Mirage 2000B two-seat trainer; the 2000D precision strike aircraft and the 2000N nuclear-strike platform, which also has a conventional role. These variants are used only by France, but most export fighters have a ground-attack capability with "dumb" or laser-guided bombs, or AS-30L laser-guided missiles. The Armat anti-radiation missile (ARM) is also an option.

Above: The baseline Mirage 2000C has been largely replaced by the Mirage 2000-5 in Armée de l'Air service, as illustrated by this EC.2 aircraft with its avionics bay door open.

Sukhoi Su-27 "Flanker"

The massively powerful, manoeuvrable and long-ranged Su-27 helped to change Western perceptions of Soviet aircraft. Since the end of the Cold War, exports of Su-27s have helped to keep both Sukhoi and the Russian aerospace industry alive.

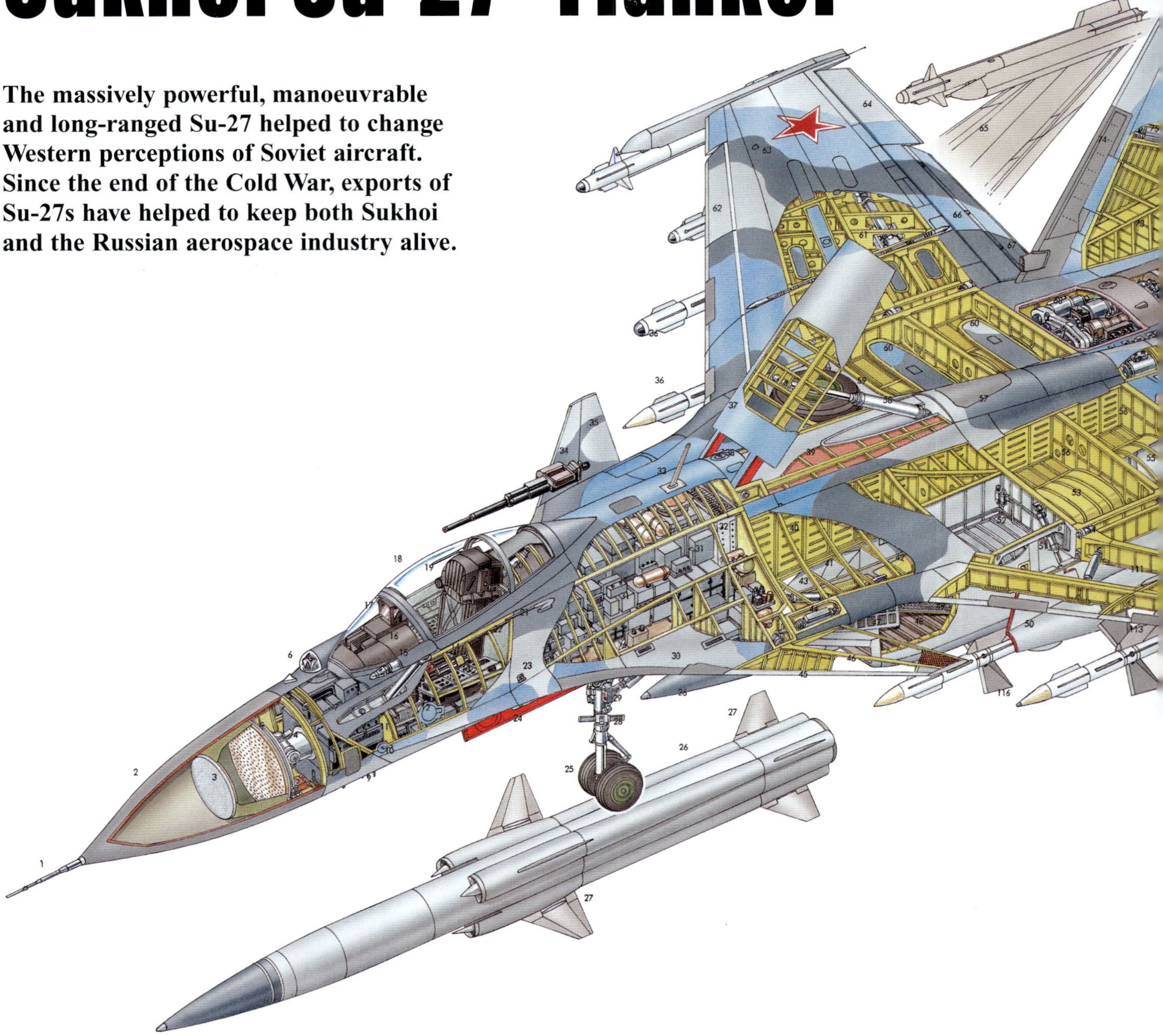

Cutaway Key

1 Pitot head
2 Upward-hinging radome
3 Radar scanner
4 Scanner mounting
5 Radome hinge point
6 Infrared search and tracking scanner
7 Refuelling probe housing
8 Radar equipment module; tilts down for access
9 Lower SRO-2 "Odd-Rods" IFF aerial
10 Incidence transmitter
11 Cockpit front pressure bulkhead
12 Retractable spotlight, port and starboard
13 Cockpit side console panel
14 Slide-mounted throttle levers
15 Flight-refuelling probe, extended
16 Instrument panel shroud
17 Pilot's head-up display
18 Upward-hinging cockpit canopy
19 K-36MD "zero-zero" ejection seat
20 Canopy hydraulic jack
21 Dynamic pressure probe, port and starboard
22 Cockpit rear pressure bulkhead
23 Temperature probe
24 Nosewheel door
25 Twin nosewheels, forward-retracting
26 ASM-MSS long-range ramjet and rocket-powered anti-shipping missile
27 Missile folding fins
28 Nosewheel hydraulic steering jacks
29 Deck approach "traffic lights"
30 Leading-edge flush EW aerial
31 Avionics equipment bay
32 Ammunition magazine, 149 rounds
33 HF aerial
34 Starboard fuselage GSh-30-1 30-mm cannon
35 Canard foreplane
36 Starboard wing missile armament
37 Dorsal airbrake
38 Gravity fuel-filler cap
39 Centre fuselage fuel tank
40 Forward lateral fuel tanks
41 ASM-MSS missile carrier on fuselage centreline station
42 Variable-area intake ramp doors
43 Ramp hydraulic jack
44 Foreplane hydraulic actuator
45 Port canard foreplane
46 Engine air intake
47 Boundary layer bleed air louvres
48 Segmented ventral suction relief doors
49 Retractable intake FOD screen
50 Mainwheel door
51 Door hydraulic jack
52 Port mainwheel bay
53 Intake trunking
54 Wing panel attachment joints
55 Engine compressor face
56 Wing centre-section integral fuel tanks
57 ADF antenna
58 Airbrake hydraulic jack
59 Starboard mainwheel, stowed position
60 Fuel-tank access panels
61 Wing-fold hydraulic jack
62 Leading-edge flap, down position
63 Starboard outer, folding, wing panel
64 Outboard plain flap, down position
65 Starboard wing, folded position
66 Inboard double-slotted flap segments
67 Engine bleed air pre-cooler air intake
68 Engine accessory equipment gearbox
69 Central auxiliary power unit

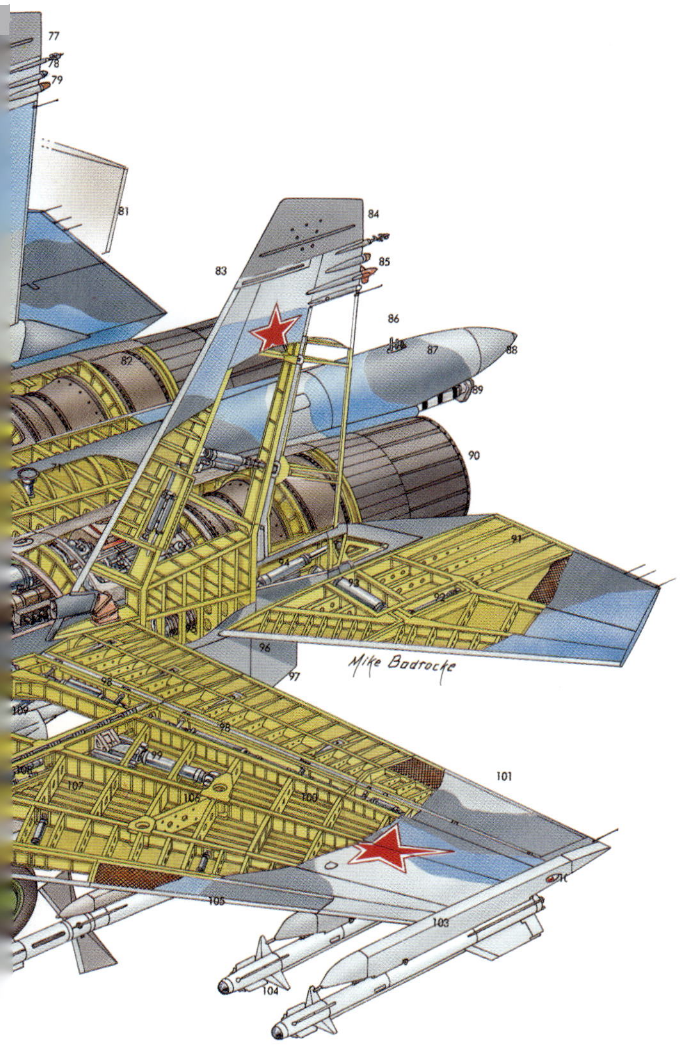

70 Chaff/flare launchers
71 Rear fuselage integral fuel tank
72 Engine oil tank
73 Fin structure
74 Leading-edge HF aerial
75 Rudder hydraulic actuator
76 Fintip UHF/VHF aerial
77 ILS aerial
78 Tail navigation light
79 Radar warning antenna
80 Starboard rudder
81 Starboard tailplane folded position
82 AL-31F afterburning turbofan engine
83 Port tail fin
84 ILS aerial
85 ECM antenna
86 Upper SRO-2 "Odd Rods" IFF aerial
87 Tailcone fairing
88 Rear EW antenna fairing
89 Deck arrestor hook
90 Variable-area afterburner nozzle
91 Port tailplane
92 Tailplane fold joint rotary actuator
93 Tailplane pivot bearing
94 Hydraulic actuator
95 Hydraulic accumulator
96 Ventral fin
97 Port inboard double-slotted flap segments
98 Flap hydraulic actuators
99 Wing-fold hydraulic jack
100 Outer wing panel structure
101 Outboard plain flap segment
102 Port navigation light
103 Wingtip missile launch rail
104 Vympel R-73 (AA-11 "Archer") air-to-air missiles
105 Leading-edge flap
106 Pylon attachment hardpoints
107 Port wing integral fuel tank
108 Wing-fold locking mechanism jack
109 Main undercarriage hydraulic retraction jack
110 Mainwheel leg strut
111 Wing-fold hinge joint
112 Leading-edge flush EW aerial panels
113 Missile pylon
114 Vympel R-27 (AA-10 "Alamo-B") infrafred-homing air-to-air missile
115 Port mainwheel
116 Vympel R-27 (AA-10 "Alamo-C") radar-homing air-to-air missile

SU-27P "FLANKER-B" SPECIFICATION

Dimensions

Fuselage length (including probe): 72 ft 0 in (21.94 m)
Wingspan over tip missile launch rails: 48 ft 3 in (14.70 m)
Wing aspect ratio: 7.76
Tailplane span: 32 ft 5 in (9.88 m)
Wing area: 667.8 sq ft (62.04 m^2)
Horizontal tail area: 131.75 sq ft (12.24 m^2)
Total fin area: 165.76 sq ft (15.40 m^2)
Distance between fintips: 14 ft 1¼ in (4.30 m)
Overall height: 19 ft 6 in (5.93 m)
Wheel track: 14 ft 3 in (4.34 m)
Wheelbase: 19 ft 4 in (5.88 m)
Maximum wing loading: 93.4 lb/sq ft (456.2 kg/m^2)

Powerplant

Two Saturn Lyul'ka AL-31F afterburning turbofans each rated at 16,755 lb st (74.53 kN) dry and 27,558 lb st (122.59 kN) with afterburning

Weights

Empty operating: 36,112 lb (16,380 kg)
Normal takeoff: 50,705 lb (23,000 kg)
Maximum takeoff: 62,391 lb (28,300 kg)

Fuel and load

Internal fuel: normal 11,620 lb (5270 kg); maximum 20,723 lb (9400 kg) or 3,170 U.S. gal (12,000 litres) in three main fuselage tanks, with additional tanks in outer wing panels; the basic Su-27 has no provision for inflight refuelling or for the carriage of external fuel tanks (see under individual variant briefings for exceptions)
Maximum theoretical weapon load: 17,636 lb (8000 kg)
Normal weapon load: 8,818 lb (4000 kg)
g limits: 8–9 at basic design gross weight

Performance

Maximum level speed at sea level (estimated): 743 kt (850 mph; 1370 km/h)
Maximum level speed "clean" at altitude: 1,236 kt (1,418 mph; 2280 km/h)
Limiting Mach number: 2.35
Absolute ceiling: 60,700 ft (18,500 m)
Practical service ceiling (est.): 58,070 ft (17,700 m)
Takeoff run: 1,640 ft (500 m) or 1,476 ft (450 m)
Landing roll: 1,968 ft (600 m) or 2,297 ft (700 m)
Landing speed: 121–124 kt (140–143 mph; 225–230 km/h)

Range

Maximum range: 1,987 nm (2,285 miles; 3680 km) at altitude; 740 nm (851 miles; 1370 km) at low level
Radius of action (high-altitude): 590 nm (677 miles; 1090 km)
Radius of action (low-altitude): 227 nm (261 miles; 420 km)

Armament

One 30mm GSh-30-1 cannon with 275 rounds
Up to 8,000 kg (17,600 lb) on ten external pylons
Up to six medium-range R-27 missiles, two short-range heat-seeking R-73 missiles

"Those who design, develop or fly fighters know that Sukhoi has succeeded at Paris in making Western fighter aerodynamics look very conventional."
– British test pilot John Farley, at the 1989 Paris Air Show

SUKHOI SU-27 "FLANKER" – VARIANTS

T10 ("Flanker-A"): Initial prototype configuration.

T10S: Improved prototype.

P-42: Special version built to beat climb time records.

Su-27: Pre-production series built in small numbers with AL-31 engine.

Su-27S (Su-27/"Flanker-B"): Initial production single-seater with improved AL-31F engine.

Su-27UB ("Flanker-C"): Initial production two-seat operational conversion trainer.

Su-27SK: Export Su-27 single-seater.

Su-27UBK: Export Su-27UB two-seater.

Su-27K (Su-33/"Flanker-D"): Carrier-based single-seater with folding wings.

Su-27PD: Single-seat demonstrator with improvements such as inflight refuelling probe.

Su-27PU (Su-30): Limited-production two-seater.

Su-30M/Su-30MK: Next-generation multi-role two-seater.

Su-30MKA: Export version for Algeria.

Su-30MKI ("Flanker-H"): Substantially improved Su-30MK for the Indian Air Force, with canards, vectored-thrust engines, new avionics provided by several nations, and multi-role capability.

Su-30MKK ("Flanker-G"): Su-30MK for the Chinese Air Force, with updated Russian-built avionics and multi-role capability.

Su-30MKM: Copy of Su-30MKI with special configuration for Malaysia.

Su-30KN ("Flanker-B" Mod. 2): Improved single-seater.

Su-30KI ("Flanker-B" Mod. 2): Improved single-seater with Su-30MK.

Su-27M (Su-35/-37, "Flanker-E"/"Flanker-F"): Improved demonstrators for an advanced single-seat multi-role Su-27S derivative.

Su-27SM ("Flanker-B" Mod. 1): Upgraded Russian Su-27S, featuring technology evaluated in the Su-27M demonstrators.

Su-27SKM: Single-seat multi-role fighter for export.

Su-27UBM: Comparable upgraded Su-27UB two-seater.

Su-32 (Su-27IB): Two-seat long-range strike variant with side-by-side seating in "platypus" nose. Prototype of Su-32FN and Su-34 "Fullback."

Su-27KUB: Essentially an Su-27K carrier-based single-seater with a side-by-side cockpit, for use as a naval carrier trainer or multi-role aircraft.

Su-35BM/Su-35S: Also dubbed the "Last Flanker." The latest development from the "Flanker" family. It features newer avionics and new radar.

SUKHOI SU-27 "FLANKER"

This Su-27 "Flanker-B" served with the Russian Air Forces Training Centre at Lipetsk in the 1990s. The unit mainly trains qualified weapons and tactics instructors. The so-called "Lipetsk Shark" was one of the first Russian aircraft to be seen in the West with non-standard markings, although they were not unknown in the Soviet era. Other "Flankers" of the unit wore a shark's mouth on the intake, but not the full-length shark silhouette seen here. The aircraft is armed with AA-11 "Archer" dogfight missiles on the wingtip and outer pylons, and the AA-10 "Alamo-A" semi-active radar-homing missile on the underfuselage pylons. The infrared-guided "Alamo-B" is fitted on the inner wing pylons.

FACTS

- The Su-27 had the first fly-by-wire system in an operational Russian aircraft.
- The Su-27 has been the mount of the "Russian Knights" and "Test Pilots" display teams.
- The engines are protected from foreign objects by intake screens that close when the wheels are on the ground.

In 1969, the Soviet military formulated a requirement for a new fighter, calling for a long-range interceptor to replace various older types, a counter to airborne warning and control system (AWACS) aircraft and something that could meet the McDonnell Douglas (now Boeing) F-15 Eagle on equal terms. At the time, the F-15 all-weather tactical fighter was still in development, as was Boeing's E-3 Sentry AWACS aircraft.

The desire for extreme manoeuvrability combined with long range could not be met in one airframe. The requirement was split into heavy and lightweight projects, the latter eventually leading to the Mikoyan-Gurevich MiG-29. Sukhoi proceeded with its T10 design – a large aircraft with plenty of internal fuel capacity, two widely spaced engines and large leading-edge root extensions that blended into the wings, which had curved tips.

The T10-1 prototype flew in May 1977, followed by several others that differed in detail. These proved less than completely satisfactory, but the revised T10S series of prototypes, which began test flights in April 1981, were to become the true predecessors of the Su-27. The T10S-3 prototype was stripped of all uneccessary weight. Also known as the P-42 "Streak Flanker," it set a number of records for the fastest climb to altitude, beating those set by a similarly modified F-15.

TEETHING PROBLEMS

There were further developmental troubles before the production Su-27, by now known in the West as "Flanker-B," began to enter service in 1986. The wing planform had changed to a more squared-off shape and the nose profile had altered, with a large radome housing a multimode radar. An infrared search-and-track sensor ball was mounted ahead of the windscreen. ECM equipment was fitted in a large tail "stinger" that protruded from between the engines.

Above: Two prototypes of the Su-35 show the wide range of armament available on modernised "Flankers," as well as the canard foreplanes.

Above: The baseline Su-27's cockpit was a product of the 1970s, with a plethora of conventional instruments.

Armament included an internal 30-mm cannon and ten pylons for missiles, including AA-10 "Alamo" beyond-visual-range weapons and AA-11 "Archer" dogfight AAMs.

The Su-27 first appeared in Western skies at the 1989 Paris Air Show, impressing observers with its agility for such a large aircraft and by not crashing, unlike the MiG-29. When the Soviet Union collapsed shortly afterwards, several former republics such as the Ukraine, Belarus and Uzbekistan inherited sizeable numbers of "Flankers." Some of these aircraft, as well as Russian examples, found their way to places such as Angola, Eritrea and Syria. In fighting between Ethiopia and Eritrea that began in 1998, the former country's Su-27s got the better of the latter's MiGs on a number of occasions.

NAVAL VERSION

Russia developed a naval version, the Su-27K (later redesignated Su-33), for use on its first conventional aircraft carriers. In the end, only the *Admiral Kuznetsov* was completed by Russia, but China, which acquired its sister ship *Varyag* and is refurbishing it for service, plans to purchase further Su-33s. China bought a number of Su-27s for its air force and is building more under licence as the Shenyang J-11.

The Su-30 is a fully combat-capable version of the two-seat Su-27UB with added strike capabilities. India's Su-30MKIs incorporate thrust-vectoring engines and canards for extra manoeuvrability. The Su-35 designation was initially used for a relatively modest upgrade plan; however, a new model Su-35BM with many internal and external improvements flew in 2008 and is to form the basis of a production model for use by the Russian Air Force.

Above: Late 1980s appearances at Farnborough and Paris air shows of Sukhoi's Su-27 demonstrators gave the West its first close views of the new "superfighter."

Panavia Tornado ADV

The Tornado Air Defence Variant (ADV) is a fighter derived from a bomber design, which perhaps made it less efficient than a purpose-built fighter. Still, it has served well as the United Kingdom's principal air-defence asset for more than two decades.

TORNADO F3 SPECIFICATION

Dimensions

Length: 61 ft 3½ in (18.68 m)
Height: 19 ft 6¼ in (5.95 m)
Wingspan spread: 45 ft 7½ in (13.91 m)
Wingspan swept: 28 ft 2½ in (8.60 m)
Aspect ratio spread: 7.73
Aspect ratio swept: 2.96
Wing area: 286.33 sq ft (26.60 m²)
Tailplane span: 22 ft 3½ in (6.80 m)
Wheel track: 10 ft 2 in (3.10 m)

Powerplant

Two Turbo-Union RB.199-34R Mk 104 turbofans each rated at 9,100 lb st (40.48 kN) dry and 16,520 lb st (73.48 kN) with afterburning

Fuel and load

Internal fuel: 12,544 lb (5690 kg)
External fuel: up to 12,800 lb (5806 kg) in two 495-Imp gal (2250-litre) and two 396-Imp gal (1500-litre) or four 330-Imp gal (1500-litre) drop tanks
Maximum ordnance: 18,740 lb (8500 kg)

Weights

Empty operating: 31,970 lb (14,502 kg)
Maximum takeoff: 61,700 lb (27,986 kg)

Performance

Maximum level speed "clean" at 36,000 ft (10,975 m): 1,262 kt (1,453 mph; 2238 km/h)
Operational ceiling: 70,000 ft (21,335 m)
Combat radius: more than 300 nm (345 miles; 556 km) supersonic or more than 1000 nm (1,151 miles; 1852 km) subsonic

Armament

One 27-mm IWKA Mauser cannon fitted to the starboard side. Main armament is four BAe SkyFlash semi-active radar-homing or four AIM-120 AMRAAM active-radar AAMs with a range of 31 miles (50 km), carried semi-recessed under the fuselage. Four AIM-9L Sidewinders or four ASRAAMS are also carried for short-range combat. Self-defence is provided by a Bofors Phimat chaff dispenser carried on starboard outer Sidewinder pylon or Celsius Tech BOL integral chaff/flare dispenser in Sidewinder rail. Vicon 78 chaff/flare dispensers under rear fuselage. GEC-Marconi Ariel towed-radar decoy can be carried on outboard wing pylon

Cutaway Key

1 Starboard taileron construction
2 Honeycomb trailing-edge panels
3 Compound sweep taileron leading edge
4 Taileron pivot fixing
5 Afterburner ducting, extended 14 in (36 cm)
6 Thrust-reverser bucket door actuator
7 Afterburner nozzle jack
8 Starboard fully variable engine exhaust nozzle
9 Thrust-reverser bucket doors, open
10 Dorsal spine and fairing
11 Rudder hydraulic actuator
12 Honeycomb rudder construction
13 Rudder
14 Fuel jettison pipes
15 Tail navigation light
16 Aft passive ECM housing/radar warning antenna
17 Dielectric fintip antenna housing
18 VHF aerial
19 Fuel jettison and vent valve
20 ILS aerial, port and starboard
21 Underside view showing semi-recessed missile positions
22 Extended fuselage section
23 Extended radar equipment bay
24 Radome
25 Secondary heat exchanger intake
26 Wing pylon-mounted missile rails
27 External fuel tanks
28 Port taileron
29 Fin leading edge
30 Fin integral fuel tank
31 Tailfin construction
32 Vortex generators
33 Heat shroud
34 Fin spar root attachment joints
35 Engine bay central firewall
36 Starboard airbrake, open
37 Airbrake hydraulic jack
38 Taileron actuator, fly-by-wire control system
39 Turbo-Union RB.199-34R Mk 104 three-spool afterburning turbofan
40 Hydraulic reservoir
41 Hydraulic system filters
42 Engine bay bulkhead
43 Bleed air duct
44 Heat exchanger exhaust duct
45 Primary heat exchanger
46 Ram air intake
47 HF aerial fairing
48 Engine compressor faces
49 Rear fuselage bag-type fuel tank
50 Intake trunking
51 Wingroot pneumatic seal
52 KHD/Microtecnica/Lucas T312 APU
53 Engine-driven auxiliary gearbox
54 APU exhaust
55 Flap drive shaft
56 Starboard full-span double-slotted flaps, extended
57 Spoiler housings
58 Starboard wing, fully swept position
59 Flap guide rails
60 Flap screw jacks
61 Wingtip fairing
62 Starboard navigation light
63 Structural provision for outboard pylon attachment
64 Full-span leading-edge slats, extended
65 Starboard external fuel tank, capacity 594 U.S. gal (2250 litres)
66 Fuel-tank stabilizing fins
67 Swivelling wing stores pylon
68 Missile launching rail
69 AIM-9L Sidewinder air-to-air missiles
70 Leading-edge slat screw jacks
71 Slat guide rails
72 Wing rib construction
73 Two-spar wing torsion box construction
74 Swivelling pylon mounting
75 Starboard wing integral fuel tank
76 Main undercarriage leg strut
77 Starboard mainwheel
78 Mainwheel door
79 Undercarriage breaker strut
80 Wing pivot sealing fairing
81 Telescopic control linkages
82 Pylon swivelling link
83 Main undercarriage hydraulic retraction jack
84 Wing sweep actuator attachment joint
85 Starboard wing pivot bearing
86 Flexible wing seals
87 Wing pivot carry-through (electron beam–welded titanium box construction)
88 Wing pivot box integral fuel tank
89 Pitch and roll control non-linear gearing mechanism
90 Air-conditioning supply ducting (Normalair Garrett system)
91 Dorsal spine fairing
92 Anti-collision light
93 UHF aerials
94 Port wing pivot bearing
95 Flexible trailing-edge seals
96 Spoiler actuators
97 Port spoilers, open
98 Port wing, fully swept back position
99 Full-span double-slotted flaps, extended
100 Port wing, fully forward position

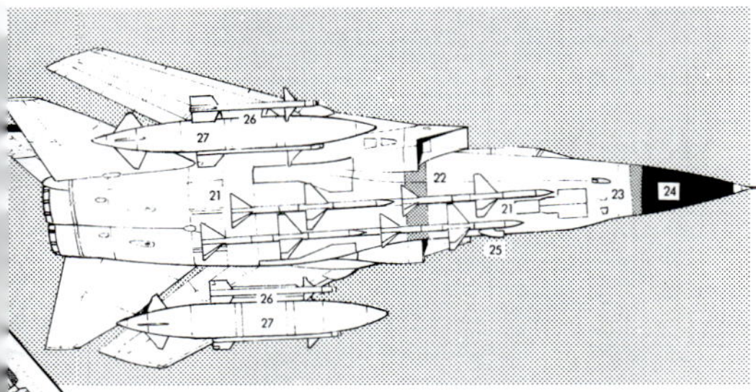

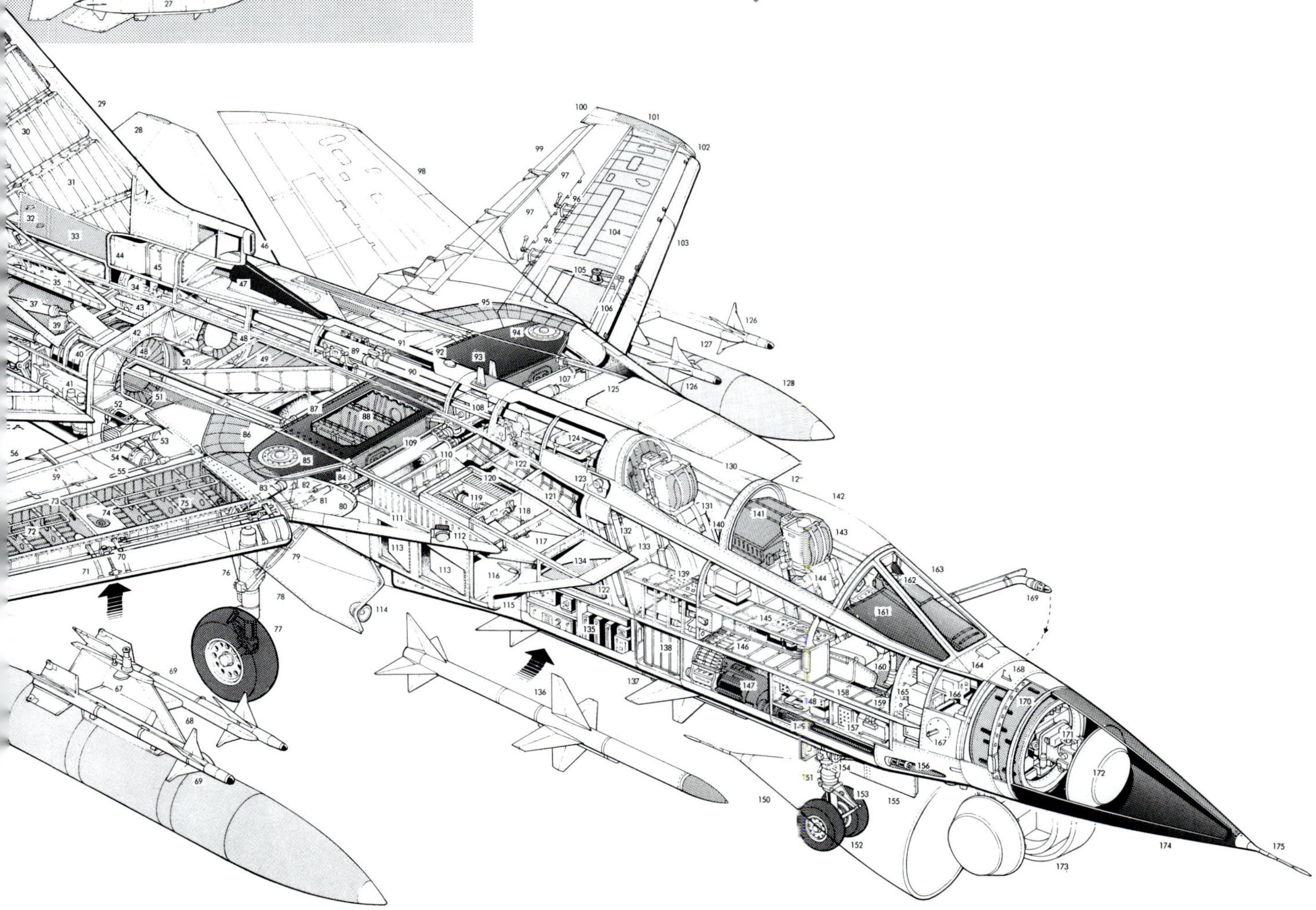

101 Wingtip fairing
102 Port navigation light
103 Full-span leading-edge slats, extended
104 Port wing integral fuel tank
105 Swivelling pylon mounting
106 Pylon angle control link
107 Port wing sweep actuator
108 Wing flap and leading-edge slat drive motors
109 Starboard wing sweep actuator
110 Hydraulic drive motor and gearbox
111 Extended wingroot glove fairing
112 Forward radar-warning receiver, port and starboard
113 Supplementary "blow-in" intake doors
114 Landing lamp, port and starboard
115 Starboard fully variable engine air intake
116 Navigation light
117 Variable-intake ramp
118 Ramp control linkage
119 Ramp hydraulic jack
120 Bleed air exit louvres
121 Boundary layer spill duct
122 Enlarged forward fuselage bag-type fuel tank
123 Cockpit canopy pivot mounting
124 Air and fuel system ducting
125 Port intake bleed air outlet fairing
126 AIM-9L Sidewinder air-to-air missiles
127 Missile launching rail
128 Port external fuel tank
129 Intake lip
130 Navigator's cockpit enclosure
131 Navigator's ejection seat (Martin-Baker Mk 10A "zero-zero" seat)
132 Canopy jack strut
133 Cockpit rear pressure bulkhead
134 Engine air intake curved inboard sidewall
135 Starboard avionics equipment and flight control system equipment bay
136 BAe SkyFlash air-to-air missile
137 Ventral semi-recessed missile housing
138 Cartridge case and link collector box
139 Navigator's side console
140 Canopy centre arch
141 Navigator's instrument console
142 One-piece cockpit canopy cover
143 Ejection-seat headrest
144 Pilot's ejection seat
145 Side console panel
146 Ammunition feed chute
147 Mauser 27-mm cannon, starboard only
148 Instrument pressure sensor
149 Cannon barrel
150 Radome, open position
151 Nosewheel leg strut
152 Twin nosewheels
153 Torque scissor links
154 Taxiing lamp
155 Nosewheel doors
156 Cannon muzzle blast tube
157 Electrical system equipment and ground test panels
158 Cockpit pressure floor
159 Rudder pedals
160 Control column
161 Instrument panel shroud
162 Pilot's head-up display
163 Windscreen panels
164 Windscreen rain-dispersal duct
165 Cockpit front pressure bulkhead
166 Avionics equipment, communications and navigation systems
167 Angle-of-attack transmitter
168 Blade antenna
169 Inflight refuelling probe, extended
170 Marconi-Elliot "Foxhunter" airborne interception radar
171 Scanner tracking mechanism
172 Cassegrain radar antenna
173 Radar unit hinged to starboard for replacement of line replaceable units (LRUs)
174 Extended radome
175 Pitot tube

"As a pure interceptor, the F3 performs well against medium and low-level non-agile threats. Where it falls down is against high-flying targets or agile fighters."
– Ian Black, former RAF Tornado F3 pilot

FACTS

- The Tornado ADV is a dedicated interceptor variant of the Tornado IDS bomber
- The ADV replaced the English Electric Lightning in Royal Air Force fighter squadrons and in turn is being replaced by the Eurofighter Typhoon
- A detachment of Tornado F3s provided air defence for the Falkland Islands for nearly 20 years

PANAVIA TORNADO ADV – VARIANTS & OPERATORS

VARIANTS

Tornado F2: Two-seat all-weather interceptor fighter aircraft, powered by two Turbo-Union RB.199-34R Mk 103 turbofan engines. Initial production version. 18 built.

Tornado F2A: F2 upgrade to F3 standard, but retaining F2 engines. One built.

Tornado F3: Improved version, powered by two Turbo-Union RB.199-34R Mk 104 engines, with automatic wing sweep control, increased AIM-9 carriage and avionics upgrades.

Tornado EF3: Unofficial designation for F3 aircraft modified with ALARM missile capability.

OPERATORS

Italy

12º Gruppo, 36º Stormo, Aeronautica Militare, 1995–2003.

1º Gruppo, 53º Stormo, Aeronautica Militare, 1995–2001.

Saudi Arabia

No. 29 Squadron, Royal Saudi Air Force, 1989–present.

United Kingdom

Operational

No. 111 Squadron RAF – F3. Based at RAF Leuchars, Fife, Scotland, 1990–present.

Disbanded

No. 5 Squadron RAF — F3. RAF Coningsby, Lincolnshire, England, 1987–2003.

No. 11 Squadron RAF — F3. RAF Leeming, North Yorkshire, England, 1988–2005.

No. 23 Squadron RAF — F3. RAF Leeming, North Yorkshire, England, 1988–1994.

No. 25 Squadron RAF — F3. RAF Leeming, North Yorkshire, England, 1989–2008.

No. 29 Squadron RAF – F3. RAF Coningsby, Lincolnshire, England, 1987–1998.

No. 43 Squadron RAF — F3. RAF Leuchars, Fife, Scotland, 1989–July 2009.

No. 56 (Reserve) Squadron RAF — F3. RAF Coningsby, England and RAF Leuchars, Scotland, 1992–2008 (Operational Conversion Unit).

No. 229 Operational Conversion Unit (No. 65 (Reserve) Squadron) RAF — F2 and F3. RAF Coningsby, Lincolnshire, England, 1984–1992.

No. 1435 Flight RAF— F3. RAF Mount Pleasant, Falkland Islands, 1992–2009.

TORNADO ADV

As part of a giant arms deal with the United Kingdom in the 1980s, Saudi Arabia purchased 24 Tornado ADV fighters and 48 Tornado IDS bombers, as well as spare parts and a training and maintenance package. The ADVs served initially with No. 29 Squadron, Royal Saudi Air Force, at Tabuk. Delivered from 1989 onwards, they flew patrols in the 1991 Gulf War, but did not see combat with any Iraqi aircraft. Unlike the RAF's Tornados, the Saudi aircraft had a working automatic wing sweep system. They used the same armament of four Skyflash semi-active radar-homing AAMs and four Sidewinders. The ADVs are being replaced with an order of 72 Eurofighter Typhoons and were withdrawn from use in 2007.

Above: Seen on an East Asia sales tour, this F3 has its wings in the forward position and its leading-edge flaps down. The Tornado was built with an automatic wing sweep system, but this was disconnected on the Royal Air Force's F3s.

The Tornado Air Defence Variant (ADV) came about as a development of the Tornado Interdictor Strike (IDS), a dedicated bomber designed to meet the needs of Germany, Italy and the United Kingdom. The Germans and Italians had a requirement for only a ground-attack aircraft, but the United Kingdom wanted to replace the English Electric Lightning F 6 and the McDonnell Douglas Phantom FG.1 and FGR.2 in the air defence role. The British solution was to stretch the basic airframe, adding an air interception (AI) radar in a lengthened nose radome and medium-range missiles in recesses under the aircraft's fuselage.

The original Tornado prototype flew in 1974 and the ADV in October 1979. The first fighter version was intended to be the Tornado F2, but there were significant delays with radar development and the 18 F2s built did not enter full RAF service. Some of them flew with ballast in the nose instead of radars. Once problems with the Marconi AI.24 Foxhunter radar were worked out, the ADV was delivered to the Royal Air Force as the Tornado F3 from 1986.

Above: The ADV's primary armament was four Skyflash recessed into the belly, as seen on this F3 of No. 229 Operational Conversion Unit.

Like the Phantom, the ADV can carry eight missiles: four semi-active radar-homing Skyflash or AIM-7 Sparrow rounds semi-recessed under the belly and four AIM-9 Sidewinders on wing pylons. On RAF aircraft, the AIM-9s have been replaced by the AIM-132 ASRAAM (Advanced short-range air-to-air missile). The integration of the AIM-120 AMRAAM (advanced medium-range air-to-air missile) was delayed until quite late in the F3's RAF career. Unlike the baseline IDS, the ADV has one 27-mm Mauser cannon, rather than two. A retractable refuelling probe was fitted on the port side of the forward fuselage, unlike the removable starboard-side probe used on the IDS. The ALARM (air-launched anti-radiation missile) has been cleared for use on the F3 for the SEAD (suppression of enemy air defences) role, but it is not thought any squadrons are currently trained in its use.

VARIABLE GEOMETRY

The Tornado ADV is a variable-geometry, or "swing-wing," design, which allows the aerodynamic configuration to be changed for high- and low-speed flight. The wings sweep from 25 degrees to 67 degrees, allowing a maximum speed of more than Mach 2, while providing good handling characteristics for takeoff and landing.

The ADV is regarded as something of a compromise as a fighter. Its intended function was as an interceptor, able to meet incoming Soviet bombers approaching the United Kingdom at a distance greater than the bombers' missile ranges. As such, it emphasized speed, climb rate and endurance, rather than dogfighting ability, and usually comes off second-best in air combat training with more modern fighters.

RAF F3s were deployed in Saudi Arabia for the 1991 Gulf War, and in Italy for operations over the Balkans in the 1990s, but have never engaged in actual combat.

OPERATORS OUTSIDE THE UK

Saudi Arabia was the only country to purchase the ADV outright, taking 24 in 1989 as part of the huge al-Yamamah weapons deal with Britain. They serve alongside McDonnell Douglas (now Boeing) F-15Cs in the air-defence role with the Royal Saudi Air Force. Despite not being a part of ADV development, Italy acquired surplus F3s from Britain in a lease deal to bridge the gap between the phasing out of the Lockheed F-104 and service entry of the Eurofighter Typhoon. The F3s served the Aeronautica Militare from 1995–2004, before being returned to the United Kingdom and replaced by leased Lockheed Martin F-16As.

Above: The ADV was one of the last Western fighters built without multifunction display screens and hands-on-throttle-and-stick (HOTAS) controls.

McDonnell Douglas/ BAe AV-8B Harrier II

Often thought of as purely an attack aircraft, the Harrier has impressive abilities as a fighter, particularly in its radar-equipped Harrier II Plus form.

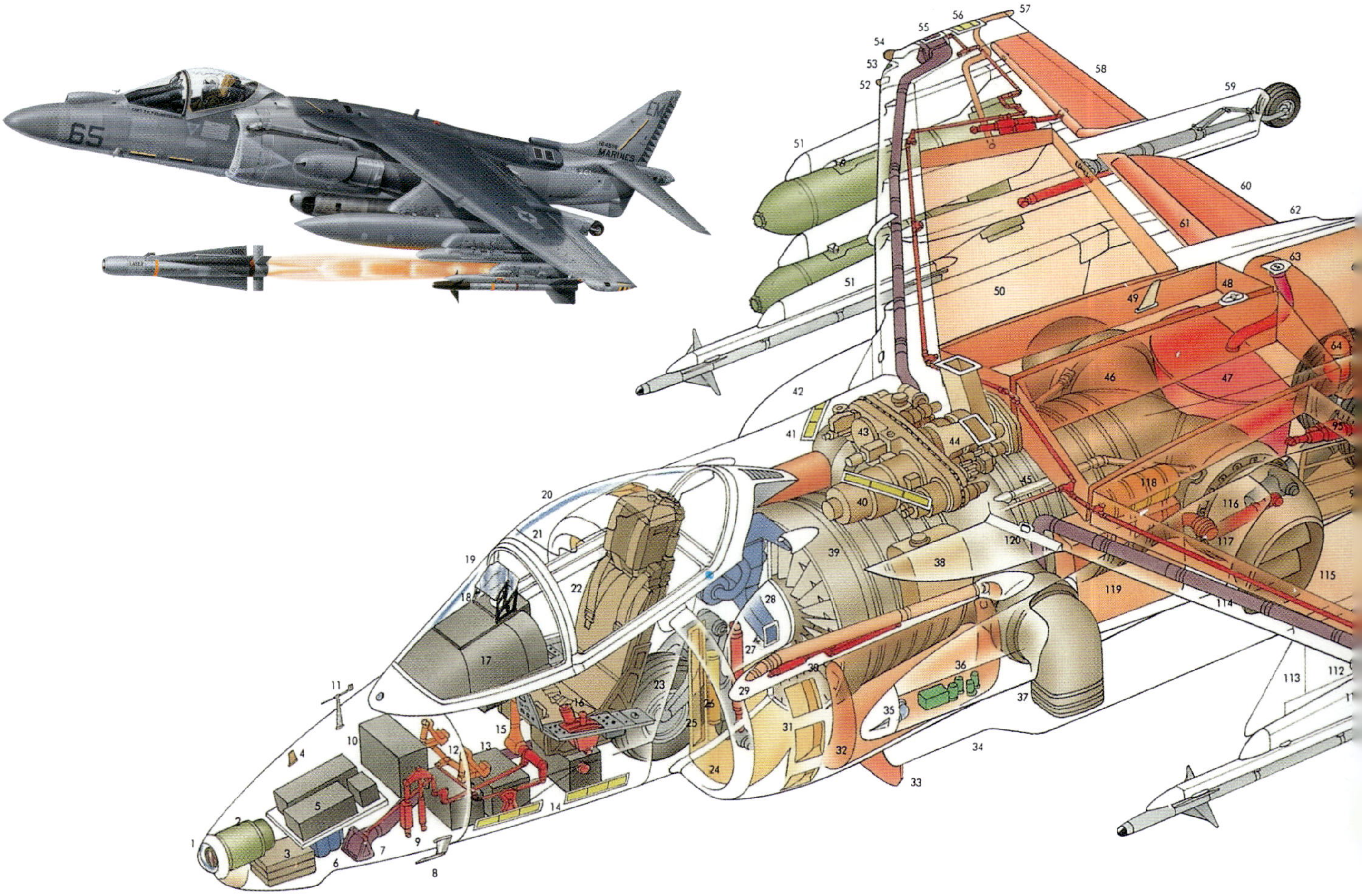

Cutaway Key

1 Glazed nose aperture
2 Hughes Angle Rate Bombing Set (ARBS)
3 Nose ballast in place of MIRLS
4 IFF aerial
5 Nose avionics equipment
6 ARBS heat exchanger
7 Pitch control reaction air valve
8 Pitot head
9 Pitch feel and trim actuators
10 ARBS signal data converter
11 Yaw vane
12 Rudder pedals
13 Air data computer and inertial navigation system equipment
14 Formation lighting strips
15 Control column and linkages
16 Engine throttle and nozzle control levers
17 Instrument panel shroud
18 Pilot's head-up display
19 Single-piece "wraparound" windscreen
20 Rearward-sliding cockpit canopy cover
21 Miniature detonating cord canopy breaker
22 Martin-Baker Mk 12 ejection seat
23 Nose undercarriage wheel bay
24 Engine air intake
25 Boundary layer bleed duct
26 Hydraulic accumulator
27 Nosewheel hydraulic jack
28 Cockpit air-conditioning system
29 Flight refuelling probe stowage
30 Probe hydraulic jack
31 Intake suction relief doors
32 Forward fuselage flank fuel tank
33 Lift augmentation retractable cross-dam
34 Fuselage strakes, port and starboard
35 Engine bay venting air intake
36 Hydraulic system ground connectors and engine monitoring equipment
37 Zero scarf forward (fan air) swivelling nozzle
38 Engine oil tank
39 Rolls-Royce Pegasus Mk 105 engine
40 Alternator
41 Formation lighting strips
42 Leading-edge root extension (LERX)
43 Engine-driven accessory equipment gearbox
44 Gas turbine starter/auxiliary power unit
45 Nozzle bearing cooling air duct
46 Wing centre-section integral fuel tank
47 Water-methanol tank
48 Anti-collision light
49 VHF/UHF aerial
50 Starboard wing integral fuel tank
51 Starboard wing pylons
52 Radar-warning antenna
53 Starboard navigation light
54 Starboard/forward missile-warning antenna
55 Roll control reaction air valve
56 Wingtip formation light
57 Fuel jettison
58 Starboard aileron
59 Outrigger wheel fairing
60 Starboard slotted flap
61 Drooping flap vane
62 Wing root fairing
63 Water/methanol tank filler
64 Engine fire-suppression bottle
65 Rear fuselage fuel tank
66 Aft avionics equipment bay
67 Electrical distribution panels
68 Heat exchanger ram air intake
69 Rudder hydraulic actuator
70 Starboard all-moving tailplane
71 Formation lighting strip
72 MAD compensator
73 Temperature probe
74 Upper broadband communications antenna

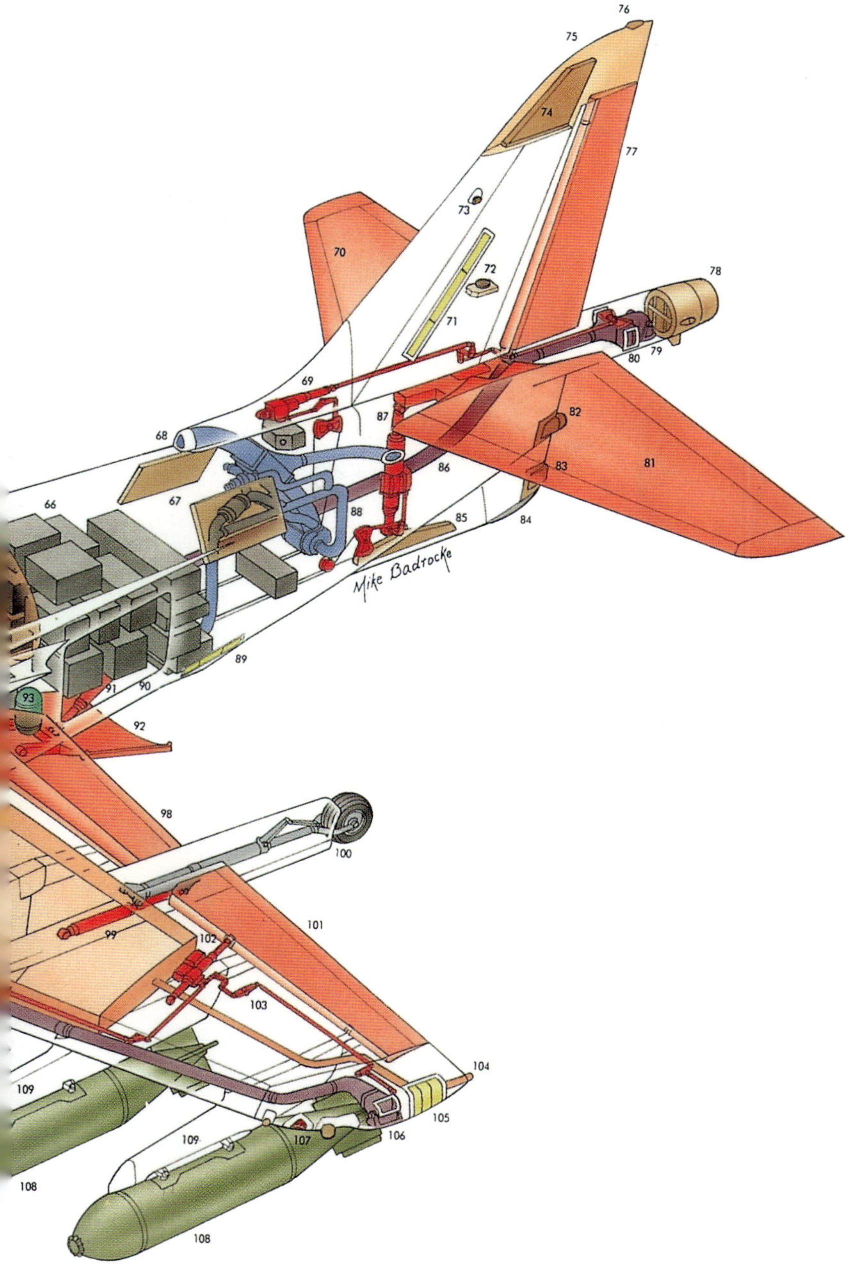

75 Fintip aerial fairing
76 Radar beacon antenna
77 Rudder
78 ECM equipment module
79 Pitch control reaction air valve
80 Yaw control reaction air valves
81 Port all-moving tailplane
82 Rear missile-warning antenna
83 Radar-warning antenna
84 Tail bumper
85 Lower broadband communications antenna
86 Reaction control air ducting
87 Tailplane hydraulic actuator
88 Avionics air conditioning equipment
89 Formation lighting strip
90 Avionics equipment bay access door, port and starboard
91 Airbrake hydraulic jack
92 Ventral airbrake panel
93 Hydraulic system nitrogen pressurization bottle
94 Main undercarriage wheel bay
95 Flap hydraulic jack
96 Fuselage heat shield
97 Port wing integral fuel tank
98 Port flap
99 Outrigger wheel hydraulic jack
100 Port outrigger wheel
101 Port aileron
102 Aileron hydraulic actuator
103 Aileron/air valve interconnection
104 Fuel jettison
105 Wingtip formation light
106 Port roll control reaction air valve
107 Port navigation light
108 BL755 cluster bombs
109 Outboard weapons pylons
110 AIM-9L/M Sidewinder air-to-air missile
111 Intermediate missile pylon
112 Wing fence
113 Inboard weapon/fuel tank pylon
114 Reaction control air ducting
115 Rear (hot-stream) swivelling exhaust nozzle
116 Main undercarriage hydraulic jack
117 Pressure refuelling connection
118 Hydraulic reservoir
119 Centre fuselage flank fuel tank
120 Engine bay venting air intake

HARRIER II GR7 SPECIFICATION

Dimensions

Length overall (flying attitude): 47 ft 8 in (14.53 m)
Wing span: 30 ft 4 in (9.25 m)
Wing aspect ratio: 4.0
Tailplane span: 13 ft 11 in (4.24 m)
Overall height: 11 ft 7¾ in (3.55 m)
Outrigger wheel track: 17 ft 0 in (5.18 m)

Powerplant

GR Mk.7: one Rolls-Royce Pegasus Mk 105 vectored-thrust turbofan rated at 21,500 lb st (95.6 kN)

Weights

Empty operating (including pilot and unused fuel): 15,542 lb (7050 kg)
Basic flight design gross weight for 7-g operation: 22,950 lb (10,410 kg)
Maximum takeoff: [after 1,430-ft (435-m) short takeoff] 31,000 lb (14,061 kg); (sea level vertical takeoff, ISA conditions) 19,180 lb (8700 kg); (sea-level vertical takeoff, 32°C) 17,950 lb (8143 kg)
Design maximum landing weight: 25,000 lb (11,340 kg)
Maximum vertical landing weight: 19,937 lb (9043 kg)

Fuel and load

Total fuel capacity: 2340 U.S. gal (8858 litres)
Total usable internal fuel: 1,141 U.S. gal (4318 litres)/ 7,759 lb (3519 kg)
External fuel: up to four 300-U.S. gal (1135-litre) auxiliary fuel tanks on four inner underwing stations; single-point refuelling plus optional retractable bolt-on flight refuelling probe above port air intake
Maximum useful load: (including fuel, water injection for engine, stores, guns and ammunition) approx. 6,750 lb (3062 kg) with vertical takeoff and 17,000 lb (7,710 kg) with short takeoff

Performance

Maximum level speed at altitude: 645 mph (1041 km/h)
Maximum level speed at low level: 661 mph (1065 km/h)
Service ceiling above: 50,000 ft (15,240 m)

Range

Operational radius: (after short takeoff with 12 500-lb/ 227-kg bombs, internal fuel and 1-hour loiter) 103 miles (167 km); (hi-lo-hi profile after short takeoff with seven 500-lb/227-kg bombs, two external fuel tanks, no loiter) 684 miles (1101 km)
Combat air patrol endurance: (at 115 miles/185 km from base) 3 hours

Armament

Fixed: two underfuselage pods each housing a single 25-mm Aden 25 cannon with 100 rounds
Weapon stations: centreline station stressed for 1,000 lb (454 kg), four stations under each wing stressed for loads up to 2,000 lb (907 kg) inboard, 1,000 lb (454 kg) intermediate and 630 lb (286 kg) outboard, additional weapon station ahead of outrigger wheel fairing for air-to-air missile

"Landing a Harrier on a ship can be both a real pleasure and quite terrifying, depending on the circumstances."
– Major John Hicks,
U.S. Marine Corps AV-8B Plus pilot

FACTS

- The Harrier can use its thrust nozzles to alter its direction or vector in flight.
- Spain's Harrier IIs are locally known as the VA.2 Matador II.
- The AV-8B+ added an extra hardpoint for an AIM-9 on each outrigger undercarriage fairing.

MCDONNELL DOUGLAS/BAE HARRIER AV-8B HARRIER II – VARIANTS & OPERATORS

MCDONNELL DOUGLAS VARIANTS

AV-8B Harrier II: "Day Attack" variant; no longer in service.

AV-8B Harrier II Night Attack: Fielded in 1991; incorporates a navigation forward-looking infrared camera (NAVFLIR).

AV-8B Harrier II Plus: Similar to the night-attack variant, with the addition of an APG-65 radar.

EAV-8B Matador II: Designation for the Spanish Navy version.

MCDONNELL DOUGLAS OPERATORS

The Italian Navy (Marina Militare) has 15 AV-8B aircraft in service. Gruppo Aerei Imbarcati "The Wolves."

The Spanish Navy has 13 AV-8B+ aircraft in use as of January 2010, with 9 Escuadrilla of the Spanish Navy Air Arm at Naval Station Rota.

The U.S. Marine Corps has 99 AV-8B+ aircraft in operation as of January 2010 in the following Marine Attack Squadrons:

VMA-211, Marine Corps Air Station Yuma, Arizona
VMA-214, Marine Corps Air Station Yuma, Arizona
VMA-223, Marine Corps Air Station Cherry Point, North Carolina
VMA-231, Marine Corps Air Station Cherry Point, North Carolina
VMA-311, Marine Corps Air Station Yuma, Arizona
VMA-513, Marine Corps Air Station Yuma, Arizona
VMA-542, Marine Corps Air Station Cherry Point, North Carolina
VMAT-203, Marine Corps Air Station Cherry Point, North Carolina
VX-31, Naval Air Weapons Station China Lake, California
VX-9, Naval Air Weapons Station China Lake, California

BAE VARIANTS

GR5: The Royal Air Force's first second-generation Harrier, entering service in July 1987. The GR5 differed from the U.S. Marine Corps AV-8B in many ways, including when it came to avionics fit, weapons and countermeasures. 41 GR5s were built.

GR5A: A minor variant of the Harrier that incorporated changes in the design in anticipation of the GR7 upgrade. 21 were built.

GR7: The GR7 made its first operational deployment in August 1995 over the former Yugoslavia.

GR7A: The first stage in an upgrade to the Harrier GR9 standard with an uprated Rolls-Royce Pegasus 107 engine.

GR9: An avionics and weapons upgrade of the standard GR7, known as the Integrated Weapons Programme (IWP).

GR9A: The Harrier GR9A is an avionics and weapons upgrade of the uprated engined GR7As.

BAE OPERATORS

United Kingdom
Royal Air Force
No. 1 Squadron
No. 3 Squadron (until 2006)
No. 4 Squadron
No. 20 Squadron
RAF SAOEU (Strike Attack Operational Evaluation Unit)
Royal Navy Fleet Air Arm
Naval Strike Wing

MCDONNELL DOUGLAS/BAE AV-8B NIGHT ATTACK HARRIER II

The AV-8B Night Attack Harrier II had an infrared unit mounted over the nose, giving it the ability to find targets at night, as did the addition of night-vision goggles (NVGs) for the pilot. The U.S. Marine Corps' VMA-214 "Blacksheep" at MCAS Yuma, Arizona, was the first unit to receive this model, in September 1989, and this aircraft from the squadron is shown carrying AIM-9Ls on the outboard pylons, AGM-65 Mavericks and Rockeye cluster bombs. Under the port side of the fuselage is a 25-mm GAU-12 Equalizer cannon pod, which took its ammunition from the pod on the starboard side. Many night-attack Harriers were later rebuilt to AV-8B Plus standard.

Within a few years of the Harrier GR1's entry into RAF service as the first operational VTOL (vertical takeoff and landing) combat aircraft, studies were already under way into a bigger, more powerful successor. British Aerospace (BAe) had partnered with McDonnell Douglas to supply the U.S. Marine Corps with a version of the GR1 called the AV-8A for use from the Marines' amphibious ships.

Above: In Operation Iraqi Freedom from 2003, the Harrier has provided essential close air support for Marines and Coalition forces on the ground.

Unlike British Harriers, the AV-8A was equipped to take Sidewinder AAMs from the outset, allowing it to self-escort attack Harriers during amphibious landing operations. RAF

Above: The early AV-8B featured a laser spot tracker in the extreme nose, as seen in this view of a U.S. Marine Corps aircraft on a transoceanic ferry flight.

Above: The AV-8B Plus gives organic air defence and close air support to USMC landing forces from platforms such as the "Wasp"-class amphibious ships.

Harrier GR3s were hastily wired to take AIM-9s during the Falklands War, and served as the main air defence for the islands after the war until the new airfield at Mt. Pleasant was completed, allowing the operation of Phantoms. Spain and Thailand used their early Harriers for fleet air defence.

A "BIG WING" AIRCRAFT

McDonnell Douglas led the development of a "big wing" Harrier, testing a composite wing on an airframe dubbed "YAV-8B" in 1978. A true AV-8B with an all-new fuselage and only a passing resemblance to the earlier model flew in 1981. British studies inspired the addition of leading-edge root extensions (LERXs), which improved turning ability. During Harrier II production, several different sizes of LERX were introduced.

The production AV-8B incorporated significant amounts of non-metallic composite materials such as carbon-fibre. The new wing had four pylons rather than two, and could carry AIM-9s on double racks. A podded 25-mm cannon could also be carried. A larger canopy with improved rear view and increased the AV-8B's air combat abilities, although there was no radar.

From 1984, the AV-8B replaced the U.S. Marines' earlier Harriers and was used largely in the attack role, as was the next development, the Night Attack Harrier II with a forward-looking infrared (FLIR) housed above the nose. The Royal Air Force's Harrier IIs, the GR5, GR7 and GR9 have remained radarless and have limited air combat utility, particularly in the fleet air-defence role with which they have been tasked since the retirement of the Sea Harrier FA2.

The Harrier II became a true fighter when the AV-8B Plus flew in the early 1990s. This was a development of the Night Attack Harrier II with a Hughes APG-65 multimode radar in an extended nose. This radar was the same as that in the McDonnell Douglas (now Boeing) F/A-18 Hornet. Spain and Italy contributed to the development of the "Plus."

A MIX OF "OLD" AND NEW

The U.S. Marine Corps re-equipped some of its squadrons with the newest model through a mix of new-builds and conversions. Spain purchased a mix of Harrier IIs with and without the radar, but all of Italy's single-seaters were equivalent to the AV-8B Plus. Spain and Italy have integrated AMRAAM missiles on their radar-equipped Harriers, giving them true beyond-visual-range capability, and more recently Spain upgraded all of its "day" Harriers to "Plus" standard.

The AV-8B first saw combat in the 1991 Gulf War, with subsequent action by Harrier GR7s and GR9s over the Balkans, Iraq and Afghanistan. To date, no air combat claims or losses have been made. The U.S. Marine Corps, Royal Navy, Royal Air Force and Italian Navy all plan to replace the Harrier with the F-35 Lightning II.

Saab JAS 39 Gripen

Sweden's JAS 39 Gripen is the multi-role successor to the several different versions of the Saab 37 Viggen. Changes in world affairs and Swedish policies have allowed the Gripen to evolve into a much more "international" fighter and one with considerable export success and potential.

Cutaway Key

1 Pitot tube
2 Vortex generating strakes
3 Fibreglass radome
4 Ericsson PS-05 multi-mode radar (hidden)
5 Single-piece windscreen
6 Instrument panel shroud
7 Instrument panel
8 Wide angle head-up display (HUD)
9 Martin-Baker Mk 10L zero-zero ejection seat
10 Ejection-seat operating handle
11 Forward nosewheel door
12 Formation lighting strip
13 Starboard nosewheel
14 Nosewheel scissor link
15 Nosewheel main strut
16 Brake hydraulic lines
17 Hydraulic steering jacks
18 Port nosewheel
19 Nosewheel door retraction strut
20 Nose undercarriage main door
21 Muzzle for Mauser 27-mm cannon
22 Throttle lever
23 Intake splitter plate
24 Port engine intake
25 Canopy
26 Ejection-seat head box
27 Avionics shelf
28 Starboard canard foreplane
29 Refuelling probe door
30 Port canard foreplane
31 Foreplane hinge point
32 Starboard inboard manoeuvring flap
33 Starboard outboarc manoeuvring flap
34 Carbon-fibre composite wing skin
35 Dorsal VHF antenna
36 TACAN antenna
37 Starboard outboard elevon
38 Starboard inboard elevon
38 IFF antenna
40 Flight-control system dynamic pressure sensor
41 Radar warning antenna
42 ECM transmitting antenna
43 Fin cap UHF/VHF antenna
44 Instrument landing system (ILS) antenna
45 Strobe light/anti-collision beacon
46 Rudder
47 Formation lighting strips
48 Engine compressor face
49 Engine accessory wiring
50 Volvo Aero RM12 afterburning turbofan
51 Afterburner petal actuators
52 Variable-area afterburner nozzle
53 Port airbrake, open
54 Port airbrake actuator fairing
55 Port inboard elevon hydraulic actuator fairing
56 Port inboard elevon
57 Port outboard elevon
58 Carbon-fibre composite wing skinning

59 Port outboard leading-edge manoeuvring flap
60 Port inboard leading-edge manoeuvring flap
61 Central fuselage fuel tanks (hidden)
62 Port mainwheel
63 Port mainwheel main strut
64 Hydraulic mainwheel retraction jack
65 Mainwheel leg drag/breaker strut
66 Port mainwheel bay
67 Starboard mainwheel bay
68 Starboard mainwheel (retracted)
69 Port canard carbon-fibre skin and structure
70 Port mainwheel door
71 AIM-9M Sidewinder short-range air-to-air missile
72 AIM-120 AMRAAM medium-range air-to-air missile
73 MBDA Meteor beyond-visual-range air-to-air missile
74 Litening targeting pod
75 GBU-32 1,000-lb (454-kg) laser-guided bomb
76 Mk 82 500-lb (227-kg) free-fall bomb
77 IRIS-T close-range air-to-air missile
78 Rafael Python IV close-range air-to-air missile

SAAB JAS 39 GRIPEN SPECIFICATION

Dimensions

Length: 46 ft 3 in (14.1 m)
Height: 14 ft 9 in (4.5 m)
Wingspan: 27 ft 7 in (8.4 m)
Wing area: 323 sq ft (30 m^2)
Wheel track: 7 ft 10 in (2.4 m)

Powerplant

One Volvo Aero RM12 afterburning turbofan rated at 12,100 lbf (54 kN) dry thrust and 18,100 lbf (80.5 kN) with afterburner.

Weights

Empty operating: 14,600 lb (5700 kg)
Normal takeoff: 18,700 lb (8500 kg)
Maximum takeoff: 31,000 lb (14000 kg)

Fuel and load

Internal fuel: 794 US gal (3,008 liters)
External fuel: 290 US gal (1,100 liters)
Maximum weapon load: 7,942 lb (3600 kg)

Performance

Maximum level speed at altutude: Mach 2 (1, 372 mph/2470 km/h)
Maximum combat radius: 432 nm (500 miles; 800 km)
Ferry range: 2,000 miles (3200 km) with drop tanks
Service ceiling: 50,000 ft (14,240 m)
Wing loading: 66.8 lb/sq ft (336 kg/m^2)

Armament

One 27-mm Mauser BK-27 cannon with 120 rounds; six Rb.74 (AIM-9) or Rb 98 (IRIS-T) missiles; four Rb.99 (AIM-120) or MICA; four Rb.71 (Skyflash) or Meteor; four Rb.75; two KEPD.350; four GBU-12 Paveway II laser-guided bombs; four rocket pods with 5.31-in (135-mm) rockets; two Rbs. 15F anti-ship missiles; two Bk.90 cluster bombs; eight Mark 82 bombs and one ALQ-TLS ECM pod.

"The traditional Swedish emphasis was on air defence and the anti-ship mission, but now we need more than that – and Gripen does it."
– Major General Jan Andersson,
Chief of Staff of the Swedish Air Force

FACTS

- The pilot boards the Gripen from the right-hand side, unlike almost all other jet fighters.
- The Gripen's datalink allows radar and sensor imagery to be passed from one aircraft to another with the receiver keeping his own systems "silent."
- With a few button presses, a Gripen pilot can change from one role to another within a single mission.

SAAB JAS 39 GRIPEN – VARIANTS & OPERATORS

VARIANTS

JAS 39A: Fighter version that first entered service with the Swedish Air Force in 1996. A modification programme has started, and 31 of these will be upgraded to C/D standard.

JAS 39A+: Upgraded single-seat fighter with PS-5/A radar and MACS D96 computer, monochrome cockpit displays.

JAS 39B: Two-seat version of the A variant. This variant is 2 ft 2 in (0.62 m) longer than the single-seat version.

JAS 39C: NATO-compatible version of Gripen with extended capabilities in terms of armament and electronics. Capable of inflight refuelling.

JAS 39D: Two-seat version of the C variant.

AS 39E/F: Designation reserved for proposed upgraded version with an AESA electronically scanned radar.

JAS 39G/H: Designation reserved for further upgraded version at some point in the future.

JAS 39X: Generic designation for export version.

Gripen Demo: A two-seat technology demonstrator for improvements slated for the Gripen NG.

Gripen NG/IN (Next Generation): Proposed version with new engine (F414G), increased fuel capacity, higher payload, upgraded avionics and other improvements. The Gripen IN version is a contender for the Indian MRCA competition.

CURRENT OPERATORS

Czech Republic
Czech Air Force: 14 Gripens on lease, including two two-seaters.

Hungary
Hungarian Air Force: 14 Gripens on a lease-and-buy arrangement, including two two-seaters (C/D versions). The final three aircraft were delivered in December 2007.

South Africa
South African Air Force: 26 aircraft ordered (down from 28), nine two-seater Ds and 17 single seat-Cs. The first delivery, a two-seater, took place on 30 April 2008.

Sweden
Swedish Air Force: 204 aircraft originally ordered, including 28 two-seaters (138 in service). Sweden leases 28 of the aircraft, including four two-seaters.

United Kingdom
Empire Test Pilots' School: Under the agreement, ETPS instructor pilots and students undergo simulator training with the Swedish Air Force, and go on to fly the two-seater Gripen at Saab in Linköping, Sweden, in two training campaigns per year (spring and autumn).

ORDERS

Thailand
Royal Thai Air Force: Six aircraft, four of them two-seaters, have been slated for delivery in 2011.

SAAB JAS 39 GRIPEN

The Saab JAS 39A first entered service with F 7 Såtenäs, Skaraborgs Flygflottilj (Air Force Wing), of the Flygvapnet (Swedish Air Force) at Såtenäs, near Lidköping, in central Sweden. The Såtenäs base is the centre of Sweden's Gripen programme, and it is also where all Gripen pilots, including those with foreign operators, are trained. Aircraft "54" was part of the second production batch, delivered in June 1998. It carries AIM-9Ls on wingtips, AIM-120s on the outer pylons and German-designed BK 90 Mjoelnir weapons on the inner pylon. The Mjoelnir can be "tossed" at the target from up to 14 miles (22 km) away, then glides to the target, dispensing 24 bomblets against armoured or soft targets.

The Saab JAS 39 Gripen stemmed from a 1980 requirement for a multi-role aircraft to replace the different versions of the Saab 37 Viggen. Having decided not to seek tenders from foreign manufacturers, the Swedish government invited proposals from within Swedish industry. In practice, this meant choosing Saab for the airframe, with the assistance of Ericcson (radar), Volvo Flygmotor (engine) and many smaller component manufacturers.

Above: The Gripen fulfills all of the roles of the Viggen in a single airframe.

The project was designated "JAS," for "Jakt" (fighter), "Attack" (attack) and "Spaning" (reconnaissance), three roles that the one aircraft was expected to perform with a change of external stores and software modes. Advances in electronics, particularly computer processing power, allowed new capabilities to be fitted into a smaller airframe than the Viggen's. An important driver of the design was that it could be maintained in combat by one specialist and five conscripts with basic training and limited equipment. In wartime, the Flygvapnet (Swedish Air Force) would disperse from fixed bases to pre-prepared stretches of highway.

FAMILIAR DELTA CANARD

Like the Viggen, the Gripen is a canard delta, although the wingtips are cropped and mount missile launchers. The canards are fully movable and can act as powerful speed brakes on landing, replacing the complicated thrust-reverser in the Viggen. The Volvo RM 12 engine was a licence-built General Electric F404 as used in the McDonnell Douglas (now Boeing) F/A-18 Hornet, but with improvements including a larger fan and a new afterburner.

CLOSER NATO LINKS

The prototype Gripen flew in December 1988. The JAS 39A and two-seat B entered Flygvapnet service in 1995 and were declared fully operational in 1997. These models were very keyed in to the Swedish defence system with its datalink and command-and-control systems. Relatively few Swedish combat aircraft had been exported before the 1990s. Political concerns about arms sales to nations likely actually to engage in anything but self-defence largely restricted foreign users to Nordic and neutral countries. Although remaining

Above: Two-seat JAS 39Ds can be used in combat roles as fighters, forward air control platforms and even to control unmanned air combat vehicles.

Above: The JAS 39C cockpit is typical of the Fourth Generation fighter, with all information needed by the pilot presented on multifunction display screens and the HUD, rather than via individual instruments.

neutral itself, Sweden moved closer to NATO in the 1990s, conducting joint exercises and joining the Partnership for Peace programme. The JAS 39C and D were designed to conform more closely to international and NATO standards, with Link 16 datalink, instruments with imperial measurements and compatibility with a wider range of weapons.

These modifications and effective marketing has helped the Gripen to make several breakthroughs in the international market. South Africa became the first export customer with an order in 1999. Hungary signed an innovative deal in 2001 to lease Gripens for 14 years with an option to buy at the end. The Czech Republic made a similar arrangement. Thailand has bought Gripens and Saab 340-based Erieye radar aircraft.

COMPETING ON THE OPEN MARKET

To compete with aircraft such as the Eurofighter Typhoon and Boeing F/A-18E/F Super Hornet for several large fighter orders, Saab has proposed a Gripen NG (Next Generation) and built a demonstrator aircraft called the Gripen Demo, which first flew in May 2008. Although outwardly similar, the Demo has a GE F414 engine as used in the Super Hornet, increased internal fuel and more weapons hardpoints. A Selex ES-05 Raven AESA was added in later testing.

The Gripen NG with these and other new features is aimed squarely at markets such as Brazil and India, and at customers wavering at the high price and political baggage attached to the F-35 Joint Strike Fighter.

Boeing F/A-18E/F Super Hornet

The Super Hornet is an evolutionary rather than a revolutionary development of the successful F/A-18 Hornet. More than 400 examples have been delivered to the U.S. Navy, replacing several older types in different roles, including the F-14 Tomcat, S-3 Viking and EA-6B Prowler.

Cutaway Key

1 Composite radome
2 Raytheon AN/APG-73 multimode radar (hidden)
3 Cannon blast-diffuser vent
4 Port for M61A1 cannon
5 Refuelling probe access door
6 Formation lighting strip
7 Lower VHF/UHF D-band antenna
8 Pitot head
9 Incidence transmitter
10 Retractable refuelling probe (extended)
11 Refuelling probe extension jack
12 Upper combined interrogator IFF antenna ("pizza box")
13 Frameless windscreen
14 Instrument panel shroud
15 Head-up display (HUD)
16 Nosewheel door
17 Pilot's control column
18 Pilot's throttle levers
19 Pilot's port control console
20 Port wingroot leading-edge extension
21 Catapult engagement bar
22 Deck approach signal lights
23 Hydraulic nosewheel steering unit
24 Port nosewheel
25 Torque scissor links
26 Catapult holdback fairing
27 Nosewheel retraction strut door
28 Nosewheel retraction strut
29 Retractable boarding ladder (extended)
30 Pilot's Martin-Baker NACES zero-zero ejection seat
31 Ejection-seat head box
32 Canopy frame
33 Rear instrument panel shroud
34 NFO's Martin-Baker NACES zero-zero ejection seat
35 Radar control joystick
36 Boarding ladder hatch door
37 NFO's port control console
38 Canopy jettison handle
39 Canopy actuator unit
40 Starboard mid-wing stores pylon
41 Inner starboard leading-edge flap segment
42 Starboard outer stores pylon
43 Outer starboard leading-edge flap segment
44 Wingtip missile launch rail
45 Wing fold hinge fairing porous panel
46 Wing carbon-fibre composite skin panelling
47 Starboard aileron
48 Starboard trailing-edge flap
49 GPS antenna
50 Canopy frame
51 IFF antenna
52 AN/ALQ-165 electronic warfare antenna (hidden)
53 Upper VHF/UHF D-band antenna
54 Environmental control system (ECS) intake door
55 Starboard tail fin
56 Carbon-fibre composite fin skin
57 Carbon-fibre composite fintip fairing
58 Rear position light
59 Aft AN/ALQ-165 receiving antenna
60 Starboard AN/ALR-67 RWR antenna
61 Fuel jettison outlet
62 Starboard rudder
63 Starboard all-moving tailplane
64 Engine bay venting air exit
65 Starboard variable-area afterburner

BOEING F/A-18E/F SUPER HORNET SPECIFICATION

Dimensions

Length: 60 ft 1¾ in (18.31 m)
Height: 4.88 in (16 m)
Wingspan: 44 ft 8½ in (13.62m)
Wing loading: 92.8 lb/sq ft (453 kg/m^2)

Powerplant

Two General Electric F414-GE-400 turbofans rated at 14,000 lbf (62.3 kN) dry and 22,000 lbf (97.9 kN) each with afterburner

Weights

Empty operating: 30,600 lb (13,900 kg)
Normal takeoff: 47,000 lb (21,320 kg)
Maximum takeoff: 66,000 lb (29,900 kg)

Fuel and load

Internal fuel: F/A-18E: 14,400 lb (6530 kg); F/A-18F: 13,550 lb (6145 kg)
External fuel: five 480-U.S. gal (1817-litre) tanks, totalling 16,380 lb (7430 kg)

Performance

Maximum level speed: Mach 1.8+ (1,190 mph/1900 km/h at 40,000 ft (12,190 m)
Maximum combat radius: 390 nm (449 miles; 722 km)
Maximum combat range: 1,275 nm (1458 miles; 2346 km)
Service ceiling: 50,000-plus ft (15,000-plus m)

Armament

One 20-mm M61 Vulcan nose-mounted Gatling gun with 578 rounds. 11 hardpoints (two wingtip; six underwing; three underfuselage) with a capacity of 17,750 lb (8050 kg) external fuel and ordnance. Typical armament four AIM-9 Sidewinder or AIM-120 AMRAAM and two AIM-7 Sparrow or AIM-120 AMRAAM air-to-air missiles; AGM-65 Maverick, Standoff Land Attack Missile (SLAM-ER), AGM-88 HARM anti-radiation missile and AGM-154 Joint Standoff Weapon (JSOW) air-to-surface missiles. Also AGM-84 Harpoon anti-ship missile and bombs

exhaust nozzles
66 Heat exchanger exhaust duct
67 Front compressor fan
68 General Electric F414-GE-400 afterburning turbofan
69 Engine accessory section
70 Afterburner section
71 Fuel venting ram air intake
72 AN/ALQ-165 high-band transmitting antenna
73 AN/ALQ-165 low-band transmitting antenna
74 Port AN/ALR-67 RWR antenna
75 Fuel jettison outlet
76 Port rudder
77 Formation lighting strip
78 Afterburner nozzle sealing flaps
79 Variable-area afterburner nozzle
80 Port all-moving tailplane
81 Port flap
82 Port aileron
83 Port missile launch rail
84 Formation light
85 Port outboard leading-edge flap
86 Port outer stores pylon
87 Port mid-wing stores pylon
88 330-gal (1249-litre) external fuel tank
89 Port inner stores pylon
90 Undercarriage shock-absorber strut
91 Main landing gear trailing-leg axle beam
92 Main landing gear strut
93 Main landing gear door
94 Port inner leading-edge strut
95 Wing-fold hinge fairing porous panel
96 Port wing carbon-fibre composite wing skinning
97 GBU-16 1,000-lb (454-kg) laser-guided bomb
98 GBU-31 laser-guided bomb
99 AIM-9M Sidewinder short-range air-to-air missile
100 GBU-24 2,000-lb (907-kg) laser-guided bomb
101 Advanced targeting forward-looking infrared (ATFLIR) pod
102 D-704 "buddy" refuelling pod
103 Impeller
104 Super Hornet Advanced Reconnaissance Pod (SHARP)
105 AGM-88 HARM

"More power; more capability; better radar; lower radar cross section; more manoeuvrability … empty space for future upgrades and magic boxes; made from fewer parts and able to carry more weaponry."
– Major Chris "Elwood" Evans, Super Hornet pilot

FACTS

- Nicknames for the F/A-18 Super Hornet include "Rhino" and "Super Bug."
- The most obvious distinguishing feature of the Super Hornet when viewed from the front and underneath is the angular shape of the engine intakes.
- The F414 engines each have 35 per cent more power than the F404s in the "Baby Hornet."

BOEING F/A-18E/F SUPER HORNET – VARIANTS & OPERATORS

VARIANTS

F/A-18E Super Hornet: Single-seat variant.

F/A-18F Super Hornet: Two-seat variant.

EA-18G Growler: The electronic-warfare version of the F/A-18F Super Hornet, slated to begin production in 2008, with fleet deployment in 2009. The EA-18G will replace the U.S. Navy's EA-6B Prowler.

OPERATORS

Australia

Royal Australian Air Force (24 aircraft on order).

United States

United States Navy

Pacific Fleet

VFA-2 "Bounty Hunters" (F/A-18F) (Strike Fighter Squadron 2), Naval Air Station Lemoore, California.
VFA-14 "Tophatters" (F/A-18E) (Strike Fighter Squadron 14), Naval Air Station Lemoore, California.
VFA-22 "Fighting Redcocks" (F/A-18F), Naval Air Station Lemoore, California.
VFA-27 "Royal Maces" (F/A-18E), Naval Air Facility Atsugi, Japan.
VFA-41 "Black Aces" (F/A-18F), Naval Air Station Lemoore, California.
VFA-102 "Diamondbacks" (F/A-18F), Naval Air Facility Atsugi, Japan
VFA-115 "Eagles" (F/A-18E), Naval Air Facility Atsugi, Japan.
VFA-122 "Flying Eagles" (Fleet Replacement Squadron, operates F/A-18E/F), Naval Air Station Lemoore, California.
VFA-137 "Kestrels" (F/A-18E), Naval Air Station Lemoore, California.
VFA-147 "Argonauts" (F/A-18E), Naval Air Station Lemoore, California.
VFA-154 "Black Knights" (F/A-18F), Naval Air Station Lemoore, California.

Atlantic Fleet – all based at Naval Air Station Oceana, Virginia
VFA-11 "Red Rippers" (F/A-18F)
VFA-31 "Tomcatters" (F/A-18E)
FA-32 "Swordsmen" (F/A-18F)
VFA-81 "Sunliners" (F/A-18E)
VFA-103 "Jolly Rogers" (F/A-18F)
VFA-105 "Gunslingers" (F/A-18E)
VFA-106 "Gladiators" (Fleet Replacement Squadron, operates F/A-18A/B/C/D/E/F)
VFA-136 "Knighthawks" (F/A-18E)
VFA-143 "Pukin' Dogs" (F/A-18E)
VFA-211 "Fighting Checkmates" (F/A-18F)
VFA-213 "Black Lions" (F/A-18F)

TEST AND EVALUATION UNITS

VX-9 "Vampires" (Air Test and Evaluation Squadron, operates F/A-18E/F and other aircraft), Naval Air Weapons Station China Lake, California

VX-23 "Salty Dogs" (Air Test and Evaluation Squadron, operates F/A-18E/F and other aircraft), Naval Air Station Patuxent River, Maryland

VX-31 "Dust Devils" (Air Test and Evaluation Squadron, operates F/A-18E/F and other aircraft), Naval Air Weapons Station China Lake, California

NSAWC (Naval Strike and Air Warfare Center), received F/A-18F, also operates other aircraft), Naval Air Station Fallon, Nevada

BOEING F/A-18E/F SUPER HORNET

As the West Coast Super Hornet Fleet Readiness Squadron (FRS), the U.S. Navy's VFA-122 "Flying Eagles," with its 37 aircraft, is larger than operational units. Of these aircraft, 11 are F/A-18Es such as the one here. The weapons loadout depicted includes the AIM-9 (wingtip pylons), AGM-88 HARM anti-radiation missile (outer wings) and the Joint Standoff Weapon (JSOW) on the mid-wing pylons. Toed-out weapons pylons were found to be necessary to ensure clean weapons separation, even though this type of pylon increases drag and reduces performance. Some of the radar cross-section (RCS) features of the Super Hornet can be seen, such as the alignment of intakes and tail fins, and the shape of panels, which produce fewer sharp angles that cause radar "hot spots."

Above: The "Super Bug" has considerably more power than the "Baby Hornet," giving better performance in the vertical plane.

The F/A-18 Super Hornet arose from two separate requirements to replace the U.S. Navy's aging combat aircraft in the 1990s. During the 1991 Gulf War, the A-12 Avenger II carrier-based stealth bomber was cancelled, mainly for budgetary reasons. The A-12 was intended to replace the A-6 Intruder in the attack role.

Proposals to replace the Grumman F-14 Tomcat with a new-build "Super Tomcat 21" derivative were shelved in favour of giving existing F-14s an attack capability. McDonnell Douglas proposed an improved version of the F/A-18 Hornet in 1991, to provide fleet air defence and medium attack missions, and the go-ahead was given the following year to begin engineering development of the single-seat F/A-18E and twin-seat F Super Hornets. The first Super Hornet (an E) flew in November 1995, and began to enter service in 1999.

MAKING THE MOST OF DIFFERENCES

The Super Hornet has the same configuration as the original Hornet, but is 25 per cent larger and has few common airframe components. The wings, tailplanes and intakes are completely redesigned. One of the Super Hornet's major advantages is the increased "bring back" of ordnance. The F/A-18C can carry an impressive ordnance load from a carrier deck, but on close air support missions in today's conflicts, where weapons are not expended on every sortie, a returning fighter can easily exceed the allowable landing weight. The much greater power of the Super Hornet's General Electric F414 engines allows up to 9,000 lb (4100 kg) of weapons and fuel to be brought back to the carrier without the need for dumping. In practice, this means more can be carried on a given sortie.

The Super Hornet also includes a number of features to reduce its radar signature. The angles of the intake sides match that of the tail fins, helping to reduce right angles, which cause major "hot spots" on radar when seen from the frontal aspect. Wing leading edges and other surfaces are coated with radar-absorbent material (RAM). The edges of various panels and vents are angled so as to scatter radar waves, rather than reflect them back at the source.

Radar and other avionics on initial production Super Hornets were mostly the same as those on later-production "legacy" Hornets. The "Block 2" Super Hornets have replaced the old APG-73 radar with the APG-79 AESA (Active Electronically Scanned Array) radar, and there is a new onboard jamming system.

The Super Hornet has an extra mission of refuelling other aircraft. With a "buddy store" refuelling pod under the centerline, the Super Hornet (usually an E model) can top up aircraft before they set off on a mission, thus allowing higher weapons loads, or if they return low on fuel or make multiple landing attempts. This role was inherited from the Lockheed S-3 Viking, which was retired in 2008.

FULFILLING THEIR NEW ROLE

Although in theory the F/A-18E replaced Grumman's A-6E Intruder and some F/A-18Cs in the U.S. Navy's VA (attack) and VFA (fighter-attack) squadrons, and the F/A-18F replaced the Grumman F-14's VF (fighter) squadrons, in practice the two Super Hornet types are largely interchangeable.

The "Super Bug" has seen air-to-ground action over Iraq and Afghanistan, but no air-to-air combat to date. An electronic attack version called the EA-18 Growler is entering service to replace the EA-6B Prowler. Australia became the first export customer when it ordered 24 F/A-18Fs in 2007. Half of those ordered will be wired to take the jamming pods and other avionics of the EA-18G, although this equipment will not initially be purchased by the Royal Australian Air Force.

Above: F/A-18Es have replaced some Grumman F-14 Tomcat squadrons, the Grumman A-6 Intruder and some F/A-18Cs on the U.S. Navy's carriers. They have also taken on the "buddy" refuelling role of the Lockheed S-3 Viking.

Above: A two-person crew shares the heavy workload in the F/A-18F's strike and air-defence missions.

Dassault Rafale

The Rafale is the latest in a succession of French fighters stretching back to before World War II. With its airframe, engines and systems all French designed and built, it is the product of one of the few nations that still has an indigenous combat aircraft industry.

DASSAULT RAFALE C SPECIFICATION

Dimensions

Length: 50.1 ft 1.1 in (15.27 m)
Height: 17 ft 6¼ in (5.34 m)
Wingspan: 35 ft 4¾ in (10.80 m)
Wing area: 492 sq ft (45.7 m^2)

Powerplant

Two Snecma M88-2 turbofan engines rated at 11,250 lbf (50.04 kN) each dry and with M-88-Eco 17,000 lbf (90 kN)

Weights

Empty operating: 20,944 lb (9500 kg)
Maximum takeoff: 54,000 lb (24,494 kg)

Fuel and load

Internal fuel: 10,300 lb (4700 kg)
External fuel: 16,500 lb (7500 kg)
Maximum weapon load: 20,950 lb (9500 kg)

Performance

Maximum level speed at high altitude: Mach 2 (1,290 kt)
Maximum combat radius: 1,000 nm (1151 miles; 1852 km)
Range: 2,000 nm (2299 miles; 3700 km)
Service ceiling: 55,000 ft (16,800 m)

Armament

One 30-mm GIAT 30/719B cannon with 125 rounds. Missiles include air-to-air missiles MICA IR/EM or Magic II; and air-to-ground missiles MBDA Apache or SCALP EG or AASM, or GBU-12 Paveway II or AM 39 Exocet or ASMP-A nuclear missile

Cutaway Key

1 Kevlar composite radome
2 Radar scanner array
3 Thales RBE2 electronically scanned multimode radar
4 Airflow sensors
5 IR scanner/tracker
6 Low-level TV (LLTV) passive visual sight
7 Formation lighting strip
8 Frameless windscreen panel
9 Instrument panel shroud
10 Wide-angle holographic head-up display (HUD)
11 Martin-Baker Mk 16 zero-zero ejection seat
12 Catapult launch bar
13 Twin forward-retracting nosewheels
14 Main undercarriage strut
15 Nosewheel scissor link
16 Nosewheel hysdralulic steering
17 Forked nosewheel retraction strut
18 Nosewheel main door
19 Nosewheel aft door
20 Spectra RWR antenna
21 Port engine air intake
22 Port forward Spectra ECM antenna
23 Ejection-seat firing handle
24 Port control console
25 Canopy mid-arch
26 Lateral avionics bay (hidden)
27 Starboard canard foreplane

28 Dorsal avionics bay (covered)
29 Starboard navigation light
30 Starboard automatic leading-edge slat
31 Heat-exchanger exhaust duct
32 RWR antenna
33 Starboard wingtip missile pylon
34 MBDA MICA air-to-air missile
35 Wing carbon-fibre skin panelling
36 Starboard outboard elevon
37 Starboard inner elevon
38 Auxilary power unit (APU) intake grilles
39 Anti-collision beacon
40 Starboard airbrake panel
41 Fin leading edge
42 Formation lighting strip
43 Forward ECM transmitting antenna
44 Spectra ECM system pod
45 Radar warning receiver
46 VHF/UHF antenna in fintip
47 Rear position light
48 Aft ECM transmitting antenna
49 Rudder
50 ILS aerial
51 Carbon-fibre skin panelling
52 Fin with carbon-fibre main structure
53 ECM antenna fairing
54 Brake parachute housing
55 Variable-area afterburner nozzle
56 Afterburner petal actuators
57 Chaff/flare dispenser (hidden)
58 Flight-control system equipment bay
59 Port outboard aileron
60 SNECMA M88-2 afterburning turbofan engine
61 Engine accessory section
62 Starboard outboard elevon
63 Starboard wingtip missile pylon
64 MATRA MICA air-to-air missile
65 Port forward RWR antenna
66 Port automatic leading-edge slat
67 Port outboard missile pylon
68 Port intermediate wing pylon
69 Port mainwheel and tyre
70 Port mainwheel strut
71 Mainwheel torque scissor link
72 Port navigation light
73 Port canard foreplane
74 Carbon-fibre foreplane skin
75 MATRA MICA air-to-air missile
76 MBDA SCALP standoff weapon
77 Folding wings
78 External fuel tank
79 Giat DEFA 791B 30-mm cannon
80 Ammunition tank with 125 rounds

"Dassault's battle-proven Rafale is the best and most complete combat aircraft our test pilot has ever flown, delivering an 'incredible' level of performance."
– *Flight International* magazine 2009

FACTS

- The Rafale A technology demonstrator was slightly larger than the aircraft that followed.
- The Rafale was intended to replace seven French types: the F-8 Crusader, Super Étendard, Jaguar, Mirage F1, Mirage 2000D/N and Mirage IV.
- The SPECTRA electronic warfare system includes an active cancellation system to disguise it from enemy radars.

DASSAULT RAFALE – VARIANTS

Rafale A: A technology demonstrator that first flew in 1986. It has now been retired.

Rafale D: Dassault used this designation (D for *discreet*, or "stealthy") in the early 1990s for the production versions for the Armée de l'Air (French Air Force), to emphasize the new semi-stealthy features it had added to the design.

Rafale B: This is the two-seat version for the Armée de l'Air; delivered to EC 330 in 2004.

Rafale C: This is the single-seat version for the Armée de l'Air; delivered to EC 330 in June 2004.

Rafale M: This is the carrier-borne version for the Aéronavale (the air arm of the Marine Nationale, or French Navy), which entered service in 2002. The Rafale M weighs about 1,100 lb (500 kg) more than the Rafale C. Very similar to the Rafale C in appearance, but with a longer nose gear leg and a deleted front centre pylon.

Rafale N: Originally called the Rafale BM, the Rafale N was planned to be a two-seat version for the Aéronavale. Budget constraints and the cost of training extra crew members have been cited as the grounds for its cancellation.

DASSAULT RAFALE M

The Rafale M of the Marine Nationale (French Navy) is notable for its strengthened undercarriage with a unique "jump strut" nose leg, which propels the nose upwards on catapult launch, giving the same boost to lift as the "ski jump" on the STOVL carriers used by the United Kingdom, Spain, Italy and India. Rafale Ms serve with Flotille 14 (14F), based at Landivisiau in Brittany, and aboard the nuclear carrier *Charles de Gaulle*. Rafale M prototype M01 is shown here with wingtip Magic 2 missiles, but the Rafale can also carry the infrared and radar-guided MICA medium-range missiles. The AM39 Exocet anti-ship missile is a primary weapon for the Rafale M, and the ASMP A nuclear standoff missile and the Apache cruise missile can also be employed.

The Rafale programme began as part of the effort to field a European fighter aircraft (EFA) for the early 1990s. The United Kingdom built an EFA demonstrator aircraft and France the ACX (for "Avion de Combat experimental"), which flew in July 1986 as the Rafale ("squall") A, fitted with General Electric F404 engines.

In 1985, France withdrew from the EFA project over differences in programme leadership and because the other partners, notably Germany and the United Kingdom, were focusing on air-to-air, while France wanted to replace several attack and strike aircraft such as the Mirage 2000N and Super Étendard, as well as fighters.

DELAYED PRODUCTION

A long test programme and funding difficulties delayed development of the production-standard Rafale, which did not fly until 1998. The Marine Nationale (French Navy) introduced the Rafale to service in 2004. The initial version was delivered to F1 standard, which had a basic air-to-air capability. Production models were built in C (*chausser* – fighter), B (*biplace* – two-seat) and M (*marine* – naval) forms.

The Armée de l'Air's initial Rafale Bs and Cs were of "omnirole" F2 standard, which allowed carriage of a variety of air-to-ground weapons. In 2008, new aircraft for both the Armée de l'Air and Marine Nationale were delivered as F3s, with the capability to carry reconnaissance pods and the ASMP-A nuclear standoff missile.

Above. The Rafale uses a sidestick controller rather than a central joystick. The Rafale M is the only carrier-based aircraft to use this arrangement.

Above: The French use American-built catapults and the Rafale M is compatible with U.S. Navy carrier systems.

Above: Many French-designed weapons such as these AASM air-to-surface modular missiles (on triple racks) are available for export customers of the Rafale.

With the back seat systems shut down, the two-seat Rafales can be flown exactly like single-seaters. The two-seater's combat role is mainly the nuclear mission. The balance of two-seat and single-seat aircraft to be purchased by the Armée de l'Air has changed during the course of production. The initial plan was to have only a few B models mainly for use as trainers, then to have a majority of Bs for the strike role, but the final plan is to have three-quarters B models and a quarter Cs.

NEAR-IDENTICAL VERSIONS

There is about 80 percent commonality between the naval and land-based versions of the Rafale; the only significant difference between the C and the M F3 is the landing gear and tailhook of the latter. Designed for the stresses of carrier operations, the M's beefier undercarriage adds about 661 lb (300 kg) to the empty weight. The M loses some weight, though, by having one fewer weapons hardpoint.

The Rafale has a sidestick controller, which, in the case of the Rafale M, is the only one fitted to a carrier-based aircraft. The instrument panel includes three screens, a huge wide-angle HUD and no conventional instruments at all. The central MFD screen uses touch-screen technology and a track pad to control radar and other sensor data. The cockpit is extremely snug compared to those of its contemporaries.

COMBAT DEBUT

Rafales made their combat debut in 2007 when both air force and navy Rafales flew close air support missions over Afghanistan, employing laser-guided bombs designated by "buddy' aircraft such as Dassault Mirage 2000s and Dassault-Breguet Super Étendards. Self-designating capability has come only with the F3 Rafales. Despite being lighter than its closest competitor, the Eurofighter Typhoon, the Rafale has less thrust and is reportedly outperformed at every level in a dogfight.

A total of just under 300 Rafales have been ordered by France, with 60 of those destined for the Marine Nationale. Dassault has heavily marketed the aircraft in its quest for export orders, with the most likely prospects being in North Africa, the Middle East, India and Brazil.

Eurofighter Typhoon

The Eurofighter Typhoon is an example of successful international industrial cooperation, although its development has not been without problems – most of them political, rather than technical.

EUROFIGHTER TYPHOON SPECIFICATION

Dimensions

Length: 52 ft 5 in (15.96 m)
Height: 17 ft 4 in (5.28 m)
Wingspan: 35 ft 11 in (10.95 m)
Wing area: 538 sq ft (50 m^2)

Powerplant

Two Eurojet EJ200 afterburning turbofan rated at 13,500 lbf (60 kN) dry and 20,250 lbf (90 kN) with afterburner

Weights

Empty operating: 24,250 lb (11,000 kg)
Normal takeoff: 34,280 lb (15,550 kg)
Maximum takeoff: 51,800 lb (23,500 kg)

Fuel and load

Internal fuel: 1,506 US gallons (5700 liters)
External fuel: two 1,000 litre (264 US gallon) tanks
Maximum weapon load: 16,500 lb (7500 kg)

Performance

Maximum level speed: In excess of Mach 2 (1,550 mph/2495 km/h)
Maximum combat radius: Ground attack, lo-lo-lo: 373 miles (601 km); ground attack, hi-lo-hi: 863 miles (1389 km); air defence with 3-hr CAP: 115 m (185 km); air defence with 10-minute loiter: 863 miles (1389 km)
Maximum combat range: 1,840 nm (1802 miles; 2900 km)
Service ceiling: 65,000 ft (19,810 m)

Armament

One 27-mm Mauser BK-27 cannon with 150 rounds. 13 hardpoints: eight underwing; five underfuselage stations. Air-to-air missiles: AIM-9 Sidewinder, AIM-132 ASRAAM, AIM-120 AMRAAM, IRIS-T. Air-to-surface missiles: AGM-84 Harpoon, AGM-88 HARM, ALARM, Storm Shadow, Brimstone, Taurus KEPD 350, Penguin. Also carrying bombs, flares, and electronic countermeasures.

Cutaway Key

1 Glass-reinforced plastic radome
2 Air data sensors
3 Starboard canard foreplane
4 Port canard forepane
5 Foreplane pivot mounting
6 Single-piece windscreen
7 Wide-angle head-up display (HUD)
8 Martin-Baker Mk 16A zero-zero ejection seat
9 Upward-hinging canopy
10 Cockpit pressurization valves
11 Lower VHF antenna
12 Starboard engine intake
13 Fuselage strake
14 Intake ramp bleed air spill louvres
15 Conditioning systems heat-exchanger exhaust
16 Formation lighting strip
17 Nosewheel
18 Starboard leading-edge manoeuvring flap
19 Wingtip defensive aids system pod
20 Fixed inboard leading edge
21 Port mainwheel and tyre
22 Undercarriage scissor link
23 Port main undercarriage door
24 Port navigation light
25 Carbon-fibre composite wing skin
26 Auxiliary power unit (APU) exhaust
27 Fuel filler cap
28 Carbon-fibre composite fuselage panels
29 Port leading-edge manoeuvring flap
30 Dorsal airbrake (closed)
31 Anti-collision strobe light
32 Starboard outboard elevon
33 Starboard inboard elevon
34 Heat exchanger ram air intake
35 Engine compressor intake
36 Eurojet EJ200 low-bypass turbofan engine
37 Engine fuel control system
38 Wing root trailing-edge fairing
39 Laser warning receiver (LWR)
40 Tailpipe sealing plates
41 Engine nozzle shroud panels
42 Variable afterburner nozzle
43 Port inboard elevon
44 Port outboard elevon
45 Brake parachute door
46 Missile approach warning sensor
47 Engine bleed air heat exchanger outlet
48 Rudder
49 Fuel jettison outlet
50 UHF/IFF antennas in fintip
51 Carbon-fibre composite fin skin
52 Metal alloy fin leading edge
53 Formation lighting strip
54 AIM-9L Sidewinder infrared-guided air-to-air missile
55 Air-launched anti-radiation missile (ALARM)
56 GBU-16 1,000-lb (454-kg) laser-guided bomb
57 AIM-120 advanced medium-range air-to-air missile (AMRAAM)

"The plane flies with one finger. I took the controls myself and I can tell you that this plane is like a drug. I didn't want to come down."
– Antonio Martino, Italy's Secretary of Defence, 1 November 2005

FACTS

- All Typhoons are fitted with a 27-mm Mauser cannon. Initially the United Kingdom chose not to make its operational for cost reasons, but has since done so.
- The Typhoon has a direct voice input system that allows hands-off control of many systems, although not weapons launch.
- A helmet-mounted sight system projects flight and radar information anywhere the Typhoon's pilot looks.

EUROFIGHTER TYPHOON – VARIANTS

DEVELOPMENT AIRCRAFT

DA1 (Germany): DA1's main role was handling characteristics and engine performance. DA1 first flew on 27 March 1994. The aircraft was retired on 21 December 2005.

DA2 (United Kingdom): DA2 undertook envelope expansion, flight control assessment and load trials. The aircraft first flew on 6 April 1994. The flight control assessment included development of the Eurofighter's "carefree handling."

DA3 (Italy): Weapons systems development.

DA4 (United Kingdom): Radar and avionics development.

DA5 (Germany): Radar and avionics development, being upgraded to Tranche 2 standard.

DA6 (Spain): Airframe development and handling. DA6 was lost in a crash in Spain in November 2002 after both engines failed.

DA7 (Italy): Navigation, avionics and missile carriage.

INSTRUMENTED PRODUCTION AIRCRAFT (IPA)

IPA1 (United Kingdom): Defensive Aids Sub System (DASS).
IPA2 (Italy): Air-to-surface weapons integration.
IPA3 (Germany): Air-to-air weapons integration.
IPA4 (Spain): Air-to-surface weapons integration and environmental development.
IPA5 (United Kingdom): Air-to-surface and air-to-air weapons integration.
IPA6 (United Kingdom): Converted Series Production Aircraft (BS031) – Tranche 2 Computer Systems.
IPA7 (Germany): Converted Series Production Aircraft (GS029) – Full Tranche 2 Standard.

SERIES PRODUCTION AIRCRAFT

EdA aircraft
The Spanish Air Force (Ejército del Aire) has one squadron of aircraft. The aircraft is designated the C.16 Typhoon.

Luftwaffe aircraft
Germany has two active EF-2000 fighter wings, Jagdgeschwader 73 and Jagdgeschwader 74. JG 73 began converting to the Eurofighter in April 2004. JG 74 received its first aircraft on 25 June 2006.

RAF aircraft
T1: The Typhoon will replace the Royal Air Force's Panavia Tornado F3 (fighter) and SEPECAT Jaguar (ground-attack) forces.

T1A: A two-seat trainer.

F2: Single-seat fighter variant.

T3: Two-seat Block 5 or later aircraft (built or upgraded from T1).

FGR4: Single-seat Block 5 or later aircraft (built or upgraded from F2). Feature increased capabilities of fighter/ground-attack/reconnaissance aircraft. The FGR4 has from June 2008 achieved the required standard for multi-role operations.

EUROFIGHTER TYPHOON

Rather than a single prototype, the Eurofighter partners built a series of instrumented production aircraft (IPA) for development work. The first to be completed was DA2, the first British aircraft, although Germany's DA1 made the first flight in March 1994. DA2, serial ZH588, flew in April 1994 and is seen here fitted with a pair of AIM-9L Sidewinders. A sensor for the PIRATE infrared tracking system is mounted below the left of the windscreen, although this was not fitted to production aircraft until the end of the first tranche. An air data probe above the radome was used for measurements as part of the test programme. It continued flying on various trials until January 2007, after which it was retired to the Royal Air Force Museum at Hendon in London.

As far back as the early 1970s, studies were under way in Britain and Germany for a highly manoeuvrable fighter aircraft along the lines of the U.S. F-16 and F/A-18 Hornet. These, together with French, Italian and Spanish requirements, merged in 1983 as the Future European Fighter Aircraft programme. Politics interceded at every stage, and France dropped out in 1985 to pursue development of its Rafale technology demonstrator into an operational fighter. Across the Channel, British Aerospace flew its own Experimental Aircraft Prototype (EAP) in August 1986.

The eventual industrial agreement followed the model of the Panavia Tornado programme, where aircraft were assembled in each of the partner nations using components built in different countries. For example, the Eurofighter Typhoon's forward fuselage, canards and tail fin are built in the United Kingdom; the central fuselage is made in Germany; the starboard wing and both leading-edge flaps are Spanish; and the port wing and flaperons come from Italy. The major systems include EJ200 engines from Eurojet and the CAPTOR radar from Euroradar. Each of these suppliers are consortiums of partner nation companies.

Workshare is allocated based on aircraft to be ordered: 232 for the United Kingdom; 180 for Germany; 121 for Italy; and 87 for Spain. Each partner nation has sales responsibility for a particular part of the world. For example, Saudi Arabia's Typhoons 72 will be built by BAE Systems (48 of them in collaboration with a local partner), while Austria's 15 jets have come from German production.

THREE-PART PRODUCTION

Known as the EFA 2000 at the time of the first (German) aircraft's maiden flight in March 1994, the name "Typhoon" was adopted in 1998 for the Royal Air Force and export aircraft. The first country to order the Typhoon outside of the partner nations was Greece, but it withdrew from the deal due to the cost pressures of the 2004 Olympic Games.

The Typhoon has a cropped delta wing, canard foreplanes and a ventral air intake with hinged flaps to regulate the airflow to the engines. There is a total of 13 weapons stations under the wings and fuselage. A sophisticated fly-by-wire control system allows carefree handling throughout the flight envelope.

Production is divided into three distinct groups, or tranches, each adding new capabilities. Tranche 1 offers basic air-to-air capabilities, with missiles including the AIM-9 Sidewinder, AIM-120 AMRAAM and AIM-132 ASRAAM. Later Tranche 1 aircraft have the PIRATE (Passive Infra Red Airborne Tracking Equipment) sensor forward of the cockpit. Tranche 2 aircraft will have a wide range of air-to-surface and air-to-air weapons options, and Tranche 3 may incorporate features such as electronically scanned radar and thrust-vectoring engines.

COMING TO FRUITION

Budgetary considerations led to delays in signing contracts for the later tranches. The nature of the original agreement

Above: Weapons, navigation, radar and systems data can be shown on any of the Typhoon's MFD screens.

means that there are large penalties for the respective countries not taking the originally allocated share of production, but it is possible that Tranche 3 aircraft will not be delivered to some or all of the partner air forces.

Typhoons have seen operational service in the air-defence role, providing combat air patrols over the Turin Winter Olympics in 2006, as well as during several international summits. They have also performed quick reaction alert (QRA) duties over the partner nations and the Falkland Islands. In addition to this, Typhoons have supplied air cover for Albania and the Baltic States, which currently have no operational fighter aircraft of their own.

Right: The Typhoon F2 was the RAF's initial single-seat version. Tranche 2 aircraft are designated FGR4, emphasizing their multi-role capabilities.

Above: Weapons options have expanded during Typhoon production. Even the "austere" capability allows carriage of precision weapons such as these LGBs.

Lockheed Martin/Boeing F-22 Raptor

The F-22 "Air Dominance Fighter" outclasses all previous and existing fighters. Its enormous price tag, however, means that it will not be fielded in great numbers and politics means that it cannot be sold to the United States' allies.

LOCKHEED MARTIN/BOEING F-22 RAPTOR SPECIFICATION

Dimensions

Length: 62 ft 1 in (18.9 m)
Height: 16 ft 8 in (5.08 m)
Wingspan: 44 ft 6 in (13.56 m)
Wing area: 840 ft² (78.04 m²)

Powerplant

Two Pratt & Whitney F119-PW-100 Pitch Thrust vectoring turbofans each rated at 29,300 lb (130 kN) dry thrust and 35,000 lb (156 kN) thrust with afterburner

Weights

Empty operating: 43,430 lb (19,700 kg)
Normal takeoff: 64,460 lb (29,300 kg)
Maximum takeoff: 83,500 lb (38,000 kg)

Performance

Maximum speed at altitude: Mach 2.25 (1,500 mph/ 2410 km/h)
Maximum combat radius: 410 nm (471 miles; 759 km)
Maximum combat range: 1,600 nm (1,840 miles; 2960 km) with two external fuel tanks

Armament

One 20-mm M61A2 Vulcan Gatling gun with 480 rounds. Air-to-air missiles: six AIM-120 AMRAAM and two AIM-9 Sidewinder. Air-to-ground: two AIM-120 AMRAAM and two AIM-9 Sidewinder and either two 1,000-lb (450-kg) JDAM or two Wind Corrected Munitions Dispensers (WCMDs) or eight 250-lb (110-kg) GBU-39 Small Diameter Bombs. Four hardpoints to carry for 600-U.S. gal (2271-litre) drop tanks or weapons, each with a capacity of 5,000 lb (2268 kg)

Cutaway Key

1 Composite radome
2 Northrop Grumman/Raytheon AN/APG-77 radar (hidden)
3 Composite fuselage chine skin panels
4 Pitot head
5 Formation lighting strip
6 Nosewheel door
7 Nosewheel and tyre
8 Forked nosewheel strut
9 Instrument panel shroud
10 Head-up display (HUD)
11 Starboard engine intake
12 Pilot's ACES II ejection seat
13 Canopy actuator strut
14 M61A2 Vulcan 20-mm cannon
15 Flush starboard electronic warfare antenna
16 Starboard communication/ navigation/ identification (CNI) antenna
17 Starboard leading-edge flap
18 Starboard wingtip navigation light
19 Port rear EW antenna
20 Formation lighting strip
21 Starboard aileron
22 Starboard flaperon

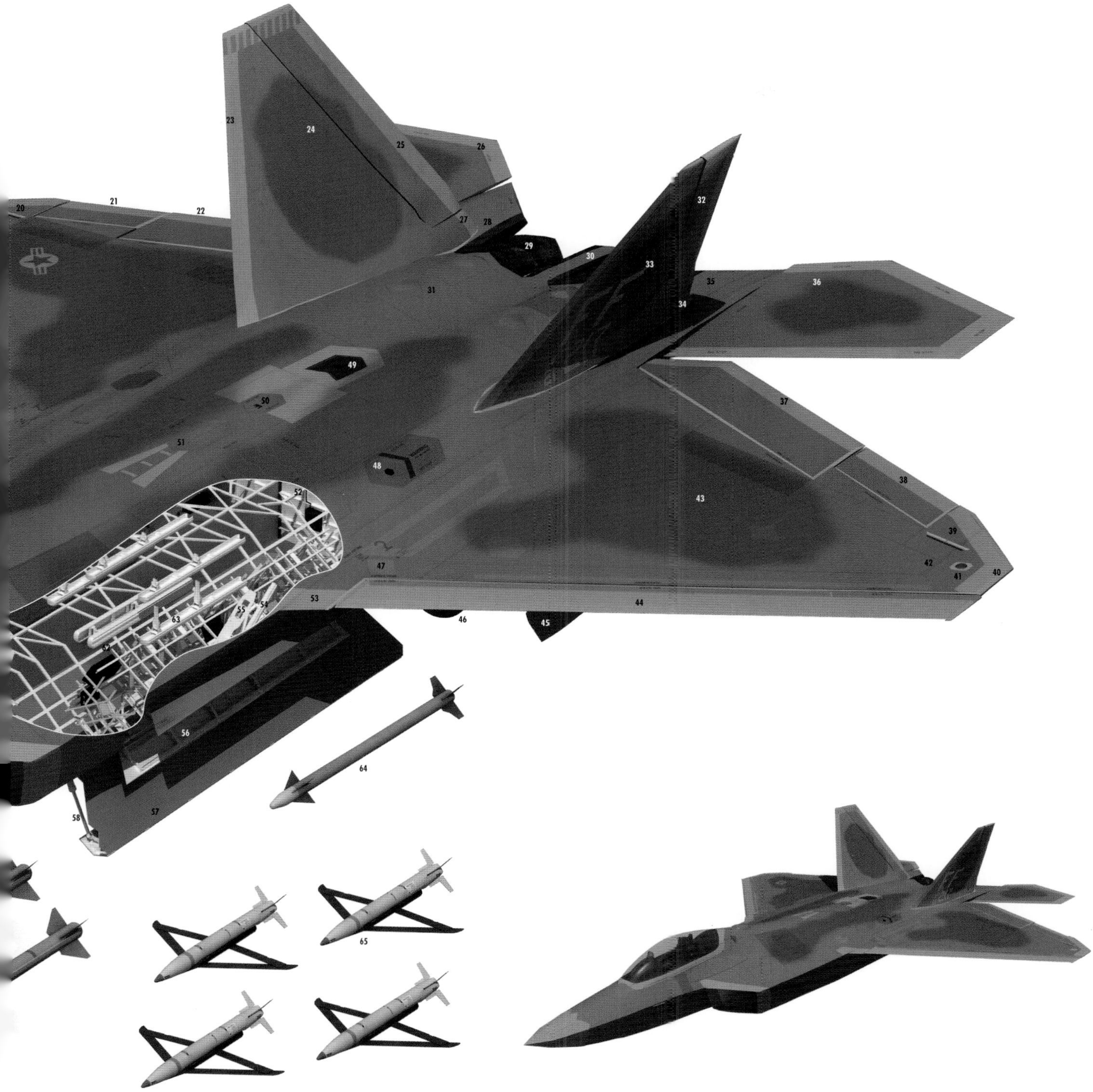

23 Fin leading edge containing CNI antenna
24 Starboard fin
25 Fin trailing edge containing CNI VHF antenna
26 Starboard all-moving tailplane
27 Rudder lower fixed fairing
28 Starboard rear CNI antenna (hidden)
29 Two-dimensional thrust vectoring afterburner nozzle
30 Runway arrestor hook fairing
31 Pratt & Whitney F119-PW-100 afterburning turbofan engine
32 Port rudder
33 Port fin
34 Rudder lower fixed fairing
35 Port rear CNI antenna (hidden)
36 Port all-moving tailplane
37 Port flaperon
38 Port aileron
39 Formation lighting strip
40 EW antenna (hidden)
41 Port navigation light
42 EW equipment (hidden)
43 Carbon-fibre wing skin
44 Port leading-edge flap
45 Inboard stores pylon
46 Port mainwheel tyre
47 Port CNI UHF antenna
48 Auxiliary power unit (APU) exhaust
49 Engine bleed air heat exchanger
50 GPS antenna
51 In-light refuelling receptacle (covered)
52 Weapons bay rear bulkhead
53 Flush port EW antenna
54 Mainwheel retraction strut
55 Mainwheel retraction jack
56 Lateral weapons bay door
57 Ventral weapons bay doors
58 Weapons bay door retraction strut
59 Port engine intake
60 Throttle controls
61 Port side cockpit console
62 Ventral weapons bay
63 Missile launch trapeze
64 AIM-9X Sidewinder short range air-to-air missile
65 GBU-39 Small Diameter Bomb
66 AIM-120 AMRAAM medium-range air-to-air missile

"The F-22 is a revolutionary, not evolutionary, leap very, very far forward."
– Lieutenant Colonel Mike "Dozer" Shower, U.S. Air Force F-22 pilot

FACTS

- The operational F-22A was accepted for U.S. Air Force service in December 2005.
- During simulated combat exercises in Alaska in 2006, 12 F-22s of 94 FS "shot down" 108 adversaries for no loss.
- In a Red Flag exercise in Nevada, 14 Raptors of 94 FS established air superiority over greater numbers of F-15 and F-16s.

LOCKHEED MARTIN/BOEING F-22 RAPTOR - OPERATORS

The U.S. Air Force is the only operator of the F-22 Raptor, with a total of 145 aircraft in inventory at the time of writing. These are operated by the following commands:

Air Education and Training Command
325th Fighter Wing, Tyndall Air Force Base, Florida
43rd Fighter Squadron – The first squadron to operate the F-22 and continues to serve as the Formal Training Unit. Known as the "Hornets," the 43rd was reactivated at Tyndall in 2002.

Air Combat Command
1st Fighter Wing, Langley Air Force Base, Virginia
27th Fighter Squadron – The first combat F-22 squadron. Began conversion in December 2005 and flew the first operational mission (January 2006 in support of Operation Noble Eagle).
94th Fighter Squadron
49th Fighter Wing, Holloman Air Force Base, New Mexico
7th Fighter Squadron
8th Fighter Squadron
53rd Wing, Eglin Air Force Base, Florida
422rd Test and Evaluation Squadron – The "Green Bats" are responsible for operational testing, tactics development and evaluation for the F-22.
57th Wing, Nellis Air Force Base, Nevada
433rd Weapons Squadron

Air Force Materiel Command
412th Test Wing, Edwards Air Force Base, California
411th Flight Test Squadron – Conducted competition between YF-22 and YF-23 from 1989–91. Continues to conduct flight test on F-22 armaments and upgrades.

Pacific Air Forces
3rd Wing, Elmendorf Air Force Base, Alaska
90th Fighter Squadron – Converted from McDonnell Douglas/Boeing F-15Es; first F-22A arrived 8 August 2007.
525th Fighter Squadron
477th Fighter Group, Elmendorf Air Force Base, Alaska – Air Force Reserve Command (AFRC) unit.
302nd Fighter Squadron – Associate AFRC squadron to the 3rd Wing.

Air National Guard
192nd Fighter Wing, Langley Air Force Base, Virginia
149th Fighter Squadron – Associate Air National Guard squadron to the 1st Fighter Wing.

Future bases and units will include:
154th Wing, Hickam Air Force Base, Hawaii (2009/2010)
199th Fighter Squadron, Hawaii Air National Guard
531st Fighter Squadron, Hickam Air Force Base, Hawaii – Associate squadron to the 199th Fighter Squadron
44th Fighter Group, Holloman Air Force Base, New Mexico – Air Force Reserve Command (AFRC)
301st Fighter Squadron – Associate AFRC squadron to the 49th Fighter Wing

LOCKHEED MARTIN/BOEING F-22 RAPTOR

The U.S. Air Force's 1st Fighter Wing at Langley Air Force Base, Virginia, became the first operational unit to receive the F-22A Raptor in March 2006. The wing shares its 40 F-22s with the pilots of the Virginia Air National Guard's 149th Fighter Wing. The two units were declared operational in December 2007. This F-22A wears the "FF" ("First Fighter") tail codes of 1 TFW. With weapons mounted internally in bays, the armament configuration can be kept secret until the moment of use. An F-22 carrying bombs appears no different and nor does it give away any performance to one equipped only with air-to-air missiles. The only stores regularly seen on F-22s are external fuel tanks for ferry missions.

The Advanced Tactical Fighter (ATF) requirement issued in 1981 set in train a long process that led to the service entry of the F-22 Raptor some 26 years later. In that time, the world and technology changed greatly. Computer modelling of the 1970s and 1980s could guarantee stealth performance only for faceted shapes and straight lines. The F-117 "stealth fighter" was not a fighter at all, with no provision for air-to-air weaponry. Its defence was not to be detected at all, but even before 1999, when one was brought down by an older-generation surface-to-air missile over Kosovo, it was clear that future combat aircraft would need stealth protection of a whole different magnitude and without having their combat capability compromised by the stealth features.

In 1986, Lockheed (partnered with Boeing) and Northrop (with McDonnell Douglas) were invited to build two airframes each to demonstrate and validate their concepts. In August 1990, the Northrop/McDonnell Douglas YF-23 flew and the Lockheed/Boeing YF-22 was unveiled. The YF-22 flew a month later. Many observers believe that the larger YF-23 was technically better, and "won" the fly-off part of the evaluation. In April 1991, however, Lockheed/Boeing were chosen to build the ATF, as much for their perceived ability to manage and deliver a complex programme as on technical merit.

FULL-SCALE DEVELOPMENT

The journey from the YF-22 to the full-scale development (FSD) F-22, which bore only a passing resemblance to the original, took until 1997. In the meantime, the Cold War had ended. In stages, the Pentagon cut planned production rates and the total requirement from the original 750 to 339.

On first viewing, the F-22A does not appear radically different to the F-15 that preceded it, but just on the surface

Above: Getting in the cockpit of the F-22 is the goal of most American fighter pilots. With fewer than 200 to be built, it will be a position of privilege.

Above: The sun catches the unique surface finish of a U.S. Air Force 1st Fighter Wing F-22A. The Raptor's coatings have unique and expensive radar and infrared absorbtion characteristics.

and under it are many unique features. Key to its incredible manoeuvrability are the Pratt & Whitney F119 engines with two-dimensional thrust-vectoring engines, which work in the vertical plane. Used in a turn, they allow the pilot instantly to turn the nose onto the target. Stealth features include special coatings, diamond shapes or serrated edges on panels and doors, and alignment of intake edges and tail fins. A gold-tinted metallic coating to the frameless canopy reflects radar energy. Weapons are carried internally, in bays under the fuselage and along the intake sides.

The incredible cost per airframe, which reached $138 million by 2008, saw production eventually capped at 187. The final figure for airframes delivered is likely to be 183, to equip seven operational squadrons, plus training and test units.

Above: One of the F-22 development aircraft flies over the California desert. It took ten years from the Raptor's first flight to service entry.

FOR THE UNITED STATES ONLY

Several nations would be natural customers for the F-22, such as Japan, Israel and Saudi Arabia, and others such as Australia would consider it – if it were available. A 2007 U.S. law actually prohibits the export of the Raptor and its sensitive technology. This has boosted the export chances of aircraft such as the Eurofighter Typhoon and Dassault Rafale in the short term, and given impetus to several nations' own fighter programmes. South Korea and Japan are among those working on indigenous stealth fighter projects for the next decade, as is Russia with its own Sukhoi T-50 or PAK-FA, an aircraft with a strong outward resemblance to the F-22.

Lockheed Martin F-35 Lightning II

The F-35 Lightning II is the most ambitious fighter programme in history. Designed in three distinct versions, the F-35 promises much and numerous air arms are depending on its success, but it also faces many technical and political challenges.

Cutaway Key

1 Radome
2 APG-71 AESA radar (hidden)
3 Datalink antenna
4 Distributed aperture system window
5 Nosegear door
6 Single nosewheel
7 Nosewheel torque link
8 Nosewheel leg
9 Fuselage chine
10 Forward-opening canopy
11 Electro-optical targeting system (EOTS) window
12 Starboard instrument panel
13 Canopy frame
14 Martin-Baker Mk 16 zero-zero ejection seat
15 Lift fan vertical drive shaft
16 Starboard engine intake
17 Port engine intake
18 Lift fan
19 Lift fan door
20 Starboard leading-edge flap
21 Formation lighting strip
22 Engine auxiliary air vent door
23 Engine auxiliary air vent
24 Lift fan horizontal drive shaft
25 Starboard navigation light
26 Starboard flaperon
27 Pratt & Whitney F135 afterburning turbofan engine
28 Roll post
29 Starboard horizontal tailplane
30 Starboard vertical fin
31 Starboard rudder
32 Nozzle bearings (hidden)
33 Exhaust fairing
34 Convergent/divergent exhaust nozzle in down position
35 Port vertical fin
36 Port rudder

F-35A LIGHTNING II SPECIFICATION

Dimensions

Length: 51 ft 2/5 in (15.67 m)
Height: 14 ft 2 in (4.33 m)
Wingspan: 35 ft (10.7 m)

Powerplant

One Pratt & Whitney F135 afterburning turbofan rated at 28,000 lbf (125 kN) and 43,000 lbf (191 kN) with afterburner

Weights

Empty operating: 29,300 lb (13,300 kg)
Normal takeoff: 44,400 lb (20,100 kg)
Maximum takeoff: 70,000 lb (31,800 kg)

Fuel and load

Internal fuel: 18,480 lb (8382 kg)

Performance

Maximum speed: Mach 1.67 (1,283 mph; 2065 km/h)
Service ceiling: 60,000 ft (18288 m)
Maximum combat radius: 610 nm (689.7 miles; 1110 km)
Maximum combat range: 12,000 nm (1,374 miles; 2220 km)

Armament

One GAU-22/A 25-mm cannoon with 180 rounds. Hardpoints with six external pylons on wings with a capacity of 15,000 lb (6800 kg) and two internal bays with two pylons each for a total weapons payload of 18,000 lb (8165 kg) to carry combinations of AIM-120 AMRAAM, AIM-132 ASRAAM, AIM-9X Sidewinder air-to-air missiles and AGM-154 JSOW and AGM-158 JASSM air-to-ground missiles. Bombload could include Mark 84, Mark 83 and Mark 82 GP bombs, a Mk.20 Rockeye II cluster bomb, Wind Corrected Munitions Dispenser, Paveway-series laser-guided bombs, Small Diameter Bomb (SDB) and JDAM-series

37 Port tailplane
38 Port flaperon
39 Port navigation light
40 Port leading-edge flap
41 Formation lighting strip
42 Port mainwheel and tyre
43 Weapons bay door
44 Weapons bay structure
45 AIM-120 AMRAAM (advanced medium-range air-to-air missile)
46 GBU-38 Joint Direct Attack Munition (JDAM)

"The [F-35] brings persistent stealth over the battlefield for the first time and will enhance the lethality and survivability of American and allied combat air, sea and ground forces."
– General John Jumper,
U.S. Air Force Chief of Staff

FACTS

- The F-35C carrier-based version has a larger wing of a different design to the other versions with folding tips.
- The U.S. forces require 2,443 F-35s to replace a number of older aircraft types.
- On the F-35B, nine intake and exhaust doors need to open and close for the lift fan system to work.

LOCKHEED MARTIN F-35 LIGHTNING II – VARIANTS & JSF PROGRAM

VARIANTS

F-35A: Conventional takeoff and landing (CTOL) variant intended for the U.S. Air Force and other air forces. It is the smallest, lightest F-35 version and is the only variant equipped with an internal cannon, the GAU-22/A.

The A variant is primarily intended to replace the U.S. Air Force's Lockheed Martin F-16 Fighting Falcon, beginning in 2013, and replace the Fairchild-Republic A-10 Thunderbolt II starting in 2028.

F-35B: Short takeoff and vertical landing (STOVL) variant. Similar in size to the A variant, the B sacrifices some fuel volume to make room for the vertical flight system. Unlike the other variants, the F-35B has no landing hook; the "STOVL/HOOK" button in the cockpit initiates conversion instead of dropping the hook. The first test flight was on 11 June 2008. The B variant is expected to be available beginning in 2012.

F-35C: Carrier variant with a larger, folding wing and larger control surfaces for improved low-speed control, and stronger landing gear and hook for the stresses of carrier landings. The larger wing area allows for twice the range on internal fuel compared with the McDonnell Douglas (now Boeing) F/A-18C Hornet, achieving much the same goal as the heavier F/A-18E/F Super Hornet.

The U.S. Navy will be the sole user for the carrier variant. The C variant is expected to be available beginning in 2014. The first production F-35C was rolled out on 29 July 2009.

INTERNATIONAL PARTICIPATION UNDER THE JOINT STRIKE FIGHTER (JSF) PROGRAM

United Kingdom: Level 1 partner in the development of the aircraft. To purchase three F-35Bs.

Italy: Level 2 partner. To purchase 109 F-35As and 22 F-35Bs.

Netherlands: Level 2 partner. To acquire 85 F-35As.

Canada: Level 3 partner.

Turkey: Level 3 partner. Plans to order 116 F-35A CTOL versions.

Australia: Level 3 partner. Expected to order 72 or more F-35As.

Denmark: Level 3 partner. Is considering replacing F-16s with F-35s.

Norway: Level 3 partner. Has stated that it will support buying F-35s for the Royal Norwegian Air Force and will develop Joint Strike Missiles for the F-35 and other aircraft.

Israel: Security Cooperative Participant (SCP). Intends to buy more than 100 F-35A Fighters.

Singapore: Security Cooperative Participant (SCP).

LOCKHEED MARTIN F-35B LIGHTNING II

The first F-35B Lightning II flew in June 2008. Of the planned 16 flying F-35 prototypes, five are Bs, three of which would clear the flight envelope and two to test the mission systems. The front and side views depict the F-35B configured for a vertical landing, showing the lift fan doors and auxiliary doors open, and the main exhaust nozzle in the down position. In operational service, the F-35B may use a rolling vertical landing technique, rather than a pure vertical descent, when space is available, such as the on the new Royal Navy carriers. This would put less stress on the engine, increasing its lifespan, and also allow greater landing weights.

Several schemes for proposed fighters to replace a variety of fighter and attack aircraft were merged in the early 1990s to meet requirements by the U.S. Air Force, U.S. Navy, U.S. Marine Corps and the Royal Navy and Royal Air Force.

Under the banner of Joint Advanced Strike Technology (JAST), the new aircraft would be a low-cost replacement for numerous types, including the Fairchild-Republic A-10, Lockheed Martin F-16, McDonnell Douglas F/A-18C and D, Grumman A-6 Intruder and McDonnell Douglas/BAe AV-8B Harrier. The British were looking for both a Harrier and a Sea Harrier replacement. To this end, the same basic airframe would be built in three versions: a conventional takeoff and landing (CTOL) model for the air force; a version for aircraft carriers (CV); and a short takeoff and vertical landing (STOVL) variant to replace Harriers on amphibious ships and British carriers.

Above: A unique helmet-mounted sight system allows the F-35 pilot to cue weapons to any target the sensors can track, even when hidden from his view by aircraft structure.

JOINT STRIKE FIGHTER

A fly-off competition was organized in 1996 to choose a winner between competing designs by Boeing and Lockheed Martin, McDonnell Douglas having been eliminated at an earlier stage. The project was now called the Joint Strike Fighter (JSF), reflecting its joint (multi-service) procurement and multi-role capabilities.

Boeing (which absorbed McDonnell Douglas in 1997) and Lockheed Martin took different approaches. Boeing built two X-32 demonstrators characterized by a huge intake under the nose. The wing was of a roughly diamond planform with large flaperons. There were no tailplanes. Lockheed Martin's X-35s were more conventional, with side-mounted intakes and tailplanes. The CV X-35A flew in October 2000, followed by the CTOL X-35C two months later. The X-35A was later modified to create the STOVL X-35B, which flew as such in June 2001. These aircraft demonstrated technologies rather than serving as strict prototypes for the JSF.

CONTRACT SUCCESS

Lockheed Martin was awarded the contract to proceed with a series of F-35A (CTOL), F-35B (STOVL) and F-35C (CV) development aircraft in October 2001. Boeing's X-32s became museum pieces (as did the X-35s).

Above: The F-35A made its maiden flight in December 2006. The flight envelope was expanded past Mach 1 in November 2008.

Above: The demonstrator X-35 underwent numerous changes in its evolution to the F-35 The more obvious ones include the shape of the nose and the tail fins, and the configuration of the canopy.

The manufacturer envisages sales of more than 4,000 F-35s, many of them replacing export F-16s. An extremely complicated industrial programme was launched with the United Kingdom, Italy, the Netherlands, Canada, Turkey, Australia, Norway and Denmark sharing the development and testing, in exchange for the chance to supply components to all customers. These nations did not initially commit to purchasing any F-35s. The degree to which the United States will allow technology transfer to the partners and other customers remains an unknown and controversial factor.

Surfaces and panel edges on the production F-35 are aligned to reduce the radar cross section. Weapons will be carried internally in weapons bays. The F-35A will have an internal 25-mm cannon. The other versions will carry the cannon as a gun pod. The canopy is hinged at the forward end. All versions will use the Pratt & Whitney F135 turbofan, with the addition of a Rolls-Royce lift fan and a reaction control system for the F-35B. The U.S. Marine Corps requires the F-35B for use from its amphibious ships; Italy and the United Kingdom are expected to also be customers.

DELAYED SERVICE ENTRY

The first F-35A Lightning II flew in December 2006 and began testing towards a planned service entry in 2012. Progress after that slipped greatly, however, with subsequent aircraft being late to enter testing. This has caused in-service dates for the F-35 with U.S. forces and signature of export contracts to be delayed by at least two years.

Glossary

AAM: Air-to-Air Missile
ADV: Air Defence Variant (of the Tornado)
AEW: Airborne Early Warning
Afterburning (reheat): method of increasing the thrust of a gas turbine aircraft engine by injecting additional fuel into the hot exhaust duct between the engine and the tailpipe, where it ignites to provide a short-term increase of power.
Aileron: an aerofoil used for causing an aircraft to roll around its longitudinal axis, usually fitted near the wingtips. Ailerons are controlled by use of the pilot's control column.
ALARM: Air-Launched Anti-Radiation Missile
All-Up Weight: the total weight of an aircraft in operating condition. Normal maximum AUW is the maximum at which an aircraft is permitted to fly within normal design restrictions, while overload weight is the maximum AUW at which an aircraft is permitted to fly subject to ultimate flying restrictions.
Altimeter: instrument that measures altitude, or height above sea level.
AMRAAM: Advanced Medium-Range Air-to-Air Missile
Angle of Attack: the angle between the wing (airfoil) and the airflow relative to it
Aspect Ratio: the ratio of wing span to chord
ASV: Air to Surface Vessel – airborne detection radar for locating ships and submarines
ASW: Anti-Submarine Warfare
ATF: Advanced Tactical Fighter
AWACS: Airborne Warning and Control System
Basic Weight: the tare weight of an aircraft plus the specified operational load
CAP: Combat Air Patrol
Centre of Gravity: point in a body through which the sum of the weights of all its parts passes. A body suspended from this point is said to be in a state of equilibrium.
Centre of Pressure: point through which the lifting force of a wing acts
Chord: cross-section of a wing from leading edge to trailing edge
Delta Wing: aircraft shaped like the Greek letter delta
Disposable Load: the weight of crew and consumable load (fuel, missiles etc.)
Electronic Countermeasures (ECM): systems designed to confuse and disrupt enemy radar equipment
Electronic Counter-Countermeasures (ECCM): measures taken to reduce the effectiveness of ECM by improving the resistance of radar equipment to jamming
Elevator: a horizontal control surface used to control the upward or downward inclination of an aircraft in flight. Elevators are usually hinged to the trailing edge of the tailplane.
EW: Electronic Warfare
FAC: Forward Air Controller. A battlefront observer who directs strike aircraft on to their targets near the front line
FGA: Fighter Ground Attack
FLIR: Forward-Looking Infra-Red. Heat-sensing equipment fitted in an aircraft that scans the path ahead to detect heat from objects such as vehicle engines.
FRS: Fighter Reconnaissance Strike
Gas Turbine: engine in which burning fuel supplies hot gas to spin a turbine
GPS: Global Positioning System. A system of navigational satellites.
GR: General Reconnaissance
HOTAS: Hands on Throttle and Stick. A system whereby the pilot exercises full control over his aircraft in combat without the need to remove his hands from the throttle and control column to operate weapons selection switches or other controls.
HUD: Head-Up Display. A system in which essential information is projected on to a cockpit windscreen so that the pilot has no need to look down at his instrument panel.
IFF: Identification Friend or Foe. An electronic pulse emitted by an aircraft to identify it as friendly on a radar screen.
INS: Inertial Navigation System. An on-board guidance system that steers an aircraft or missile over a predetermined course by measuring factors such as the distance travelled and reference to 'waypoints' (landmarks) en route.
Interdiction: Deep air strikes into enemy areas to sever communications with the battlefield
IR: Infra-Red
Jet Propulsion: method of propulsion in which an object is propelled in one direction by a jet, or stream of gases, moving in the other

Laminar Flow: airflow passes over an aircraft's wing in layers, the first of which, the boundary layer, remains stationary while successive layers progressively accelerate; this is known as laminar flow. The smoother the wing surface, and the more efficient its design, the smoother the airflow.

Landing Weight: the AUW of an aircraft at the moment of landing

Lantirn: Low-Altitude Navigation and Targeting Infra-Red for Night. An infra-red system fitted to the F-15E Strike Eagle that combines heat sensing with terrain-following radar to enable the pilot to view the ground ahead of the aircraft during low-level night operations. The information is projected on the pilot's head-up display

LWR: Laser Warning Radar. Equipment fitted to an aircraft that warns the pilot if he is being tracked by a missileguiding radar beam.

Mach: named after the Austrian Professor Ernst Mach, a Mach number is the ratio of the speed of an aircraft or missile to the local speed of sound. At sea level, Mach One (1.0M) is approximately 1226 km/h (762mph), decreasing to about 1062 km/h (660mph) at 30,000 feet. An aircraft or missile travelling faster than Mach One is said to be supersonic. Mach numbers are dependent on variations in atmospheric temperature and pressure and are registered on a Machmeter in the aircraft's cockpit.

Maximum Landing Weight: the maximum AUW, due to design or operational limitations, at which an aircraft is permitted to land

Maximum Take-Off Weight: the maximum AUW, due to design or operational limitations, at which an aircraft is permitted to take off

MG: Machine gun (Maschinengewehr in German, hence MG 15)

NATO: North Atlantic Treaty Organization

NBC: Nuclear, Chemical and Biological (warfare)

Operational Load: The weight of equipment necessarily carried by an aircraft for a particular role

Phased-Array Radar: A warning radar system using many small aerials spread over a large flat area, rather than a rotating scanner. The advantage of this system is that it can track hundreds of targets simultaneously, electronically directing its beam from target to target in microseconds (millionths of a second).

Pulse-Doppler Radar: a type of airborne interception radar that picks out fast-moving targets from background clutter by measuring the change in frequency of a series of pulses bounced off the targets. This is based on the well-known Doppler Effect, an apparent change in the frequency of waves when the source emitting them has a relative velocity towards or away from an observer. The MiG-29's noted tail-slide manoeuvre is a tactical move designed to break the lock of a pulse-Dopper radar.

Rudder: movable vertical surface or surfaces forming part of the tail unit, by which the yawing of an aircraft is controlled

RWR: Radar Warning Receiver. A device mounted on an aircraft that warns the pilot if he is being tracked by an enemy missile guidance or intercept radar.

SAM: Surface-to-Air Missile

SHF: Super High Frequency (radio waves)

Spin: a spin is the result of yawing or rolling an aeroplane at the point of a stall

SRAM: Short-range Attack Missile

Stall: condition that occurs when the smooth flow of the air over an aircraft's wing changes to a turbulent flow and the lift decreases to the point where control is lost

Stealth Technology: technology applied to aircraft or fighting vehicles to reduce their radar signatures. Examples of stealth aircraft are the Lockheed F-117 and the Northrop B-2.

STOVL: Short Take-off, Vertical Landing

Take-Off Weight: the AUW of an aircraft at the moment of take-off

Turbofan Engine: type of jet engine fitted with a very large front fan that not only sends air into the engine for combustion but also around the engine to produce additional thrust. This results in faster and more fuel-efficient propulsion.

Turbojet Engine: jet engine that derives its thrust from a stream of hot exhaust gases

Variable-Geometry Wing: a type of wing whose angle of sweep can be altered to suit a particular flight profile. Popularly called a Swing Wing.

VHF: Very High Frequency

VLF: Very Low Frequency

V/STOL: Vertical/Short Take-off and Landing

Wild Weasel: code name applied to specialized combat aircraft tasked with defence suppression

Yaw: the action of turning an aircraft in the air around its normal (vertical) axis by use of the rudder. An aircraft is said to yaw when the fore-and-aft axis turns to port or starboard, out of the line of flight.

Index

Picture Credits

Art-Tech/Aerospace: 6, 8, 14 both, 20-21 all, 27, 32, 33 bottom, 36, 44, 48, 50 bottom, 51, 54, 56, 62 bottom, 63, 66, 68-69 all, 74, 75 top, 81 both, 86-87 all, 92 top, 93, 98, 110-111 all, 117 bottom, 129 bottom, 134-135 all, 146-147 all, 158-159 all, 160, 168-169 all, 174 both, 184-187 all, 191, 192 bottom, 193, 198 bottom, 199, 208, 210 top, 211, 216 top, 217, 222-223 all, 228, 241, 246 top, 247, 264, 265 top, 270 both, 294 top

Art-Tech/MARS: 75 bottom, 216 bottom, 240 top, 271

BAE Systems: 312 top

Cody Images: 7 top, 33 top, 38, 39 bottom, 92 bottom, 240 bottom, 265 bottom

Dassault: 162, 259 top, 295

Steve Davies: 181 top

Dryden Flight Research Center: 140 top

Eurofighter: 161 top, 300, 301

Gripen: 282-283 all

Lockheed-Martin: 26 top, 99 top

U.S. Air Force: 15, 26 bottom, 45 bottom, 50 top, 57, 60, 62 top, 80, 117 top, 152 bottom

U.S. Department of Defense: 7 bottom, 9, 39 top, 45 top, 96, 99 bottom, 104-105 all, 116, 122-123 all, 128, 129 top, 140 bottom, 141, 152 top, 153, 161 bottom, 163, 180, 181 bottom, 204-205 all, 210 bottom, 214, 229 both, 234-235 all, 246 bottom, 252-253 all, 258, 259 bottom, 276-277 all, 288-289 all, 294 bottom, 306-307 all, 312 bottom, 313

Jim Winchester: 175, 192 top, 198 top